*The Christology
of Jesus*

BEN WITHERINGTON, III

The Christology
of Jesus

FORTRESS PRESS   MINNEAPOLIS

THE CHRISTOLOGY OF JESUS

Interior design: Karen Buck

Library of Congress Cataloging-in-Publication Data

Witherington, Ben, 1951–
 The christology of Jesus / Ben Witherington III.
   p.   cm.
 Includes bibliographical references.
 ISBN: 0-8006-2430-0 (alk. paper)
   1. Jesus Christ—Knowledge of his own divinity.   2. Jesus Christ—
 Person and offices—History of doctrines—Early church, ca.
 30–600.   3. Bible. N.T. Gospels—Criticism, interpretation, etc.
 I. Title.
 BT216.5.W57   1990
 232.9′.08—dc20   90-34896
                                                           CIP

Manufactured in the U.S.A.   AF 1-2430
94   93   92   91   90   1   2   3   4   5   6   7   8   9   10

"WHOEVER HE WAS or was not, whoever he thought he was, whoever he has become in the memories of [people] since and will go on becoming for as long as [we] remember him—exalted, sentimentalized, debunked, made and remade to the measure of each generation's desire, dread, indifference—he was a man once, whoever else he may have been. And he had a man's face, a human face. . . . *Ecce homo* Pilate said—Behold the man—yet whatever our religion or lack of it, we tend to shrink from beholding him and play our game instead with Shakespeare's face or Helen of Troy's because with them the chances are we could survive almost anything—Shakespeare's simper, say, or a cast in Helen's eye. But with Jesus the risk is too great; the risk that his face would be too much for us if not enough, either a face like any other face to see, pass by, forget, or a face so unlike any other that we would have no choice but to remember it always and follow or flee it to the end of our days and beyond.

"So once again, for the last time or the first time, we face that face . . . Take it or leave it, if nothing else it is at least a face we would know anywhere—a face that belongs to us somehow, our age, our culture; a face we somehow belong to. Like the faces of people we love, it has become so familiar that unless we take pains we hardly see it at all. Take pains. See it for what it is and, to see it whole, see it too for what it is just possible it will become . . . He had a face . . . [that was] not a front for him to live his life behind but a frontier, the outermost visible edge of his life itself in all its richness and multiplicity . . . The *faces* of Jesus then—all the ways he had of being and being seen. The writers of the New Testament give no description of any of them because it was his life alive inside of them that was the news they hawked rather than the color of his eyes.

F. Buechner

Contents

Preface   ix

1. Methodological and Historical Considerations   1
   Formal Arguments   3
   Methodological Matters   22
   Caveats and the Criteria for Authenticity   27

2. Christology and the Relationships of Jesus   33
   Jesus and the Baptist   34
       The Beginning of the Gospel   36, Vipers and
       Vituperation   39, Doubts and Distinctions   42
       Queries from Prison   42, The Greatest Man
       Alive   45, Attack upon the Realm   46,
       Contrasting Styles of Ministry   49, Jesus the
       Judean Baptizer?   53, Conclusions   54
   Jesus and the Pharisees   56
       Who Were the Pharisees?   56, Purity and
       Purpose   59, The Sabbath — Rest or
       Restoration?   66, Fasting or Feasting?   71,
       Banqueting with the Bad   73
   Jesus, Revolutionaries, and Romans   81
       Josephus and the Revolutionaries   81, How
       Revolutionary Was Galilee?   88, Jewish Messianic
       Movements   90, Jesus as a Revolutionary   96,
       Revolutionary Disciples?   96, Revolt in the
       Wilderness?   98, Testing Jesus' Metal   101, A
       Grand Entrance?   104, A Temple Tantrum?   107,
       Conclusions   116

Jesus and the Disciples 118
    Jesus the Charismatic Leader 118, Jesus' Sense of
    Purpose 120, Jesus' Sense of Mission 121, Jesus and
    the Twelve 126, Fishing for Followers 129, Two by
    Two 132, A Radical Renunciation 137, You Be the
    Judge 140, Conclusions 142

3. Christology and the Deeds of Jesus 145
   Jesus the Visionary 145
       The Fall of Satan 146, The Rise of the Son 148
   Miracles and Mighty Signs 155
       Miracles and Magic in Antiquity 156, Jesus
       and the *"theios aner"* Concept 160,
       The Handling of Miracles in Mark and Q 161, Jesus'
       Interpretation of His Miracles 164, No Sign of
       Approval 168, Eyesight to the Blind 170,
       Unseasonable Expectations? 173
   Conclusions 175

4. Christology and the Words of Jesus 179
   Jesus as Teacher and Preacher 179
       Jesus' Hermeneutics 185, "Amen, I Say" 186,
       David's Son or David's Lord? 189
   Jesus and the Dominion of God 191
       What Is the *Basileia?* 192, The Coming and Power
       of the Dominion of God 198, The Mystery of
       the *Meshalim* 206
   Abba and Filial Consciousness 215
       Abba 216, Inside Information 221,
       Heaven Knows 228
   The Son of Man 233
       Background Issues: Enoch and His Kin 234,
       Jesus' Language 236, *Bar enash* in Daniel 7 and
       1 Enoch 238, Possible Gospel Allusions to
       Similitudes and Daniel 240, The Son of Man and His
       Itinerant Lifestyle 243, The Son of Man
       Manhandled 250, A Ransom for Many 251,
       "Trailing Clouds of Glory" 256, Conclusions 261

5. Afterword and Conclusions 263
   Wrede's "Messianic Secret" Motif 263
   Jesus' Self-Perception 267
Abbreviations 279
Bibliography 285
Index 302

Preface

BECAUSE IT HAS been now almost 40 years since E. Käsemann and others launched the new quest for the historical Jesus, and because some modern scholars continue to be skeptical about the possibility of saying anything significant about the historical Jesus' self-understanding, it may rightly be asked, Why this book and why now? The reasons are several.

First, we are only now in a position to assess the relevance for the study of Jesus and benefit from the tremendous amount of work that J. H. Charlesworth and others have done on the extracanonical literature of early Judaism. This data is especially germane to the study of the Son of man material and to helping us to see the scope and character of messianic expectations in early Judaism.

Second, a renewed optimism exists in many parts of the scholarly guild today that something significant can indeed be known about the historical Jesus and even about his self-understanding. This is shown by a host of recent scholarly works on Jesus by R. A. Horsley, M. Borg, H. Boers, J. Charlesworth, M. de Jonge, and R. Leivestad to mention but a few.

Third, as will become clear in chapter 1 of this study, some of form criticism's older assumptions about the Jesus material no longer will stand close scrutiny. The more scholarship becomes convinced of the essentially Jewish character of the Jesus material and the likelihood that for several decades it was handled and passed on at least to some extent like Jewish tradition, the less convincing arguments become that suggest the synoptic material developed rather like pure folklore. M. Hengel has also reminded us that in the main the dilemma of the gospel writer was not how to create enough material to present a reasonably full portrait of Jesus but rather how to edit a considerable array of sources and types of material down to manageable size (cf. Luke 1:1-4).

Finally, the scholarly work currently being done in the Jesus Seminar and in Q studies has in various ways raised once again questions about the portrait of Jesus that arises especially from the sayings material. Yet it is not sufficient to pursue this matter simply by examining the sayings material, or the titles, or for that matter any other single type of material in the Jesus tradition. Perhaps the most significant problem with some of the most recent studies on Jesus is the tendency to focus too much on one or another type of material to the exclusion of the rest of the evidence. Thus, for example, E. P. Sanders bases too much on what he takes to be the reasonably certain facts about Jesus' life. It would seem, then, that the time is propitious for presenting a broad-scale study on the self-understanding of Jesus, approaching the matter from different angles and seeing what all the evidence that can be reasonably argued to go back to a *Sitz im Leben Jesu* will reveal to us.

Throughout this study I have sought to provide a good sense translation of quotes from German, French, or other languages, rather than a more literal rendering. Unless otherwise indicated, all translations are my own. In addition to the usual system of abbreviations, short titles keyed to the bibliography are used. Because of this both abbreviations and bibliography are grouped at the end.

This book has been made possible only through the aid of many people. I would like to express my appreciation to C. K. Barrett, Richard Hays, N. T. Wright, as well as the late John Hollar of Fortress Press for their scholarly advice. Also, I should like to thank Brad Weidenheimer, our librarian, who diligently sought out many necessary books and articles not available at Ashland Theological Seminary Library. For the preparation of the bibliography I am grateful to Lori Lower of ATS. Finally, I must give credit to my wife, Ann, who carefully types, edits, and critiques my work. On a personal level, this book is dedicated to my parents, Ben and Joyce Witherington. On an academic level, this study is dedicated to John Hollar (in memoriam), who guided me and made possible the publication of this book, and to C. K. Barrett, to whom I owe a great debt as my mentor.

Ben Witherington, III

Methodological and Historical Considerations

STRANGE AS IT may seem, the question whether Jesus himself had a Christology has not been explored in a systematic way. This lacuna has not been for a lack of approaches. Since the beginning of the new quest for the historical Jesus in the 1950s, both exegetes and theologians have been preoccupied with Christologies in and of the New Testament—the Gospels, Paul, Q, or other sources. Some have sought to isolate the Christologies of individual communities, even though there is little evidence that any community had a pure form of Christology as characterized by the use of one title or type of thinking or preaching.[1] Exploring the Christologies of the New Testament is important, but doing this in place of a Christology of Jesus is a fundamental mistake because, as de Jonge says, "any survey of the early Christian response to Jesus should start with at least a brief outline of what Jesus thought and told about himself. How did he understand his relation to God and his role in God's dealings with Israel and humanity?"[2]

Persons familiar with the historical-critical approach to the New Testament might not find this lack of studies on Jesus' Christology strange, since some form critics, because of their assumptions as to how the church had handled the Jesus tradition, virtually ruled out all possible concrete knowledge about the historical Jesus' views on various subjects. The resurrection of Jesus—or the resurrection experiences of Jesus' first followers, as they maintained—generated a christological approach to Jesus and the Jesus

---

[1] M. de Jonge, *Christology in Context*, 19, following N. Dahl. On the matter of the Christology of the so-called Q community, cf. pp. 223–24 below.

[2] Ibid., 20.

material. Thus, a great chasm was fixed between the historical Jesus and the church's later views of Jesus as Christ, Lord, or Son of God. This is a serious error because, as de Jonge notes:

> Jesus is at the center of all early (and later) Christology. This presupposes some degree of continuity between what he said and did and people's reactions. It also presupposes some continuity between the situation of his followers before Jesus' cross and resurrection and their situation after those events.[3]

In a similar way, L. W. Hurtado concludes: "a key factor that must be taken into account in understanding the rise of early Christian devotion to Jesus is the pre-Easter ministry of Jesus and its effects upon his followers."[4] In other words, it is no longer necessary nor sufficient simply to assume that historically there must have been a radical difference between the way Jesus viewed and presented himself and the way the early church interpreted him.[5]

In this book, I intend to state as much as I think is plausible about how Jesus viewed himself, particularly with respect to christological matters, in an attempt to associate Christian faith with the life of the Jesus of history.[6] It is one thing, however, to say Christian faith is based on the facts of Jesus' life and quite another to maintain that faith is based on our ability to establish, much less prove, the reality of those facts by the historical-critical method. Because Christian faith long antedated the historical-critical method, no necessary dependency can be posited of faith on this method. Historical-critical method functions to cast doubt on or provide support for the authenticity of various historical traditions. In this sense, I remain committed to the historical-critical method, including the possibilities and limitations of form criticism.[7] What follows, therefore, should be seen as an attempt to underscore the value of the study of the forms in which the

---

[3] Ibid., 21.

[4] L. W. Hurtado, *One God, One Lord,* 116.

[5] Cf. R. Morgan, "The Historical Jesus and the Theology of the New Testament," 193. Some scholars have even assumed that accepting such a radical gulf between Jesus as he presented himself and as the post-Easter Christians viewed him is the prerequisite to being considered rational in the modern era. Cf. H. Conzelmann, *Jesus,* 5: "The historical and substantive presupposition for modern research into the life of Jesus is emancipation from traditional Christological dogma on the basis of the principle of reason."

[6] Cf. H. Boers, *Who Was Jesus?* 94: "The question of whether a particular saying was actually pronounced by Jesus is not only impossible to answer but, from the point of view of the developing Christian religion, irrelevant. What was important about Jesus for the developing Christian religion was not so much the concrete facts of his life but the impact he had made on his followers, as reflected in the tradition of his life and teachings and in the legends of his birth and childhood." Thus, on Boers's view, we arrive at the anomaly that the Christian faith is only directly based and dependent on the historical impressions the disciples had of Jesus, whether those impressions were true or false.

[7] Ben Witherington, "Principles for Interpreting the Gospels and Acts," 35–70.

synoptic material was passed down. I also value related sorts of literary criticism, including rhetorical and genre criticism.

FORMAL ARGUMENTS

Particular assumptions about the nature and transmission of the gospel material congruent with Bultmann and Dibelius's formal analyses need to be contested.[8] Bultmann claims that the early church did not perceive (or at least did not make) a distinction between the pre-Easter sayings of Jesus and the post-Easter inspired utterances of (anonymous?) Christian prophets which, he claims, were accepted as the words of the ascended Jesus, and were sometimes accidentally, sometimes deliberately, retrojected into settings in Jesus' ministry.[9] Whereas Bultmann thinks the tradition moved from general fluidity to general fixation, he nonetheless posits that the sayings material was more freely handled in the middle (when a saying of a prophet was accepted as a saying of the ascended Lord), or near the end of the fixation process (when the saying of a prophet or the ascended Lord became a saying of the historical Jesus). The Book of Revelation indicates there were utterances of the ascended Christ spoken through prophets in the early church, but this does not prove either that such utterances were indiscriminately collected with other utterances of Christian prophets, or that sayings of the exalted Lord became sayings of the historical Jesus. Indeed, the evidence from Revelation points in the opposite direction because the sayings of the exalted Lord spoken through a Christian prophet (who is named) are identified precisely as such. This indicates that such sayings were distinguished from the sayings of the historical Jesus.[10]

Even more doubtful is Bultmann's appeal to Odes of Solomon 42.6, not only because it is still widely held that the Odes should be dated after the Gospel material.[11] When one examines the relevant non-Gospel material, we find that Paul distinguishes between his own authoritative utterances and those of his Lord (cf. 1 Cor. 7:10, 12, 25, 40), and 1 Cor. 14:29 indicates that the utterances of the prophets were to be weighed and tested, not accepted as of unquestionable authority as were the Lord's words (cf. 7:10, 12). Even when such prophetic utterances were approved, it is still not clear from this material that they were accorded the same status as, or were indistinguishable from, the words of the historical Jesus. As J. D. G. Dunn

---

[8] Ibid., 44–50. See also, Witherington, "Women and Their Roles in the Gospels and Acts," 59–65.

[9] R. Bultmann, *The History of the Synoptic Tradition*, 122–28.

[10] J. D. G. Dunn, "Prophetic 'I'-Sayings and the Jesus Tradition," 175–98; W. Grudem, "The Gift of Prophecy in 1 Corinthians," 229–35; D. H. Hill, *New Testament Prophecy*, 160–85.

[11] Hill, *Prophecy*, 11ff.

has shown, in both the New Testament and other early Christian literature, there is evidence that Christians, like their Jewish forebears, had a healthy suspicion about prophetic oracles and subjected them to close scrutiny, inquiring about their source. Note that Luke carefully mentions the prophet's name when he cites an oracle (Acts 11:27, 28; 13:1, 2; 21:10).[12]

If the utterances of Christian prophets were valued as highly as the sayings of the earthly Jesus, then the rationale for retrojecting them back into the ministry of Jesus is lacking.[13] Further, how has it happened, if the early church retrojected prophetic material into a ministry setting, that we have little or no Gospel material dealing with some of the major crises of the early church over circumcision, baptism, the relationship of Jews to Gentiles—including table fellowship with Gentiles, and the basis for acceptance among Jesus' people? Can we legitimately assume that all these matters were settled when the Gospels were written or that none of them was an issue for the evangelists?[14] Although it is possible that the sayings of Christian prophets or the exalted Lord were at some point (accidentally?) attributed to the earthly Jesus, the evidence is not convincing and cannot be used to argue that the original *Sitz im Leben* of much of the Gospel sayings material is the post-Easter Christian community.[15]

Certainly M. E. Boring has made a case that we have a substantial number of sayings of Christian prophets in the Synoptics.[16] Boring candidly admits that "we have no primary sources except whatever sayings from Christian prophets may be contained in the Synoptic tradition itself. [And] it is a defective method to identify prophetic logia in the tradition on the basis of a characterization construed from this same tradition."[17] How, then,

---

[12] Dunn, "Prophetic 'I'-Sayings," 179.

[13] W. Grudem, "Gift of Prophecy," 230, points out that there is no evidence outside the Gospels of inspired prophetic speech being transformed into a historical narrative whether we examine the other New Testament documents or extant Jewish writings.

[14] C. F. D. Moule, *The Phenomenon of the New Testament*, 43–81; T. W. Manson, *Studies in the Gospels and Epistles*, 7, points out: "The Pauline letters abound in utterances which could easily be transferred to Jesus and presented to the world as oracles of the Lord. How many are? None. It seems a little odd that if the story of Jesus was the creation of the Christian community no use should be made of the . . . Pauline material."

[15] Even in the case of the "I am" discourses in the Fourth Gospel, what we may have is theological elaboration of certain motifs from the ministry of the historical Jesus. To elaborate the meaning of Jesus' life work, his words and deeds, is not the same as claiming to speak *as* Jesus or the risen Lord under inspiration. Theological elaboration must not be confused with prophetic speech. Even in the case of prophetic speech, it is one thing to speak for God with the qualifier, "thus sayeth the Lord," it is another thing to speak *as* God or the risen Lord without such qualifiers. I would not rule out Schürmann's suggestion that the Johannine discourses have as their point of departure the private discussions Jesus had with his disciples before Easter about his life and purpose. Nevertheless, I shall neither build anything on such a conjecture nor treat these discourses as a source of historical information.

[16] Especially in "How May We Identify Oracles of Christian Prophets in the Synoptic Tradition?" 501–21, where Boring sets out his methodology; and in *Sayings of the Risen Jesus*, where he develops his case in detail.

[17] Boring, "Oracles," 503.

does one get around such an impasse? First, Boring suggests that one should sift the rest of early Christian literature both within and without the canon to discern the character and form of early Christian prophecy. Second, if one has a saying that on other grounds is widely regarded as secondary, one should examine it to see if it might be an utterance of a Christian prophet.[18] Boring believes that such oracles of the risen Lord arose separately from and were combined with the sayings traditions in the period A.D. 30–70. After that period, he believes, prophecy and Gospel tradition became literary phenomena in their own right, and thus the intermixing of the materials ceased.

Because we have already discounted some of the evidence from Revelation that might support Boring's case, we will now examine the rest of his evidence. First, Boring points to several sayings in the Pauline material that he thinks are or point to prophetic oracles of Paul himself— Rom. 11:25–27; 1 Cor. 15:51–52; 1 Thess. 4:15–17. In two of these sayings the key material is introduced with a reference to a mystery that is now being disclosed, which sets the utterance off from other pronouncements. This word *mystery* occurs only once in the whole of the synoptic tradition in the obscure saying about the purpose of Jesus' parables (Mark 4:11; Matt. 13:11; Luke 8:10)! Many scholars consider that saying secondary. Thus the use of the word *mysterion* helps us find only one possible Christian prophetic utterance in the Synoptics. Furthermore, the eschatological or even apocalyptic content of the two sayings in Romans does not distinguish them from other sayings we find in the synoptic tradition, some of which likely go back to a *Sitz im Leben Jesu*.

The most plausible Pauline example is 1 Thess. 4:15–17, a teaching about the parousia and events surrounding it. Paul does not say that this material is a prophecy, but that it is *en logo kyriou*, which may mean "in the teaching of the Lord." Paul could be alluding to the teachings of the earthly Jesus or to those of the risen Lord. Certainly, there are some eschatological utterances that may have come from the earthly Jesus about the future coming of the Son of Man and the circumstances surrounding that event.[19] Recall also that in 1 Corinthians 7 Paul clearly distinguishes between his own utterances and those of the Lord. Thus, even in the most plausible of the examples from the Pauline literature there is room to doubt that Paul is claiming these teachings came ultimately from the risen Lord rather than the

---

[18] Boring follows this methodology not only in his older articles on prophecy but also in his most recent work, *Sayings of the Risen Jesus*, 55–57. Notice he also adds that a Synoptic saying must be seen to have existed independently from a narrative context, as a prerequisite to seeing it as a possible example of early Christian prophecy. This is a crucial point and means that by and large, Boring's approach has to do with the Q material and *not* Mark, whom he thinks was opposed to the type of detached sayings collection that Q represents (230–34).

[19] See pp. 256–61 below on Mark 14:62–63.

earthly Jesus.[20] Nor do these sayings encourage us to think he confused or made no distinction between the two sorts of utterances.[21]

Boring also cites the classic example of Agabus found in Acts 11:27-29; 21:10-11. Unfortunately for Boring's case, Luke explicitly tells us that Agabus's prophecy came to him not from the risen Lord, but from the Holy Spirit (21:11; cf. 11:28). Thus Boring argues unconvincingly that Luke has changed an original reference to the risen Lord so that the Holy Spirit is now credited as the source of this utterance—a conjecture without textual basis but with a thematic basis because Luke does stress the Holy Spirit in his two-volume work.[22]

Besides eschatological content, Boring lists three other features that he believes distinguish Christian prophetic speech—initial Amen, chiasmus, and legal form.[23] Jesus probably spoke, Boring admits, on some eschatological matters and used the initial Amen to introduce these and other kinds of sayings. Because Boring allows that Jesus himself probably spoke some prophetic oracles, a prophecy cannot be taken automatically as an utterance of a later Christian prophet. In fact, Boring candidly admits that "since Jesus was himself something of a charismatic figure, who is frequently portrayed in the Gospels as a prophet . . . authentic sayings are also likely to manifest prophetic traits."[24]

In regard to chiasmus, New Testament scholars frequently are unable to agree whether or not a certain saying, hymn, or passage manifests this structuring device. It seems that chiasmus is more in the eye of the beholder than in the text itself. In regard to the so-called law words that E. Käsemann and others have categorized, I neither focus on these sayings nor base any conclusions on them. Some of these law sayings may not go back to the historical Jesus and may have come from Christian teachers or other authority figures rather than from early Christian prophets. There is nothing in such sayings, however, that strongly leads us to think they came from prophets.

Thus, although Boring has made a case for finding sayings of Christian prophets in the Synoptics, his criteria for discerning such sayings and his results are disputable. Boring concludes: "Has it been demonstrated in the preceding pages that sayings of Christian prophets can be identified within

---

[20] The mere use of the term *kyrios* of the historical Jesus whether in the Synoptics or in the Pauline material does not prove that an author was incapable of or uninterested in distinguishing what Jesus said before Easter and after Easter. The use of *kyrios* only makes clear that the author identifies the historical person Jesus with the risen Lord. All utterances and actions of the risen Lord are not automatically predicated of Jesus during his earthly ministry.

[21] The more detailed investigation of this matter and arguments against the sort of case that Boring wants to make may be found in E. Cothenet, "Prophetisme dans le Nouveau Testament"; cf. G. Delling, "Gepragte Jesus-Tradition im Urchristentum."

[22] Boring, "Oracles," 508-9.

[23] Ibid., 515.

[24] Boring, *Sayings*, 57.

the Synoptic tradition? No."[25] I would agree. He has neither given us any sure means by which to detect that a synoptic saying may come from a Christian prophet nor provided convincing evidence that the early church intentionally transferred sayings of the risen Lord (which Revelation shows were extant) to the earthly Jesus in the synoptic material. In view of Boring's admission that his study may lead to the verdict of *non liquet,* the burden of proof should be on those who claim there are early Christian prophetic utterances in the Synoptics. Granted, there is secondary or redactional material in the Synoptics. It is one thing, however, to demonstrate that a saying is secondary and quite another to demonstrate it is an early Christian prophecy.

What, then, is the character of the Gospel tradition and how did it develop? The contention that it developed in a manner analogous to the growth of folk literature has rightly been subjected to close scrutiny. Although comparisons of this kind are natural and needful, similarities in form or content do not prove that the origin or development of the two sets of material are the same. A selective comparison leads to questionable conclusions, as is the case with the studies of Dibelius and Bultmann. Neither scholar, as E. P. Sanders has shown, made a systematic attempt to see how various sorts of folk stories developed over a period of time, perhaps because of the difficulties of finding, dating, and relating various versions of a story. Instead, the form critics apparently derived their laws of transmission by assuming that purity of form indicates relative antiquity and by examining how the first evangelist and Luke used Mark and Q and how later Christian literature used the canonical Gospels. Sanders notes, "the form critics did not show, outside of the Synoptic Gospels, that there was a body of tradition which had at first existed in pure forms, but whose purity of form had been corrupted by the passage of time."[26] Further, the majority of the synoptic data seems to be of mixed form. Thus, it is not clear whether the so-called pure forms were earlier and then corrupted or later and the result of good editing.

Dibelius clearly derives his laws of development by analyzing the needs and activities of the Christian communities and by positing that a certain need requires a certain form of material. Any variation from that form indicates development. In practice, Dibelius admits that comparisons with folk literature are hard pressed to reveal how Christian material developed because folk literature does not grow out of the same kind of community with the same kind of needs.[27] More consistently, Bultmann distinguishes between laws of formation and laws of transmission. The former he discovers by analyzing comparative literature, the latter almost exclusively

---

[25] Ibid., 230.

[26] E. P. Sanders, *The Tendencies of the Synoptic Tradition*, 22–26.

[27] Cf. M. Dibelius, *From Tradition to Gospel*, 288–89; Sanders, *Tendencies*, 14–15.

by studying the Gospels and their interrelationships. In the work of both Bultmann and Dibelius, then, "the laws of transmission have not been established outside the Christian material itself."[28]

The problem of selective use of examples arises even when Bultmann draws conclusions about how the Gospel material developed from his study of the Gospels' interrelationships. For instance, Bultmann argues that details (names, places, and so on) often were added to the tradition as it developed. His explanation for the many cases in which Mark includes, and the parallels omit, such details is usually an appeal to an *Ur-Markus* hypothesis. In fact, although the evidence is mixed, Sanders shows that Mark is usually more detailed than the parallels.[29] Thus, the assumption is suspect that the Gospel traditions originally were rather bland and anonymous, and that names and details later were attached to give life to the story in order to connect it with figures important to the history of early Christianity or at least to some part of the early church.

The appropriateness of appealing to the laws of formation of folk literature to explain the formation of the Gospel material is questionable for five reasons: (1) usually the material used as a basis of comparison developed over a much longer period of time than the Gospel's 40- to 70-year gestation period; (2) the folk literature appealed to seldom is dealing with historical events to the same degree, if at all, that the Gospels are; (3) various factors—eyewitnesses, reverence for the historical figure being written about—probably acted as a restraint on the degree of embellishment of the Gospel material, unlike the case with much of folk literature; (4) even in the rabbinic literature that provides the closest parallels there is nothing comparable to the Gospel's focus on, proclamation of, and belief in one person;[30] and (5) it is more probable that the first disciples of Jesus and the earliest post-Easter community would have passed on his words and deeds in a way that showed as much respect for the tradition as Jewish students showed their teachers' words and deeds in the first century than have allowed the tradition to undergo radical transformation in ways analogous to folk literature.[31]

It is plausible that Jesus' first disciples used techniques of transmission common in their milieu, for example, memorization, repetition, and even brief note taking. There is evidence that Jesus used various mnemonic

---

[28] Sanders, *Tendencies*, 19, who adds on pp. 21–22, "To my knowledge this has never been done."

[29] Ibid., 151–83.

[30] Cf. R. E. Brown, "After Bultmann, What?"; P. Benoit, "Réflexions sur la Formgeschichtliche Methode"; and, E. E. Ellis, "New Directions in Form Criticism."

[31] Cf. H. Riesenfeld, *The Gospel Tradition and Its Beginnings*; B. Gerhardsson, *Memory and Manuscript*; B. Gerhardsson, *Tradition and Transmission in Early Christianity*; and for a valuable critique of the Gerhardsson theory, cf. W. D. Davies, *The Setting of the Sermon on the Mount*, 464–80.

devices, suggesting that he sought to make his teaching both memorable and memorizable.[32] Yet one must be cautious in assuming that Jesus' sayings were treated in the same way later rabbinic material was handled. As Schürmann has pointed out, Jesus was both more and other than a rabbi because it appears he intended his words to be taken as a revelation of God's eschatological plans. This would make the preservation of the form of the material important if the contents were to be passed on intact to other believers.[33] The disciples, however, seemed to be more concerned to conserve, pass on, and apply to new situations Jesus' meaning than his exact words. That is, the material is dependent on the *Sitz im Leben* for its specific formulation. Translation of the sayings tradition from Aramaic into Greek at an early date shows that the preservation of the exact form of the words and linguistic idiom was not essential for the early Christians. This factor, along with theological purpose, may account for many of the divergences in wording in parallel Gospel traditions. Nevertheless, the traditions that the Gospel writers employed were community property; the evangelists were not as free in shaping them as they would have been had they created these materials. As G. Hughes puts it, "for those who lived as contemporaries with the transmission process, there was a genuine possibility of testing the information given by the writer . . . over against the traditions, [which are] the public property of the community within which the traditions have been received . . . ; but this implies, in turn, that his [the biblical writer's] picture of Jesus is not at his beck and call but is subject to some degree of historical scrutiny."[34]

The question then becomes: To what degree of historical scrutiny? M. Hengel has demonstrated that the categories of Hellenistic and Palestinian are no longer adequate guides for distinguishing the earlier and later strata in the Gospel material.[35] In particular that a saying or tradition has a Hellenistic flavor is no certain sign of its lateness.

Furthermore, J. N. Sevenster, R. H. Gundry, and recent studies on the character of Galilee in particular make clear that Greek was widely known in first-century Palestine, especially in Galilee.[36] In fact, the archaeological evidence indicates that both literate and basically illiterate Jews (both scribes and fishermen) would have known at least enough Greek to do business in a mixed-language milieu. Galileans in particular had considerable contact with Greek-speaking people. Sevenster concludes that "no matter how very

---

[32] For instance, C. F. Burney, *The Poetry of Our Lord.*

[33] H. Schürmann, "Die Vorosterlichen Anfange der Logientradition," 65.

[34] G. Hughes, *Hebrews and Hermeneutics: The Epistle to the Hebrews as a New Testament Example of Biblical Interpretation.* SNTS Monograph 36 (Cambridge, 1979), 92. Hughes, to be sure, focuses on Hebrews, but what he says applies even more to the Gospels and especially the Synoptics.

[35] M. Hengel, *Judaism and Hellenism.*

[36] Cf. J. N. Sevenster, *Do You Know Greek?* 176–91; R. H. Gundry, *The Use of the Old Testament in St. Matthew's Gospel,* 178–204. I will discuss the more recent works of S. Freyne in chap. 2.

superficial and sketchy that knowledge was, many from all layers of society understood it [Greek] and were able to speak and write it."[37] Thus, it is possible that Jesus' disciples, even before Easter, began to translate Jesus' sayings into Greek for the benefit of people in Palestine. Indeed, Jesus himself may have spoken publicly in Greek, if the crowd being addressed was sufficiently diverse. Further, as H. C. Kee has suggested, it was likely part of Jesus' plan to address a wider audience than simply small-town and Aramaic-speaking Galileans, as both his taking up residence in the cross-roads town, Capernaum, and various traditions about his travels and contacts beyond the scope of Israel suggest.[38]

These considerations do not yield the conclusion that Jesus mainly spoke Greek (the Aramaic phrases from Jesus found in Mark suggest otherwise), even though he may well have done so in the Decapolis or when encountering a Syro-Phoenician, for example. My point is that neither the language nor time factor can any longer be claimed as a significant barrier between the New Testament critic and some of the earliest stages of the tradition. That the Jesus material comes to us in Greek is no sure indication that this material has gone through a long or convoluted process of evolution. If proclamation of the life and sayings of Jesus began shortly after Easter—or, in the case of some of Jesus' words and deeds, even before Easter—then translation of Jesus' sayings and the stories about him may have begun even in the A.D. 30s. Both Dodd and Stanton have shown that there was an interest not only in Jesus' words but also in his deeds in early Christian preaching.[39]

The assumption that the translation of the Gospel material into Greek was not undertaken for a long time after its proclamation in Aramaic made plausible the assumption that considerable changes and corruption took place in the material before it was ever rendered into Greek. Such an assumption, however, ignores or too easily dismisses the careful work of Jeremias and M. Black on the Aramaic background of the sayings tradition in the Gospels. When such work is taken seriously, then it appears likely either that there was a substantial and relatively fixed Aramaic tradition from an early date which lies behind much of the sayings material we find in the Gospels, or that this Aramaic material if not fixed at a very early date, was nonetheless translated at a very early date into Greek. This would account for the fact that a great deal of the sayings material can be readily

---

[37] *Do You Know Greek?* 185–86.

[38] "The Import of Archaeological Investigations in Galilee for Scholarly Reassessment of the Gospels." Paper delivered at the SBL Meeting November 1989.

[39] Cf. C. H. Dodd, *The Apostolic Preaching and Its Development*. London: Hodder and Stoughton, 1944; G. N. Stanton, *Jesus of Nazareth in New Testament Preaching*, SNTS Monograph 27 (Cambridge, 1974).

translated back into Aramaic and manifests various sorts of Semitisms. After pursuing the matter for many years, Black reevaluated his work:

> For the sayings and teachings of Jesus, however, there is little doubt that the bulk of Semitisms are translation phenomena and have arisen in the process of translating and paraphrasing the *verba ipsissima* of Jesus. . . . I have seen no reason to change the conclusions which I reached in my *Aramaic Approach to the Gospels and Acts* that an Aramaic tradition (oral or written) lies behind the sayings of Jesus (in the Fourth Gospel as well as the Synoptics).[40]

Significantly, those New Testament scholars in the modern era who have been the most well-versed in both Aramaic and Greek have tended to draw rather conservative conclusions about the state of the sayings material as we find them in the Gospels.[41]

Determining the *Sitz im Leben* of a pericope by analyzing its Gospel and pre-Gospel form(s) needs to be discussed. Often the form of a saying or pericope will give only a clue to its original *Sitz im Leben*, especially in cases when the same form was used in different situations for various reasons. The variety of views about the original *Sitz im Leben* of most pericopes alone demonstrates that only in a minority of cases does form clearly indicate the *Sitz im Leben*. Form criticism has been useful primarily in the study of pronouncement and miracle stories. In the remainder of the Gospel material, the form categories suggested (for example, legends) tell us little about a narrative's form, dealing instead with content and implying a judgment on the material's historical value.[42]

As Bultmann recognized, Dibelius's statement, "in the beginning was the sermon," was unduly restrictive in his attempt to encapsulate the situation that gave rise to the various Gospel forms. A variety of activities led to a variety of forms of tradition. As Schürmann has shown, it is also unwarranted to restrict the potential *Sitz im Leben* of a Gospel pericope to the post-Easter community. The inner life of Jesus' itinerant followers, as well as the outer life of that group who apparently went out to proclaim the good news during the ministry of Jesus, provided the sociological conditions in which Jesus' words and deeds could have begun to take on a somewhat fixed form

---

[40] M. Black, "Second Thoughts 9. The Semitic Element in the New Testament," *ET* 77 (1965): 20–23.

[41] The judgment of Jeremias is by now famous (or infamous): in the Synoptics it is the inauthenticity not the authenticity of the sayings material that must be demonstrated, *New Testament Theology*, 37. This study, however, will not presume the authenticity of the material with which we are dealing, because many scholars do not share Jeremias's optimism.

[42] V. Taylor, *The Formation of the Gospel Tradition*, 32. Even in the miracle stories it is hard to see how certain elements such as the statement of the illness, the fact and nature of the cure, the proof or result of healing, could have been omitted and there still be a miracle story. One must be open to the possibility that the course of events necessitated that certain elements be included in the account of the events.

prior to Easter.[43] It is necessary to distinguish between the situation or event that gave rise to a tradition and the conditions in which a tradition was *actualized,* that is, collected and passed on in a relatively fixed form by Jesus' disciples.[44] In the case of a saying, it is possible that Jesus himself formed the tradition. In the case of a narrative, what *Sitz im Leben Jesu* normally means is that the tradition, although formed after Easter, arose out of the pre-Easter events and the discussion and relating of those events by Jesus' disciples. No one is contending that narratives (apart from the *meshalim,* if one wants to call them narratives) came from Jesus' lips. Even if the tradition was not actualized until after Easter, it does not follow that the church created the narrative out of non-historical material. To form a tradition about certain events is not the same as inventing the circumstances narrated.

My view of the origins of the Gospel tradition is based on some of the earliest New Testament documents (Paul's letters to Thessalonica and Corinth). At various places in his letters, Paul adopts the technical language used when the transmission and reception of authoritative traditions was being referred to in later rabbinic Judaism (cf. 1 Cor. 11:2, 23; 15:1, 3; 1 Thess. 2:13; 4:1; 2 Thess. 3:6). Paul also speaks of Christian traditions as *paradosis* (cf. 1 Cor. 11:2; 2 Thess. 2:15; 3:6). These facts, although they do not lead to the conclusion that the Jesus tradition was passed on in exactly the same manner as the Jewish material, do establish one point:

> Early Christianity is conscious of the fact that it has a tradition of its own including many traditions which the Church teachers hand on to the congregations, which the congregations receive, and which they then are to guard and to live after. In Paul's times there existed a conscious, deliberate . . . transmission in the early Church.[45]

What sort of traditions were being passed on in Paul's day? A variety of traditions may have included: narrative and sayings material involving the last supper (cf. 1 Cor. 11:23ff. which supports the view that the passion narrative was fixed relatively early); credal summaries and lists of witnesses to Jesus' appearances (1 Cor. 15:1, 3, 4); important sayings of Jesus (1 Cor. 7:10, 11); and ethical exhortations to follow Jesus' or Paul's example, or the church's ethical teaching (1 Thess. 2:13; 4:1, 2; 2 Thess. 2:15; 3:6; Gal. 1:9). This shows that not only the sayings of Jesus but also other traditions – some ethical, some credal, some narrative – were being passed on by Paul and others in the early church.[46]

---

[43] Schürmann, "Die Vorosterlichen," 39–45.

[44] The term actualized is Gerhardsson's in *Memory and Manuscript,* 331–32.

[45] B. Gerhardsson, *The Origins of the Gospel Tradition,* 28.

[46] It is possible that some of these traditions could have been fused or confused, resulting in some things being attributed to Jesus that ought not to have been. This does not seem to have happened often, probably because the early church *on the whole* does not seem to have manufactured new sayings about the kingdom or Son of man. Further, Jesus' teachings do not seem

Combining the above considerations with Schürmann's work on the pre-Easter *Sitz im Leben* of much of the Gospel material and Dunn's argument about the use of criteria to test and sift early Christian prophecy, a general picture emerges of a tradition that was relatively fixed at an early date, especially in the case of Jesus' sayings. Two factors may have led even in the case of the narrative material to a rather conservative handling of the material: the interest of early Christian preachers in Jesus' deeds as shown by C. H. Dodd and G. N. Stanton; and the concern of Luke and other Hellenistic Christians to convey historical information accurately.[47] Even though it is probably true that Riesenfeld, Gerhardsson, and Riesner have gone too far in stressing both the fixing process and the fixed result in early Christian transmission,[48] W. D. Davies is right to stress that the Jewish milieu of the earliest tradition and a respect in the community for Jesus, his words, and deeds probably exercised a conserving and conservative influence on the tradition.[49]

Two additional factors militate against a radical chasm between the historical Jesus and the faith of the early church. First, we need to reckon, according to Hengel, with the editing and condensing of a vast amount of source material by the evangelists (cf. Luke 1:1ff; John 20:30).[50]

> The earliest stage was not the isolated individual tradition, but the elemental wealth of impressions called forth by the meteoric appearance of Jesus. Then still during Jesus' lifetime, there began a process of collection which at the same time meant selection and restriction.[51]

The process of editing and limiting is shown, for example, when we examine how the first evangelist handles his Markan source material. Some expansion of the source material is also in evidence and here we may learn about the concerns of the evangelists and the early Christians. This does not warrant the assumption, however, that the evangelists or their early Christian predecessors were the creators of the Gospel tradition, or especially of the sayings tradition. As I. H. Marshall says:

> It is clear that the basic tradition of the sayings of Jesus was *modified* both in the tradition and by the Evangelists in order to re-express its significance for new situations; it is by no means obvious that this basic tradition was created

---

to have provided a precedent for the church's ethical teaching, such as the household codes. We do not find relevant sayings on the lips of Jesus during the ministry about many things important to the early church, such as Christian baptism or circumcision, which suggests there was some care in separating the traditions of Jesus from later church traditions.

[47] Witherington, "Women in the Gospel and Acts," 69–70, 73–74, 77–80.

[48] Cf. below, pp. 16–17.

[49] Cf. *Setting*, 464–80, and his "Reflexions on Tradition" 127–59. The Q material especially comports in its form with what we might expect from a Jewish milieu.

[50] Cf. *Acts*, 11.

[51] Ibid., 25.

by the early church. Similarly, it is unlikely that the stories about Jesus and the narrative settings for his teaching are [all] products of the church's *Sitz im Leben*. The fact that such material was found to be congenial for use in the church's situation is no proof it was created for this purpose.[52]

Second, the assumption that we may attribute the Jesus tradition to *Gemeindetheologie* is faulty according to P. G. Müller.[53] Jesus spoke not in a historical vacuum but in a very particular (social, economic, political, and religious) setting with others who lived in the same milieu, including disciples, sympathizers, large and small crowds, and even opponents. How could a *Gemeindetheologie* arise that, unlike rabbinic literature, focused on one particular Jew—and a crucified one at that—and was concerned with his ongoing significance?[54] How did it happen that a collection of Jesus' logia was made if his words were not remembered and preserved by some? Müller maintains that this sort of collection was made because "Jesus must be seen as a factual participant in the communication process . . . of his time, his preaching was no monologue, but the result of social interaction in a speech process in which Jesus himself was a Sender as well as a Receiver."[55] Furthermore, Jesus spoke not only in the midst of an esoteric and private group of disciples but also in public. Much of what he said we moderns would deem *mass communication*.[56] In such a setting was it possible for some sort of radical amnesia to take place about Jesus' actual words and deeds not only for his adherents but also for his opponents? In view of the later antagonistic relationship between Judaism and Christianity, surely the early church took care about what they placed on Jesus' lips because others besides his followers heard him speak. Jesus himself was a speech event that was a challenge to his immediate context—to ongoing discussion and interpretation. Thus, Müller stresses that:

> the speech of Jesus (. . . in both word and deed . . .) methodologically can not be severed from the speech of the Community focusing on him. . . . [Rather] . . . the linguistic explication in the *Gemeindetheologie* stands in genetic connection with the speech of Jesus in Word and Deed. [Thus] the line from the historical Jesus as speaker to the Community concerned with speaking about Jesus in a Christological fashion must . . . be borne in mind more if the question about the historical Jesus and his authentic presence in the text of the New Testament is put.[57]

---

[52] *The Gospel of Luke: A Commentary on the Greek Text*, NICNT (Exeter: Paternoster Press, 1978), 33.

[53] P. G. Müller, *Der Traditionsprozess im Neuen Testament*.

[54] Cf. E. P. Sanders, *Paul and Palestinian Judaism*, 70.

[55] *Der Traditionsprozess*, 128.

[56] Ibid., 129.

[57] Ibid., 116–17.

What Jesus said was not fully understood until after Easter, but, as Müller stresses, this very lack of understanding led to more reflection on the actual words and deeds of Jesus.

What, then, was the role of the Easter events in regard to the origins of the Gospel traditions? On the one hand, to argue that most of the synoptic corpus arose as a response to and reflection on the Easter experiences is not convincing, especially when the disciples' experiences are seldom the focus in the Gospel tradition. Furthermore, the resurrection is only rarely alluded to before the passion narrative, and then either in the context of the Jewish debate about such matters (cf. Mark 12:18–27 and par.),[58] or a cursory reference is made without clear reference to Jesus' coming vindication beyond death (e.g., Mark 8:38). On the other hand, what happened as a result of the Easter experiences was not the creation of the Gospel tradition; rather, "through the Easter experiences a new horizon of understanding was opened up."[59] The Easter experiences led to a deeper understanding and appreciation of what Jesus said and did during his ministry, as the later Gospel traditions admit (e.g., John 16:4). As Müller puts it, there was a speech continuity before and after the Easter experiences, and the earlier hearing and reflecting on the speech event of Jesus did not cease but was enhanced by such experiences. Thus, the alleged chasm between the speech event of the historical Jesus and the post-Easter speaking about Jesus probably never existed. This, however, does not prove a christological continuity between Jesus and the early church.[60] That possibility can be explored only through a detailed investigation of the synoptic material—the aim of this study. Nevertheless, the warning of E. Hoskyns and N. Davey should have been heeded long ago:

> The final task of the historian is to gather up the evidence and to describe that event in such a manner that it is shown to lie within the structure of human life and to be intelligible in that context. Further, it must be described in such a manner that the emergence of the primitive church is also intelligible on the basis of the life and death of Jesus of Nazareth. For any historical reconstruction which leaves an unbridgeable gulf between the faith of the primitive

---

[58] In regard to this tradition, it probably was not a later invention of the church because the interlocutors are the Sadducees, not the Pharisees and because we have no evidence of ongoing discussion by Christians with such a group—a discussion not even possible after A.D. 70.

[59] Müller, *Der Traditionsprozess*, 135.

[60] I am also fully cognizant that one ultimately cannot present a comprehensive view of the way that the historical Jesus informs and should inform Christology without taking fully into consideration both his death and its sequel. Cf. Morgan, "The Historical Jesus," 195. In this study, however, our aim is to investigate the ministry itself to see what it may tell us about Jesus' self-understanding. In short, whatever Jesus' death tells us about his self-concept, his life also must be allowed to contribute to the overall picture. The detailed investigation of his death by crucifixion itself deserves a study. I am also aware that the historically reconstructed Jesus provides at most only a partial picture of the so-called real Jesus. Therefore, the phrase 'historical Jesus' needs to be distinguished from the idea of a historically reconstructed Jesus.

church and the historical Jesus must be both inadequate and uncritical: inadequate, because it leaves the origin of the church unexplained; and uncritical, because a critical sifting of the evidence of the New Testament points towards the life and death of Jesus as the ground of primitive Christian faith, and points in no other direction.[61]

The Gerhardsson theory about the origin and transmission of the Gospel materials has been put forward in a revised version by R. Riesner.[62] Rather than proceeding anachronistically and comparing the formation of Gospel material to that of the later rabbinic material, Riesner bases his argument on what can be demonstrated about the nature of learning in the first century, particularly in settings such as the Jewish home and synagogue. Comparison with the rabbinic material was suspect because there is nothing quite comparable in rabbinic literature to the fixation in the Gospels on one teacher's words and deeds and because of the serious problem of projecting practices of Judaism after A.D. 70 back on Jesus' era.

Furthermore, Jesus was not a professional rabbi and in many ways he acted differently from those who later were called rabbis. There is no evidence that he set up a Torah school. Indeed, Jesus' idea of discipleship is more than being a student or *tradent* of a great teacher, although that role was part of discipleship. Whether or not his sayings were treated like Holy Writ can be determined only by examining the Gospel data, not by a priori arguments.

Riesner has obviated a good deal of this sort of criticism by focusing on ancient educational practices that were not confined to settings such as a Torah school. He has shown that learning by heart was the mainstay of education in Jewish homes, synagogues, and elsewhere in the Mediterranean crescent in the early first century. Riesner reminds us that the focus of synagogue worship even in early Judaism was the reciting of Scripture and the exposition of that text, very much like what we find in Luke 4:16–30 (whatever the historical value of that text as a record of an event in Jesus' life). He has also shown, based on the work of S. Freyne and E. Meyers,[63] that in Galilee there was a commitment to the Torah, synagogue training, and the usual staples of a Jewish education. Further, he appears to be correct that up to 80 percent of the synoptic sayings material bears evidence of

----

[61] E. Hoskyns and N. Davey, *The Riddle of the New Testament*, 170.

[62] See his impressive and lengthy study, *Jesus als Lehrer*. A summary of his argument can be found in his "Der Ursprung der Jesus-Überlieferung." Cf. Gerhardsson's reassertion of his own case, although in part using Riesner's work, in "Der Weg der Evangelientradition." For a recent and careful critique of the Gerhardsson theory, see P. H. Davids, "The Gospels and Jewish Tradition: Twenty Years after Gerhardsson." Reference should also be made to Riesner's detailed study of Jewish elementary education and its bearing on the Gospel tradition in "Judische Elementarbildung und Evangelien-Überlieferung."

[63] Cf. pp. 88–90 below.

being cast in poetic form in the Aramaic original,[64] making it both memorable and memorizable. Moreover, Jesus cast his utterances in short and sometimes mnemonic form to aid in the learning.

How, then, do we evaluate these arguments? First, the arguments of Riesner and Gerhardsson are based on general observations about the form of some of the shorter sayings material, but notably not on the *meshalim*, which was perhaps Jesus' most characteristic form of public utterance. Whether this theory fits the facts can only be determined by a detailed study of the Gospel material itself. Gerhardsson did not undertake such a study and Riesner only partially analyzes the synoptic evidence while concentrating on the material that bolsters his case.[65] Gerhardsson admits:

> It is clear that the Jesus tradition is elaborated. The adherents of Jesus have influenced the tradition of Jesus' words, in that they have laid out their meaning and have undertaken certain corrections in wording—through omissions, additions, and reshaping—and for all the sayings they have formulated and reformulated narrative traditions. . . . There is also apparently reason to question, whether or not certain . . . logia and parables in the spirit and style of Jesus were formulated. . . .[66]

This is no small series of qualifications, and it means that any sort of rigid application of the Gerhardsson theory fails when the Synoptics are closely analyzed.

W. Kelber, in reaction to the form critics and the Gerhardsson school, has written a provocative book in which he asserts that oral speech and written texts should be sharply distinguished both in their nature and in what he calls their hermeneutics.[67] Kelber agrees with the theories of A. B. Lord, a specialist in orality, that the spoken and written media are so distinct that the two need to be analyzed very differently.

> Oral and written compositions come into existence under different circumstances. A speaker addresses an audience in front of him, and its presence in turn affects the delivery of his speech. There is a sense in which performer and audience share in the making of the message. An author, by contrast . . . exercise[s] controls over his composition in a manner unknown to the performer of live speech.[68]

Kelber repeatedly talks about oral speech as involving "living words," as opposed to written speech that is seen as a dead abstraction, separable from

---

[64] Cf. Riesner, "Der Ursprung," 507. Here he is relying on the older works of Burney, Jeremias, and others.

[65] Cf. Riesner, *Jesus als Lehrer*, 352ff.

[66] Gerhardsson, "Der Weg der Evangelientradition," 82–83.

[67] W. Kelber, *The Oral and the Written Gospel*.

[68] Ibid., 14–15.

the speaker. He seems to think that written words can be understood apart from a socio-historical context of meaning in a way that is not true of oral speech. He insists that "oral transmission is controlled by the law of social identification rather than by the technique of verbatim memorization."[69] Things are transmitted, he urges, only if the hearer can identify with or appropriate the message heard. Furthermore, there is no such thing as repeating oneself when one speaks orally; "each oral performance is an irreducibly unique creation . . . each moment of speech is wondrously fresh and new."[70] Finally, Kelber claims that oral transmission tends to preserve the essential information but to abandon features that are not met with social approval.[71]

Here only a summary critique of Kelber is possible. First, his criticism of Bultmann and Gerhardsson is correct at various points. Against Bultmann, he is right that there is no speech chasm between Jesus and the early church.[72] Against Gerhardsson, he is right that we do not have any clear evidence that notetaking was a characteristic response of the disciples to their teacher's words during the ministry of Jesus. Kelber is also correct in showing that what we often have in the Synoptics is simply a written record of various sorts of oral traditions; in other words, we are dealing with material that the evangelists did not by and large create out of whole cloth.[73] But Kelber is probably wrong in stating that we have no evidence of pre-gospel textuality because both the Q material and documents such as the Gospel of Thomas seem to offer such evidence.

Second, Kelber tries too hard to distinguish early Christianity as an oral community from the Qumran community as a people grounded in written documents and words. It seems more plausible that, because early Christianity was a development of early Judaism, one must reckon not only with the effect of both the oral and the written sayings on Jesus' followers but also with the interaction of the oral and written on each other. This conclusion has been recently confirmed by L. Hurtado who also points out that Kelber has not done a historical investigation of the level of literacy in Palestine in particular or the Roman empire in general, that Mark seems to be patterned after oral speech and was likely intended for oral performance, and that even texts once written were subject to some modifications due to later editing and copying.[74]

---

[69] Ibid., 24.

[70] Ibid., 30–31.

[71] Ibid.

[72] It is strange that Kelber, after criticizing Bultmann for various matters, proceeds to follow him at particular points by assuming that a vast number of Gospel stories can be treated straightforwardly as folklore.

[73] Kelber's case seems strongest when he is dealing with the Markan healing and exorcism narratives; cf. ibid., 46–57.

[74] L. W. Hurtado, "Textual Fixity in the Synoptic Tradition? A Critique of Werner Kelber" (Paper delivered at the SBL meeting November 1989). On the oral environment and the

That the early followers of Jesus were still in many ways people of the Book is adequately shown both by the overwhelming number of allusions to the Old Testament in some of the earliest written sources (for example, the Markan passion material) and by the primitive catenas of Old Testament texts found in the New Testament. The reality of that sacred tradition surely affected how the early Christians thought about and handled their own new traditions that Jesus and others generated. Frankly, too much of what Kelber wishes to assert is based on research about how oral transmission especially of Balkan folk ballads and epic poetry operates in the modern era. But what we have in the New Testament is not the ancient equivalent of folklore or Aesop's fables, but the story of a historical figure, Jesus of Nazareth. It is also questionable whether the early handlers or proclaimers of the Jesus tradition, including the evangelists, were attempting to mythologize a historical figure. For example the attempt to find a *theos aner* Christology in Mark would seem to have failed.[75] Only in the case of the synoptic parables is the analogy sufficiently close to folklore to warrant the sort of comparisons Kelber would like to make.

Third, too much of Kelber's work exudes a romanticism about oral speech as more living than written speech. Indeed, it is not because words are spoken but because one has direct contact with a living speaker that oral communication can be distinguished from written speech. For instance, it is the gestures and intonation of the speaker, and the possibility of adjusting one's words on an ongoing basis to suit the occasion and audience that gives oral communication certain advantages over written words and not the fact that an encoder's words are spoken. Furthermore, there are varieties of oral speech. Not all varieties are couched in such a way to make them socially acceptable, nor are all forms strongly affected — much less conditioned — by the audience. Various of the minatory sayings in the Gospels suggest confrontation rather than social adaptation to the audience at hand. If the so-called preventive censorship stressed by Kelber was fully operational at the level of oral tradition,[76] then how do we explain so many uncomfortable and enigmatic words of Jesus passed down in the sayings material?

Fourth, Kelber also overemphasizes the low level of literacy in Jesus' environment. The evidence of Sevenster and others shows that even Jewish fishermen had a rudimentary reading knowledge both of their native tongue and of the language of commerce, Koine Greek. The evidence we have from early Judaism does not suggest that only the elite could read and write in Jesus' day. Rather, it suggests that a goodly number of Jews, especially

---

interrelation of the oral to the written in Jesus' age one should also consult P. J. Achtemeier's presidential address given at the SBL meeting in November 1989 (*"Omne verbum sonat:* The New Testament and the Oral Environment of Late Western Antiquity," *JBL* 109 [1990]: 3–27).

[75] Cf. pp. 160–61 below on *theos aner* Christology.

[76] *The Oral and the Written Gospel,* 28–29.

males who did business in a multilingual society and who would be called upon to recite Torah on the Sabbath, had learned such skills in synagogue school and in the home. Remember that Israel was an occupied land, having been influenced by Hellenization and now by the Roman presence. Kelber also overplays the idea that Jesus' movement was a rural one, removed from contexts where writing might be valuable or even required. Lower Galilee was no remote backwater in Jesus' day.[77]

Finally, too much of what Kelber assumes about the Gospel tradition is based on doubtful interpretations of key texts like Luke 10:16 that can easily be understood in the context of Jewish language about the *Shaliach*.[78] If Jesus did commission some of his followers to act as his agents, then this text is perfectly plausible on the lips of Jesus himself.[79] It is not necessary to see this as a text created by a Christian prophet who assumed his words were the very words of the risen and exalted Christ and, thereby, equivalent to the words of the earthly Jesus.

Kelber's work has been influenced in many ways by the more substantial study of E. Güttgemanns.[80] Note that Güttgemanns, like Kelber, is heavily dependent on Lord's work on Balkan epic poets and the way they orally created poetry.[81] Both Kelber and Güttgemanns dismiss the more proximate and Jewish analogies to Gospel traditions in favor of a Balkan folklore analogy. They too hastily claim that epic poetry, particularly oral epic poetry and ballads, is closer in genre or nature to the oral source material that lies behind the written Gospels than any other sort of material. This overlooks not only the long gestation period that epic tales undergo, which is so very different from the Gospel traditions, but also the hints that our Gospel writers are not free-form composers of their material but are limited to a significant degree by the historical substance of what they record, in other words, that their material is based on the testimonies of things actually seen and heard (cf. Luke 1:1-4).

Both Güttgemanns and Kelber overplay the degree to which early Judaism could be called an oral culture. They also disagree with the judgment of Bultmann and others that the composition of the Gospels is simply the completion of the process begun with the first oral traditions. In other words, both authors insist on the discontinuity between oral and written material. Güttgemanns especially stresses the way "the written 'simultaneously objectifies the information' and makes it more easily communicable."[82]

---

[77] Cf. pp. 88-90 below.

[78] Kelber, *Oral and Written Gospel*, 25ff.; cf. J. Fitzmyer, *Luke 10-24*, 856-57.

[79] Cf. below pp. 132-37.

[80] E. Güttgemanns, *Candid Questions Concerning Gospel Form Criticism*.

[81] The key works of A. B. Lord are *Slavic Folklore*, *The Singer of Tales*, and "The Gospels as Oral Traditional Literature."

[82] *Candid Questions*, 198.

Yet the truth is that oral communication also objectifies a speaker's thoughts and is just as subject to misuse and misunderstanding by one's audience as written words are. Oral words can be filtered and dealt with as abstractions or taken out of their original context just as written words can be. The loss of original *Sitz im Leben* happens to both oral and written communication. Furthermore, a great deal of the contrast Güttgemanns wants to make between listener and reader is based on the assumption that oral speech is by nature dialogical.[83] But there are various sorts of oral performances besides dialogue, for example, monologue, prophetic proclamation, instruction, and recitation for the purpose of learning and memorization. Güttgemanns's case requires that there be something inherently dialogical about oral speech that is not true of written words, but he has failed to demonstrate such an extreme claim. Paul's letters are as dialogical as many forms of oral speech.

Güttgemanns's conclusions stress that as a result of Lord's work "for the first time the sociological discontinuity between the oral and the written mode of tradition has been empirically demonstrated with respect to oral literature."[84] This conclusion oversteps the limits of the evidence. What one can say is that in an environment where only oral communication is used (and thus there is no interaction between oral and written media), or when one is using a purely oral medium (such as singing), there are certain traits that distinguish that sort of communication from written communication. The Gospel material, however, neither arose in a purely oral environment nor remained in the transmission of material purely oral at the pre-synoptic stage of development. If the Qumran community is any analogy at all, then probably some of the Gospel material was written down early in order to provide a tangible record of the oral tradition. I am willing to accept the older form-critical suggestion that, at the earliest writing stages of the Gospel material, what we have is a record of or surrogate for the oral tradition. Thus, we are able to find various traits of oral tradition in Mark and Q (for example, the use of mnemonics).[85] This means that there is a continuity between the oral and written at the earliest stages of the written form of the Gospel material. It also means that one should see Mark and the collector(s) of the Q material as more recorders than composers of their material, although in the case of both Mark and Q there is some creative arrangement of the smaller units of tradition as well as some redactional modification and provision of a framework in which to put those smaller units.

Following a traditional critical approach to the Gospels, I am willing to say that by examining the way the first evangelist and Luke handled Mark and Q, the following conclusions can be reached. Not only does the Gospel

---

[83] Ibid., 201–2.
[84] Ibid., 401.
[85] Ibid., 402.

material seem to have been handled rather conservatively but also there is no reason to think it was otherwise when this material was in the oral stage of transmission. Indeed, at the oral stage things may have been less fluid because there was no fixed written text on which one could elaborate. If the analogy with Jewish, non-Christian literature is any guide, then elaboration was more likely to come once there was a relatively fixed and recorded corpus from which to work. Thus, reliance on one's recall of what had been memorized, which would have had a very fixed form, was no longer necessary. Haggadic and Midrashic treatments of a narrative are possible when there is a fixed text in writing and when losing the original is no longer a perceived danger. If Luke's prologue is any guide, then there was an attempt to sift the multiple sources of information available about Jesus' words and deeds. To be sure, each pericope or saying must stand on its own so far as whether or not it goes back to a *Sitz im Leben Jesu,* and in this study *we will not assume the authenticity of any key text.*

METHODOLOGICAL MATTERS

Methodology, according to Robert Funk, is not an indifferent net — it catches what it intends to catch.[86] In many recent efforts to investigate the life of Jesus to see if anything remotely unique much less messianic could be found, not surprisingly the answer has been largely negative. To a great degree this is caused by a failure to fish with a sufficiently large or multi-faceted net. On the one hand those who insist on finding the real Jesus only in certain aphorisms and a small collection of parables that have had to survive an overzealous filtering process to be proclaimed authentic, not surprisingly arrive at the conclusion that Jesus was largely silent about himself. On the other hand, those who insist on relying on certain key actions of Jesus, to the exclusion of the vast majority of his sayings, in order to discover who Jesus really was, are able to conclude that Jesus was simply another Jew interested in restoration theology.

   Although I agree that certain undisputed *facta* — such as Jesus' crucifixion and his relationship with the Baptist — can serve as the lynchpins of an argument that otherwise depends on examining the words, deeds, and relationships of Jesus, these undisputed *facta* are too few to provide an adequate foundation on which to build much of a case. In fact, as the recent criticisms of E. P. Sanders's *Jesus and Judaism* have pointed out, accepting only sayings that seem to cohere with these few accepted facts of Jesus' life are likely to produce a somewhat distorted view of Jesus.[87] The vast majority

---

[86] R. Funk, "Beyond Criticism in Quest of Literacy," 151.

[87] Cf. the critique of B. D. Chilton, "Jesus and Judaism": "Sanders's emphasis on the *facts* . . . about Jesus leads him to take certain short cuts in the exegesis of *logia* whose significance is

of Jesus' sayings, including the ones that most scholars consider authentic, do not have to do with matters such as the Baptist, or Jesus' crucifixion, or his final trip to Jerusalem and the events that ensued.[88]

With the majority of scholars, I suggest we give the most attention to the sayings material if we are to understand how the historical Jesus viewed himself. It is the logia that have obtained a relatively fixed form earlier than any of the other Jesus material and have been passed down in a more fixed form than all the narrative material (with the possible exception of the passion narrative). Nevertheless, in terms of the order of dealing with material it is wise to begin with what is less controversial. In order to provide a general frame of reference, we will begin our study with Jesus' relationships to some of his contemporaries, the Baptist being the first of these, and then examine some of Jesus' deeds and how he evaluated them. Finally, we will focus on some of the more controversial sayings material dealing with the *basileia*, the Son of man, and other related matters.

Still another example of fishing with too small a net is the attempt to interpret Jesus almost solely in light of either his Jewish background or a certain *religionsgeschichtliche* approach. With this approach we end up with a simple Galilean hasid, a peripatetic Cynic philosopher, or even a Hellenistic or Jewish magician.

Another sort of methodological mistake is made when there is an attempt to discern what Jesus thought about himself simply by examining those passages that include some so-called title which Jesus may or may not have used. In all of these cases less is not necessarily more. It is refreshing to find a scholar like Gerd Theissen who freely admits that applying his methodology to the data will not give us the key to understanding Jesus and the movement he initiated.[89] Nonetheless, in the vast majority of recent studies of Jesus there seemingly has been so much specialization, and so many attempts to rule the majority of available data out of bounds from the outset, that any progress in the discussion of Jesus and Christology has been rendered virtually impossible due to a too abrupt methodological foreclosing of the field of focus. In short, the fallacy of mistaking the part for the whole, or ignoring the whole for the sake of concentrating on the part, however superbly and correctly that part has been analyzed, has led to significant distortion. B. F. Meyer stressed that it is wrong to decide

---

central to his thesis." Cf. C. Rowland, "Sanders's Jesus"; and D. Senior, "Jesus and Judaism."

[88] It is too early to assess the results of the famous Jesus Seminar (founded by Robert Funk) which has been voting on the authenticity of various sayings attributed to Jesus in the Gospel tradition. But if preliminary information is any guide, there is good reason for the 1986 critique by the Jerusalem School for the Study of the Synoptic Gospels that the Jesus Seminar, due perhaps to an over reliance on the criterion of dissimilarity to determine authenticity of a saying, has denuded Jesus of his essential Jewishness.

[89] *The First Followers of Jesus.*

historicity questions . . . in peremptory fashion by a single acid test . . . dealing with the data atomistically. Questions of historicity are not reasonably handled in this way. On the whole it is rare that a solid judgment of historicity can be made *prior to and apart from a large frame of reference.*[90]

We will try to use that broader frame of reference by examining Jesus' words and deeds in the context of his relationships. We will be attempting to heed the needed warning of S. Freyne:

> The historian must constantly pay attention to the data—all the data—available, irrespective of how disparate the pieces may appear to be and how resistant they are to being fit into a plausible pattern . . . we [should] take seriously the fact that Jesus both taught and did certain actions that were seen by his contemporaries as works of power. . . . It is this very combination of deeds and words that makes it so difficult to fit Jesus neatly into any of the roles that can be documented—teacher, oracular prophet, prophet of liberation, aspirant to popular kingship, man of deeds (*hasid*) despite the clear similarities with all of them, and even though he is sometimes hailed in one or other of those roles by his audience.[91]

Some contend that the Gospels present no firm, historical material even of an indirect nature on which to judge the matter of whether or not Jesus had a Messianic self-consciousness.[92] Such a skeptical judgment will be challenged in this book. This does not mean I think there is sufficient evidence in the Gospels to psychoanalyze much less psychologize Jesus. As B. Malina points out, the way people were presented in antiquity was almost never by offering a cradle-to-grave picture of personality development, much less a psychological profile of what made this or that individual tick. Rather, a portrait was painted by relating certain things the person said or did, or by focusing on certain relationships that person had.[93] It was believed that one could judge the tree by the fruit it bore.

Malina convincingly argues that moderns in the West operate with a different model of personality than was the case in first-century Palestine. In Jesus' day, personal identity was established and grounded in one's religious, ethnic, social, familial, and economic group.[94] Thus, it was widely believed that a person could be known chiefly through his or her interpersonal behavior, that is, through speech, actions, and forms of interrelating. For us this might seem to be an indirect way of knowing someone, especially

[90] *The Aims of Jesus*, 84, emphasis mine.
[91] *Galilee, Jesus and the Gospels*, 222–23.
[92] Cf. the remark of M. Borg, *Jesus*, 10: "Whether Jesus thought of himself as having any special exalted identity—as 'Messiah' or 'the Son of God'—we can not know because of the very nature of the documents. When we do find such statements in the gospels . . . they may not be taken as historically accurate statements of what was said during the ministry itself."
[93] Cf. *The New Testament World*.
[94] Ibid., 54–55.

if it amounted to presenting many sayings in which the speaker does not speak directly about him- or herself. But in some ways the best way to get to know someone is by listening to his or her indirect testimony that is not self-conscious. I suspect that one reason for the modern counsel of despair – that we can not know anything about how the historical Jesus viewed himself – is because we too often come to the Gospels with our modern paradigms of how we may come to know something about a particular person. These paradigms are overly influenced, however, by modern psychological theories about human individuality.

The study of any historical person is risky, and this is certainly true when one is assessing from indirect evidence how a historical person like Jesus evaluated himself. The evidence is primarily indirect because Jesus seldom spoke directly about himself and because we have no documents from his hand. What we do have is a record that concentrates on three years of his life. There is insufficient data to analyze in any modern way Jesus' character development or most of the significant influences on his life, especially his pre-adult life, which modern psychology often deems the most crucial period for character formation. Thus, we should not attempt a psychoanalysis of Jesus because his Gospel portraits do not allow us to do so. Does this mean that any attempt to discern something of what the adult Jesus thought of himself is doomed to failure? I think not for several reasons.

First, we intend to investigate the Gospel material with a very specific question in mind: Does this material reveal what the adult Jesus thought of himself during his earthly ministry with regard to the questions of his messianic, or filial, or transcendent, or even divine consciousness?[95] In short, does the evidence warrant the deduction that Jesus thought of himself in categories that go beyond normal human self-perceptions?[96] We are interested in investigating Jesus' self-understanding in these matters, not his self-consciousness. As D. Wells rightly says of the term *self-understanding*, it is

> less psychological and more cognitive. It has to do with the value we place on ourselves and the meaning we draw from our lives. Our self-understanding

---

[95] Divine consciousness can mean either consciousness of the divine or, in the narrower sense, consciousness that one thinks oneself to be divine. I prefer the term transcendent self-concept to the term divine consciousness because the latter can be understood to mean different things. I would stress that human consciousness is one thing, human *being* is another. By this I mean that what one thinks oneself is or is aware of being, and what one actually is, may be two different things. Epistemology and ontology are two different, although related, matters.

[96] Here it is important to explain what I mean by normal. If by normal one means how an average person *does*, or how most people *do* perceive themselves, then the term abnormal simply means beyond or out of the ordinary. If, however, by normal one means how one *ought* to perceive oneself to be a normal human being, then that is something quite different. In this context, by normal I mean ordinary. Thus, a person with an exceptional self-concept is not necessarily *abnormal* if by that one means less than truly human, or even psychotic. That person, however, would be abnormal on my definition, that is, out of or beyond the ordinary.

answers the questions as to who we are and why we do what we do. There will be psychological components in our answers, but self-understanding differs from self-consciousness as interpretation does from fact. Our self-consciousness is the raw material upon which we work; what we make of it is our self-understanding.[97]

Because the Synoptics do claim that Jesus was more than an ordinary mortal, it follows that if there were any data available from the early first century which warranted such a claim, the evangelists would probably have assembled it. Thus, happily, the data we seek is not other than what can be found in the Synoptic Gospels. The first three evangelists were indeed interested in Christology, and the texts suggest they were also interested in Jesus' views on christological matters. The available sources and our specific focus correspond in subject matter sufficiently to give hope of concrete results. Furthermore, we shall avoid theorizing about Jesus' birth, early childhood, youth, or possible afterlife. Rather, our concern is to focus on the material that recounts various aspects of Jesus' earthly ministry. With this focus and given the apparent character of the Gospels as well as the interests of their authors in answering the question of who Jesus was and who he thought himself to be, there is some real prospect of success in our investigation, provided there is historical substance to the Gospel material we intend to investigate.

In Jesus' case especially, who a person is, who he claims to be, what he thinks of himself, and what others claim about him can all be different. On the one hand, Jesus' disciples could have claimed Jesus to be the Christ and could have been wrong. Or Jesus' critics could have claimed he was an instrument of the Devil and they too could have been mistaken. It is also historically possible that Jesus thought himself to be the Messiah or Son of God but was mistaken. On the other hand, various of these claims could be true. It is not our purpose to assess the truth of these claims of or about Jesus made by the evangelists, Jesus himself, or his critics. Theological evaluation of such claims is a second-order question that can only be addressed after one establishes what the claims actually amounted to historically. It is crucial, however, that we not rule out in advance that Jesus could have made some extraordinary claims, or at least understood himself in a manner that went beyond ordinary human self-understanding. C. F. D. Moule was correct to urge that we must allow for the "sheer originality of Jesus" including not only "the originality of what Jesus may have said, but also of what he was."[98]

Then, too, it is not sufficient to evaluate only claims, whether explicit or implicit, but all the data that may suggest an answer to the question of

---

[97] *The Person of Christ,* 36.
[98] *The Origins of Christology,* 8.

how Jesus viewed himself. We will devote ourselves to the task of evaluating how Jesus understood himself in regard to christological matters, using all the tools of the historical-critical method. Until the biblical texts are seen in their proper context and are clearly understood, the question of the veracity of this material cannot be posed.[99]

A further problem for our study arises because it has been maintained that "knowledge of the historical Jesus is not *essential* . . ." to Christian faith.[100] If by this one means that Christian faith could ultimately survive without a historical Jesus that substantially corresponds with the church's portraits of him, as both Jesus of Nazareth and the Christ of faith, then I disagree, especially since Christianity purports to be a historical religion and not a philosophy of life. What the historical Jesus was actually like matters tremendously in this particular sort of religion. E. Sjöberg is much nearer the mark when he insists that "the question about the historicity of the messianic self-understanding of Jesus is the central question in the investigation of early Christianity. Everything hangs on that."[101] It is because of this central importance that I have undertaken the difficult task of searching out from the Synoptics whether or not Jesus had a messianic self-concept, or at least some sort of transcendent self-understanding.

CAVEATS AND THE CRITERIA FOR AUTHENTICITY

With B. Chilton, I agree that the way to begin a historical analysis is with the text as we have it. Then, "if one can isolate what the redactor has brought to a given passage, one can infer that the residue of the passage stems from the tradition prior to the Evangelist."[102] The residue must then be examined to see if it goes back to a *Sitz im Leben Jesu*. One should peel the onion from the outside in.[103] Unfortunately, because of the size of the task I cannot always present the results of my redaction-critical analysis of a

---

[99] The one exception to what I have just said would be if our study led to the conclusion that Jesus historically made no extraordinary claims and had no transcendent self-concept. Such a conclusion would directly affect the issue of the veracity of these supposed claims or ideas. In short, the historical-critical method could at most establish a negative conclusion in regard to truth claims, that is, there is no point in raising the question of the veracity of Jesus' claims or self-concept because he made no such claims and because the historical evidence suggests he had a perfectly ordinary self-concept. Herein we see the limits of the historical-critical study of the New Testament.

[100] Borg, *Jesus*, 13.

[101] *Der verborgene Menschensohn*, 239.

[102] *God in Strength*, 22.

[103] Cf. N. J. McEleney, "Authenticating Criteria and Mark 7:1–23," 432: "Logically, the first step in attributing materials to different stages of the Gospel tradition is to begin with the end product, the Gospels as they now stand, and to discover in them the work of the evangelists themselves."

passage or of the themes and tendencies of a given evangelist before I deal
with a text in what is probably its earliest form. Often I can only present
some evidence for the reason I think this or that form of a saying or passage
is the most primitive. Considerably more time, however, is spent dealing
with the basic question of the authenticity of the earliest layer of tradition.
This is necessary if we hope to say anything with confidence about Jesus'
views of himself.

Concerning the criteria for authenticity, one would hope that we are
beyond the point of limiting authentic material only to those traditions that
can pass that most stringent of all tests—the criterion of dissimilarity.
Although this is an important criterion, sometimes it is not the most accurate
gauge of authenticity because Jesus did share some things in common with
early Judaism and early Christianity. Often more useful are the criteria of
multiple attestation of the core (in various sources or, less frequently, in
various forms) and coherence around that core. The criterion of dissimilarity
serves to confirm the authenticity of a saying; it generally cannot be used to
rule out the authenticity of other sayings because Jesus had some coherence
with his predecessors and successors. Only when we find material that can
be shown to clearly contradict the core established by the criterion of dissimilarity can a negative verdict be pronounced on a tradition that does not
meet the criterion of dissimilarity.

The criterion of style or characteristic motifs also is helpful as a
secondary criterion, employed after other data have been analyzed and a
core group of material pronounced authentic.[104] I place considerable weight
on whether or not a given saying or tradition goes back to an Aramaic
original, or whether or not it plausibly fits into a Palestinian context of Jesus'
era. Finally, scholarly consensus should be considered, although, because
it may be wrong, a scholar has the right to differ on individual sayings or
pericopes.

The criteria for authenticity recently outlined by D. Polkow are quite
compatible with my own.[105] In a preliminary stage of the investigation, he
first discounts redaction and then discounts tradition. Then he applies the
primary criteria for authenticity (dissimilarity, coherence, multiple attestation) followed by secondary criteria like style and scholarly consensus.[106]

In this study we will focus on the primary and secondary criteria, mentioning occasionally how the preliminary criteria have been applied. These
primary and secondary criteria work better with sayings material than with
narratives, although they may be used in the latter case as well. In general,
more redactional elements may be expected in the narratives and narrative

---

[104] Meyer, *Aims,* 86, speaks of "irreducible personal idiom" such as Jesus' use of Abba or
Amen as another index to historicity.

[105] Cf. D. Polkow, "Method and Criteria for Historical Jesus Research."

[106] Ibid., 342.

frameworks than in the sayings material, even though the sayings do also manifest the work of the evangelists because the narratives were transmitted mainly by his followers and not by Jesus himself (unless we are talking about *meshalim*).[107]

From my siftings, I present only the material that, using the historical-critical method, reasonably goes back to a *Sitz im Leben Jesu*. Thus, I avoid two methodological errors: ruling out prematurely any particular kind of material—for example, sayings, *meshalim*, miracle tales, pronouncement stories, and arguing for the authenticity of all of the Gospel material. A reasonable explanation of the data is not only a possible one but also is a sufficient and coherent one in light of all the other evidence.

To be limited by the scope of the data, we will need to forego asking some interesting questions that the texts themselves do not address. This study is an exegetical analysis of texts—focusing on the exegetical and historical tasks before proceeding to second-order questions; it is not an exercise in systematic theology. Thus, some christological questions are not discussed here. For example, I am not interested in Jesus' views of God (that is, Jesus' theology) except as it has bearing on his views of himself. Nor do I seek either a theology of Jesus or a study of his views about himself as an ordinary human being. I am interested in evidence that Jesus thought of himself as more than an ordinary human being. I recognize that, strictly speaking, the term Christology applies only to ideas about the Messiah. I use the term to refer, however, not only to messianic self-understanding but also to any sort of transcendent self-concept out of which may have arisen a christological view of self.

This is not a life of Jesus, although an understanding of the salient elements of that life are necessary to our inquiry. I am well aware of A. Schweitzer's warnings that each epoch since Jesus' time has found its own thoughts in him, and so to speak has recreated him in its own image.[108] I hope I am not guilty of that; some of the things I discovered in this study disturbed my own predispositions and prior understanding of Jesus.

To be a good historian and exegete it is necessary to evaluate the data on its own terms. R. L. Wilken was right to insist that "we have no license to judge the distant past on the basis of our present perception of events of more recent times."[109] After all, our times are very different from the days

---

[107] That some of the narratives were initially transmitted before Easter is possible if Jesus did have a circle of followers whose task was to be fishers of human beings even *during his ministry* (on this cf. pp. 129–31 below). Some sort of account not only of Jesus' words but also of his *deeds* had to be given if more people were to come and follow Jesus. Such a narrating of words and deeds was especially necessary when dealing with those who had little or no previous contact with Jesus. On the pre-Easter *Sitz im Leben* for the learning and transmitting of some of Jesus' sayings during the ministry, cf. H. Schürmann, *Das Geheimnis Jesu*, 14–72.

[108] *The Quest for the Historical Jesus*, 4ff.

[109] *John Chrysostom and the Jews*, 162.

of Jesus in many ways, and our own personal experiences may also be different from his. What we normally experience cannot be assumed to encompass the full range of possible human experiences. I do not intend to foreclose such issues on the basis of any sort of modern a priori judgment that such things do not and cannot happen. The evidence for all sorts of events and claims both usual and unusual need to be examined by the historian. If an ordinary explanation cannot be found, then an extraordinary one cannot be ruled out.

I wish to stress that in this book I am basically raising the first-order questions about the meaning of texts and their larger historical context and behind both of these, the way Jesus understood himself. Interpreting texts and presenting their probable meaning is not the same as asserting truth claims. Thus, it is perfectly possible for someone to conclude that my analysis about how Jesus viewed himself is correct, but that Jesus was wrong about himself. What Jesus either explicitly or implicitly claimed about himself is one matter; whether those claims are true or not is another matter altogether. G. B. Caird is also right to say, "It is one thing to ask what the New Testament teaches, and quite another to ask whether that teaching is credible to ourselves or to others."[110]

Most of my material, with rare exception, is taken from Mark or Q. Thus, I will start with what are probably our earliest sources and go into later material, if it confirms hints in the authentic synoptic material or if it helps make sense of that data. I will not be dealing with material such as the "I Am" discourses in the Fourth Gospel because it is difficult to argue on the basis of the historical-critical method that they go back to a *Sitz im Leben Jesu*. Even when we can get back to such a *Sitz im Leben* from Mark or Q, what can be recovered is often only the substance of what Jesus said or did, although sometimes we are able to recover his very words. The success of this investigation, I would like to stress, does not hinge on any one piece of data, but rather on the overall picture that emerges from an investigation of the relevant relationships, deeds, and words of Jesus. Thus, even if I am wrong about a particular saying, action, or relationship being authentic, the overall results of the study will still stand.

I am indebted to the recent scholarly efforts of Charlesworth, Riches, Horsley, Sanders, Meyer, O'Neill, Borg,[111] Harvey, and Vermes to name but a few. They cannot be blamed for deficiencies found in this study. Most of

---

[110] Quoted in Morgan, "The Historical Jesus," 205 n.18.

[111] Borg's work I have found particularly helpful at various points and I quite agree with him that the Schweitzerian assertion concerning Jesus' proclamation being given in the context of a delusion that the world was going to end imminently should rightly be challenged. I would demur, however, from the *way* Borg seeks to challenge this still widely held assumption—by evacuating the historical Jesus' life and teaching of eschatological content. To say that Jesus had an eschatological worldview is not the same as to say his eschatology was what Schweitzer thought it was. Cf. Borg, "An Orthodoxy Reconsidered," 207–17.

these scholars did not address the question of Jesus and Christology directly, and where it was discussed it was in light of the particular approach and slant the writer pursued. In short, the topic has not recently been tackled head-on in any full way in the English-speaking world using all the resources of the historical-critical method. I am quite convinced that this is a task, however, that must be undertaken because as F. Mussner and W. Kümmel have pointed out, "Christology hangs in the air if it is not grounded in Jesus' own self-consciousness."[112] With L. E. Keck I urge that "though the historical Jesus is but a part of the whole of Christology, it is the crucial part without which nothing else has validity or significance in the long run."[113]

What is needed, then, is an effort to analyze the relationships, deeds, and words of Jesus in their historical context, drawing not only on the usual tools of historical criticism but also on recent gains in the sociological study of the New Testament period, as well as the literary analysis of various types of ancient literature. Attempted here is this broad approach, which has as its basis exegesis and historical analysis. The extent of success in my efforts needs to be decided by the reader.

---

[112] "Ein Jahrzehnt Jesuforschung (1965–1975)," *ThR* n.s. 40 (1975): 289–336, here 319, where Kümmel is quoting and endorsing the words of F. Mussner.
[113] L. E. Keck, *A Future for the Historical Jesus*, 38.

2

Christology and the Relationships of Jesus

JESUS' RELATIONSHIPS APPEAR at first to be a promising avenue to get a fix on his self-conception. There is, however, a problem that emerges. Not all of Jesus' relationships extend over his whole adult life. For instance, what we can discern from his relation with John may be helpful in understanding Jesus before or at the beginning of his ministry, but it may not be helpful in evaluating Jesus at the climax of his ministry.

If Jesus' general knowledge, self-understanding, and wisdom increased or developed over the course of his lifetime (Luke 2:52), then any fixation with only the Jesus whom John knew, or only the Jesus whom the Romans encountered at the conclusion of Jesus' life, or only the Jesus with whom the Pharisees interacted in the Galilean ministry will give us but a partial picture. To treat Jesus like other historical figures, we cannot accept such an approach. Granted, the material that we have deals mostly with the last one to three years of his life, and there may have been little development in Jesus' self-conception during so short a span. Because of the dramatic turns that his life took during this last period, we should not draw such a conclusion prematurely without first examining all of the evidence that reflects a *Sitz im Leben Jesu.*

We will focus first on Jesus and John and then on Jesus' relationships with several groups he encountered during the Galilean ministry—the Pharisees and the sinners, the revolutionaries and the Romans, and the disciples. In this manner, we hope to discern, first, how Jesus viewed himself over the course of his adult life and, second, to what extent his process of self-definition is revealed in the last years of his life.

JESUS AND THE BAPTIST

In the wake of the new quest for the historical Jesus and the Qumran literature, the exploration of the synoptic pericopes and logia that deal with Jesus and John the Baptist has yielded diverse hypotheses: (1) John was an Essene and perhaps so was Jesus; or (2) Jesus was only a disciple of John; or (3) Jesus, although initially a follower of the Baptist, developed his own style and message for ministry to Israel that significantly differed from John's; or (4) Jesus saw both John's and his own ministry as part of a single final attempt by God to bring a wayward people back into proper relationship with God in the light of the inbreaking dominion, which meant judgment or redemption depending on how one responded to the summons of John and Jesus. One's view affects how one answers many christological questions. If, for instance, Jesus was no more than a disciple of John or a prophet who continued John's ministry (the second view), then it may be improper to speak of a Christology of or about Jesus.

W. Wink's detailed redaction critical study of the Baptist traditions offers a beginning because, if we can separate redactions from sources, then a less biased historical perspective on John and Jesus is opened. Wink maintains that "the history of John the Baptist has . . . served as the seemingly secure bedrock on which the reconstruction of the history of Jesus could proceed."[1] A great deal of the Baptist material might also reflect the polemics of the Christian church against the Baptist sect in the period A.D. 70 and afterward. Wink shows, however, that the Gospel tradition, far from being polemics against John and his followers, claims John for the Christian cause. Thus, progressing chronologically from Mark to the Fourth Gospel, generally speaking John's words about Jesus become increasingly confessional.[2]

Even in Mark's Gospel, John is "the beginning of the Gospel," the one who sets things in motion and prepares Israel for the coming of God's dominion. The Gospel writers were hardly guilty according to Wink of "anachronistically projecting back into its origin the later conflict between Christians and John's disciples."[3] The evidence of a conflict between the followers of Jesus and John in the later period seems scant. It is unlikely that the early church, which was increasingly concerned to indicate the uniqueness of its Savior, created a group of traditions that not only connected Jesus to John, but also gave John a significant role.

Wink argues that it is Jesus' own positive evaluation of the Baptist which accounts for the subsequent appreciation of John by the evangelists.[4] We

---

[1] W. Wink, *John the Baptist,* ix.

[2] Luke however is somewhat less confessional on the whole than Mark.

[3] Wink, *John the Baptist,* 109.

[4] Ibid., 111.

may add that they were concerned to state how the Jesus movement and the Gospel events got started. The evangelists' unity on John's connection to "the beginning of the Gospel" results from historical realities that could not be ignored if the evangelists were to be fair to their source material.

Wink's redaction-critical work yields the following conclusions: (1) Mark portrays John as Elijah incognito, which parallels the Messianic-secret motif; (2) Matthew uses John as an ally of Jesus against the hostile front of opposition Jesus encountered in Judaism; (3) Luke accepts the Markan picture of John as forerunner and adapts it to his conception of *Heilsgeschichte;* and (4) the fourth evangelist offers a John portrayed as the ideal witness to Jesus as God's Christ, the Lamb.[5] From the Markan and Q material, de Jonge concludes that:

> although John is clearly described as Jesus' forerunner, and the new dispensation in God's dealings with Israel and the world only begins with Jesus, there is no indication that John is expressly relegated to an inferior position. John was important . . . and there was no need to put groups of disciples of John (Luke 7:18) right concerning the true status of their master.[6]

Keeping these tendencies and conclusions in mind makes differentiating redaction from source material much easier.

What is the Baptist's historical context? Is he an isolated prophet, a manifestation of the Qumran sect, or another leader of a reform movement in Judaism? On the one hand, John appears like an Old Testament prophet in both his oracles of doom and his ascetical behavior. On the other hand, his practice of baptizing has no precedent in the Old Testament prophetic literature and is like the practices of Qumran and other baptist-type sects (Ebionites, Elkasites, Nasoreans, or an individual like Banus). John cannot be seen as simply a reformer of society like the Pharisees because he calls even the ritually pure and the righteous to repentance and baptism and he threatens that one's descent from Abraham was neither a protection from the coming judgment nor a guarantee of one's place in God's final dominion, and because he did not write off the nation as the sons of darkness—he calls them to repentance. Yet John, unlike Jesus, apparently performed no miraculous deeds or signs. John's water rite, however, seems to have a different focus than the practices of Qumran, coming closer to what we know of Jewish proselyte baptism.[7] Nevertheless, despite the differences from the Qumran practice, J. Becker asserts, "the Baptist belongs together much more with the Teacher of Righteousness."[8]

---

[5] Ibid., 110–11.

[6] de Jonge, *Christology in Context,* 76.

[7] Cf. G. Bornkamm, *Jesus of Nazareth,* 47.

[8] J. Becker, *Johannes der Taufer,* 105.

In conclusion, although John may have been a part of the Qumran community, he is no longer a member when we encounter him in the Gospel literature because (1) he calls the nation to repentance, (2) he allows both the unclean and the clean, the sinners and the righteous, to come into contact with him, and (3) his water rite is not merely a repeatable ritual ablution. Second, Jesus recognized John as a prophetic figure, and there is no reason to dispute this identification. There is also no reason to see John as the founder of a messianic movement because neither in the Gospels nor in Josephus (*Ant.* 18.5.2) is there any evidence that John viewed himself in such a light. Nevertheless, he seems to have felt that the final and decisive judgment of God was about to fall on Israel. Finally, John should not be seen as a reformer in the same manner that the Pharisees or Zealots were reformers. He urges neither a levitical nor a revolutionary program to cure the nation's ills. He was in many ways a unique figure that caused a stir amongst the religious and in the halls of power in the region because he was perceived to be a threat to various authority figures, a threat to the religious and political status quo. We must investigate the relevant data in Mark, Q, and to some extent John to determine the relationship of Jesus and John: Mark 1:1-11, 14, 15;[9] Matthew 3/Luke 3:1-22; Matt. 11:2-19/Luke 7:18-35; and John 3:22−4:3.[10]

THE BEGINNING OF THE GOSPEL (MARK 1:1-11)

That John preached in the chalk wilderness adjacent to the Jordan River and baptized in that river is little disputed. According to Luke (3:1), John appeared during the fifteenth year of the reign of Tiberias, which dates him somewhere between autumn A.D. 27 and the summer of A.D. 29.[11] If we couple Luke's information with what we find in Josephus (*Ant.* 18.109-19), which implies that John was executed by Herod Antipas around A.D. 32,[12] we are able to date rather precisely when Jesus was in contact with John. Apparently, the wilderness setting was not created out of the composite citation that introduces the Gospel of Mark (Exod. 23:20a; Mal. 3:1 MT; Isa. 40:3 almost verbatim from the LXX), especially because scholars agree that John baptized Jesus in the Jordan. John's ministry probably was mainly in, or near, Judea, with some ventures into Perea and possibly into Galilee.[13] The likelihood of this is shown by three considerations: (1) Mark 1:5 tells us that those who were coming to John were from Judea in general and

---

[9] The fascinating material in Mark 6 is omitted from this discussion partly because so many scholars find it legendary and partly because it sheds no new light on Jesus' relationship to John compared with the pericopes under discussion.

[10] E. Linnemann, "Jesus und der Taufer," 219-36.

[11] Cf. B. F. Meyer, *The Aims of Jesus*, 115.

[12] See B. Reicke, "Setting of John's Baptism," 210.

[13] In either Perea or Galilee he would have been in Antipas's domain.

Jerusalem in particular; (2) if John had contact with or formerly had been a member of the Qumran sect, then we might expect to find him in this region; (3) the relevant material in Josephus also suggests a setting of Judea and Perea for John's ministry.[14] Thus, Jesus was probably baptized by John in or near Judea, and if there was a period when Jesus was with John, or perhaps assisted him, or was engaged in a parallel activity, it also was probably in Judea. In short, there is a possible Judean period in Jesus' life prior to his public Galilean ministry. This is supported by John 3:22—4:3, if that material has any historical substance.

Although Mark 1:6 may be drawn from the portrait of Elijah (the leather girdle, cf. 2 Kings 1:8), the rest of the description is plausible, and John's diet comports with what was available in the Judean wilderness.[15] If John viewed himself as a prophet, then it should not be surprising that he dressed and acted in a way that reflected his awareness of prophetic literature.

Opinions as to the purpose of John's baptism are varied. Josephus suggests that it was for the purification of the body "when the soul had previously been cleansed by righteous conduct" (*Ant.* 18.117). Yet he seems aware of its association with the forgiveness of sins because he asserts that this baptism was not to be used to beg off from sins previously committed, unless there was that previous cleansing of the soul. This suggests a parallel with the assertion of the Gospel of Mark: repentance and confession were necessary before or with the act of baptism in order for the act to be authentic (the outward act symbolizing the inner cleansing). Mark 1:5 mentions the audible confession of sins, and the previous verse says that this baptism was "for the remission of sins." Recent study suggests that there may not have been proselyte baptism in pre-Christian times, so John's practice may have been novel.[16]

Whatever Mark contributed to this summary, it is historically plausible that John's baptism was for the forgiveness of sins. By the criterion of dissimilarity this motif seems to be authentic because Christians associated forgiveness of sins with Jesus and what he accomplished on the cross. Furthermore, they would hardly have invented the idea that Jesus underwent a baptism for the forgiveness of sins because Jews associated forgiveness with the activities and sacrifices offered in the temple and because Christians had a high view of Jesus' character. John offered something radical and different—an alternative way to forgiveness apart from the fulfillment of all the legal requirements of the law.[17] No wonder the Lukan

---

[14] Cf. Reicke, "Setting of John's Baptism," 213, "The evidence implies that his activity was concentrated in the Jordan valley and the Dead Sea region . . ."

[15] Cf. H. B. Swete, *The Gospel according to St. Mark* (London: Macmillan & Co., 1898), 4–5.

[16] Cf. D. Smith, "Jewish Proselyte Baptism and the Baptism of John," *ResQ* 25 (1982): 13–32; K. Pusey, "Jewish Proselyte Baptism."

[17] So rightly Linnemann, "Jesus und der Taufer," 228ff., and H. Boers, *Who Was Jesus?* 34.

tradition asserts that tax collectors and even (Roman?) soldiers came to John for baptism (Luke 3:12-14).[18] This tradition seems to be confirmed by the criterion of multiple attestation, for Matt. 21:31-32 asserts that John baptized tax collectors and harlots (cf. Luke 7:29-30). If this was the case, then John too was at odds with both the temple establishment and the Pharisees on the means of procuring forgiveness—something they thought only God could dispense through the proper legal channels. Could Jesus have obtained his idea about forgiveness of sins from John?

In reference to Mark 1, did John proclaim a coming one whose baptism he contrasted with his own water baptism? On the surface one can deduce that this is a Christian addition to the historical tradition meant to cast John into Jesus' shadow. Bultmann sees vv. 7-8 as a later addition to the passage.[19] This overlooks that Q had its own version of this tradition (Matt. 3:11/Luke 3:16).[20] Bornkamm puts it this way:

> The preaching and baptism of John the Baptist . . . is confirmed by the fact that the Christian message no longer presented the work of the coming judge of the world in terms of a baptism of the Spirit *and fire,* and that a strong tension exists between its presentation of Christ and the picture of the Messiah as announced by John.[21]

This means that John did not see himself as the definitive revealer of God but expected a sequel to his ministry. From Mark and Q, it is not clear whether he expected that judge to be Yahweh's self-intervention or some lesser and perhaps human agent of God bringing judgment on God's people—as had happened so often before in Israel's history. If the saying about the sandals is authentic, then it might suggest a human agent, but it could be a metaphor stressing John's servant status in relationship to the coming one.[22]

In terms of the Markan outline, Wink argues that the material we have just discussed is seen by Mark as the beginning of the gospel—the good news begins with John and his ministry.[23] Against this V. Taylor urges that this overlooks seeing Mark 1:1 as a title for the whole Gospel, and he claims that this underestimates the importance of the Scripture citation in 1:2-3.[24]

---

[18] The interesting material in Luke 3:11-14, which may well be the background for Jesus' own stipulations when he sent out his disciples in pairs, will not be treated here because we are focusing on the material that may have some christological weight. In any case, Boers, *Who was Jesus?* 34ff. has recently cast doubts on the historicity of this material. He asks whether it is probable that Roman soldiers would have sought advice from an ascetic preacher in the wilderness.

[19] R. Bultmann, *Die Geschichte,* 261.

[20] Cf. I. Havener, *Q—The Sayings of Jesus,* 123.

[21] Bornkamm, *Jesus of Nazareth,* 48; italics mine.

[22] The possibility of a human agent or the Messiah doing the works God promised to do was apparently conceivable in early Judaism. Cf. J. C. O'Neill, *Messiah,* 3-4.

[23] Wink, *John the Baptist,* 1ff.

[24] *Mark,* 152.

As both Cranfield and Lane point out, however, 1:1-4 are probably one long introductory sentence that asserts that, although the good news concerns Jesus Christ, it begins with the wilderness prophet. The good news was bound up with the preparatory role and work of John.[25]

VIPERS AND VITUPERATION (MATTHEW 3/LUKE 3:1-22)

Havener states: "Although John appears or is mentioned only a few times in Q, nonetheless, he is second only to Jesus in importance, and about a tenth of Q is devoted to materials concerning him."[26] Thus John the Baptist played an important role in the pre-Gospel traditions about Jesus, and there were probably good historical reasons that John was included in the collections of Gospel traditions and even in the logia of Jesus. The anomaly of this must be stressed—in the midst of the church's collection of Jesus' sayings were also included sayings of John!

Following Polag's reconstruction of the *Vorlage* behind Matthew 3/Luke 3:1-22, we arrive at the following sermon in miniature:

> You brood of vipers! Who warned you to flee from the wrath to come? Bear fruit that befits repentance, And [do] not . . . say to yourselves "We have Abraham as our father"; For I tell you that God is able from these stones to raise up children to Abraham. Even now the axe is laid to the root of the trees; every tree therefore that does not bear good fruit is cut down and thrown into the fire. I baptize you [with] water but he who is mightier than I is coming. . . . He will baptize you with the Holy Spirit and with fire. His winnowing fork is in his hand, and he will clear his threshing floor and gather his wheat into the granary, but the chaff he will burn with unquenchable fire.[27]

That John is addressing Israel is beyond cavil because of the reference to Abraham,[28] but was this sermon addressed to the multitude (as Luke avers), or to some specific group of Jews (as Matthew suggests)? Marshall contends that the Matthean specification of the narrower audience seems to comport with his redactional tendencies elsewhere (cf. Matt. 16:1, 6, 11f.).[29] This overlooks that in Luke 7:29-30 there is a testimony about antipathy between John and the Pharisees, and as J. Fitzmyer points out the address

---

[25] Cf. C. E. B. Cranfield, *Mark*, 34-35; W. Lane, *Mark*, 42-43.

[26] Havener, *Q—The Sayings of Jesus*, 62.

[27] A. Polag, in Havener, *Q—The Sayings of Jesus*, 123-24. The portions in brackets are not in both Matthew and Luke, and so it is unclear what was in the *Vorlage*.

[28] R. Bultmann, *Synoptic Tradition*, 123, 134, has maintained that it is pure chance that this speech, a Christian composition, was put on John's lips rather than Jesus' lips. Against the view that this is a Christian composition is the fact that this speech is full of Semitisms. Also, as Wink, *John the Baptist*, 19 n.1, points out, it is unlikely that the church would either transfer a word of Jesus to John or create a speech for John that suggests salvation could be had by repentance, not by repentance plus faith in Jesus.

[29] Marshall, *Luke*, 139, following Creed and Schürmann.

"brood of vipers" suggests some specific group that displeased John.[30] Indeed the sermon suggests that there was some particular group that John was surprised to find coming for baptism in order to flee the wrath to come, whereas this was not his reaction to all those who came. He did expect some response by some Israelites but not by this particular group.

The answer to the question "Who told you to flee?" would be John himself if the addressees were simply the multitudes who came to hear John at the Jordan! But John seems to think that someone else had told the Pharisees and Sadducees about his message of imminent judgment, and apparently they had come to hear it for themselves.

Is this speech an apocalyptic fragment or more generally an eschatological judgment oracle, perhaps not unlike what we find in some of the minor prophets? Becker has rightly concluded that "Jesus shares with the Baptist the same relationship to Apocalyptic. Neither are Apocalypticists and they only use Apocalyptic material to a limited extent."[31] John is using metaphorical speech; clearly he expects some act of divine judgment to fall on Israel soon, unless there was an about face in the nation's character. Although wrath is emphasized, John allows that the winnower will gather some wheat. John should not be viewed as only a prophet of doom.

Once again John does not specify who will come after him. The figure of the winnower gives us no clue as to whether or not John expects a human agent of divine judgment. Matthew 13:41, for instance, specifies angels of the Son of man being sent out to do the gathering of the evildoers. Possibly John has some Messianic figure in view as the coming one, but more cannot be said with the evidence we have.[32] If the evidence of 1QS 4:20-21 is germane, then God is seen as the agent who will sift humanity, but there the focus is not on separation but the purifying of certain individuals.

David Catchpole compares this material to the parables of the tares and of the dragnet. He demonstrates striking parallels between the teaching of Jesus and John and concludes:

> In the earliest form of the parable of the tares (Matt. 13:24b, 26b, 30b) there is documented the overlap and therefore the continuity between the preaching of the historical John and that of the historical Jesus. Both preachers affirmed the imminent and challenging reality of God's future and final kingship implemented in judgment, and both called for an immediate response so that the disaster of belonging to the category of chaff or weeds might be averted and replaced by the security of belonging to the category of the wheat.[33]

The many points of continuity between Jesus and John reveal a great deal about Jesus' self-conception.

---

[30] Fitzmyer, *Luke 1–9*, 467; cf. Linnemann, "Jesus und der Taufer," 227–28.

[31] Becker, *Johannes der Taufer*, 105.

[32] Cf. Hill, *Matthew*, 95.

Matthew 3:9 talks about being children of Abraham. D. Allison has pointed out that Isa. 51:1–2 is the background for these verses: "Look to the rock from whence you were hewn . . . Look to Abraham your father and Sarah who bore you."[34] Because the verb translated "to raise up" probably has the sense of "to cause progeny to come forth" the point of the saying is that God can give even to the rocks the power to bring forth children of Abraham—physical descent is no longer a guarantee of salvation, if it ever was. Here is, as Allison avers, as strong an attack on what Sanders calls covenantal nomism as one could wish to find. The children of Israel are being told that repentance and conversion is required of them if they are to avert personal disaster, and this is true even of the Pharisees and Sadducees. It is the content of their character, not their physical lineage, that will determine whether they are cut down at the root or survive the coming judgment. Even D. Daube, a Jewish scholar, has remarked that this passage means that "you must acquire him [Abraham] like strangers."[35]

John seems to believe that Israel, or at least its leadership, is deeply corrupt and requires conversion to avert judgment. It could be argued that John saw as his task the gathering of a remnant to weather the storm of the coming wrath of God. But he had not reckoned on the current leadership of Israel being part of that remnant, hence his response here.

What did John think about this coming one? Besides the idea that he will bring judgment, which may correspond to the idea that he will baptize with fire, the contrast is made between John's own baptizing with water and the coming one baptizing with the Holy Spirit. Various scholars have maintained that this reference to the Holy Spirit can hardly be authentic, but before accepting this view we should ask what John meant if he said such a thing, and whether such an utterance could have been made at all in a pre-Christian *Sitz im Leben*.

First, seeing the phrase "in/with the Holy Spirit" as a purely Christian addition is difficult because Jesus did not baptize anyone with or in the Holy Spirit. Yet this utterance sets up the expectation that we will see Jesus doing what John suggested. In fact, the Synoptic Gospel writers do not portray Jesus, even in purely redactional summaries or remarks, as baptizing anyone or even talking about doing so. He seems to speak only of his own (coming) baptism (Luke 12:50). In the one saying that does mention Jesus' disciples undergoing a baptism similar to his own, it seems that the Holy Spirit is not the subject and that Jesus is not the bestower of the baptism in

---

[33] D. Catchpole, "John the Baptist," 570.

[34] D. C. Allison, "Jesus and the Covenant," 59.

[35] D. Daube, *Ancient Jewish Law*, 10. E. Schillebeeckx, *Jesus*, 134, is even more strident in tone: "The possibility of escape from God's wrath is separated from its connection with the Abrahamic promise to the whole nation and is individualized by a new bond, that is the baptism of John, engagement with a total change, a transformation. . . . Implicit therefore in John's whole movement is an unprecedented disavowal of the Jerusalem Temple cult and propitatory sacrifices."

question (Mark 10:38-39). Although it can be argued that the reference is to the bestowal at Pentecost, remember that this reference to the Holy Spirit needs to make sense within the outline of Mark and Matthew, not in Luke-Acts only. All three of the Synoptic Gospels refer to this baptism with the Holy Spirit and it must make sense within their narrative structure.

Second, the term Holy Spirit was known in the Old Testament and other early Jewish literature (cf. Ps. 51:11; Isa. 63:10f.; *Pss. Sol.* 17:42; 1QS 4.20, 8.16; *C.D.* 2.12). The coming of the Spirit in the last days was also a familiar concept (Joel 2:28-30; Isa. 32:15; 44:3; Ezek. 18:31; cf. 1QS 4.20-21). Even the contrast between water and Spirit is known (Isa. 44:3; Ezek. 36:25-27; 1QS 4.21). Thus, the ingredients existed in the Old Testament and the thought world of John for such an utterance to be made. What precisely he meant by it, and in particular whether it is a reference to coming salvation perhaps with purgation (hence the reference to fire?) or simply a coming judgment, is hard to say. One thing does seem clear: John is contrasting his baptism to the later Spirit baptism with the implication that his baptism will not have the same efficacy or effect as the later one.

DOUBTS AND DISTINCTIONS (MATT. 11:2-19/LUKE 7:18-35)

The Q material in Matthew 11/Luke 7 dealing with Jesus and John should be seen as three separate sets of traditions: Matt. 11:2-6 and par.; Matt. 11:7-11 and par.; and Matt. 11:16-19 and par. We will also look at the saying about violence and the *basileia* (Matt. 11:12-13/Luke 16:16).

Queries from Prison (Matt. 11:2-6/Luke 7:18-23) The first subsection is structured as a pronouncement story, culminating in Jesus' reply to John's disciples. Although Bultmann regards the saying of Jesus that climaxes the story as authentic,[36] he regards the setting as inauthentic. Against this view, Kümmel has rightly pointed out that: (1) the setting of the story, had it been created by the early church, would surely have placed a different title than the vague "coming one" on John's lips (there is no evidence that this was ever a title for Jesus in the early church); (2) in view of the tendency for the tradition to stress John's role as a witness to Jesus (John 1), the expression of doubt by John is surely not the invention of the Christians who passed on these traditions.[37] Marshall makes the point that Jesus' reply does not directly answer John's question; indirect responses are characteristic of Jesus when confronted with questions about his identity.[38] Furthermore, the evidence is weak for a supposed antagonistic relationship between the disciples of Jesus and John in the latter part of the first century as a significant

---

[36] Bultmann, *Synoptic Tradition*, 22, 115, 135.
[37] Cf. W. G. Kümmel, *Promise and Fulfilment*, 110-11.
[38] Marshall, *Luke*, 288.

factor affecting the shape of the Baptist traditions in the Gospels.[39] D. Lührmann points to the "scandal" of a description of Jesus' work without any reference to his death and resurrection as an indication that this material can be seen as a saying of Jesus.[40] We may confidently state that this material derives from a *Sitz im Leben Jesu.*

Matthew more nearly gives us the original form of this saying. In view of the Lukan additions about the sending of two disciples and the account of Jesus' healings in the presence of the two requisite messengers (witnesses?), apart from the redactional *"tou Christou"* in Matt. 11:2, the Matthean version seems more primitive.[41] Matthew tells us that John's query comes from the period after he was incarcerated by Herod. The question relates to John's previous proclamation about a coming one, whom he saw as bringing about God's definitive judgment on Israel, although not without rescuing a certain remnant. Fitzmyer has urged that the allusion is to Mal. 3:1 in light of Luke 3:15–17, and that John probably saw Jesus as Elijah *redivivus.*[42] If so, then Jesus seems to be rejecting such an identification and replacing it with a more Isaianic vision of his role. As Fitzmyer demonstrates, however, "the coming one" could just as well be an allusion to Zech. 9:9 (*erchetai* LXX) and to the Qumran literature using such language to talk about the future Messiah(s) (cf. 1QS 9.11, 4QPBless. 3).[43] Furthermore, in the Malachi passage it is God who finally comes and judges after the messenger has come and refined God's people.

Yet John seems to have expected his successor, "the Coming One," to be a judging figure. Here is the clue to explaining John's quandary. Jesus did not seem to be carrying out judgment on the people; rather, he seems to be about the business of healing and helping them.[44] Jesus makes clear that he did not come to live up to John's expectations but to God's call upon his life. If the emphasis in John's message was coming judgment, then the emphasis in Jesus' words and deeds was that the inbreaking of the dominion of God meant liberation and healing, although if one rejected that liberation, judgment would follow.

What does Jesus' response indicate about his self-understanding? First, note that Jesus' response consists of six brief parallel clauses and a closing remark that has a poetic form in Aramaic.[45] Such use of Aramaic poetry seems to have been characteristic of Jesus. Second, this is a composite

---

[39] Wink, *John the Baptist,* 107ff.; Fitzmyer, *Luke 1–9,* 663ff.

[40] D. Lührmann, *Die Redaktion,* 25–26.

[41] The reference to 'the Christ' is probably the addition of the first evangelist, but a reference to the deeds of Jesus could well have been in the evangelist's source.

[42] Fitzmyer, *Luke 1–9,* 663–64.

[43] Ibid., 666.

[44] So also Dunn, "Matthew 12:28/Luke 11:20," 44. Jesus then would be correcting John's rather one-sided expectations about the role of the Coming One.

[45] J. Jeremias, *New Testament Theology,* 20–21.

citation from Isa. 29:18–19; 35:5–6; 61:1; 26:19, with the addition of the allusion to lepers, but perhaps 2 Kings 5 lies in the background of that portion of the saying. This citation suggests that Jesus saw himself as more than a prophet. "He sees in his ministry something which does not merely revive prophecy but 'fulfills' it."[46] The emphasis here is on the present fulfillment of Old Testament hopes for the messianic or eschatological age.[47] The evidence that in early Judaism the Messiah was expected to be a healer is slender. Thus, if Jesus did see himself in that role, then it seems he had his own vision of what being a messiah would entail. As Fitzmyer points out, Jesus seems to have deliberately left out the references to vengeance in Isa. 29:20; 35:5; 61:2, which could have been quoted with the material we have.[48] Jesus instead sees himself as a bearer of eschatological blessing, perhaps one who brings about the conditions associated with the final eschatological dominion of God. The final blessing formula is also significant. In light of the way *skandalidzo* is used in the Gospel material (Luke 17:2; Mark 4:17; 6:3; 9:42–47; 14:27, 29; "to stumble," or in the passive "to take offense"), what is probably meant is that how one reacts to Jesus will determine one's standing at the eschatological judgment.

The negative form of this blessing is probably conditioned by the fact that John seems to be having doubts about Jesus, perhaps even losing confidence in him.[49] To this Jesus replies in effect: blessed is the one who does not give up faith in me. Flusser assesses this tradition:

> What is important is that Jesus affirmed in principle the Baptist's question about the eschatological meaning of his activities, but without explicitly declaring he was the coming Messiah. He establishes his claim to the eschatological office by pointing to his preaching of salvation and to his supernatural works of healing. Jesus saw these as an unmistakable sign that the era of salvation had already dawned.[50]

Clearly this story is not told for its own sake because we are not told how John responded to Jesus' answer. It should be added that this saying, if it is a response to John's query from prison, suggests that Jesus began his ministry before John's death.

---

[46] C. H. Dodd, "Jesus," 66.

[47] Cf. R. T. France, "Old Testament Prophecy," 56. France's detailed study of the use of the Old Testament by Jesus has led him to the following significant conclusion: "I have found no instance where Jesus expects a fulfilment of Old Testament prophecy other than through his own ministry, and certainly no suggestion of a future restoration of the Jewish nation independent of himself" (58). The one possible exception to this might be some of the future Son of Man material, but we shall see reasons to doubt that it referred to someone other than Jesus. Cf. pp. 256–61.

[48] Fitzmyer, *Luke 1–9*, 667.

[49] Marshall, *Luke*, 292.

[50] D. Flusser, *Jesus*, 36.

The Greatest Man Alive (Matt. 11:7–11/Luke 7:24–28) According to the Q tradition in Matt. 11:7–11/Luke 7:24–28, Jesus was by no means stinting in his praise of John. He is called the greatest person ever born and said to be more than a prophet. It seems impossible to maintain that Matt. 11:9, 11 and parallel are anything other than the very words of Jesus, for the church would never have invented them.

It is possible that the Scripture quotation is an editorial addition, and some would argue that Matt. 11:11b should be seen as such. On this view, these verses were added by the church to put John in his place—as Jesus' forerunner.[51] Schweizer, who argues against the authenticity of the Scripture quotation, argues in favor of 11:11b because Jesus could hardly have praised John so highly without qualifying his remarks in relationship to the coming dominion of God. Purely on literary grounds, the formulation of 11:11a seems to require 11:11b for what we seem to have here is antithetical parallelism. It can also be maintained that the argument for the later addition of 11:11b rests on the uncertain assumption that it must be seen as a derogatory remark about John.[52]

Several elements in this pericope simply confirm what we have already surmised about John from Mark 1: that he was to be found in the wilderness and that his raiment was far from that of royalty's. This gives independent confirmation from Q to the motifs in the Markan narrative we examined earlier.

The reference to a reed shaking in the wind also probably relates to John's setting, not his character, because such vegetation did grow around the Jordan.[53] There may also be an allusion to Herod Antipas in 11:8, in which case John is being contrasted with him and this remark was made after John was imprisoned. It is possible that Matt. 11:11ff. did originally go with what precedes it, although we will not contend for this view.

What is of importance is that Jesus calls John more than a prophet. What could that possibly augur not only about John but also about how Jesus viewed himself? Jesus includes John not only in the prophetic category but also in a higher one as well. This suggests that Jesus saw him as the last and greatest eschatological prophet—preparing God's people for God's final and climactic act of redemptive judgment. This is what John's own words would suggest because he did foresee a coming one; Jesus' estimation may have been based in part on John's own words. If this assessment is correct, then the citations of Mal. 3:1 and Exod. 23:20 are accurate insights into what Jesus thought of John, even if these Scriptures were added later. Surely Jesus did not see himself in any category less than John. The idea that Jesus saw

---

[51] Cf. Schweizer, *Matthew*, 257–62.

[52] Marshall, *Luke*, 293.

[53] Hill, *Matthew*, 199. Why should Jesus wish to stress John's frailty when Jesus was about to praise him highly? No, the crowds went out to see a great man—John the Baptizer.

himself as a prophet is well attested in at least two different layers of the tradition (Luke 13:33–34; Mark 6:4 and par.). If, however, Jesus saw John as the final great prophet, then this implies that he saw himself either as the coming one or as some sort of messianic figure that went beyond purely prophetic categories, without making the prophetic label entirely inappropriate.

What are we to make of Matt. 11:11/Luke 7:28? These sayings suggest that Jesus saw John either as a transitional figure with one foot in the age of the law and the prophets and the other foot in the new age or as the one who initiates the process at the outset of the turn of the eons.[54] In either case, John is not excluded from the inbreaking dominion of God and may be included in it. If so, then the antithetical statements in Matt. 11:11 are probably not meant to contrast John who is outside the kingdom with those who are within it. Rather, the comparison is between two ways of evaluating the human condition: those born of women and those in the dominion of God. These two categories are not mutually exclusive. The point is that even the greatest person in terms of human origins does not have as great a status as the least of those who has been transformed by and included in God's inbreaking dominion. The latter has an origin from God which eclipses all purely human or physical categories, origins, or estimations. As Marshall puts it, "possession of a place in the kingdom is more important than being the greatest of the prophets."[55]

Some have conjectured that *ho mikroteros* should be seen as a comparative, not a superlative, and thus refer to Jesus himself.[56] Against this is the very structure of the utterance, which contrasts those born of women and the least in God's dominion. Were there an intended contrast between John and Jesus here, then *mikroteros* might refer to Jesus being younger, but this seems unlikely on Jesus' lips at this point. The focus is not on Jesus and John but on those born of women and anyone in the dominion, even the least participant in it. The two realms in Jesus' mind are of qualitative difference in significance; the one derives from physical generation, the other is a result of God's supernatural intervention in human events and lives. All else pales in light of the possibilities of participating in God's dominion. Here Jesus seems to have picked up and expanded John's contrast between physical descent and repentance and faith as a prerequisite of participating in the coming dominion.

Attack upon the Realm (Matt. 11:12–13/Luke 16:16)   Most difficult of the logia from Q is Matt. 11:12–13//Luke 16:16. Yet it is important because it appears to give substantial support to M. Borg's contention that "there is much in the Gospels that suggests conflict as a context for interpreting the teaching of

---

[54] So Boers, *Who Was Jesus?* 44–45.

[55] Marshall, *Luke*, 296.

[56] O. Cullmann, *Christology*, 24, 32.

Jesus."[57] The saying is not located in its original context either in Matthew or Luke, which makes discerning its meaning more difficult.[58] In general, E. Bammel's argument that we should see two different sayings has met with little acceptance, not least because of the special vocabulary about force in both versions of this saying.[59] In view of the difficulty of the saying and its apparent placing of the Baptist and his work alongside of (or of a piece with) Jesus' work, the argument against the authenticity of the saying does not prevail.[60]

In discerning the saying's original form, four considerations are crucial: (1) the Matthean form is more difficult and thus probably nearer to the original, at least in 11:12; (2) this view is supported when we note the typical Lukan vocabulary about preaching the *basileia* (cf. 4:43; 8:1) and the *apo tote*;[61] (3) it appears that Matthew, in order to connect the statement about prophets and law with 11:14, which refers to Elijah, has reversed the original order of the saying, which Luke does preserve; and (4) Matthew seems to have added the word "prophesied" to 11:13. Thus, the original form of this saying is likely to be as Polag has reconstructed it: The law and prophets were until John; since then the *basileia* has suffered violence and the violent take it by force.[62]

Commentators generally agree that *biadzo* should be taken *in malem partem*, a conclusion that is supported by E. Moore's detailed investigation of both *biadzo* and *harpadzo* in Josephus. Especially in combination they are used "to signify the direct employment of physical violence as a means of coercion, and . . . they carry with them a strong overtone of censure."[63] The question still remains whether we should take *biadzetai* as middle or passive. If it is a middle, then the sense would be that the *basileia* overpowers by force, presses hard, or even acts with violence, whereas in the passive it would mean that the dominion itself suffers violence. The Matthean form of this part of the saying favors the idea that the dominion is suffering violence because we are immediately told that violent men plunder it (*auten*: the dominion itself). This fits with the usual negative connotation of the main verbs in question.

To what, then, would Jesus be referring? At least three conjectures are possible, and a preference is linked to whether or not one sees John as a part

---

[57] M. Borg, *Conflict*, 24, a thesis we will explore more thoroughly when we discuss the Pharisees. In general, I agree with Borg on Jesus' conflict with his context, but I find the attempt to de-eschatologize Jesus unconvincing. Part of the conflict arose precisely because of a difference about eschatology—Jesus thought the *basileia* was breaking in, in his ministry.

[58] So J. Schlosser, *Le Regne*, 510, whose in-depth analysis is most helpful with this passage.

[59] Cf. E. Bammel, "Luke 16:16-18," 101-6. The fact that John is mentioned in the third person here speaks against Bammel's attempt to see this as a tradition from a Baptist community.

[60] Cf. Schlosser, *Le Regne*, 509ff.; Marshall, *Luke*, 627; Kümmel, *Promise and Fulfilment*, 121-23.

[61] Cf. Fitzmyer, *Luke 10–24*, 1115.

[62] Cf. Schlosser, *Le Regne*, 511ff.; Polag, in Havener, *Q–The Sayings of Jesus*, 143.

[63] E. Moore, "BIADZO," 540.

of or initiator of God's inbreaking activity/realm. One meaning is that both John (at the hands of Herod Antipas) and Jesus (perhaps at the hands of the crowds) had suffered from those who would use violence to achieve their aims. In the case of John that meant silencing him; in the case of Jesus, attempting to force his hand and make him a political ruler.[64] A second possible meaning is that local revolutionaries were attempting to force the dominion of God to emerge by undertaking acts of violence against the Romans. Such a statement on Jesus' lips is possible, especially in view of his own comments about violence (Luke 22:49–51; Matt. 26:52). A third possible meaning is that sinners and outcasts were taking the dominion by storm, so to speak, ever since the possibility of right standing with God had first been offered through baptism by John and then later by Jesus' preaching of the good news. The only difficulty with this last view is that it makes various negative verbs, and a noun that usually has a negative sense, serve a positive purpose—describing an activity Jesus wholly condoned. Thus, the first or second view seems the more probable.

Nevertheless, we can draw five conclusions from this saying. First, Jesus sees the dominion as a present reality that can be acted upon.[65] Second, Jesus sees John either as a transitional figure straddling the old era of law and prophets and the new eon, introduced by his preaching and baptizing,[66] or as the first in the new era. The preposition *mechri* (or even *heos arti*) is susceptible to such an interpretation. In either case, this would explain how Jesus would interpret John's and his own experience together. Third, the rather volatile atmosphere in which John and Jesus preached and worked is attested. In such a setting, care was needed in order not to be co-opted by violent men for their own more political causes. Fourth, Jesus did not see his work as merely a continuation of the agendas of the previous age—the time of the law and prophets was ceasing to be (or, if John was already dead, had ceased to be). The inbreaking of the dominion meant a new—indeed an eschatological—state of affairs for God's people. Fifth, it is hardly possible here to take *basileia* to mean what B. D. Chilton wants it to mean—God in his activity—because Jesus was not saying that God was under attack or suffering violence! Here is a saying that shows that the *basileia* must be seen not merely as a reign but also as a realm.[67]

---

[64] For a detailed attempt to put forward this view cf., P. W. Barnett, "Jewish Prophets," 145-210, and my discussion of this possibility, pp. 98-101 below.

[65] Kümmel, *Promise and Fulfilment*, 122-24; this will be confirmed when we discuss Luke 11:20. Boers, *Who Was Jesus?* 46ff., also draws this conclusion. In fact he would urge that Jesus saw John as ushering in the dominion of God, and thus Jesus is to be seen as a post-eschatological figure.

[66] So Fitzmyer, *Luke 10–24*, 1117-18.

[67] For the detailed discussion on the dominion material and Chilton's hypothesis, cf. pp. 192-98.

Contrasting Styles of Ministry (Matt. 11:16–19/Luke 7:31–35) That Jesus perceived John as a man of God with divine authority is also clear from such texts as Mark 11:27–33 and parallels that probably contain an authentic utterance of Jesus.[68] Various texts suggest that Jesus was willing to parallel his own work and divine authority with John's. These same texts suggest that Jesus saw himself as having divine authority and a divine commission. None of the texts that suggest parallels or even the indebtedness of Jesus to John, should cause us to overlook those texts that suggest Jesus distinguished himself and his work from John in various regards. One such text is the Q material of Matt. 11:16–19/Luke 7:31–35.

Even the most stringent sifters of the Gospel tradition agree that the substance of this material, a wisdom saying in the form of a modified similitude, should be accepted as coming from a *Sitz im Leben Jesu*.[69] Two difficulties are the saying of or about Wisdom at the end of the pericope and the use of Son of man. The latter may be an original "I" that has been replaced with the Son of man.[70] But if *bar enasha* was sometimes used by Jesus as a circumlocution when referring to his own present ministry, then there is no good reason to doubt its originality here.[71] With regard to the wisdom saying, scholars are evenly divided on its original form. Almost certainly Luke has added *panton* at 7:35, but it could also be argued that Matthew altered the original to speak of Wisdom's deeds in light of Matt. 11:2. Against such a conclusion, Hill is probably right that "deeds" is the original reading at this point since "children" is suspect on the grounds of harmonization with Luke 7:35.[72] This, however, does not decide what was in the *Vorlage* behind the present forms of this saying. The reading "deeds" should probably be seen as original because in Luke's Gospel there is an attempt even in the birth narratives to show how John and Jesus are closely linked together in life and in God's plan. The allusion in Luke to Jesus and John as Wisdom's children would fit this redactional agenda nicely.[73]

This saying comments on "this generation," a phrase often used pejoratively in the Gospels to mean this wicked or faithless generation (cf. Luke 11:29–32 and par.; 11:50f. and par.; 17:25; Mark 8:12, 38, passim). In the Old Testament, it is also used to criticize the immorality or faithlessness of Israel (cf. Deut. 32:5, 20; Judg. 2:10; Pss. 78:8; 95:10; Jer. 7:29). The phrase in its present context suggests a basic rejection of Jesus by the majority of his potential audience in Israel. Thus, this saying derives from late in the

---

[68] Cf. Taylor, *Mark*, 468–69; Cranfield, *Mark*, 362.
[69] Cf. N. Perrin, *Jesus*, 41; J. Breech, *Silence*, 9–10.
[70] A. J. B. Higgins, *Jesus*, 121–23.
[71] On the Son of man material, see pp. 233ff.
[72] Cf. Schweizer, *Matthew*, 264–65.
[73] Hill, *Matthew*, 202.

ministry when it was evident that the vast majority were to reject the good news Jesus offered as they had rejected John's ministry.

Even though it is possible to interpret the similitude otherwise, we should recognize the standard Jewish introduction of a parabolic saying, so that the comparison is between the whole situation described in the saying and the behavior or case of "this generation." The comparison is not suggesting that "this generation" is like the children first mentioned in the similitude, but that they are like the playmates who respond to the children calling them to play.[75] Thus, we are to see the children, who are inviting the others to play first at a wedding and then at a funeral, as Jesus and John. Both Jesus and John performed for them but they would neither dance nor mourn, refusing to be drawn into the events Jesus and John were heralding.

To be sure, it might be pressing the comparison too far to correlate the dancing with Jesus and the mourning with John. Nonetheless, in Matt. 11:18 and parallels, we hear of John's ascetical behavior (neither eating nor drinking, which Luke has expanded), and in 11:19 of Jesus' full participation in the fellowship of breaking bread and drinking wine, even with sinners and toll collectors.[76] Neither extreme of behavior pleased "this generation" — they labeled John a fanatic or a madman (he has a demon) and Jesus as immoral and a libertine (not only a glutton and a sot, but a friend of those who should be shunned — sinners and traitors). This is a caricature: John did eat and drink some things and we have no evidence that Jesus was famous for overindulgence. Nevertheless, the perceived difference in the way John and Jesus went about ministry is aptly reflected. Jesus says in effect that it does not matter which extreme of behavior was suggested or what reaction to life was encouraged because nothing pleased this faithless audience; they would not play either John's or Jesus' game.

What is striking about this similitude is that, although Jesus groups himself with John as a performer before Israel (notice the "we"), he definitely distinguishes their behavior. They had different visions about how to go about their ministries. Jesus neither carried the efforts of John a step

---

[74] Reicke, "Setting of John's Baptism," 222, has even suggested that in view of the Baptist's possible connections with the Qumran community, Luke may be intertwining Jesus and John because in the Qumran community two Messiahs were expected, one from the tribe of Levi, and one from the tribe of Judah. Thus Luke stresses at the outset that John is from Levi (1:5) while Jesus came from Judah and was born in David's city (1:27; 2:11). The problem with this view is that in the end, Luke recognizes only one Messiah, Jesus, whom he calls Lord in his redactional summaries and whom even in the birth narratives he sees as the one Savior.

[75] Cf. Jeremias, *Parables of Jesus*, 101.

[76] W. Farmer, *IDB* 2:957, s.v. "John the Baptist," has pointed out that "a person who eats and drinks" in a pejorative context like this refers not to excessive eating but to unlawful eating — eating unclean food and eating with unclean people. Thus the interpretation of Jesus' eating and drinking in the second half of the verse is understandable, the reference to excess presumably being a pejorative exaggeration. It appears quite plausible that Jesus did not observe all the Old Testament dietary restrictions. Cf. below pp. 56ff., on Jesus and the Pharisees.

further nor adopted the same modus operandi. Jesus preached good news of the dominion's arrival; John baptized and warned of coming judgment and the need for preparation. The difference between these two men was not simply that Jesus ministered after John, and thus saw the inbreaking of what John only looked forward to in his lifetime (Mark 6:14–29; Josephus *Ant.* 18.5.2, 1.116–119). What besides sequence made for this difference? Matthew 11:19b reads "but Wisdom is justified by her works." "Works" is probably the original reading especially in view of the reference to children in the similitude. It is more probable that "works" would be changed to "children" to make the saying fit neatly with what precedes. The meaning would be that despite the rejection by the general public, which has been the subject of discussion up to this point, Wisdom will be vindicated by her deeds.

A significant tradition in early Judaism developed about wisdom as "a quasi-personal hypostasis in heaven, a divine agent expressing the mind of God, who preaches to men and longs to dwell among them but is rejected by them"[77] (cf. Job 1, 28; Prov. 1, 8; Sir. 1, 24; 11QPs-a 18; Bar. 3f.; 1 En. 42; 4 Ez. 5; 2 Bar. 48; Wisdom, passim). Especially in Proverbs 8, Wisdom cries out in the public places urging the people to listen. The striking parallel to the setting of our similitude suggests that Jesus had this text in mind.

Let me introduce a rather speculative notion to make sense of aspects of the Jesus tradition that suggest his self-understanding. Hurtado has demonstrated the widespread use of the concept of divine agency in early Judaism, applied to everything from personified divine attributes, to patriarchs, to special angels.[78] Let us suppose that Jesus saw himself as God's *Shaliach* or agent, someone endowed with divine authority and power, the very authority and power of the sender.[79] This idea is found rather frequently in recent scholarly discussions of the historical Jesus. The *Shaliach* must be endowed with a divine commission and instructions. He must have a certain knowledge from and of the sender, indeed wisdom to carry out the sender's instructions and purposes. He must know key aspects of the sender's mind. This profile describes the portrait of Wisdom we find in Proverbs 8 and elsewhere in the Wisdom literature. Is it not conceivable that a Jesus who saw himself as God's agent might also have seen himself as divine Wisdom incarnate or as a figure such as the Enochian Son of man?[80] J. Breech, no

---

[77] Marshall, *Luke*, 303.

[78] Hurtado, *One God, One Lord*, 17–92.

[79] Cf. pp. 133–37.

[80] The wide variety of forms that speculation took in early Judaism about the matter of divine agency and agents is amply shown by Hurtado, *One God, One Lord*, 17–92. It is crucial to note that as Hurtado says, the idea of God having a chief agent "was widely shared and cannot be described as the exclusive property of any one type of Judaism" (18). It is thus not a major leap to suggest that Jesus also may have engaged openly in such speculation. Nor is it the case that this speculation only had to do with personified divine attributes because there was also

conservative, argues: "The appended saying interprets Jesus as the heavenly Wisdom who comes down to earth and calls men in the marketplace but they do not heed (Proverbs 8)."[81]

This Wisdom theme could be part of the first evangelist's christological redactional work.[82] Two things, however, count against this conclusion. First, this does not blend in well with other christological redaction of the first evangelist, or even with his overall christological presentation that involves both source and redactional material.[83] Second, it is Luke, not Matthew, who tells us that Jesus is the one who will dispense wisdom to his followers in their hour of trial (Luke 21:15). If Matthew had a Wisdom focus in his redactional work, then we might have expected to see the evidence of it in his apocalyptic discourse, but in fact we find it only in the parallel material in Luke. Thus, the conjecture of seeing the wisdom motif in Matt. 11:19//Luke 7:35 as going back to Jesus has more to commend it than Suggs's view. This conjecture must find support in other texts because one text is insufficient to draw a firm conclusion.[84]

If Jesus did see himself as God's Wisdom in the flesh, then it would explain: (1) a saying such as Matt. 12:42/Luke 11:31, which may well be authentic;[85] Solomon had wisdom, but Jesus was greater by being the manifestation of Wisdom in the flesh; (2) the reason that Jesus preferred the parable or similitude as a mode of speech—one characteristic form or genre of wisdom literature; (3) the reason that he felt free to vary not only from conventional wisdom but also from Torah in the manner he did ("but I say to you"); (4) his felt-closeness to the Father (abba) and his apparent belief that he had special knowledge of the Father that only Jesus could reveal;[86] (5) a saying such as "foxes have holes" in Matt. 8:20/Luke 9:58; which is like

---

speculation about exalted patriarchs and special angels as God's divine agents (cf. 51–92). We will discuss the material in the parables of *1 Enoch* (cf. pp. 234–48 below). Thus, what Jesus may have implied about himself could have been understood as a form of speculation about a notable person of faith (who was believed to have been a real person, like an Enoch, or another figure from the patriarchal period), assuming the role of God's divine agent—his *Shaliach*. The only daring aspect of this would be that Jesus would have been applying such speculation to himself while he was ministering, not to someone else long dead.

[81] Breech, *Silence*, 25.

[82] Cf. M. J. Suggs, *Wisdom*.

[83] Cf. M. D. Johnson, "Reflections on a Wisdom Approach to Matthew's Christology," *CBQ* 36 (1974): 44–64.

[84] Cf. pp. 221–28, on the sapiential material. The discussion of our text by C. E. Carlston ("Wisdom and Eschatology," 102–3) in relationship to other wisdom material in the Gospels confirms the wisdom character of this material. Cf. F. Christ, *Jesus Sophia*, 63ff. There are many texts with wisdom overtones. If any of them are authentic, then they also would bolster the case that Jesus may have seen himself as Wisdom incarnate, or the embodiment of divine wisdom. Cf. Matt. 11:25–27 and par.; Matt. 11:28–30; Matt. 23:34–36 and par.; and Matt. 23:37–39 and par. Note that not all this material is from Q and that as we have argued elsewhere in this study, Q is not simply to be seen as "Logoi Sophon." See pp. 223–24.

[85] Cf. B. Witherington, *Women in the Ministry*, 44–45 (and notes).

[86] This depends on the authenticity of sayings such as the so-called Johannine thunderbolt

1 En. 42.2 and Eccles. 24:6–22 where Wisdom has no dwelling place; (6) how, as early as ten to fifteen years after Jesus' death, the church was already singing Christ hymns such as Phil. 2 that apparently manifested a belief in the preexistence of the Son; and (7) the reason' that Jesus distinguishes himself from John in various crucial ways.

Whatever one thinks of Matt. 11:19b, Jesus did see himself as taking on a task like that of Wisdom in Proverbs 8. Distinguishing himself from John is his modus operandi for ministry because Jesus viewed himself in a different light and perhaps in a different category than he viewed John, whom Jesus said was more than a prophet. It may be asked, Why did Jesus not call himself Wisdom more directly or more often than in this one saying (Matt. 11:19b)? The explanation at hand is that he used the Son of man terminology in place of Wisdom.

JESUS THE JUDEAN BAPTIZER? (JOHN 3:22–4:3)

Many believe the controversial material from John 3–4 has little historical substance to it. Nevertheless, it is worth a brief look, bearing in mind that our conclusions to this point stand regardless of one's view about the nature of the Fourth Gospel vis-à-vis historical matters.

Linnemann's challenging study on Jesus and John led her to the following conclusions on the basis of the historical substance behind John 3:22–4:3: (1) Jesus worked as a baptizer, or at least allowed and encouraged his disciples to do so (4:2), during the lifetime of John;[87] (2) Jesus drew greater crowds as a baptizer than John; (3) Jesus stayed for a long time with John beyond the Jordan in Perea, allowing himself not only to be baptized by John but also to become a disciple of John; (4) the later side by side baptizing of two groups became a problem; (5) Jesus abandoned his baptizing when he heard that the Pharisees had learned Jesus was having more success than John, for it was not his intention to weaken or compromise John's position in the eyes of his opponents (the Pharisees); (6) Jesus learned from John of this new way of right standing with God—through repentance and baptism apart from detailed fulfillment of the law's requirements; (7) this led Jesus to the conclusion that the event of the repentance of sinners and tax collectors was the sign of the final inbreaking of God's mighty dominion. Coupled with John's imprisonment, it prompted Jesus to take up a ministry of preaching the inbreaking dominion in his native region of Galilee.[88]

(Matt. 11:27), which is set in the midst of several obvious wisdom sayings in 11:25 and 11:28ff. On Matt. 11:25–30, see pp. 221–28.

[87] Various scholars have seen 3:22 as being contradicted by 4:2. Cf. R. E. Brown, *The Gospel according to John 1–12* (New York: Doubleday, 1966), 164.

[88] Cf. Linnemann, "Jesus und der Taufer," 226–33.

What are we to make of these suggestions? First, 3:22–23 does not indicate that Jesus was in the Baptist's circle, or that he baptized with or under his tutelage.[89] What is suggested is a parallel practice in the same general region during the same general time period. Jesus endorsed John's work, as being baptized by John implies. Definitely, Mark 11:27–33 (and par.) indicates that Jesus saw John's baptism as having divine approval. This suggests that Jesus got the idea for a brief baptizing ministry from John because Jesus saw John's effectiveness in calling people to repentance and preparation for the coming divine activity.

Second, it is quite plausible that Jesus, out of respect for John, ceased his own parallel ministry so as not to compromise John's work. Perhaps he saw his own efforts as an attempt to supplement, not supplant, John's efforts. Perhaps when it became apparent that John would not minister anymore due to imprisonment, Jesus had to carefully evaluate the call of God on his life to see if God was urging him to go a step further than the Baptist, perhaps with a somewhat different emphasis or modus operandi. Jesus would preach, heal, and fellowship directly with the people rather than wait for them to come to him.

Both points six and seven are believable although they cannot be verified. Perhaps Jesus did gain some insight into the new work to which God was calling him by observing the method and message of John. Nevertheless, when he began his Galilean ministry he no longer saw his work as an extension or supplement of John's, if he had ever done so. Allowances must be made for both the similarities and the differences between Jesus' and John's ministries because these indicate that Jesus did not see himself as another prophet like John, although John was the closest and nearest point of comparison on the contemporary Judean scene. Thus, even though Jesus saw both John and himself as prophetic figures, nonetheless he saw John as more than just another prophet and himself as more than and other than John.

CONCLUSIONS

One key insight drawn from the material is that Jesus saw himself as not merely announcing but bringing about the eschatological blessings promised in Isaianic prophecies. Unlike John, Jesus apparently did not expect a coming one, a successor. He himself was bringing the final eschatological message and work of God for God's people Israel.[90] This explains the

---

[89] R. Schnackenburg, *The Gospel according to St. John* (London: Burns and Oates, 1968), 1:410–11.

[90] In general R. B. Gardner's distinctions are correct. Cf. his *Jesus' Appraisal*, 190: "Jesus is conscious, however, not only of an *eschatological solidarity* between John's work and his—but of a *soteriological difference* as well . . . In Jesus' mission, however, it is not only the time of the End

strident, urgent tone to much of what Jesus said. Salvation for Israel hinged on how it responded to Jesus' call and, before that, to John's.

A second insight is that Jesus may have seen himself as divine Wisdom in the flesh, or at least as carrying out the tasks and roles that the Wisdom literature portrays Wisdom as doing. This, when coupled with Jesus' understanding of himself as the *Shaliach* of God, may go a long way toward explaining Jesus' exalted sense of authority, power, and mission. It may explain why he felt free to say and do striking things that did not match up with common expectations about either a prophet or a Messiah.

Jesus said John was the greatest of those born of women and, thus, is the one figure in the Gospel tradition to whom Jesus seems to compare and contrast himself, both in his words and deeds. Although Jesus could have compared himself to various other contemporaries (Herod Antipas, Caesar, the Pharisees, the Sadducees, the priests and Levites, the revolutionaries), or with prophetic or kingly figures in Israel's past (David, Solomon, Moses, Jonah), he chose to mention such figures only in passing, or with less frequency than he mentions John. Although the chronological placement of many of Jesus' sayings about John is not clear, Jesus was comparing and contrasting himself to John from early on to near the very end of Jesus' ministry (cf. Mark 11:27–33 and par.). John was the main human touchstone for Jesus, the one figure who helped him sort out his own sense of identity and mission.

A third insight by inference is that Jesus manifested a normal progressive historical consciousness. Although it appears that Jesus early on saw himself acting parallel to and perhaps even as a supplement to John's ministry (if the material in John 3:22—4:3 has any historical substance), when John was imprisoned—or perhaps even shortly before then, when John appeared to be in some danger—Jesus reevaluated God's call on his life, leading to his all too short ministry in Galilee. The seeds of that "something greater than John" self-understanding may have been planted as early as Jesus' baptism by John, which seems to have coincided with some sort of charismatic experience or vision that Jesus had about being God's unique Son.[91] Jesus may have seen himself as the coming one of whom John spoke, although clearly Jesus saw his task and message as placing more emphasis on the good news about God's inbreaking activity than on the bad news of judgment that John stressed when speaking of the coming one. Certainly the eschatological consciousness of both men, their understanding of the crucial and decisive time that was dawning for Israel, is very similar in nature and orientation. Jesus saw John as a transitional figure, the last of the old style prophets, or the decisive eschatological prophet of God, who has one foot

---

which is dawning, but the Endtime *salvation* as well. Herein lies the christological otherness of Jesus" (emphasis his).

[91] Cf. pp. 148–55.

in and introduces the new eon. Of both John and Jesus it was said the dominion suffers violence.

JESUS AND THE PHARISEES

The debate about Jesus' relationship with the Pharisees is crucial to our study because of its bearing on christological questions. At stake is Jesus' relationship with the most prominent and popular of the Jewish parties of the pre-A.D. 70 period and his view of Torah with its oral extrapolations in the "traditions of the elders." In short, at stake is Jesus' relationship with the form of Judaism that survived the destruction of the temple and became the font of all later forms of Judaism.

WHO WERE THE PHARISEES?

Pharisaism was, at least for many in the pre-A.D. 70 period, the religious *vox populi* as well as the group most revered by the people. Examining Jesus' reaction to the Pharisees and what it says about his self-concept gives us significant clues about Jesus' view of: (1) the moral condition of early Judaism and its popular leadership; and (2) how Jesus saw himself relating to and fitting in with his own people.

The subject of Jesus' relationship with the Pharisees appears frequently in the Synoptic Gospels, although seldom as the focus of a given pericope in its final form. Information about the Pharisees is also given in Josephus's works and in the rabbinic material of the two Talmuds and the Mishnah. Unfortunately, the initial impression that it will be easy to access that relationship is deceptive because of some complex issues raised by these sources.

First, the relationship between the *perushim*, the *sopherim*, the *hakamim*, the *haberim*, the scribes, and the group the New Testament calls the Pharisees is not clear. E. Rivkin explains this relationship with a series of equations: the *perushim* = the Pharisees = the *haberim* = the *hakamim* = the *sopherim*.[92] Rivkin sees the Pharisees as a scholarly class dedicated to the twofold law. Unlike J. Neusner, Rivkin does not see such issues as purity and sabbath observance as the primary focus of the Pharisees. Rather, "the Pharisees were teachers of salvation for the individual through a community of true believers in the two-fold law, and not nationalists focusing on the land, or on the temple or on the sovereign state."[93]

There are problems with Rivkin's assessment. First, as Neusner's work on the rabbinic material concerning the pre-A.D. 70 Pharisees shows, most

---

[92] Cf. E. Rivkin, "Pharisees."
[93] Ibid., 661.

of the legal pericopes in that corpus involving Pharisees "deal with dietary laws: ritual purity for meals and agricultural rules governing the fitness of food for Pharisaic consumption. Observance of sabbaths and festivals is a distant third."[94] This squares with the overall impression the Synoptics give concerning what preoccupied the Pharisees and what issues they argued with Jesus. As Neusner repeatedly asserts, broadly speaking the rabbinic and New Testament literature agree on what were the prevailing issues for Pharisaism, and these were the very matters about which Jesus took issue with this group.

Second, particularly in Mark but also elsewhere in the Gospel tradition, scribes and Pharisees are associated but still distinguished, even to the point of being mentioned separately (cf. Mark 3:22; Matt. 8:19; 9:14; 13:52). Most interesting is the phrase in Mark that speaks of "the scribes of the Pharisees" (Mark 2:16). I share Bowker's view that "the references to *Pharasaioi* in Mark . . . appear to reflect, with very great precision indeed, the transition from the *Pharasaioi* of Josephus to the *perushim* attacked as extremists, of the rabbinic sources."[95] In the rabbinic literature *hakamim* is the term used to describe the Pharisees of the pre-A.D. 70 period as a whole, but occasionally the term *perushim is used*. Rivkin plausibly suggests that *perushim* in the rabbinic literature is used only of the Pharisees of the earlier period writ large when they are juxtaposed with the Sadducees.[96] Together all the references to *perushim* suggest that this term is used sometimes as a noun meaning separatists and sometimes as a label for the group we know as the Pharisees, although in later rabbinic literature it may sometimes refer to a particular group of Pharisees—the ultraorthodox. In fact, if one compares M. Hag. 2.7 and Dem. 2.3, a solution to our dilemma suggests itself, as Danby and Moore saw long ago.[97]

Third, the term *perushim* is used in the post-A.D. 70 rabbinic literature basically as a polemical term (the Separatists) to refer to the *haberim*, except when the term was needed to distinguish *hakamim* from the Sadducees as a particular religious group or ongoing movement.[98] This probably means that the term *haberim* ("associates" or "companions") refers to a group within the Pharisaic movement—an ultraorthodox wing that may have led a semi-cloistered existence a good deal of the time in order to insure full obedience

---

[94] J. Neusner, *Rabbinic Traditions* 3:304.

[95] J. Bowker, *Jesus*, 39. This suggests that Mark accurately reflects the *Sitz im Leben Jesu* on this matter, rather than simply his own situation.

[96] Rivkin, "Pharisees," 659; cf. his more lengthy study, "Defining the Pharisees."

[97] Cf. H. Danby, ed., *The Mishnah*, 214 n. 1; G. F. Moore, *Judaism in the First Centuries of the Christian Era* (New York: Schocken, 1971), 2:26.

[98] Apparently, Jesus had little contact with the Sadducees, probably because he was seldom in Jerusalem and seldom in contact with landed aristocracy; thus, we will not deal with his relationship to this group. Cf. J. Le Moyne, *Les Sadducéens*, esp. 401–6.

to their interpretation of the Old Testament laws about ritual purity. They were sectarian, not unlike the Qumranites.

Supporting this view is Rivkin's admission that the *haberim* were not a scholarly class but individuals who had voluntarily taken upon themselves extra religious duties, such as tithing from produce above what was required.[99] Sanders is surely right in saying, "It is generally granted on all hands . . . that before 70 there were *haberim*—lay people who maintained themselves in a relatively high state of ritual purity. What is important to note is that such groups were small, voluntary associations which accepted special rules for special reasons."[100] They should not be equated with the larger group the New Testament calls Pharisees (who may have numbered as many as 6000).[101]

To sum up, the pre-A.D. 70 Pharisees are the group that later rabbinic literature calls the *hakamim* or sometimes the *sopherim* (although the latter may refer to Pharisaic leaders or teachers of the larger movement). The *haberim* cannot simply be equated with the Pharisees; more and less strict Pharisees existed in and before Jesus' day, as the controversies between the houses of Shammai and Hillel make clear. Because it was the more lenient, Hillel group that prevailed in most regards in Judaism,[102] the ultraorthodox *haberim* are not surprisingly labeled separatists in the later tradition in a somewhat polemical sense. Among the Pharisees of Jesus' day were *haberim*, scribes (the Torah copiers and scholars who would be expected to give the interpretation of the Torah), and ordinary observant lay people and teachers who were part of the movement (some of whom were among the *haberim*, some of whom were not). In the New Testament, the term Pharisee refers variously to the *haberim* among the movement, the non-*haberim*, and the movement as a whole; only the context may give clues. That the New Testament term Pharisee already has its more polemical reference to the ultraorthodox among the movement—the *haberim*—is less likely. In any event, Jesus was confronted by Pharisees of varying degrees of rigidity about matters of the law and especially ritual purity.[103]

Several general observations about the Pharisees now can be made. First, it is true that one of the overarching goals of the Pharisees was to "spread Scriptural holiness throughout the land"—to borrow a phrase from another era of religious history. "In a very specific way the Pharisees claimed to live

---

[99] Rivkin, "Defining the Pharisees," 245. This explains how it is that the *haberim* are always juxtaposed with the *am ha 'aretz*, not with the Sadducees. The *am ha 'aretz* were those who were not superscrupulous about observance of halakic requirements, although this did not make them sinners or bad Jews.

[100] E. P. Sanders, *Jesus and Judaism*, 183.

[101] E. Schürer, *History of the Jewish People* 2:389 n. 20.

[102] Neusner, *Rabbinic Traditions* 3:301ff.

[103] Cf. the conclusions of Bowker, *Jesus*, 29ff. M. J. Cook, "Jesus and the Pharisees," 441–60; D. Smith, "Jesus and the Pharisees."

as if they were priests, as if they had to obey at home the laws that applied to the Temple."[104] Second, the Pharisees claimed to be those who passed on oral Torah that originally, in their way of thinking, was passed on to Moses at Sinai along with the written Torah and was preserved through passing on the tradition intact by a succession of faithful tradents. By claiming to have the correct interpretation and ability to explain (and expand) the law according to oral tradition to meet new situations, they asserted implicit and sometimes explicit authority over all Jewish people. Not surprisingly, they did not easily tolerate anyone who threatened the assumptions upon which that authority was based. As the Mishnah later explained: "It is more culpable to teach against the ordinances of the scribes than against the Torah itself" (M. San. 11.3).

What is surprising is how Hellenized even the Pharisees could be, in many ways appearing like a Hellenistic philosophical school or movement.[105] Hillel may have steered the Pharisaic movement in a more quietistic and Hellenistic (philosophical and sectarian rather than political or revolutionary) trajectory. At the group's inception, however, they were not only involved in the political positions during part of the Hasmonean period but also were a bit revolutionary in their approach to some matters.[106] Politics certainly was not the dominant concern of the Pharisees of Jesus' day, except insofar as it affected their ability to carry on their religious movement as they saw fit. Their agenda was the hallowing of everyday life in all its aspects within the existing structure of society, not apart from it, as was the case with the Qumranites.

PURITY AND PURPOSE

Was Jesus a Pharisee, or at least inclined to be one of their adherents? Evidence such as Jesus' involvement with the structure of the existing Jewish society and his lack of withdrawal from that society for any length of time favors such a suggestion. Further, there are texts in which Jesus seems to commend to his audience the teachings of the Pharisees along with their right to positions of teaching authority (Matt. 23:3) and concedes that the Pharisees maintain a certain standard of righteousness (Matt. 5:20). If one maintains the authenticity of Matt. 5:17–18 or Luke 16:17, then it could even be urged that Jesus was a rigorist in regard to observance of Torah, a posture that various Pharisees definitely took toward the law. Finally, Jesus

---

[104] J. Neusner, *Judaism,* 42.

[105] For his striking comparison of the Pharisees and a Hellenistic philosophical school, see M. Smith, "Palestinian Judaism," esp. 81.

[106] Rivkin, "Pharisees," 661: "The ultimate revolutionary act of the Pharisees was to insist that the high priest follow Pharisaic procedures on the Day of Atonement."

seems to have affirmed a belief in resurrection (cf. Mark 12:18ff.), which comports with Pharisaic teaching.[107]

There are several problems with this line of reasoning, however. First, drawing this picture of Jesus relies too heavily on Matthew to the neglect of the earlier material in Mark and Q. Second, it ignores some of the stringent criticism of the Pharisees even within Matthew, not all of which is likely to be later polemics of the Christian church (cf. Matthew 23). Third, Jesus not only had table fellowship with those whom the Pharisees considered unclean (e.g., sinners and tax collectors) but also felt free to touch and be touched by, discourse with, and even have as traveling companions people who were sometimes ritually or morally unclean.[108] When we add to this the fact that the Pharisees always appear in controversy settings with Jesus in our earliest Gospel (twelve times),[109] we have a picture at variance with that of Jesus, the Pharisee. Finally, the work of two scholars completes our picture.[110] M. Borg confirms that one of the essential characteristics of Jesus' ministry was controversy, particularly over holiness issues. Finally, D. Catchpole has also rightly pointed to some of the likely authentic Sabbath controversy material, some of the Q antitheses, Jesus' divorce ruling which is at odds with Mosaic law, and the fact that controversy with the Pharisees seems to lie behind many of the parables as evidence that Jesus could not have been a Pharisee or even largely in agreement with them.

Thus, the impression of Jesus in constant controversy with the Pharisees cannot be dismissed as polemical ax grinding by Mark. The majority of scholars still believe that Mark was written prior to or very near the fall of Jerusalem and the temple. This means that Mark was written long before the *Berkat ha minim,* and thus before the Christians could no longer actively participate in synagogue services. In short, Mark's Gospel was written in a period when the Christian community was still sorting out its relationship with Judaism and would not be generating a programmatic attack on the Pharisees, the most prominent and popular party within Judaism.

Let us evaluate the Markan material that focuses on Jesus' relationship to the Pharisees. Mark 7 is a collection of Jesus' teachings probably given on more than one occasion and grouped here due to thematic similarity (dealing with the issues of ritual and moral purity). This material may already have been grouped by catchword connection in Mark's source. It is plausible that Jesus had discussions with the Pharisees on two vital topics—the matters of handwashing and of clean and unclean food.

---

[107] On this passage, cf. Witherington, *Women in the Ministry,* 32ff.

[108] That this sort of fellowship, particularly with unclean women, was characteristic of Jesus' ministry is shown in Witherington, *Women in the Ministry,* 11ff.; cf. also Witherington, "On the Road."

[109] Cf. B. Chilton, *God in Strength,* 40 n.12; Taylor, *Mark,* 57.

[110] M. Borg, *Conflict,* 229ff.; D. Catchpole, "The Problem of the Historicity of the Sanhedrin Trial," in *Trial,* 48–50.

The *haberim* among the Pharisees most likely criticized Jesus in regard to a failure on his or his disciples' part to wash their hands.[111] This would have been a controversy over what Mark calls the "tradition of the elders" (Mark 7:5), which probably refers to the oral Torah or oral expansions on Torah that the Pharisees accepted as binding in addition to the written Torah. R. Booth, in his detailed work on tradition and legal history, concludes that *haberim* did practice supererogatory handwashing before A.D. 70 and before the *hakamim* made a decree on the subject.[112] There is, then, nothing improbable about Jesus discussing such a matter with the *haberim*.

When one analyzes Mark 7:15ff., however, the matter at issue is clean and unclean food. At stake here is not merely a supererogatory practice but the Torah's teaching. Certainly, in his redactional and parenthetical comment at 7:19b, Mark believes that Jesus is setting aside the Old Testament laws about clean and unclean food.

Yet there is still another historical objection to the plausibility of Jesus having such discussions in Galilee. On the one hand, such scholars as Jeremias and Farmer seem confident that there was a considerable Pharisaic presence in Galilee.[113] On the other hand, M. Smith avers, "There is strong evidence that there were practically no Pharisees in Galilee during Jesus' lifetime."[114] Several things count against Smith's view. First, there are the examples of Johanan ben Zakkai who moved to Galilee from the south and Eleazar from Galilee who seems to represent the Pharisaic point of view and is involved in the conversion of the royal house of Adiabene (*Ant.* 20.34–49).

Second, many Pharisees felt strongly about convincing other Jews of their viewpoints because they wanted Jewish society as a whole to reflect the holiness of the temple, and the Jesus tradition mentions their penchant for proselytizing (cf. Matt. 23:15; *Ant.* 20.34–49).[115] One should not be misled by the fact that the Pharisees are not focused on by Josephus in his narratives. As A. J. Saldarini says:

> The minor role played by the Pharisees in Josephus is explained by his concentration on the governing class and its political and military fortunes. . . . Neither the priesthood, the aristocrats, nor the peasants are treated except when they have an impact on the fortunes of the nation as a whole. The Pharisees are mentioned at times of change, crisis, or transition in government because when power shifted they and many other social and political forces in Jewish society became active in competition for power and influence.[116]

---

[111] Cf. Sanders, *Jesus and Judaism*, 198ff.

[112] R. Booth, *Purity*, 194ff.

[113] Cf. J. Jeremias, *Jerusalem*, 267; and W. R. Farmer, *Jesus and the Gospel*, 30.

[114] M. Smith, *Jesus the Magician*, 157; cf. the caution of M. Hengel, *The Charismatic Leader*, 55 and 45 n.26.

[115] A. Segal, "The Cost of Proselytism," 336–69, has more than amply demonstrated that the Pharisees were very interested in proselytism. Cf. esp. 353–60.

[116] A. J. Saldarini "Pharisees and Scribes," 203.

Third, in view of S. Freyne's detailed study, lower Galilee cannot be characterized as some cultural backwater cut off from the major movements of Judaism in the first century.[117] Indeed, as J. A. Overman indicates, what is striking is the degree of urbanization in Galilee.[118] The very existence of numerous synagogues in Galilee makes it likely that there were resident Pharisees in the region.

Fourth, Mark suggests that the Pharisees and scribes at least once came from Jerusalem to discuss matters with Jesus (7:1; cf. 3:22). This has suggested to some that they may have been retainers of the temple leadership so far as it was represented in Galilee.[119] Mark realizes that the center of the Pharisaic movement was in the south, but this would not prevent members of the movement from traveling north to hear what a notable teacher like Jesus had to say on subjects of importance to them (ritual purity or sabbath observance). Thus, Jesus probably had ongoing discussions with the Pharisees in Galilee whether or not those debating with him actually lived in Galilee.

Finally, it is right to point out that "since Mark writes just before or after the war against Rome, he is not anachronistically reading the later Pharisees/rabbis back into Jesus' life. His traditions reflect at least the mid-first century. . . ."[120] I would argue that they ultimately go back to the experience of Jesus himself.

Turning to the discussion on handwashing in Mark 7:1–8, it sometimes is urged that Jesus does not seem to respond to the question as to why the disciples eat with defiled hands. As Taylor points out, however, the quotation of Isa. 29:13 is very apposite on this occasion,[121] especially when coupled with the saying in Mark 7:8. I judge the challenge to the authenticity of the response in 7:6–8 to have failed. For our purposes, only 7:7–8 need represent the gist of Jesus' response, and here it is clear that Jesus is criticizing the upholding of oral Torah as the expense of written Torah. Interestingly, Jesus calls the oral Torah the teaching or precepts of human beings. Inherent in this is a lower assessment of oral tradition than seems to have been characteristic of the Pharisees. Besides calling such traditions human, Jesus seems to believe that oral Torah and written Torah could be in

---

[117] Cf. S. Freyne, *Galilee*, 41ff. Indeed, as J. H. Charlesworth, *Jesus within Judaism*, 105, says, we now know that lower Galilee had a close relationship with Judea.

[118] Cf. J. A. Overman "First Urban Christians?" 160–68. Overman disputes Theissen's stress on the itinerant nature of the Jesus movement, pointing out that in most locations in Galilee, Jesus and his followers could simply have walked home at the end of the day!

[119] Saldarini, "Pharisees and Scribes," 204–5. "The Pharisees' stress on tithing and priestly piety for the laity could have been attractive to the Jerusalem authorities who desired to collect tithes from all Jews in Palestine and who could have met resistance from Jews in Galilee outside their political control" (205). Saldarini thus explains the lack of significant mention of the Pharisees in Galilee outside the Gospels by the view that they were retainers of the Jerusalem authorities.

[120] Ibid., 204.

[121] Taylor, *Mark*, 334.

conflict with one another. At least in the case of the *haberim*, Jesus states that their priorities are askew, putting oral before written Torah. Now, it appears Jesus rejects the "traditions of the elders" at least on this point and thus does not manifest a Pharisaic attitude toward oral Torah. This suggestion is confirmed by some of the probably authentic material among the famous antitheses (cf. Matt. 5:21ff.).[122]

We now turn to Mark 7:15, widely regarded as an authentic Jesus logion (although independent of the earlier discussion in Mark 7:1-8). Some doubts, however, have been expressed by Sanders and Harvey.[123] Sanders doubts that if Jesus had made such a clear pronouncement, then Peter and James could hardly have contended for the maintenance of food laws in the earliest church. This sort of critique ignores several key factors. First, the Gospel tradition is clear that many things Jesus said were not immediately understood either by the disciples or others. Second, the metaphorical nature of this saying lends itself to several possible interpretations. Third, even Mark feels it necessary to explain the saying in 7:15 to his much later Christian audience, suggesting that the meaning cannot be assumed to be obvious. Fourth, if Mark is writing to a predominantly gentile audience, then there would have been no need to create such a saying because his audience would not assume the uncleanness of food. In short, the saying must be at least pre-Markan and thus have been passed on at some point by the Jewish Christian community, which assuredly did not invent such a saying. Finally, Paul, a Pharisee, would not have come up with the principle he states in Rom. 14:14 about nothing being unclean of itself, had there not been some Jesus tradition or precedent in the earliest period of the church for such a remark.[124] More likely, Paul's remark goes back to the saying in Mark 7:4-15 than he came up with the same idea independently. I conclude that the arguments against the authenticity of this saying are strained.

Bultmann tells us that in form this saying is probably a wisdom utterance,[125] more specifically, a *mashal* or metaphorical utterance in two parts.[126] As Daube puts it, "it is deliberately obscure. In fact to the public at large . . . it must sound like an allusion to some strange piece of magic."[127] The first half of the saying must refer to food, with the point being that no food that

---

[122] On the authenticity of some of the antitheses, see the arguments of J. Jeremias, *New Testament Theology*, 204ff.

[123] Sanders, *Jesus and Judaism*, 266ff.; A. E. Harvey, *Jesus*, 39.

[124] Cf. S. Westerholm, *Jesus and Scribal Authority*, 81-82.

[125] Bultmann, *Synoptic Tradition*, 74.

[126] J. Riches, *Transformation*, 137.

[127] D. Daube, *New Testament*, 142-43. Daube sees in Mark 7 a fundamentally Jewish pattern of argumentation involving: a question put by an opponent; public retort of a mysterious sort sufficient to silence the questioner; request for explanation by followers; and private explanation later to the followers.

goes into a person can make him or her unclean. This member of the twofold saying could stand on its own, but probably should not. Nonetheless, even if only this part of the saying is authentic, it presents a strong case for the view that Jesus judged the laws in Leviticus 11 and Deuteronomy 14, as well as oral expansions on them, no longer were valid. Perhaps Jesus said this because he believed that a new situation prevailed for believers because the kingdom was now breaking into human history.

Booth tries to negate the force of the usual interpretation by contending that we have here a relative rather than an absolute contrast, the *ou/alla* construction, meaning "nothing outside a person defiles that person as much as things that come from within it."[128] This is possible, and a Semitic dialectical comparison using contrastive terms could lie behind the text here, but there are serious problems with this view. First, whatever the text originally meant, in light of 7:19b Mark obviously understands the Greek construction in 7:15 to indicate a clear contrast, and it may well be that Mark has formulated this saying in Greek for the first time. Second, we do not have here the simple *ou/alla* formula but rather *ouden/alla*. The word *ouden* here must mean "nothing," and I can find no examples where *ouden simpliciter* means "not so much." Nor can *ouden* simply mean "not" or "no" here because the point refers to some object or lack of it that enters the human being from outside. The United Bible Societies Greek New Testament suggests a colon before the saying introduced by *alla*, not the comma one might expect if a simple *ou/alla* construction was in view here. Third, the difficulty of this saying favors its authenticity, in view of the tendency in later Gospel material to depict Jesus as a law-abiding Jew. It stands in contrast to the positions of both early Judaism and the earliest Jewish Christian church. On the basis of the criterion of dissimilarity, its claims to authenticity are impeccable if the clear contrast is the intent of the saying.

The second half of the saying is more enigmatic than the first. The phrase "but that which goes forth from a person is the thing that makes a person unclean" might refer to the emission of bodily fluids or waste such as semen, urine, excrement, or spittle.[129] If this saying was originally given by Jesus to the Pharisees, then this is how the second half of the saying would have been understood. In fact, 7:19a might favor this interpretation with the reference to that which goes into the stomach and then out into the latrine. It is not until we get to 7:21–22 that we can deduce a ritual/moral impurity contrast, and some contend that this material is Mark's own moralistic expansion on the original saying. Regardless, one conclusion seems firm on the basis of Mark 7:15: Jesus was no Pharisee, and he seems to have assumed the authority to declare some portions of Torah invalid. Westerholm says that Jesus

---

128 Booth, *Purity*, 69, 219.
129 Cf. Riches, *Transformation*, 137.

did not recognize scribal authority as binding. . . . It seems clear that he conceived the will of God and the nature of biblical law in a different fashion . . . whereas Pharisaic halakhah found the will of God in the divinely ordained statutes of scripture, all of which had to be carefully obeyed, Jesus shows an apparent indifference toward certain aspects of the scriptural law. . . . His repeated statements that purity is an inner, not external, matter make the observance of scriptural rules of ritual purity for their own sake . . . religiously indifferent. . . . His attacks against the tradition are not motivated by the view that it is extrabiblical and thus lacking in authority, but by a fundamentally different conception of the will of God. Jesus did not define the will of God in terms of the careful fulfillment of scripture's statutes; for him the attitude of the heart was critical.[130]

This is not merely a matter of priorities or of repeating the prophetic message of getting back to the heart of the law—*sediqa* and *hesed*.[131] Jesus seems to assume an authority over Torah that no Pharisee or Old Testament prophet assumed—the authority to set it aside. What is striking about the way Jesus relates to the law is that his response in the authentic material seems varied. Sometimes he affirms the validity of some portions of the law.[132] Sometimes he intensifies the law's demands (e.g., portions of the Sermon on the Mount), a point of view that does not violate the law but goes beyond it.[133] Sometimes he adds new material, apparently of juridical force, to the law (e.g., his teaching on adultery and divorce in Mark 10/Matthew 19).[134] Sometimes he sets aside the Torah as he does in Mark 7:15.[135] In short, he feels free not only to operate with a selective hermeneutic but also to add and subtract from Scripture.

All of this suggests that Jesus did not see himself as a Galilean hasid or another prophet, even one like Elijah. He saw himself in a higher or more authoritative category than either of these types familiar to Jewish believers,

---

[130] Westerholm, *Scribal Authority*, 90–91. He concludes: "It seems apparent that Jesus was not a Pharisee . . ."

[131] B. J. Malina, *New Testament World*, 144–45, suggests the following analysis of Jesus' views: "The emphasis ought not to be on how Israel should approach God, but on how God in fact approaches Israel. The purpose of interaction with God . . . is to replicate and reveal how God acts towards his people (openness to all . . .), not to replicate and support how Israel has acted toward God in the past (selective defensiveness . . .) . . . What results is the embedding of the purity rules of the Torah within the Torah as a whole instead of fitting Torah as a whole into the purity rules, as the elites would insist."

[132] Cf. Witherington, *Women in the Ministry*, 11ff., esp. on the Decalog command to honor parents.

[133] Sanders, *Jesus and Judaism*, 267–69, is right to stress that intensifying the law is not the same as abrogating or contradicting it.

[134] Cf. Witherington, *Women in the Ministry*, 20ff.

[135] There are numerous other places in the Gospel tradition that point to Jesus' rejection of the clean/unclean distinctions, such as staying in the house of Simon the Leper (Mark 14:3). This implied a rejection of the approach to holiness that identified holiness with ritual cleanliness or, to put it another way, saw cleanliness as next to godliness. Cf. Charlesworth, *Jesus within Judaism*, 73.

but we cannot substantiate this conclusion without first looking at texts where Jesus interacts with the Pharisees and then at texts indicating his view of the law. At this point, we can say with Westerholm:

> the centre of Jesus' ministry was not his understanding of the law of God, but the message of divine intervention in the history of God's people: . . . Jesus' message for "sinners" was not that a true understanding of God's law showed them to be either more or less sinners than the Pharisees made them out to be; sinners they were but God's salvation had come near to them as well![136]

THE SABBATH – REST OR RESTORATION?

Mark depicts Jesus at odds with the Pharisees over what he or his disciples are doing on the Sabbath (Mark 2:23–28 and par.; healing on the Sabbath, Mark 3:1ff. and par.; and the unique Luke 13:10–17). On the basis of multiple attestation we may be rather certain Jesus did have such controversies in regard to Sabbath behavior.

Yet Sanders suggests that a story like Mark 2:23–28 is too unrealistic to be considered an authentic report of Jesus' behavior. He parodies the narrative: "Pharisees did not organize themselves into groups to spend their Sabbaths in Galilean cornfields in the hope of catching someone transgressing."[137] This caricature makes the story seem too fantastic to be believed. Sanders's skepticism is based on the belief that there were few if any Pharisees in Galilee before A.D. 70 and that it is unlikely that the Judean Pharisees made long expeditions to catch Jesus as a lawbreaker. Reasons to believe that there were Pharisees in Galilee have already been given. Further, if Jesus really was a controversial teacher and healer, then he would have been precisely the kind of person the Pharisees would have investigated to see whether he agreed with or was a threat to their ideas and authority.

I grant that Galilee was probably looked upon by the Pharisees rather like a mission field, for Freyne has shown that in some regards (such as on the matter of paying the temple terumoth, the half shekel) Galileans apparently followed Sadducean rather than Pharisaic practice, and so would have been considered lax by the stricter Pharisees. But even allowing for this fact, Freyne's careful conclusion is warranted: "It still does not seem possible to eliminate completely a genuine confrontation between Jesus and Pharisaism. . . . When all these passages have been subjected to a thorough form- and redaction-critical analysis they still leave no reasonable doubt that Jesus was at odds with the Pharisees on a number of crucial points in their piety."[138]

---

[136] Westerholm, *Scribal Authority*, 131.
[137] Sanders, *Jesus and Judaism*, 265.
[138] Freyne, *Galilee*, 321; cf. 280–81, on the temple tax.

As Mark 2:23–28 is presented, there are various views of what happened, none of which require us to envision Pharisees lurking in cornfields on the Sabbath waiting to catch Jesus. In fact, the story says nothing of them even being in the fields. Verse 24 simply says that the Pharisees spoke to Jesus about the conduct of his disciples. While *Ide* could mean that the Pharisees observed the disciples' behavior on that Sabbath, it may mean no more than "Look here, why are your disciples acting in this fashion?" a question that could have been raised after the occurrence as well as during it. Mark's account is elliptical and does not explain the location of the Pharisees. In any case, Sanders has to read more into the location of the dispute than is warranted.

Its form is a conflict-speech that ends with a final pronouncement to silence the critics. Should we see v. 28 as part of the original story, or as a redactional summary to bring out the christological import of the story? In view of the grammatical awkwardness of the verse being tacked onto verse 27 by means of a *hoste* clause, even such a conservative commentator as Cranfield is willing to grant that the verse is an editorial conclusion.[139]

The remainder of the pericope seems authentic. First, the reference to Abiathar as high priest creates difficulties and probably was not invented by the early church because it appears to place an error in Jesus' mouth. Second, this story is about the behavior of the disciples, not Jesus, although Jesus accepts responsibility for his disciples' behavior. Later polemic was more likely to make this a direct *tête à tête* between Jesus and the Pharisees about Jesus' behavior in which he is vindicated. In short, a direct christological focus might be suspect, but not the narrative itself as presented in Mark. Third, this pericope does not elaborate on the possible parallels between Jesus and David. Daube stresses that this narrative reflects the ordinary dynamic between disciples and their teacher, in which the latter assumes responsibility for his followers' behavior. The implication is that he either passively accepts or actively endorses such behavior because he does not correct it.[140] "So powerful is a master's position that an action he condones may be imputed to him just as much as one he initiates."[141] In short, this narrative depicts a relationship between Jesus and his followers which is believable in Jesus' pre-A.D. 70 Jewish *Sitz im Leben*.

The bone of contention in this story is neither the plucking and eating of standing corn—the Old Testament specifically permits this (cf. Deut. 23:24–25; Lev. 19:9–10, 23:22; Deut. 24:19ff.)—nor the length of the disciples' Sabbath journey, but the time when these actions transpire—on the Sabbath. Several approaches have been taken to the appeal to David's example in this pericope. First, possibly it is meant to establish a precedent

---

[139] Cranfield, *Mark*, 118.
[140] D. Daube, "Master and Disciples."
[141] Ibid., 5.

in extremis for the disciples' behavior. Against this there is no indication in the text that eating was a life or death matter for the disciples in this case. Even strict Pharisees seem to have agreed that life-threatening situations overrode the prohibition against work on the Sabbath. No such situation is found here.

Second, it might be an example of Jesus' selective hermeneutic and prioritizing—stressing that moral matters take precedence over ritual ones. Although possible, this does not fully explain why the story proceeds as it does. Is the issue that there are special circumstances that—or special persons who—can change the rules of the game? In view of the climax (2:27), the implicit issue is Jesus' interpretation of the Sabbath which allows behavior seemingly in violation of Exod. 16:25-26, which rules out gleaning and plucking. Thus, the issue in this case, as in Mark 7:15, is neither oral Torah nor the traditions of the elders but the written Torah itself. R. Banks sees here "a novel use of the Old Testament, christological in character, so striking that it must stem from Jesus himself."[142] Given his reading of 7:27–28, Banks is probably right to suggest that by this quote Jesus "is insisting that if only the Pharisees had understood something of the nature of his mission they would not have condemned his disciples for their action."[143]

Third, an attempt can be made to fend off the apparent radical direction of Jesus' permission to glean and the accompanying saying by quoting Mekil. Exod. 13.14 or *B.T. Yom.* 85b: "the Sabbath is delivered to you and not you to the Sabbath." These quotes are from a later period of Jewish history, and H. Braun is probably right to point out that "this rule of conduct . . . only signifies that the Sabbath might be violated only to rescue a human life."[144] The thrust of 2:27 is rather different from this. Jesus' point of view seems to be that human beings do not exist for the sake of the law, but rather the converse. The function of the Sabbath is to restore and renew creation to its full capacity, just as leaving the land fallow for a sabbatical year might do.

The disciples' eating was a means of restoration and renewal for them. Thus, they should be permitted to eat, even at the expense of specific, clear prohibitions in the law. In short, Jesus sees it as part of his mission to interpret matters according to their true or original intention, no longer making allowances for the hardness of human hearts. This is especially clear in Jesus' teaching on marriage in which he appeals to the creation order and the fact that "from the beginning it was not so."[145] This approach seems to be implicit in both the allowance of the disciples to glean and the response in 2:27. This does not amount to appealing to one part of Scripture over another. Rather, there is in the midst of the Pharisees a distinctive person

---

[142] R. Banks, *Law*, 116.
[143] Ibid., 117-18.
[144] H. Braun, *Spätjudisch-Haretischer* 2:70 n.2.
[145] Cf. Witherington, *Women in the Ministry*, 26-27.

uniquely authorized by God who, like David, might do something creative and new. This meant that at least some of the old rules no longer applied, for a new situation was dawning, a divine dominion was breaking in through the ministry of Jesus. Jesus was offering new commandments or possibilities in light of the new eschatological situation.[146]

The explanatory power of this view of Jesus' actions is evident when we apply it both here and in the healing-on-the-Sabbath stories. Because I have already treated two of these stories in detail,[147] it is sufficient to quote Banks's conclusion that they

> give an invaluable insight into Jesus' attitude towards the sabbath. For him it is not only a day upon which it is appropriate to heal, it is the day on which one must do so. . . . His practice is a direct consequence of his understanding of his mission, not in the first instance, an attempt to provoke the Pharisaic opposition by transgressing either the oral or written Law. Inasmuch as it may run counter to the Mosaic Law it is indicative again of his position *above it, not an explicit stand against it.*[148]

From this conclusion a question arises: What sort of person takes such a stance in relation to the law?

The categories of teacher or prophet are inadequate to explain such a stance: We have here either a lawbreaker or one who stands above the law and uses it to fit his mission and the new situation that results from that mission. The latter seems more probable because of Jesus' careful regard for some aspects of the law. Infidels are not concerned about scrupulous observance of some laws when they feel free to violate others with impunity. All of this suggests that whether or not Jesus was right about himself, he did conceive of himself as being in a special and perhaps almost unprecedented (with the exception of David?) category vis-à-vis the Old Testament law and other institutions of Judaism. Although he does not make this clear in so many words, it is implicit in both his actions and words, especially in the controversies with the Pharisees.

Possible confirmation for this interpretation of Jesus' view of the law comes from the sayings of a near contemporary of Jesus, Johanan ben Zakkai, who is reported to have been a disciple of Hillel and who migrated north to Galilee during the period when Jerusalem and the temple were about to fall. After a lengthy discussion about the matters of clean and

---

[146] K. Berger, *Die Gesetzesauslegung Jesu*, 588, connects this newness with Jesus' repentance preaching as follows: "The validity of the conversion, according to the view of Jesus—so far as we are able to conclude anything about it—-is closely connected with the acknowledgment of his being God's Sent One. His help after conversion can only be grounded in the fact that Jesus maintained that he had received Revelation, i.e., God's Word. Because he is a genuine Revelation-bearer, his commandments are something new."

[147] Witherington, *Women in the Ministry*, 66–71.

[148] Banks, *Law*, 130.

unclean, the passage in Numbers Rabbah 19.2 concludes: "It is not the dead that defiles nor the water that purifies. The Holy One, blessed be He merely says: 'I have laid down a statute . . . I have issued a decree. You are not allowed to transgress My decree.'" In Strack-Billerbeck, a volume that must be used with caution, it is suggested that this was Johanan's polemic against Jesus' novel attitude toward the law,[149] in particular Mark 7:15. This is conceivable and suggests that some in Johanan's day were actually questioning the validity or at least the applicability of some of the law. Jesus was the sort of person who would have received Johanan's censure, whether or not he actually responded to Jesus in this famous dictum.

Harvey's treatment on the constraints of history has suggested that there was a particular set of parameters within which Jesus must have operated in order to be understood, much less accepted, by his Jewish contemporaries. I agree that he had to communicate in understandable terms and categories, although he did not have to agree with current or popular uses of such terms and categories. As N. T. Wright pointed out, one needs to be fairly flexible when using such an approach because it is impossible to say with certainty that Jesus could or could not have said or done one thing or another.[150] We do not know enough about pre-A.D. 70 Judaism to be certain what the outer limits of comprehensibility or acceptability might have been.

From what we do know, however, it appears that, for both the Pharisees and the ordinary observant Jew, Jesus' actions and sayings as depicted in Mark 2:23ff. and 7:15 suggest that he sometimes stepped beyond what was normally perceived to be the acceptable limits of Jewish diversity. His actions, however, were at least partially comprehensible even to nondisciples because he does frequently talk and act in ways that seem to communicate to an audience wider than the Twelve.

Did Jesus see himself as the dispenser of a new Torah in the messianic age? W. D. Davies showed with reasonable certainty that the rabbinic material that talks in terms of a new Torah in the messianic age post-dates A.D. 70. Nevertheless, the evidence, especially from the intertestamental and early rabbinic literature, allows Davies to conclude:

> We can at least affirm that there were elements inchoate in the Messianic hope of Judaism, which could make it possible for some to regard the Messianic Age as marked by a New Torah, new indeed . . . not merely in the sense that it affirmed the old on a new level, but in such a way to justify the adjective *HDSHH* that was applied to it.[151]

---

149 Hermann L. Strack and P. Billerbeck, *Kommentar zum Neuen Testament aus Talmud und Midrasch* (Munich: Beck'sche, 1974–), 1:719.

150 Cf. Harvey, *Jesus*, 1ff.; N. T. Wright, "Constraints."

151 W. D. Davies, *Torah*, 85.

What this means is that it is conceivable, in a setting like pre-A.D. 70 Palestine, where there was considerable messianic fervor among various elements of the population, for Jesus to have introduced a *lex nova,* or at least a novel approach to the old law supplemented by his own teaching, especially if he felt that the messianic age was being ushered in by his own ministry. We have yet to show that Jesus believed this.

FASTING OR FEASTING?

In our discussion of Jesus' relationship to the Baptist we discerned that there were elements of continuity and discontinuity between John's movement and that of Jesus. In Mark 2:18-22 we find yet another element of discontinuity—Jesus' disciples do not fast as a regular practice. It is possible that the reference to the Pharisees here is redactional. This is not a necessary inference on several accounts. Fasting was one of the pillars of Pharisaism. The Pharisees made a practice of fasting on Mondays and Thursdays (cf. Luke 18:12; *M. Taan.* 1.4-5; *B.T. Taan.* 10a). The Old Testament required fasting only on Yom Kippur (cf. Exod. 20:10; Num. 29:9-11; Lev. 35:9), but at the end of the prophetic period other fast days were being practiced (cf. Zech. 7:5; 8:19; cf. *J.T. Taan.* 68a-d). Note that, as in the Sabbath controversy story, at issue is the behavior of Jesus' disciples, which may suggest the earliness of this narrative because there appears to have been a tendency to give Gospel stories more of a christocentric focus as the tradition developed.

Reference to Jesus' death in this pericope is unlikely, it is objected, at so early a point in the ministry. Mark has probably not presented this material in its original chronological setting. This story reflects a time when John was already dead and his disciples were mourning and fasting as a result. More likely, the placement of this story is due to Mark's (or his source's) desire to group together various narratives about Jesus' controversies with the Pharisees.[152] The reference to "the disciples of the Pharisees" is another objection to this story's authenticity. This may refer to nothing more than the lay adherents of the Pharisaic teachers. Pharisees taken as a group did not have disciples, but some of their individual scribes or teachers did.

The sayings in 2:21-22 were originally a separate unit, as is suggested by the absence of any linking words at the beginning of 2:21. Focusing our attention on 2:18-20, the form is a pronouncement story. It has been argued that 2:19b-20 because of its allegorical element is likely to reflect a later Christian creation, and thus is not part of the original material. Against this, as Cranfield noted, there is already an element of allegory in 2:19a. In any case, as R. E. Brown has shown, various Jewish *meshalim* had allegorical

---

[152] Cf. Taylor, *Mark,* 208; Lane, *Mark,* 107-9.

elements so that a hard and fast distinction between a parable and supposed later allegorical accretions cannot be made. Parables in Jesus' day and before often had allegorical elements.[153] Yet, there is no explicit reference here to Jesus as the bridegroom. Later Christian tradition was not reluctant to make this idea more explicit (cf. Eph. 5:22-32; 2 Cor. 11:2; Rev. 19:7, 9; 21:2, 9; 22:17). Lane says, "Although the image of the wedding feast was sometimes used by the rabbis to express the joy of the messianic era, neither in the Old Testament nor in later Jewish literature was the Messiah represented as the bridegroom."[154] Thus, whatever Jesus intended by this reference, it would not likely have been immediately understood as any sort of explicit messianic claim. There was no conventional notion of messiah as bridegroom. Thus, 2:19b-20 fit the pattern that we have noted all along—Jesus, when making claims about himself through word or deed, employed an indirect and allusive (and some might say elusive) manner to avoid identification with various popular notions of the day.

The question about fasting is raised by the Baptist's followers and the Pharisee's adherents. Jesus' disciples did not make it a habit to fast.[155] Jesus' response is by analogy—the situation is like the circumstances of a Jewish wedding. Are "the sons of the bridechamber"[156] to fast as long as the bridegroom is with them? While the bridegroom is with them, they are not able to fast.[157] But days will come when he will be taken away from them, and then they will fast in that day.

No explicit mention is made as to how the bridegroom will be taken away. We might expect a more explicit reference to crucifixion or a violent death if this were a later church creation. The passive *aparthe* implies that God will conclude the bridegroom's life at some future time (an example of a divine passive in which God is the implied agent of the action). The verb itself means to take away or remove, although there is no strong sense of a violent removal (cf. Isa. 53:8 LXX where the context implies violent removal). Here Jesus implies that the time of his life and ministry is a time for joy and celebration—for feasting, not fasting. Fasting is and will be appropriate at a time of mourning after the bridegroom is removed from the earthly scene. This might be analogous to the present situation of the

---

[153] Cf. Cranfield, *Mark*, 135-36; Brown, *New Testament Essays*; and pp. 206-15 below.

[154] Lane, *Mark*, 110.

[155] That the narrative implies a deduction made after a period of observation also implies a *Sitz im Leben* for this story later in the ministry of Jesus.

[156] The Semitic form of expression, which refers to the wedding guests (or perhaps more correctly the bridal guests), favors the earliness and authenticity of this utterance. The Hebrew would be *bene hahuppah*.

[157] Here again we see a Semitic element—parallel construction—saying the same thing twice in two slightly different manners. The Old Testament is replete with this, e.g., Ps. 8:4; Gen. 3:16; 4:23. It is especially characteristic of poetic material.

Baptist's followers who are fasting as part of their mourning for their departed leader.

Thus, Jesus seems aware of bringing about a new or different set of affairs that are cause for celebration. The celebration is not only because the kingdom is breaking in but also because Jesus is dwelling in the midst of his disciples. This saying also reinforces our earlier conclusion that Jesus was no Pharisee. But there is a further point – if the text does not imply John is dead, then perhaps we are meant to see a distinction between what characterizes the disciples of Jesus while he is present and the disciples of John. In any event, the appropriateness of celebration due to a special occurrence or person should not be missed. What Jesus was about prompted, if not required, an appropriate response. The failure of the inquisitors to see something special in the situation, or perhaps even in Jesus, caused their failure to understand the behavior of Jesus' disciples.

BANQUETING WITH THE BAD

Jesus most certainly directed his attention to the least, the lost, and the last among Israel's populace.[158] In particular, Jesus had a reputation of sharing in table fellowship with such people, as is confirmed by the criterion of multiple attestation (cf. from L, Luke 7:36–50; 19:1–10; from Q, Matt. 11:19// Luke 7:34; and our present text, Mark 2:15–17 and par.). But who were these people?

Biblical scholarship tends to identify the sinners with the *am ha 'aretz* and to assume *telonai* refers to those who worked for the Romans, when it may refer to customs officials who worked for Herod Antipas or Philip. Sanders's work establishes clearly that the *am ha 'aretz* cannot simply be equated with the sinners of the New Testament.[159] Nor should the poor be equated with the sinners. When Jesus associated with the outcasts of society, it is not that he associated with the common folk who did not observe all the ritual purity rules of the *haberim*. The rabbinic sources urged Pharisees (in particular, the *haberim* among them) not to have table fellowship with the *am ha 'aretz*.[160] Yet this does not make the *am ha 'aretz* sinners; it means they are not as ritually observant as the Pharisees or, in particular, the *haberim*.

In the sixty or so Old Testament references to this phrase, *am ha 'aretz* is not a technical term of either a polemical or negative nature. Indeed, it is not a technical term at all.[161] The phrase varies in reference from context to context with *eretz* meaning everything from a particular village and its

---

[158] Cf. Sanders, *Jesus and Judaism*, 326.

[159] Ibid., 188–99.

[160] Cf. *M.Demai* 2.2–3. Nor may scholars eat with them, cf. *B.T.Ber.* 43b. *J.T.Shab.* 3c seems clearly to indicate that it is the Pharisees in general who should not eat with such people.

[161] Cf. E. W. Nicholson, "*Am Ha Aretz.*"

surrounding area, to a region, to the nation as a whole. Yet, the term is not used to indicate a particular kind of people. There is a distinction in some intertestamental documents like the *Psalms of Solomon* between the sinner (or wicked) and the righteous (or devout), but this is a moral distinction without any connection between this usage and the idea of the *am ha 'aretz* (cf. *Pss. Sol.* 2:34ff.; 3; 12:6). This moral distinction is relevant to our discussion of Mark 2:15–17, especially 17b.

Examining the uses of the term sinner in the Synoptics discloses that it is used differently in various contexts. In Mark 14:41 the term sinner refers to Jesus' enemies who are coming to arrest him. Here also the word means something like "immoral people" (cf. Luke 24:7). But in Luke 13:1–3 we find the term referring to everyone, much like the usages of later Christianity and some early Jewish literature (cf. *Pss. Sol.* 17:21–22). Again the term here does not mean the ritually non-observant but appears to have a more general moral sense: All fall short of God's righteous moral requirements.[162] Thus, neither the biblical, extrabiblical, nor rabbinic evidence suggests that "sinner" designates the ordinary people of the land, the common folk who were not as ritually observant as the Pharisees or, especially, the *haberim*. Rather, the term sinner always has a moral connotation, and varies in meaning from a broad reference to all humans in their moral inadequacy in the sight of God to a more specific reference to a notable group of moral failures. In the later case, the term is a virtual equivalent to the wicked and refers to those considered morally suspect or even openly immoral.[163]

It is this last group, the morally suspect and openly immoral, that Jesus says he came to call and with whom he had table fellowship. Not surprisingly, this behavior was considered scandalous by the Pharisees and especially by the *haberim*, who would have seen such table fellowship as the antithesis of their own. Examining Mark 2:15–17 and 14:41 together, it is striking that Jesus classified his arrestors in the same category as the openly

---

[162] Cf. R. A. Horsley, *Spiral of Violence*, 218–23.

[163] J. D. G. Dunn, "Pharisees," questions Sanders's conclusions on this matter. Dunn admits that in some contexts, sinner equals the wicked, for instance in the Old Testament, but urges that the Pharisees used the term to refer to those whose behavior was what they considered beyond the pale or boundaries of proper behavior for an Israelite. Thus the term sinner could refer to another Jew who was not necessarily notoriously sinful or to a Gentile in the same condition. The real questions are: (1) did the Pharisees really call all those outside their sect sinners, perhaps along the line of the Qumranites? and (2) if so, is it their definition of sinner that we find not only on Jesus' lips but from the pen of the evangelists? On the basis of Mark 2:16–17, one might conclude that Jesus did indeed adopt the Pharisees' definition of sinner, at least for the sake of argument on that occasion. Yet the contrast he makes in 2:17, if it is an authentic saying, and many doubt it, suggests the language of the Old Testament and the intertestamental usage. This is further supported by the fact that Jesus agrees that the sinners are not morally well. This being the case I think Sanders's argument probably stands. Even if it was the case that "the Pharisees . . . did the religious 'naming' in their society, and they were the ones who, by calling others 'sinners' set themselves up as 'righteous' . . . Jesus is presented as engaged in rearranging the Pharisees' categories" (J. H. Gill, "Irony," 143).

immoral—the wicked—with whom Jesus was accused of associating. In Mark 2:15-17 note that Jesus agrees with his adversaries in calling his table companions sinners, although his use of righteous may be ironic in his final reply.

A. Oppenheimer's detailed study shows that the term *am ha 'aretz* cannot refer to a particular class of persons such as the poor. Rather, both poor and rich can be classified in this way if they are neglectful of strict observance of various rules of ritual purity. Indeed, even a priest can be classified as an *am ha 'aretz* (M. Hor. 3.8). Furthermore, the *am ha 'aretz* cannot be said to be the dominant social group in Galilee as distinguished from the case in Judea. As Oppenheimer states: "The sources . . . do not testify to a sparseness of the knowledge of Torah and of the observance of the commandments in Galilee, nor to its having been inhabited by 'ammei ha-aretz.' The evidence in the New Testament about the Sages who came to Galilee from Jerusalem do not prove that in Galilee itself there were no Sages."[164] Oppenheimer even dismantles the assumption that Jesus' followers can be identified as or with the *am ha 'aretz*. The characteristic of the *ammei ha 'aretz*—that they neglected various strict rules about ritual purity—can be distinguished from Jesus' attitude, namely, that such rules cannot merely be neglected but even declared no longer applicable (Mark 7:15). In contrast, the *ammei ha 'aretz* neither opposed nor denied the validity of such rules; they just did not fully observe them. Thus, although it may be the case that Jesus had various *ammei ha 'aretz* among his followers, the two groups should not be identified. Oppenheimer's summary definition is instructive: "the ammei ha-aretz . . . were not a sect with its own principles but rather a social stream that had neither social institutions nor frameworks, and that were not scrupulous in the observance of all the commandments and in the study of the Torah in accordance with the outlook of the Sages and the teachers of the Torah."[165] The image of Jesus leading a sort of disgruntled peasant group from Galilee that was opposed to the Pharisees finds no basis in the material about the *am ha 'aretz*. It might be nearer to the mark to say Jesus focused on the *anawim* in his ministry, which no doubt included some who were neglectful of strict Torah observance.

Further insight into the meaning of Mark 2:15-17 is gained from the Qumran material.[166] On the basis of 1QSa 2.17-21 and 1QS 6.4-5, the table fellowship Jesus was sharing with sinners was not merely a foreshadowing but a foretaste of the messianic banquet, when those from all sorts of places

---

[164] A. Oppenheimer, '*Am Ha-Aretz*, 203-4. Indeed, it is possible to list various sages from Galilee from the days of both the Second Temple and Jamnia period. To mention only a few: R. Jose the Galilean, R. Halafta of Sepphoris, R. Hanina b. Teradion, abba Jose Holikofri of Tiv'on.

[165] Oppenheimer, '*Am Ha-Aretz*, 229.

[166] Cf. Horsley, *Spiral of Violence*, 179-80.

and walks of life would sit down at table together. The Qumran evidence suggests that "the Qumranites were . . . celebrating their regular community meals as if the messiahs were already there, that is, were celebrating in anticipation of the future consummation."[167] Jesus' views of who would be included in the consummate banquet differed from the Qumranite views. Nonetheless, it is notable that the Qumran text reads "when Messiah shall summon them . . . they shall gather for the common [tab]le, to eat and [to drink] new wine . . . Thereafter the Messiah of Israel shall extend his hand over the bread, [and] all the Congregation of the Community [shall utter a] blessing . . . It is according to this statute that they shall proceed *at every me[al]* at [which] at least ten men are gathered together."[168] Apart from the last line, one might think the subject was purely the future messianic banquet, but the last line makes clear that the banquet is being shared in the present as well.

It is uncertain whether Mark 2:13-14 should be included with 2:15-17, or whether the two stories have been associated because of the common theme of the calling of customs or tax collectors to follow Jesus or have fellowship with him. Thus, we shall not contend for the unity of this material. In regard to 2:13-14, the Synoptics are unanimous that Jesus had at least one deliberately called customs official among his inner circle. There is no reason to doubt the authenticity of this testimony even if the tradition is not completely clear on the name of this individual — Levi or Matthew. It is striking, however, that the "sinners and tax (or customs) collectors" are found together in a variety of sources in the Gospels (cf. Luke 15:2; Matt. 11:19 and par.; Mark 2:16 and par.), suggesting an association of groups that goes back to a *Sitz im Leben Jesu*. Furthermore, the evidence from the *Psalms of Solomon* makes the contrast of sinners and righteous in the final pronouncement of 2:17b believable on the lips of Jesus. Thus, there are no significant obstacles to taking vv. 2:15-17 as reflecting a situation in the life of Jesus and his response to it.

It is uncertain from 2:15 whose house Jesus is in, but because the connection with 2:13-14 is probably not original, it may even be that Jesus' own house is in view. If this is the case, then we see him not merely attending a banquet with the wicked and the customs collectors but hosting one. Because the Greek text is not clear on this point, we will build nothing on that suggestion. We are told that this was no private affair with an isolated Zaccheus, but a dinner with many tax collectors and sinners. There may also be reference to numerous disciples as well, even though the text is ambiguous on this point. The reference to the scribes of the Pharisees appears to reflect a viable distinction, revealing a knowledge that not all Pharisees were

---

[167] Ibid., 180.

[168] Cf. E. Lohse, ed., *Die Texte aus Qumran*, 50-51, the emphasis is mine. Cf. G. Vermes, *Dead Sea Scrolls*, 121.

experts in or copiers of Torah. This same distinction, found in another source (Acts 23:9), suggests its historical accuracy. That the scribes object to Jesus' behavior (and here it is his behavior that is at issue, although his disciples are confronted about it) is quite understandable in view of some of the things the Old Testament says about the wicked (cf. Ps. 10:15; 141:5; and esp. Prov. 2:22; 10:30; 14:9: "God scorns the wicked, but the upright enjoy his favor").

How could Jesus be a godly man, much less sent by God, if he acted in contrast to what the Scriptures said about the wicked and about God's attitude toward the wicked? Again Jesus' behavior would be seen as deliberate disobedience to Torah and its warning about the wicked. This is why more than one commentator has urged that Jesus' view of the law threatened the national existence, hence the strong negative reaction by Pharisees and others.[169] Borg has put it this way:

> Holiness as the cultural dynamic shaping Israel's ethos had originated as a survival strategy during the exile and afterward as the Jewish people pondered their recent experience of destruction and suffering. They were determined to be faithful to God in order to avoid another outpouring of divine judgement. Moreover, as a small social group—a conquered one at that, bereft of kingship . . . they were profoundly endangered by the possibility of assimilation into the surrounding cultures . . . The quest for holiness addressed both needs. It was the path of faithfulness and the path of social survival . . . The laws regarding purity and tithing were the major focus of the Pharisaic intensification of holiness. The Pharisaic program thus addressed the greatest source of non-observance, that created by the double system of taxation.[170]

Thus, Jesus' behavior on the Sabbath, his behavior toward sinners, and his pronouncement about clean and unclean would certainly have been perceived by the Pharisees as a direct threat to Jewish survival and, in fact, a form of unfaithfulness to God. Not surprisingly, they are depicted as openly hostile toward Jesus. The irony is that Jesus saw the Pharisaic approach to holiness as the real threat to both the internal cohesion of God's people and to their survival—because such a strict approach to holiness left most people on the outside.

Mark 2:17a is likely a conventional or proverbial saying (cf. *Mekil. Exod.* 15:26; Pausanias ap. Plutarch Apophthegmata Laconica 230F). Jesus, like many others, could occasionally draw on conventional material. This saying gives us clear insight into how Jesus viewed himself and his ministry—

---

[169] W. D. Davies, *The Gospel and the Land*, 346, in the context of examining J. Klausner's view that Jesus was an anarchist. As Davies puts it, "The Law, it cannot be sufficiently emphasized, was inextricably bound up with the land and with the culture of the Jews: it was the means of national as well as religious integration. Rightly or wrongly, the Pharisees and others sensed that Jesus' attitude to the Law involved the destruction of the Jewish people as a people."

[170] Borg, *Jesus*, 87, 89.

like a doctor whose task is to help those who are ill or in need of treatment. This image of Jesus as physician is also found in another layer of the tradition in Luke 4:23 where once again it is coupled with a conventional or proverbial saying.

The physician analogy suggests two things: Jesus understood his life task as helping and healing the least, the last, and the lost; and he knew that inherent in that agenda was a setting aside or transcending of any observance of certain Old Testament laws about ritual purity and the proper separation of the wicked and the righteous. To reclaim the wicked for God, Jesus had to be willing to at least abrogate or transcend certain provisions of the Old Testament law, not unlike a doctor who when assuming the responsibilities of a physician also assumes the risk of contracting the patient's condition, even though this is not intended. Thus, it was an inherent byproduct of Jesus' ministry that strict obedience to the written Torah, much less to the oral Torah, was an impossibility. This ministry to sinners and tax collectors (who here were probably customs officials of Herod Antipas, not Rome) also resulted in his being reckoned as one of the wicked in some minds. Now, when we investigate some of the likely authentic sayings of Jesus that depict him as upholding some portions of the law,[171] it will become apparent that probably in Jesus' own mind he saw himself in his ministry to sinners as transcending the old restrictions in light of the new situation created by the Kingdom breaking-in in his ministry. In short, it is doubtful he saw himself as a lawbreaker, but surely various of those who did not interpret Jesus' ministry as he did would have seen him as such. As Dodd once said of the Pharisees' attitude about Jesus, "It was that they discerned in Him an attitude in religious matters which was fundamentally inconsistent with their presuppositions."[172]

One final issue from Mark 2:15–17 remains: Are we to assume that v. 17b is meant to be serious or ironic? How we read the tenor of the remark will determine how it should be interpreted. If it is ironic, then the term *dikaios* would mean something like the so-called righteous. In some texts, however, Jesus seems to allow that the scribes and Pharisees did maintain a laudable standard of righteousness (e.g., Matt. 5:20), although there is also plenty of polemical material which could suggest the contrary (cf. Matt. 23:1–7, esp. v. 2, and Mark 12:38–40). The problem in evaluating this varied polemical material is that we cannot always be sure that Jesus is addressing the same group of Pharisees or scribes or *haberim* in each case, and further some texts possibly reflect an earlier, some a later, perspective during the ministry. Some of these remarks may have come after the Pharisaic evaluation of Jesus had changed or had become unreservedly negative, and some texts are held

---

[171] Cf. Witherington, *Women in the Ministry,* 11ff.
[172] Dodd, "Jesus," 55.

to reflect a Christian polemical viewpoint dating to after A.D. 85. For this reason we will not be including the more polemical material in our discussion of Jesus and the Pharisees as its authenticity is difficult to establish.

Taking Mark 2:17b on its own, we need to concentrate on the focus of the text, not on its possible implications about the righteous. The point is Jesus came to call sinners, and this meant that he was directing his ministry *especially* to a particular type of Israelite—the least, last, and lost. This did not rule out others from aligning themselves with Jesus, indeed when Jesus uses the phrase lost sheep of Israel, he seems to refer to all of Israel. The term *hamartolos* in Mark 2:15–17 should not be assumed to have its later Pauline meaning where it refers to all fallen human beings. Rather, the usage here is more in line with earlier Jewish literature, especially the Wisdom literature. What then does it mean to "call" sinners? Presumably this means to invite them to become disciples, or possibly to summon them to repentance in view of the inbreaking kingdom or both. What is striking about this behavior is that Jesus does not require repentance or changed behavior in advance of having table fellowship with the sinners. Rather, he seeks them out as they are, and without prerequisites calls them to face the implications of his ministry and the inbreaking Dominion of God. This interpretation comports with two other important pieces of data about Jesus' ministry. First, among his disciples or the wider circle of his followers were various sorts of people from the fringes or outcasts of society—a tax collector, possibly a Zealot, some fishermen, some women, and some sinners. Second, Jesus' vision of guests at the messianic banquet appears to have included such people (cf. the Q saying Matt. 8:11–12/Luke 13:29). Possibly then he saw meals with sinners and tax collectors as a foreshadowing or foretaste of that banquet in the kingdom. This may imply that he saw himself as fulfilling a messianic mission. Schürmann argues that on occasion, Jesus performed not "prophetic symbolic actions" so much as "eschatological fulfillment signs."[173] Banqueting with the bad may have been one such sign that the eschatological reign of God had broken in.

We have now come to the end of our discussion of Jesus' relationship to the Pharisees. B. Lindars has summed up his impressions of the data this way:

> On the one hand Jesus preaches the crisis of the coming kingdom, and draws attention to the piercing moral challenge which this entails. On the other hand he practices a compassionate ministry, which frequently involves him in setting aside the strict application of the law, so that he runs the risk of incriminating himself with the scribes and Pharisees.[174]

From a very different starting point U. Luz concludes:

---

[173] H. Schürmann, "Die Symbolhandlung Jesu," 86.
[174] B. Lindars, "Pharisees," 62.

> Jesus was certainly also rejected by many Pharisees. His liberal interpretation
> of the Sabbath laws and especially his freedom regarding the regulations
> governing ritual cleanliness must have appeared problematic to the Pharisees,
> one of whose chief concerns was the ritual purity of the *whole* people of God
> (Israel). . . . I for one do not consider the numerous scenes in the Gospels
> which speak of conflict between Jesus and the Pharisees have all been
> fabricated . . .[175]

I see little reason to disagree with these assessments. Surely Jesus was no
Pharisee, but rather in the arguably authentic Gospel material he is always
depicted as being in controversy with them.

In terms of the christological implications of this material, we have seen
indirect evidence that Jesus viewed himself as more than just a prophet or
teacher. How he handles Torah, especially in terms of his own ministry's
priorities, suggests a person who thought of himself in ways that a Galilean
hasid never did. In fact, texts such as Mark 2:18–22 suggest that Jesus
believed he and his ministry represented something distinctive and special,
which were cause for special celebration—an idea that comports with the
feasting with sinners and tax collectors. The analogy with David and his
situation in Mark 2:23–28 suggests at least a special person and special
circumstances are the explanation for the disciples' behavior. *Implicit* messianic implications may be here. Mark 7:15 makes quite clear that Jesus'
attitude toward the law is not one that a typical teacher or prophet would
assume. Not only does Jesus appeal to one part of the law against another,
but he also deems some of the law no longer applicable or, to put it another
way, abrogated in view of the new situation of the Kingdom's coming in his
ministry. He believes that he is implementing God's true intentions for
humanity in institutions such as the Sabbath, even though the way he acts
is at variance with the usual understanding in early Judaism of the Old
Testament Sabbath texts.

Who, then, did Jesus think he was? In this section we have seen an
individual who thought he had authority over and above the Torah, a person who did not agree with the Pharisees about oral Torah, a person who
felt that the new situation caused by his ministry was reason for celebration
and special responses. In short, he was a person who appears to have
thought that 'new occasions teach new duties.'

Later we will examine in more detail the possibility that Jesus also saw
himself as God's *Shaliach,* or special agent imbued with the full authority of
the Father and sent on a special mission of limited duration to reclaim what
belonged to the Father. We have already seen some indications that this is
how Jesus may have viewed himself. Indeed, the material we have examined so far seems to point in this direction for two reasons: (1) the way Jesus

---

[175] P. Lapide and U. Luz, *Two Perspectives,* 141.

takes an independent line, acting in accord with how he perceived his own task, *even if* it meant going against either the Traditions of the fathers or the Torah or both; (2) the way Jesus is held responsible for his disciples' actions and how they are queried about his actions suggest a relationship of agency as well as discipleship. Clearly the relationship of Jesus and his inner circle is a close one in terms of word and deed.

JESUS, REVOLUTIONARIES, AND ROMANS

Obtaining an adequate historical perspective on a matter is often difficult, and nowhere is this more the case than in trying to assess how Jesus felt about the revolutionary response to Rome by some Jews. Bound up with this is the issue of what form or forms that revolutionary response actually took from A.D. 6 until the fall of Jerusalem and beyond. This means we need to assess both Gospel data and the accuracy of the historian Josephus. What are we to make of his various and apparently contradictory references to Zealots, brigands, revolutionaries, bandits, robbers, and the sicarii to mention only some of the terms he uses to describe those who were willing to take weapons in their hands during the period A.D. 6–74? We need to deal with Josephus and his perspective on the revolutionaries before we can assess Jesus' response to them, so that we will have a clear notion of that to which he was reacting. One of Jesus' followers was apparently called Simon the Zealot. How are we to assess this if, as some aver, there was no party of the Zealots until the outbreak of the Jewish War in the 60s?

JOSEPHUS AND THE REVOLUTIONARIES

The student of Josephus is confronted with the same sort of problems in dealing with his works as the biblical scholar faces with the synoptic Gospels, because the two versions of Josephus's account of Jewish history, *The Jewish Wars* and *Jewish Antiquities,* differ significantly. Take, for example, the varying perspective on the Pharisees in these two works. From *Antiquities* one can deduce that the Pharisees were a significant factor in social and political matters in pre-A.D. 70 Judaism. Not only are they mentioned first among the three major "philosophies" of Judaism but they are also given more discussion than in the *Wars* (cf. *Ant.* 18.11ff. and *Wars* 2.163ff.). In the *Wars* the mention of the Pharisees is brief, and this brevity is especially striking given the lengthy discussion of the Essenes which begins the section on the three more ancient philosophies. It might be possible to deduce, with M. Smith and J. Neusner, that the Pharisees were a rather minor sect, or at least not a leading or dominant one in the pre-A.D. 70 period, and that in *Antiquities* Josephus has magnified their role in light of post-A.D. 70 developments.

But it is equally possible to draw another conclusion. Dunn urges that: (1) although the reference to the Pharisees is briefer, in the crucial section of *Wars* they are called the "leading" sect (*ten proten*, 2.163); (2) it is probable that Josephus, who was writing the *Wars* in Rome in the 70s under the patronage of Vespasian and as a propaganda piece, that is, in part an apologia of the Jewish people to be read by Romans and other non-Jews, deliberately downplayed the role of the Pharisees in his earlier work so as not to draw attention to and suspicion upon them.[176] In *Antiquities*, written considerably later, Josephus not only had the benefit of a longer time to assess the matter but surely felt more certain that Judaism and Pharisaism had survived the disaster of the 70s.

This observation is important for our study of the revolutionaries because it seems likely that the later work, *Antiquities*, gives us a clearer perspective as to what was actually the case with these Jews. When Josephus wrote *Wars*, he was concerned to cast blame for the disasters of the 60s and 70s on the more militant Jews. In the later work he does this as well, but he is writing less out of bitterness and the heat of the moment because *Wars* was composed only shortly after the end of the debacle in Israel. In fact, Josephus states explicitly that the purpose of *Wars* is "to deter others who may be tempted to revolt" (3.108). This is not the case with *Antiquities*, a work apparently composed gradually and under some external urging (it was not finished until A.D. 93–94 during the reign of Domitian and shortly before Josephus's death). As H. St. J. Thackeray observed, "The author thus severs his connexion with Roman political propaganda and henceforth figures solely as Jewish historian and apologist."[177] Bear in mind that *Antiquities* deliberately concludes at the onset of the Jewish Wars in A.D. 66.[178]

The tone differs between the *Wars* and *Antiquities* on the subject of revolutionaries. When speaking of Judas the Galilean and the so-called fourth philosophy he founded among the Jews in A.D. 6 at the time of the census of Quirinius (*Wars* 2.118–119), Josephus mentions no connection between Judas and the Pharisees. In fact he says that Judas founded a group that had nothing in common with the other major parties of Judaism (Pharisees, Sadducees, Essenes). By contrast, *Ant.* 18.23 says that the group founded by Judas "agrees in all other respects with the opinions of the Pharisees,

---

[176] J. D. G. Dunn, "Pharisees."

[177] Cf. H. St. J. Thackeray's introduction in *Josephus IV, Jewish Antiquities Book I-IV* (Cambridge: Harvard University Press, 1930), vii.

[178] The literature on the subject of either Josephus's or Jesus' view of the revolutionaries is vast. Some of the more helpful studies are: M. Hengel, *Die Zeloten*, which includes his response to his critics; M. Black, "Judas of Galilee"; M. Smith, "Zealots and Sicarii"; S. G. F. Brandon, *Jesus and the Zealots*; M. Smith, "Jesus and the Zealots: a Correction," 453; H. P. Kingdon, "Zealots"; M. Smith, "Origins of the Zealots"; H. Merkel, "Zealots"; E. M. Smallwood, *Roman Rule*; M. Avi-Jonah, ed., *Herodian Period*; P. W. Barnett, "Jewish Prophets."

except they have a passion for liberty . . ." Further, in *Ant.* 18.3-4 Josephus says that Judas enlisted the aid of one Saddok, a Pharisee. These connections with Pharisaism are missing in the *Wars* in the parallel passages. This is likely because Josephus wanted Pharisaism to survive the disasters of the Jewish wars, and its survival was still in doubt when he wrote the *Wars*. Keep in mind that Josephus tells us in his *Life* 11−21 that at one point he resolved to join the Pharisees and went into basic training in order to do so. His sympathies were clearly with this group. He even admits that the revolutionary government in Jerusalem during the Jewish War sent two Pharisees to Galilee in an action directed against Josephus himself, then provincial commander (*Life* 197[39]). Surely it follows that his references in the *Antiquities* to the associations of Pharisaism and Judas's so-called philosophy are historically accurate because Josephus would hardly have invented such an idea. This is all the more the case in view of the fact that Josephus was at one time a rebel commander in Galilee and would likely have wanted to cover his tracks, disassociating himself from the failed revolutionary movement especially in his earlier work (*Wars*).

Another comparative example further illustrates our point. In *Wars* 2.56, Josephus only briefly mentions Judas's breaking into the armories at Sepphoris. Here Judas seems to be nothing more than a bandit. By contrast in *Ant.* 17.271-72, Josephus candidly admits that the act at Sepphoris was part of Judas's "zealous pursuit of royal rank." In short there is more involved than mere banditry or anger with the powers that be. R. A. Horsley and J. S. Hanson in fact point out "that there were several mass movements composed of Jewish peasants from villages or towns such as Emmaus, Bethlehem, Sepphoris−people rallying around the leadership of charismatic figures viewed as *anointed kings* of the Jews. These movements occurred in all three principal areas of Jewish settlement in Palestine (Galilee, Perea, Judea), and just at the time when Jesus of Nazareth was presumably born."[179] We will have more to say on the subject of messianic figures and movements in Jesus' era shortly.

A further difficulty, especially in regard to *Wars*, is that Josephus seems to contradict himself at various points. In *Wars* 2.253-54, Josephus dates the rise of the sicarii to the procuratorship of Felix (A.D. 52-60), whereas later in the same work (*Wars* 7.253-54) he seems to date the origins of this group to the time of Judas himself (*tote gar hoi sikarioi*). As Hengel points out, in the *Wars* Josephus only once (2.254ff.) mentions the new tactics of the sicarii from which they got their name (apparently a label first applied to them by the Romans), but this sort of information occurs more frequently in *Antiquities*.[180] Thus, it is wiser to give preference to the later and less

---

[179] R. A. Horsley and J. S. Hanson, *Bandits*, 117.
[180] Hengel, *Die Zeloten*, 405, e.g., the reference to sicarii being forcefully put down by Albinus

polemical evidence of Josephus in *Antiquities* on these matters, than to the material in the earlier work. To be sure, all the data needs to be critically evaluated and used, but preference will be given to *Antiquities* in matters of historical accuracy about the Zealots, the sicarii, and revolutionaries in general.

When we focus on *Antiquities*, note immediately that Josephus does not intend to treat Judas and the events of A.D. 6 as an isolated incident with no relationship to later revolutionary activities, a fact that the New Testament confirms (cf. Acts 5:34-35).[181] On the contrary, Josephus states explicitly that Judas and Saddok planted the seeds of the later troubles, which probably is an allusion to the events of the 60s and 70s (cf. *Ant.* 18.9-10). Josephus freely admits the popularity of the movement that Judas and Saddok started and connects it with what he calls the later ruin or destruction of early Judaism. Also, at *Ant.* 18.5ff., the author makes quite clear that this is a theocratic movement because they rely on the help of the divine (*theion*). This is confirmed at *Ant.* 18.23ff., where Josephus says that Judas and his followers admit only God as their true leader and master. If Josephus is right in connecting the sicarii with both Judas and Masada, then the evidence is germane that the inhabitants were religiously observant Jews—as the ritual bath and synagogue at Masada indicate. It is thus impossible to characterize this movement as purely social or political. As was so often the case, politics and religion were intertwined in first-century Judaism, and this was especially true with the movement Judas started. Josephus admits this, despite his apparent distaste for the group's violent tactics and his willingness to call them bandits or brigands or self-aggrandizing insurgents on various occasions (cf. *Ant.* 18.24ff.; 18.4-7, noting the reference to *lesterion*).[182]

Also probable was a family link between Judas and some of the major later leaders of the revolutionaries. For instance, Josephus mentions Menahem as the son(?) of Judas the Galilean, and one who seems to have assumed leadership among the sicarii (*Wars* 2.425, 433), taking them off to Masada. He was killed by the partisans of another group of insurgents identified with a man called Eliezer. Notably, the theocratic ideology is again mentioned by Josephus (*Wars* 2.433). Thus, although Josephus willingly calls the sicarii *lestas,* nonetheless he does not try to make their motives for action purely personal, political, or social. Furthermore, we read at *Wars* 2.444 that Menahem was followed or attended by *tous zelotes*. Possibly, Josephus is not referring to some particular party called "the Zealots" that was led by Menahem, but simply uses the term in a more generic sense to

---

in *Ant.* 20.208ff. which is omitted in *Wars* 2.272-276. More evidence could be produced, but this should suffice.

[181] M. Black, "Judas of Galilee," 5.

[182] Cf. H. G. Woods's conclusion in "This Time," 266: "Judas the Galilean . . . was clearly inspired by something more than hope of personal gain."

refer to a group of zealous persons, or even "fanatics" as Thackeray would have it.[183] Later there is reference to Eliezar son of Simon and "the *zelotes* under him" (*Wars* 2.564-5), which suggests that the term could be or was also applied to a group with more priestly connections.[184]

Nevertheless, *Wars* 2.444 plausibly indicates that for Josephus, there was an integral connection between Judas, Menahem, the sicarii, and at least some of those who in the 60s were called Zealots. Although it is true that Josephus does not use the term Zealot of anyone before he begins narrating the events of the Jewish War, this observation may not be very significant.[185]

The family connection with Judas seems to go even further, if we are to believe *Wars* 7.253-56. Here we are told that the sicarii at Masada are led by a descendant of Judas, a man by the name of Eleazar. This is surely the same Eleazar mentioned in *Wars* 2.444 as escaping from the temple area at the time of Menahem's murder and later becoming the despot of Masada. He is called in the earlier passage the son of Jairus. Thus, a clear familial line is traceable from Judas to at least one group of the insurgents during the Jewish War.[186] At *Ant.* 20.102, Josephus indicates Judas's sons were crucified by Tiberius Alexander about A.D. 45. In view of the history of this family, it would seem likely that their crucifixion was due to some sort of political unrest they had caused, not mere banditry. As Rengstorf argues, "The Romans themselves did not in fact treat as *lestai* the Zealots whom they captured. Their punishment was crucifixion, and this alone was enough to show that they were regarded and treated as political offenders."[187] Further, as Hengel has

[183] Josephus, *Jewish Wars 1-3*, 496-97.

[184] H. P. Kingdon, "The Origins of the Zealots," *NTS* 19 (1972-73): 74.

[185] Cf. the considered judgment of Smallwood, *Roman Rule*, 154: "Even if the triple identification of Judas's sect, the terrorists, and the Zealots of the war years cannot be proved definitely, the clear connexion between the motives and beliefs of the three groups at any rate indicates a development of one group out of another. Even though the title Zealot was apparently not taken by Judas's sect or by the terrorists, the Zealots were inspired by the same attitude to the Law, the same dream of the recovery of independence, and the same hostility to foreign domination and hence to Jewish collaboration with Rome, which was rooted in the tradition of Jewish nationalism going back to the days of the Maccabees."

[186] Barnett, "Jewish Prophets," 13ff., wants to insist that this was only a clan movement, without wide support, and that even when the Zealots arose in the 60s it was a small faction. His basic argument is that it was only in the second procuratorial period that there was significant unrest (A.D. 44-66). He seems to have bought Josephus's apologetic attempt to minimize the source of the problem and present one particular group as the main scapegoat for the disastrous results of the Jewish War. Barnett is correct that the first procuratorial period was considerably more stable than the second, but then this is a relative comparison that should not be turned into a contrast between the two periods. The crucifixion of Jesus suggests that the Romans were more than a little edgy even in the first procuratorial period and with good reason.

[187] K. Rengstorf, "*lestes*." Rengstorf also maintains that Josephus views the Zealots through Roman eyes or at least presents them from a Roman point of view as an armed political movement of rebels and malcontents. This is truer of the presentation in *Wars* than in *Antiquities*, where Josephus is less pejorative about this group.

insisted of both groups of A.D. 6 and 73, they are said to recognize only God as their leader and Lord.[188]

Josephus explicitly connects Judas to the ensuing woes of the 60s and 70s which began after Gessius Florus, the procurator of Judea in A.D. 64–65 (*Ant.* 18.24). This may be either because his family carried on the cause or because the ideals he espoused were continued by a significant contingent of the insurgents in the 60s. In any case, Josephus seems to insist on connecting Judas to the later events and to indicate that his ideology provided the underpinnings to this movement.

That various separate robber bands decided to take advantage of the chaos during the Jewish war to advance their own personal gain or purposes need not be doubted. Simon bar Giora may be one such person, even though he apparently attempted to make common cause with the sicarii at Masada (*Wars* 4.503ff.). Josephus says that the sicarii could not be tempted to join him. Thus, it must have been with others that Simon marched on Jerusalem and opposed the priestly Zealots and their allies the Idumaeans (cf. *Wars* 4.509ff.). It needs to be granted that Josephus does not use the term Zealot of anyone prior to the Jewish War itself. Yet, it also seems correct to say that Josephus does not use *zelotes* as a technical term for a unified party, but as a character reference for all the insurgents during the Jewish War whose motives could be associated with zeal for the law or monotheism or some theocratic ideal. It is striking that when with some venom Josephus writes of the (priestly) Zealots, he does so in terms similar to the way he describes the sicarii—their religious claims and their actions (cf. *Wars* 7.268–70; *Ant.* 18.1ff.).

Thus, it appears that despite the protests of M. Smith and others,[189] Hengel's careful conclusions are fully warranted: "the Jewish Freedom movement between 6 and 70 A.D. had a certain uniform ideological basis. They stood near to Pharisaic piety and bore the impression of a strongly eschatological [outlook]."[190] They may also have patterned themselves on the zealous deeds of Phineas and the Maccabees, as Kingdon strongly urges.[191]

In the face of this, R. Horsley has recently maintained that "there is simply no evidence for any violent resistance movement at the time of Jesus."[192] In order to maintain such a view, Horsley must: (1) ignore or dismiss the remarks of Josephus that indicate the religious motifs for some

---

[188] Hengel, *Die Zeloten*, 394ff.

[189] Smith, "Zealots," 1ff. It may be granted that Josephus does not identify the priestly Zealots with the sicarii. Furthermore, there may not have been a party called the Zealots before the Jewish War. It does not follow from this that there was no revolutionary movement during the period A.D. 6–70. The evidence of Josephus suggests the contrary.

[190] Hengel, *Die Zeloten*, 412.

[191] Kingdon, "Origins of the Zealots," 74ff.

[192] Horsley, *Spiral of Violence*, 262; cf. esp. 20–120.

of the actions of various insurgents; (2) dismiss or ignore the family connection between Judas the Galilean and those apparently in the forefront of resistance after Jesus' day and especially in the events of the Jewish War; (3) ignore that Josephus uses the term "bandit" pejoratively because of his attempt to distance himself from the resistance movement, despite the fact that in such texts as *Ant.* 18.23ff. and 18.4ff. Josephus admits that these so-called bandits were not mere robbers, but those who had a theocratic vision of how Israel should be; and (4) distinguish between Judas and the later sicarii. Horsley attempts to dispose all of this by saying, "The Fourth Philosophy, however, had focused its opposition on the tribute to Rome, whereas the Sicarii focused exclusively on the Jewish high-priestly aristocracy."[193] This ignores that an attack on the aristocracy was also an attack on Rome and its collaborators, so there is hardly a real distinction in aims of the two sorts of actions. Furthermore, his case rests at crucial points too heavily on the more polemical and apologetical work *Wars*.[194] One must also add that Horsley's distinction between the early and middle decades of the first century, although having some truth to it, does not lead to the conclusion that there was an essential difference in kind or character between say A.D. 30 and 60. Rather the difference was a matter of degree. What had long been festering in Judea and Galilee erupted in the 60s. The eruption in the 60s was not the result of a sudden change in attitude toward Rome, or the sudden organization of resistance to Rome.

For our purposes, what is crucial is that: (1) during the months in which Jesus ministered, although perhaps fewer outbursts of violence occurred than before and after the third decade of the Christian era, nonetheless an ongoing movement of zealous people existed, who for religious as well as other reasons were prepared to take revolutionary action against Rome, and its collaborators; and (2) while there may not have been a party specifically called the Zealots in Jesus' day,[195] the ideals of Phineas and the Maccabees were still much alive and had significant popular support.[196] The fact that the movement begun by Judas the Galilean seems to have been a family affair should not lead us to see it as an isolated phenomenon without

---

[193] Ibid., 41.

[194] Ibid., 56–57.

[195] I tend to agree with Black, "Judas of Galilee," 51, when he suggests that "Zealot" was probably "Josephus's Jewish Greek term for Jewish irredentists of whatever faction." Several, however, have tried to limit the term to just the priestly Zealots (see Merkel, "Zealots,"), but this seems not to work in view of its application not only to Menahem's followers but also its association with John of Gischala. In the last case it could be argued the term is applied to the latter figure because he united with the priestly Zealots.

[196] W. Klassen, "Jesus and Phineas," sees the Phineas model as much alive in Jesus' day, but concludes, "The name of Phineas, while prominent in many writings of the first century is missing in the New Testament. The reason for this is to be found in the rejection by Jesus of his story. He did not find Phineas congenial to his program although he must at the outset have been very deeply attracted to Phineas" (499).

popular support. To the contrary, Josephus says that many and especially the young were affected and infected by the potent ideology Judas had offered the people when he insisted that paying taxes to Rome was a violation of Jewish religion.[197]

Thus, the question needs to be raised, Was Jesus like his fellow native of Galilee, Judas, a revolutionary? If Jesus had a messianic understanding, could he have seen himself in terms that the sicarii and others would have found appealing? Could he have made claims or held views like those Josephus predicates of Judas (he sought "Basileios time," *Ant.* 17.272; on messianic pretenders of the period, cf. *Ant.* 17.273ff.; *Wars* 2.57ff.)?

HOW REVOLUTIONARY WAS GALILEE?

We have been discussing the larger contextual issue of whether or not there even *was* a revolutionary movement in Israel during and after the time of Jesus. A related issue is whether or not Galilee was a hotbed of revolutionary fervor, perhaps the epicenter of such sentiments. This issue is raised not least because Jesus was a Galilean and ministered in Galilee but also because Josephus keeps referring to people such as Judas the Galilean, and events such as Judas the son of Ezechias's raising of a considerable group of followers at Sepphoris and raiding the royal arsenals there (*Wars* 2.56). This raid happened either shortly after Jesus was born or when he was a small boy only a few miles from his home town.

In our investigation of the revolutionary potential of Galilee we are aided by the detailed works of E. Meyers, S. Freyne, G. Theissen, and Barnett.[198] What these studies show is that while there were insurgents from and in Galilee, "the widely held view of the Galilean as a revolutionary, a boor or am-ha'ares or a speaker of poor Aramaic . . . is open to considerable doubt."[199] Nevertheless, all Israel was in a state of considerable tension after the death of Herod the Great not least because of the shifting political scene, with client kings or governors in turns ruling parts of the promised land,[200] and, as de Jonge says, the "longing for decisive change was intense."[201]

Meyers stresses that one must distinguish sharply between the character of upper and lower Galilee, Jesus being from the latter, while a figure like John of Gischala would be associated with the former. Further, Josephus admits that Judas the so-called Galilean was from Gamala, a city in lower

---

[197] Cf. the interesting, even novel, presentation on this point by G. Theissen, *Shadow of the Galilean*, 67ff.

[198] Cf. Freyne, *Galilee*, passim; E. M. Meyers, "Galilean Regionalism"; E. M. Meyers and J. F. Strange, *Archaeology*; G. Theissen, *First Followers*, passim.

[199] Meyers, "Galilean Regionalism," 220.

[200] Theissen, *First Followers*, 76, although his remarks are more applicable to the Judean scene than that of Galilee so far as political instability is concerned.

[201] de Jonge, *Christology in Context*, 163.

Gaulinitis on the Transjordanian side of the Galilean Sea (*Ant.* 18.4). Meyers adds, "The hills of lower Galilee present no effective barrier to communication. Indeed Lower Galilee is closely tied to the busy trade of both the Mediterranean and the Sea of Galilee . . . On the other hand, Upper Galilee . . . is a self-enclosed area defined by the awesome slopes of the Meiron massif."[202]

The evidence Meyers produces is sufficient to show that Jesus grew up in the most developed area in both Galilees. Furthermore, Jesus' ministry seems to have been largely confined to lower Galilee, yet a survey of the Gospels shows him avoiding (deliberately?) the major cities of the region such as Sepphoris and Tiberias. His ministry seems directed primarily to the smaller towns and villages, especially around the Sea of Galilee, with Capernaum as his base of operations. Jesus, then, lived in a region where there was a more cosmopolitan and open environment than was true in upper Galilee and the evidence supports the view that lower Galilee, while maintaining Aramaic as its main spoken language at least among the Jews dwelling there, had a substantial Greek component in its linguistic character, in contrast to upper Galilee.[203] This strongly suggests that in terms of culture and cultural attitudes, lower Galilee was more Hellenized than either upper Galilee or the Transjordan region from which Judas the insurgent came.

Lower Galilee, because its soil was much more fertile than that of Judea, was highly valued during Jesus' age. This may have bearing on the revolutionary potential of the region because it was subject to the abuses of absentee landlordism, as well as double taxation—both civil and religious. This may have been counteracted because lower Galilee was not a rural backwater; parochialism was not likely a major factor.

Freyne, after a detailed study of Galilee during our period, draws the following conclusions. First, the potential and factors for lower Galilee to become a cauldron bubbling over with revolutionary ferment were not absent, but striking is the little clear evidence for such a conclusion except at the beginning and end of the first procuratorial period.[204] Even these examples can be explained because the Jews frequently tried to take advantage of transitions in power to regain some of their former position and power in the region. Second, the only places where we clearly see revolutionary activity in lower Galilee in the relevant period seem to have been Tiberias and Sepphoris, both of which Jesus seems to have avoided. Third,

---

[202] Meyers, "Galilean Regionalism," 95. As a result of still ongoing digs in upper Galilee, there now appears to be some evidence to dispute this conclusion. It appears upper Galilee was open to the north and felt influence from that direction.

[203] Meyers and Strange, *Archaeology*, 90–91.

[204] So also Barnett, "Jewish Prophets," 14f.; and his article, "Under Tiberius All Was Quiet," *NTS* 21 (1974–75): 564–71.

revolutionary activities associated with Judas in the early period and with his descendants during the Jewish War focused not in Galilee but Judea and particularly Jerusalem. Fourth, despite a few scattered large cities, Galilee had a predominantly peasant ethos, and the Galilean peasant fared better than his Judean counterpart, although his situation was far from ideal. Fifth, the crucial political and social events or circumstances that might provoke revolution to arise in Galilee were apparently absent in Jesus' day, even though the potential was there.[205] Was Jesus' appearance, perhaps due to some of his "signs and wonders," seen by the revolutionaries as a signal for them to arise and throw off the yoke of Rome? This question will be raised when we examine the Gospel material itself.

JEWISH MESSIANIC MOVEMENTS

G. Theissen, in his sociological study of the Jesus movement, points to certain critical factors in Galilee that were conducive to such a movement and could have led to it being messianic in character. First, a significant number of people in Galilean society seemingly had become marginalized for political, social, or religious reasons. These were people such as over-taxed fishermen, tax collectors, harlots, the diseased, tenant farmers, and day laborers. Messianic movements characteristically draw on such marginalized people to build a cohesive resistance to the status quo. Those who have least to lose by change also have the most to gain. Now, it cannot be denied that the Jesus movement at least in part oriented itself toward and included various of these sorts of people.[206]

Second, after referring to the cases of Judas the Galilean, Jesus, John of Gischala, and the Qumranites, Theissen argues: "The programmes of all renewal movements suggest a detachment from the Hellenistic cities and an ambivalent attitude towards Jerusalem."[207] This remark is striking because Jesus not only avoided Hellenistic cities like Tiberias and Sepphoris, but the Jesus tradition, if it is reliable at this point, indicates both Jesus' love for Jerusalem and his belief in its impending doom.[208]

Third, such movements manifested a theocratic vision, believing God was or would soon intervene and establish direct, divine rule because God alone is King. This we can see not only in Judas the Galilean and later in the

---

[205] Freyne, *Galilee*, 208–47.

[206] Theissen, *First Followers*, 45ff.

[207] Ibid., 50.

[208] His avoidance of Tiberias and Sepphoris should not lead to the picture of Jesus as only frequenting bucolic settings. As Josephus reminds us, there were numerous villages in Galilee in the first century, and many of them had a considerable population. *Wars* 3.41–43 refers to villages of fifteen thousand residents. Cf. A. N. Sherwin-White, *Roman Society*, 130–31.

sicarii but also in Jesus who proclaimed the inbreaking of the Dominion of God.[209]

Fourth, Barnett has discerned a particular pattern suggesting that the Jesus movement, even during Jesus' own ministry, already had an intentionally messianic character. Its character was not unlike that of other such movements of the day, as indicated by the messianic character of particular symbolic acts. Consider the following chart:[210]

Ruler	Mes. Figure	Mes. Activ.	Location	Audience
Pilate	Jesus	feeding 5,000	wilderness	5,000 men
Pilate	Samaritan	reveal temple vessels	Mt. Gerizim	great crowd
Fadus	Theudas	divide Jordan	Jordan	great crowd
Felix	the Egyptian	Jerus. walls to collapse	wilderness to Mt. Olives	4,000 men

One other figure, John the Baptist, might fit on this chart because he certainly performed symbolic acts of baptism in the wilderness at the Jordan, preached a coming judgment, attracted significant crowds, and led what W. D. Davies calls a repentance movement of which many feel Jesus was at one time a part.[211] Nevertheless, John apparently disclaimed any messianic status. This chart suggests that particular sorts of symbolic acts, relating to religious and often Old Testament matters, would have been construed by early Jews as a signal that the messiah or the messianic age was at hand. Jesus is credited with performing such a symbolic act in all four Gospels. Indeed, the Feeding is the only miracle recorded in all four Gospels. Thus, if the Gospels are accurate in recording that Jesus performed some sort of symbolic act before a large crowd which could have conjured up messianic visions and hopes, then his ministry would fit into a pattern that seems characteristic of early Jewish messianic movements.

It has been pointed out that early Jewish messianism was more often focused on a "Salvation hope" rather than a "central Saving person" because such messianism was essentially theocentric in orientation.[212] I would put the matter somewhat differently. It is clear from sources as diverse as the Qumran literature and the *Psalms of Solomon* that before and during Jesus' day, a significant focus was on one or more messianic figures, who are properly understood in the larger context of messianic hope. In short, although messianic hope involved more than an interest in a coming anointed one, such a coming one was often the focal point of that hope both during and

---

[209] Cf. pp. 198–201, to Theissen, *First Followers*, 59ff.
[210] Barnett, "Jewish Prophets," 182–83.
[211] W. D. Davies, "From Schweitzer," 535.
[212] L. Wachter, "Messianismus," 125.

before Jesus' day. Furthermore, the longing for God's anointed did not cease after the disasters of A.D. 70 and the disappointment with various failed messianic movements in the first and early second century A.D., as is shown by P. Schafer's review of the relevant data from the Tannaitic and Amoraic period.[213]

We are reminded by G. Scholem that in Judaism redemption has always been conceived as having a public character, involving historical events, and not merely as having internal and purely spiritual changes within individuals, although those sorts of change were also involved in the messianic hope.[214] He also stresses, "When the Messianic idea appears as a living force in the world of Judaism . . . it always occurs in the closest connection with apocalypticism."[215] By this he means that messianism is almost always associated with ideas that the end, or at least the messianic age, is about to break in abruptly at any moment, and it presupposes a fundamentally pessimistic assessment of the present state of affairs of God's people. "Jewish Messianism is in its origins and by its nature . . . a theory of catastrophe. This theory stresses the revolutionary, cataclysmic element in the transition from every historical present to the Messianic future."[216]

Although a Jew might prepare for its coming and in a sense provide a climate of readiness for the intervention, a Jew did not expect to personally bring in the messianic age by any set of historical actions. The usual belief seems to be that the messianic age could be hindered from coming by unpreparedness, but it could not be forced into happening because it entailed the intervention of God. This needs to be borne in mind when assessing the revolutionaries and their possible connections to messianic movements. Also, it needs to be remembered that in a good deal of the literature, "the figure of the Messiah, in whom fulfillment of redemption is concentrated, remains peculiarly vague."[217] This means a range of possibilities of what messiah might be like were circulating, although there was a strong expectation that messiah would rectify the societal injustices God's people faced and throw off the yoke of any foreign rule.

It is instructive to consider the nature of a Jewish messianic movement other than the Jesus movement. Davies has brought to bear the insights from a later Jewish messianic movement and its interpreters. The study of the movement that was spawned as a result of the life and activities of Sabbatai Svi led Scholem to deduce the following as a general paradigm:

---

[213] P. Schafer, *Rabbinischen Judentums*, 214ff. He is right that that messianic hope oscillated between "Naherwartung und religiosem Pragmatismus" (214).

[214] G. Scholem, *Messianic Idea*, 1-2.

[215] Ibid., 4.

[216] Ibid., 8.

[217] Ibid., 17.

First there is the emergence of a messianic figure. He serves as a catalyst, negatively, for the radical criticism of the existing order; positively, of dreams at long last come true, of barriers long-standing being broken down, of a new creation – all this accompanied by an impulse to propagate the good news. And then secondly, this messianic figure must meet a widespread need and be understood to satisfy that need in terms of an interpretative ideological structure of magnitude and depth.[218]

Now, this description gives us some possible clues for interpreting Jesus and his ministry because: (1) as we saw in our discussion on the Pharisees Jesus not only radically criticized the laws of clean and unclean (cf. Mark 7) but he also associated with tax collectors and sinners, as well as with the diseased, making him a clear threat to the existing religious and social order of Judaism; (2) Jesus clearly served as the catalyst for a movement that long outlasted his earthly lifetime; (3) Jesus' preaching of God's inbreaking dominion seems to have offered much not only to the disenfranchised but also to some of the enfranchised, if they would change their life and follow him (e.g., Joanna of Chuza, Lazarus's family); (4) Jesus undoubtedly was one who felt compelled to proclaim his message to the public; and (5) Jesus couched his proclamation in terms of the familiar terminology of the *malkut* that was coming, thus like the revolutionaries providing a religious framework to interpret his actions and ministry in general. In the setting of occupied Palestine such a proclamation coupled with various direct actions for the disenfranchised would have been seen to meet deeply felt needs of God's people. F. C. Grant observed that in the context of God's people "where political depression exists Messianism flames up as a political hope, centered in a royal-divine person; where economic depression exists (without political unrest), Messianism looks forward to an age of economic exaltation . . ."[219] This suggests that whatever Jesus' public claims for himself may or may not have been, clearly his actions and preaching would likely have raised messianic questions and expectations in the context and environment of early Judaism that manifested both political and economic unrest.

These remarks are all the more likely to be correct in view of what Theissen points out about the close of the reign of Herod the Great: He even went beyond the bounds of Jewish monotheism, having

himself celebrated as a god (OGIS 415) . . . He succeeded in finding a prophet who promised him the kingdom in God's name (*Ant.* 15.373ff.). He probably also wanted to promote himself as messiah, the new David. Whereas David had only made preparations for building the temple, and Solomon carried them out, Herod did both . . . Thus Herod usurped not only power, but the messianic hopes of Israel. This must have had a devastating effect and aroused

---

218 This is Davies's summary of Scholem's assessment in "From Schweitzer," 541.
219 F. C. Grant, "Economic Significance," 197.

even greater longing for the true Messiah, who would not hand the Jewish people over to the power of Rome. . . . This longing must have increased during Herod's long reign. After his death, messianic pretenders appeared everywhere: Judas in Galilee, Simon in Perea, Athronges in Judea. . . . "Such madness seized the nation at that time because they had no king of their own . . ." (*Ant.* 17.10.5–7, par. 277).[220]

Davies points out that it turned out to be more crucial who Messiah was in the case of Christianity, than in some messianic movements, because the focus was on Jesus and his teaching in ways that were not true of the movement set in motion by Sabbatai Svi.[221] Davies stresses one other element about such messianic movements—their eschatological and sometimes apocalyptic orientation, an orientation that exists in the Jesus tradition even from its point of origin.

We have briefly pointed to some indicators in the environment and in Jesus' ministry that could have led to the interpretation of Jesus and his movement in messianic categories, in view of both the revolutionary sentiments and the messianic expectations evident in early Judaism. Whether such an interpretation actually transpired and whether Jesus saw his ministry in this light can only be determined by a close examination of the relevant Gospel data.

Most students of the New Testament are aware that there was no single normative set of expectations involving the messiah that existed in early Judaism. Thus, for instance, not only at Qumran (1QS 9.11) but elsewhere as well (cf. *Test. Levi* 18; *Reuben* 6.8) Messianic hopes focused on not one but two figures—a priestly and a kingly anointed one. Also at Qumran were some who anticipated an eschatological or messianic prophet, perhaps one like Moses (cf. 4QTestim; 1QS 9.11). This form of messianic hope seems to be reflected in the Fourth Gospel (John 1:31; 6:14). One major problem in evaluating the evidence is that only a small portion of texts actually mentions an anointed one using the specific term *Mashiach* (or in Greek *Christos*). Various texts express future hope without focusing it on the coming of one or more human individuals.

Nevertheless, perhaps the most prevalent and popular form of messianic expectation was for a ruler of Davidic descent, and nowhere is this better expressed than in *Psalms of Solomon* 17, which C. Rowland says is "typical of the central characteristics of messianic beliefs with its emphasis on the human descendant of David, the vanquishing of Israel's foes and the establishment of a reign of justice and peace on earth under the direction of the King."[222] This text also makes two other things evident. First, messianic expectation basically focused on one or several *human* figures, not divine

[220] Theissen, *First Followers*, 74–75.
[221] Davies, "From Schweitzer," 554.
[222] C. Rowland, *Christian Origins*, 94.

ones, although there is some evidence from 4 Ezra 13–14 and 1 Enoch 37–71 to suggest that some expected a preexistent divine figure to come. The former work seems to be late first century, while the latter is much debated, although it may have been produced as early as the lifetime of Jesus.[223] Second, messianic expectation did not include, according to the evidence available, a suffering much less a crucified messiah. On the contrary, the normal expectation was that the messiah would come and vanquish the oppressors of God's people. There were other sorts of expectations, such as the Samaritan expectation of the Ta'eb or restorer.[224] Mention may also be made of the Jewish discussion about Elijah as a forerunner, although the focus is not specifically on a *messianic* figure (cf. *M. Sotah* 9.15; *Eduyoth* 8.7; *Jub.* 23.9).[225]

Caution is needed when discussing what terms or titles could and could not have been used by or of Jesus during his lifetime. This is shown by the recent striking parallels to Luke 1:32 from an unpublished Aramaic text from Cave 4 of the Qumran findings. This fragment reads in part: "He shall be great on the earth . . . he shall be called the Son of the Great God . . . they shall call him the Son of the most high."[226]

What the evidence tends to show is the presence of a variety of terms and concepts which Jesus could have employed, if he wished to express to his audience that he was a messianic figure of some sort. The absence from his lips of such a term as *Mashiach* or *Ben Dawid* would by no means be decisive in determining whether he had a messianic consciousness. It might indicate that he did not wish to identify with the most common or popular forms of messianic expectation of his day. The terms and ideas used to express messianic hope were sufficiently fluid that Jesus could have indicated messianic status in other ways, if he wished to do so. We are constantly reminded that "the creativity of Judaism in the period before and after Christ may well be its outstanding feature."[227] Whether he did express himself in any messianic terms can only be determined by a careful exegesis of the relevant data, as we have already seen in our study of the words of Jesus.

---

[223] The consensus of the SNTS Pseudepigrapha Seminar was that the *Similitudes* were from the first century, and if they were included in the larger *Enoch* document by the end of the first century A.D., then they must have been extant in some form prior to then. Cf. J. Charlesworth, ed., *Pseudepigrapha* 1:7; and on the date of 4 Ezra, 1:520. Cf. pp. 238–48, of this study on the importance of the *Similitudes* for the Son of man issue.

[224] Witherington, *Women in the Ministry*, 166–67 nn.65, 67; S. Mowinckel, *He That Cometh*, 293.

[225] S. Mowinckel, *He That Cometh*; J. Klausner, *Messianic Idea*; K. Berger, "Messiastraditionen," 1–44.

[226] Fitzmyer, *Luke 1–9*, 347; and reconfirmed orally in Fitzmyer's Qumran lecture in Boston at SBL, 1987.

[227] M. E. Stone, "Judaism," 79.

At this juncture we will examine evidence that Jesus might have conceived of himself in terms congenial to the hopes of the revolutionaries of his day, or terms like those of *Psalms of Solomon 17:* "Behold, O God and raise up unto them their king, the son of David . . . And gird him with strength that he may shatter the unrighteous rulers, and that he may purge Jerusalem from nations that trample her down to destruction."

JESUS AS A REVOLUTIONARY

In the new quest for the historical Jesus, one major debate centers on the extent to which Jesus can be characterized as a revolutionary. In the West, although this seems related to the rise of the counterculture movements of the 60s, the question has gained additional interest because of the increasing influence of developing-nation liberation theologies. Today we hear the insistent cry that a political key is the one that unlocks the door to the real historical Jesus.[228] Our interest lies not with modern hermeneutical attempts to bring the life of Jesus to bear on various situations, but rather with the prior historical questions of what Jesus actually thought of himself. In particular, we will focus here on how Jesus' self-understanding becomes evident in his relationship to or with the first-century Jewish revolutionaries.

In the past two decades important contributions have been made by S. G. F. Brandon, O. Cullmann, and M. Hengel.[229] In fact, the impact of Brandon's study is still being felt because, as recently as 1984, a full-scale response to Brandon appeared under the title *Jesus and the Politics of His Day.*[230] Although Brandon was the catalyst for the modern discussion of the matter, H. S. Reimarus in his *Von dem Zwecke und seiner Junger* (1778) had already labeled Jesus a revolutionary. Brandon does not go as far as Reimarus but Brandon does see Jesus in essential agreement with the revolutionaries' goals and perhaps even with their methods. Our task is to investigate the relevant New Testament data.

Revolutionary Disciples? If it is true that a person may be judged by the company he or she keeps, then a case can be made for Jesus being a revolutionary on the basis of some of the names and nicknames of the Twelve. For

---

[228] J. Luis Segundo, *Historical Jesus*, 71ff., 178ff. Segundo is very careful to distinguish Jesus from the first-century Jewish revolutionaries. He rightly maintains that Jesus' argument was not with the Romans, but with "the religio-political authorities of Judaism" (72). "All recent attempts to prove Jesus politically linked with the Zealots . . . can hardly be taken seriously. They are threadbare. . . . Examining the written documents concerning Jesus, we do not find in them the slightest approval of the Zealot cause even though the opportunity was presented to Jesus (see Luke 13:1)" (73).

[229] S. G. F. Brandon, *Jesus and the Zealots;* O. Cullmann, *Jesus and the Revolutionaries;* M. Hengel, *Was Jesus a Revolutionist?*

[230] E. Bammel and C. F. D. Moule, eds., *Jesus and Politics.*

instance, it is conjectured that *Ioudas ho Iskariotes* is really a somewhat poor Greek rendering for "Judas who was one of the sicarii." Simon bar Jona was long ago thought by R. Eisler to mean "Simon the anarchist," or revolutionary.[231] Calling the Zebedees "sons of Thunder" (Mark 3:17) has been taken to mean that they were men who favored military action against the Romans, a suggestion that might be combined with such texts as Luke 22:49-50 to produce a plausible conjecture. Finally, the most important conjecture is that Simon the *zelotes* (Luke 6:15), which in Mark as well as in Matthew is Simon *ho Kananaios* (Mark 3:18; Matt. 10:4) means "Simon the revolutionary."

Turning to this last suggestion, the Markan and Matthean forms of Simon the *zelotes* do not likely mean Simon the Canaanite because it is simply the Greek rendering of the Aramaic word for a person who has zeal (from the verb *qna*).[232] Even granting this, however, we must raise the question whether the verb *qna*, perhaps in its noun form, had become a technical term during Jesus' day for a revolutionary, or whether we may not rightly make a distinction between an "Eifer" and a "Zelot" — the former being a person perhaps like Paul who was zealous for the law but not against the Romans, and the latter being a person who was a revolutionary opposed to Rome.[233] Whether one was an "Eifer" or a "Zelot," either designation could go back to known uses of the verb *qna*. Indeed, one detailed investigation of the *qannaim* concludes: "*qannaim* cannot always be regarded as the rabbinic equivalent to the Greek *zelotai*."

Further, B. Salomonsen insists that the term can be used of a private individual who may have been zealous for the law or who may have been a racial fanatic, but in any case cannot be certainly linked to the Zealots of the 60s that Josephus discusses.[234] Remember that even the term *zelotes* is not used of any group of the revolutionaries in Josephus's accounts prior to his discussion of the 60s. Thus it is not necessary to conclude on the basis of linguistic evidence that even Simon was a revolutionary against Roman rule.

Moreover, according to all the synoptic accounts (cf. Mark 2:13-17; Matt. 9:9-13; Luke 5:27-32), Simon was banded together with at least one tax collector or customs official, whatever his name may have been. Whether Matthew/Levi was simply a toll collector for Herod Antipas or one who collected directly for the Romans, his job entailed collaboration with the governing authorities. How could such a person openly cooperate in a group with a revolutionary? This problem cannot be dismissed or passed over. Even Brandon admits, "The inclusion of Simon the Zealot in the apostolic

231 R. Eisler, *The Messiah Jesus*, 65ff.

232 Cullmann, *Jesus and the Revolutionaries*, 62 n.11.

233 Hengel, *Die Zeloten*, 154ff.

234 B. Salomonsen, "Zealots," 175.

band actually points to the probability that Jesus was not a Zealot, and that his movement was not an integral part of the Zealot resistance against Rome."[235] Notably, only Simon is called a Zealot, which suggests that in this regard he differed from the other members of Jesus' inner circle. Beyond this we must insist that if Simon had been a revolutionary, to work harmoniously with a tax collector he surely must have been only formerly a Zealot, or else Simon was zealous for the law perhaps like Paul but not against Rome, that is, he was an "Eifer" not a "Zelot."[236]

In regard to Simon bar Jona, Hengel has shown that evidence convincingly favors taking this name as a simple Aramaic patronymic—Simon son of John.[237] In regard to Judas Iscariot, the more plausible derivation is "man of Kerioth," and some of the variants in the manuscript tradition favor seeing Iscariot as a reference to a place of origin.[238] More importantly, in John 6:71 Judas is said to be "son of Simon Iscariot" (cf. 13:26). Are we to think of Judas's father as one of the sicarii as well? It is more plausible that we are dealing with a place name—Simon "of Kerioth." The conjecture in regard to Boanerges can equally well be understood as referring to their temperament, not their political loyalties. In any case, both with Simon and with the Zebedees we still need to ask how they could have worked together with one who had collaborated with the occupation powers if they were revolutionaries? The present evidence persuades that Jesus' disciples should not be seen as a revolutionary band, although formerly some of them may have had such an orientation—Simon, in particular. Therefore, we can tell little about Jesus' attitude toward the revolutionaries from these conjectures.

Revolt in the Wilderness?   A more promising avenue of investigation is to test how revolutionary Jesus was by examining the one miracle pericope that all four Gospel writers share,[239] which likely goes back to the period of the Galilean ministry—the feeding of the five thousand. If the Fourth Gospel is independent of the Synoptics,[240] then on the criterion of multiple attestation there is a good prospect that the story of the feeding of the five thousand in some form goes back to a *Sitz im Leben Jesu*. This is more likely if we also note that Matthew and Luke agree against Mark in various details of this

---

[235] Brandon, *Jesus and the Zealots*, 355.

[236] Brandon was unrepentant of his conclusions on this subject even after severe criticism. He says in "Jesus and the Zealots: a Correction," 453, "the inclusion of a professed Zealot in the apostolic band also indicates that Jesus did not regard the profession of Zealot principles as incompatible with intimate participation in his own mission." Cf. the criticism in the reviews by W. Wink, "Jesus and the Revolution"; M. Hengel, "Reviews."

[237] Hengel, *Die Zeloten*, 55–57.

[238] Cf. aleph, theta, and family 13 at John 6:71, and D at 12:4; 13:2, 26; 14:22; Taylor, *Mark*, 234.

[239] We shall examine other miracle pericopes in the next major section of our study. Cf. below pp. 158–68.

[240] Cf. Witherington, "Principles."

story, which may well suggest that there was also a Q version.[241] An additional possibility is that Mark has preserved two *different* forms of this story (the feeding of the four thousand and of the five thousand being variants of one ancient tradition). This can only mean that the story was deeply imbedded in the tradition. Another factor favoring the basic authenticity of the core of this story is that it does not fit neatly into the normal form-critical categories. Although Bultmann included this story among his list of miracle stories,[242] as Taylor points out, "It has not yet attained the rounded form of a Miracle-story proper and stands nearer the testimony of eyewitnesses."[243] He points especially to Mark 6:37 as an indicator that this story is based on eyewitness tradition, because it is unlikely that the church would later invent such a question.

Interestingly, features of the Johannine version seem likely to reflect a *Sitz im Leben Jesu*. For instance, Brown says of John 6:14–15, "If John was written toward the end of the first century when Roman persecution of Christians under Domitian was all too real, then the invention of the information in vss. 14–15 seems out of the question . . . we believe that in these verses John has given us an item of correct historical information."[244] The later tradition would not likely add political overtones to the story, indeed it is easier to believe that Mark may have downplayed such aspects. Dodd agrees:

> In the known conditions under which primitive Christians lived in the Roman Empire it would be far easier to account for the toning down of apparently political features if the tradition originally contained such features . . . If there was a tradition of events belonging to this period of the Ministry which suggested that he was in danger of being made the centre and leader of a movement of popular revolt . . . we can well understand why in Mark this dangerous feature was glossed over.[245]

Nevertheless, this story, when it begins to speak of the actual act that is seen as miraculous, uses language that is deliberately reminiscent of the material from the Last Supper narrative, so as to make a theological point about the eucharistic significance of this story (cf. esp. 1 Cor. 11:23–25; Mark 14:22–24; 8:6–8).[246] This may be attributed to the Christian community recasting the story somewhat to make it more useful for church purposes. Strikingly, "the Johannine account agrees more closely with the synoptic parallel than any other pericope of the Gospel."[247] This, however, does not

---

[241] Brown, *John 1–12*, 238.
[242] Bultmann, *Synoptic Tradition*, 231f., 251.
[243] Taylor, *Mark*, 321.
[244] Brown, *John 1–12*, 249, 250.
[245] C. H. Dodd, *Fourth Gospel*, 215.
[246] Dodd, *Fourth Gospel*, 201; Brown, *John 1–12*, 236ff.
[247] E. Bammel, "The Feeding," 215.

effect the essential historical points that interest us: (1) that Jesus somewhere in the Galilean wilderness was involved in an event of feeding with
a large crowd;[248] (2) that the crowd took this feeding to imply Jesus was
making certain messianic or eschatological claims, perhaps that he was the
latter day Mosaic prophet of whom the Pentateuch had spoken (Deut. 18:15;
Num. 27:17) and thus they sought to compel or at least urge Jesus to become
leader of a movement having direct political implications for their situation;
(3) that Jesus would have none of this and withdrew from the crowd; (4) that
this event likely climaxed the Galilean ministry, a fact that both Mark and
John independently attest;[249] and (5) that Jesus probably intended this
feeding as an eschatological sign that the Dominion of God had broken in
through his ministry, possibly along the lines that he interpreted his breaking bread with tax collectors and other outcasts of society. He may also have
seen it as a foreshadowing of the messianic banquet, but this is less certain.[250] What is more certain is that the parallels between John 6/Mark 6 and
the story of the Egyptian in Josephus's *Wars* 2.261 and *Ant.* 20.169, which
Barnett has stressed, are rather impressive.[251] They strongly suggest that
Jesus was implying something about the significance of his person and work
by this "sign" in the wilderness, although apparently what he intended and
what the crowd took him to mean were two different things, hence his
withdrawal.

What, then, was Jesus implying by this feeding, and what prompted him
to respond as he did to the crowd? First, Jesus never disclaimed the label
prophet, indeed on more than one occasion he seems to have owned it
(Mark 6:4; Matt. 23:37).[252] Thus, it is not difficult to believe that Jesus might
have performed a sign meant to indicate that he was a prophet, the final
eschatological prophet because he did not seem to have expected any successors. As Bammel rightly points out, however, "The proof a person has
given of his prophetic status raises the expectation of a forthcoming political
role"[253] (cf. Luke 24:19-21). If the Johannine version of this story is correct
on this point, then Jesus' sign in the wilderness raised the expectation that

---

[248] For our purposes it is not necessary to demonstrate that this story is about a miracle at
its most primitive level, only that there was a notable feeding that at least some in the crowd
understood to have a certain kind of theological and political significance. Nevertheless, it seems
to me that a miracle of some sort better explains this crowd reaction as well as the motives for
preserving this story in the church.

[249] I agree with Barrett, *The Gospel according to John,* 2d ed. (Philadelphia: Westminster, 1978),
271-72, that Montefiore has overplayed the political significance of the story, at least in regard
to certain details and Jesus' intention, but cf. H. Montefiore, "Revolt in the Desert (Mark 6:30ff.)"
NTS 8 (1961-62): 135-41. Barnett, "Jewish Prophets," 38ff., makes the most of Montefiore's
suggestion.

[250] Taylor, *Mark,* 321, follows A. Schweitzer in saying that Jesus was deliberately anticipating
the messianic feast at which, in his view, all sorts of people would participate.

[251] Barnett, "Jewish Prophets," 29-30.

[252] Bammel, "The Feeding," 230.

[253] Ibid., 231.

he would assume the role of *basileus,* perhaps even throw off the yoke of Roman rule, or, because this was in Galilee, that of the client-ruler Herod Antipas. Yet Jesus rejects this suggestion, and it may be that the fading of mass support for Jesus was the result of his refusal to accept the acclamation or suggestion of the crowd on this occasion.[254] H. G. Wood stresses that after compelling the disciples to leave, Jesus pacifies and dismisses the crowd and withdraws from Galilee. This likely means, "Jesus refuses to be the warrior-Messiah of popular expectation [cf. *Psalms of Solomon* 17] . . . the farewell to the crowd and the night of prayer may point to a decision to break off the public ministry, at least for the time being. Jesus then withdrew from Galilee . . . because of the popular enthusiasm which followed the feeding of the multitude."[255]

This can be taken to mean that although Jesus may well have seen himself as the Mosaic prophet of the eschatological age, or at least the one who brings in God's dominion and so foreshadows the coming messianic feast, nevertheless he rejected the application of popular messianic expectation to himself. He had not come to be the warrior messiah. This does not mean he simply rejected any sort of messianic idea when applied to himself, but clearly he rejected this form of it. Yet it was apparently this form of messianism that was most often associated with the house of David in Jesus' day, and he was likely a "scion of the house of David."[256] Thus, although we cannot conclude from this story that Jesus had a nonmessianic self-understanding, it must surely count against his having seen himself in the mold of the Davidic Messiah that was to come as a warrior king. It must also count strongly against the view that Jesus was in sympathy with the goals and theology of the revolutionaries.

Testing Jesus' Metal   Another passage from the ministry period that gives insight into Jesus' view of the revolutionaries and Rome is Mark 12:13–17 (and par.). Here we have a classic example of a pronouncement story where everything prepares the way for a climactic saying. The narrative is reduced to the bare minimum, and in regard to the saying itself Bultmann avers: "There are no grounds to think this is a Community product."[257] In any case, it is altogether believable that Jesus would be questioned on what was for many Jews, especially the revolutionaries, one of the burning issues of the day: Should the Jews pay tribute money to Caesar and so implicitly acknowledge his authority over them?

It is probable that the coin was one of the second series of denarii that Tiberius issued, one side of which read, *PONTIF MAXIM,* and the other, *TI*

---

[254] Ibid., 232 n.145.

[255] H. G. Woods, "This Time," 265.

[256] Bammel, "The Feeding," 237.

[257] Bultmann, *Die Geschichte,* 25.

CAESAR DIVI AVG F AVGVSTVS.[258] For many Jews to even use such a coin, much less to use it to pay tribute to Caesar, amounted to recognizing his claims made on the coin to be Pontifex Maximus and divine Augustus. As Bruce says, the most likely setting for this incident is Judea where "the tribute question was one of practical moment, with the risk of an impolitic answer being construed as seditious."[259] Thus, it is likely that this question and Jesus' answer came in the context of his final visit to Jerusalem.[260] Remembering the principle established by Judas the Galilean that it was immoral and indeed sacrilegious to pay tribute to Caesar, this question would seem to be meant to reveal the extent to which Jesus was in sympathy with the so-called Fourth philosophy of Judas.

The question posed to Jesus requests an opinion concerning the legality of the tribute; the phrase, "is it permitted," refers to permission in the Mosaic law (cf. Mark 3:4, *exestin* as here; 1 Cor. 14:34). Jesus' response depends on the acknowledgment by his audience that these coins do belong to Caesar, who has minted them and whose picture appears on them. It is well known that there are various sayings in the Jesus tradition that suggest he did not have much regard for money, or mammon as he called it (cf. Matt. 6:24; Luke 16:9, "unrighteous mammon"). Furthermore, he saw the accumulation of money as a positive impediment to entering the dominion of God (Mark 10:25; Luke 16:19–31). Thus, Jesus' response hardly means simply to be civic minded and pay your taxes. This saying probably has little to do with modern theories of two spheres of influence or the separation of God and state. Rather than being a counsel of submission to earthly rulers, it is more likely to be a comment on the relative insignificance of the issue in the light of the inbreaking dominion of God.

Notice that Jesus has no such coin on his person, but his inquisitors do. If there were any revolutionaries in the audience this would only be seen as a plus for Jesus because the revolutionaries apparently felt it was impious even to carry or use Caesar's coins at all, not least because they often bore "graven images." In light of Jesus' view about the inbreaking of God's reign, it is unlikely that Jesus would have given any sort of wholehearted endorsement to Rome or supported its legitimacy. Yet the way he frames his response would have seemed to revolutionaries "a deplorable compromise."[261] Such people, however, did not think on the same plane as Jesus, who believed that God was directly bringing in the divine dominion and that whether one paid tribute to Caesar neither helped nor hindered the coming of that dominion.

---

[258] H. St. J. Hart, "The Coin," 241–48.

[259] F. F. Bruce, "Render to Caesar," 249–63.

[260] Sherwin-White, *Roman Society*, 126–27.

[261] Cullmann, *Jesus and the Revolutionaries*, 45.

In short, Jesus disagreed that the paying of tribute was a litmus test deter-mining one's loyalty to the biblical God. In fact, giving Caesar back his meaningless pieces of metal that bore his image could even be seen as a religious duty, thus refusing to have or use anything that ultimately belonged to Caesar. As Bruce suggests, Jesus was counseling "the handing back to a Gentile ruler of coins which bore his name and image, coins which for that very reason no truly pious Jew ought to possess . . ."[262] By putting the matter this way, although Jesus would surely have disappointed the revolu-tionaries, he would have given his other opponents (notice that Mark men-tions the Herodians and Pharisees here) no cause to report him to the Romans. This saying could certainly not be construed as seditious, whatever its precise nuances.

What should one render, or give back to God? Jesus does not say here, but it is unlikely that he is here referring to the paying of the temple tax, although that is not completely impossible.[263] It is more probable that here again we have an example of Jesus being concerned with ultimate issues — the giving of one's whole self to God, for after all we are created in God's image,[264] we are God's, and in Jesus' view the situation was urgent because of the inbreaking of the dominion (cf. Mark 10:6).[265] Now was the time to render God's own proper due.

Once again we see no encouragement for the view that Jesus was either a revolutionary or in sympathy with them. Why should he align himself with a group whose methodology for bringing in God's reign stood in such contrast to his own? His approach was to pursue a ministry of preaching, teaching, healing, and having table fellowship even with tax collectors and sinners. If anything, his vision was even more directly theocratic than the

---

[262] Bruce, "Render unto Caesar," 262; Daube, "Master and Disciples," rightly notes the subtlety of Jesus' response. "Jesus' solution is indeed far from a strightforward 'Yes'. He takes the view that he and his are not liable to the tax any more than the sons of an earthly king would have to offer tribute. Only he does not wish to give offence" (13). He goes on to note that Jesus gives up nothing of his own, since the coin that was used to pay would have been ownerless, not belonging to Jesus or anyone. Thus, they do and they do not pay. "They do by handing the temple the coin. They do not in that the coin is not genuinely theirs" (14).

[263] Independent confirmation of the rightness of the interpretation of this passage would seem to come from a close examination of Matt. 17:24–7, if it is dominical, as W. Horbury avers in "The Temple Tax." In this passage Jesus does not endorse the paying of the Tyrian half-shekel levy, rather, "he only pays in a manner not admitting liability" (282). The actual point Jesus wishes to make is "that God's people should not be taxed in the name of their divine king" (285). His radically theocentric perspective causes him to evaluate this levy, not from a pragmatic standpoint but in light of the true status of the children of a divine king. Nevertheless, Jesus takes no revolutionary action against the levy, nor does he refuse to pay. Although he does not feel obligated to pay, he does so in order not to give unnecessary offense, having made his point.

[264] G. Bornkamm, *Jesus of Nazareth*, 123, says, "This means: the coin belongs to Caesar, but you to God. Probably it contains an even more specific thought: the coin which bears the image of Caesar, we owe to Caesar. We, however, as men who bear the image of God, owe ourselves to God."

[265] Witherington, *Women in the Ministry*, 26–27 nn.132–37.

revolutionaries' stance. No wonder the choral response at the end of this pericope in its Markan version is the amazement of the audience; they had never heard teaching like this before, not even from a "sophist" (to use Josephus's term) like Judas the Galilean.

A Grand Entrance?   If there is a strong case to be made that Jesus had sympathy with the cause of the revolutionaries and thus saw himself in that sort of light, then its basis is the last week or so of Jesus' life. For those who prefer a nonmessianic interpretation of Jesus they must be able to explain how it was, if Jesus was an interesting but nonthreatening Galilean *hasid*, that he ended up being crucified and that, according to strong tradition, the *titulus* read "King of the Jews." The form and nature of Jesus' death raise a major objection against any purely nonmessianic interpretation of Jesus' words and actions and at the same time seems to give substantial support to a theory like Brandon's. Thus, when scholars try to evaluate what it was about Jesus' last week that may have led to crucifixion the focus usually is on: (1) his entry into Jerusalem; and (2) his actions in the temple, perhaps coupled with certain oracles about the future of the temple.

Immediately we face difficulties when we focus on Mark 11:1-11 (and par.) because significant doubt exists as to whether this event happened, especially in light of D. Catchpole's study.[266] Bultmann also concluded that this is a messianic legend, although perhaps based on an account of Jesus' entry into Jerusalem with a crowd of expectant pilgrims.[267] Thus, we must examine this material carefully to see whether we can deduce anything about the historical Jesus.

First, Catchpole appears to be guilty of a common fallacy when pursuing a *formgeschichtliche* approach to a narrative: He assumes that because the narrative seems to fit a particular formal pattern, one can therefore draw conclusions about the historical authenticity of the narrative's essential content. But the fact that this story may be in the form of a legend of the entry of a king into his city does not rule out the possibility of a historical basis for the story.[268]

Furthermore, Catchpole's formal analysis attempts to place Zech. 9:9 into a category that speaks of a king arriving after having achieved a victory. Although Zech. 9:1ff. does speak of victory over foes, these foes are beaten outside the holy city, at which according to v. 8 the king will encamp "as a guard so that none may march to and fro." Thus, as he comes to the city he is indeed triumphant. The final victory, however, has not been achieved. Indeed, it appears that the holy city has not yet been liberated. Verse 10 says, "I will cut off the chariot from Ephraim, and the war horse from

---

[266] Catchpole, "The 'Triumphal' Entry," 319–34.
[267] Bultmann, *Die Geschichte*, 281.
[268] M. Dibelius, *Die Formgeschichte*, 118–22.

Jerusalem; and the battle bow shall be cut off, and he shall command peace to the nations." Thus, the king is not being welcomed into a city already at peace, prepared for his coming. Nor does his coming inaugurate the era of peace.[269] Rather, the war horses must first be cut off from Jerusalem. Jerusalem's people should rejoice because their liberator has come, not because the liberation has already been completely accomplished. In short, this text probably does not fit the pattern Catchpole has discerned of a king returning to his city after the final victory and with the acclamation of his people. Even though the Markan text may be related to Zech. 9:9, it does not fit the perceived formal pattern.[270] Even if it did fit such a pattern, one could not make a value judgment on the historical substance of Mark 11:1-11 (and par.) simply because it has been written in light of a recognized pattern and particular Old Testament texts.

Second, Derrett has gone to some lengths to show that various people including the disciples of rabbis could and did commandeer animals in Jesus' era and afterward, following the rules for *angaria*, the impressing of means of transportation for some specific limited time and purpose.[271] There is no good reason that Jesus and his disciples could not have utilized such a recognized practice.

Third, the Markan form of the story does not show the elaboration on Zech. 9:9 that we find in Matthew and John, although the implicit allusion seems to be present in Mark as well. Furthermore, Jesus is not hailed as Lord; at most he is hailed as the one coming in the Lord's name.[272] Indeed, it can be argued that Jesus is simply being accompanied by various pilgrims who are singing the pilgrim songs, one of which is based on Ps. 118:26ff. and was certainly used during the Feasts of Tabernacles and Passover.[273] (Psalm 118:26 may be no more than a greeting used to address pilgrims as they approached the holy city.) In short, the Markan form of the story is primitive and does not capitalize on the christological potential of the text, unlike the later versions of this story. Taylor concludes:

> In favor of the historical worth of the narrative are the local expressions at the beginning, the vivid character of the account, including the instructions to the two disciples, the description of what happened, the restrained nature of the

---

[269] Catchpole, "The Triumphal Entry," 319.

[270] As H. Schürmann, following E. Schweizer, says, if Mark 11:1-10 had been spun out of Zech. 9:9, then the allusion would surely have been made clearer. Cf. Schürmann, "Die Symbolhandlungen Jesu," 93. Schürmann suggests that we see in Jesus' ministry a series of eschatological signs among which may be included: (1) eating with sinners and tax collectors; (2) feeding the five thousand; (3) the triumphal entry; and (4) the cleansing of the temple. All these are in his view to be taken as signs of the in-breaking of the dominion and are, at least by implication, messianic acts.

[271] J. D. M. Derrett, "Law in the New Testament."

[272] This may or may not relate to the idea of the "coming one" if that was a messianic designation; cf. pp. 43-44.

[273] Taylor, *Mark*, 456; Marshall, *Luke*, 715; D. Flusser, *Jesus*, 105.

acclamation, and the strange manner in which the account breaks off without any suggestion of a "triumphal entry" (as in Mt). These characteristics suggest the eyewitness rather than the artist. . . . We must conclude that it comes from the best tradition, with embellishment only in the phrase concerning the colt: "whereon no man ever yet sat." With good reason we may assign it to the Petrine tradition.[274]

Whether there was in Jesus' day or before a messianic expectation that involved Zech. 9:9—and the Jewish literature usually cited appears to come from a later era[275]—there is no reason that Jesus could not have conceived of himself in such terms, in contradistinction to the normal Davidic messianic expectations. The Fourth Gospel independently gives us a version of this story, that includes the association with Zech. 9:9. Here again, the criterion of multiple attestation applies. For our purposes the historical substance of the story needs only to be the fact that Jesus requisitioned an ass or the foal of an ass[276] and rode into Jerusalem upon it accompanied by various people, presumably including the disciples. It may also be historical that there were with Jesus pilgrims, presumably from Galilee, who were singing or shouting some of the Hallel psalms. But even if only the event of Jesus riding into the city on an ass is historical, then there can be little doubt that Jesus associated himself with Zech. 9:9.[277]

We must now inquire into the possible meaning of such an event. Notice that nowhere else in any of the Gospel stories has Jesus ridden, and this riding seems to go against the tradition of pilgrims walking into the holy city together at feast time. Thus, Jesus is deliberately distinguishing himself from those with whom he was traveling; here he deliberately elevates himself above his companions, by this symbolic action of self-elevation. That he intended this to be a symbolic act, one might call it a prophetic sign,[278] seems likely.

That the sign was meant to say something about Jesus' intentions and self-revelation seems certain. It is not clear however, that either the crowd or the disciples (cf. John 12:16) took the hint at least until later, although the event itself was remembered.[279] Skepticism about the possibility of such an

---

[274] Taylor, *Mark*, 452–53.

[275] Fitzmyer, *Luke 10–24*, 1245–46, and *B.T.San.* 98a; cf. Moore, *Judaism in the First Centuries of the Christian Era* (New York: Schocken Books, 1971), 2:334–35.

[276] That *pwlos* need not mean horse here, but rather an ass as the other Gospels interpret the matter, see F. F. Bruce, "Book of Zechariah," 339 n.1.

[277] Kümmel, *Promise and Fulfilment*, 116–17, who says there can be no doubt.

[278] Borg, *Jesus*, 174.

[279] If the waving of the palm branches is an authentic remembrance, then this may suggest that the crowd at least saw Jesus in the light of the Maccabean military heroes, Judas and Simon, and thus would have anticipated some direct political action by Jesus while in the city (cf. 2 Macc. 10:1–9; 1 Macc. 13:52). Cf. W. Farmer, "Palm Branches." If so, then Jesus' chosen form of mount reveals his rejection of this form of messianic expectation.

occurrence, based on the supposition that the authorities would have acted against Jesus, is grounded on the assumption that this event was of much greater magnitude than it likely was. Furthermore, if this event happened outside the city and in the press of the festival crowd, then it may well have gone unnoticed by the authorities, unless it was later reported to them. One must not envision an authority under every bush watching Jesus' every move.[280]

If Jesus did see himself in terms of Zech. 9:9, then this action might even be called an antirevolutionary act, meant to delimit clearly what sort of messianic figure was not consistent with his self-understanding and what sort of self-image he intended to project. He would not ride into town on a war horse. Rather, he chooses the route of the peaceable kingly figure or "Israel's shepherd-king."[281] This certainly comports with some of his likely authentic utterances (Matt. 5:9, 38–48).[282]

Thus, Jesus does at the end of his career deliberately reveal his self-perception, but not in the terms of the most popular form of messianic expectation.[283] Indeed, it may be that Jesus was the first one to base messianic expression on Zech. 9:9. In any event, Jesus cannot be seen as a revolutionary on the basis of this action; his intent and action were otherwise, and it is unlikely that an action such as this led to his demise. For the historical antecedents of the crucifixion we must look to the temple traditions.

A Temple Tantrum?   Assessing Jesus' view of early Judaism entails examining his view of the three fundamental foci points of that religion: Torah, temple, and territory (the promised land). The Torah was discussed when we considered Jesus' relationships with the Pharisees.[284] Here, however, we must examine what Jesus said about and did in the temple. Careful examination is crucial because Brandon has argued that Jesus, accompanied by disciples and a crowd, went into the temple and that upon seeing Jesus' action in the temple, the excited crowd attacked and pillaged the temple.[285] Although the Gospels say nothing about a crowd pillaging the temple, making Brandon's case largely an argument from silence, even if Jesus acted alone "it is this event that comes nearest to revolutionary activity and it is

---

[280] Marshall, *Luke*, 710.

[281] Bruce, "Book of Zechariah," 347. There is further evidence that Jesus saw his actions in the light of Zechariah, as we will see in the next section on the temple; cf. O'Neill, *Messiah*, 57–58.

[282] R. Guelich, *Sermon on the Mount*, 90ff., 250ff.

[283] Grant, "Economic Significance," 288–89: "Our Lord did not take over the Messianic hope *just as it stood*, without revision or reinterpretation . . . the economic, political, mundane, nationalistic details which prophetic and apocalyptic Messianism had elaborated, [Jesus] did not take over. . . ."

[284] Cf. pp. 59–81.

[285] Brandon, *Jesus and the Zealots*, 333.

this narrative that contains the watchwords indicating Zealotism: *zelos* and *lestes.*"[286]

Various attitudes about the temple existed in Jesus' day, ranging from the views expressed in some parts of the Enoch and the Qumran literature that the temple was corrupt and would be judged or destroyed (cf. *1 Enoch* 89.73−90.29; 4QFlor. 1.1–12),[287] to very positive assessments. Part of the difficulty lay in the fact that Herod the Great was the one largely responsible for the present state of the temple building, and even leaving aside the notorious examples of his immorality, violence, and self-aggrandizing behavior, his family heritage was Idumean. It is clear that attitudes in Galilee were rather different from those in Judea. Freyne has assembled data to show that: (1) many of the Galileans probably did not follow Pharisaic regulations in regard to the paying of the half-shekel temple tax, but instead followed the Sadducean position on the matter; and (2) the Galileans were not scrupulous about tithing. Freyne conjectures that this was not caused by an antitemple attitude, but in part from the fact that "their attitude can be interpreted as conservative rather than neglectful, reflecting a refusal to adopt new ideas in religion any more than in other walks of life, in line with peasant attitudes everywhere."[288] Some of Freyne's evidence is post-A.D. 70, but it does reflect a trend that existed well before the destruction of the temple. One should not conclude from this evidence that the Galileans as a whole were antitemple because both Josephus and the New Testament attest that Galileans made regular pilgrimages up to Jerusalem (cf. *Ant.* 118–120; Luke 13:1).

The point is that there was precedent in Jesus' day for differing from both the Pharisees and the temple hierarchy about the Herodian temple and its worth. Even if one supported the concept of temple worship, one might be critical of corrupt practices within it. Such differing from the Judean or Jerusalem views of these matters apparently was not unusual in Galilee.

Jeremias has drawn our attention to some extrabiblical material that suggests there was an association in early Judaism between the coming and enthronement of Israel's final shepherd king and the renewal of the temple.[289] Besides interesting evidence from outside Jewish circles, Jeremias points to a text such as *1 Enoch* 90.28–30 which reads, "Then I stood still, looking at that ancient house being transformed: All the pillars and all the columns were pulled out . . . I went on seeing until the Lord of the sheep brought about a new house, greater and loftier than the first one, and set it up in the first location . . . All the sheep were within it." From what follows in *1 Enoch* 90.40, it appears that the reference to the Lord is not to a messianic

---

[286] Bammel, "The Poor and the Zealots," 124.

[287] Cf. The reconstruction of the fragments in D. Juel, *Messiah and Temple*, 180.

[288] Freyne, *Galilee*, 277ff., here 281.

[289] J. Jeremias, *Jesus als Weltvollender*, 32ff.

figure but to Yahweh. Nevertheless, Jeremias is correct to point to texts such as *Ant.* 18.85ff. and *Wars* 6.283ff. where some eschatological expectation is present in Jesus' setting for a messianic figure to do something about the temple as a means of making or legitimating a messianic claim.[290]

Two further preliminary remarks are necessary before examining the Gospel material. First, there is an interesting passage in the *M. San.* 9.6 which states that the *qannaim* may fall upon anyone who steals a sacred vessel, presumably from the temple. This indicates that zeal for the temple was assumed to be justified, even if it involved violence against the defiler or violator. Acts 21:28-29 attests to mob violence against one who was perceived as violating the sanctity of the temple, in this case, Paul, by bringing a non-Jew into the temple precincts.

Another important matter is what Jesus might have been directing his wrath against if he did perform some sort of violent act in the temple. It cannot be assumed that it was directed purely against the sacrificial system and its support mechanisms such as the selling of pigeons or the changing of money.

N. Hamilton has urged that Jesus' wrath was directed against "the whole economic function of the temple,"[291] which included not only the sale of birds for sacrifice and the money changing operation but also those who delivered goods to the vendors, merchants who sold and bought cattle,[292] as well as those who would simply be coming to make a deposit in the temple, which served as the bank for Jewish people. Any or all of these activities could have been the object of his action.

In regard to the historicity of Jesus performing some kind of action in the temple, the following considerations seem decisive. First, the later church, either in its early days when it was still involved in the temple prior to A.D. 70 (cf. Acts 2:46) or later when it was seeking to present itself as a religion that was not an inherent threat to the empire, would have been unlikely to have invented a tradition about Jesus taking some sort of violent action in the temple. Temples of all sorts were protected by the Romans during the age of the empire, not least because sacrifices for the emperor were to be offered in these temples.[293] As Sanders says, withholding sacrifices was taken by the Romans as the final sign of a revolt.[294] Second, the outer court of the temple served as the agora for Jerusalem and was very large, some 300 meters wide by 450 meters in length.[295] If, as the Gospels

---

[290] Ibid., 39.

[291] N. Q. Hamilton, "Temple Cleansing," 370-71.

[292] Cf. Mark 11:15, and J. Jeremias, *Jerusalem*, 33ff.

[293] Sherwin-White, *Roman Society*, 35ff.; J. Juster, *Les juifs*, 1:459-60, says that desecration of a temple was regarded as a capital offense by the Romans.

[294] Smallwood, *Roman Rule*, 148ff.

[295] Hengel, *Was Jesus a Revolutionist?* 15.

all agree, Jesus acted on his own, then it is possible that a major disturbance was not created and the Roman soldiers in the adjacent Antonia Fortress would not have been summoned. If any action was taken at all as a result of the minor disruption, then it could have been handled by a few temple police who, if Jesus did not persist in his action for long, could easily have helped to set matters right and reported the incident to the temple authorities.

Third, even Bultmann allows that a historical background to this story may be postulated whatever redactional additions may have been made to the basic tradition. He calls the story (at least Mark 11:15b–d, 16, 17) a biographical apophthegm.[296] Fourth, as Fitzmyer says, the main objection to the historicity of this story is the difficulty some scholars have in seeing how Jesus could have cleaned out the whole court of the Gentiles without opposition from the temple police. But this objection fails if Jesus did not cleanse the whole court but took an action limited in time and space, meant as a prophetic sign and not as an actual attempt at an effective cleansing.[297] Fifth, according to the majority of scholars the criterion of multiple attestation here again applies because John's version of this story seems clearly to stem from a non-Markan tradition and most certainly has a non-Markan placement that surely suggests the Fourth Evangelist is not following Mark here.[298] Sixth, if Jesus' anger was directed against the trade going on in the temple, no good evidence attests that such commercial use of the court of the Gentiles was a practice of long standing. Indeed, V. Eppstein has argued that the practice originated in the lifetime of Jesus, perhaps instituted as late as A.D. 30 by Caiaphas, and that there was great controversy during this period over this innovation because markets already existed on the Mount of Olives for the same purposes.[299] Jesus' action then would be comprehensible as a response to a recent abuse introduced into the temple precincts, presumably for the profit of the temple hierarchy. We know that the high priest received a share of the temple tax, so other forms of revenue raising may also have been introduced (cf. *M. Shek.* 3.1).[300] We also know that later the so-called shops of the House of Annas were rebelled against by the people.[301]

If we grant that an action by Jesus in the temple is both possible and plausible, the question then becomes which form of text, the Markan or Johannine, is more likely to preserve the original historical substance of the event. Most scholars are convinced that the Johannine placement of the story is likely to be secondary, but this does not settle the question of which

---

[296] Bultmann, *Synoptic Tradition*, 36, 56.

[297] Fitzmyer, *Luke 10–24*, 1264.

[298] Brown, *John 1–12*, 116–20.

[299] V. Eppstein, "Cleansing of the Temple." This may perhaps be coupled with the observation that there were those who in Jesus' day were zealous to exclude Gentiles altogether from the temple. Cf. 4QFlor.; and Juel's discussion in *Messiah and Temple*, 172ff.

[300] Jeremias, *Times of Jesus*, 49.

[301] J. D. M. Derrett, "The Zeal of the House," 86.

account is closer in substance to the original events. Both accounts mention the overturning of the moneychangers' tables and both mention the driving out of those who sold the birds and animals (John adds the driving out of the animals as well, while Mark mentions the driving out of those who bought). This seems likely to have been the nature of the original action that stands behind both accounts.

In John we hear the pronouncement, "You shall not make my Father's house a house of trade," which may be the Johannine version of, "Is it not written, 'My house shall be called a house of prayer' . . . but you have made it a den of robbers." It is also possible that John's saying is not just an alternate form of the same saying (cf. Mark 11:16 on traders in the temple), in which case the background to the Johannine sayings is more likely to be Zech. 14:21 rather than Isa. 56:7/Jer. 7:11 which stands behind the Markan saying. Some sort of word or words of interpretation to make the action intelligible likely goes back to a *Sitz im Leben Jesu.* The Johannine version seems to have incorporated an additional temple saying, John 2:19, from some other context.

Next the question about the meaning of this action and Jesus' word of interpretation needs to be raised. Again there are various possibilities. Was this action a symbolic cleansing of the temple as it is so often interpreted to be, or are Jesus' words and deed more a symbolic judgment sign, foreshadowing a coming judgment on the corrupt institution? To what extent is Jesus rejecting the temple per se or only some aspect of it, or is this action more a statement against the corruption in the temple? Should this action be seen as messianic, perhaps interpreted in light of various traditions that anticipated that the Davidic messiah would build the eschatological temple (cf. 2 Sam. 7:13), or is it simply the action of a reformer, one wishing to restore the original or proper purity of the present temple? These issues are made more complex because there are various forms of the saying, suggesting that Jesus predicted the destruction of the temple. These sayings also need to be evaluated.

Most scholars are in agreement that in the case of the saying about the destruction of the temple, John 2:19 preserves the more primitive form, and Mark 14:58 may be seen either as a somewhat garbled version of this saying or, more likely, as the misunderstanding of the saying by those who sought to bear false witness against Jesus before the Jewish authorities (cf. Mark 14:57). Jesus apparently did predict the demise of the temple (cf. Mark 13:1-2 and par.). If the original form of the saying is along the lines of John 2:19 or Mark 13:1-2, then Jesus does not suggest that he himself will tear down the temple, but he may be suggesting that he will raise up the new eschatological temple. It is thus unlikely that Jesus' action in the temple should be seen as an attempt to destroy the temple. This comports with the messianic traditions of early Judaism because "in none of the messianic texts is the Messiah expected to destroy the temple, even as the prelude to the building of a new temple."[302] If Jesus saw himself as in some sense messiah, then it is unlikely that his action in the temple was meant to be literally destructive, although it might well have prophetically depicted the coming destruction. By contrast two texts (2 Sam. 7:13 and Zech. 6:12) were understood in pre-Christian Jewish circles to refer to the messiah building the final temple, although probably the majority of Jews in Jesus' day held the view that God would build the final temple (cf. esp. Exod. 15:17).[303]

Theissen has encouraged us to see Mark 14:58 in the light of the tensions between those who dwelt in the city of Jerusalem, a good many of whom depended on the temple and in particular the ongoing building of the temple for their livelihood, and those who dwelt elsewhere in the land, perhaps particularly in Galilee.[304] He argues that the early church would not have created a saying like Mark 14:58 because Jesus did not build a new temple in that era and because the Romans, not Jesus or the Jews, destroyed the temple.[305] He draws attention to the resistance not only at Qumran, but also among the ordinary people, to the temple Herod built, especially in light of the heavy tax burden. Notably, all those prophets who criticized the temple in the past were from among the people of the land, not from Jerusalem—Micah, Jeremiah, Uriah (Jer. 26:20). In an already nervous city closely watched by the Romans, any words or actions perceived to be a threat against the temple, would be taken as a threat against such groups as the priesthood, the aristocracy, and the construction and maintenance workers employed at the temple. Jesus might easily be construed as deliberately whipping up the visiting pilgrims against the establishment and the city dwellers. After all, had he not arrived with a crowd of out of town (Galilean?) pilgrims?

He would have been perceived as all the more dangerous if it was known that he was preaching the arrival and even inbreaking of the dominion of God, which had political and social as well as religious implications, especially for Jerusalem. Any sort of radically theocratic preaching was bound to make the present human intermediaries between God and God's people nervous because their positions would be threatened by such a vision of history. They had most to lose if things could not be maintained as they were. Furthermore, there was the matter of right standing with God. "The Jerusalemite had interest on the grounds of the holiness of their City, that is on the ground of the Temple. Any questioning of the religious status of the City must also place therefore the material status of its inhabitants in question."[306] These factors make clear that much more was at stake than just

---

[302] Juel, *Messiah and Temple*, 200.
[303] Ibid., 150ff.
[304] G. Theissen, "Die Tempelweissagung Jesu."
[305] Ibid., 145.
[306] Ibid., 154.

spiritual matters, especially if Jesus performed a prophetic sign in the temple and perhaps said something sounding like a threat against the temple.

Although Jesus' action in the temple could be interpreted in various ways, it probably should not be seen as an attempt to interrupt or condemn the temple cultus per se. This is so because: (1) even as a symbolic act, Jesus' action would have been singularly ineffective because at least four markets were on the Mount of Olives where commerce was not interrupted by him[307]; (2) various traditions including Matt. 5:23–24 and Acts 2:46 argue against such an interpretation;[308] and (3) the direction of the sayings in both John and Mark is against some sort of action or trading in the temple, not against the temple per se.

How, then, should we understand Jesus' action? One possible view would be that Jesus' action was a prophetic judgment sign.[309] J. Roloff maintains: "The action of Jesus was accordingly a prophetic sign, that the repentance and conversion of Israel in the Endtime will be brought about."[310] This view is plausible not only because of the independent saying about the coming demise of the temple but also because of the variety of Jewish groups in Jesus' age, especially at Qumran, who felt the Herodian temple was radically tainted and corrupt and thus doomed. This conclusion recently has been supported by C. A. Evans who refutes the views of Sanders.[311] Jesus may well have been like-minded, especially if he, like some of his fellow Galileans, was not enamored with such means as the temple tax and tithes to obtain money from the populous for the temple and its hierarchy. Money, particularly the changing of money so that the half-shekel tax could be paid, seems to be part of what Jesus is attacking in the temple.

A second possibility is broached by Hamilton. He argues that because the wealth of Judea was concentrated in the temple bank, which functioned like a state exchequer, and because those who interfered with the economic affairs of the temple—often appropriating money from it—were always the kings or rulers of the land, Jesus' action suggested a kingly claim. "Without the authority of the sanhedrin or Roman procurator such sovereign interference in the economic affairs of the temple must have been taken as a direct claim to be king."[312] Only royalty would dare interfere as Jesus did. The only problem with this rather impressive argument is that Jesus does

---

[307] Furthermore, the old objection that there would have been nowhere to keep animals in the temple precincts has been shown to be invalid in light of the discovery of stables and a passageway from the Double Gates, an area where the merchants likely would have been, to these stables. Cf. Charlesworth, *Jesus within Judaism*, 117.

[308] W. D. Davies, *The Gospel and the Land*, 349 n.45, item 1.

[309] Borg, *Jesus*, 175.

[310] J. Roloff, *Das Kerygma*, 95.

[311] Cf. C. A. Evans, "Jesus' Action in the Temple and the Evidence of First Century Corruption in the First-Century Temple," *SBL Seminar Papers* (Atlanta: Scholars Press, 1989), 522–39.

[312] Hamilton, "Temple Cleansing," 371.

not actually appropriate anything here; the mere interference with the cultus in itself was probably not peculiarly regal. Certainly the later actions of the sicarii and the priestly Zealots in the temple could not all be interpreted in this fashion.

A third view is that the messiah was expected on the basis of such texts as *Psalms of Solomon* 17 to come and cleanse the land, thus creating "the purified conditions in which Redemption would be possible."[313] This view coheres with Eppstein's with the additional component that Jesus would be taking on a messianic function, not merely offering a prophetic critique in cleansing the temple.

A fourth view centers on the fact that this action seems to have taken place in the court of the Gentiles. The argument is largely based on Mark 11:17, particularly the phrase "for all nations." The point would be that Jesus was trying to clear the outer court so that the Gentiles too could worship in God's house. It should be noted that none of the other Gospels includes this phrase, not even Luke, and most scholars would agree that Mark was directed toward a predominantly gentile audience. Most scholars would urge that this phrase is Mark's redactional comment.

A fifth view depends on which form of the saying or sayings was likely Jesus' original comment on his action. If John 2:16 (or something quite like it) was Jesus' word of interpretation, then it is plausible that Jesus would be alluding to Zech. 14:21 and would be seeing himself as bringing in that final holy time when there would no longer be a trader in the house of the Lord. This interpretation gains credence if Jesus interpreted himself and his role in light of the prophecies of Zechariah. In fact, O'Neill has intimated that Zechariah's oracles could have had a major influence on Jesus' thinking about some of the matters climaxing during the last week of Jesus' life.[314] The problem with seeing the saying in Mark 11:17 (and par.) as original has been pointed out by A. E. Harvey: Neither half of this saying is apposite when translated back into Hebrew or Aramaic. The word translated "robber" means "raider," not "swindler," and so it could refer to a revolutionary but not someone like a money changer or a simple trader.[315] Thus, the Johannine saying more likely captures the sense of how Jesus originally interpreted the event.

---

[313] C. Roth, "The Cleansing of the Temple," 176.

[314] O'Neill, *Messiah*, 56–58. This would also include the possibly authentic saying of Jesus where he quotes Zechariah's oracle about smiting the shepherd. It should be noted that Zech. 6:12 is one of the oracles that refers to the messianic building of the temple, which could be behind John 2:19b and Mark 14:58b. Cf. Bruce, "Book of Zechariah," 343ff. In reference to Mark 14:27, he says, "I have no doubt at all that Mark is right in ascribing this interpretation of the prophecy to Jesus; it is all of a piece with Jesus' presentation of Himself as the Shepherd of Israel—a presentation which can be traced in most of the Gospel strata."

[315] Harvey, *Jesus*, 132, nn.

What may we conclude from all this? The most plausible interpretations of Jesus' action in the temple suggest that Jesus performed a prophetic sign that was meant either as a signal of coming judgment on the temple or more probably as a symbolic action of cleansing, perhaps like that of Nehemiah's (cf. Neh. 13:4–9, 12–13),[316] in which case Jesus was saying that God's final action was upon the people of Israel and that Jesus was bringing it in.[317] If the interpretive word in John 2:16b goes back to a *Sitz im Leben Jesu*, then Jesus would once again be indicating that he saw himself as the messianic figure of Zechariah who not only brought the final cleansing to Israel at its center of being, the temple, but who also brought in the dominion of God that was expected on "that day." In addition, John 2:19 comports with this view, further suggesting that Jesus saw himself as the one who would build the eschatological house/temple of God, whatever Jesus may have meant by such an idea. Thus, we see two attempts, the entry and the cleansing, by Jesus during the closing days of his life to present himself in a messianic light, not in accord with popular expectation, but in accord with his own self-perception, which seems to have been based on the oracles of Zechariah.

That Jesus' action was not revolutionary in the sense that Brandon would have it is clear from two facts: (1) *pace* Brandon, none of the Gospels suggests that this action was anything other than an individual act of Jesus himself; and (2) neither Jewish sources nor the Gospels record any response by the temple police against Jesus at the time, which strongly supports the view that this was not a large-scale action but rather a prophetic, symbolic gesture. Jesus had not come to destroy the heart of Judaism, but rather to cleanse it and so make it possible for Jews to see their state of affairs in a true light. Then the Jews would be prepared to enter the dominion of God, which was already in their midst through Jesus' own actions and preaching. Yet by this time Jesus already saw that by and large Judaism was not responding to his message and methods, so that an oracle about the doom of the temple or God's judgment upon it was also possible. Nevertheless, this was not Jesus' last word on the matter. If we are to believe John 2:19b, then Jesus saw himself as the one to bring in the final day, indeed, to raise up the final temple of God.

Here we see an individual who had a very different view of messianism than many of his contemporaries including the revolutionaries. His vision was chiefly shaped by Zechariah, not the Davidic traditions and their successors in texts like *Psalms of Solomon* 17. He had a messianic self-understanding, but it was precisely this that distinguished him from various popular expectations and the hopes of the revolutionaries, from the Pharisees, and even from the Baptist. Jesus was in many ways unique, although

---

[316] Derrett, "The Zeal of the House," 93.

[317] Cf. R. Pesch's conclusion that Jesus was setting in motion the eschatological collection of Israel by cleansing the temple: "Der Anspruch Jesu," esp. 56.

not entirely novel, for he too interpreted his life in the light of the age-old Scriptures, like his fellow pious Jewish contemporaries. Because his self-perception was based in the Scriptures, his self-expression in word and deed would not have been totally opaque but certainly new and challenging, even threatening to the status quo approaches to Torah, temple, and territory.

CONCLUSIONS

That Jesus was crucified, and that the *titulus* likely read "King of the Jews" is one of the most well-assured results of the historical critical study of the life of Jesus.[318] One will likely fail to explain this outcome to Jesus' earthly life without seriously entertaining the likelihood that what Jesus said or did that was perceived as a messianic claim, unless one holds that both the Jews and the Romans completely misunderstood Jesus' nature and intentions. Yet a good deal of Gospel evidence suggests that Jesus was crucified because of what he said and did, indeed because of who he was, rather than in spite of these factors. Jesus had said something about the coming demise of the temple, he had talked about being involved in the setting up of the eschatological temple, and perhaps most importantly, he had cleansed Herod's temple or at least performed a prophetic sign that indicated the need for this. It was these sayings and the final dramatic act in the temple that both implied certain claims on Jesus' part and led to his demise. It is not accidental that in the Jewish interrogations of Jesus, questions come up about what Jesus said about the temple and his identity, while in the trial before Pilate Jesus is asked about his identity, and in Luke 23:2 we hear that some thought Jesus had forbidden the paying of tribute to Caesar. All of these issues were involved in Jesus' teaching and actions during the last few weeks of his life, and we have sought to treat each of these matters in some depth in this chapter.

The point is not that one can simply take the various trial accounts of Jesus as straightforward history writing. Indeed, these are some of the most complex and difficult traditions in the Gospel. Rather, the point is that the charges made against Jesus do have echoes from and are in part based upon what he actually said, did, and claimed at least implicitly in the last few weeks of his life, however much the accounts have been theologically elaborated. Indeed, I think we can now present a coherent picture of the last few weeks of Jesus' ministry.

Jesus lived in an age when there was an ongoing revolutionary movement, when his own home region was a place where there may have been

---

[318] Bammel, "*Titulus*," 363: "The wording of the *titulus* as it is reported in the Gospels is in all likelihood authentic."

some real revolutionary ferment. Jesus seems to have partaken in some of the disaffection that many of his contemporaries felt with the religious and political authorities of his day. He seems to have strongly identified with the outcasts of his society, and he manifested some of the same qualities and attitudes that other renewal movements of his day shared: a critical attitude toward Jerusalem, an avoidance of Hellenistic cities of the region, and a theocratic vision coupled with the conviction of the near or present eschatological action of God. Indeed, it appears that the eschatological meal he shared with his fellow countrymen in the Galilean wilderness was interpreted by many to mean that Jesus was the messianic figure for whom many were looking—either the sort of Messiah the revolutionaries were hoping for, or at least the Davidic Messiah in the mold of *Psalm of Solomon* 17. Yet Jesus rejected this sort of evaluation of himself and his ministry. Although he agreed with some of the radical critique of his nation's malaises, he did not agree with the revolutionaries or even the dominant Davidic hopes about what the solution to these problems should look like. It appears likely that the feeding of the five thousand was the last act of his Galilean ministry because after that he withdrew, not wanting to be evaluated in those terms. Jesus, like many others who sought to lead messianic movements in the first century, did perform particular, even symbolic actions, which raised messianic expectations. The sort of expectations they raised, however, were not what Jesus had in mind, hence his withdrawal.

There is no good evidence that anyone in Jesus' inner circle was a revolutionary. That Simon is singled out as the Zealot distinguishes him from the other disciples and may indicate either his former loyalties or his zealousness (like Paul's) for the law. That there was a customs official or tax collector among the Twelve counts against the revolutionary theory. So too does Jesus' saying about paying the tribute money to Caesar—Jesus does not reject outright the claims of Caesar on the money Caesar minted, although Jesus sees such claims of little significance in comparison to the claim God has on his people. The money may be minted with Caesar's image, but human beings are minted with God's, and God's claim is both higher and prior to Caesar's, especially in light of the inbreaking dominion of God. It could be argued that it was a duty for a pious Jew to return Caesar's money to him, in order to have nothing to do with one who claimed to be Pontifex Maximus and divine. Jesus then was no revolutionary. Although his messianic movement definitely had political and social implications, Jesus did not give in to a purely political solution to Israel's dilemmas. There was no need; God was already intervening in Jesus' own ministry and God's hand did not need to be forced.

During the final weeks of Jesus' life, when he foresaw both his own and the temple's demise, Jesus still pressed forward his case to be a different sort of Messiah, one after the image that Zechariah had in mind. To this end, he rode into Jerusalem on the foal of an ass and performed a prophetic and symbolic cleansing of the temple. This last action, coupled with what Jesus had said about the temple, led to Jesus' death, a death by crucifixion.[319] Although undoubtedly Jesus' interlocutors during the last day of his life did not understand the term in the same way, ironically it was a correct assessment when Jesus was crucified as "King of the Jews." If the narrative of the interrogations are correct in this one point, then Jesus did not refuse the title of *Mashiach* of *Christos* on the lips of the Jewish or Roman authorities.[320] Still the most plausible thesis about the *titulus* is that it refers to the crime of *laesa majestas*.[321] As H. Windisch once said, if Jesus stated or accepted an assertion about his messianic status, Pilate probably had little choice but to condemn him.[322] It remains to be seen how these assessments fit into Jesus' vision of his overall mission to Israel and to his community that he had called out to be his disciples.

JESUS AND THE DISCIPLES

Perhaps no set of relationships better reflects how Jesus viewed himself than those he had with his followers. Some of Jesus' followers were apparently with him throughout his ministry, and they are the group with whom he was most likely to disclose his innermost thoughts and feelings. Conzelmann points out that "in the relationship of Jesus to his disciples what is specific in his self-understanding is documented."[323] Before we study Jesus in relationship to his followers, however, we need to review the modern sociological study of "charismatic leaders."

JESUS THE CHARISMATIC LEADER

We will discuss the possibility that Jesus saw himself as a *theios aner* when we examine the miracle traditions. This discussion runs into difficulties because there are no clear cut paradigms for such a person. There are, however, rather striking parallels between what commitment meant for a follower of Pythagoras (Iamblicus *Pythag.* 17.73) and what it meant for a follower of Jesus (cf. Matt. 8:21–22/Luke 9:59–60).[324] Caution should be exercised in applying modern paradigms or models of leadership, such as the

---

[319] Sanders, *Jesus and Judaism*, 330–32.

[320] Cf. D. Catchpole's detailed analysis, "The Answer of Jesus to Caiaphas (Matt. 26:64)," 213–26: "Hence in Matt. 26:25 *su eipas* contains an affirmation modified only by a preference for not stating the matter *expressis verbis*."

[321] Bammel, "Titulus," 357.

[322] H. Windisch, *Imperium and Evangelium*, 22.

[323] H. Conzelmann, *Jesus*, 35.

[324] Cf. pp. 137–40; and Hengel, *The Charismatic Leader*, 25.

Weberian model of the charismatic leader, to Jesus. Nonetheless, the modern sociological discussion has led to some worthwhile insights.

B. J. Malina, in his critique of the Weberian model of the charismatic leader,[325] suggests that Jesus ought to be seen as a "reputational legitimate leader." This sort of person is neither invested with authority by the powers that be (Jewish authorities in either Jerusalem or the Romans) nor is the authority based on the sheer force of the person's personality, rather, such a person is "recognized as wielding authority due to reputation rooted in socially verifiable influence (teaching) or beneficial power (healing), not on illusory charisma."[326] The reputational leader:

> normally emerges in situations where cultural values cannot be realized in normal human living. This authority derives from the successful criticism and dislocation of the higher order norms which legitimate the authority prevailing in a given society. This sort of authority . . . is rooted in a person's ability to influence change in the broadly encompassing norms that constrain the recognition of legitimate authority."[327]

What is persuasive about Malina's analysis is that most of the recognition Jesus received and the authority he was perceived to have seem to be based on his teaching and healing. The first problem with completely accepting this model as applicable to Jesus, however, is that the reputational leader, according to Malina, is one who does not fully believe in himself or in his ability to effect change. He does not seek to bind people to himself, he is just "a 'collective representation,' a visible symbol of the values and tendencies of his society rather than a *source* of those values and tendencies. Jesus thus personifies the values and goals of those who followed him."[328]

A second problem with this conclusion is that as Malina himself admits, early Jewish culture was disdainful of glorifying a human individual unless that person could be seen as the messiah of God. The Jewish culture did not give complete deference to higher human authority, indeed every form of human power was very carefully scrutinized and critiqued.[329] The question then becomes, If Jesus was simply a reputational leader, how could an attitude of reverence and a fixation on the person of Jesus develop so quickly after his death? How did he come to be crucified as "King of the Jews"? How could traditions develop that suggest Jesus' absolute authority even over the

---

[325] Cf. B. J. Malina, "Charismatic Leader," and, M. Weber, *Economy and Society,* 241. The charismatic leader is defined by Malina following Weber, as "a great person of authoritarian bent who is dedicated exclusively to radical change on the basis of his own . . . exceptional powers or qualities . . . in a situation of social crisis, especially one of political and/or normative vacuum" (56).

[326] Malina, "Charismatic Leader," 57.

[327] Ibid.

[328] Ibid., 61.

[329] Ibid., 58.

law prior to the writing of the Gospels? Why do so many layers of tradition suggest that Jesus did not embody the values of many of the opinion shapers in his society with whom he had various controversies, or even the values of some followers who seem to have expected him to restore Israel to its Davidic glory, an expectation that he disappointed?

Third, there are traditions suggesting that Jesus bound the inner circle of his disciples closely to himself and exercised personal authority that went beyond the category of reputational leader, leading to his demise. In short, there are too many traditions suggesting that Jesus was something more than a reputational leader and that the later portrait of Jesus by the Gospel writers was a development out of factors present in the *Sitz im Leben Jesu*, not a creation of the early post-Easter Christian community.

A fourth problem with Malina's theory is that Jesus proclaimed that the dominion of God was breaking into history through Jesus' ministry. A person who believes that such a thing is happening through his own activities surely perceives himself in ways that go beyond the description of a reputational leader. Jesus not only proclaimed the dominion, he brought it in as was evident from the changed lives of individuals. The blind see, the lame walk, and, as Jesus implied to the messengers of John the Baptist, this should lead one to see him as a fulfiller of Old Testament promises. He was not just the man of the hour who arose when a difficult circumstance required a response. He was one who saw himself as sent by God to accomplish specific tasks. Thus, while I agree that Jesus was neither a Hellenistic divine man nor a charismatic leader as Weber defines it, Jesus' personal charisma and the fact that he bound disciples to himself needs to be given due weight in an evaluation of what Jesus was like and how he viewed himself. We turn now to evidence that allows us to see whether our criticism of Malina is justified, and whether our alternative to his view can be substantiated.

JESUS' SENSE OF PURPOSE

Some of the most important material for assessing Jesus' sense of purpose is the various *elthon* sayings. Bultmann's[330] scruples against sayings that begin "I came" or "I have come" seem unfounded in view of two factors: (1) the form of *elthon* plus the infinitive probably goes back to *ata* (*ba*) *le* plus the infinitive, which means, as does *elthon* plus the infinitive, "I intend" or "I have the task"; (2) there are various examples from the Qumran literature where the Teacher of Righteousness speaks in a similar manner in the first person about himself (cf. 1QH 2.11-12 ["I became"]; 1QH 2.14-15; 1QH 2.32-33 ["my steps proceeding from you"]).[331]

---

[330] Bultmann, *Die Geschichte*, 167.
[331] On the interpretation of these, see Fitzmyer, *Luke 10-24*, 995-96. To this we may add a

Particular reasons for accepting the authenticity of Luke 12:49-50 (and also Matt. 10:34b) are as follows. To "cast fire" seems to be a literal translation of an Aramaic phrase meaning "to kindle fire," and furthermore the use of *ti* here is very Semitic and used like *Mah* introducing a rhetorical question.[332] Also the expression *Balein eirenen* seems to be a Semitism (cf. *Lev. R.* 9 [111b], *Mekilta to Exod.* 20,25; *Sifre Num.* 16). The *ouk/alla* structure of Matt. 10:34b speaks for its being the earlier form of this saying, and indeed it can be translated back into Aramaic.[333] In any case, the unusual form and difficulty of both sayings (Luke 12:49, Matt. 10:34b) favor their authenticity, and the same applies to Luke 12:50a, although Luke has made some changes of diction. Matthew 10:34b makes sense in a setting late in Jesus' ministry when hostilities against him prevented him from being accepted by many of his peers.[334] Two facts favor the authenticity of some form of the baptismal saying (Luke 12:50): (1) it probably does not refer to water baptism, and thus is not likely a church creation; and (2) it suggests that Jesus is limited or constrained by larger historical forces or factors—something must happen to him for him to accomplish his purpose.[335] It is possible that Luke 12:49 and 50 are parallel sayings, which reflect two different ways of getting the same point across. An independent tradition (Mark 10:38b) also seems to attest to the ideas that Luke 12:50 expresses. Further, the "not peace but a sword" tradition seemingly goes against the Gospel portrayal of Jesus as a man of peace, and this favors its authenticity (contrast Matt. 26:52 and 10:34). Finally, Matt. 10:34a has the same form as Luke 12:49: *elthon Balein.*[336] Thus, we need to ask, What are the meanings of Luke 12:49, 50, and Matt. 10:34a-b?

First, both Luke 12:49 and 50, in contrast perhaps to Matt. 10:34, refer to a *future* activity. Second, there is the contrast between the first and second saying—one referring to fire, the other apparently to water. Third, the first saying seems to refer to an activity that Jesus will perform, while Luke 12:50 refers to something that must happen to him, although this could be a means by which he fulfills his purpose. Before we can settle this issue, however, we need to determine what is meant by fire.

As A. von Harnack points out,[337] when used in a religious sense fire can have either a positive or a negative connotation. On the one hand it can refer

---

text to which J. Carmignac (*Teacher of Righteousness,* 142) points: "For because of thee (do I continue on) my course" (1QH 2.22ff.).

[332] E. Arens, *The ELTHON-Sayings,* 64ff., although I find him overly skeptical about the authenticity of some of the *elthon* sayings.

[333] W. F. Albright and C. S. Mann, *The Gospel According to Matthew* (New York: Doubleday, 1971), 130.

[334] Arens, *The ELTHON-Sayings,* 86.

[335] T. W. Manson, *Sayings of Jesus,* 120-21; Kümmel, *Promise and Fulfilment,* 70 and n.168.

[336] Marshall, *Luke,* 545-46; Fitzmyer, *Luke 10-24,* 993-96.

[337] A. von Harnack, "'Ich bin gekommen,'" 12.

to the fire of judgment (Luke 9:54; Matt. 13:30), or on the other hand, to a cleansing or purifying force, or to the cleansing action of God's Holy Spirit, rather than a purely destructive one (1 Cor. 3:13). Here it seems to refer to something that has not yet transpired.[338] There is also the problem of whether we should translate *gen* as earth or land (i.e., Israel). It is hard to avoid the impression that this saying is about some form of (coming) judgment, in particular on Jesus' fellow Jews. Certainly nothing in the context supports the idea of a reference to the cleansing work of the Holy Spirit. Even Luke 3:16–17 suggests a distinction between the work of the Spirit and fire, the latter being associated with the winnowing of God's people. It appears that we have a prophetic judgment oracle: Jesus has come to bring God's decisive judgment upon the land.[339] That it has not yet come to pass suggests that now is the time for final repentance, for turning to God, for preparation for the coming maelstrom.[340]

This comports well with the apparent meaning of Matt. 10:34a–b, which suggests that now is the hour of decision and that how one decides about the work and person of Jesus and his proclamation of the dominion of God will affect one's present human relationships and one's final standing with God (cf. Matt. 10:32–33, 39–40). Furthermore, the use of the sword metaphor to suggest the inbreaking of eschatological times and particularly eschatological judgment can be found in numerous Jewish texts (cf. Isa. 34:5; 66:16; Ezekiel 21; *1 Enoch* 63.11, 91.12, 100.1f.; *2 Bar.* 70.6). As Arens points out, it was widely believed that the time of Messianic peace would be preceded by judgment when the righteous would be vindicated and sinners judged (cf. *Psalms of Solomon* 17).[341]

---

[338] A contrary-to-fact wish; cf. BDF, par. 299.4, 156–57 and 360.4, 182; Moule, *IB*, 137, 187. As Zerwick (*BG*, sec. 405, 138–39) makes clear, *ei* plus a clause like we have here does not in Greek express an impossible situation, simply one not yet realized. Behind *ei* may stand a Hebrew *lu* or the Aramaic equivalent, meaning "would that it were already kindled."

[339] This is one of the few places where Jesus has anything to say about the land, or the so-called doctrine of the land. After a careful study of Jesus' attitudes toward the land, W. D. Davies is able to come up with only one passage that might suggest Jesus subscribed to some sort of territorial doctrine: Matt. 19:28 and par. Yet Davies is forced to conclude due to the actual nature of the evidence, "Jesus, as far as we can gather, paid little attention to the relationship between Yahweh, and Israel and the land" (*The Gospel and the Land*, 365). I am willing to further say that Jesus links the dominion of God to God's activity and to people, in particular, to Israelites who respond to Jesus, but not to the land. The Beatitude about inheriting the earth (land?) cannot be used to claim Jesus had a territorial doctrine. This explains why Davies must also conclude, "the Christian faith is, in principle, cut loose from the land, . . . the Gospel demanded a breaking out of its territorial chrysalis" (336).

[340] Sanders, "Jesus and the Kingdom," 225–39, wishes to insist that Jesus could not possibly have said something like this oracle. Rather he insists, "Jesus affirmed the value and permanence of the nation of Israel as nation." It would be much better to say as Davies does that Jesus' positive concern was for Israel as a people, in view of his belief in the coming final judgment on the land and nation. Cf. Davies, *The Gospel and the Land*, 336–54.

[341] Arens, *ELTHON-Sayings*, 80–81.

If this is correct, then perhaps Jesus saw his ministry as preparation for or bringing in the messianic woes. Because Jesus addresses all or some part of Israel, judgment is beginning with the household of God. In these utterances Jesus is going beyond John, not merely proclaiming judgment's coming but also seeing himself as the one who will "cast fire upon the land" causing division, decision, and finally judgment on those who do not respond properly. Arens sums up the meaning of Matt. 10:34a-b by saying that this text reveals:

> a Christological outlook wherein Jesus appears as Messiah. His coming was the dawn of the messianic times which are marked by acceptance/rejection and consequent judgment. It is a time of decision. To bring the sword appears as a circumlocution for the end-times which precedes peace itself. The perspective is therefore highly eschatological. It assumes the understanding of the "who" who speaks and concentrates on the "what" he provokes. With the inauguration of the Kingdom come the adversities: a messianic paradox brought about by a paradoxical figure.[342]

This saying is of particular importance to our study because an investigation of the wisdom material and other relevant Jewish literature shows that although the wise man may be called God's son, he is not said to be sent by God, and although human messengers may be sent by God, they are not called sons of God, and although angels may be called sons of God, this is always in a collective context.[343] If Jesus saw himself as God's sent one as well as God's Son, this would set him apart from these other categories.

But lest Jesus sound merely like an angry young man grieved with his people for their lack of response to him, we must now examine Luke 12:50. The fact that the saying is future oriented and comes from the time of Jesus' ministry surely rules out the idea that this is about Jesus' baptism by John. If this saying is a pair with Luke 12:49, then the question arises whether there is some sort of sequence envisioned here such as that which Leivestad has in mind when he comments, "Before he can carry out this lifework, he must experience a 'baptism' and that must also be a 'baptism with fire.'"[344] There is evidence from the later Greek versions of the Old Testament (cf. Ps. 42:7; 69:1-2) and in Hellenistic sources that baptism here could refer to being overwhelmed by a catastrophe.[345] Thus, we see how Luke 12:49-50 may be linked together. Jesus himself came to cause a trial by fire for Israel, but he himself must undergo trial by water ordeal.

It would seem that this baptism can refer only to Jesus' sufferings, and in a context of discussing messianic woes it may be implied messianic

---

[342] Ibid., 86.

[343] de Jonge, *Christology in Context*, 169.

[344] R. Leivestad, *Jesus in His Own Perspective*, 103.

[345] A. Oepke, *"Bapto," TDNT* 1:530, 538; and Marshall, *Luke*, 547.

sufferings. As Marshall avers, Luke 12:50 "conveys the idea that the death envisaged by Jesus . . . is no mere fate or accident but a destiny to be fulfilled; cf. especially 13:32; 22:37 . . . The thought is thus 'How I am totally governed by this until it be finally accomplished!' "[346] It appears that at some point Jesus came to see death as both inevitable and as God's plan for his life. Yet by challenging Israel to force it to make a choice, he was also bringing a time of division followed by judgment on at least some in Israel, and he included himself as one of those who would undergo the ordeal of God's judgment.[347]

There is some justice in the assessment that Jesus saw his task in life to come and die, enduring God's overwhelming wrath. This text, however, gives no clue as to the reason that Jesus thought this way or what possible good enduring such a fate might do. There is the slight hint that Jesus thought by going through his baptism he and his mission would no longer be constrained or distressed.[348] This hints that he envisioned some sort of triumph for him or his mission beyond the baptismal ordeal. We must now ask directly, what did Jesus see as his mission?

JESUS' SENSE OF MISSION

Jesus was a devout individual who believed he had a mission in life. It appears that having observed the Baptist's work and subsequent imprisonment, Jesus chose to pursue his calling during what turned out to be the last three years of his life. This sense of mission is perhaps best encapsulated in Matt. 15:24 (cf. 10:6), but we need to ask whether such a saying is authentic.

It has been argued by scholars like F. W. Beare that Matt. 15:24 and 10:6 reflect early Palestinian Christian missionary preaching.[349] But where is the evidence that such early Jewish Christian preaching prohibited going to the Gentiles, as Matt. 10:6 does? At most it might be argued that the focus was on fellow Jews and that there was no thought of a positive Gentile mission. Early Judaism was evidently not opposed to proselytism (cf. Matt. 23:15, *Ant.* 20.38–48), indeed some Jews were zealous about making converts, although an organized effort to get Gentiles into the synagogue is doubtful. My point is that early Jewish Christians would not have prohibited approaching Gentiles, although they may not have encouraged it. Furthermore, this apparent particularism in Matt. 15:24 and 10:6 seems to be at odds with the universalistic thrust of the First Gospel (cf. Matt. 2:1ff.; 4:15; 12:18–21; 8:11ff.; 15:21ff.; and especially 28:19).[350] Jeremias

---

[346] Marshall, *Luke*, 547.

[347] Meyer, *Aims of Jesus*, 213.

[348] BAG, s.v. *"sunecho."*

[349] F. W. Beare, *Matthew*, 341–42; cf. 242.

[350] Schweizer, *Matthew*, 238; Hill, *Matthew*, 185.

argues that this saying goes back to an Aramaic original. He notes that the use of the divine passive *apestalen*, which is characteristic of the early tradition, means "God has sent me" or "my God given commission is to . . ." Also, *eis* is seen by Jeremias as a rendering of the Hebrew *Bu*; thus, the phrase is a Semitism.[351] I conclude that neither Matt. 15:24 nor 10:6 originated either in early Jewish Christianity or from the pen of the first evangelist, and most certainly did not come from Hellenistic and gentile Christianity.

The case for the essential authenticity of this material is bolstered when we discover that a similar viewpoint is reflected in other layers of the tradition such as in Luke 19:9-10. But what does Matt. 15:24 mean?

The image of Israel as sheep is traditional and found in various places in the Old Testament (e.g., Psalm 23, Ezekiel 34), and the image of Israel as a nation of lost sheep is also well-known (e.g., Ezekiel 34 and especially Jer. 50:6). Is Jesus referring to one particular group of Israelites, the lost among Israel (a view perhaps supported by sayings like Mark 2:17b), or does he believe all the people of Israel are lost sheep in need of shepherding? The present contexts of both Matt. 10:6 and 15:24 favor the conclusion that all Israel is meant.[352] In the former saying the lost sheep of Israel is distinguished from Samaritans and Gentiles, in the latter from a "Canaanite" woman from the district of Tyre and Sidon.[353] The conclusion that all Israel is meant is also favored by Ezekiel 34 and Jer. 50:6, which surely stand in the background here.

Although Jesus gave special attention to the "sinners" in Israel, traditions suggest he had some followers who were good pious Jews, who were neither poverty-stricken nor outcasts (cf. Luke 8:1-3; 10:38-42, and one may also note the traditions that Jesus dined with a Zaccheus or a Simon the Pharisee). The fact that Jesus chose twelve disciples suggests that his focus was not on a particular segment of Israelites but on all of them. This conclusion is favored by a text such as Mark 6:34/Matt. 9:36, even though this text is an editorial comment.

Several important points may now be made about Matt. 15:24. First, Jesus has a sense of urgency about his mission not least because he believes all Israel is lost and unprepared for the current inbreaking of the dominion of God. Even his gathering of the Twelve is meant to better reach out to all Israel with his message and ministry. This is precisely the sense of Matt.

---

[351] J. Jeremias, *Jesus' Promise to the Nations*, 26-27 and n.2. "Matthew's only reason for preserving the logion in spite of its repellent implication was that it bore the stamp of the Lord's authority."

[352] H. Schürmann, "Mt. 10:5b-6," 279. Schürmann sees Matt. 10:5b-6 as part of an old narrative piece that reported the messianic act of Jesus for Israel (280). Jesus is attempting a messianic rescue of Israel and enlists the aid of the twelve in this vital task.

[353] On this pericope and its original form and general authenticity, cf. Witherington, *Women in the Ministry*, 63-66.

10:6. The disciples are Jesus' agents, given a specific task of limited duration and the necessary authority and power to carry it out, and working in the name of their master for the sake of all Israel. His mission is their mission.

Second, the fact that Jesus uses this imagery to describe his mission suggests that he sees himself as taking on a task that Yahweh is said to undertake in Ezekiel 34. This implies that Jesus saw himself in elevated categories because he is undertaking a task previously attributed to Yahweh. (This phenomenon will also be seen in our discussion of some of Jesus' *meshalim*.) This elevated self-understanding is also present in Luke 19:10, about which Fitzmyer points out, "Thus the Lucan Jesus is depicted as one sent . . . even to act as Yahweh told Ezekiel he would act toward his scattered people as a shepherd."[354] Is this a purely redactional motif? Because the idea is independently attested in Matt. 15:24, this is unlikely. The authenticity of Luke 19:10 can be disputed. But if one leaves out the use of "Son of man" (a circumlocution for "I" in this case), there is every reason to conclude that the saying goes back to a *Sitz im Leben Jesu*. As Marshall and Fitzmyer point out, 1 Tim. 1:15 is what the saying would have looked like, if it had been derived from a Hellenistic source.[355] Thus, what we see in Matt. 15:24 is that Jesus viewed himself as Israel's shepherd, which implies he believed he was called to lead, oversee, and even rescue God's people. The image of Jesus as a or even the shepherd of Israel is widely attested in a variety of Gospel traditions, both in sayings and summaries (Mark 6:34; 14:27 and par.; Matt. 15:24; 25:32; John 10:15–27). The question is not whether Jesus saw himself in such a role—he probably did—but whether he understood himself as fulfilling the role of a human shepherd of Israel or perhaps something more.

JESUS AND THE TWELVE

That Jesus had a circle of adherents during his ministry is "self-evident."[356] Not self-evident is the nature and extent of that group. The matter becomes more complex when one tries to discern the relationship of Jesus' disciples in general to the Twelve in particular. Although there are some who doubt that Jesus gathered a group of twelve closer disciples around him, the following factors strongly support the historicity of this idea: (1) by A.D. 50 the concept of the Twelve is already a fixed idea for Paul (1 Cor. 15:5), even to the point that they are called the Twelve when apparently there were only eleven immediately after the Easter events; (2) that Judas the betrayer is regularly mentioned in the Gospel tradition as one of the Twelve is something no Christian would have invented (Mark 3:14–19; Luke 6:13–16; Matt.

---

[354] Fitzmyer, *Luke 10–24*, 1226.
[355] Marshall, *Luke*, 698–99; Fitzmyer, *Luke 10–24*, 1226.
[356] Conzelmann, *Jesus*, 33.

10:2-4; John 6:67);[357] (3) references to the Twelve are also found in the double tradition (cf. Matt. 19:28; Luke 22:30), meaning that it was present in the tradition apart from Mark, as John 6:67 also shows.[358] Certainly the evidence that Jesus had twelve disciples is compelling.

Somewhat more controversial is whether the Twelve were seen by Jesus or the Gospel writers as the only disciples. Despite the impressive case made by R. P. Meye that the Twelve equals the disciples,[359] on balance it falls short of proof. Meye might have proven his case in Matthew, where it is apparently part of the author's redactional agenda,[360] but not in Mark, the focus of his study. Clearly, not only are the Twelve chosen from among a group of Jesus' disciples (Luke 6:13-17 and perhaps Matt. 10:1, 5), but others including women are mentioned as itinerating with him (Luke 8:1-3).[361] But for our concerns it is critical to state the reasons that the Twelve do not seem to be equated with Jesus' disciples or followers in Mark, the earliest Gospel.

Mark uses the term disciple forty-two times to refer to the followers of Jesus, the twelve we find only ten or eleven times (depending on how one reads the text of 3:16), and the term apostle only once (6:30). Mark 4:10 is critical because it refers to *oi peri auton sun tois dodeka,* and these are all asking about the explanation of the parable. Now this is rather awkward Greek and Mark probably did not create the whole phrase, although he could have added "the twelve" to "those around him" which he found in his source, or vice versa. As Best points out "those around him" contrasts with the reference to "those outside" mentioned in the next verse.[362] As Freyne admits, there is nothing particularly Markan about the style of 4:10.[363] Thus, we conclude that this verse is a piece of tradition Mark found in his source.

As to the meaning of Mark 4:10, the most natural interpretation is that it refers to a group with the Twelve, not a group that is the Twelve. Even if we translate it "those around him including the twelve,"[364] it would still imply a larger group of which the Twelve was a portion.

Further support for the view that the Twelve are not seen by Mark as all the disciples can be found in at least three places. First, Mark 3:31-35 implies that Jesus' brothers and sisters would be those who do God's will, which in

---

[357] Ibid., 34.

[358] E. Best, *Disciples and Discipleship*, 132ff.

[359] R. P. Meye, *Jesus and the Twelve.*

[360] S. Van Tilberg, *Jewish Leaders*, 112ff.; G. Strecker, *Der Weg der Gerechtigkeit*, FRLANT 82 (Göttingen: Vandenhoeck and Ruprecht, 1966), 191ff.

[361] Witherington, *Women in the Ministry*, 116-18.

[362] Best, *Disciples*, 139; cf. 137-40.

[363] S. Freyne, *The Twelve: Disciples and Apostles* (London, 1968), 111, although he excepts the reference to the Twelve. However, as Best urges (*Disciples,* 140 n.39), even that is not necessarily evidence of Markan redaction here.

[364] Best, *Disciples*, 140.

view of the context probably does not refer just to the Twelve.[365] Second, Mark 10:32 implies a larger group of followers going up to Jerusalem with Jesus, although he draws the Twelve apart. It may be that this is a redactional formulation, but it suggests at least two groups of followers—a wider circle out of which Jesus draws aside the Twelve. This is possibly also true of Mark 3:14.[366]

Thus, we have seen that although in Mark 4:10, this distinction is pre-Markan, here it recurs even if it is redactional. Third, and perhaps most important, although Mark places no stress on women following Jesus in Galilee in the narration of Jesus' ministry, he clearly mentions such a group at 15:40-41 and describes them as functioning as disciples.[367] I conclude that not only at the level of Mark's own presentation but also in the sources behind his Gospel, there was no equation of the Twelve and the disciples.

This is important especially if this distinction goes back to a *Sitz im Leben Jesu* (and who, in any case, would invent women disciples in early Jewish Christianity and insert them into the text?). It would seem to imply: (1) that the Twelve were not seen by Jesus as a sort of righteous remnant of Israel, gathered to the exclusion of others benefiting from his ministry or being disciples (the others including women, sinners, tax collectors, etc.);[368] and (2) that although the number twelve says something about Jesus and his followers in relationship to Israel,[369] it does not necessarily indicate he was attempting to establish an exclusive community involving just himself and the Twelve that would symbolically be the basis of a new Israel. Yet, by symbolically choosing Twelve and sending them out to Israel, he may have been implying that he was the one to fulfill the task of the eschatological gathering of Israel.[370] G. Lohfink puts it more strongly: "For Jesus the idea of the reign of God automatically implied the gathering of Israel."[371] Schnackenburg emphatically says that if one denies that Jesus intended to gather some sort of community, then one "misunderstands the messianic-eschatological thought of Israel, in which eschatological salvation cannot be separated from the people of God and in which the community of God necessarily belongs to his reign."[372]

---

[365] Witherington, *Women in the Ministry*, 85–88.

[366] Fitzmyer, *Luke 1–9*, 254.

[367] Witherington, *Women in the Ministry*, 118–23.

[368] Cf. Meyer, *Aims of Jesus*, 153ff.

[369] I will argue that the Twelve were called not to be Israel, but to free Israel by going forth and sharing in Jesus' ministry to Israel, which called the nation to task and to decision in light of the in-breaking dominion of God.

[370] H. Schürmann, *Ursprung und Gestalt*, 45–60, reprinting his well-known study on "Der Jungerkreis Jesus als Zeichen für Israel." I do not share his view that we may see in the Twelve a justification for later Catholic orders; cf. his "Jesus' Disciples: Prototype of Religious Life," *Theology Digest* 15 (1967): 138–43, which is a condensed and translated version of the above study.

[371] G. Lohfink, *Jesus and Community*, 26.

[372] R. Schnackenburg, *Gottes Herrschaft und Reich*, 150. I have followed Lohfink's translation

It is seldom noted that Jesus never identifies himself as one of the Twelve in any of the Gospel traditions. This suggests that Jesus did not symbolically identify himself as or with Israel, any more than he identified the Twelve in this fashion. Jesus ministered *to* Israel; he was not and did not see himself *as* Israel. One can maintain that Jesus saw himself as a shepherd to and over Israel and that the twelve were extensions of such a ministry, but not that either Jesus or his followers saw themselves as Israel proper. Hengel says, "The instituting of the Twelve itself, who included Matthew the taxgatherer and Simon the 'man of zeal,' and who cannot have been identical with the number of disciples called by him . . . points to this openness for all Israel. . . ."[373] Jesus' claim was on all of Israel, and he does not operate with Isaiah's notion of a remnant.[374]

FISHING FOR FOLLOWERS

Best points out that what distinguishes the disciples from the Twelve is that the Twelve are given the opportunity to participate in Jesus' ministry.[375] Indeed, if Mark 1:17 (and par.) is any indication, that commission came with their initial call to follow Jesus.[376] But is this saying authentic? Several things favor such a conclusion.

First, there is no evidence apart from the Gospel material that the early church referred to missionary work in terms of fishing for human beings. Neither in Acts nor in the Pauline or Petrine literature is there anything along these lines. Portions of John 21 can be read in this way because it is post-Easter material, but when the discussion actually turns to the matter of converts, they are called sheep, not fish. Second, if indeed any of Jesus' chosen Twelve were fishermen, this explains the use of the metaphor to a large extent and provides a rather unique *Sitz im Leben* for the saying. It is doubtful that we can find an equally plausible *Sitz im Leben* after Easter.

Third, this saying suggests that Jesus recruited followers or disciples, something Jewish teachers of Jesus' day apparently did not do. "There are no rabbinical stories of 'calling' and 'following after' analogous to the pericope

---

here, but cf. J. Murray's English translation in Schnackenburg, *God's Rule and Kingdom*.

[373] Hengel, *Charismatic Leader*, 60.

[374] Lohfink, *Jesus and Community*, 34. One must be careful how one phrases this. It is clearer to say that while Jesus intended to approach all Israel, giving special attention to the least, last, and lost, his community turned out to be smaller than Israel as a whole due to the nature of the response. His intention was to "re-form" or gather Israel as community; he did not intentionally set out to rescue only a part of it.

[375] Best, *Discipleship*, 128ff. Best thinks this differentiation may be redactional, but against this is the saying we are about to investigate.

[376] G. Buchanan, *Jesus the King*, 96: "Those who were called to be 'fishers of men' were expected to recruit still more men into the program." Thus, this saying is to be seen as a call to mission, not just a call to follow.

in Mark and Q, nor did the summons 'follow me' resound from any rabbinical teacher in respect of entry into a teacher-pupil relationship."[377] Rather, the student came to the teacher, for example, Paul went to Jerusalem to study with Gamaliel, if Acts 22:3 is to be believed.[378] Jesus' action is to be seen along prophetic lines, possibly in the tradition of Elijah (1 Kings 19:19–21).[379] Fourth, it appears this saying was passed down independently in a somewhat different context and variant form (Luke 5:10). Bultmann regards Mark 1:16–20 as a biographical apothegm, an ideal scene based on a saying or metaphor about fishing for human beings.[380] However, even if the narrative framework is ideal, the saying could still be an authentic logion of Jesus, reflecting his call of one or more of the Twelve. In any event, Taylor, Fitzmyer, and others argue for the authenticity of this saying and of the motif of Jesus calling an inner circle to himself that at some point was limited to twelve.[381]

I conclude that the arguments for the authenticity of Mark 1:17 prevail. The sudden response of the fishermen in the story may reflect the editing of the original tale, but if some of these men had been involved with the Baptist and had known Jesus in that context, even the sudden response is not improbable.

What, then, is the meaning of the saying? If we start with the Lukan formulation and work our way back to the more primitive version in Mark, we may find a clue. Luke uses the verb *zogron* which with *ese* means literally "to take alive." This certainly suggests a rescue operation, that is, the Twelve shall be in the business of rescuing human beings. Based on what we have already seen of how Jesus accepted the message of the Baptist, the Twelve will rescue people from the wrath to come—the fire that was soon to be kindled upon the land. Luke presents the saying in a positive way. Even if he is presenting an independent version of what we find in Mark 1:16–20, because he does not reproduce that Markan pericope elsewhere, this would mean that we have here the manner in which Luke interpreted the original saying, changing the original verb to make clear its positive focus.

Such a positive focus is much less clear in Mark 1:17, where the text reads, "Come after me, and I shall make you become fishers of human beings." In light of the possible Old Testament background to this saying (in Jer. 16:16; Ezek. 29:4ff.; 38:4; Amos 4:2; and Hab. 1:14–17), there may have

---

377 Hengel, *Charismatic Leader*, 50–51.

378 Neither the rabbis nor the master teachers are castigated in Matt. 23:15, but only the experts in the Law and the leaders of the lay movement called Pharisaism. These are not to be confused with rabbis or hasids. Cf. Josephus *Ant.* 20.38–48. On proselyting practices in early Judaism, see Daube, *New Testament*, 336–61.

379 Hengel, *Charismatic Leader*, 16ff.

380 Bultmann, *Synoptic Tradition*, 562.

381 Taylor, *Mark*, 167–88, a Petrine reminiscence; Fitzmyer, *Luke 1–9*, 562–63; Marshall, *Luke*, 199–201.

been an ominous overtone to this saying. Especially in the Jeremiah and Ezekiel sayings, the connotation is one of catching people for judgment, with either God or an agent of God doing the catching. This led C. W. F. Smith to say that this phrase is "inappropriate if the mission of the disciples is thought of as rescuing men or bringing them to salvation."[382] This comment might be apropos, if we ignore the fact that "to win back, to gather, or to fish a Jew meant to bring him back under the wings of the Shekinah, which is another way of saying that the omnipresence of God was to become a living, life-shaping reality to him again."[383] J. Manek has reminded us that in Semitic thought, water, particularly the chaos waters, is seen as the enemy of God (cf. Ps. 74:13). "In the background of Jesus' picture of 'fishers of men' it is therefore necessary to see that the waters . . . are the underworld, the place of sin and death. To fish out a man means to rescue him from the kingdom of darkness, out of the sphere which is hostile to God and remote from God."[384] Possibly, when Jesus spoke of his baptism he was thinking of the chaos waters flooding over him causing his death.

Part of the problem here may be in the way this saying is perceived. If Jesus sent the Twelve only to the house of Israel and saw his mission limited in that way, then the best way to interpret a saying such as this is that Jesus envisions not the winning of proselytes but the winning back or rescuing of Jews. Daube has demonstrated that in regard to a verb like *kerdaino* (cf. Matt. 18:15), the meaning is not to convert but to win back.[385] If Jesus saw his basic program as winning back the lost sheep of Israel, not converting the world, in light of the fire from heaven that was hovering on the horizon, then the use of the metaphor is quite understandable. I wish to stress that the call to follow entails a call to mission, to being involved in the rescuing operation that Jesus saw as his own task in life. The metaphor, which had overtones of judgment, and the urgency may be explained by G. B. Caird:

> Jesus was working against time to prevent the end of Israel's world, that the haste of the mission was directly connected with the many sayings which predict the fall of Jerusalem and the destruction of the temple. He believed that Israel was at the crossroads, that she must choose between two conceptions of her national destiny . . .[386]

Thus, we have seen in Mark 1:17 (and par.) a call to discipleship and to mission. Apparently the Twelve was formed not to be Israel, but rather to free Israel in light of what was to come.

---

[382] C. E. F. Smith, "Fishers of Men," 187.

[383] On this whole saying and its *religionsgeschichtliche* treatment, see W. H. Wuellner, "Fishers of Men," 114.

[384] J. Manek, "Fishers of Men," 139.

[385] Daube, *New Testament*, 358–59.

[386] G. B. Caird, *Jesus and the Jewish Nation*, 8.

TWO BY TWO

Implicit in the calling of the disciples to be fishers of humans is the idea that at some point they would undertake such a task. This commissioning comes to us in two different forms and from at least two different sources.[387] That Matthew and Luke agree on various points of the charge over against Mark, for example, in the matter of carrying a staff (Mark 6:8; Matt. 10:10/Luke 9:3), indicates that there was a Q version of this charge.[388] Thus, on the criterion of multiple attestation this charge in some form probably goes back to a *Sitz im Leben Jesu*. Luke may even have known yet a third version of the same charge that he has recorded in the commission to the Seventy (Luke 10:1-12). Certainly the structure of the charge in Luke 9 and 10 is closely parallel. In any case, numerous scholars have argued that the commission of the Twelve is "one of the best attested facts in the life of Jesus."[389]

In terms of form-critical judgment of the material, it may be that several of Jesus' sayings are clustered together on the basis of a similar theme. Yet it is hard to miss the logical progression from conferral of authority and power, to commission, to instructions for carrying out that commission. As Marshall says, "These instructions give the impression of being meant for a particular time and place; a missionary enterprise in a restricted area of Palestine among Jews is indicated."[390] The way that Luke 22:35-38 refers back to this commissioning strongly suggests that this material was a unity in Luke's source, even in Q. Luke seemingly has used material from Mark and Q in Luke 9 and 10, although some assimilation occurred, but Matthew has conflated the material from Mark and Q into one passage (Matt. 10:1-14). The material in Matt. 10:15ff., coming from a later period, will not be considered. The first evangelist has also inserted into his material the list of the Twelve (Matt. 10:2-4). Matthew 10:5-6 will be discussed further because it was probably an original part of the Q charge.[391] Otherwise, Mark's form of the charge appears to be the most primitive, especially with its reference to the disciples being sent out in twos (Mark's largely gentile audience would not have known about Jewish rules of a twofold testimony).

In the Markan and Q form of the charge to the Twelve, we are told that the disciples are to assume, even if for a limited time, the same functions Jesus was performing, such as exorcism, healing, and preaching (cf. the summary in Luke 9:11, although there is some variation in Mark and Q as

---

[387] Manson has urged that even L had a commissioning pericope as well; *Sayings*, 73-74.

[388] Havener, *Q—The Sayings of Jesus*, 130-31.

[389] Manson, *Sayings*, 73; cf. J. M. Creed, *St. Luke* (London: Macmillan, 1930), 125; Marshall, *Luke*, 349-50; E. Schweizer, *Das Evangelium nach Markus* (*Das Neue Testament Deutsch 1*) (Göttingen: Vandenhoeck & Ruprecht, 1975), 71ff.; more tentatively, Fitzmyer, *Luke 1-9*, 753.

[390] Marshall, *Luke*, 351.

[391] Havener, *Q—The Sayings of Jesus*, 130.

to what preaching by the disciples entailed). Accordingly, we need to decide whether Jesus saw the Twelve as his agents—*shalihim*.[392]

What was the nature and function of a *shaliach* according to the Jewish evidence? Manson gives us a useful summary:

> First, that he performs on behalf of someone else, whether an individual or a corporate body, functions which his principal is himself entitled to perform. Second, that the nature of his activities, and in some cases their duration, is defined, so that his authority does not go beyond the terms of his commission. Third, that his commission is not transferable. When he ceases to exercise it, the authority reverts to the principal. Fourth, that *shaliach* is not a term of status but of function. Fifth, that in so far as the *shaliach* has a religious commission it is always exercised within the borders of Jewery, and does not involve what we should call missionary activity.[393]

We should consider the charge in light of these concepts because it is only in connection with the narrative of the charge that the first evangelist calls the twelve *apostoloi* (Matt. 10:2; cf. Mark 6:30).[394]

The important evidence about the *shaliach* is not to be found in the Old Testament where, apart possibly from 1 Kings 14:6, the *shaliach* is never referred to, but in later Jewish sources such as the Mishnah. *M. Rosh Ha-Shanah* 4.9 records a saying of R. Gamaliel (probably the first, but even if it is the second it still comes from the period A.D. 80–120) about the agent of the congregation who fulfills the obligation that rests upon the group. *M. Rosh Ha-Shanah* 1.3 states that *shalihim* were sent out to settle calendrical matters in the Diaspora even while the temple stood. Likewise *M. Yoma* 1.5 refers to *shalihim* of the court prior to A.D. 70. It is true that in the Jewish evidence there is no reference to missionaries as *shalihim*, but note that the Twelve are not in the charge passage functioning strictly speaking as missionaries. Their commission involves Jews only, within the Holy Land at that, and their work should be seen along the lines of a reclamation or

---

[392] B. Lindars, "Jesus as Advocate," 492: "They spoke as themselves the agents of him who was God's agent. . . ." Lindars argues for the view that Jesus did believe he had a role at the final judgment of advocate and accuser, and parallels this to a saying like Luke 22:30, suggesting the disciples would also have such a role. Thus, he carries the *shalihim* idea even unto the eschaton. It might be interesting on the basis of such sayings as Mark 8:38 to pursue the possibility that Jesus saw himself as final accuser and judge because he saw himself as replacing Satan in his role as accuser in the heavenly court. Is this related to the saying in Luke 10:18 about Satan being seen falling from heaven? Of course, he also saw himself as final advocate for those who faithfully followed him.

[393] T. W. Manson, *The Church's Ministry* (London: Hodder and Stoughton, 1948), 43–44.

[394] There is considerable reason for doubt about the reference to *apostoloi* in Mark 3:14 on text critical grounds. As is admitted by the textual committee (Metzger, *TC*, 80), we may have a case of assimilation here from Luke 6:13. Luke has a different approach to the matter of apostles. The reference to apostles is omitted by such diverse witnesses as A, C^2, D, K, L, P, Byz Lect, and Diatessaron, as well as numerous minuscules. Even if it is original, it only supports our case that Jesus saw the Twelve as *shalihim* because we are told that the Twelve were designated to be *apostoloi*, indicating a function they were to assume.

restoration project. Note there was no precedent in Greek to account for the widespread use of *apostolos* in early Christianity. As Barrett says, "There is only one reasonable explanation of the data: the noun was already current in some Hellenistic-Jewish circles as an established rendering of *Shaliach*."[395] Rengstorf makes the point about the Syriac church translating *apostolos* by *shaliach*.[396] In view of this evidence, the reference to the Twelve as Jesus' *apostoloi* becomes significant. The Twelve were Jesus' *shalihim*.

Barrett assumes that the Twelve were to be officials and administrators over the community that Jesus brought into being – the eschatological Israel.[397] Against this, note that the commissioning of the Twelve has to do with the Twelve and the rest of Israel who were not yet disciples, the lost sheep to whom the disciples were sent. This becomes clear when we examine Matt. 19:28 (and par.). The disciples will not be judged by the Twelve; the disciples are not called Israel, much less the Twelve tribes of Israel in the Gospels. We are now prepared to examine the charge in greater detail.

First, in the commission the Twelve are sent out two by two. This fact seems to be independently confirmed by noting that the first evangelist groups his list of twelve in six groups of two (10:2–4; cf. Acts 1:13), prior to recording their commission. Also, Jeremias has demonstrated that it was the custom in early Judaism for teachers to send out their disciples in twos on errands or missions of importance, a fact attested in the Gospels (Luke 7:18; 19:29; Mark 11:1; 14:13; Matt. 21:1). There were two reasons that Jesus might have used this custom in sending out the Twelve: "The Message was better protected through two Messengers. Moreover, one can certainly see a second motive, that out of the Old Testament instructions it is to be concluded that, for all cases of capital crimes [or acts], the harmonious testimony of two or three witnesses to the charged action shall be a prerequisite for legal condemnation."[398] This suggests that Jesus saw the mission of the Twelve as part of something vital, even a life and death matter.

Second, note that this mission is directed to the lost sheep of Israel. This phrase is contrasted to going on a road that might lead one to Gentiles or Samaritans. Thus, this term is a general one used in no fixed manner to single out one group of Israelites from another. It is not, for instance, a technical term for the Jewish poor in the land, and it is unlikely that the phrase is a synonym for the *am ha 'aretz*.[399] The latter phrase referred to those that were not as scrupulously observant of the law (as were, for instance, the Pharisees or *haberim*) usually as a result of ignorance of the law

---

[395] Barrett, "Shaliah and Apostle," 99; and *Signs of an Apostle*, 32ff.; K. Rengstorf, *TDNT* 1:420ff., s.v. "*apostolos.*"

[396] Rengstorf, "*apostolos*," 414.

[397] Barrett, "Shaliah," 101.

[398] J. Jeremias, "Paarweise Sendung," 138.

[399] E. W. Nicholson, "*Am Ha Aretz*," 66.

or inability to follow it due to poverty.[400] Thus the mission or tasks assigned to the Twelve are limited in scope, and in view of texts like Mark 6:30, they must be seen as limited in duration, exactly as was the case with the Jewish *shaliach*.

Third, we need to comment on the content of the message the twelve were to proclaim. Mark mentions that they called the people to repentance (6:12). However, the Q form apparently entailed speaking about the dominion of God and its nearness (Luke 10:11; Matt. 10:7). It is likely that both of these subjects were broached by the disciples because we know: (1) that Jesus did follow in the footsteps of John preaching repentance to Israel for a time; and (2) that he did proclaim the coming dominion of God. Thus both of these ideas may have been a part of the original message of the Twelve, and as such they were speaking for Jesus. If the message was about the dawning dominion of God, then the urgency of the mission is readily apparent. That dawning dominion meant salvation for some, but it meant fire from heaven for those who did not repent and respond properly to the message.

As most commentators urge, the more primitive form of the instructions about what to take on the mission tour is probably found in Q where various items including the staff are prohibited, unlike in Mark. It is possible that Matt. 10:9 preserves the original form of the instructions,[401] in which case the instruction amounted to a warning not to make any additional preparations for the tour (*ktesethe*, meaning obtain), but simply to go as they were and rely on the system of standing hospitality in Israel as they visit each village. It is possible that the original instructions prohibited the taking of a staff or two shirts among other things. Perhaps there may be some merit in Manson's conjecture that Jesus is sending out the Twelve like an invading army meant to live off the land, in view of the urgency of the situation with no time for detailed preparations or the gathering of provisions.[402] If so, then the Twelve would have been sent out late in the Galilean ministry, perhaps just before the feeding of the five thousand.

Now, it may be possible that Jesus had two different groups of disciples—wandering charismatics (i.e., the Twelve and some others), and sympathizers

---

[400] Oppenheimer, '*Am Ha-Aretz*, 20–22. Oppenheimer is also clear that the view that Galilee was a place where people were largely ignorant of Torah, perhaps due to a lack of sages, is simply untrue (204ff.). "Nor can Galilee in the days of the Second Temple and the generation of Jabneh be described as devoid of the Torah and as an exclusive abode of the *ammei ha-aretz la-Torah*. There were important Sages in the days of the Second Temple and in the generation of Jabneh who were Galileans" (210; citing R. Jose the Galilean, R. Halafta of Sepphoris, R. Hanina b. Teradion, among others). Or again he says, "The evidences as a whole show that the Jewish character of Galilee was not less than that of Judaea. Nor is there any justification for associating the concepts of the '*am ha-aretz le-mitzvot*' and the '*am ha-aretz la-Torah*' with Galilee to the exclusion of Judaea" (215).

[401] R. T. France, *The Gospel according to Matthew* (Grand Rapids: Eerdmans, 1985), 179.

[402] Manson, *Sayings*, 181.

who were perhaps not called disciples but who did support Jesus financially or otherwise.[403] Some of Jesus' instructions, such as the material we are now evaluating, would apply only to the former group, but it is possible that Jesus envisioned the supporters in the villages as the ones who would provide the hospitality when the Twelve arrived in the various areas of Galilee.[404] The Twelve are not called to asceticism, because they are to have food and shelter, although it is not to be provided out of their own pockets. The disciples are to expect, as Jesus' *shalihim,* that they will be treated as Jesus himself would be treated, whether for good or ill. Since the Twelve are *shalihim,* such texts as Matt. 10:40 become understandable—the acceptance or rejection of Jesus' *shalihim* amounts to the acceptance or rejection of Jesus because they are endowed with his authority and mission (*M. Berak.* 5.5). But Matt. 10:40 also makes clear that Jesus saw himself as the *shaliach* of God, God's agent or sent one, given a specific commission and mission to God's people.[405] This is especially true if the saying refers to receiving hospitably or receiving in hospitality, thus relating to the remarks made in Matt. 10:11–14.[406]

We have here a crucial clue that Jesus viewed himself as one endowed with divine authority and sent forth on a divine mission of reclaiming Israel for God. Jesus saw himself as God's final and thus unique agent on an eschatological mission to proclaim and bring in God's dominion. Since that dominion had to do with the hopes and expectations of God's people, Jesus concentrated his mission upon them. Yet there were consequences to rejecting God's *shaliach,* or even Jesus' *shalihim.*

Fourth, besides the various judgment sayings (Matt. 10:15/Luke 10:12; and another Q saying Matt. 11:21/Luke 10:13) that indicate rejecting Jesus or his mission led to divine judgment, we will now consider the implication of the gesture of shaking dirt off one's feet. There is little dispute over the authenticity of Mark 6:11.[407] In fact, Caird is willing to say, "The Mission Charge is better attested than any other part of the Gospel record."[408] There are generally two schools of thought about what the gesture of "shaking the dust off of one's feet" means. On the one hand, it is similar to what Jews would do when they left a gentile land because such lands were considered unclean and thus defiling. On the other hand, it might be a simple gesture of repudiation, a symbolic severing of an association with that town from

---

[403] Theissen, *First Followers,* 8-23.

[404] G. Lohfink, *Jesus and Community,* 54. I agree with Lohfink about the community nature of Jesus' ethic, as opposed to his repentance preaching to the general public.

[405] As Schweizer admits, the original form of this saying could well go back to Jesus (*Matthew,* 253); Hill, *Matthew,* 195.

[406] Hill, *Matthew,* 195.

[407] E. Schweizer, *Das Evangelium nach Markus* (Göttingen: Vandenhoeck and Ruprecht, 1968), 72; Marshall, *Luke,* 354.

[408] G. B. Caird, "Uncomfortable Words," 41.

henceforth. In light of Acts 13:50, this latter view is a plausible conjecture.[409] The evidence, however, not only of the judgment sayings but also of the extrabiblical material would seem to favor the former view.[410] The point of the gesture then would be that this town was to be considered heathen and defiled and thus no Jew should associate with it.[411] Caird has put this thesis in its most stark form:

> The astonishing thing about Jesus' instructions to his disciples is that this Jewish gesture is now to be employed against Jews, whether as a warning or threat. The burden of the disciple's message is that God is now establishing His long-promised reign over Israel, and that every community in the country must decide whether or not to join with Jesus in this new chapter of their national history. . . . Jesus, like John the Baptist before Him, believed that Israel was facing the great national crisis to which all the Old Testament prophecy pointed, and that she must choose either to follow Jesus in his pro-gramme of national renewal under the rule of God or else to follow the policy of nationalism to its inevitable and disastrous climax of war with Rome.[412]

This view comports with our conclusions in our study of Jesus and the revolutionaries. It also suggests that a repudiation of Jesus meant a repudiation of one's chosen status by God, and hence subjected one to God's judgment. These drastic consequences are conceivable on Jesus' lips if he viewed himself as God's *shaliach* and the twelve as his *shalihim*. It also explains why Jesus made such radical demands of renunciation of those who would be among his traveling followers.

A RADICAL RENUNCIATION

The major differences between following Jesus and following a rabbi are evident in some of the radical statements about the call to discipleship such as the Q saying found in Matt 8:21–22/Luke 9:59–60. As Manson puts it:

> The life of a *talmid* as *talmid* was made up of study of the sacred writings, attendance on lectures, and discussion of difficult passages or cases. Discipleship as Jesus conceived it was not a theoretical discipline of this sort, but a practical task to which men were called to give themselves and all their energies. Their work was not study but practice. . . .[413]

---

[409] Fitzmyer, *Luke 1–9*, 754.

[410] F. J. Foakes Jackson and Kirsopp Lake, *Beginnings of Christianity 5* (London: Macmillan & Co., 1933), 269–71.

[411] Marshall, *Luke*, 354–55.

[412] The validity of this assessment is not dependent on accepting Caird's view that each village must and will decide by means of decision of a town meeting or council. Cf. "Shaking the Dust," 41.

[413] T. W. Manson, *Teaching of Jesus*, 239; cf. C. K. Barrett, *Gospel Tradition*, 10–11.

Of all the sayings about the cost of discipleship, Matt. 8:21–22/Luke 9:59–60 has the best claims to authenticity. Here Jesus seems to be counseling a violation of one of the Ten Commandments, which apparently he elsewhere affirms.[414] Both the harshness of the logion and its obscurity count strongly in favor of at least the saying of Jesus in Matt. 8:22 (and par.) being authentic.[415] In regard to whether or not this saying goes back to a *Sitz im Leben Jesu,* Bultmann maintains that we have an ideal scene, created as a setting for the authentic saying. Against this is the fact that the saying requires some sort of context or setting to make sense; it cannot stand on its own because it is not a general maxim but a reply to some sort of statement or question. Someone had to have said something about burying someone, in order to prompt such a reply. Bultmann admits that this saying was handed down in a concrete setting, but gives no reason that the context we are given for the saying in Q cannot be original.[416] Hengel, who has given the saying its most thorough treatment, maintains that the original form of the material included an introduction to the saying such as the following: "Another said 'Permit me first to go and bury my father.'"[417] This view is supported in the latest treatment of Q, which has the saying prefaced by: "But another said to him 'Lord, let me go and bury my father.'"[418] Thus the objection to the setting of the saying does not prevail. As to whether Luke or Matthew is closer to the original form, the Matthean form must be given the edge. Luke has probably shifted the command "Follow me" to the beginning to introduce the saying and to make Jesus the initiator of the dialog.[419] Furthermore, the command that follows the saying about burying the dead (Luke 9:60b) is usually judged to be Lukan as well.[420]

It is possible that the first evangelist has made an originally anonymous interlocutor into a disciple at Matt. 8:21. However, because normally only those who are disciples address Jesus as *kyrie* in the Gospel tradition (and this is always the case in the First Gospel),[421] the first evangelist probably believed that his source material was referring to someone who was already in the broad sense a disciple, and thus he made this clearer by adding *ton matheton.*[422] This saying then would be about the claim of Jesus over one who

[414] On the authenticity of this passage, cf. Witherington, *Women in the Ministry,* 11–13.

[415] A. Plummer, *A Critical and Exegetical Commentary on the Gospel according to St. Luke* (Edinburgh: T. & T. Clark, 1922), 267; Fitzmyer, *Luke 1–9,* 833. On the ethics of the early church, and 1 Tim. 5:8 and Eph. 6:2-3, see Witherington, *Women in the Earliest Churches,* 42ff.; cf. Bultmann, *Die Geschichte,* 27ff., 58–60.

[416] Marshall, *Luke,* 409.

[417] Hengel, *Charismatic Leader,* 4.

[418] Havener, *Q—The Sayings of Jesus,* 129. The emphasized material is not common to both Matthew and Luke.

[419] Marshall, *Luke,* 411.

[420] Banks, *Jesus and the Law,* 97.

[421] Schweizer, *Matthew,* 21.

[422] It is noteworthy that a few manuscripts simply have *tis* here (1230, 1253) and there are

was already among his disciples. This comports with the fact, too seldom noticed, that the interlocutor simply asks that he may go and bury his father first, which implies that he intends to heed the call thereafter. This is the attitude of one who already considered himself a disciple of Jesus. If the word "first" is crucial, then this would be a saying about priorities, not a general remark about the meaninglessness of burial customs and honoring parents. Jesus would be suggesting that following him was a higher priority than obeying one of the Ten Commandments—honoring parents was understood to entail giving them an honorable burial.

The radical nature of Jesus' demand is demonstrated by Hengel's detailed treatment of burial customs and attitudes about the unburied especially among the Jews in the first century A.D.[423] For instance, *M. Berak.* 3.1 insists that attendance to the duty of burying the dead supersedes even the most binding of religious obligations (cf. Tobit 4:3; 6:13). Even a priest was expected to fulfill his filial duty in this regard (*S.Lev.* 21.3).[424] Only two sorts of persons in the Old Testament were considered exempt from the duty of burying one's father—a Nazirite and the high priest (Lev. 21:11; Num. 6:6–7).

We cannot conclude from this saying that Jesus judged this burial duty to be insignificant. Rather, as Beare says, the more weight one gives to such an obligation, the clearer it becomes how urgent and imperative an absolute response to Jesus' call was. Such duties were important, but the urgency of the response to Jesus' call took precedence over all else.[425] Thus, Jesus' call to follow him is even more stringent than the call of Elisha by Elijah. Even Elisha was allowed to make a farewell gesture to his family (1 Kings 19:20). The conclusion is hard to avoid that someone and something greater than Elijah and his work is presented here. Hengel urges us to judge this narrative "in the light of the messianic authority of Jesus."[426]

Supporting this view is the fact that Jesus sees his mission and that to which he is calling his disciples as taking precedent over duties found in the Mosaic law. He thus exercises a certain sovereign freedom over the Mosaic law. Even Sanders, who does not think that Jesus took such a radical stance in relation to Torah, is forced to admit:

What is important here is to see the force of the negative thrust: Jesus *consciously* requires disobedience of a commandment understood by all Jews to

---

variations between "the disciples" and "his disciples" in the other manuscripts. Hill, *Matthew*, 165, conjectures that a scribe could be meant, especially if the original reading was not "his disciples."

[423] Hengel, *Charismatic Leader*, 8–15; cf. Beare, *Matthew*, 214.

[424] Banks, *Jesus and the Law*, 97.

[425] Beare, *Matthew*, 214; Banks, *Jesus and the Law*, 98. On the priority of the family of faith and its duties over the physical family, see Witherington, *Women in the Ministry*, 11–28, 86–88.

[426] Hengel, *Charismatic Leader*, 15.

have been given by God. . . . At least once Jesus was willing to say that following him superseded the requirements of piety and the Torah. This may show that Jesus was prepared to challenge, if necessary, the adequacy of the Mosaic dispensation.[427]

Turning to a detailed interpretation of this saying, the probable basic meaning is, "Let the spiritually dead bury the physically dead—you come and follow me." The use of the term death in a metaphorical sense was well known in Judaism,[428] and we have an example of such usage here. The implication is that those who do not follow Jesus are spiritually dead. This comports with what we have learned elsewhere: Jesus thought Israel was like a flock of lost sheep; he had come to shepherd and rescue them in the face of the coming dominion and judgment of God. This saying also comports with some of the conclusions we drew in our discussion of Jesus' relationship to the Pharisees: Jesus felt he had the divine authority to supersede or replace portions of the Mosaic law, especially in view of the inbreaking dominion of God.

Whether Jesus made such a radical demand of all his disciples may be debated. It might be argued that such a demand was made only of those who desired to (or those he had called to) travel with him. Even if this is so, it would still mean that Jesus was urging a whole group of people to accept demands that went beyond and sometimes even against Old Testament law. This implies Jesus thought of himself in categories different from any other prophet or teacher of the law. I conclude that Hengel is fully warranted in seeing an example of Jesus' messianic authority coming into play in this pericope. This authority is also evident in another saying where Jesus assigns his own inner circle definitive roles in the final judgment over Israel.

YOU BE THE JUDGE

Matthew 19:28 and Luke 22:30 are critical for understanding Jesus' view of and relationship to the Twelve. Here Jesus expresses his view of the future along lines that strongly suggest he shared his people's hope for an earthly kingdom. For instance, H.-W. Bartsch says, "Behind any messianic hope stands the vision of the reestablished twelve tribe rule as the center of the Kingdom of God."[429]

Despite the strong protest of Beare,[430] this saying in some form has good claims to authenticity for the following reasons. First, it is doubtful that the early church would have made up a saying that seems to envision an earthly kingdom, which did not appear in the first century, and suggests roles that

---

427 Sanders, *Jesus and Judaism*, 254–55.
428 Hengel, *Charismatic Leader*, 7–9.
429 H. W. Bartsch, *Jesus*, 68.
430 Beare, *Matthew*, 400.

the Twelve did not assume in relationship to Israel in that same period. An origin in early Palestinian Christianity might be plausible, as Beare maintains, if the Gospel of Matthew was written extremely early in the first century and grew out of such a community. It is certainly not plausible that the first evangelist would pass along, much less create, such a saying after 70 A.D. when Israel had been shattered and the church was already pursuing a separate existence. Second, this tradition suggests a role for the Twelve in contrast to the various sayings about them being servants like Jesus, rather than *dominii* like gentile rulers. In view of the importance of the servant traditions in the early church, this contrasting saying may well reflect a *Sitz im Leben Jesu*. Third, Kümmel argues that this saying is authentic because it comports with other authentic material in which Jesus envisions a coming eschatological judgment linked with the present.[431] Fourth, Manson protests how hard it is to imagine the early church inventing a saying which, because it is placed on the lips of Jesus during his ministry, envisions a throne for Judas. This may explain why Luke has dropped the word *dodeka* before the word throne in his version of the saying.[432] Thus, Bultmann and others do not prevail in seeing this saying as a church creation.[433] The commentators are fairly evenly divided over which saying is more primitive, with some even urging that it was the last saying to be found in Q. Whether or not this is the case, it does appear to be an isolated logion that has found different placement in Matthew and Luke, and thus the context of either version does not help us much in grasping the original intent. In regard to the original form of the saying, the Matthean version should be given the edge because of its reference to "twelve thrones."

In regard to the meaning of the saying, several points require discussion. First, the reference to the twelve tribes favors seeing Israel as a reference to the nation of Israel, which comports with what we are told about the limitations of the mission of the Twelve (Matt. 10:5–6). If the saying goes back to Jesus, it could not have been understood in any other way originally. Second, this saying is clear that Jesus does not identify the Twelve as Israel. The Twelve may symbolically represent Jesus' design to gather all Israel and may even make clear how Israel ought to respond to Jesus, but they do not constitute that whole Israel. Third, it is not clear how we should take the verb *krino*. It could refer to ruling or acting as the Old Testament judges did,[434] in which case this saying envisions some sort of eschatological age in the future on earth when the Twelve will rule. On the other hand, *krino* could easily refer to the final judgment, as the somewhat similar saying in

---

[431] Kümmel, *Promise and Fulfilment*, 47–48.

[432] Manson, *Sayings of Jesus*, 217.

[433] Bultmann, *Synoptic Tradition*, 158; contrast, Fitzmyer, *Luke 10–24*, 1413.

[434] Beare, *Matthew*, 399, who cites some apparently late evidence that there was an expectation that in the age to come God would restore Israel's judges, i.e., rulers.

1 Cor. 6:3 suggests. Matthew 25:31ff. would also favor this. On this inter-pretation we here learn of a special role the Twelve will have in relation to the nation Israel at the final judgment. This would strongly suggest that the call Jesus places on the lives of the Twelve is not entirely temporal or tem-porary. It will continue to function even at the last judgment. Jesus sees the Twelve as fulfilling some leadership role over Israel both in the present and at the eschaton. But if the Twelve have a claim on and over the nation of Israel, gathered together for the final judgment, note how much more claim Jesus has who chose the Twelve and gave them their commission. Implicit in this saying, then, is a self-estimation on the part of Jesus that suggests he saw himself as the one sent to gather the twelve tribes in the final activity of God.

Note that this saying probably alludes to Dan. 7:22.[435] This suggests that Jesus conceived of his own role in light of that crucial Old Testament chapter and that he envisioned the role of his inner circle of followers as shaped by his understanding of that eschatological and apocalyptic material.

CONCLUSIONS

We began this section by examining Malina's view that Jesus was a reputa-tional legitimate leader. There are significant problems with this view. Although many people viewed Jesus as having authority because of his teaching or healings, there are indications that he saw himself as having authority quite apart from his performance of such functions. This is evident in the material dealing with Jesus' calling the disciples, the radical demand he made upon them (even in contravention of the Mosaic law), and his choosing of the Twelve for a special mission to Israel that had both imme-diate and eschatological components. Such demands and actions point to a person who was certain of the personal authority he had over people and, in particular, over Israel. I agree with Barrett that the Gospel "tradition originated . . . in the impression made by a charismatic person."[436]

A more adequate model for evaluating Jesus' self-image and explaining his sense of authority over both the law and Israel is that of the *shaliach*. Jesus saw himself as God's agent endowed with divine authority and sent on a divine mission to rescue Israel from impending disaster, while at the same time offering them one last chance to accept the rule of God and God's claim on their lives. On such a model we can see the reason that Jesus assumed his words were God's words for Israel, that his agenda was God's agenda for Israel, and that how one reacted to Jesus would determine one's

---

[435] Manson, *Sayings of Jesus,* 217.
[436] Barrett, *Gospel Tradition,* 10. Barrett rightly cautions that this should not amount to simply transferring Jesus from the category of rabbi to that of prophet when he does not belong wholly in either category (n.19).

final standing with God. But Jesus did not see himself as an agent of God, but as the *final* eschatological agent of God who brings in God's reign, and even casts fire upon the land if God's people do not respond properly to that inbreaking reign in the ministry of Jesus.

It is striking how Matt. 10:40 confirms that Jesus saw the Twelve as his own *shalihim,* and that he saw himself as God's *Shaliach.* Here we see both an identification of the Twelve with Jesus in mission and a distinction between them and him in status. Although Jesus and the Twelve function similarly in relationship to Israel, the Twelve are only Jesus' sent ones, while Jesus is God's agent. This explains why Jesus never identifies himself as one of the Twelve or even as Israel, but assumes authority over both. Thus, Jesus had a more than ordinary sense of self-importance. It is appropriate to talk about his messianic self-concept, although even that well-worn phrase is not wholly adequate to express how Jesus viewed himself. It is not surprising that he was reticent to use such familiar labels of himself as *mashiach* because the possibility of misunderstanding was indeed great, especially in view of the nationalistic expectations that existed in Jesus' day.

The material suggests Jesus saw Israel as God's lost sheep, and that he saw himself as their divinely sent and divinely endowed shepherd. Here, too, Malina's paradigm falls short because Jesus did see himself as both commissioned and endowed to be a leader of and over Israel, indeed their final leader who brought in the eschatological reign of God. If Jesus saw himself in light of such texts as Jer. 50:6, then he may have believed he was not just another human shepherd of Israel, but one who takes on the divine role or task of finally gathering the people of God. They must be rescued by Jesus and his helpers before judgment falls even upon Israel. This sort of understanding of one's life task implies at least a messianic self-concept.

Jesus neither was, nor considered himself to be, an ordinary person. He did not conceive of himself merely in terms of a prophet or teacher. Rather, he saw himself as God's *Mashiach* and *Shaliach,* as the final Shepherd of God's people. It was this self-perception expressed in word, deed, and especially symbolic action during the last week of his life, that led to Jesus' death as "King of the Jews."

3

Christology and the Deeds of Jesus

ONE STRIKING OUTCOME of the nineteenth-century quest for the historical Jesus was that Jesus became so modernized he sounded like an advocate for the liberal Protestantism of Schleiermacher, Ritschl, and others. This image, when it became evident that it was hardly an accurate description of the historical Jesus, was replaced, according to Schweitzer, by the image of Jesus as an apocalyptic seer who expected the end of the world most any time. Jesus the apocalyptic seer dominated the discussion of the historical Jesus in the twentieth century often because it was assumed Schweitzer was right, and there was little more to be said on the subject. The liberal Jesus was replaced by a Jesus so remote from current experience and the church's portrait of him that he became little more than a historical curiosity in some circles.

JESUS THE VISIONARY

Since the beginning of the new quest for the historical Jesus in the 1950s, there has been an increasing uneasiness about Schweitzer's Jesus. One of the major trends in the new attempt to envision the person of Jesus has come from both Christian and non-Christian scholars who conclude that Jesus should be seen in light of *charismatic Judaism.* According to this interpretation, Jesus was a Galilean sage and *hasid* with extraordinary spiritual gifts, not unlike Hanina ben Dosa or possibly Honi the Circle Drawer.[1] This

---

[1] Cf. G. Vermes, and to some extent J. D. G. Dunn's *Jesus and the Spirit;* but now even more emphatically M. Borg, *Jesus.*

145

image is posited to replace the portraits of eschatological prophet or apocalyptic seer.

One warrant for this is the textual evidence that Jesus was a visionary, that is, that he had what might be called ecstatic experience. This should not surprise us because the "pneumatic" nature of early Christianity is clear from Acts and 1 Corinthians, and because Paul clearly did have such visionary experiences (cf. 2 Cor. 12.1ff.). There is no reason to think Paul invented this sort of pneumatic approach to religion, and thus it may reflect the original orientation of Jesus himself. Several texts support this view.

Unfortunately, whenever one begins to deal with paranormal experiences, it is frequently assumed that such experiences are purely subjective, that is, they bear no relationship to objective reality. Borg rightly complains,

> Texts that report "paranormal" happenings, whether they be visions of another realm or miracles, are either largely ignored or else interpreted in such a way that they do not violate our sense of what is possible or real. Thus because we do not know what to do with the world of the Spirit, we tend not to give it a central place in our historical study of biblical tradition. But the reality of the other world deserves to be taken seriously. Intellectually and experientially, there is much to commend it. The primary intellectual objection to it flows from a rigid application of the modern worldview's definition of reality. Yet the modern view is but one of a large number of humanly constructed maps of reality. . . . To try and understand the Jewish tradition and Jesus while simultaneously dismissing the notion of another world or immediately reducing it to a merely psychological realm is to fail to see the phenomena, to fail to take seriously what the charismatic mediators experienced and reported. For many of us, this will require a suspension of our disbelief.[2]

It also will not do to characterize persons as psychotic just because they have visions that go beyond ordinary human experience. That diagnosis was offered by some of Jesus' contemporaries, perhaps even his family members who appear to have failed to understand him (Mark 3:21).[3] Thus, we must ask in earnest whether Jesus was a visionary, without allowing our modern preconceptions of normality to prejudice the discussion.

THE FALL OF SATAN (LUKE 10:18)

One of the most puzzling of Jesus' sayings is Luke 10:18 which sounds like a quote from the seer of Revelation (cf. Rev. 12:9–12). It is possible that Luke 10:18 is drawing on the same myth of the casting out of Satan from heaven as is found in Revelation 12.[4] Certainly it is a vignette from a larger

---

[2] Borg, *Jesus*, 33–34.
[3] Witherington, *Women in the Ministry*, 85–87.
[4] Cf. Marshall, *Luke*, 429. Cf. John 12:31; Rev. 20:1–3; Isa 14:12.

conceptual world that is distinctly Jewish. It presupposes Satan's role in the heavenly council, as is found in Job 1:6–12; 2:1–7 where he is seen as the accuser, troubler, and general adversary of God's creatures (*Ha Satan* meaning "the adversary"). We know that by the first century A.D., there was a rather well-developed Satanology, as is reflected in the New Testament and other Jewish writings (*T. Levi* 18.12; *T. Jud.* 25.3; *T. Ash.* 7.3; *T. Dan* 5.10–11; *Assum. of Moses* 10.1.; *Jub.* 23.29). Another passage of relevance is *1 Enoch* 55.4 which reads, "You would have to see my Elect One, how he sits in the throne of glory and judges Azaz'el [i.e., Satan] and all his company, and his army, in the name of the Lord of Spirits."[5] There is good reason to ascribe Luke 10:18 to Jesus; its very strangeness strongly favors its authenticity.[6] The real problem is what sense to make of it.

First we must determine whether Luke 10:18 is a freefloating logion that Luke has placed here, or whether it actually goes with v. 17. Most scholars argue that v. 17 goes with v. 20, and that v. 18 was not attached to v. 17.[7] Therefore, we must take it as a general assessment by Jesus about his success against the strong man (cf. Luke 11:20 and par.).

As to grammatical problems, although it is argued that the imperfect tense of *theoreo* represents a continuous or repeated experience,[8] if this saying goes back to an Aramaic utterance of Jesus then there is only one Aramaic past tense that lies behind this Greek rendering of the original saying.[9] Further, the aorist of *theoreo* was not a common usage, and so the imperfect may be used here in its place.[10] Second, the participle *pesonta* is a constative or timeless aorist expressing a fact, or punctiliar action without any indication of the timing.[11] Thus, the reference is to Satan's fall, not his falling. Third, the question remains as to what the phrase "from heaven" modifies – Satan's fall, or "like lightning." If it modifies "like lightning," then we may not be told from where Satan fell. Yet even if we translate, "I saw Satan fall, like lightning from heaven," it could still be implied that Satan's fall is from the same place from which lightning falls. In any case, the present Greek word order leads to the following literal translation, "I saw (watched) Satan as lightning from heaven fall."

In regard to the meaning of the saying, commentators are rather equally divided as to whether this is to be seen as a visionary experience of Jesus' or whether he is using a mythical metaphor to describe his (and perhaps his

---

[5] Following the translation in *OT Apoc.* 1:38.

[6] Cf. Fitzmyer, *Luke 10–24*, 859; and Jeremias, *Sprache*, 187–88. Bultmann, *Synoptic Tradition*, 158, says this saying is derived by Luke from tradition.

[7] Cf. Marshall, *Luke*, 428; Fitzmyer, *Luke 10–24*, 859.

[8] Cf. J. M. Creed, *Luke*, 147; and Moule's translation, "I have been seeing how Satan is overthrown," in Moule, *I-B*, 206.

[9] Cf. K. G. Kuhn, "*theoreo*," *TDNT* 5:346 n. 161.

[10] Cf. BDF, sec. 101, p. 52; Marshall, *Luke*, 428.

[11] Cf. Robertson, *Grammar*, 843, 910, 1114; Zerwick, *Biblical Greek*, par. 269, p. 90.

disciples') triumphs over the powers of darkness through exorcisms and other means. But if Jesus believed in a real Satan, demons, and heaven, then there is no reason to see this saying as merely a dramatic way of referring to the cures that were being worked. Another reliable tradition strongly suggests that Jesus believed he was in a literal battle with Satan for the lives of the people he was trying to help and that he had to bind the strong man in order to loosen his captives (cf. Mark 3:23–27 and par.). Luke 10:18 is of a piece with those parabolic utterances, suggesting that Jesus saw victories on earth through his ministry, perhaps through exorcisms in particular, which indicated that the strong man was already bound, that he had already lost his former heavenly place and role as troubler of God's creatures.

This saying suggests that Jesus had apocalyptic visions.[12] Two other narratives could be put in that category: the story of Jesus' baptism, and the story of his temptation. The former has a historical basis in John's baptism of Jesus; the latter is much more difficult to claim as a historical account. This is especially so because Mark does not give us the elaborate description of those temptations that we find in Q, and we have no hint that Jesus may have related such an experience to his disciples, especially if it came before the ministry period and was highly personal.

My point is that on the basis of the usual criteria for authenticity, it is difficult to argue for the historicity of an event that was a private and personal experience with no outside witnesses. Dunn cautions that most of the Gospel tradition does not describe Jesus as an ecstatic, "although he did have one or two experiences which could be called ecstatic, whether visionary or moments of high exultation. But he did not attempt to stimulate ecstasy or work up inspiration."[13] Thus, we will only examine the baptism narrative as a source of information about Jesus' experiences.

THE RISE OF THE SON (MARK 1:9–11 AND PAR.)

When Jesus was confronted about his authority he offered a counterquestion about the authority of John's baptism (Mark 11:27–33 and par.). This tradition surely preserves an authentic memory in the life of Jesus because it is doubtful that the church created a saying to suggest either that John had equal authority to Jesus or that Jesus derived his authority from the baptism of John. Yet, Jeremias has argued, "If his counter question is meant seriously, it means: 'My authority rests on John's baptism,' and that again will mean in concrete terms: 'My authority rests on what happened when I was baptized by John.'"[14] This suggests that Jesus saw his baptism as a definitive turning point at which he got authorization or at least empowerment for the

---

[12] Creed, *Luke*, 147; E. E. Ellis, *Luke*, 157; Borg, *Jesus*, 43.

[13] Dunn, *Jesus and the Spirit*, 87.

[14] Jeremias, *New Testament Theology*, 56.

ministry he had undertaken. If Jesus did even in part consider himself a prophetic figure, then it should hardly be surprising either that he had some sort of prophetic call experience as did various Old Testament figures or that when queried about the source of his authority or the reason for his ministry he referred back to that experience. But what we are dealing with in this narrative seems to be not merely a prophetic call narrative, although it is at least that, but also the account of some sort of apocalyptic vision Jesus had.[15]

The student of apocalyptic literature will recognize that Mark's account of the baptism has several features typical of apocalyptic literature: the rending of the heavens, the voice from heaven, and the reference to the Spirit coming down suggesting communication or even some form of communion being established between heaven and earth. One need look no further than the canonical apocalypse to find similar ideas, "I was in the Spirit on the Lord's day, and I heard behind me a loud voice like a trumpet . . ." (Rev. 1:10); "After this I looked, and lo, in heaven an open door! And the first voice, which I heard speaking to me like a trumpet said, 'Come up here, and I will show you what must take place after this. At once I was in the Spirit'" (Rev. 4:1-2); "Then I saw another mighty angel coming down from heaven, wrapped in a cloud, with a rainbow over his head, and his face was like the sun, and his legs like pillars of fire" (Rev. 10:1); "And I saw the holy city, new Jerusalem, coming down out of heaven from God, prepared as a bride adorned for her husband; and I heard a loud voice from the throne saying, 'Behold, the dwelling of God is with human beings'" (Rev. 21:2-3).

There are three notable connections with our text. First, in both Mark and Revelation, we have an example of the rending or opening of heaven preceding the hearing of the voice. Second, notice the sequence in both Mark 1 and Revelation 1 of the Spirit and then voice. In both it is when the seer is in the Spirit that he hears the voice from heaven. It is no accident that we are told in Mark 1 that the Spirit came down upon Jesus and then he heard a voice from heaven. Third, beings, objects, or messages can all come forth from heaven when the heavens are opened, as is attested by both Mark and Revelation. This should be sufficient to show that what we have in Mark is a summary account of an apocalyptic vision.

---

[15] The interpretation we are about to offer is supported by C. E. B. Cranfield's careful analysis of this story. Cf. Cranfield, "The Baptism," 56: "The subject of *eiden* ('saw') is Jesus, and there is nothing in Mark's account that necessarily implies that anyone besides Jesus saw the heavens opened and the Spirit descending or heard the voice. It is therefore open to us to assume that Mark intended to record not externally objective phenomena but a vision – albeit a vision that was no empty dream but a *real communication* from God. That Jesus did at this time experience such a vision seems likely enough, and we may suppose that the account of it derives ultimately from Himself." More than one *Sitz im Leben* is plausible when Jesus would have had occasion to recount this experience: (1) when he was questioned about his authority; or (2) when his disciples wanted to know about how he had come to take up his ministry.

Further, the Markan account of the baptism, as opposed to the later elaboration in Matthew, is depicted as a private communication and event between Jesus and God. No crowd is mentioned, although doubtless there were some people at the Jordan with Jesus and John on this occasion (Luke certainly thinks so; cf. 3:21; John 1:29–34). The address from heaven is to Jesus personally ("You are my beloved Son"), whereas the first evangelist has made it a matter of a public attestation to Jesus from heaven ("This is my beloved Son," Matt. 3:17; cf. Luke 3:22). Certainly, the Markan account is more primitive at this point and summarizes a visionary experience—the *eiden* in Mark 1:10 indicates that only Jesus saw the Spirit coming down and heard the voice.

What is the probability that we have here an accurate summary, ultimately from Jesus, of a visionary experience he had at the Jordan when he consented to be baptized by John? First, we have noted that Jesus seems to point to his baptism as the time when he received his authorization or empowerment for ministry.[16] Some explanation needs to be given for the fact that Jesus, a grown man, felt compelled to begin a ministry after being baptized by John, considering the lack of evidence that others baptized by John felt such a compulsion. Second, we must explain why the synoptic Gospels say that Jesus did not begin his public ministry in Galilee until after his baptism—a sequential connection seems to be posited.

Third, there is no attempt in Mark 1:9–11 to portray Jesus' baptism as a prototype of Christian baptism. Fourth, as Dunn says "To associate Jesus' anointing with his baptism by John played into the hands of Baptist sect apologetic."[17] Fifth, after Jesus began his ministry and gathered his disciples, there would have been good reason for Jesus to recount this experience to his followers at least in summary form, in order to explain how he came to take up this ministry. Unlike the story of the temptation, here there was a built-in need for the ongoing recounting and interpretation of this event and its significance for Jesus and his followers. Sixth, if there was a Q version of this event, as many Q experts contend,[18] then we have two accounts of Jesus' baptism,[19] both of which say that Jesus was baptized by John, that the Spirit descended on Jesus, and that a voice from heaven indicated he was God's beloved Son.[20]

Seventh, why does Mark state that John's baptism is one of repentance for the remission of sins (cf. Mark 1:4–5), and then immediately recount Jesus' baptismal experience? It is doubtful that the early church would have

---

[16] If we are to take seriously the implications of Mark 11:27–33 (and par.). Notice the reference in that dialog to *exousia* coming *ek ouranou*.

[17] I owe these last two points to Dunn, *Jesus and the Spirit*, 63.

[18] Cf. Havener, *Q–The Sayings of Jesus*, 64, 124.

[19] There may be a third account in the *Gospel according to the Hebrews*; cf. Taylor, *Mark*, 158.

[20] Cf. Dunn, *Jesus and the Spirit*, 62.

sanctioned either that Jesus underwent a repentance baptism or that his authorization and empowerment for ministry came during such a baptism. Barrett rightly notes that the closest parallel to John's baptism is proselyte baptism, not the Qumran lustrations. Further, if we give some credence to Josephus's account (*Ant.* 18.116–19), then John's baptism had to do with uniting oneself to a group of people, perhaps to those duly prepared to face and avoid the wrath to come.[21] Jesus identified with John's message and call for preparation to face the coming judgment. This text hardly reflects later Christian theologizing.

Eighth, in regard to the voice from heaven, although Mark does not give us the full text of Ps. 2:7, he is probably quoting part of this well-known verse about the elevation of an individual to the position of king over Israel, "You are my son, today I have begotten thee."[22] It is more probable to conclude that Jesus believed that in his vision these words had been spoken to him and that the church later felt it had to pass on the words from this sacred occasion in spite of their possible adoptionist implications, than to deduce that the early church without any precedent would have chosen an adoptionist text to express its theology. None of the evangelists interpret the text in adoptionist fashion. For them we have here a simple confirmation of who Jesus is without any statement as to when he became the Son. My point is that if the evangelists or the early church were the creators of this scriptural reference, then another text would have been chosen.

Last, would the early church really suggest that Jesus received the Spirit only when he was baptized by John? We know from the birth narratives that such an idea was rejected by some early Christians. Yet there is a clear sign the early church had to admit that in a sense, this was true. In one of the most primitive fragments of early Christian preaching, we find: "The word which was proclaimed throughout all Judea, beginning from Galilee after the baptism which John preached: how God anointed Jesus of Nazareth with the Holy Spirit and with power; how he went about doing good and

---

[21] Cf. C. K. Barrett, *Holy Spirit*, 32–33.

[22] There is probably an allusion to Isa. 42:1 and to the *Akedah*, and thus to Gen. 22:2 in the LXX. If so, then our text has sacrificial overtones. The problem lies in determining how much the ideas about the *Akedah* had developed by Jesus' day. I am not as confident as G. Vermes and R. J. Daly that the ideas expressed in *Targ. Neof.* and the *Frag. Targ.* were influential in Jesus' day. Even if they were, it should be noted that: (1) in the Targum the heavenly voice is the angels speaking to one another; (2) the address to Abraham by Yahweh is about *his* son, not God's, unlike our text; (3) the word "beloved" alone, since it is common in the Old Testament, is not sufficient to establish a link between Genesis 22 and Mark 1; (4) there is no hint of any sacrificial motif otherwise in the Markan text; and (5) the mention of a voice from heaven is simply a stock item in texts affected by apocalyptic and establishes neither a literary dependency, nor a dependency of ideas between Mark 1 and Genesis 22. Nevertheless, cf. Vermes, *Scripture*, 193–227, esp. 222–23; and R. J. Daly, "Sacrifice of Isaac," 67–71. In *T. of Levi* 18.6ff. we find more clearly some of the motifs present in the Markan baptismal story, but this material may well be a Christian interpolation into this testament—so, for instance, H. C. Kee, who thinks the reference to water is a Christian insertion at 18:7 (*OTP* 1:795).

healing all who were oppressed by the devil, for God was with him" (Acts 10:37–38).[23] Notice the clear sequence: baptism of John, anointing with Spirit and power, and ministry including healing.

I conclude that Mark 1:9–11 is a very primitive summary about the decisive turning point in Jesus' life, which goes back to Jesus himself. The only real evidence of Markan redaction is in the introductory phrase in v. 9 ("and it happened in those days") and the use of *euthys* in v. 10.

Note again that Ps. 2:7 seems to be part of what could be called a coronation hymn.[24] What is significant is that an individual, when assuming the tasks and functions of king, is at that point called "my Son" by the authorizing voice, who perhaps was the priest speaking as the *vox dei*. This psalm, then, is about investiture into a royal office and the divine approval being placed on an individual who would be king. In short, the allusion to Ps. 2:7 in Mark 1:11 brings royal overtones to our passage.

Perhaps here is the best point to discuss the terms *mashiach* and *christos*. We will first summarize the work of M. de Jonge.[25] I agree that in *Psalms of Solomon* 17–18 and elsewhere, when the coming king is referred to, there is no rigid distinction between a political-national figure and a spiritual one. In the evidence we do have, however, the political-national component of the expectation is a prominent, in some cases a dominant, part of the expectation about the coming king. What was mysterious to many was that Jesus eschewed the political-national aspects of the aspirations about messiah, refusing to engage either the nations in general or the Romans in particular during his ministry. Nevertheless, Jesus' ministry did have a definite social component, as R. Horsley has argued.[26]

Secondly, de Jonge rightly points out that we find little use of the absolute term *ha Mashiach* in the literature.[27] Normally, it is "his Anointed" or "God's Anointed" with a qualifying word (usually possessive); for instance, in *Ps. of Sol.* 18.5 we find, "He brings back His Anointed." Another striking passage is *1 Enoch* 48.10 where we read, "For they have denied the Lord of Spirits and His Anointed. The name of the Lord of Spirits be blessed." From the Qumran literature we may cite 4QPatr 3, which proclaims

---

[23] In view of such texts as Luke 1:34–35 and 2:49–52, it is hardly possible to argue that this preaching summary in Acts 10 is a piece of Lukan theologizing about Jesus.

[24] Cf. P. Craigie, *Psalm 1–50* (Waco: Word, 1983), 62–69; A. Weiser, *The Psalms*, trans. H. Hartwell (Philadelphia: Fortress Press, 1962), 108–16; M. Dahood, *Psalms 1: 1–50* (New York: Doubleday, 1965), 7–14.

[25] Cf. M. de Jonge, "Anointed"; also his "*Christos*."

[26] R. Horsley, *Spiral of Violence*, 167ff.

[27] Which raises the question of how *christos* has virtually become a proper name along with Jesus even in the earliest Gospels and Paul. Something happened during Jesus' life to warrant this plentiful use of *christos*, in view of how seldom the term is used outside the New Testament, and certainly never as a name. My view is that Jesus was crucified as king of the Jews, but he did not refuse the suggestion he was *mashiach* during his ministry, although the use had to be clarified with such terms as *bar enasha*.

the coming of *Mashiach Ha Sedek,* while commenting on Gen. 49:10. Special attention should also be given to 4QFlor. 1.18–19 which, after alluding to 2 Samuel 7 and the "Scion of David," quotes Ps. 2:1–2. There is, of course, also the Cave 4 fragment, which seems to address the son of the king and reads, "He shall be called [son of] the [g]reat [God] and by his name he shall be named. He shall be hailed (as) the Son of God. . . ."[28] Reference should also be made to 1QSam. 2.12 where we do have the absolute usage *Ha Mashiach,* and to 1Q161.8–10, which quotes Isa. 11:1–5. In the latter we find the assurance that the Spirit of the Lord will be on the future descendant of David. De Jonge reminds us (on the basis of *Ant.* 6.166–68, among other texts), that there is some evidence that suggests David was thought to be a prophet and perhaps an exorcist.[29] Although the number of uses of *Mashiach* are few in the relevant literature, they are sufficient for de Jonge to conclude,

> It denotes the special relationship to God of various figures which are expected in God's future. . . . There is clearly a tendency to connect the expression especially with the expected king and it is on the way to becoming a standard expression. Not the person as such, but his calling and function are of importance.[30]

This material suggests the following: If Jesus had a visionary experience at his baptism in which he was convinced he was anointed with the Spirit and was called God's Son with allusion to Psalm 2, then it would be difficult for him not to conclude that he was God's *Mashiach.* If he did have such an experience and drew such conclusions, then a clear explanation can be given for the course that Jesus chose and for the reason that he acted as one with sovereign authority and power.

Vermes and Borg attempt to relate Jesus' sense of special sonship to that experienced by such charismatic Jews as Hanina ben Dosa or Honi the Circle Drawer.[31] The material about Hanina is drawn from a later period, however, when Christianity and Judaism were already at odds with one another, but even in the case of Honi the Circle Drawer (first century B.C.) all that is said is that he is a "son of the house" before God. Although connoting closeness to God, messianic overtones are not given, as the reference to all God's sons in the same text makes clear.[32] By contrast, here and elsewhere in the Synoptics sonship means something distinctive, even messianic. One further piece of background material may help us to understand the baptismal narrative. J. A. Davis traced the connections of Spirit and wisdom in the

---

[28] Cf. the reconstruction in Fitzmyer, *Luke 10–24,* 347; and pp. 221–23 below.

[29] de Jonge, "Christos," 334–35.

[30] de Jonge, "'Anointed,'" 147.

[31] Vermes, *Jesus the Jew,* 58ff., 210ff.; Borg, *Jesus,* 40–41.

[32] See Borg, *Jesus,* 31; and my discussion of the sonship material in the Hanina and Honi traditions pp. 182–85, 216–21.

relevant Jewish literature, such as Philo, Qumran, and Sirach.[33] He concludes:

> The highest degree of sapiential attainment in the literature that we have surveyed may be seen to be consistently attributed to the person who has had an experience of inspiration, and gained wisdom with the help of the Spirit. In Sirach it is attributed to the scribe who has been filled with the divine Spirit of understanding and is enabled, as a result of his experience, to perceive and pour forth words of wisdom as a sage. At Qumran, it is attributed to the teachers and leaders of the sect who receive a knowledge of the hidden meaning of the law and the Prophets through such divine revelation . . . the person of higher sapiential status is said to have obtained the wisdom that differentiates him from others through the assistance of God's Spirit.[34]

This is relevant for two reasons. If Jesus believed he had received a special anointing by God's Spirit, then it would explain the messianic overtones of his words, deeds, and relationships, especially the reason he often speaks like a sage using the genre of Jewish sages to convey God's truth (e.g., *meshalim*).

We are now prepared to examine the baptismal narrative. First, note what might be considered an odd juxtaposition of the Spirit coming down on Jesus coupled with a *bath qol*—a daughter of a voice. In normal Jewish thinking the latter was given because of the lack of the former. Dunn, however, thinks it misleading to connect this voice from heaven with the *bath qol*.

> To link the voice with the *Bath qol* is to miss the whole point. For the "daughter of the voice" was believed to have taken the place of direct inspiration of the prophets by the Holy Spirit. And it is at this moment above all that the long drought of knowing the Spirit comes to an end. It is not simply that the age of prophecy returns . . . but rather that the age of the Spirit has now come.[35]

Dunn is correct, and the voice from heaven can be explained by the fact that this is an apocalyptic vision. There is no need to explain the voice in terms of the *bath qol*.

Second, although there are certain similarities to prophetic call narratives (cf. Isa. 6:1-13; Jer. 1:5-19; Ezekiel 1-2), the differences are more striking: There is no description of Jesus' inner reaction to this experience, no specific mention of a commission (although calling him son with reference to Ps. 2:7 alludes to his assuming messianic functions), and no reply on the part of Jesus even at the earliest stage of the tradition.[36] Mark 1:9-11 (and par.)

---

[33] J. A. Davis, *Wisdom and Spirit*.
[34] Ibid., 61.
[35] J. D. G. Dunn, *Baptism*, 27.
[36] Fitzmyer, *Luke 1-9*, 480.

describes the unique vision that confirmed Jesus' identity and by implication, his task in relation to God's people. He was to be God's *Mashiach*.

Third, little should be made of the fact that the Spirit is said to have descended like a dove. This could be a reference to Gen. 1:2, but it is equally plausible that in light of the connections to which we have already alluded between wisdom and Spirit in early Jewish literature, our text is closer to what we find in Philo *Q.R.D.H.* 126 where the dove represents divine Wisdom and elsewhere also the Logos (cf. 234). The reference to the Spirit being like a turtledove is from a later period (cf. *Targ.Song* 2.12), as is *B.T.Bab.Hag.* 15a, which examines Gen. 1:2 and talks of the Spirit hovering over the waters. It is germane to point out that Jesus' anointing with the Spirit is not directly connected with the waters or the physical baptism, but happens afterward (when "he came up out of the waters").[37] Thus, the allusion to the dove may be a wisdom motif, which should not be pressed because we are talking about an analogy (*"like* a dove").

In this brief text that summarizes Jesus' apocalyptic vision, we are given the impression that Jesus had his identity confirmed, his life task set, and the necessary empowerment granted for him to carry out what God intended for him to be and do. It may be true that Jesus' visions were infrequent—certainly what happened to him at his baptism was a singular experience. Thus, it is going too far to call Jesus an apocalyptic seer; most of his utterances, although often having a wisdom or eschatological bent, are hardly apocalyptic in the sense of representing the communication of a revelation that came to Jesus in the form of a vision. We may wish to call Jesus a charismatic, one endowed with full measure of the Spirit, but perhaps not an ecstatic.[38] What our text tells us is that "Jesus thought of himself as God's son and as anointed by the eschatological Spirit. . . ."[39] Bear in mind also the insight of A. F. C. Wallace who points out that revitalization movements typically come into being through a prophet's "revelatory visions."[40]

MIRACLES AND MIGHTY SIGNS

How Jesus used the empowerment he received at baptism needs to be examined. That Jesus performed deeds that were perceived as miracles by both him and his audience is difficult to doubt. Whether we are dealing with a case of raising the dead or healing the blind or exorcising a demon, we find evidence in various sources and layers of the tradition that Jesus was noted

---

[37] Dunn, *Baptism*, 29ff.
[38] Cf. Dunn, *Jesus and the Spirit*, 84ff.
[39] Ibid., 67.
[40] A. F. C. Wallace, "Revitalization," 512.

for performing such acts. Borg's conclusion is typical: "Jesus was one of these 'men of deeds.' Indeed to his contemporaries it was the most remarkable thing about him. During his lifetime he was known primarily as a healer and exorcist."[41] If Jesus was endowed with the Spirit, then it should hardly surprise us that he performed activities like those of Elijah, for example, who was similarly endowed according to biblical tradition. Herein lies a problem, however. If Jesus' deeds were no different from those of a great prophet or Hellenistic wonder worker, then how can they be said to have any christological weight? One could argue that if raising the dead or healing the sick proves Jesus to be the messiah, then these same activities prove Elijah to be the messiah.

It could also be argued that exorcisms, or giving of sight to the blind, were a sign that the messiah had come, since there was no real precedent for such acts in the Old Testament. Furthermore, apart from the Aramaic incantation bowls and the *Testament of Solomon* that post-date the New Testament, there is evidence from Qumran Cave 11 that Solomon, Son of David, was associated with exorcisms. The fragment in question is of a recension of Psalm 91 and probably dates to the late first century B.C.[42] Later rabbinic literature is known to have seen this psalm as a song for exorcising demons (cf. *J.T.Sabb.* 6.8b; *B.T.Sheb.* 15b; and especially *J.T.Erub.* 10.26c). Even more striking is what Josephus says about Solomon in *Ant.* 8.45:

> And God granted him knowledge of the art used against demons for the benefit and healing of human beings. He also composed incantations by which illnesses are relieved, and left behind forms of exorcisms with which those possessed by demons drive them out, never to return. And this kind of cure is of very great power among us to this day. . . .

This knowledge of exorcism is associated with Solomon's wisdom. These examples raise the possibility that Jesus' exorcisms may have been intended or seen as making some sort of messianic claim.[43] Isaiah 35:5ff. supports the idea that from at least the late prophetic period there was an expectation that in the messianic age there would be healing of the blind.

MIRACLES AND MAGIC IN ANTIQUITY

People in antiquity were so primitive, it has been maintained, that they believed almost everything that happened could be attributed to supernatural forces. This supposed lack of critical faculty to discern the difference between natural and supernatural causes has led many moderns to seek naturalistic explanations for most of Jesus' deeds. Dunn has argued: "There

---

[41] Borg, *Jesus*, 60.
[42] Cf. D. C. Duling, "Solomon," 238–39.
[43] de Jonge, *Christology in Context*, 167–68.

is no instance of a healing miracle which falls clearly outside the general category of psychosomatic illnesses."[44] This is a very dubious deduction. The raising of the widow of Nain's son, much less Lazarus, and the healing of a man born blind can hardly be categorized as the curing of psychosomatic illnesses. More to the point, È. Yamauchi shows that in various Near Eastern civilizations such as those in Mesopotamia, Egypt, and Israel both before and during the New Testament era, various people could distinguish between illnesses that were naturally or supernaturally caused or cured.[45] My point is that miracle stories, whatever their historical substance, that cannot be explained in a reductionistic fashion occur even in the Synoptics. I suspect that this reductionism is based in part on a false premise about the powers of critical discernment in antiquity.[46] Schillebeeckx rightly cautions:

> Anyone who recounts miracle-stories [especially in conjunction with stories that do not contain miracles] is already living in what is plainly a "transitional world"; he is no longer a primitive for whom everything in fact is "miraculous" and accounts of individual miracles make nonsense—even though he too recognizes gradations in the world of miracles; but he is not, on the other hand, a member of a secularized, technological welfare state in which there can no longer be any room for "miracles."[47]

Bear in mind that modern assumptions about the nonexistence or impossibility of miracles are as uncritical as the assumption that everything is miraculously caused. Rather, the evidence for the miraculous must be weighed and sifted like any other historical evidence, and an explanation adequate to account for the phenomena needs to be given.

Schillebeeckx reminds us that even Jesus' opponents did not dispute that he worked miracles, but they attribute them to the powers of darkness (cf. Mark 3). Apparently, there were two verdicts about Jesus' mighty deeds—of God or of the devil. "Such extreme verdicts are not reached in respect of any old nondescript 'average person'; they presuppose some sort of 'marvellous phenomenon' perceived and acknowledged as such by all parties."[48] The people of Jesus' day were prepared to believe in such phenomena, but was any distinction made between magic and miracle?

Here we are helped by J. M. Hull and H. C. Kee, who seek to place the Gospel material in the larger context of ancient miracles and magic.[49] These

---

[44] Dunn, *Jesus and the Spirit*, 71.

[45] E. Yamauchi, "Magic or Miracle?"

[46] Barrett, *Gospel Tradition*, 69, says, "In most instances the narratives given to us by the Evangelists cannot be rationalized without being completely transformed. Jesus is represented not as using natural laws and forces but as transcending and overriding them."

[47] Schillebeeckx, *Jesus*, 182.

[48] Ibid.

[49] J. M. Hull, *Hellenistic Magic*; H. C. Kee, *Miracle*.

studies are more useful than those of M. Smith who has a polemical ax to grind that skews his handling of the evidence.[50]

Hull suggests that a miracle is and would have been considered partly or wholly magical if (1) the miracle has no cause but the will of the miracle worker, (2) cause and effect are indicated, their interconnection being based upon a theory of *mana* or sympathetic bonds; or (3) the cause of the miracle is believed to be the performance of certain rituals that are efficacious in themselves. The basic idea behind magic seems to be an interpersonal, inter-subjective transaction, with or without intermediary means.[51] The ancients had a difficult time separating miracles from magic, and if one performed the former, then one could have used the latter to bring it about. One of Smith's claims seems to have substantial support: Jesus was perceived by some to be a magician, especially when he performed exorcisms or used clay or spittle to heal a person (cf. Mark 7:33; 8:23; John 9:6). These activities and means were the stock and trade of magicians. Barrett reminds us, "It is true Jesus must have presented a . . . 'pneumatic' figure as with authority he rebuked the unclean spirits, but so did the legendary Solomon, and the half-legendary Apollonius . . . so too did the perfectly real Rabbis who exorcised demons, and the equally real magicians who hawked the magical spells."[52] This larger context, not just the Old Testament background, needs to be kept in mind when we weigh whether Jesus' mighty deeds have any christo-logical significance.

It appears from the Gospel data that Jesus does not qualify as a magician for the following reasons. First, there is clear evidence that he believed he performed exorcisms by personally using the power of God's Spirit (cf. Luke 11:19–20/Matt. 12:27–28), not by merely exerting his own will against that of the forces of darkness. Second, there is no clear evidence of Jesus using spells or magical words to perform his miracles; usually his miracles result from his spoken word. The Aramaic words Jesus uses in Mark 5:41 are not an incantation formula but a simple direct address. The use of clay or spittle does not necessarily amount to a ritual; it may have been Jesus' way of making clear to his audience that he was in the process of healing someone. Clearly, he is portrayed as being able to perform the same miracle without such a procedure, so that he was not dependent on a ritual.[53]

Third, with rare exception Jesus' actions cannot be explained by the use of such concepts as *mana* or various forms of sympathetic magic.[54] Fourth,

---

[50] Cf. Smith, *Jesus the Magician*, which contains much valuable material.

[51] Hull, *Hellenistic Magic*, 54–55.

[52] Barrett, *Holy Spirit*, 57.

[53] Notice in John 9:6 clay and spittle are used; in Mark 8:23; 7:33 only spittle; in Matt. 12:22 neither are mentioned; and Matt. 9:32–34 treats dumbness as a case to be treated like exorcism.

[54] There is a possible exception to this in Mark 5:30 (cf. Luke 8:46). The summary in Luke 6:19 can be explained as editorial, but the material in Mark 5:30 seems to be of the essence of the story. It could be argued that Mark has written this story using the conventional language

the frequent association of Jesus' miracles with faith distinguishes them from the extrabiblical traditions,[55] and particularly the *theios aner* material. But it is also striking how *pistis* in the synoptic miracle material has the sense of trust in Jesus' ability to help, and it is not used in the later post-Easter sense of faith in Jesus.[56] Fifth, there is a striking absence of the use of rings, holy water, herbs, incantations, or various aids especially when performing an exorcism, although Jesus does follow the usual procedure of addressing, obtaining the name, silencing, and dismissing the demon.[57] Sixth, Jesus never gives instructions or directions about natural cures.[58] Seventh, in the Synoptics Jesus does not follow biblical or later Christian precedent in performing his cures; he does not pray nor does he invoke the sacred name.[59] Eighth, Jesus performs neither a punishment miracle (unless one counts the cursing of the fig tree), nor what may be called a liberation from human bonds (cf. Acts 16:25ff.), nor any purely gratuitous miracle. Ninth, Jesus does not perform miracles to draw a crowd or draw attention to himself, in fact, he specifically refuses to do this (cf. Mark 8:11ff. and par.). It is not surprising that Kee concludes after his study of the Gospel miracle material that Mark presents Jesus' miracles "within a framework very different from that of the Magical Papyri."[60] This is true because even at the earliest level of the tradition Jesus was not perceived by Christian tradents to be a magician and did not intentionally present himself as such. Hull concludes, whatever others may have thought, "Jesus did not think of himself

---

and modes applied to Hellenistic magicians, but there seems to be some evidence that Mark downplays the miraculous. Nonetheless, it is quite believable that Mark might write in a fashion that his predominantly gentile audience would understand. On *mana* and Mark 5:30, cf. Barrett, *Holy Spirit*, 75.

[55] This remark requires some qualification because in the Hellenistic material, there is in some cases a response of an individual who hears about or sees a healing that might be called belief or trust of a sort. Yet, as Horsley, *Jesus*, 226–27, indicates, there is a difference because "in the Hellenistic sources . . . faith is individualistic and cognitive, whereas in the gospel traditions it is relational and integral to the healing events themselves. In the Hellenistic literature and inscriptions, faith is basically an attitude of the listener or onlooker as a consequence of the story or incident. In the gospel stories, faith is a basic trust or even persistent seeking by the principal actors in the story and is a condition, sometimes almost a cause, of the healing itself."

[56] Dunn, *Jesus and the Spirit*, 75, says, "It is this *dependence* on winning a response, on winning people to faith, which distinguishes Jesus' *dunameis* from the possible parallels in Jewish or Hellenistic circles, where faith plays no part." Especially helpful is Roloff's study on faith in the synoptic material in *Das Kerygma*, 153–73: "But before everything, Faith stands out in the . . . synoptic material, [and] although it has to do with the person of Jesus, never [do we find it] in the post-Easter sense of faith in Jesus . . . [This shows] 'how faithful had the Synoptic tradition proved in this respect to the original report'" (173; in the latter quote, Roloff endorses G. Ebeling).

[57] Hull, *Hellenistic Magic*, 61ff.

[58] Ibid., 75. As Hull notes, even in Mark 5:43 the eating is not part of the cure but rather proof of the return to normality.

[59] J. Neirynck, "Miracle Stories," 866–67. He points out that the most characteristic note found in the Gospel miracles that is not found in Acts is faith, while "The use of the *nomen sacrum* and prayer distinguishes an apostle or a missionary from Jesus as the divine-man. These features are traditional and pre-Lucan in character."

[60] Kee, *Miracle*, 170.

as a magician."[61] He may have seen himself as a prophetic or even messianic healer, but only an examination of the evidence will bear this out. Here we can conclude that there are features in the synoptic miracle material that suggest Jesus was not and did not intend to be seen as a magician.

JESUS AND THE "THEIOS ANER" CONCEPT

At one time, many thought Jesus was being depicted as a *theios aner* in some of the Markan miracles. When Leander Keck wrote his important article on Markan Christology in 1965, he was surprised that one such as Cullmann would reject the suggestion that the *theios aner* concept might be of relevance to understanding Jesus as a miracle worker or, at least, the presentation of him as such by the evangelists.[62] Since that time, two studies have caused a major reevaluation of this theme's relevance for the analysis of Gospel miracle material.[63] In 1987, G. Downing could say on the basis of these two studies, "I take it that D. L. Tiede and C. H. Holladay between them have shown that there was no composite role of inspired teacher-and-worker-of-miracles with the title *theios aner* waiting around for Jesus to be cast in it."[64] E. Best is also willing to say, "It is not as certain as it is sometimes alleged that there was a clear concept of a divine man in the contemporary world; even if there was, it is less clear that the early Christians would have consciously formalized their teaching along its lines."[65]

What can we say about the *theios aner* concept? First, "many scholars have been operating under the false impression that the term *theios aner* was a fixed concept in the Hellenistic world."[66] It was not; rather, it was an umbrella concept incorporating disparate and sometimes even contradictory elements.[67] The concept has been pressed into a variety of uses. Thus, a divine-man Christology "that can encompass the christologies of the four gospels and the pre-gospel miracle cycles would have to be too broad a concept to have much interpretative value."[68] Second, when one examines Plato's Socrates or Plutarch's Alexander or Philo's Moses or even Dio of Prusa's Diogenes, the real basis for calling any of these individuals a *theios aner* or recognizing any of them as having divine status "rests upon his

---

[61] Hull, *Hellenistic Magic*, 144–45.
[62] L. Keck, "Mark 3:7–12," 330–31 and n.63.
[63] Cf. D. L. Tiede, *Charismatic Figure*; C. H. Holladay, *Theios Aner*.
[64] G. Downing, "Social Contexts," 444.
[65] Best, *Disciples*, 183.
[66] Tiede, *Charismatic Figure*, 289.
[67] Ibid., 255; cf. B. L. Blackburn, "THEIOI ANDRES," 188. He indicates there is no evidence it was a *terminus technicus*. In fact, the term *theios aner* is expressly used of only three figures who were thought to have performed some sort of miracles and were considered in some sense divine: once of Epimenides, once or possibly twice of Moses, and four times of Apollonius.
[68] Ibid., 265 n.63.

characterization as a sage and possessor of virtue who can serve as a paradigm for moral edification."[69] In short, it does not rest on their abilities as wonder-workers. Furthermore, the record of Apollonius's deeds comes from a much later period than the New Testament material. Accordingly, this concept is not going to help us much in discerning what sort of miracle worker Jesus was, or was perceived to be, or was portrayed as being by the evangelists. Hellenistic wonder-workers or charismatic figures were numerous (Simon Magus, for example), but in the last analysis, these figures are not exactly the same thing as a *theios aner*. I conclude that the *theios aner* concept is too amorphous and will not help to understand how Jesus viewed himself as a wonder-worker.

THE HANDLING OF MIRACLES IN MARK AND Q

Even in the case of John, the Gospel writers do not play up the miraculous element in the traditions of Jesus' mighty works that they present to us. The Fourth Gospel does not dwell on the miracles in the sign narratives; in fact, sometimes they are not even described. Rather, the focus is on their effects and christological significance. Often, however, there is a stress on the magnitude (not the nature) of the miracle—the quantity of water changed, the fact that a man was born blind, the number of days Lazarus was dead. But this is mentioned in order to magnify the miracle worker, not because of an interest in the miracle itself. Käsemann says:

> For John, too, miracles are indispensable. They are not mere concessions to human weakness. . . . Human need is, to be sure, the occasion for the miracle, but the meeting of human needs is at most a subsidiary aim. . . . It is indeed correct to point out that John attacks a craving for miracles. This is not done, however, on the basis of a criticism of miracles in general, but in the interest of his one and only theme, namely his christology. His dominant interest . . . is that Christ himself may not be overshadowed by anything, not even by his gifts, miracles and works.[70]

When we turn to the material in Mark and Q, we discover a considerable restraint being exercised in comparison to various extrabiblical and apocryphal tales about miracles. In the case of Mark, almost all the miracles are clustered in the first half of the Gospel, making up about forty-seven percent of that half. The dominant interest seems to be in *exorcisms*—in a miracle related to the eschatological inbreaking of God's dominion and possibly to a messianic figure, but also in a miracle that does not seem to have been the focus of most of the miracle tales about early church figures (cf. Acts). It is possible that Mark has drawn on a pre-Markan miracle cycle

---

[69] Ibid., 291.
[70] E. Käsemann, *Testament of Jesus*, 21.

for some of this material.[71] It is also possible that "Mark contains two streams of miracle material: one closely related to the Palestinian scene and the message of Jesus in its native setting; the other relatively unrelated to Jesus' message."[72] Keck suggests that the material found in Mark 3:7–12; 4:35–5:43; 6:31–52; and 6:53–56 comes from a later, more Hellenistic source that does not reflect the concerns of the ministry. Yet this material's focus is on Jesus' travels in the region around the Sea of Galilee and on his use of a boat to reach many of these places. A more helpful distinction for our purposes might be between miracles of an epiphanic nature, such as some of the nature miracles that seem directly to reveal something about Jesus, and those of a more indirect nature, such as exorcisms that could be evaluated variously. We will not study the epiphanic miracles because most scholars believe they reflect later church interests.

In any event, Mark is clearly interested in miracles, as both the quantity and the summaries show (1:32–34; 3:7–12; 6:53–56; 8:14–21), but it is hard to find evidence of Markan redaction that intends to heighten the miraculous.[73] We see throughout the first half of the Gospel that these miracles can be variously evaluated. However, although they raise the question of who Jesus is, they do not provide a clear answer—other than attesting Jesus is a man with divine power. Best explains:

> On the one hand the healing narratives attract men to Jesus; on the other, they do not reveal his true nature and the real claim he makes on them; this only comes from the cross. Hence Mark's ambivalent attitude. So he retains the miracles, but sets them within the framework of a story dominated by the passion.[74]

Achtemeier sees the matter a little differently. He, too, claims that the miracles are deliberately set in a larger framework, but his contention is that Mark uses the miracle material to aid in portraying Jesus as a teacher. This is seen in the very first miracle story, Mark 1:21–28. "Here, plainly, Mark wants us to be clear on the fact that the power inherent in Jesus' teaching is precisely the power that enabled him to overcome demonic forces."[75] Achtemeier suggests that Mark wants to state clearly that Jesus is not just another Hellenistic wonder-worker. "The Jesus who performed mighty acts is the Jesus who is preeminently the teacher. . . ."[76] Whether one prefers the analysis of Best or Achtemeier, the point is that Mark was not in the business of playing up the miraculous or inventing miracle tales. Rather, he was

---

[71] Cf. P. Achtemeier, "Isolation" and his "Origin and Function."

[72] Keck, "Mark 3:7–12," 50–51.

[73] Best, *Disciples*, 182.

[74] Ibid., 190.

[75] P. Achtemeier, "He Taught Them," 478.

[76] Ibid., 480.

trying to place the miracle tales he found in his source(s) in a larger context so that Jesus would be understood. The issue of the context in which the Markan miracles are placed is important in another regard as well. What Barrett says about exorcisms can be said of all the miracles to some extent. They "draw their significance not from their content, which is commonplace enough, but from their context; it is the Christological setting in which they are placed which completely differentiates them from other narratives."[77] One may say these miracles gain their christological significance from the interpretation that Jesus (and others) give to such events. Achtemeier's suggestion that Mark presents the miracles in the context of depicting Jesus as a teacher may be explained by what we have just noted.[78] For now it would appear that the only uninterpreted miracles that might have raised messianic questions would have been exorcisms and possibly giving sight to the blind. Nevertheless, Mark is careful to warn his audience that miracles could be ambiguous. After all, they lead Pharisees and Herodians to oppose Jesus (3:6); cause scribes to think of Jesus as possessed (3:22); leave people from his hometown unimpressed (6:2-3); cause Herod to imagine that Jesus is John the Baptist *redivivus* (6:14-16); and do not eliminate the disciples' misunderstanding (6:52; 8:17-21).[79] Yet miracles are neither dismissed nor denied nor demythologized, but simply presented in a larger context.

Turning to Q, we discover that miracles are mentioned only occasionally—hardly surprising in what is primarily a sayings source. Nevertheless, we do find the intriguing story of the healing of the centurion's servant (Matt. 8:5-13; Luke 7:1-10), which may have been placed right next to Jesus' response to the Baptist in Q (Matt. 11:5/Luke 7:22).[80] In addition, there is the important woe saying about three Galilean cities in Matt. 11:21-24/Luke 10:13-15. Thus, we find in Q the solicitation of a miracle, the interpretation of miracles, and also the effect of rejecting miracles. Note, however, that even in Matt. 8:5-13/Luke 7:1-10, the real interest is in the dialogue between Jesus and the centurion, not in the miracle itself.[81] In the important sayings in Matt. 12:27-28/Luke 11:19-20 the focus is on explaining the significance of Jesus' exorcisms, as opposed to those performed by others.

I conclude that in Q, as well as in Mark, no real evidence of any desire or interest to play up the miraculous aspects of Jesus' ministry is exhibited. Their reality is recognized, and they are considered integral to the ministry. The focus, however, is on their interpretation and significance as well as on the implications of responding positively or negatively to them. What I want

---

[77] Barrett, *Holy Spirit*, 57.

[78] Achtemeier, "He Taught Them," 480. His power as a teacher is made visible in his mighty deeds, i.e., the two are related.

[79] Ibid., 477.

[80] Cf. Havener, *Q—The Sayings of Jesus*, 127-28.

[81] Ibid., 100.

to stress about the miracle material and the references to miracles in both Mark and Q is that neither source evidences any interest in novelistic expansion or creation of miracle stories. Both found the material in their sources, yet they tried to give it neither too much nor too little weight. Thus, we may learn something indirectly about how Jesus viewed himself because this material appears in our earliest sources with relatively little redactional expansion or modification of a specifically christological nature.

JESUS' INTERPRETATION OF HIS MIRACLES

Arguments for the authenticity of Matt. 12:28/Luke 11:20 will be dealt with later. It is doubtful, however, that Matt. 12:27/Luke 11:19 is a creation of the early church in view of its admission that other Jewish exorcists among Jesus' opponents were successful and that Jesus, according to words placed on his lips, might be casting out demons by the prince of demons (Beelzebul). Nevertheless, we can discern something of Jesus' view of miracles from these two, perhaps originally separate, sayings.[82]

Jesus freely admits that his power to perform exorcisms is not his own, but is derived from a higher supernatural power. This point cannot be overstressed because it makes clear that Jesus does not perform exorcisms simply by exerting his will against that of the demons. There is no interpersonal battle going on between him and the powers of darkness. Thus, Jesus distinguishes his work from what Hull has defined as magic.

Second, Jesus claims that it is by God's power, not Satan's, that he casts out demons. This implies a direct consciousness of God's power resident in Jesus so that he may draw on it whenever necessary, but especially to help others since exorcisms are always miracles of compassion.

Most important for our purposes is the connection with the dominion of God. This connection distinguishes Jesus' exorcisms from all others, with the possible exception of his followers', whom he endows with God's power to pursue the same purposes. These exorcisms are not just random examples of God's help to the suffering, but herald the breaking in of the eschatological reign of God. The importance of this should not be minimized. As Theissen has put it,

> Jesus is unique in religious history. He combines two conceptual worlds which had never been combined in this way before, the apocalyptic expectation of universal salvation in the future and the episodic realization of salvation in the present through miracles . . . Before Jesus there was no comparable combination of apocalyptic and the charism of miracle-working. . . . The eschatological view of miracles is generally and rightly held to be a peculiarity of Jesus' preaching. Because the negative web of evil has already been broken it is

---

[82] Cf. Marshall, *Luke*, 474–75; Fitzmyer, *Luke 10–24*, 921.

possible for salvation to come in individual instances. Because individual instances of salvation occur, the presence of the end can be proclaimed here and now.[83]

Jesus sees his miracles as bringing about something unprecedented – the coming of God's dominion. Note that Jesus interprets God's reign in terms of changed human lives, not cosmic or political change. He sees himself as one who is bringing in and bringing about change within the lives of individual human beings so that they can relate to God and others as God intends them to do. This is God's final will for God's creatures. Here we see a person who believes he has been endowed by God with the power to bring about God's final transformation of human lives. In view of some of the late prophetic texts that associate such changes with the messianic age and sometimes specifically with God's anointed one (cf. Isa. 61:1ff.; 35:5), it does appear that Jesus is making an implicit messianic claim. Who else had the power to bring in God's final reign over human lives?

Equally important is Jesus' response to the Baptist. The following factors point to the authenticity of Matt. 11:4-6/Luke 7:22-23: (1) in view of the growing tendency in the tradition to make John a witness for Jesus, the doubts here expressed are surely an authentic note; (2) the absence of any concluding response of or reply by the Baptist points to the primitiveness of the narrative; (3) the reference to Jesus as the Coming One is a "very rare title which is not usual either in Judaism or in later Christianity";[84] (4) Jesus' pointing to his miracles, rather than answering the question directly, seems to be characteristic of the way he responds to questions about who he is; (5) the lack of reference to exorcism suggests that the narrative has not been touched up to conform to the actual course of Jesus' activities; (6) other traditions outside of Q also suggest that Jesus saw his job as announcing good news to the poor (cf. Luke 4:16ff.; also the Q Beatitude, Luke 6:20/Matt. 5:3);[85] (7) in view of the fact that neither early Judaism nor the church would have characterized the messiah as one who simply comes and heals and preaches good news to the poor, this too must count in favor of the authenticity of this material.[86]

In Matt. 11:2-19/Luke 7:18-35, we clearly see that Jesus believes he is on a mission to fulfill God's promises concerning the final state of God's people. Jesus came to preach and bring the eschatological blessings of God; how one reacts to Jesus determines whether or not one will be blessed by these activities (the negative side of this will be seen when Matt. 11:21/Luke 10:13 is examined). Jesus is willing to allow his preaching and his miracles to

---

[83] G. Theissen, *Miracle Stories*, 278-80.
[84] A. George, "Paroles de Jesus," 289, my translation.
[85] Ibid., 291.
[86] Ibid.

indicate who he truly is. Here is someone conscious of being more than just a proclaimer or prophet, although he is certainly that. Rather, Jesus sees himself as one who rescues people, bringing about the condition of eschatological *shalom* or salvation in their lives. To be sure, the miracles involve physical healing, but in view of the frequent stress in the healing stories on the necessity of faith or trust in Jesus as one who can bring God's help, clearly something more than mere physical restoration is at issue here. The larger context of the Old Testament text Jesus cites, Isa. 35:4–6/61:1, also suggests this. It is doubtful that Jesus made the sort of neat distinctions between the physical and spiritual realms that moderns do. Here again we see a claim that, although indirect, suggests Jesus saw himself as more than a prophet or ordinary miracle worker. He was one in whom and through whom the promises of God came to pass. This is surely some sort of transcendent claim, whether or not we call it messianic.

Luke 10:13–15/Matt. 11:21–23a is a Q saying that may be categorized as a woe oracle like those we find in the Old Testament (cf. Amos 6:4–7; Mic. 2:1; Hab. 2:6–7; Zeph. 2:5).[87] Its original setting has probably been lost because the first evangelist and Luke present this material in different contexts. Most scholars argue that the Matthean form is more primitive, although it appears that 11:23b–24 was later added by the first evangelist because this material is not found in Luke.[88] In favor of the authenticity of the earliest form of this saying, Matt. 11:21–23a, is the fact that it records the failure of at least one part of Jesus' ministry.[89] Furthermore, the mention of Chorazin must count in favor of its authenticity because the city is mentioned nowhere else in the Gospel tradition and an early Christian mission was evidently not undertaken at this tiny village.[90] The saying presents various hints that it was originally an Aramaic oracle—parallelism, the use of the divine passive, assonance between Bethsaida and Sidon.[91] Also in favor of its authenticity is the note of eschatological judgment even on the people of God, as well as the appeal to repentance, both of which seem to characterize at least the early period of Jesus' Galilean ministry shortly after Jesus had contact with the Baptist (who preached in similar fashion).

For our purposes several key insights are gained from Luke 10:13–15/ Matt. 11:21–23a. First, Jesus expected the citizens of these villages to see his miracles as more than just deeds of compassion. They were a visible form of calling people to repentance in view of the coming dominion of God. Notice, there is no mention of preaching along with the mighty signs,

---

[87] Cf. J. A. Comber, "Matt 11:20–24."

[88] George, "Paroles de Jesus," 293–94; Schweizer, *Matthew*, 266–67.

[89] George, "Paroles de Jesus," 295.

[90] Jeremias, *Jesus' Promise*, 50 and n.1.

[91] Cf. Jeremias, *New Testament Theology*, 15; and George, "Paroles de Jesus," 294–95.

although that may have been the case. The point of this saying is that the deeds themselves should have been sufficient to lead to repentance.[92] Second, however, Jesus admits that the mighty deeds themselves do not automatically produce the proper response that he desires. These deeds may raise questions about who Jesus is and what he is doing, but they do not in themselves transform the hearts of their eyewitnesses and lead them to understand Jesus and his deeds. Yet it is right to see this oracle as a comment primarily on the hardheartedness of Jesus' audience because he indicates that if he had performed the same miracle in famous pagan cities like Tyre and Sidon, repentance and the signs of repentance would have resulted.

Third, notice that how one reacts to Jesus and his actions now will affect one's status at the last judgment. This saying, like the previous two we have examined, suggests that Jesus saw his miracles as evidence of the inbreaking dominion of God that should lead people to humble themselves before their God.[93] Jesus, then, is the one who brings the final decisive action of God upon God's people. How one responds will determine one's final status with God. This suggests that Jesus saw himself as the final and decisive mediator between God and God's people.

In conclusion, Jesus saw his miracles as part of his overall effort to bring in the dominion of God, both as part of the final eschatological blessing upon God's people and as part of the call to repentance and response of faith to what was happening in and through the ministry of Jesus. All of this suggests a transcendent evaluation by Jesus of the importance of his ministry, including the mighty deeds. Even at the historical level, Barrett's conclusion is fully warranted:

> The general purport of the sayings about miracles which we have so far considered is that they are acts of divine power wrought through God's representative. As such they are signs of the coming New Age of God's salvation, and as such they may be recognized by all who have eyes to see. It is true that many, even the disciples, are blind, but God's power is nevertheless prodigally expended in miracles the significance of which might be grasped by those whose minds are enlightened. Behind the figure of Jesus as a "pneumatic" person (as he is portrayed in the miracles themselves) we see the root of his power—his Messiahship, and his connection with the Kingdom of God.[94]

---

[92] Dunn, *Jesus and the Spirit*, 71, sees the lack of mention of preaching in this logion as an indicator of the authenticity of the saying because "this feature is without real parallel in the Jewish (Palestinian) mission of the early church. . . ."

[93] Cf. R. Latourelle, "Authenticité historique," 248: "These miracles are the signs of the advances of God, the call to repentance and conversion before the imminent coming of the Kingdom of God."

[94] Barrett, *Holy Spirit*, 90.

NO SIGN OF APPROVAL (MARK 8:11; LUKE 11:29)

There is little benefit in investigating various healing narratives in detail when it is not their content but their context that is of christological significance. The questions we want to answer at this point are: (1) was Jesus willing to perform miracles upon request to authenticate his work and nature? (2) did Jesus perform miracles that might have been evaluated as uniquely messianic? and (3) did Jesus perform what might be called prophetic sign-miracles? These questions will be addressed in each of the next three sections.

Attempting to discern the earliest form of Mark 8:11 (and par.) about Jesus' refusal to provide a sign from heaven is difficult. Most scholars are convinced that we have in Mark and Q at least one authentic minatory saying that indicates Jesus refused to produce a sign.[95] The majority of scholars now think that the Q form is more primitive and that Mark has edited the saying, leaving out the material about the sign of Jonah due to his messianic-secret theme. Thus, the Jonah material in some form (perhaps Luke 11:29b) is probably original. For our purposes it is not necessary to focus on this part of the saying. If the reference to Jonah is a vague allusion either to Jesus' death (made explicit in later handling of the saying, cf. Matt. 12:40), or to some other event in the future after Jesus' earthly ministry, then it is irrelevant to our discussion. It would still mean that Jesus absolutely refused the request for a sign during his ministry. It is also difficult to discern the original audience for this saying, although it may be the Pharisees and some of Jesus' other adversaries who asked him for the sign (cf. Mark 8:11/Matt. 12:38). It is doubtful whether this saying is a response to any request by a follower of Jesus because the saying responds to those who might be classified among this (evil) generation.

It may be that Mark intensified the negativeness of the response—the absolute negative seems to represent a Hebrew oath formula which does not exist in Aramaic.[96] In addition, we have the solemn asseveration formula, "Amen, I say to you," to introduce the saying in Mark but not in the parallels. It must be stressed that Jesus is being asked for an *oth*, or a legitimating sign from heaven. Schillebeeckx suggests that they were asking Jesus for his credentials as a prophet.[97] It also is possible that they were asking him to demonstrate his messianic status (cf. Matt. 16:1).[98] In either case, Jesus refuses to produce such credentials.

Let us stress that the request is for what is called in Greek a *semion* which, unlike the case in the Fourth Gospel, is a word never used in the synoptic

---

[95] Cf. Bultmann, *Synoptic Tradition*, 112, 117–18; Schweizer, *Matthew*, 290–92.

[96] Cf. MHT 2:468–69. However, if Jesus was responding to scholars or even lay experts in Torah, then he might have used an Hebraic oath formula.

[97] Schillebeeckx, *Jesus*, 190.

[98] Cf. Hill, *Matthew*, 220.

Gospels to refer to Jesus' mighty works or miracles.[99] What apparently is being requested is some flamboyant sign in the heavens or a gratuitous and visible miracle that would indicate Jesus' transcendent status. This request surely comes after Jesus had performed various miracles that already had been interpreted as to source and nature (benevolent or malevolent).

It is doubtful that Jesus had been requested to perform an *oth* if he had not already done something that raised the question of his possible transcendent status. Schweizer aptly sums up the possible reason for Jesus' refusal: "The demand for a sign spells the end of faith. Where guarantees are demanded, confidence has vanished."[100] Paul tells us it was characteristic of Jews to ask for signs (1 Cor. 1:22). Certainly there was a great craving for the miraculous and the visibly spectacular in Jesus' day. Jesus, however, does not see it as his task to meet people's expectations or even their requests, but rather to minister to their needs and to do the will of the Father.

How, then, do we evaluate Jesus' clear refusal to produce an *oth*? Apparently Jesus refuses not because he could not perform such an act, not because he did not think of himself in prophetic or messianic categories, but because the questioners were approaching Jesus in a manner that precluded seeing him and his work with eyes of faith. The philosophy of his interlocutors was "prove it to us — seeing is believing." Jesus, however, operated on the principle that believing leads to seeing and receiving miraculous help, among other things. The key element in this interchange is the spiritual condition of the inquisitors and the motives behind their request. They are part of "this evil generation" who are not willing or prepared to receive what Jesus has to offer.

There is no contradiction here to the narratives where Jesus heals upon request — an *oth* and a mighty work are not the same in any case. Nor is there any contradiction to the fact that Jesus performed certain prophetic and symbolic acts like cleansing the temple. Remember that when Jesus did the latter it was not due to anyone's demand, but because he felt led by the Father. Whatever else one may make of this saying, it has a certain similarity to the temptation narratives, where again Jesus refuses to produce a stupendous and gratuitous deed on demand.

Perhaps Jesus did keep his messiahship secret from those who were hostile and unwilling to approach him with trust and open-mindedness.[101]

---

[99] Cf. Fitzmyer, *Luke 10–24*, 935.

[100] Schweizer, *Matthew*, 292.

[101] Cf. Barrett, *Holy Spirit*, 120: "But he kept his Messiahship secret, and knew himself to be a Messiah destined for suffering and death; hence it might be expected that the Spirit which rested upon him would not be openly and entirely manifest. And so it was. The miracles were not unmistakeable portents. . . ."

In any event, this narrative says nothing against the thesis that Jesus had a transcendent self-concept.

EYESIGHT TO THE BLIND (MARK 8:22-26)

The study of extrabiblical miracle stories certainly enlightens the New Testament scholar in his or her quest to understand the biblical text. For instance, when one studies the exorcism narratives and finds that the demons are the only ones who recognize Jesus for who he is, the scholar familiar with the Hellenistic miracle material will not immediately conclude that this reflects the later confession of the church.[102] There are notable parallels from the *Magical Papyri*, e.g., *PGM* 8.13: "I know you, Hermes, who you are and whence you come and which your city is."[103] Such parallels suggest that the biblical scholar should not be so confident in thinking that the narrative has been significantly altered in light of later christological concerns. Such addresses to the exorcist or key figure in the story are common in these stories. In fact, B. D. Chilton argues that the demons attempt to bind or control Jesus by using his name, thus attempting to produce an exorcism of the exorciser![104]

The same caution applies to the story about Jesus healing the blind, which has no parallels in the Old Testament but some parallels outside it. The reason for considering the possibility that Jesus really did heal at least one blind person is that this type of miracle is attested (1) in the uniquely Markan material found in 8:22-26; (2) in the Bartimaeus story (Mark 10:46-52; Luke 18:35-43; Matt. 20:29-34); (3) in the Matthean summary in 15:30; (4) in John 9; and (5) in Jesus' allusion to Isaiah 35 and 61 in his response to John (Luke 7:22/Matt. 11:5). By the criterion of multiple attestation, at least some of this material likely goes back to a *Sitz im Leben Jesu*, and none of these stories appears to be more primitive than Mark 8:22-26.

The healing of the blind is found in the intertestamental Book of Tobit. At 11:10-14, Tobit is healed by what appears to be a magical ritual.[105] One may also point to the now familiar tale of the healing of a Roman soldier with an eyesalve made of honey and cock's blood (*Syll.* 1173.15-18).[106] Taylor also points to *SIG* 3.1168 which refers to a blind man who saw a vision of Asclepius the god of healing and "the first thing he saw was the trees in the

---

[102] It has always struck me as peculiar that some scholars can be so confident that the address of the demons to Jesus is simply a reflection of later church theology. Mark 3 makes clear that Mark is trying to exonerate Jesus of the claim of being in league with the Devil—would he or his source really have placed the only true confession of Jesus on the lips of Jesus' opposition? That could only help to support the case that Jesus was in league with Beelzebul.

[103] Cf. Hull, *Hellenistic Magic*, 67.

[104] B. D. Chilton, "Exorcism," 6:261.

[105] Ibid., 48.

[106] Found in A. Deissmann, *Ancient East*, 135-36.

temple precincts."[107] Consider also the famous story about the Emperor Vespasian curing a blind man with the use of spittle (Tacitus *Hist.* 4.81; Suetonius *Vesp.* 7).[108] These parallels show there was widespread belief that a miracle such as healing the blind was possible, perhaps through using a concoction applied to the eyes. As Dunn says, the more credence one gives to the extrabiblical parallels, "the less significance can be attributed to Jesus' miracles as 'proofs' of his uniqueness. But then Jesus himself never used them in this way."[109] But this comment overlooks one important factor. In Palestine, Jesus' actions would be interpreted in light of the Old Testament, and we already have seen that Jesus himself interpreted his healings in light of the Isaianic prophecies in Isaiah 35 and 61. The healing of the blind was not unprecedented, but when interpreted in light of the prophecies of the Old Testament about the eschatological and messianic age, they can be seen in a new light. We turn, then, to these key Old Testament texts.

In the promise about a coming day of redemption the Isaianic prophet says in 29:18, "The deaf, that day, will hear the words of a book and, after shadow and darkness, the eyes of the blind will see." At Isa. 35:5, after referring to Yahweh's intervention for vengeance and vindication, we are told that when intervention happens, "then the eyes of the blind shall be opened." In the address to the Ebed at 42:7, the Ebed is commissioned "to open the eyes of the blind, to free captives from prison." In some cases, such as Isa. 42:18ff., the reference is to spiritual blindness; nevertheless, there is enough here to suggest that in the messianic age there would be transformation of the physically and spiritually blind. This transformation is not ascribed to any Old Testament prophet; thus, if Jesus did heal the blind, it would have raised messianic questions. E. Hoskyns suggests that there may have been a tradition that physical contact by the messiah could bring God's salvation to an individual.[110]

As Taylor shows, the form of Mark 8:22–26 is closely parallel to the story in 7:32–37, the cure of the deaf mute.[111] This has led to the conjecture that they are variants of one original tradition. Given the striking differences in the story, however, we probably have an example of how certain kinds of miracle stories tended to take on a relatively fixed form as the tales were told and retold.

The following factors favor the authenticity of Mark 8:22–26. First, note that both Matthew and Luke omit this story, probably because they found it too difficult given that Jesus heals the man, not instantly but through a

---

[107] Cf. Taylor, *Mark*, 371.

[108] Cf. C. K. Barrett, *The Gospel according to St. John*, 2d ed. (Philadelphia: Westminster Press, 1978), 358.

[109] Dunn, *Jesus and the Spirit*, 74.

[110] Cf. E. Hoskyns, *Cambridge Sermons* (London: SCM, 1938), 172; but cf. the needful caution of R. H. Fuller, *Interpreting the Miracles*, 61.

[111] Taylor, *Mark*, 268–69.

process. Second, the statement about seeing men walking like trees may go back to an Aramaic original.[112] Third, that same statement suggests that the man was not originally blind. Thus, there is no attempt here to heighten the miraculous as in John 9, and the statement by the man in v. 24 opens the door to the suggestion that this might have been the curing of a real but nonetheless psychosomatic ailment. Fourth, Jesus lays his hands on the man twice. A later church redactor with a christological focus, much less Mark, would probably not invent the idea of a cure being partially effected by the first touch. As Taylor says, "The story itself warrants us in speaking of tradition, since its realism shows it to be anything but a product of invention."[113] The fact that Jesus takes the man aside also counts in favor of its authenticity because there is no tendency in this story to turn it into some sort of public demonstration.

Of all the miracles in the Gospels, this story comes closest to being a popular miracle tale. Here we see Jesus using a means of gradual cure, like a Hellenistic wonder-worker. Spittle was almost considered to be a medicine with curative powers.[114] In any event this tale, if it has not been cast into Hellenistic garb by Mark, which I would not rule out, suggests that Jesus was not afraid to be perceived as a popular wonder-worker if it meant he could help someone. While Jesus had power to cure, it did not always work automatically or instantly. Other factors affected the outcome, including faith, as other miracle stories indicate (cf. Mark 5:34; 6:5-6).[115] The conclusion of the story at v. 26 suggests that Jesus did not want publicity for what he had done in this case. This verse may be due to Mark's messianic-secret theory, but it is equally possible that it reflects Jesus' concern that the man be allowed to return to a normal existence without a lot of fanfare.

This story only takes on larger significance when seen in light of the contextual interpretation Jesus gives such miracles in his response to the Baptist. But if Jesus healed even one blind person, then his response to John must be taken as more than just rhetorical flourish. Jesus sets his miracles in their proper context, in a context his Jewish audience would recognize and understand. He sees them as a means of bringing in the long promised dominion of God that would bring blessing and healing to God's people. As such, there is an implicit claim to being the one who brings in the final reign of God—a messianic claim. What makes the healing of the blind unique is not the act in itself, but the larger Old Testament context in which Jesus interprets the act. Not only is such a deed promised in the eschatological age, but the act is set against the backdrop of the fact that no Old Testament

[112] Cf. M. Black, *Aramaic Approach,* 371.
[113] Taylor, *Mark,* 370; cf. Cranfield, *Mark,* 263–64; Lane, *Mark,* 284ff.
[114] Cf. Hull, *Hellenistic Magic,* 76–78.
[115] On the story of Jairus and the Jewess and its likely authenticity, see Witherington, *Women in the Ministry,* 71–75.

prophet, not even Elijah, performed such an act. Such a healing suggests that Jesus was more than a prophet.

UNSEASONABLE EXPECTATIONS? (MARK 11:12-14, 20-25)

The story of Jesus cursing the fig tree is thought by many scholars to be historically, if not also morally, problematic. Here is the only example in the Gospels of an intentionally destructive miracle. More than one commentator has concluded on the grounds of moral improbability alone that it does not go back to Jesus, being so out of character for him. Yet such an assessment ignores other Gospel traditions that relate that Jesus pronounced judgment on various people and even destroyed part of the temple. Thus, I conclude that Jesus was not always gentle and mild, but sometimes in both word and deed treated the theme of judgment; therefore, our text should not be thought historically improbable on the grounds of inconsistency with Jesus' known character.

The second major obstacle to seeing this narrative as historical is that it seems both pointless and mean-spirited. If it was not the season for figs, as Mark admits, then what would prompt Jesus to curse the tree? This objection ignores several factors. First, this action could be an acted parable, a symbolic prophetic act meant to visibly depict a larger, more important matter. It is probably not just an example of what happens when Jesus gets irritated with an unproductive part of God's creation. Second, if, as both Mark and the first evangelist suggest, this event transpired during Jesus' last trip to Jerusalem for Passover, then note that in late March and early April there are already leaves on the fig trees on the Mount of Olives and the green figs appear even before the leaves. While it is true that the fruit that is eaten from the fig tree is not harvested until autumn (hence Mark's correct comment that the first evangelist omits), nonetheless there is edible green fruit in the spring that Jesus might have expected to find, but did not.[116] Jesus may have expected to find the first spring crop of figs on this tree when he came to Jerusalem, but he did not, perhaps because the tree was sterile.

The proper matrix for understanding this story is twofold. First, the prophets frequently used the fig tree as a metaphor for Israel's status before God (cf. Jer. 8:13; 29:17; Hos. 9:10, 16; Joel 1:7; Mic. 2:12; 7:1-6; Isa. 34:4). Jesus apparently also used this metaphor (cf. Luke 13:6-9). Second, later prophets were known to have performed symbolic actions, and in some cases what they symbolized was coming judgment on Israel (cf. Ezek. 4:1-15; Jer. 13:1-11; 19:1-13; Isa. 20:1-6). Jesus' act becomes clear in light of these prophetic traditions: he was symbolically indicating the coming

---

[116] Cf. Lane, *Mark,* 401; M'Neile, *Matthew,* 302, says these figs are quite edible and some people even prefer them.

judgment on Israel. Thus Mark, who has divided up the original story into two parts using his sandwich technique, was nonetheless right to associate this act with another prophetic symbolic act that possibly hinted at the destruction of Israel—the cleansing of the temple.[117]

Some scholars suggest that Mark 11:12–14, 20–25 is a development of the parable in Luke 13:6–9. Against this is the fact that the parable is governed by the theme of delay in judgment—the tree was to be cut down if it did not produce after one more year.[118] In our narrative, judgment comes, if not instantaneously (as in Matt.), then nonetheless quickly and without opportunity to produce the fruit required. Jesus may have been familiar with the Q saying in Luke 3:9/Matt. 3:10, an oracle of the Baptist about coming judgment on Israel. If so, he may have decided symbolically to provide his own version at the end of his ministry when it became clear that Israel essentially had rejected him.

Probably, the sayings in Mark 11:22–25 should be seen as later additions to the end of the story, and so we will not treat them here.[119] Although I would not rule out Beare's suggestion that this story developed out of a saying of Jesus that Israel was like a sterile fig tree with lots of leaves and no fruit,[120] the offensiveness of the story speaks for its authenticity. Because there are no other miracles of intentional destruction by Jesus, there is no basis in the tradition to suggest that the Gospel writers would create a story that could be misunderstood to mean (1) that Jesus was given to fits of rage; or (2) that he used his power irresponsibly by expecting a tree to provide fruit out of season and then cursing it for not doing so. Thus, the arguments in favor of the essential authenticity of this story outweigh those against it.

According to the text, Jesus was hungry and looking for something to eat from a fig tree, but when he found no fruit, he made a solemn pronouncement, "May no one ever eat fruit from you again." The use of the optative here indicates a strong prohibition,[121] which is made milder by the first evangelist who uses the subjunctive. Thus, the saying probably goes back to a strong curse formula in the Aramaic. Taylor says, "The words are the equivalent of a sentence of death upon the tree."[122] Mark 11:21 indicates just such a curse formula in Jesus' words.

In view of the context, Mark indicates that Jesus meant this as a lesson to teach his close followers about the impending doom facing Israel and Jerusalem in particular. This gloomy oracle comes at the end of Jesus'

---

[117] Cf. pp. 107–16.
[118] Cf. Hill, *Matthew*, 294.
[119] Cf. Cranfield, *Mark*, 360, Taylor, *Mark*, 465.
[120] Cf. Beare, *Matthew*, 419.
[121] Cf. MHT 1:165; Moule, *I-B*, 136.
[122] Taylor, *Mark*, 460.

ministry when it was clear he had been rejected or ignored by the vast majority of Israelites. The story also may show Jesus' awareness of his own parallel fate—that the destiny of the nation and Jesus were intertwined. In any event, this significant act places Jesus within the line of those messengers of God who performed various symbolic acts foreshadowing the dark future of God's judgment against the people.[123] This text should not be seen in isolation from the various times when Jesus proclaimed good news, but it should make clear that his message was not simply the opposite of John's. Sometimes he could sound and act much like the Baptist.

CONCLUSIONS

Some evidence suggests that Jesus was to some extent an apocalyptic seer. Schweitzer was right at least in part. Yet the apocalyptic element is not central in the synoptic evidence about Jesus' deeds or even his words.

In regard to Christology, we have discovered indications that Jesus saw his baptismal experience as the starting point for a messianic career of sorts. Possibly we can consider it a point of confirmation about his identity and empowerment for mission. The primitive baptismal tradition in Mark 1 suggests that Jesus' sense of sonship contained a messianic component at least as early as his experience at the Jordan. This is not surprising given that other figures of Jesus' era claimed messianic status (e.g., Theudas and the Egyptian) and that some went into the wilderness and had dealings at the Jordan. We also find in Luke 10:18 that Jesus believed he was involved in a supernatural struggle with Satan, but that Satan's fall or defeat had been foreseen and was indicated by the exorcisms and perhaps other activities of his ministry. (This comports with the material on the *basileia* in Luke 11:20/Matt. 12:28.)

Our discussion of the miracles of Jesus focused on the christological interpretation of his mighty deeds. Both the exorcisms and the healing of the blind could have led to certain messianic expectations about Jesus. It may be that Jesus was cognizant of such implications when he performed these deeds, although his main motive for performing miracles was not to draw attention to himself but to help others. Much depends on how early connections were being made between the Son of David and exorcism traditions.

---

[123] Cf. P. Fredricksen, *Jesus to Christ*, 112–13, urges that we see the gesture in the Temple as likewise a symbol of destruction, the impending apocalyptic destruction of the temple. She rightly connects it with Jesus' ongoing proclamation of the coming dominion of God. Thus the sequence—proclaiming the kingdom, triumphal entry, threatening prophetic gesture in the temple, preaching in temple about coming destruction (Mark 13)—leads in her estimation to Jesus' downfall. While agreeing Jesus' stance and preaching were not directly confrontational with Rome (she allows he is a pacifist), nonetheless, his words and deeds about the coming kingdom clearly had social and political implications which got him in trouble (cf. 124–25).

The evidence of Josephus and other early Jewish sources indicates that these ideas were already alive in Jesus' day.

The concepts and expectations about God's *Mashiach* were rather fluid in Jesus' day, as de Jonge's studies propose. On the one hand, caution is needed when insisting that all Jews were expecting a national-political messiah. On the other hand, this seems to have been a prominent part of the expectation in some quarters. Nonetheless, the fluidity of messianic expectations would have allowed room for Jesus to chart his own course for his messianic movement. It was not necessary for Jesus to conceive of his task as confronting the Romans. Thus, that he did not confront the Romans does not necessarily count against the idea of his having a messianic self-understanding.

We also observed that Jesus expected his audience to respond to his works in faith and with repentance. This suggests his duty was more than just performing acts of compassion. Rather, he was calling God's people back to their source in view of the inbreaking dominion of God and of the potential bad news on the horizon for those who rejected the manifestation of that dominion in Jesus' ministry. The cursing of the fig tree shows that Jesus foresaw doom for those who did not bear fruit full of repentance. Jesus was willing to perform prophetic warning signs, but not legitimating miracles on the demand of his skeptics. The power of God must be used to help people. Jesus felt no need to make a demonstration of who he was; the words and deeds would speak for him if one had eyes of faith. Gratuitous miracles would have been an irresponsible use of the *exousia* God had bestowed on him. Jesus had a mission and a message to proclaim, and the response of faith was necessary to understand both what he was about and who he was.

Thus, our evidence about Jesus' self-image comes indirectly through his words and deeds. This indirection, or willingness to allow his actions to speak for him, seems to be characteristic of Jesus. J. H. Gill explains: "This use of 'indirect communication' serves as a mark of authenticity within the gospel narratives of a crucial feature of Jesus' historical posture vis-à-vis other persons."[124] There was a certain veiledness to all of Jesus' claims, but perhaps especially his messianic claims. The purpose of this indirection seems to have been: "to allow sincere hearers the freedom to . . . decide for themselves . . . the kerygma . . . must necessarily be sought and engaged in order to be discerned and appreciated."[125] We have seen this indirection in examining Jesus' deeds, but it is fully in evidence in his words, and nowhere is this more obvious than in the fact that characteristically Jesus conveyed his message in *meshalim*. But if a Chorazin or a Bethsaida did not

---

[124] Gill, "Jesus, Irony," 145.
[125] Ibid., 150.

draw the proper conclusions from his deeds and words, then it became evident that more was at stake in how one responded to Jesus than just receiving momentary physical aid. As we turn to discuss Jesus and his teaching on the *basileia, abba,* Son of man, and related matters, these factors should be borne in mind.

4

Christology and the
Words of Jesus

MOTIFS FROM THE sayings material, especially Jesus' teaching and preaching, tell us more than a little about his self-understanding. We will first consider the distinctive ways Jesus spoke and the ways he handled Scripture. In particular we will examine Jesus' rather unique way of relating Scripture to his own experience, his use of Amen as a means of confirmation of the truth of his own remarks, and finally his discussion of the Christ using a form of expression that might be called haggadic. This will be followed by a detailed discussion of *abba*, filial consciousness, and finally the Son of man material.

JESUS AS TEACHER AND PREACHER

C. H. Dodd once urged students of the New Testament to observe that although the Gospels were written under the influence of a "high" Christology, nonetheless they all represent Jesus as a teacher with a circle of disciples.[1] Actually, this should not be surprising. After all, there is an overlap in what a teacher, a prophet, or even a leader of a messianic movement would do in early Judaism; one commonality would be to convey a message that one felt God would have God's people know.

Doubtless, Jesus was perceived to be a great teacher by his intimates and others, and thus he was honored with terms of respect like *Rabbouni*, Rabbi, or just Teacher. The evidence for these forms of addressing Jesus is found

---

[1] Dodd, "Jesus," 53–66.

in various layers of the traditions (cf. Mark 5:35; Luke 6:40/Matt. 10:24; John 20:16). Furthermore, with only two exceptions (Matt. 23:5–7; John 3:26), no one else but Jesus is called by the term rabbi or *Rabbouni* in the Gospels.[2] In addition, it does not appear that the title rabbi or teacher had any christological weight for the earliest Christians during the period when the Gospel material was being formed and gathered. The idea that Jesus was a notable teacher is, therefore, an authentic motif.[3] Jesus was also perceived to be a teacher by those Jews who were not necessarily sympathetic to what he said and stood for, even in the period after Jesus died. *B.T.San.* 43a says, "Jesus had five *talmidhim:* Mattai, Naqai, Netser, Buni, and Todah" (cf. also *Aboda Zara* 16b–17a). Furthermore, the forms in which Jesus gave his message were thoroughly in keeping with how a Jewish teacher would teach — using *meshalim,* maxims, various forms of wisdom utterances, relying on various allusions to the Old Testament.[4]

Few would dispute that the major mode of Jesus' teaching was *meshalim,* and this in itself raises certain christological questions because considerable evidence from early Jewish and Samaritan literature indicates that many Jews expected the messiah to be a teacher of godly wisdom.[5] In chapter 1, we pointed out how Jesus made his teaching not only memorable but also memorizable by using both poetic and other mnemonic devices. We stressed that the disciples of Jesus probably passed on the Jesus tradition in the same fashion as other Jewish tradents passed on their masters' words.[6] The system of elementary education for children six to twelve (or thirteen) years of age was widespread in early Judaism, and in that context as well as in the synagogue, certain skills in learning and passing on valued religious traditions would have been inculcated.[7] The acceptance of these facts does not lead us to adopt either the view that Jesus set up some sort of formal school when he instructed and trained the disciples or the extreme form of what has been called the Gerhardsson theory. Nonetheless, Gerhardsson's approach is much nearer the truth and historically more believable in a Jewish setting than analogies with the development of pure folklore. Jesus was not a purveyor of fables or short stories as we know them, and even in the case of his *meshalim,* Jeremias, Dodd, and others have shown that

---

[2] So Pelikan, *Jesus through the Centuries,* 11.

[3] Cf. Riesner, "Der Ursprung," 503.

[4] Cf. Bultmann, *Die Geschichte,* 20–23, 64, passim.

[5] Cf. *C.D.* 6,11; 7,18; 4QFlor. 1,11; 11QMelch. 18–20; *Test. Jud.* (A) 21,1–4; *Test. Lev.* 18,2–6; *Ps. Sol.* 17.42–3; 18.4–9; *1 Enoch* 46.3; 49.3–4; 51.3; Memar marqa 4.12; *Targ.Isa.* 53.5, 11; *Targ.Gen.* 49.10; *Midrash Ps.* 21.90a; Riesner, "Der Ursprung," 505. This evidence is significant because there are various authentic Jesus *logia* where we find a connection between wisdom teaching and a person who exercises divine authority through his words and deeds. Cf. for example, Matt. 12:42/Luke 11:31; Matt. 11:16–19/Luke 7:31–35.

[6] Riesner, *Jesus als Lehrer,* 29ff.

[7] Cf. Borg, *Jesus,* 39–40, on Jesus' own training; also, see Riesner, *Jesus als Lehrer.*

considerable restraint was exercised by the Christian community in the ways they embellished or expanded such material.

As our discussion goes forward we will see evidence that Jesus' basic indebtedness is to Jewish wisdom, prophetic, and eschatological traditions, and to a lesser extent apocalyptic traditions (cf. Mark 13). Apparently Jesus was not and did not set out to be like a "teacher of the Torah" per se, passing along legal judgments or exegesis of various texts. Rather, he spoke and preached about the inbreaking dominion of God using *meshalim*, wisdom utterances, riddles, and other Jewish forms to get this message across. This is one of the reasons that Hengel sees Jesus as "a messianic Teacher of wisdom and the beginning of Christology."[8] Riesner remarks, "Jesus did not teach under the call of an external authority, but can lay claim [to expounding] the will of God directly."[9] Even if some of the famous antitheses of the First Gospel are a product of Matthean redaction,[10] some are not, and the form seems to go back to an authentic contrast or motif that characterized the way Jesus taught – distinguishing his own teaching from that of others and allowing his to stand on its own authority.[11] Borg rightly says, "Thus the language of Jesus indicates an awareness of a tradition-transcending authority, one from the mouth of the Spirit."[12] This may be true because Jesus believed that what he taught and preached was not something he had learned from Jewish teachers, but an eschatological revelation given by God. Properly speaking, the disciples had been instructed to pass along both his teaching and his preaching, and apparently this happened even during his ministry, if the sending out of the twelve during Jesus' lifetime is a historical fact.[13] It is because of this event that

---

[8] To borrow the title of Hengel's famous article, "Jesus als messianischer Lehrer der Weisheit und die Anfange der Christologie."

[9] Riesner, *Jesus als Lehrer*, 499; cf. Jeremias, *New Testament Theology*, 14ff.

[10] That at least some of the antitheses go back to Jesus has been shown by Guelich, *Sermon on the Mount*, 178ff; cf. Jeremias, *New Testament Theology*, 251–53; Bultmann, *Synoptic Tradition*, 134–36.

[11] Thus Guelich says (*Sermon on the Mount*, 185), "Neither Qumran nor the rabbis set their teaching over against that spoken to those of old, the generation at Sinai. . . . One never finds a parallel in Judaism for authoritatively setting a demand against the immutable Law. . . . Jesus does not merely 'hedge' one from transgressing the Law (rabbis) nor does he offer the true meaning of the Law (Qumran). Rather Jesus' demand actually transcends that of the Law. It is this uniqueness that sets Jesus' demand apart and speaks most forcibly for the authenticity of the antithetical format. . . . Furthermore, one must not shy away from the startling antithesis between *God has said to those of old/But I say to you* since here lies not only the key to the antitheses but to Jesus' ministry."

Berger, despite his skepticism about the authenticity of most if not all the antitheses, nonetheless remarks that Jesus urged his audience to make an absolute choice between his teaching and his way, on which hung redemption, and anything else. Jesus' approach required one to decide whether he or his opponents were false teachers or false prophets (*Die Gesetzesauslegung Jesu*, 590).

[12] Borg, *Jesus*, 47.

[13] Cf. pp. 132–37.

both Schürmann and Riesner have argued that already during Jesus' lifetime, there was the impetus and need to learn and pass on Jesus' words. Because of these factors, I am optimistic that we can learn something about Jesus from his teaching and preaching material.

Let us first consider what sort of teacher Jesus was, based on our understanding of Jesus' social context. We have already noted some reasons that Jesus does not fit into the category of rabbi. In the main he does not engage in disputations about the Scripture and in particular the Law, but rather directly declares the will of God for the present. There also are difficulties in seeing Jesus simply as a Galilean *hasid,* or charismatic teacher. For one thing Jesus does not seem to teach in the same fashion or with the same focus as someone like Honi or Hanina apparently did (and neither of them gathered disciples).[14] Perhaps here is the place to define *hasid* and to note similarities and differences between Jesus and the *hasidim.*[15]

The term *hasid* in early Jewish literature refers to a pious person, one especially known for his deeds. They are sometimes referred to as or associated with the "men of action" in the Mishnah (cf. *M.Suk.* 5.4; *M.Sotah* 9.15; *T.Suk.* 5.2). Figures like Honi the Circle-Drawer and Hanina ben Dosa were numbered among the *hasidim,* not only because of their piety but also because they did such remarkable things as healing people or bringing rain through fervent prayer. Safrai notes other features of the *hasidim,* for example, their rigor in observing the Sabbath (e.g., *B.T. Niddah* 38a, *B.T.Shab.* 150b), their insistence on wearing the ritual fringes (*B.T.Men.* 41a), their prohibition against killing snakes and scorpions on the Sabbath (*B.T.Shab.* 121b), and their noncompliance with all the *halakah* about matters of ritual purity (*J.T.Av Zarah* 22, 11b). Safrai rightly stresses, "The individual character of the *Hasidim* and of their *Halakhoth,* were not reconcilable with the general outlook of the rabbis."[16] They were both more and less rigorous than the Pharisees and the later rabbis in various matters,[17] and just because they were very strict in some matters does not mean we should place them among the *haberim.*

The *hasidim* were noted for being first to visit those in mourning (*Trac.Semahoth* 12), and for redeeming individuals who had been taken captive (*B.T.Shab.* 127a). It appears that the *hasidim* were pacifistic in nature, being ready for martyrdom (cf. *J.T.Ter.* 8.46b). They were noted for their protracted periods of fervent prayer.[18] The *hasidim,* then, were individuals especially dedicated to acts of piety and charity.

---

[14] F. G. Downing, "Social Contexts," 440–43.

[15] I am indebted to the detailed work of S. Safrai, conveniently summarized in "Teaching of the Pietists."

[16] Ibid., 26.

[17] Ibid., 33: "Among all the austerities practised by the *Hasidim* there is no trace of austerity in *halakhoth* concerning ritual purity."

[18] Ibid., 31–32.

On the surface there are parallels with the synoptic picture of Jesus. Did he not also perform miracles and various deeds of piety and charity? Was he not noted for taking an independent line from various of the Pharisees on several matters, sometimes being more strict, sometimes less? Did he not also disdain certain restrictions about ritual purity? Was he not a pacifist? Are there not traditions that suggest Jesus saw it as part of his task to redeem people (cf. Mark 10:45)? Did Jesus not visit and help those in mourning? Is there not a tradition that Jesus wore fringes (cf. Matt. 9:20)? There are enough parallels to prove that Jesus would have been seen by many as a *hasid*. Note that the *hasidim* were thought by some to be heretics and were investigated by the successors of the Pharisees (cf. *T.Shab.* 11.4). Much depends on whether the relevant traditions in the Gospels actually go back to a *Sitz im Leben Jesu*.

Differences also can be shown between the synoptic portrait of Jesus and that of the *hasidim*. First, the *hasidim* are said to bring about miracles only through fervent prayer; this is not the case with Jesus. Even a text like Mark 4:34 does not clearly mention prayer.[19] Second, none of the *hasidim* ever made messianic claims, even indirectly. The traditions about the *hasidim* do not even raise such an issue, whereas the synoptic traditions do so at least implicitly. Third, the *hasidim* are not said to reject the intrinsic "traditions of the elders," but are selective in how they follow them, unlike the case with Jesus.[20] Further, the tradition preserves not a single ruling in the names of Hanina or Honi or even Phineas ben Ya'ir.[21] The focus is always on their actions. This stands in contrast to Jesus at various points. Perhaps, most importantly, the much discussed passage about Honi the Circle-Drawer, where he is called a *ben bayith* (a son of the house), should not be taken to indicate a parallel sense of sonship to that of Jesus. As Safrai shows,[22] this phrase refers to a royal slave, the term "house born" or "son of a house" referring to a domestic slave. Honi is simply being called a slave in God's house. The same applies to the tradition about Hanina ben Dosa in *B.T.Ber.* 34b, where Hanina is said to be "like a slave before a king." The sonship material in the Synoptic Gospels does not even suggest such a connection. Thus, although Jesus may have appeared to be like a *hasid*, this category is insufficient to explain all of the arguably authentic material in the Synoptics. In particular, Jesus' sense of sonship seems unlike that of the *hasidim*.

---

[19] In Mark 9:29 and 11:34 Jesus is telling his disciples how they may produce the desired exorcism or receive the object of their longing—through prayer. It may, but does not necessarily, follow that Jesus would also have to use prayer to accomplish such things.

[20] Did Jesus also selectively follow the tradition of the elders? If he did wear tassels, this might be concluded, so we will not stress this point (although only Matthew suggests that he did, and this may be an example of Semitizing of the tradition).

[21] Safrai, "Teaching of the Pietists," 19.

[22] Ibid., 19.

Some scholars have sought to determine whether certain non-Jewish models of pedagogy might better characterize Jesus. For instance, V. Robbins suggests that Jesus might be like various itinerant preachers and teachers of the Hellenistic world who come and challenge people to adopt a new way of thinking and living.[23] Part of the problem with Robbins's examples (from Xenophon, Plato, and Philostratus) is that they come from either a much earlier or later period than the Gospel material, not to mention a rather different social context.[24] Furthermore, Jesus is not portrayed in the Gospels as "a paidagogos, or school-teacher, or sophist . . . [or] as a metaphysical philosopher, Academic, Peripatetic, Stoic, Epicurean, or any other such."[25] This drives Downing to the conclusion that the popular Cynic preacher is the closest parallel. Granted, there are certain parallels both in chosen lifestyle and, to a lesser extent, in message. Yet the teaching material in the Gospels frequently refers to Jesus' function as a healer, and some of the healing stories contain important teaching material. This is important, if, as Downing admits, there are no models or examples of a Cynic healer, and if Apollonius who is in some ways parallel to Jesus was a Pythagorean.

R. Horsley has pointed out the following problems with casting Jesus as a Cynic preacher or teacher: (1) the instructions given in the mission charge (Mark 6:8, cf. Luke 9:3; 10:4) make a clear distinction between what Jesus' disciples are allowed to carry and the usual equipment of wandering Cynics; (2) the Cynics appeared primarily in the cities while Jesus seems to have avoided the cities; (3) the Cynics saw themselves as called to be individual moral examples for other individuals, but did not feel called to form a movement, much less a community; (4) the Cynics had no community base, but were truly vagabonds and beggars, whereas Jesus apparently expects there to be a communal base of support or hospitality for his followers.[26]

Thus, there are no comprehensive paradigms or parallels to Jesus as a teacher—not even the Teacher of Righteousness provides a full parallel.[27] One needs to reckon with the fact that Jesus the teacher was, if not *sui generis*, nonetheless a complex combination of influences, and no one parallel model is adequate to categorize him. It seems clear that although there may have been Hellenistic influences on Jesus' teaching style, content, and lifestyle, nonetheless these were mediated to him through early Judaism, which had been affected in various ways by Hellenization. In short, the primary matrix for understanding Jesus as a teacher is the constellation of Jewish parallels. But if we admit that to some degree Jesus was

---

[23] Robbins, *Jesus the Teacher*.

[24] Downing, "Social Contexts," 443.

[25] Ibid., 445

[26] Horsley, *Spiral of Violence*, 230–31.

[27] So rightly Carmignac, *Teacher of Righteousness*, 127–31; also 5–15.

a unique teacher, we should not be surprised that even the Jewish parallels fall short of describing the nature of Jesus as a pedagogue.

JESUS' HERMENEUTICS

One of the more distinctive aspects of Jesus' use of Scripture is that by and large,

> neither Jesus nor his followers was concerned to produce an extended exposition [of Scripture] of the order of midrash, pesher, or targum. In its own way each of the latter three serves as a commentary on a book of scripture. But Jesus seems to have broken new ground, not in contemporizing scripture . . . but in making God's present activity, not the text, his point of departure . . . he did not use the circumstances of the present to explain the meaning of scripture; he rather used the scripture to assert God's meaning for the present.[28]

In short, Jesus used Scripture as a commentary on and means of expressing God's present activity in his ministry; he did not use the present circumstances of God's people or his followers to interpret Scripture. Perhaps the most obvious example of this phenomenon in a Q passage is Matt. 11:2–6/ Luke 7:18–23.[29] Here Jesus answers John's disciples by indicating that various Isaianic texts are coming to fulfillment in the present ministry of Jesus.

This example suggests Jesus believed that he was living in the age of Scripture fulfillment, or the eschatological age, and that he was bringing it about. His creative use of Scripture was prompted by his awareness of the *kairos*—that God was right now breaking into human history and fulfilling both God's promises and threats concerning redemption and judgment.[30] The fact that Jesus uses this sort of existential starting point in his understanding and handling of Scripture leads us to ask, Did he also see Scripture as a commentary on himself as well as on God's present activity? Did he use Scripture and scriptural language to explain, perhaps both to himself as well as to others, who he really was and why he had to be the person he was? In short, did Jesus begin with his own self-awareness and then go back to certain Old Testament texts to provide a commentary on that awareness? Did he see himself as in some sense the reality of which Scripture had only previously given verbal foreshadowings?

There are certain Old Testament texts to which Jesus did seem to turn to express or serve as a commentary on his self-understanding, for example, Dan. 7:13–14 (which seems to explain his use of *bar enasha*), the Daniel text

---

[28] B. D. Chilton, *Galilean Rabbi*, 187. Due attention should be paid to the last few words of this quote. The Qumran community used its own situation to interpret the Old Testament, but Chilton distinguishes Jesus' approach from that way of proceeding.

[29] For the arguments in favor of its historicity, see pp. 164–67.

[30] For detailed information on the Jesus' view of the *malkut* see pp. 192ff.

combined with Ps. 110:1, or Ps. 110:1 by itself. Various texts in Zechariah about the shepherd or Coming One seem crucial to Jesus' sense of identity or, at least, to his means of expressing who he thought he was. It is hard to say whether Jesus' self-understanding affected more the way he looked at these texts, or the texts themselves affected more how Jesus viewed himself and his mission. Likely there was influence by the Scriptures on Jesus' self-awareness as well as use of the Scripture to express current self-concepts.

After demonstrating Jesus' use of various passages from Daniel and Zechariah, among others, in ways that show that he thought these texts could be used to speak about himself and his mission, France concludes:

> In his use of the Old Testament Jesus stood alone among his Jewish contempo-
> raries, and that not because he took unusual liberties with the text, . . . but
> because he believed that in him it found its fulfilment. It is from this basic fact
> that all the differences [in Scripture usage] spring.[31]

For now it is sufficient to point out that Jesus' rather distinctive way of using Scripture should alert us not to be surprised if Jesus had a rather unique self-concept.

"AMEN, I SAY"

Sometimes one learns more about a person by observing how they speak, than by what they say. Whether or not this is true in Jesus' case, something can be learned about his self-image by the way he addressed his contem-poraries. To date no one has successfully cast doubt on Jeremias's study of Jesus' use of *amēn*.[32] Thus, for instance, K. Berger's efforts to explain a prepositive use of *amēn* as being like an oath particle in Greek (such as *naí*) have convinced very few scholars.[33]

Although there may be one other example of a prepositive use of *amēn* from before Jesus' day,[34] this has been disputed. In this particular case, it is plausible that the *amēn* concludes the previous line in the letter, rather than

---

[31] R. T. France, *Jesus*, 201.

[32] Cf. Jeremias, *New Testament Theology*, 35–36.

[33] Cf. Berger, *Die Amen-Worte Jesu*, to the comments of Hasler, *Amen*, and Fitzmyer, *Luke 1–9*, 536–37. The response of a linguist and Aramaic specialist like Fitzmyer is especially important. He says Berger's view is "almost certainly misguided" (537). Here it is crucial to point out that Jeremias had already rebutted Hasler's view that "Amen I say unto you" arose in the liturgy of the Hellenistic communities, or that Amen had lost its character of response already in Jesus' day. The usage elsewhere in the New Testament refutes the latter claim, and the fact that Amen is found in all our sources refutes the former—not all of our sources are derived from Hellenistic communities. Cf. Jeremias, *New Testament Theology*, 36 n.2.

[34] J. Naveh, "Hebrew Letter," 129–39.

introducing the following one.[35] Chilton's suggestion that the use of "in truth" to introduce certain statements in the *Targum of Isaiah* (37.18; 45.14, 15) provides a direct parallel to the Gospel use of *amēn* rests on several questionable assumptions.[36] First, we know that the *Targum of Isaiah* dates from a period considerably later than that of Jesus' lifetime.[37] Second, and just as important, this Targum is an example of later Aramaic, which differs in significant respects from middle Aramaic.[38] Third, the provenance of this document and of its form of Aramaic is not the same as the provenance of Jesus' ministry and reflects a different speech context. Last, Chilton simply asserts that *amēn* equals "in truth" in the Targum; he does not demonstrate this.

More critical is the fact that the prepositive use of *amēn* with a verb of saying is not found anywhere else in the New Testament other than on Jesus' lips,[39] and it is found there in all layers of the tradition, in all our sources: thirteen times in Mark, nine in Q, nine in M, nine in L, twenty-five times in John (as "Amen, amen").[40] In striking contrast is both the Old Testament usage where *amēn* is a word used to confirm someone else's oath or benediction or curse or blessing, and the usage of *amēn* in the New Testament outside the Jesus tradition where it always is used in assenting to another's words: 1 Cor. 14:16; 2 Cor. 1:20; Rev. 5:14; 7:12. By the criterion of dissimilarity as well as the criterion of multiple attestation, "Amen I say unto you" has the highest claims to being derived from Jesus, reflecting a unique speech trait of his.

David Daube shows that such a modification of the use of *amēn* "did not go beyond the natural possibilities of actual Hebrew speech" and thus would have been intelligible, but he provides no examples from before, during, or shortly after Jesus' era.[41] Daube shows that *amēn* in later rabbinic sources (cf. *B.T.Shab.* 119b, *San.* 111a) was taken as an abbreviation standing for "God faithful king."[42] But this seems to have no connection with the way

---

[35] Cf. Fitzmyer, *Luke 1–9*, 536. At the least, one may agree with Fitzmyer that the example cited is not prepositive.

[36] Chilton, *Galilean Rabbi*, 202. It is surprising to hear Chilton suggests *amēn* is a Hellenistic equivalent to anything. The word is clearly Semitic, and the Greek *amēn* is just an adequate transliteration.

[37] Chilton, *Galilean Rabbi*, 57, is forced to admit: "Our understanding of the development of the Isaiah Targum certainly does not permit us to assume that it was known to Jesus; even the earlier, Tannaitic framework only took shape a generation after his ministry."

[38] Cf. the discussion of *bar enasha* on pp. 236–38.

[39] Cf. J. Hempel, "Amen."

[40] There is no need to repeat all of Jeremias's detailed documentation. Cf. *New Testament Theology*, 35–36, although remember that in the Fourth Gospel the Amen is doubled.

[41] Daube, *New Testament*, 392. E. Schweizer, *Matthew*, 104, suggests that the prepositive use of *amēn* "probably derives from the usage of Greek-speaking Judaism" without giving any reasons or support for such an assertion. This is doubtful not least because we are talking about a Semitic idiomatic use of the word.

[42] Daube, *New Testament*, 390.

amēn is used in the Gospels, where it always introduces a significant statement, such as one about the coming *malkut* or the present work of Jesus.
Amēn indicates that Jesus is about to make a solemn and authoritative pronouncement, on the basis of his own authority.[43]

What, then, do we make of Jesus' habit of introducing his words with
"Amen I say to you"? It is insufficient to compare it to "thus says the Lord,"
although that is the closest parallel. Jesus is not merely speaking for
Yahweh, but for himself and on his own authority—something a prophet
did not do in any authoritative utterance addressed to God's people. He
affirms or confirms the truthfulness and authority of his own words in
advance. This strongly suggests that he considered himself to be a person
of authority above and beyond what prophets claimed to be. He could attest
to his own truthfulness and speak on his own behalf, and yet his words
were to be taken as having the same or greater authority than the divine
words of the prophets. Here was someone who thought he possessed not
only divine inspiration, like David (cf. below on Mark 12:35–37), but also
divine authority and the power of direct divine utterance. The use of *amēn*
followed by "I say unto you" must be given its full weight in light of its
context—early Judaism.

Consideration needs also to be given to what sort of sentences were introduced in this manner: usually those involving a statement about the inbreaking dominion of God or Jesus' work, that is, those things that Jesus
either proclaimed, brought about, or did. It was not just a way of affirming
the truthfulness of any kind of utterance. Dunn best sums up the significance of this phenomenon:

> His authority was charismatic also in the sense that it was immediately
> received from God, or rather *was the immediate authority of God*. This is the clear
> implication of Jesus' "emphatic *ego*" and "Amen"—a style of speaking express-
> ing a consciousness of transcendent authority. . . . When others in the tradi-
> tion in which Jesus stood expressed the immediacy of their authority, they
> prefaced their words with "Thus says the Lord." But Jesus said "Amen, I say
> to you." . . . It is this charismatic nature of Jesus' authority, the immediacy of
> his sense of authority together with the *conscious self-reference* of so much of his
> teaching, which seems to set Jesus apart from other men of comparable sig-
> nificance in the history of religions.[44]

In light of the uniqueness and context of this form of utterance, only a
person with a self-understanding that goes beyond the sort that arises out
of a prophetic consciousness would speak in this manner. Here one is confronted with a phenomenon without real precedent, nor did it spawn
attempts at imitation in the early church. This phenomenon strongly implies

---

[43] Cf. Hill, *Matthew*, 117.
[44] Dunn, *Jesus and the Spirit*, 79.

that Jesus believed he spoke not merely by inspiration and thus for God, but also with divine power and authority and for himself. This implies either a transcendent self-concept or self-deception or incredible presumptuousness. No ordinary or even extraordinary person, whether teacher or prophet, spoke this way.

The listener had to draw his or her own conclusions from this speech trait; it was not the same as a direct claim to divine speech and authority. Jesus apparently spoke in a fashion that could have led people to the conclusion that he was someone greater than even David.

DAVID'S SON OR DAVID'S LORD? (MARK 12:35-37)

There was considerable speculation in Jesus' day about the Messiah being a descendant of David. First is 2 Samuel 7, which had undergone significant modifications by the time the Chronicler got hold of it (cf. 1 Chr. 17:11, 14) so that a collective reference to "your offspring" became a specific reference to "one who shall be from among your sons."[45] Later is the prophetic material in Isa. 9:2-7; 11:1-9; Jer. 23:5f.; 30:9; 33:15, 22; Ezek. 34:23-24; 37:24; Hos. 3:5; and Amos 9:11. The precise terminology "son of David" is apparently not attested before *Psalms of Solomon* 17.23, but thereafter it seems to have become common parlance (cf. *B.T.San.* 98a; *J.T.Ta'an.* 4.8.68d; *B.T.San.* 97a). Attention also should be given to the Qumran evidence in 4QFlor. 1.11-13, where the promise to David is interpreted in light of Amos 9:11. (cf. *C.D.* 7.16; *B.T.San.* 96b), and to various Midrashim on 2 Sam. 7:1.[46]

There is some evidence of a Solomon, Son of David–exorcist tradition that may have been extant in Jesus' day, but it is uncertain to what degree this affected Jesus. Even where there seems to be a connection in the New Testament between "Son of David" and healing (cf. Mark 10:46-52 and par.), there is no connection with either exorcism or Solomon.[47] Matthew 12:23, however, is found in a context where exorcism is at issue, but there "Son of David" is redactional (cf. Mark 3) and of no relevance to our discussion of Jesus' usage of the phrase "Son of David." What this shows is that the Gospel writers are not trying to stress such a connection between Jesus and Solomon. Nevertheless, if such a tradition connecting exorcism and Solomon was extant in Jesus' day, then it is possible that Jesus' exorcisms would have raised certain messianic questions and expectations.

Mark seems to have preserved the more primitive form while the first evangelist has turned this brief passage into a conflict dialog with interlocutors. Daube presents evidence that we have here at least one question raised by Jesus that falls into the category of haggadah—the attempt to raise

---

[45] Cf. Fitzmyer, "Son of David," 118-19.
[46] Cf. Flusser, "Two Notes."
[47] Cf. Duling, "Solomon."

and resolve questions within or between nonlegal biblical texts where there seems to be a conflict. Here Jesus would be raising an apparent contradiction between the scribes' teaching on the "Son of David" and what Ps. 110:1 asserts.[48] This would count in favor of the authenticity of the saying; Jesus would be using a familiar technique to raise an important issue.

It has been urged against the authenticity of this saying that: (1) because there is no speculation about the messiah based on Ps. 110:1 in early Jewish literature, whereas this is the most used verse in the New Testament for such discussion, this must be a church creation; (2) the argument here relies on a play on words that does not exist in the Hebrew, but only in the Septuagint (*Kyrios/kyrios*); (3) the saying implies a rejection of the Son of David tradition in favor of a Son of man or Son of God as messiah tradition;[49] (4) here Jesus uncharacteristically takes the initiative.

Problems are raised by these arguments. First, although there was no known speculation about the messiah based on Ps. 110:1 in early Judaism,[50] there is no reason that Jesus could not have introduced this text into the discussion, which would account for its later frequent use in the early church. The form of the passage suggests that Jesus is introducing a new consideration that seemingly conflicts with usual scribal teaching about the messiah as Son of David. Evidence in a separate tradition (Mark 14:62 and par.) shows that Jesus probably did draw on Ps. 110:1 to discuss messianic matters.[51] If so, then this would support his usage of such a text here. It is more important to note that the way Ps. 110:1 is used here differs somewhat from its use elsewhere in the New Testament, which suggests this passage is not just another example of church usage.[52]

Jesus does not directly refer this text to himself; in fact, his indirect approach could even lead to the conclusion that he was referring to someone other than himself. Furthermore, the Davidic origin of the messiah was too well established for Jesus to dispute such a matter. Nowhere else in the Gospel tradition do we have any evidence that he did so. Rather, Jesus is showing the inadequacy, not the inaccuracy, of such an interpretation of the messiah. The point is that the messiah is more than a Son of David, not that he is other than a Son of David. Further, it is doubtful that the church would create a text that could lead to the conjecture, presently made by various scholars, that Jesus disputed the Davidic origins of the messiah.

Second, because Jesus is not reading from a Hebrew scroll but citing from memory, it is possible that he quoted this text in Aramaic, and the word play

---

[48] Cf. Daube, *New Testament*, 160–63.

[49] Cf. Bultmann, *Synoptic Tradition*, 66, 136–37; Hahn, *Titles of Jesus*, 103ff.

[50] That we have Psalm 110 in the psalter collection from Qumran makes doubtful the argument that Psalm 110 is of Maccabean date; it may even go back to the period of the monarchy. Cf. Lane, *Mark*, 436ff.; Childs, *Old Testament as Scripture*, 504–25.

[51] For a discussion on authenticity and other matters, see pp. 256–61.

[52] Cf. van Iersel, *"Der Sohn,"* 171–73, esp. n.3.

works in Aramaic as well as in Greek: *amar marya le mari*.[53] Mark uses the Septuagint version of the Old Testament text with minor modifications for his own audience.[54]

Third, there is no evidence that there is an attempt here to replace a Son of David messianism with a Son of man or Son of God one. In the former case, this requires our reading Mark 14:62 into this text; in the latter case it ignores the fact that the point at issue is the messiah being David's *kyrios* not God's Son.[55] Fourth, there is evidence in the Gospel tradition of Jesus taking the initiative (Mark 8:27ff.) and using the method of indirection to make his point (cf. Luke 7:22ff.). As Taylor says, "The allusive character of the saying favours the view that it is an original utterance; it half conceals, half reveals the 'Messianic Secret.'"[56] Here we have no clear dogmatic church identification of Jesus as either David's Son or his Lord, only a hint designed to prompt thinking on the subject.

What, then, is the meaning of Mark 12:35–37? Jesus is challenging the adequacy of simply viewing the messiah as a descendant of David. This may also imply a critique of the sort of Davidic expectation registered in *Psalms of Solomon* 17 and elsewhere in which the messiah is expected to be a political figure, throwing off alien rule. Jesus did in fact contest the alien rule of Satan over human spirits, but did not directly confront Caesar.[57] Taylor suggests that Jesus wishes his audience to consider the possibility that he might be David's Lord, and thus supernatural in dignity and origin.[58] As we shall see, in Mark 14:62 Jesus uses this same text to suggest that he will be invested with (further?) divine authority. Clearly, this text is a crucial one in Jesus' process of self-discernment and self-understanding. This text, when coupled with others, strongly suggests that Jesus did see himself in more than ordinary human categories. Neugebauer is right to caution that the text focuses on *messianology*, or the character of the messiah, and not *Christology*, or the identity of the messiah.[59] Nevertheless, the text while focusing on the messiah's character does imply something about his identity.

JESUS AND THE DOMINION OF GOD

The discussion of Jesus' teaching almost always begins and frequently ends with the debate about what the phrase *basileia tou theou* means. Most of the

---

[53] Cf. Fitzmyer, *Luke 10–24*, 1312.

[54] The article is omitted before *kyrios*, and *hupokato* seems to have been in the original text of Mark instead of the LXX's *hupopodion*. Cf. Metzger, *TC*, 111.

[55] Cf. Marshall, *Luke*, 746–47; Fitzmyer, *Luke 10–24*, 1312–13; Taylor, *Mark*, 491–93.

[56] Taylor, *Mark*, 493.

[57] Cf. pp. 101–4.

[58] Cf. Taylor, *Mark*, 493; Marshall, *Luke*, 746–49.

[59] F. Neugebauer, "Davidssohnfrage," 81–82.

scholarly world agrees that *basileia tou theou* was at the heart of and characterizes the teaching of Jesus.[60] Unfortunately, the unanimity ends there because no widespread agreement exists about what Jesus meant by this phrase and how it functioned in his authentic teaching. The protest is warranted that scholars "have internalized, de-temporalized, de-historicized, cosmologized, spiritualized, allegorized, mysticized, psychologized, philosophized, and sociologized the concept of the Kingdom of God."[61] Relatively clear, however, is that this phrase has something to do with Jesus' fundamental eschatological outlook and his belief in the intervention of God in human history.[62]

WHAT IS THE BASILEIA?

Despite the protest of Borg,[63] the attempt to reconstruct a noneschatological Jesus, or a Jesus who did not make eschatological matters important in his preaching and teaching, seems doomed to failure for at least the following reasons: (1) it requires the dismissal of all the material in the Gospels where Jesus speaks about the future coming of either the *basileia* or the Son of man; (2) it requires that one also dismiss as inauthentic numerous eschatological sayings that do not specifically refer to the *basileia* or Son of man (such as some of the collection of materials in Mark 13); (3) it requires a reductionist approach to the considerable number of parables that speak about such things as future judgment and future separation of the wicked and the righteous; (4) various symbolic and prophetic actions likely performed by the historical Jesus (cursing of the fig tree, cleansing of the temple) become difficult, if not impossible, to explain on the assumption of a noneschatological approach; and (5) the close association of Jesus and John the Baptist not only in actions but also in some of their messages must be ignored because it is difficult to deny to John an essentially eschatological message.

In contrast, I quite agree with E. Schillebeeckx that the Schweitzerian view of a Jesus who offered an interim ethic since the end of the world was immediately (or within a generation) at hand can be shown to have fundamental flaws.[64] Schillebeeckx asserts: "It nowhere appears from the texts

---

[60] With a few notable exceptions; e.g., cf. the interesting if eccentric attempt by Breech, *Silence*, passim, to read Jesus' authentic parables and teaching without reference to *basileia*. The irony of Breech's approach is he thinks he is getting back to a *Sitz im Leben Jesu* by reading his critically limited selection of material through the eyes of Sartre, Nietzsche, and Salinger, among others. It should hardly be surprising, then, that Jesus comes out sounding rather like an advocate of existentialism and the quest for authentic human existence in the face of a nihilistic world.

[61] Buchanan, *Covenant*, 55.

[62] Cf. the helpful treatment in Rowland, *Christian Origins*, 113ff.

[63] Borg, "Temperate Case."

[64] Cf. pp. 228–33; and T. F. Glasson, *Jesus and the End*.

that Jesus identifies this coming (of the kingdom of God), this drawing near, with the end of the world."[65] Already it is necessary to avoid confusion by defining some essential terms such as eschatology and apocalyptic.

Eschatology, strictly speaking, refers to the study of the events and things that conclude human history, or at least bring human history to a climax, however long the denouement after the crucial events occur. This term can legitimately be used, however, to refer to events that have to do with a messianic age that precedes "the end of the world," an age that in the relevant Jewish literature can last for a considerable period of time before the "end of the world" (cf. *Syr. Baruch* 24–30, 4 Ezra 7.29f., *1 Enoch* 91–93).[66]

Apocalyptic literature is not to be identified with eschatological literature *simpliciter*, but is a particular genre or type of eschatological literature. I find the SBL Apocalypse Seminar genre definition of apocalyptic literature, with D. Helmholm's further additions, to be essentially correct. *Apocalypse*

is a genre of revelatory literature with a narrative framework, in which revelation is mediated by an otherworldly being to a human recipient, disclosing a transcendent reality which is both temporal, insofar as it envisages eschatological salvation, and spatial insofar as it involves another supernatural world. [Normally] it is intended for a group in crisis with the purpose of exhortation and/or consolation by means of divine authority.[67]

On this definition it appears to me improper to continue to characterize Jesus' teaching as mainly apocalyptic in form or content.[68] So far as we know he never produced an apocalypse, nor did Jesus use the sort of narrative framework that can, broadly speaking, be called apocalyptic, nor did he in the main speak of visions or things that were happening in heaven or were hidden behind the visible tapestry of history. His concern was with what was happening to human lives during and through his ministry in the early first century. One may contend that there are some apocalyptic elements or fragments or even images in Jesus' teaching (Satan falling from heaven, for

---

[65] E. Schillebeeckx, *Jesus*, 152.

[66] Cf. Rowland, *Christian Origins*, 56–64.

[67] Cf. J. J. Collins, *Apocalyptic Imagination*, 1–32; and, D. Helmholm, "The Problem of Apocalyptic Genre and the Apocalypse of John," *Society of Biblical Literature Seminar Papers*, ed. K. H. Richards (Chico, Calif.: Scholars Press, 1982), 157–98.

[68] Charlesworth, *Jesus within Judaism*, 38–39, has recently argued for this same conclusion: "Certainly Jesus was not one of the apocalyptists. They were repeatedly exhorted to write down what they had seen and heard. Jesus wrote nothing. The apocalyptists were often scribes, influenced by Wisdom literature and preoccupied with encyclopedic scientific knowledge. Jesus was an itinerant teacher who, rather than debate esoterica, was obsessed with the need to proclaim to all Israel the approaching nearness and importance of God's kingdom." He goes on to point out that unlike the Apocalyptists, Jesus saw God as very near (Abba), was not world negating, and did not call down vengeance on Israel's enemies, but rather called people to love their enemies. This is not to minimize certain similarities such as concern for the oppressed and a belief that only God by intervening in history can finally rectify the difficulties God's people face in this world.

instance, or possibly some portions of Mark 13), but this material is certainly the exception and does not predominate.

As to whether Jesus shared an apocalyptic worldview, by which is usually meant a view that the world's end was necessarily imminent and that this world's structures were so inherently corrupt and evil that they were unredeemable, this assumption may also be disputed. Jesus proclaimed the good news about the possibility of redemption with the coming of God's dominion. In this regard Borg's critique of the end-of-the-world-Jesus is on target.[69] Jesus' teaching is most definitely given within an eschatological framework and has eschatological content, but this teaching only has some apocalyptic elements and images. There are disconcerting bits of teaching, such as Jesus' sayings about the family and its ongoing existence, that do not seem to fit such an outlook.[70] Also, Jesus' apparent refusal openly to condemn Roman rule or taxation does not comport with the usual apocalyptic vision of a world already gone bad and filled with evil, satanically directed empires that cause God's people to suffer. To the contrary, Jesus comes proclaiming good news that God is even now intervening in history. His dominant message is not a call to perseverance until some future time when God will act. Furthermore, the parables themselves fall into the category of wisdom, not apocalyptic, literature[71] and as such are like some of the *meshalim* of the Old Testament in form, although in content they often do have an eschatological message. Nor should Jesus' interest in *heilsgeschichtliche* matters be taken to indicate that his thought or speech patterns were essentially apocalyptic in nature. My point is not that Jesus' outlook and teaching contains no apocalyptic elements, but only that he cannot in the main be categorized as an apocalyptic seer.

Thus, I must reject N. Perrin's approach to the *basileia* material when he characterizes Jesus' use of the term as an apocalyptic symbol, or even to speak anachronistically as a steno- or tensive symbol.[72] Rather, as Hill has pointed out, the term *basileia* is not an apocalyptic symbol, if by that one means something that designates or points to something other than itself and so has a referent external to itself.

> In these terms "kingdom of God" cannot be a symbol because it has no literal meaning to point to a symbolic one. . . . Kingdom of God is not a symbol . . . it may evoke the larger myths but it does not symbolize them or anything else: rather it is something symbolized in the myth, in the narrative and in parable

---

[69] Borg, "An Orthodoxy Reconsidered."

[70] Cf. Witherington, *Women in the Ministry,* 11–35.

[71] Notice the absence of real parables in the canonical apocalypse.

[72] Notice the incorrect categorization of such material as *Assumption of Moses* 10 as apocalyptic material, as well as Jesus' teaching about the *basileia,* in Perrin, *Jesus,* 27–34. For a useful critique of Perrin's approach, cf. D. C. Allison, *End of the Ages,* 108–11.

as Perrin tacitly acknowledges when he refers to the Kingdom of God as the ultimate referent of the parable.[73]

In short, the phrase *basileia tou theou* refers to a concept or series of concepts or ideas; it does not symbolize these concepts. The phrase on Jesus' lips does, however, connote an eschatological idea—God's final intervention in history to bring it to its climax. This idea is expressed in both more traditional Old Testament oracles and also in specifically apocalyptic material in Daniel and elsewhere.

The debate about the *basileia tou theou* in Jesus' teaching has focused on two primary questions: (1) definition, and (2) its time element. J. Schlosser has sufficiently reviewed the literature and the various possible meanings of *basileia*,[74] so that we can simply summarize the various proposals here. First, *basileia* refers to the reign of God exclusively, and all texts that seem to refer to a realm can be explained by speaking of entering the sphere of the reign of God. It is generally emphasized on this view that it is God's dynamic activity intervening in human history, not some static concept of God's universal and perpetual sovereignty, to which Jesus refers.[75] Second, *basileia* refers sometimes to God's reign that is breaking into history in Jesus' ministry, sometimes to the realm over which God rules, depending on the text and context. In short, Jesus seems to have used this term in a multivalent way, although it is not meant to convey two ideas in any one text, rather, the single dominant sense changes with the context.[76] One must bear in mind that when a first-century person spoke of a king and his kingdom, "It was not monarchy in the modern sense of a ruler over a clearly defined territory. A kingdom was rather a sphere of power. Where we would say 'state' or '. . . kingdom,' the ancients said 'subjects of king (so and so).'"[77] Third, *basileia tou theou* is a circumlocution for God in strength or in God's activity or in God's self-manifestation in history.[78]

These three suggestions occur repeatedly in the literature and none are without their flaws. All of the major treatments on the subject are, however, in agreement and correct in pointing out that the term kingdom, which in English denotes exclusively a realm, is hardly adequate as a translation of *basileia*, especially in view of the Hebrew/Aramaic background (*malkut* in Hebrew, *malkutha* in Aramaic). Against the first definition there are too many texts where the *basileia* is seen as something that people enter, appropriate, or even seize, and this hardly seems to comport with the

---

[73] Hill, "Kingdom of God,'" 69.

[74] J. Schlosser, *Le Règne*, 47ff.

[75] This is Schlosser's own view, but it is perhaps fair to say that it is the predominant view today among New Testament scholars.

[76] Cf. G. E. Ladd, *Presence*.

[77] Ferguson, *Early Christianity*, 158.

[78] Chilton, *God in Strength*, 10ff.

concept of a reign, even a dynamic reign, or activity of God; how does one seize an action or activity? The second definition could be said to cover all the data, but then the translation "kingdom" becomes inadequate as the sole conveyer of the term's meaning. The third definition bypasses the whole question of timing by arguing that the phrase simply refers to God. But it will be noted that this definition runs into quite a few problems. For instance, the definition needs to be expanded to mean God in God's activity or God in God's self-manifestation, and when the matter is defined thusly, it appears to me that one is basically back to the first definition again with its liabilities. One needs to ask if Jesus really meant to convey the idea of people entering God, much less seizing God.

This criticism cannot be dismissed by arguing that what is meant is much the same as entering life (Mark 9:43) because life is not a being like God but a force or condition. It also is inadequate to begin talking about entering the sphere of God, coming into God's orbit or under God's control so to speak, for when one does this what the individual has entered is not God but God's control or reign, and so once again we are back to the same problems entailed in the first view. It seems to me that all the evangelists are quite clear that this *basileia* has something to do with events that transpire in time, such as exorcisms, not merely a timeless Being who is manifested or revealed through human history.

Consider, for instance, a saying like Luke 12:32. Here God is said to be pleased to give Jesus' followers the *malkut*. What is conceived of here is something the flock does not yet have, something that will come to them as a gift of the Father, but it is not identical with the Father or even with the Father in God's activity. Now whether or not this saying in particular is authentic,[79] it is characteristic of various sayings where God is distinguished from the *malkut*. It may be prayed for from God, but it is not the same as simply receiving God. To be sure, it is God who is involved, but the focus is on the dynamic action and its results, not on God per se in the phrase *basileia tou theou*. That God is *melek* does not mean we can simply identify God with the *malkut*. In other words, the phrase *basileia tou theou* is not simply another way of speaking about God's presence but rather the saving activity of God and its results. As a term that has to do with *Heilsgeschichte*, its temporal element cannot be ignored or simply dismissed. In view of the problems with all three definitions, it will be worthwhile briefly to review some of the relevant data again and to make a proposal of our own.

When one begins to search for relevant parallels to the Gospel phrase "*basileia tou theou*," neither in Jewish literature of the period, nor before the New Testament era, nor in many parallels in the Christian literature are they found in great abundance (cf. Acts 8:12; Rom. 14:17, 1 Cor. 6:9; 15:24).

---

[79] On which, cf. Schnackenburg, *God's Rule and Kingdom*, 190.

Nevertheless, the few examples that do exist seem instructive. First, the Greek word *basileia* seems originally to have meant the office of the king, or kingly rule in the secular literature (cf. Aristotle *Pol.* 3.1285b, 20). In other words, it could refer either to a position, a state, or an activity.[80] Similarly, the Hebrew term *malkut* and its Aramaic variant can refer either to kingship or kingdom—an activity, the exercise of an activity, or the realm or persons over whom that activity is exercised (cf. Exod. 19:6; 1 Chron. 17:14; 28:5; Dan. 2:44; 4:22; 7:27).[81] The Daniel references are especially important because in the context of the discussion it becomes obvious that *malkut* is a term that is seen as parallel to *saltan* which means rule, authority, or kingdom.[82] In the Qumran literature there are few parallels, but the usage of *malkut* in 1QM 19.8 should be compared to 1QM 12.16 (*T. Dan.* 5.13; *T. Benj.* 9.1; 10.7 also seem to refer to God's royal rule).

Of particular interest is *Psalms of Solomon* 17 which likely dates to before the end of the first century A.D. In this psalm we read: "And the kingdom of our God is forever over the nations in judgment. Lord, you chose David to be king over Israel and swore to him about his descendant forever, that his kingdom should not fail before you. But because of our sins, sinners rose up against us, they set upon us and drove us out."[83] What is especially interesting here is not only the parallel between God's and David's *basileia*, but also clearly David's *basileia* is seen as a realm, parallel to the term Israel, out of which God's people could be driven. Of course, the eighteenth benediction where the kingly reign/realm of God is invoked could also be cited, as well as the latter rabbinic parallels from Johanan ben Zakkai and others about taking up the yoke of the *malkut* (cf. *M. Berak.* 2.2; 2.5).[84]

Interestingly, the Hebrew, Aramaic, and Greek terms that we have been discussing have a range of possible meanings. Also, although in the biblical and relevant Jewish literature it is possible to surmise that the concept of God's or a human being's reign or dynamic activity is perhaps the dominant usage, the idea of a royal realm or sphere over which royal power is exercised is not entirely absent from the literature. As P. Pokorny has recently put it, "The kingdom of God is the kingdom of the God who is sovereign . . . and near . . . , but it also is a *kingdom*. The kingdom of God means not only the rule of God, thought of as the creator's rule over his creation . . . but a new social and, in a certain sense, a 'spatial' entity."[85] Thus, the term *basileia* could have meant either the reign or realm when used in reference to God, and perhaps the best English equivalent that can be used to refer to both

---

[80] Cf. Klappert, "King, Kingdom," 373.

[81] Cf. Kuhn, "Basileus," for discussion.

[82] Cf. Lattke, "Synoptic Concept," 79.

[83] I agree with and follow the translation in Charlesworth, *Pseudepigrapha*, 2:665–66.

[84] On the Old Testament and extrabiblical background to the concept of the *malkut Yahweh*, cf. Maag, "Malkut JHWH."

[85] Pokorny, *Christology*, 17, 27.

would be the word *dominion,* which can be used to refer either to a realm or to the exercise of royal authority or rule or even to an ongoing reign (have or exercise *dominion* over). In short, it can refer to divine activity or its effect or result.

THE COMING AND POWER OF THE DOMINION OF GOD

Although it is virtually undisputed that Jesus taught about the dominion of God, more than a little disagreement exists as to how to analyze his dominion teaching. Many would insist that we begin with the most characteristic or striking form of Jesus' teaching—the *meshalim.*[86] The problem with this view is at least twofold: (1) although the parables may be the characteristic mode of Jesus' teaching, they are certainly an indirect and metaphorical way of speaking on our subject, and thus it stands to reason that if there is a more direct and clearer teaching, we should begin with it; and (2) because of the opaque nature of the parables (since they are not simply allegories that can be easily decoded), christological questions concerning Jesus' employment of them are difficult to answer.[87]

Summing Up in Advance (Mark 1:14, 15) I think Chilton, Schlosser, and others are justified in their decision to focus first on the sayings material in order to discern what Jesus meant by *basileia.* Perhaps the most obvious starting point is to begin with the earliest Gospel's material that is relevant to our discussion. In view of the detailed historical-critical analyses by Chilton and Schlosser on Mark 1:14, 15,[88] we can summarize the probabilities concerning which portion(s) of this material can be considered likely to go back to Jesus. First, it appears likely that this material is meant to be a summary statement by Mark attempting to characterize the early preaching of Jesus (that is, this is a summary in advance related to the Markan unit 1:1–3:6).[89] Second, it does not follow from this that the unit is purely redactional because nowhere else is Jesus depicted as preaching a message that so clearly echoes John's (cf. 1:4 and 1:14, 15) and we know that the tradition was likely to distinguish Jesus from John as time went on. Furthermore, both F. Mussner and R. Pesch have characterized the phrase "the time is fulfilled" as echoing the prophetical herald material in the Old Testament (cf. Isa. 56:1, Ezek. 7:3, 12) and thus Pesch concludes we have here "an authentic word of Jesus."[90] Chilton has also demonstrated a close parallel to Mark 1:15 in *Targum Isa.*

---

[86] For instance, cf. Perrin, *Jesus,* 89ff. and his review of various estimates on the importance of understanding Jesus' dominion teaching by beginning with the parables.

[87] For an interesting attempt to do so, see J. R. Michaels, *Servant and Son.*

[88] Cf. Schlosser, *Le Règne,* 91ff.; Chilton, *God in Strength,* 29ff.

[89] Cf. Taylor, *Mark,* 165–67.

[90] R. Pesch, "Anfang des Evangeliums," 135; cf. F. Mussner, "Gottesherrschaft," 90ff.

53.1, which provides a plausible Aramaic background for some of the material in this verse.[91] Parallel diction to Mark 1:15 found in the Q material in Luke 10:9/Matt. 10:7 provides the confirmation of multiple attestation, which suggests this material likely goes back to Jesus. I thus conclude that although Mark 1:14 is probably Mark's editorial introduction to this saying of Jesus, there is no good reason to deny the authenticity of v. 15, at least as an authentic summary of Jesus' early preaching.[92]

The most striking thing about this saying as a whole is its focus on time — one era has been completed and another is now drawing near signaling the need to announce something about the *basileia*. Understanding the sense of this saying depends in large measure on understanding the main verbs in v. 15. The first of these, *pleroō*, probably renders the Hebrew *ml'*. The word in itself is not specifically eschatological, but it can certainly be used to that effect in eschatological contexts (cf. Tobit 14:5). It is possible, as Chilton argues,[93] that the Aramaic *slm* stands in the background here, but in any case the thought behind the use of this verb in Mark 1:15 is best illuminated by prophetic material such as we find in Isa. 60:22. There God is the one who, according to God's plan, will bring something about at the appropriate time, that is, the time God has designated. This verb suggests that Jesus discerns it is time for Jesus to begin actively pursuing his ministry of proclaiming the *basileia*, but this inherently implies that he thinks God is doing or is about to do a new thing, that one chapter of human history has finished and a new one is about to begin.

The second main verb, *heggiken*, has been the subject of enormous controversy. Again, we need to consider the Hebrew or Aramaic equivalent, which is likely to be *qrb* rather than *ng'* or *mt'*. Despite the vigorous arguments of C. H. Dodd,[94] *heggiken* normally refers to the approach or drawing near of something in time and space. In view of the other parallels of our saying with prophetic material, it should not be ignored that in the Septuagint version of Isa. 56:1 and Ezek. 7:7; 9:1, *heggiken* renders *qrb* and refers to the nearness of something. Notice also that this verb is used in the Septuagint when the nearness of judgment or of God is referenced (Deut. 4:7; Jer. 23:23; Isa. 41:21; 48:16; 51:5; 56:1). Thus, it seems to me that the conclusion of Black and Schlosser is more than warranted; without further support in the context of Mark 1:15, Dodd's translation "the kingdom of God

---

[91] Cf. Chilton, *God in Strength*, 93–95. I am not convinced by Chilton's insistence that this Targum provides the key for how Jesus would likely have used the Aramaic term *malkutha*. In fact, in J. F. Stenning's text, *The Targum of Isaiah* (Oxford: The Clarendon Press, 1949), at Isa. 53:1 *malkutha* is nowhere to be found.

[92] So Chilton *God in Strength*, 67ff., who provides many more detailed arguments including the analysis of word usage, which confirms that v. 15 does not represent typically Markan redactional diction.

[93] Chilton, *God in Strength*, 82.

[94] Cf., for instance, Dodd, *Parables*, 29–30.

has come" appears to be a matter of special pleading.[95] I hasten to add here, as does Schlosser, that it does not follow from this that Jesus is referring to a matter that is in the distant future; rather, it refers to something near at hand, something approaching.

This leads us to ask the reason that the verb *heggiken* is in the perfect here. R. H. Fuller has suggested the tense indicates that "the impending event, while most emphatically future, is nevertheless operative in advance."[96] But what would this mean? If the *basileia* is operative in advance, then in some sense it has come. In view of the use of *heggiken* in Rom. 13:12; James 5:8; and 1 Pet. 4:7, a translation such as "has drawn near" best captures the sense of the verb. In any event, the nearness proclaimed here does not preclude Jesus referring later in his ministry to the *basileia* as here. This is the case especially if this verse is no more than a summary of Jesus' early preaching, when there still seems to have been influence from his association with the Baptist.[97]

The coming of God's dominion requires a human response—repentance and faith. R. Leivestad has pointed out the following salient difference in the preaching of Jesus as opposed to the preaching of John. Although John simply warns of impending judgment and calls for repentance, Jesus calls for repentance and proclaims good news.[98] We are not told the content of this news at this point but clearly some sort of eschatological pronouncement is indicated, which may go back to Isaianic prophetic material (cf. Isa. 40:1ff.). It is also important to bear in mind a text like *11Q Melchizedek*, which likely demonstrates that the concept of bringing good tidings about an impending action of God for or among God's people was seen as one of the tasks of the *Mashiach* at least by some Jews prior to A.D. 70.[99] H. Merklein, in his detailed study of the use of the terms *metanoia/metanoeo* in the Gospel accounts of the words of John the Baptist and Jesus, also notes the differences between Jesus' and John's call to repentance.[100] John's call is always associated with the impending judgment on Israel. Not so with Jesus' call,[101]

---

[95] Cf. Schlosser, *Le Règne*, 106–7; Black, *Aramaic Approach*, 209ff.

[96] Fuller, *Mission*, 25.

[97] Cf. pp. 34–35, on Jesus and John.

[98] Leivestad, *Jesus in His Own Perspective*, 37ff., pointing also to the fact that Jesus apparently did not baptize but began a new phase of eschatological proclamation after John's demise or at least after his imprisonment.

[99] Cf. Aune, "Jesus' Messianic Consciousness." We must bear in mind that lines 15ff. of 11Q Melchizedek consist of a pesher on Isa. 52:7, in which good tidings is what God's messenger is sent to proclaim.

[100] Merklein, "Die Umkehrpredigt."

[101] Although Mark 1:14–15 may indeed be a summary of Jesus' early preaching, we have other evidence that repentance was part of that preaching. From Q we may note Luke 10:13–15 (and par.) and also 13:3, 5, which comes from Luke's special source (cf. Luke 11:31f.). Various of the parables could also be cited; cf. Merklein, "Die Umkehrpredigt," 140–41.

which is associated with Jesus' bringing in the dominion of God through words and deeds (cf. Luke 10; 13; 15; esp. 11:31–32).[102]

What, then, may we deduce from this summary about Jesus' view of himself? It appears clear not only because he picks up where John left off but also from the content of Mark 1:15 that Jesus sees himself as an eschatological messenger of God, perhaps even the final such messenger, who foresees and foretells the approaching intervention of God in the midst of God's people. This message calls for a change in the people of God in preparation for God's intervention, but it also proclaims that there is good news to be grasped and accepted.

The Finger of God (Luke 11:20/Matt. 12:28) Our second critical saying is found in Luke 11:20/Matt. 12:28. It is probable, in view of the significant role of the Holy Spirit in early Christian theology, that Luke preserved the earlier form of this saying referring to the finger of God (in contrast to the Spirit) as the agent of exorcism. A textual problem, however, exists in the Lukan form of this Q saying: should the *egō*, which precedes the verb *ekballo* in p75 B and various other witnesses, be taken as original, or is it an addition based on the Matthean parallel (or possibly on the basis of v. 19)? In view of early manuscript support for the inclusion of *egō*, it should probably be accepted as an original part of the text, although some important manuscripts such as p45 apparently omit it.

That Jesus was an exorcist, and well-known at that, is certainly one of the most incontestable facts about his ministry,[103] although significant debate exists as to what sort of cure exorcism actually is (a healing of emotional or mental illnesses? an actual casting out of supernatural entities?). Our purpose is not to debate this issue, but only to clarify in what sense he was a healer of the human spirit as well as of the human body. The fact of Jesus' acts of exorcism is attested in nearly all layers of tradition, and also by allusions to exorcism in sayings, narratives, and summaries (e.g., Acts 10:38; Mark 1:21–28 and par; Mark 3:22b and par.; Luke 10:20 and par.). Furthermore, there is little evidence that exorcism was characteristic of the ministry of early Christians (only Acts 8:7 and 16:16–18) and is notably absent from the Epistles and also from the Fourth Gospel.

Schlosser's detailed, critical study has verified both the independence and the authenticity of the saying in Luke 11:20. Furthermore, this conclusion, which was already accepted by the majority of scholars, has been reinforced recently by J. D. G. Dunn.[104] Although this saying likely had a setting other than the one given to it in Q, the saying probably arises out of controversy over Jesus' exorcisms, such as in Mark 3:20–30. Here, then, we

---

[102] Ibid., 142–43.
[103] Cf. Twelftree, "Ekballo," 363–68.
[104] Cf. Schlosser, *Le Règne*, 127ff.; Dunn, "Matthew 12:28/Luke 11:20."

seem to have a statement by Jesus intended to give his own interpretation of the significance of his exorcisms. Several aspects of the saying call for detailed analysis.

First, the anthropomorphism "the finger of God" likely alludes to the narrative about the third plague in Exod. 8:15 (cf. Deut. 9:10; Exod. 31:18; Ps. 8:3). The phrase itself seems to convey a sense of the magnitude of the actor's power—this act is performed by merely lifting a finger. As Dunn suggests, the deliberate use of the phrase "finger of God" could also imply a "claim to an action of epochal significance equivalent to the deliverance from Egypt . . . (cf. Dan. 3:10)."[105] Fitzmyer suggests that Jesus is contrasting his power with that of magicians; Jesus performs these exorcisms without the aid of such things as charms, rings, incantations.[106] A significant flaw in M. Smith's portrayal of Jesus as a magician is that he fails to weigh the many points of discontinuity between Jesus and Hellenistic wonder-workers against the few points of similarity.[107] Smith also fails to define adequately what qualifies one to be called a magician. If by the term he means one who performs magical incantations, spells, or other magical rites, or one who summons the powers of darkness to perform miracles, then there is little or no evidence to support such a view of Jesus, and various traditions deliberately dispute any connection of Jesus with anything or anyone diabolical (cf. Luke 11:14–19 and par). In summary, the reference to God's finger distinguishes how Jesus operates from the ways of those who rely purely on prayer or invoke the name of God or some other source of power or authority to perform exorcisms.[108]

Second, the meaning of the verb *ephthasen* is disputed, but here it would seem Dodd has the better interpretation.[109] For one thing, *heggiken* and *ephthasen* are not synonyms.[110] The verb *ephthasen* should be seen as a true aorist here, precisely because Jesus is making a statement about what is already true about the *basileia* as a result of what has already happened during Jesus' ministry-exorcisms.[111] The timing of the exorcism and the *basileia* need to be seen as parallel or the analogy loses its compelling force. Jesus is saying that because he is performing exorcisms, something is now true of the *basileia*—it has come in some sense. R. Schnackenburg comments,

---

[105] Dunn, "Matthew 12:28/Luke 11:20," 40.

[106] Fitzmyer, *Luke 10–24*, 922.

[107] Cf. Smith, *Jesus the Magician*, passim; and the careful critique by Goergen, *Ministry of Jesus*, 173–75 and notes.

[108] Cf. Twelftree, "Ekballo," 384–85; also 393: "His uniqueness as an exorcist may be as simple, though as profound, as his seeing his exorcisms as empowered by God, through the eschatological Spirit, yet depending on his own personal resources."

[109] Dodd, *Parables*, 44; and his article, "Kingdom of God."

[110] Cf. Kümmel, *Promise and Fulfilment*, 105–9.

[111] Note that some of the Syrian witnesses use the root *grb* at Luke 11:20 and Matt. 12:28.

"Accordingly, the reign of God is seen as an effective power (not as a kingdom, as an institution, nor as a purely interior reality)."[112]

Third, the *eph humas* needs to be analyzed. The presence of this phrase supports what we have just said because it suggests that something has already happened in regard to the dominion that Jesus' hearers could grasp or at least observe. In some sense it has come upon them! The exorcisms of Jesus are evidence that the dominion of God is already breaking into their midst. Probably, as Fitzmyer suggests, *eph humas* here means "unto you," that is, to the present audience, not to some future one.[113]

This text causes problems, on the one hand, for those like Fuller who wish to interpret all of Jesus' sayings as referring consistently to an imminent but not yet present *basileia*.[114] On the other hand, texts like Mark 1:15 cause dilemmas for those who wish to insist upon a strictly realized viewpoint.[115] It is much better to admit that the data do not fit neatly into one category or the other. This is hardly surprising, given how Jewish eschatological literature juxtaposes present and future in various ways. It is possible to construe this as a simple transition in time, that is, Luke 11:20 presupposes that Jesus has already engaged in his ministry and some exorcisms as a part of that work, whereas Mark 1:15 seems to be a comment on Jesus' early proclamation. What Mark 1:15 meant was that God's dominion was near at hand, at the door; what this text asserts is that it has arrived. These two statements dovetail nicely, as Schlosser has argued,[116] if we take seriously that Mark 1:15 means the dominion is very near and that Luke 11:20 comes from later in the ministry.

What may we deduce about Jesus' view of himself from this text? First, Jesus sees himself not merely as a herald but as one who brings in the dominion of God. This is more than a simple prophetic role. Notice that the text says Jesus himself (the *ego*, if original, is emphatic) performs these miracles "by the finger of God." This at least means by God's power, as the use of *pneuma* in the Matthean form of the saying interprets, but it is not impossible that more is being suggested. In the Old Testament usage of the phrase "finger of God," God alone performs acts with God's finger or fingers. God's human representatives such as Moses are not said to do so. This suggests a close association between Jesus and God—that Jesus saw himself as God's eschatological *shaliach*, or one endowed with the full power and authority of the Divine in order to bring about God's eschatological reign. Although there were many other exorcists, so far as we know Jesus is the only one to interpret his exorcisms as a manifestation of the inbreaking

---

[112] Schnackenburg, *God's Rule and Kingdom*, 124.
[113] Fitzmyer, *Luke 10–24*, 922.
[114] Cf. Fuller, *Mission*, 26.
[115] Cf., for instance, the attempt to revive Dodd's view in Goergen, *Ministry of Jesus*, 146ff.
[116] Cf. Schlosser, *Le Règne*, 128ff.

final dominion of God. This interconnection of eschatology and exorcism in Jesus' interpretation of these cures is distinctive.[117] Havener puts it this way: "The implications of these few words are enormous, for Jesus is claiming that the exorcisms which he performs are themselves manifestations of the kingdom of God already present. In other words, the end time has begun, and Jesus' ministry shows forth the presence of God's reign."[118] If one closely evaluates texts (such as Isa. 24:21–22; *1 Enoch* 10.4ff.; *Jub.* 23.39; 1QS 4.18–19; *T.Mos.* 10.1; *T.Levi* 18.12; *T.Jud.* 25.3; and Rev. 20:2–3), then part of the Jewish expectation was that Satan would be vanquished at the end of the age. Jesus, then, would be claiming in a saying such as Luke 11:20 (which coheres well with other similar synoptic material; cf. Mark 3:20ff.) that he was bringing in the final eschatological age. This was evidenced by his bringing about the demise of Satan's control over human lives.

"On Earth" (Luke 11:2/Matt. 6:10)   As almost all scholars admit,[119] the Lord's Prayer in some form probably goes back to Jesus himself. The petition about the *basileia* is an adaptation of the traditional Jewish prayer known as the *Kaddish,* which actually is more of an Aramaic doxology than a full prayer.[120] The part that concerns us reads: "May he establish his *malkutha* in your lifetime and in your days and in the lifetime of all the house of Israel speedily and soon." Luke 11:2/Matt. 6:10 is much more abbreviated than this, but in each case we have a prayer petition in which the *basileia* is envisioned as something that comes in the future. It probably read in the Aramaic original *tete malkutak.*[121] This is a prayer for God's final eschatological dominion or rule to break into history and set things right.

Two points about this petition are germane to our discussion. First, here the *malkutha* is something that God brings in, and thus is the object of prayer. It is not something an ordinary mortal can set up or establish, so one can only pray for its coming. But if this is the case, how striking becomes the saying we have just investigated about Jesus bringing the *malkutha* through his miraculous actions. Again, it seems clear that Jesus sees God working directly in and through him to establish God's final *basileia.* Yet, if Jesus believed this about himself, why must this dominion still be prayed for? A dimension of the *basileia* is presumably neither on the scene nor said to be immediately appearing nor just on the horizon.

It is an old, but perhaps still useful, distinction that when Jesus spoke about the *basileia* as something present or near he referred to the activity or reign of God breaking into human history, but when he spoke of entering

[117] Cf. Dunn, "Matthew 12:28/Luke 11:20," 40.
[118] Havener, *Q—The Sayings of Jesus,* 51.
[119] Cf. Perrin's list of the undisputedly authentic sayings of Jesus, in *Jesus,* 41.
[120] Cf. Beasley-Murray, *Jesus and the Kingdom,* 147.
[121] Cf. Jeremias, *New Testament Theology,* 196.

the *basileia* he envisioned the *basileia* as a realm on earth that would appear only sometime in the future. This would comport well with the Beatitudes that speak of inheriting the earth. It also fits most or all of the synoptic entrance sayings, and furthermore it comports with the few sayings we have outside the Synoptics that focus on the inheriting or being worthy of the *basileia* (cf. John 3:5; Acts 14:22; 1 Cor. 6:10; Eph. 5:5; Gal. 5:21; 2 Thess. 1:5; 2 Pet. 1:11; Rev. 11:15).

Second, as we have already stressed, here the *basileia* is seen as purely future. In light of the fact that in Jewish literature apart from the *Kaddish* prayer and in early Christian literature, there is no talk about a coming of a *basileia* as we find it in Luke 11:2/Matt. 6:10, then this idea must surely be seen as going back to Jesus.

Of the many entrance sayings in the Synoptic Gospels, the vast majority of them, whatever their authenticity, clearly refer to a future entrance into the *basileia*, although how far distant in the future is not made clear (cf. Matt. 5:20; 7:21; Mark 10:15 and par.; Mark 10:23 and par.). Mention may also be made of Mark 9:43–47 (and par.), although there the subject is entering life, still that entering clearly is seen as something that happens later—after one has severed oneself from whatever causes one to sin. Again, one may point to Matt. 16:19, and whether or not it is authentic, it certainly seems to imply that entering the *basileia* is something that was not yet happening. In Luke 12:32 the flock is promised the (future) kingdom. There are various allusions in some of the parables that may be of relevance here (cf. Matt. 7:13–14; 25:10, 21, 23, 30) but they do not suggest any different conclusion.

Luke 11:52, if it is not a variant of Matt. 23:13, really does not bear directly on the question because the *basileia* is not specifically mentioned. It can be argued that entering into knowledge equals entering the *basileia*, but this is difficult to prove so we should probably base no conclusions on this text. This leaves us with the two Matthean logia—23:13 and 21:31. It must be said that neither of these sayings clearly states that someone is currently entering the *basileia*. Thus, for instance, in 21:31 the verb *proagousin* can be taken to mean either "take your place in" (Hill) or "are ahead of you" (M'Neile), in which case we are dealing with a matter either of who obtains a place or of who comes before the other in line to enter the *basileia*.[122] If this is a saying of Jesus, then M'Neile is likely right that the present-tense verb here represents a timeless Aramaic participle, in which case it could just as easily refer to a future as to a present entering.[123] The same may be said for the use of *eiserchomai*, which is in the present tense in Matt. 23:13.[124] It may be noted that the following participle likely makes reference to those "trying to enter." The Pharisees do not allow those to enter who are trying to do so.

[122] Cf. Hill, *Matthew*, 31; and M'Neile, *Matthew*, 306.
[123] M'Neile, *Matthew*, 306.
[124] So ibid., 333.

This text, then, could be said to imply that those people might otherwise enter the *basileia* in the present, but more likely the reference is to a future entering as a result of such things as present efforts and obedience. This corresponds with those sayings that speak of feasting in the kingdom with Abraham in the future (cf. Matt. 8:11–12), and with what appears likely to be an authentic utterance of Jesus about his drinking the fruit of the vine later in the coming dominion of God (Mark 14:25).[125]

I thus conclude that no actual texts speak about entering the *basileia* during Jesus' ministry. All the entrance texts refer to a future entrance, although how distant in the future is not said. It may be added that this language comports with the general Jewish eschatological perspective about the *basileia* of God as something that happens in the future.

It has been noted that the sayings about the future of the *basileia* and the future role of the Son of man do not overlap. This observation is fundamentally a sound one, and it follows that it is likely to be difficult to determine from future *basileia* sayings anything clear about Jesus' conception of himself. This conclusion seems warranted except in two regards. First, Mark 14:25 seems to suggest not only that Jesus envisioned participating in that final dominion of God but also, if we read this saying in conjunction with a saying like Matt. 8:11–12, that he would do so with the kind of people to whom he seems to have ministered during his ministry. This does not clarify what the correlation is between involvement in Jesus' ministry or responding positively to Jesus' ministry now and participating in the *basileia* later, but there seems to be some connection. Perhaps this conjecture finds confirmation in a saying such as the Q logion, Luke 12:8/Matt. 10:32. Second, if Mark 14:25 is any guide, then it appears that Jesus at least envisioned participation in the dominion after his death (cf., for instance, Luke 23:43).

THE MYSTERY OF THE MESHALIM

Among New Testament scholars it is almost axiomatic that Jesus' *meshalim* (parabolic discourses) are not about himself but, by and large, about the *basileia*.[126] Thus, discovering Jesus' self-understanding will necessarily be a matter of inference from what certain parables may imply. Yet, several scholars are convinced, in spite of what we have just said, that this sort of inquiry is by no means fruitless. Thus, for instance, J. D. Crossan is persuaded that the parables "express and they contain the temporality of Jesus' experience of God; they proclaim and they establish the historicity of Jesus' response to the Kingdom." Indeed he is even willing to call the parables the "ontological ground" of the life of Jesus, and thus the cause not the effect

---

[125] Even Sanders is willing to grant the authenticity of this saying in some form, in *Jesus and Judaism*, 147ff.

[126] Cf. Goergen, *Ministry of Jesus*, 217.

of his other words and deeds.[127] Although this may be a bit hyperbolic, if there is any truth in Crossan's assertion it is worth exploring the matter further. A recent study has concluded that "Jesus the parabler is intimately related to the parables he told. . . . Any teller is implicitly involved in his tales, and some tellers play out their tales. Jesus belongs to the latter category."[128] A significant effort to pursue these insights at length has been undertaken by J. Ramsey Michaels who is convinced that the parables do convey some clues to understanding both Jesus' own religious experience of God and his vision of the one he called *abba*.[129]

With the application of various new methods of literary criticism to the parables, such as structuralism or the sort of analysis pioneered by A. N. Wilder, R. Funk, J. Breech, or D. Crossan, New Testament scholarship entered a new era. No longer was the old approach, which followed the lead of A. Jülicher by deleting allegorical elements and finding the one main point of a parable, seen as adequate. In fact, rather widespread agreement exists that the literary creations commonly called parables actually fall into three different but related categories: (1) the similitude, which is seen essentially as a simile; (2) the parable, which can be called an extended metaphor; and (3) the example story, which is more an extended narrative than just a comparison and is often followed by an application. The major difference between similitude and parable appears to be not length so much as focus: a similitude describes typical or ordinary occurrences, whereas a parable describes something unusual (indeed, unlikely if not impossible, humanly speaking) happening in the midst of the real and ordinary. Roughly, the similitudes appear to be deductions based on real life and fall rather strictly into the category of wisdom literature, but the parables proper seem to be constructed and based on an assumption about the nature of how God works in human history or at least on the basis of God's divine plan.[130]

If, however, we consider all three types of parabolic literature together under the general term *meshalim* (which can refer to everything from a simple proverb to a narrative like that of the Good Samaritan), then Dodd's definition still seems helpful to explain how these sorts of creations function: "At its simplest, the parable is a metaphor or simile drawn from nature

---

[127] Crossan, *In Parables*, 32–33.

[128] Cf. Chilton and McDonald, *Ethics of the Kingdom*, 70.

[129] Michaels, *Servant and Son*, passim.

[130] Crenshaw, "Determining," has made some helpful distinctions. He notes at least four different kinds of wisdom-juridical, natural, practical, and theological, and he claims that each has a distinct *Sitz im Leben*. Jesus seems in the main to have exhibited what Crenshaw calls family/clan wisdom, "the goal of which is mastering life," and perhaps also scribal wisdom, "the goal being education for all, the stance dogmatico-religious, and the method dialogico-admonitory" (130). He does not seem primarily to have used what has been called nature wisdom. It should also be noted that wisdom literature is not characterized by a nationalistic fervor, like one finds in Esther (141). This suggests that Jesus may have chosen a wisdom mode of speech because he wished to speak in a manner that did not raise nationalistic expectations.

or common life, arresting the hearer by its vividness or strangeness and leaving the mind in sufficient doubt about its precise application to tease it into active thought."[131] Hence, the meaning of the parable will not always be immediately apparent, especially in our case where we already are admittedly looking for clues to a subject on whom the parables do not seem to focus—Jesus himself. But hints seem to be given, especially in four sorts of *meshalim:* (1) those that refer to the matter of reversal, which seems to have been a major theme in Jesus' teaching and preaching; (2) those that illuminate Jesus' religious experience; (3) the parables and sayings that include metaphors and images suggesting Jesus applied Old Testament images for God to himself during his ministry; and (4) genuine parables that seem to have reflected on Jesus' view of his ministry and how it was being received.

First, in view of the reversal parables Schillebeeckx maintains:

> The fact is, a parable turns around a *scandalizing* centre, at any rate a core of paradox and novelty. A parable often stands things on their head; it is meant to break through our conventional thinking and being. A parable is meant to start the listener thinking by means of a built-in element of the "surprising" and the "alienating" in a common every day event.[132]

That Jesus had a special concern for the last, the least, and the lost, cannot reasonably be disputed, but what is even more striking is that he spoke of their being first, most, and found. This seems to have irked a considerable number of his critics because apparently Jesus not only associated with sinners and tax collectors but he even had the audacity to claim that they were going away justified or entering the dominion in front of the respectable and, in particular, ahead of those who were precise about their obedience to Torah (cf. Luke 13:28–30; 18:9–14; Mark 2:15–17). In this regard such parables as that of the Good Samaritan or the Pharisee and the tax collector immediately leap to mind. Or one may think of the rich man and Lazarus, or the prodigal son, or the great supper (Matt. 22:1–10), or the two parables about the guests (Luke 14:7–14). Some of this material may be dismissed as purely redactional, particularly in the case of Luke who seems to have a special interest in such reversal material (cf. the thematic sermon in Luke 4:18ff.). But the authenticity of all this material can hardly be denied; we only wish to contend for this theme being present in some of the authentic parables.[133] Further, the reversal theme corresponds with some of the authentic narrative material that describes those to whom Jesus gave special attention in his ministry and how he viewed the outcasts of society vis-à-vis

---

[131] Dodd, *Parables,* 5.

[132] Schillebeeckx, *Jesus,* 156–57.

[133] Cf., for instance, the critically limited lists of authentic parables in Perrin, *Jesus,* 41, and Breech, *Silence,* 1ff., both of which contain more than one parable of reversal.

the more respectable members of that society.[134] Sanders aptly sums up the probabilities that reversal was a major focus in Jesus' teaching and ministry when he says,

> The novelty and offence of Jesus' message was that the wicked who heeded him would be included in the kingdom even though they did not . . . make restitution, sacrifice, and turn to obedience to the law. Jesus offered companionship to the wicked of Israel as a sign God would save them, and he did not make his association dependent on their conversion to the law. . . . If Jesus added to this such statements as that the tax collectors and prostitutes would enter the kingdom before the righteous (Matt. 21:31) the offence would be increased.[135]

As Sanders goes on to say, here is an implied self-claim to know whom God would and would not include in the final dominion. But who knows such things except God, or perhaps a person who thinks he or she has direct access to the mind of God about such matters? In short, at the very least this new vision of who may end up in God's dominion suggests that Jesus believed he had knowledge that no one else had about God's will and plan for at least some of Jewish humanity. This implies a claim to personal reception of God's revelation, but Jesus not only envisions such possibilities and proclaims them, he also acts on such a vision. Later, when we evaluate the possibility of Jesus considering himself in some sense God's special son, we will have occasion to reflect on the so-called Johannine thunderbolt in the Q saying in Matt. 11:25-27/Luke 10:21-22.

Some such claim of special access to God and God's will seems to stand behind the parables and teachings in the Gospel about reversal. Because of the reversal parables, Crossan urges, "Jesus' parables are radically constitutive of his own distinctive historicity and all else is located in them."[136] Nevertheless, Jesus proclaimed the dominion of God and thus one should expect at most an implicit Christology in such material. The works of Funk, Crossan, Wilder, and others have led us to see that the imagery of Jesus' parabolic preaching cannot in the end be radically separated from the message it intends to convey. In short, in a real sense the "medium is the message" and the parables are Jesus' way of making people ponder the nature of the *basileia* that is breaking in through his ministry.

The idea that some parables reflect and illuminate some of Jesus' own religious experience depends on our accepting the theory that some *meshalim* reflect not a master's metaphor but a pupil's.[137] These, then, are

---

[134] Cf. the treatment of the authentic reversal material, in Witherington, *Women in the Ministry*, 35ff.

[135] Sanders, *Jesus and Judaism*, 207–8.

[136] Crossan, *In Parables*, 32–33.

[137] Cf. R. Funk, *Language*, 137; and Crossan, *In Parables*, 12, both of whom are following a distinction by C. S. Lewis.

stories or metaphors in which Jesus may be a character, not merely an omniscient and external creator, because they are images Jesus believed he received from God revealing to him something about the world, the *basileia* in the world, and his role and purpose in relationship to both of these. Michaels urges that some of the *meshalim* "may be described as stories his Father told him, or images his Father showed him."[138] Could these stories be the vehicles through which Jesus learned or discerned his own mission in life? If this is a possibility, then "parables may stand at the very root of Christology itself. If parables were a mode by which Jesus heard God addressing him, then we might expect them to have powerfully shaped his self-understanding."[139] Let us consider some examples.

Mark 4 tells the familiar story of the sower who sows seed on different types of soil, with varied results. It is possible to take this as Jesus' means of encouraging his disciples about their spreading the Word and its varying results, leaving Mark 4:14–20 out of consideration because most consider it Mark's redactional expansion. The basic parable's authenticity is, however, not seriously challenged by any known study.[140] But suppose it in fact is a story Jesus believed he had heard from God about the failures and success of his own ministry, not of the later efforts of the disciples?

Jeremias suggested such an interpretation of Mark 4 some time ago, arguing that Jesus here presents a response to the fact of opposition to and even desertions from his own ministry.[141] Here, then, Jesus draws and gives encouragement from the eschatological harvest imagery because he himself received a mixed response to his ministry. In this parable, which Jesus heard from God, he learned of himself as a sower. Naturally this does not allow us to give way to wholesale allegorizing of the parables, but when one compares parables in extrabiblical Jewish literature there is good reason for at least some of R. E. Brown's conclusion that

> Jülicher's total rejection of allegory is an over-simplification . . . there is no really sharp distinction between parable and allegory in the Semitic mind. In the Old Testament, the apocrypha, and the rabbinic writings, *mashal* covers parable and allegory. . . . Therefore, there is no reason to believe that Jesus of Nazareth in his *meshalim* even made a distinction between parable and allegory.[142]

I prefer the more limited claim that Jesus' parables could and likely do have allegorical elements occasionally, a claim confirmed by a detailed study of all the parables by P. Payne.[143]

---

[138] Michaels, *Servant and Son,* 102.

[139] Ibid., 106.

[140] Cf. the detailed verification of this fact in Payne, "Authenticity."

[141] Jeremias, *Parables,* 151.

[142] R. E. Brown, *New Testament Essays,* 323.

[143] Cf. Payne, "Authenticity," 334ff.

A second possible example may be found in the brief saying about the binding of the strong man in Mark 3:27/Matt.12:29/Luke 11:21, which, because it involves metaphorical speech, may be counted among the *meshalim*. Although it is possible that this saying was not originally part of the Beelzebul controversy material, it fits suitably in such a setting as it does appear to be a response of Jesus when challenged about his exorcisms. In view of the differences between the Lukan form and that in Matthew and Mark, it seems probable that Luke is following the Q form of this parable while Matthew simply follows Mark. The Markan form of the saying seems to be the more primitive because the Lukan version seems to allude to the Septuagint version of Isa. 53:12. Jesus may here be alluding to some popular literature that comes from before his day; the *Testament of Levi* 18:12 says, "And Beliar shall be bound by him. And he shall grant to his children the authority to trample on wicked spirits." Although this document does include some Christian interpolations, apart from the phrase "in the water," which H. C. Kee has rightly bracketed in the new translation of this document, the verse we have translated does not seem to be an interpolation but rather an original part of this document that likely dates during the Maccabean period.[144] The verse likely speaks of some future messianic priest's role. But Jesus, in his parable, is speaking of something currently happening—the plundering of the strong man's goods—which is possible only because the strong man has now been bound by a stronger one. Jeremias has argued that the binding of the strong man refers to what happened in Jesus' temptation period.[145] This may well be so, but if this saying is a comment on Jesus as a successful exorcist, as it likely is, then it clearly implies that Jesus has somehow and at some point bound the strong man in order to plunder his goods.

As Dodd points out, in some Jewish literature God's reign could only come after the demise of Satan's reign over the earth.[146] This suggests two things about the speaker of this saying: (1) Jesus saw himself as endowed by God with supernatural power so great that he could both bind Satan and liberate his captives; (2) the saying reflects a consciousness on Jesus' part that he is bringing in the final eschatological dominion of God and the salvation that comes with it for God's people. In short, this saying manifests more than a prophetic self-understanding, although I hesitate to call it a messianic self-understanding because there is no expectation in the Old Testament that *mashiach* would come as an exorcist. He would, however, come as a liberator, and perhaps in his sayings and his work Jesus redefined messianic expectations deliberately. In any event, we have seen in these two parables

---

[144] This document is translated and discussed by H. C. Kee, in *OTP* 1:795, 777-78.
[145] Cf. Jeremias, *Parables,* 122-23.
[146] Cf. Dodd, *Parables,* 23-24, 95.

alone that some of the parabolic material can be fruitfully seen as a comment on Jesus' own religious experience and so on his religious self-understanding.

Another avenue is worth exploring while we are considering the *meshalim*. Payne has argued that Jesus made an implicit claim to deity by means of the images of himself he used in the parables.[147] Some of the images to which Payne points, which are applied to God in the Old Testament, and perhaps are being used by Jesus of himself in the parables, do not necessarily lead to the conclusion Payne suggests. Thus, for instance, the explicit or implicit use by Jesus of the shepherd imagery (cf. Matt. 18:12–14; Luke 15:4–7; Mark 14:27–31), which is certainly used of God in the Old Testament (cf. Psalm 23 and passim), is also used of human leaders among God's people in the Old Testament (cf. 2 Sam. 5:2; Zech. 10:2; Exod. 34:23). Thus, at most, an image like this found in a parable—if it tells us anything about Jesus' self-concept—could just as easily suggest that Jesus saw himself as leader, perhaps a Davidic leader for and over God's people.

A further problem arises when Payne uses parables like Matt. 21:28–32 or Luke 15:11–32 to suggest that Jesus saw himself as the Father figure in these parables. Against this, for instance, is the content of Matt. 21:31, which speaks of people entering the dominion of God, not of the Christ, and this follows after the command to go and work in the vineyard. Surely it is more natural to see here a reference to the heavenly Father, of whom Jesus is the messenger.

Much more promising is the material in Mark 4:3ff. (and par.), which likely has as its background the use of the sower image of God's messianic activity in the Old Testament and the Targums (cf. Isa. 61:11; Jer. 31:27f., Exod. 15:17; *Targ. Yer.* I).[148] Here we seem to have the implication (if Mark 4:3ff. implies a self-reference as we have suggested elsewhere in this chapter) that Jesus saw himself assuming a role assigned to God in the Old Testament. Another possible example is the bridegroom material found in a variety of Gospel sources (Mark 2:19f. and par.; Matt. 25:1–13). The Old Testament background seems to be texts such as Isa. 49:14–26; 54:4–8; Jer. 2:2; Ezek. 16:8–14; and Hos. 2:16–23. There is no evidence in Jewish literature including the Old Testament that the messiah was ever called or alluded to as the bridegroom.[149] Thus, here again we have material that suggests Jesus saw himself fulfilling a role that only God is elsewhere described as assuming. Thus, it is quite possible, if the parables were meant to comment on Jesus and his mission, that Jesus saw himself as carrying out a divine role or task. What is not so clear is whether this amounts to an implicit claim to deity.

---

[147] Cf. Payne, "Jesus' Implicit Claim," which was culled from his dissertation, "Metaphor as a Model for Interpreting the Parables of Jesus" (Cambridge University, 1975).

[148] Cf. the chart in Payne, "Parables," 21–23.

[149] Cf. pp. 73ff.

A more controversial parable in Mark 12:1-9 (and par.) was widely regarded as a Christian allegory until three matters were drawn to the attention of New Testament scholars. First, the version of this parable in *Gospel of Thomas* 65 has almost no allegorical features. In *Thomas* there is no obvious connection with Isaiah 5 as there is at the beginning and end of the Markan form of this parable; rather, there is a simple telling of how a good man who owned a vineyard let it out to various tenants and sent two servants, one at a time, to collect the fruit of the vineyard. Finally, the owner sends his son, who is recognized by the tenants as the heir and is abruptly killed. Note that in this version any reference to a beloved son is absent, and the servants are not identified as prophets, nor is there an elaborate allusion to Isaiah 5 making clear the vineyard is Israel, nor are we told that the body was tossed outside the wall of the vineyard. Rather, we have a straightforward story.

The second factor that makes it likely this story is authentic at least in the simplified form, is that, as Jeremias has shown, it is true to life—a characteristic of many of Jesus' parables. The parable reflects the real hostility of Galilean peasant farmers to foreign absentee landlords who had taken over their land and demanded a share of their hard-earned crop. Jeremias and Dodd agree that the scenario is an apt description of the resentment of Galilean peasants and thus that the parable could go back to Jesus.[150] Furthermore, it was even possible for a person to exercise squatter's rights on Galilean land if the owner and all heirs were deceased; thus, the supposition of the tenants is not implausible. They act in accord with local laws about ownerless property.

Third, this parable ends abruptly with the death of the son. Were this a Christian creation we would have expected an allusion to resurrection or at least a successful resolution of the situation as Leivestad stresses.[151] We may add, too, that the parable in its simplified form follows the rule of three with a dramatic climax, and, furthermore, it perfectly suits the *Sitz im Leben Jesu* in that it alludes to a context of hostility and controversy. Nor can one delete the son from the parable, for otherwise the whole climax and the rationale for telling the story about tenants who thought they could gain control of the land by doing away with the heir is lost. I conclude this parable should be seen as authentic in its simplified form, most nearly represented in *Thomas* 65.

Now it is quite true that there is little evidence the messiah was called the Son of God in pre-Christian Jewish literature, but in the royal psalms the king might be called son by God (Ps. 2:7; cf. 2 Sam. 7:12-14), and that is what the last figure in this parable is called: simply the son. Jesus, who saw himself as God's last messenger, also plausibly saw himself as in some

---

[150] Cf. Jeremias, *Parables,* 74–75; Dodd, *Parables,* 96–102.
[151] Cf. Leivestad, *Jesus in His Own Perspective,* 112–13.

special sense God's son, a term that here perhaps would have had messianic and royal, not ontological, significance because the Jews did not expect a divine messiah. This parable is believable on the lips of Jesus from a time near the end of his ministry when, in the context of increasing rejection of his message, especially by the Jewish authorities and Pharisees, it looked rather inevitable that he would meet with a violent end if he continued to pursue the course he had chosen.

What is especially intriguing about this parable for our purposes is not only Jesus' likely allusion to himself as God's son and the final messenger sent to the tenants in the vineyard but also the issue over which the son would lose his life: the rightful claim to be heir to the vineyard. Had Jesus come to reclaim Israel for the Father? Was he doing so in a context in which that reclamation project implied a claim on his own part to have authority or even ownership in some sense over that vineyard and its tenants? If this is the case, then surely we see here an implicit messianic as well as eschato-logical claim—a claim that was both understood and rejected by the current tenants of the vineyard, for it meant their displacement from positions of ultimate authority over Israel. If this text tells us something about Jesus' self-perception and about how he was viewed by at least some of the Jewish leadership, then it is hardly surprising that the question of Jesus' authority and its ultimate source arises at various points and in various layers of the Gospel tradition (cf. Mark 11:28ff. and par.; John 5:27; Luke 10:19ff.; Matt. 28:18). Jesus believed his authority was such that he might not only proclaim the truth to Israel, but in fact claim or reclaim Israel for the truth.[152]

Let us sum up what has been discerned in this section. First, we saw Jesus as an eschatological messenger who announced the near coming and even presence of the dominion of God. More than this, however, clearly from Luke 11:20/Matt. 12:28 Jesus saw himself as in some sense bringing in the final eschatological dominion of God, insofar as it affected the human condition directly. By contrast, there is little or no evidence that Jesus thought he was bringing in that dominion in a way that would cause cosmo-logical change during his ministry. Human history and human lives are the arena into which he sees the dominion breaking, in spite of the unchanged nature of the earth, the cosmos, and even the continuing existence of "this generation" or, as Paul called it, "this present evil age." God's dominion is breaking into the midst of a dark world without immediately transforming or obliterating it all. Only those who have eyes can discern its presence.

We conjectured that Luke 11:20 (and par.) may suggest that Jesus saw himself as the *Shaliach* of God, one who acts finally and decisively with the authority and power of the one who sent him. In the parables, and

---

[152] After finishing this chapter, I discovered that Charlesworth has recently argued—almost point for point—for the same conclusions about this parable; cf. his *Jesus within Judaism*, 141-53.

particularly in the parables of reversal, we find a message that corresponds with the description at various points of the character of Jesus' ministry. This leads one to strongly suspect that the parables must be inspected not merely as self-contained metaphors or literary devices but also as vehicles to convey something about the dominion of God and what Jesus' ministry has to do with that dominion which, by implication, says something about Jesus' role and self-concept vis-à-vis the dominion. We saw that Jesus appears to have claimed that he knew whom God would and would not include in God's final dominion and, in fact, claimed that how one reacted to him and his ministry affected one's standing in that dominion. This implied not only a claim to special revelatory insight from God but also a special role in bringing in and establishing God's dominion.

Indeed, so great did Jesus conceive his power and authority to be that he saw himself as one who had bound Satan and was freeing his captives, in short, one capable of doing battle with the ultimate and supernatural sources of evil in the world. Finally, we also reviewed evidence that Jesus plausibly saw himself, perhaps in a royal or messianic sense, as God's son, sent into the vineyard to reclaim God's people for God.

This means that even dealing only with some of the likely authentic synoptic *basileia* material, a picture arises of a man who saw himself as more than just a prophet or a wise man. Here instead we see one who not merely reveals but accomplishes God's will for God's people, one who saw himself as God's climactic agent for change among his fellow Jews. Indeed, this man saw himself as having some sort of authoritative claim to the vineyard of God itself, being God's royal son and thus God's heir. Herein lies, at least, an implicit messianic claim.

ABBA AND FILIAL CONSCIOUSNESS

S. Kim urges the New Testament student to see that "both the abba-address and self designation 'the Son of Man' are the most striking of the unique features of Jesus, and they express his self-understanding more clearly than anything else."[153] If this is even remotely close to a correct assessment, then we need to give due attention to the Gospel evidence on both these topics. The Son of man material will be discussed in the final section. Here, we will examine the concept of *abba,* and two key texts which, if authentic, suggest that Jesus spoke of himself as a special son of God.

---

[153] Kim, *Son of Man*, 75. Kim's attempt to amalgamate Son of man and Son of God terminology, along with Suffering Servant material, has rightly met with critical skepticism. A great deal of valuable material, however, especially of a technical nature, is in this study.

ABBA

The detailed work of Jeremias on *abba* has met with criticism from those who claim he has overstated his case for the uniqueness of the use of *abba* in Jesus' prayer language.[154] We will first examine the evidence used to dispute Jeremias's claim. Then we will reexamine the Gospel evidence that suggests Jesus used the term *abba,* and draw some conclusions about what this usage reveals about his self-understanding.

G. Vermes, followed by Dunn among others, is convinced that Jeremias was incorrect to conclude that Jesus was unique in his use of *abba* as an Aramaic address to God.[155] The basis for this skepticism lies in the following texts: *B.T.Taan.* 23b; *Targ. Ps.* 89.27; and *Targ.Mal.* 2.10. These are the only texts from the entire later Semitic corpus that could possibly prove Jeremias wrong. Strangely, Vermes's argument ignores that Jeremias anticipated an objection being raised on the basis of *B.T.Taan.* 23b, which is certainly the most promising of the three texts.

The incident in question involves Hanin ha Nehba, the grandson of Honi the Circle Drawer, who lived near the end of the first century B.C. During a drought some school children came to Hanin, presumably because his famous grandfather had been a noted rainmaker, crying *"abba, abba habh lan mitra,"* that is, "Father, father give us rain." After their entreaty Hanin prayed, "Master of the world grant it for the sake of these who are not yet able to distinguish between an *abba* who has the power to give rain and an *abba* who has not." As Jeremias points out,[156] Hanin does not here address God as *abba* in prayer. In fact, what we have is a play on words, so typical of Jewish teachers and *hasids* of that era. God is addressed with the proper phrase "Master of the world." This text does demonstrate, however, that *abba* was used by small children of their elders, in this case a revered teacher or *hasid,* but it was more commonly used of one's father.

Jeremias also deals with *Targ. Mal.* 2.10,[157] and although interesting, the text does not invoke God using *abba.* The one tantalizing text is the *Targ. Ps.* 89.27, which reads *"hu yiqre li abba att."* Note that God promises the Davidic king, that is, God's *mashiach,* that he will call on God saying, "You are *abba* to me, my God." It is difficult to date this Targumic material, but even if it goes back as early as a *Sitz im Leben Jesu,* what could we discern from it? We would learn that a special and unique person, the Davidic messiah, is promised that he will be allowed one day to address God as *abba,* presumably because the Davidic king was thought of as being God's son in

---

[154] Jeremias, *Prayers,* 11–65, provides a convenient summary.

[155] Cf. Vermes, *Jesus the Jew,* 210ff.; his *World of Judaism,* 41–43; and Dunn, *Christology,* 24–25, and notes.

[156] Jeremias, *Prayers,* 61.

[157] Ibid., 60–61.

some unique sense (cf. Ps. 89:19–37; 2:7–9). Even here there is no prayer, but rather a promise from God. This text, if it is early, would lead us precisely to the opposite conclusion from Vermes's that various people of Jesus' era likely addressed God as *abba*. On the contrary, this text could suggest that Jesus' use of *abba* counts as evidence that he saw himself as the Davidic Messiah! Hengel conjectures: "The roots of the address *'abba'* in primitive Christianity—which certainly go back to Jesus—could lie here."[158] Furthermore, it is an argument from silence to maintain that *abba* comes from lower class Palestinian piety.[159] What little we know about lower class Palestinian piety, which has left us almost no literary sources, provides us with no evidence that ordinary Jews were addressing God as *abba*.

Dunn, however, points to other evidence to dispute Jeremias's claim: Wis. 14:3; Sir. 23:1, 4; 51:10; and 3 Macc. 6:3, 8.[160] All indications are that both 3 Maccabees and Wisdom were composed in Greek and do not go back to a Semitic original. If so, then it is fruitless to cite such evidence to show that *abba* may have been used by Jews before or during Jesus' day. What these texts may show is that there was a growing tendency in Jewish literature during the so-called intertestamental period to address God as Father, even in prayer (Wis. 14:3).

The evidence from Sir. 23:1, 4; 51:10, however, must be evaluated differently. This document was probably written in Hebrew around 180 B.C. and translated into Greek a generation or two later.[161] God is called *abi* in Sir. 51:10, not the Aramaic term of endearment, *abba*, and in the Greek of Sir. 23:4 we have *kurie pater*. Again we have intertestamental evidence for a growing use of the term father for God, even in prayer. E. H. Schuller has recently produced evidence from two as yet unpublished Qumran texts (4Q 371 and 4Q 372) for the use of *abi* as an address to God.[162] This is much closer to the use of *abba*; but even this material, strictly speaking, does not provide us with examples of the use of *abba* at all, much less *abba* in prayer language. The word *ab* with the possessive suffix *i* means "my father," not simply Father, the Father, or even Daddy.

Much more substantial are J. Barr's recent arguments.[163] Only some of his critique of Jeremias should stand. First, Barr relies on targums, in particular the *Targum of Isaiah*, to make his case. This material is representative of later Aramaic, and our critique about the use of later Aramaic in both the dominion material and Son of man material also applies here mutatis

---

[158] M. Hengel, *Son of God*, 45, n.89.

[159] Cf. M. Smith, review of *Jesus and the Spirit*, by Dunn, *JAAR* 44 (1976): 726.

[160] Dunn, *Christology*, 27.

[161] Cf. *APOT*, 291–93; and D. W. Suter, "Ecclesiasticus."

[162] E. H. Schuller, "Prayer Texts from Qumran" (paper delivered at SBL, November 1989).

[163] J. Barr, "'Abba, Father,'" and his "Daddy."

mutandis.[164] This is all the more so because with *abba* as with *bar enasha*, we are dealing with words that have the emphatic or definite termination in *-a*. Second, some of the evidence that Barr cites, in particular *Targ. Isa.* 8.4, supports the conclusion that this is the language of a child making his first attempt to speak adult language. I quite agree that Jeremias's analogy with babble is inappropriate, but so is Barr's attempt to deny that we are dealing with a language style characteristic of children. This is especially evident in the example of the incident in the life of Hanin ha Nehba. Third, Barr's attempt to deny a connection between Paul's (and other early Jewish Christian's) use of *abba* and Jesus' use is strained at best in view of the lack of other instances of the use of *abba* prior to A.D. 70. It rests at least in part on the dubious assumption that Paul knew little about the speech and sayings of Jesus. Fourth, Barr as much as suggests that *abba* is the language of intimacy, not simply the equivalent to the more formal Father when he says of the incident in the Garden of Gethsemane recorded in Mark 14:36, "Its special and intimate character caused the actual word '*abba*,' to be noted here."[165]

I suggest it is no accident that in the three cases where *abba* occurs in the New Testament (Mark 14:36; Rom. 8:15; Gal. 4:6), they are all in contexts where the intimacy of the speaker's relationship with God is being expressed in a moment of real passion, using this specific term. It is, of course, entirely likely that Jesus also used other words for God in other contexts, perhaps even *abi*. The point I would stress, however, is that Jesus' use and then the later Christian use of *abba* as a term expressing the intimacy of one's relationship to God is, so far as the evidence now stands, distinctive of Jesus and the Jesus movement. That the Matthean parallel (Mark 14:36/Matt. 26:39, 42) has 'my Father' is hardly surprising because the addition of the possessive qualifier seems characteristic of the Matthean redaction of such prayers (Matt. 6:9 and par.).[166]

Accordingly, I find no evidence to dispute Jeremias's claim that *abba* is a unique feature of Jesus' and early Christians' prayer language. But the New Testament evidence used to support this view needs further scrutiny.

The safest place historically to begin is with the material in Paul, which dates to the mid-50s if not earlier—Gal. 4:6 and Rom. 8:15–16. In both texts *abba* refers to an invocation of God as *abba* impelled or made possible by the Spirit that Jesus sent to his followers. From this evidence alone we need to allow that in early Jewish Christianity some people addressed God as *abba*. This is not the kind of address that could have arisen either from gentile

---

[164] Cf. pp. 192–98 and pp. 236–38.

[165] Barr, "'Abba, Father,'" 177.

[166] I accept Barr's critique of the translation "Daddy," but it does seem that the word *abba* in the examples we have means something like "dearest Father," not just "Father." Barr, "Daddy," 46, admits the term is not formal, but comes from the familiar or colloquial language. As we have it in the New Testament, it is in the emphatic state, used as a vocative, and is thus a term of special entreaty to God.

Christian piety or from Diaspora Jewish converts to Christianity (for whom Aramaic was probably not the language of prayer). In view of Mark 14:36, it is not plausible that Paul invented this form of address. Indeed, that Paul assumes his audience will know what he means by the use of *abba* suggests the practice was rather widespread in early Christianity.

On the one hand, it would seem difficult to argue that Mark 14:36 goes back to a saying of Jesus because it seems to be part of a prayer that Jesus made while he was alone in the Garden of Gethsemane. How would the disciples have even found out about this prayer's content? On the other hand, this example of the use of *abba* is found in the midst of a saying that it is very difficult to argue the early church would have invented. Would Christians really have invented the idea that Jesus distinguished his will about the cross from God's? This is most unlikely. Closer scrutiny of the Markan narrative reveals the following: (1) Mark says that Jesus took Peter, James, and John with him when he went off to pray, and that he was only a little way away from them when he prayed; and (2) we are not told that the disciples immediately fell asleep as soon as Jesus left the three to pray. It is possible that one or more of the three overheard the beginning of Jesus' prayer, which appears to be all we have recorded here.[167] It could be argued that the saying that includes *abba* is authentic but was placed in this setting before the Passion narrative was written down. This is also possible, but even if it is the case it does not affect the conclusion that Jesus prayed to God as *abba*.

Further confirmation that Jesus prayed in this fashion is found in Luke 11:2, which is not dependent on Markan material. Jeremias's detailed arguments show the Lukan form of the Lord's prayer is the more primitive, and it was originally given to the disciples in Aramaic beginning with the word *abba*. Jesus' prayer is probably a modification of the traditional Kaddish prayer which reads:

> Exalted and hallowed be his great name
> in the world which he created according to his will.
> May he let his kingdom rule
> in your lifetime and in your days and in the lifetime
> of the whole house of Israel, speedily and soon.
> And to this, say: amen.[168]

Luke 11:2 indicates only that Jesus taught his disciples to pray to God using *abba*; however, whatever degree of intimacy Jesus shared with God, it was a degree of intimacy the disciples could also share as his followers. Thus, while one can argue that Jesus made possible the sort of relationship to God that allows the cry *abba*, one cannot maintain that it tells us

---

[167] Cranfield, *Mark*, 430–31; cf. Taylor, *Mark*, 551, concerning the Petrine reminiscence.
[168] Jeremias, *Prayers*, 98.

something exclusively true of Jesus himself. Here, then, we do have clear evidence of an intimate relationship with *abba*, but it has no exclusively christological weight if the disciples can also share in such a form of address to God. Nevertheless, the following can be said.

First, this form of address does imply a filial consciousness on the part of Jesus that involved a degree of intimacy with God unlike anything we know of in Judaism prior to Jesus' day. So far as we can tell from our limited evidence, no one had previously addressed God as *abba*. Second, it was only by being Jesus' disciple that one could dare to take up such a form of address, for the Lord's Prayer is more properly called the disciples' prayer. There is a sense in which only through relationship with Jesus does such prayer language become possible.

There may be further significance in the fact that Jesus apparently urged the disciples not to call any person or teacher *abba* (Matt. 23:9). The practice of calling the elders of Israel "fathers" (cf. Acts 7:2; 22:1) was not unknown, and possibly certain major Jewish teachers received the honorary title of *abba* in Jesus' day, though even this is uncertain.[169] We have seen in the case of Hanin that children might address one such as him as *abba*. This suggests that Jesus made a clear creature-creator distinction, as is reflected in the exclusive use of *abba* for God. Jesus apparently also spoke of "your *abba*" to the disciples and also of "my *abba*," but never of "our *abba*."[170] Jesus apparently did distinguish between the degree of intimacy he had with God and the degree the disciples could share. The problem is that because both Jesus and his disciples may address God as *abba*, this would seem to be only a difference in degree, not a difference in kind. Again, the christological weight of such evidence is difficult to assess. Nevertheless, this material shows that Jesus saw himself as the unique mediator of a relationship with the Father that could express itself by using the intimate term *abba*. Thus, R. Bauckham rightly stresses:

> What enables us to move from the distinctiveness of his use of *Abba* to a recognition that he experienced his sonship as a unique relationship with God is the connexion between his sonship and his mission. Paradoxically, it is in its capacity to be shared that Jesus' consciousness of sonship appears most

---

[169] Barbour, "Status and Titles," 139. Barbour makes the plausible suggestion that Matt. 23:9 actually means, "Do not count the patriarchs as your fathers," that is, do not rely on your Jewish ancestry (not unlike the Baptist saying, "Do not begin to say, 'We have Abraham as our father'" [Luke 3:8]). Or he suggests it might mean, "Do not depend on the Fathers," which would amount to a rejection of the oral tradition. This would comport with what Jesus elsewhere may have said about the so-called tradition of the elders (cf. Matt. 15:2; Mark 7:5, 8).

[170] Matt. 6:9 would not count against this conclusion because even if this verse did go back to a *Sitz im Leben Jesu*, it is the way the disciples corporately are to pray, and it would not reflect Jesus praying "our *abba*" with the disciples. More likely, however, Matt. 6:9 is a later liturgical modification of the simple *abba* found in Luke 11:2. For the detailed discussion of the clear distinction of "my Father" and "your Father" in the sayings material, cf. Jeremias, *Prayers*, 38–45.

distinctive. . . . This sharing of his sonship with others belonged to his unique mission as the agent of God's eschatological salvation. He was the unique Son through whom the eschatological gift of sonship was bestowed on others . . . only as the disciples of Jesus did the disciples come to know God as *Abba*.[171]

INSIDE INFORMATION (MATT. 11:27/LUKE 10:22)

A controversial piece of evidence is found in Matt. 11:27/Luke 10:22, the "thunderbolt [a better translation might be meteorite] fallen from the Johannine sky."[172] We need to examine this saying because a special sense of being God's son is implied in Jesus' use of the term *abba*, and thus he may have on occasion called himself "the Son" (although perhaps only when he was with his disciples).[173] That this text is crucial for any christological inquiry about Jesus' view of himself is amply demonstrated by B. M. F. van Iersel's remark that "the orthodox exegete has regarded it as the cornerstone of New Testament Christology. . . . For the liberal exegete it has certainly been a stone of stumbling."[174]

In the 1950s scholars dismissed Matt. 11:27/Luke 10:22 as a creation of the early church, but with the investigation of wisdom literature in the interim, an increasing number of scholars have changed their minds on this matter. In our discussion of Jesus' relationship with John the Baptist we examined Matt. 11:16-19/Luke 7:31-35, which showed that Jesus expressed his self-understanding using wisdom language. We must at least entertain the possibility that Jesus did so on more than one occasion. Our saying seems to reflect the same sort of exclusive knowledge of God and God's will that we find in such texts as Dan. 2:20-23, where Daniel is portrayed as the truly wise man who thanks God for God's unique revelation to him.

It needs to be decided whether Matt. 11:27/Luke 10:22 was originally part of a larger group of sayings, or whether from the beginning it was a free floating logion. We must also determine the most primitive form of this saying. We first observe that the larger narrative context of the saying differs in Matthew and Luke. Thus, for instance, in Luke the saying follows the return of the Seventy from a mission (Luke 10:1-12), while in Matthew it follows the discussion about the relationship of Jesus and John (Matt. 11:1-19). In both Gospels the more proximate context is the woes on the

---

[171] Bauckham, "Sonship," 249, 250. One should also note the conclusion of Charlesworth, *Jesus within Judaism*, 134, who says that in light of the tendency in Jewish literature of the day to stress the distance of God from God's people—a God who communicated with them through angels and other intermediaries—Jesus' use of *abba* rather than *abinu* when addressing God must surely be seen as striking a distinctive note. There seems also to be some connection between Jesus' assertion of the nearness of the *basileia* and the implied nearness of God in the use of *abba*.

[172] Hase, *Die Geschichte Jesu*, 422.

[173] Cf. Marshall, "Divine Sonship," 90.

[174] van Iersel, *'Der Sohn,'* 146.

unrepentant cities (Matt. 11:20–24; Luke 10:13–15).[175] Both Matt. 11:27 and Luke 10:22 are preceded by the so-called *Jebelruf* of Jesus about the revelation of the Father to the *nepioi*. Note the various parallels in the sayings of Matt. 11:25–26 and Matt. 11:27. Both sayings seem to be about revelation, particularly to a select group of Israelites—the followers of Jesus. As Fitzmyer notes about the Lukan form of the sayings, the contrast between Father and Son in Luke 10:22 was already implicit in 21b.[176] This suggests the two sayings were originally together in Luke's source. There may also be some relationship between the *tauta* ("these things"; Matt. 11:25 and par.) and the *panta* (11:27 and par.). It thus appears plausible that Matt. 11:25–27 (and par.) was originally a unit, especially if the wisdom character of this material is kept in mind. Divine Wisdom was entrusted with the secrets or revelation of God and with the task of revealing them to humanity (cf. Prov. 8:14ff.; Wis. 2:13, 16; 4:10–15).[177] Divine Wisdom, however, was rejected by the mass of humanity, even the so-called wise, but was accepted by the poor and unlearned.[178]

Wisdom 2:13–16, an important parallel to Matt. 11:27, states, "He claims to have a knowledge of God, and calls himself a son of the Lord . . . and boasts of having God for his father" (cf. Ecclus. 4:10). This text in Wisdom 2 refers to the virtuous man who has wisdom from God. One may also point to *1 Enoch* 42.1–2 or 51.3, although these sayings are closer to a wisdom logion, such as "the son of man has nowhere to lay his head." This material could have easily arisen out of a Jewish milieu in touch with its wisdom heritage. Thus, Bultmann's conclusion that Matt. 11:27 (and par.) is a later Hellenistic revelation saying is unlikely and unnecessary.[179] The general content of this material could have derived from the era and environment of the historical Jesus.

Suggs maintains that the wisdom motifs we find here are attributable to the redaction work of the evangelists. This conclusion has been rejected by M. D. Johnson because in the case of Matthew it does not blend in with the overall Christology of the First Gospel.[180] It is not clear that portraying Jesus

---

[175] In Luke 10:16–20, we do have several intervening isolated sayings.

[176] Fitzmyer, *Luke 10–24*, 866.

[177] On the wisdom background of these parallel sayings and the fact that this background supports taking Matt. 11:25–27 (and par.) as a unity, see Suggs, *Wisdom*, 89–92.

[178] J. M. Robinson, "'*Logoi Sophon*.'" Robinson argues at some length that there is a particular *Gattung* into which Q fits. "The fact that the sayings collection as a *Gattung* tended to associate the speaker of the sayings with the sage has become audible in noting the connection between 'sayings' *logoi*, and 'sages' *sophoi*, which in substance leads to *logoi sophon*, 'sayings of the sages' or 'words of the wise,' as a designation for the *Gattung*" (111). Robinson thinks that Jesus' sayings were originally apocalyptic in nature but that they were given a wisdom context during the stage of oral tradition. There are problems with concluding that Q is simply a collection of wisdom sayings.

[179] Bultmann, *Synoptic Tradition*, 159–60.

[180] Cf. Johnson, "Reflections"; cf. J. M. Reese, "Christ as Wisdom."

as Wisdom or incorporating wisdom motifs into his christological portrait was part of Luke's redactional agenda either. What then of the so-called Q community?

Here the argument has a certain plausibility in light of the following sayings: (1) Matt. 11:16–19/Luke 7:31–35; (2) Matt. 12:42/Luke 11:31; (3) Matt. 23:34–36/Luke 11:49–51; (4) Matt. 23:37–39/Luke 13:34–35; and (5) Matt. 11:27/Luke 10:22.[181] The difficulty is that there is little evidence a Q community, for whom only certain sayings of Jesus apart from a Passion story served as the Gospel, ever existed.[182] If one points to the *Gospel of Thomas* as a parallel, we still have no evidence that it was the only authoritative presentation of the Gospel that its author or his community of faith used. Even if one could prove such a case about Thomas's community, there was a tendency in the more gnostic-oriented communities to focus on sayings rather than on narrative. What was true in the community out of which *Thomas* originated might not have been true in the non-gnostic communities that made the collection(s) we now call Q.[183] Thus, the argument that there ever was a Q community is based on silence because it is methodologically unsound to base conclusions on this matter purely on sayings from the Synoptics. One cannot first assume there was a Q community and then select certain synoptic sayings to bolster such an assumption. One must first demonstrate that either external evidence or the sayings themselves, if they are our only real evidence of the existence of such a community, suggest the existence of such a unique sayings-oriented community. Even if one could find evidence along these lines that was not purely subjective, in regard to our issue scholars have denied that a consistent wisdom Christology (Christ=Wisdom) can be found in Q.[184]

C. E. Carlston has demonstrated that various wisdom motifs and ideas found in Q also go back to a *Sitz im Leben Jesu*, that personified Wisdom was a familiar idea in early Judaism, so that Jesus may have appropriated and used that concept in his own way.[185] Furthermore, as A. Y. Collins makes clear, Q is not simply a collection of wisdom material—a good half of the material is of another genre.[186] It is interesting that Q and the earlier Jesus material both manifest a mixture of wisdom elements with eschatological and apocalyptic material, among other things.

---

[181] I am indebted here to M. Abbott, "Wisdom and Christology in Q" (unpublished paper presented in December 1984), 1–22.

[182] de Jonge, *Christology in Context*, 83: "It is extremely unlikely, however, that the communities in which the sayings of the Q collection were handed down knew no other traditions about Jesus' life, death, and resurrection/exaltation. Q's implicit Christology cannot have represented the whole understanding of Jesus by any Christian congregation."

[183] Cf. Robinson, "'*Logoi Sophon*,'" 102 and n.69.

[184] Cf. Suggs, *Wisdom*, 96; G. N. Stanton, "Christology of Q," 37.

[185] Carlston, "Wisdom and Eschatology," 117–18.

[186] A. Y. Collins, "Son of Man Sayings," 1–34.

None of this denies that collections of Jesus' sayings were made in the pre-Gospel stage of early church history by various groups of Christians. Nor does it deny that Q is a useful cipher for such collections, particularly non-Markan sayings material common to Matthew and Luke. Furthermore, the first and third evangelists may have had varying forms of Q at their disposal, which accounts for some of the differences between the Matthean and Lukan forms of various sayings. Because these sayings collections were being compiled well before the fall of Jerusalem and the dispersion or death of a significant group of eyewitnesses to the life and teachings of Jesus, the burden of proof lies with those who insist that certain themes in Q do not go back to Jesus but only to early Palestinian Christianity (e.g., the Wisdom theme).[187] We are looking at a span of only two or, at the most, three decades before such collections were available in relatively fixed forms. It is unlikely that early Palestinian Christianity deviated significantly from Jesus in its handling of such major themes as the Jewish wisdom motif in Q.[188] Thus, the authenticity of a saying such as Matt. 11:27/Luke 10:22 cannot be denied because it reflects a major Q theme. That Jeremias shows in detail how this saying goes back to an Aramaic original surely counts in favor of it going back to Jesus.[189] The major argument against its authenticity has to do with its content, not its form or wisdom theme.

It is sometimes urged that we have in Matt. 11:27/Luke 10:22 an example of early Christian gnosis. This might be plausible if we could eliminate the phrase "no one knows the Son but the Father," as Harnack tried to do on the basis of the inversion of the Father and Son phrases in some manuscripts. It is also true that this phrase is omitted in certain Lukan manuscripts (1216, 1579a). But there is overwhelming manuscript support for including this phrase and maintaining the traditional order of clauses.[190] It is easy to understand why such a phrase would be omitted by some orthodox copyists; it suggests that even Jesus' followers do not truly know him. This would have been equally offensive to orthodox Christians and the Gnostics.[191]

It is also urged against the authenticity of this saying that the term "the Son" would not be found on the lips of Jesus. As A. M. Hunter points out, there are various synoptic texts that would support the view that Jesus could have and did refer to himself in this manner (e.g., Mark 1:11 and par.; 12:6 and par.; 13:32).[192] If Mark 12:1–9 (and par.) is authentic, as we have

---

[187] That there is a wisdom theme in Q is undeniable; that it amounts to a consistent wisdom Christology is another matter.

[188] Witherington, "Principles for Interpreting," 35–70.

[189] Jeremias, *Prayers*, 45–46.

[190] Cf. Metzger, *TC*, 152.

[191] Cf. Dunn, *Jesus and the Spirit*, 29, who points out that the Gnostics would have stressed knowledge of Jesus, not his unknowability.

[192] Cf. A. M. Hunter, "Crux Criticorum," 244. One may also point to the *abba* material and such texts as Luke 2:49, which at least imply a filial self-consciousness.

argued,[193] then Jesus could have referred to himself as "the Son" in the presence of his intimate followers. Matt. 11:27/Luke 10:22 does seem to be the expression of one who feels inspired by God to pass on a revelatory word of wisdom to a select few. If Jesus offered such a revelatory word, then it would presuppose that he viewed himself as having intimate knowledge of God's nature and perhaps also of God's will.

In addition to the *abba* material, which at least implicitly supports the view that Jesus thought of himself as God's special son, there is another line of evidence from the Qumran material that removes obstacles to a conclusion that this saying may be authentic even with its reference to "the Son." The title "Son of God" has been shown to be as much at home in a Palestinian Jewish context (cf. 4QFlor. 1–2.i.10, or 10–14) as in the Hellenistic world.[194] Thus, the title "the Son," which in tandem with "the Father" can only mean "the Son of God,"[195] cannot be dismissed as impossible on Jesus' lips as being too Hellenistic.

Furthermore, the attempt to dismiss this saying as inauthentic due to its Johannine character is a weak argument. As Manson says, we cannot dismiss this text "unless we are prepared to lay down as a canon of criticism that no saying in the Synoptics which has a parallel in the Fourth Gospel can be a genuine utterance of Jesus."[196] Dunn adds that it is doubtful that a Q saying was taken from Johannine material that probably dates from the last decade or two of the first century.[197] It is possible to argue that the fourth evangelist independently provides evidence for a saying like ours in some form (cf. John 7:27), perhaps even in the form of a parable (John 5:19–20a).[198] In the end, all the traditional bases for judging this saying to be inauthentic no longer will bear close scrutiny.

Probably, the first evangelist has provided us with the more primitive form of this saying. This is so for the following reasons: (1) Luke uses *ginoskei* instead of *epiginoskei*, a simplification; (2) Luke has an indirect question in the second and third lines of this saying, making this more useful for church purposes; (3) Luke, unlike Matthew, has not repeated the verb of knowing.[199]

---

[193] Cf. p. 213.

[194] Fitzmyer, *Luke 1–9*, 206–7.

[195] I agree with Marshall, "Divine Sonship," 87–88, that it is artificial to distinguish radically between "the Son" and "the Son of God." As Marshall shows, the later New Testament writers know of no such distinction, and Mark 13:32 should probably be seen as evidence that Mark also made no such distinction, because elsewhere he uses "Son of God" to mean the same thing and person. It is also untrue that Son of God and Father are never found together (cf. Gal. 4:6; Rev. 2:18, 27; 1 John 4:14–15).

[196] Manson, *Teaching of Jesus*, 110.

[197] Dunn, *Jesus and the Spirit*, 28.

[198] Cf. Dodd, *More New Testament Studies*, 30–40.

[199] Cf. Jeremias, *Prayers*, 46.

As for the content, if Matt. 11:27 (and par.) was originally connected with 11:25–26, then we have two revelatory utterances—one given by the Father to the *nepioi*, the other by the son of the Father apparently to the same group. We must focus on the second while keeping in mind the first. Jeremias champions the theory that the essential meaning of our saying, at least in its middle lines, is a simple proverb: no one knows a father like his son and vice versa. It is "simply an oriental periphrasis for a mutual relationship: only father and son really know each other."[200]

There are several problems with this conclusion. It requires Jeremias to argue that the words father and son have been given an absolute or titular sense sometime after Jesus spoke them (originally in the Aramaic the two relational words were simply used in a generic sense). Against this, however, is the very character of the saying; it is at least in part about the revelation of the nature of a unique being—God—and a statement about God's unique relationship with Jesus. Thus the definite articles are necessary; this is not about just any sort of father-son relationship. Second, Jeremias's argument requires that we separate the middle two clauses of this verse from the first and last ones, but the two middle clauses are integrally related to the first clause. The unique relationship of Jesus with the Father is the basis for the claim of special knowledge and for the ability to be a special revealer of knowledge (clause d). Furthermore, the saying concludes that only Jesus gives access to such knowledge. If Jesus was simply stating a truism, he would hardly have claimed that the nature of the father-son relationship could only be known through a specific revelation by a specific individual. Worse than that, the statement is not even a broadly applicable truism because often wives, brothers, and friends know a person more intimately than their father.[201] This was certainly true in Jesus' day when people married young and when a son at an early age went off to study with a famous Jewish teacher.

The use of son in the opening and closing clauses is not based on a metaphor or aphorism.[202] Further, the saying in Matt. 11:27 is not grounded in an analogy with father-son relationships in general, but focuses on a revelation about God and God's special relationship with Jesus. Put a different way, the mutual knowledge Jesus and the Father have of one another cannot be predicated of just anyone, and only Jesus can share it with others.

Two factors point in favor of this saying's authenticity: it not only refers to the fact that only the Father knows the Son but also that the content of

---

[200] Ibid., 47.

[201] Schweizer, *Matthew*, 271; cf. Dunn, *Jesus and the Spirit*, 32. I agree with Dunn that we must not abstract the middle couplet of Matt. 11:27 from the rest of the saying. Notice how the first and last elements of the saying belong together, both referring to revelation. Cf. Iersel, *'Der Sohn,'* 50ff.

[202] Cf. Schweizer, *Matthew*, 271.

Jesus' revelation here is not the son himself. Rather, that Jesus is the son is the presupposition behind his being able to give such a revelation of the Father.[203] Were this a later church creation we would expect the revelation to be about the son. Further, as de Jonge points out, there is no attempt to introduce a specifically christological title, "Son of God," nor is that title made the object of special revelation. Rather, this saying is about the unique and unprecedented relationship between Jesus and God that goes beyond human imagery and imagination.[204] Fuller was right to complain against Hahn that Matt. 11:27 is not a christological contraction, "but an explicit expression of the implicit Christology of Jesus' own use of *abba*."[205]

What, then, does the saying mean? In view of the use of the language of revelation at the close of the saying and the verb *paradidonai* at the beginning, we should deduce that the "all things" passed on to Jesus by the Father refers to knowledge, not power or authority, as in Matt. 28:18. If 11:27a is connected to what follows, then the "all things" would refer to Jesus' intimate knowledge of the Father and perhaps also to his knowledge of his special relationship with the one he called *abba*, or perhaps to his special mission in life. The claim of exclusivity of mutual knowledge of Father and son should be compared to the claims that state only Wisdom knows God and vice versa (cf. Job 28:1–27; Sir. 1:6, 8; Bar. 3:15–32; Prov. 8:12; Wis. 7:25ff.; 8:3–8; 9:4, 9, 11). The middle two clauses suggest that Jesus sees his relationship to the Father in the light of wisdom ideas, and he may see himself as Wisdom incarnate here. Caution must be exercised, however, because the term wisdom is absent from this saying. At most we can argue that Jesus intended his audience to recognize that he was assuming Wisdom's place and roles—the revealer of God's mysteries who had special access to that knowledge due to his special relationship with God.

Second, the tense of *paradothe* suggests some specific point in the past when this revelation came to Jesus. One might conjecture that this revelation came at Jesus' baptism, if that tradition is in some form authentic. In any case, this does not indicate an ongoing awareness, but a very specific event of revelation in the past by the Father to Jesus, on the basis of which he may reveal some things to his followers. In short, this saying indicates that Jesus is dependent on what God has revealed to him for the content of what he reveals to his followers. This subordinationist note is probably original with Jesus rather than a creation of the church.

Third, note that there seems to be a contrast between the "all" of Matt. 11:27a and the "no one" in v. 27b. While Jesus knows all things God has revealed to him (about God or himself?), no one else knows the Father at all, or at least no one other than Jesus knows God with the intimacy that

---

[203] Cf. Dunn, *Jesus and the Spirit*, 33.

[204] de Jonge, *Christology in Context*, 81.

[205] Fuller, *Foundations of New Testament Christology*, 133 n.20; cf. Hahn, *Titles of Jesus*, 308ff.

allows one to call God *abba*. This implies a claim that Jesus is the exclusive mediator of the true knowledge of God or of wisdom from God.

Last, the final clause suggests Jesus may choose to whom he reveals this intimate knowledge of God, and in this case it is either Jesus' own followers or perhaps only the most intimate of those followers, the Twelve. The proof that Jesus bestowed this knowledge of God may be seen in the fact that the disciples also come to address God as *abba*. Jesus' revelatory wisdom given to the disciples in private apparently is not the same as Jesus' public teaching, which concentrates on *meshalim* and the dominion of God (cf. Mark 4:11).

Here, then, we have a saying that, if authentic, (1) draws out the implications of Jesus' use of *abba* for his own self-conception; (2) indicates Jesus saw himself in a unique relationship with God, possibly assuming the place and role that Wisdom had in various places in the wisdom literature; and (3) suggests Jesus was given this revelatory knowledge or wisdom for a purpose – to reveal the true nature of the Father to those whom Jesus chose. In short, Jesus saw himself as the unique mediator of the final revelation of God, and thus God's unique Son – the one who brings God's people back to a true and final knowledge of God.[206] G. Dalman explains that Jesus is God's only possible and absolutely reliable revealer.[207] Kim argues: "But for this function of revelation, which is in fact the function of Wisdom . . . he does not use the self-designation 'the Son of Man' but obliquely designates himself as the Son . . . because the latter is the proper term for a revealer."[208]

HEAVEN KNOWS (MARK 13:32/MATT. 24:36)

That Jesus' special and unique "communion"[209] with God did not include a knowledge of every truth or secret God might have unveiled to him is made clear in Mark 13:32/Matt.24:36. This text is less difficult to imagine going

---

[206] Fuller, *Mission*, 84–85, concludes after investigating the relevant texts that although Jesus meant nothing metaphysical or messianic by his use of the term Son, nonetheless "what is more likely than that Jesus explained to his disciples that the basis of his authority was that unique Sonship which the encounter of his Baptism made explicit." Fuller goes on to argue that the use of such a term by Jesus was "pre-Messianic. It is a relationship on the basis of which Jesus will perform the work which will lead men later to confess that God has exalted him as Messiah. . . . The Son-hood is the basis of his Messiahship, not the Messiahship the basis of his Son-hood." It follows from this that both Bauckham and Fuller are correct: the Sonship concept is the proper starting point for a discussion of Christology and Jesus' self-perception.

[207] Dalman, *Words of Jesus*, 283.

[208] Kim, *Son of Man*, 92.

[209] To use Manson's term for what *yada* means here; see Manson, *Teaching of Jesus*, 111. I agree that to strictly separate functional from ontological Christology is difficult if not impossible on the basis of the Gospel material – one cannot in a case like Matt. 11:27/Luke 10:22 separate Jesus' being in relationship with the Father from his mission or how he functions. The mission is grounded in the being-in-relationship. Cf. Bauckham, "Sonship," 258–59.

back to a *Sitz im Leben Jesu* than Matt. 11:27/Luke 10:22. In fact, Schnacken-burg says about the troublesome final clause of Mark 13:32, "There are no grounds for striking out the final words ('nor the Son but the Father') as long as we accept the genuineness of Matt. 11:27 = Luke 10:22."[210] Yet there are significant doubts about its authenticity. There are three basic positions: (1) that it is wholly authentic; (2) that some of its substance is authentic, but with modifications in the later handling of the saying, in particular by adding the reference to "the Son";[211] and (3) that it is not authentic but a Christian addition to an otherwise Jewish apocalypse.[212]

In terms of text-critical evidence, Luke omits this verse altogether, pos-sibly because it predicates ignorance of Jesus. It is also true that the majority of the witnesses of Matthew omit the phrase *oude ho huios*, including the later Byzantine text.[213] In fact, it is omitted by aleph-a, K, L, W, Delta, II, and numerous minuscules, and the omission is witnessed by such church fathers as Origen, Basil, and Didymus. On the other hand the phrase is included in Matthew by the best witnesses of the Alexandrian, Western, and Caesarean text types (including aleph-b, B, D, theta, and various Church Fathers). It is probable, then, that this phrase was originally present in Matthew, as it certainly was in Mark and that it was later omitted due to the doctrinal difficulties it caused the church.

Few scholars today are willing to dismiss the whole saying as inauthentic. Furthermore, if the objection to the phrase about the son is based on a lack of Jewish precedent for such a usage,[214] in our discussion of Matt. 11:27/ Luke 10:22 we found such a precedent in the Qumran literature, to which we may add such Old Testament texts as some of the so-called messianic psalms (cf. Ps. 2:7) and also 2 Samuel 7.[215] Certainly, it is difficult to believe that the early church would predicate ignorance on Jesus' part about impor-tant eschatological matters (whether "that day" means the day of judgment or the Parousia).

Yet, Cullmann mentions the possibility that the nonarrival of the Parousia during the first generation or two of Christians was the impetus for the creation of such a saying.[216] According to this logic the saying was created either to correct the false impression that Jesus was wrong about the timing of the end or to explain the delay of the Parousia. On the contrary, this saying may affirm that he simply did not know (and therefore did not

---

[210] Schnackenburg, *God's Rule and Kingdom*, 210.

[211] Cf. Bornkamm, *Jesus of Nazareth*, 226; Jeremias, *Prayers*, 37, 44.

[212] Bultmann, *Synoptic Tradition*, 130. Actually Bultmann held that v. 32 was probably a Jewish saying, perhaps part of a Jewish apocalypse to which the last six words had been added by a Christian redactor.

[213] Cf. Metzger, *TC*, 62.

[214] As seems to be the case with Kümmel, *Promise and Fulfilment*, 42.

[215] Beasley-Murray, *Jesus and the Kingdom*, 336 and notes.

[216] Cullmann, *Christology*, 289.

predict) the timing of the end. The view mentioned by Cullmann is dependent on the assumption that the so-called delay of the Parousia was a major problem for the early church, a view strongly challenged by T. F. Glasson and others.[217] But even if many were troubled by the delay of the Parousia in the early church, surely the logical way to deal with such a problem would be to create a saying of Jesus that stated he knew the end was not imminent. Creating a saying about Jesus' ignorance about such matters only solves one problem by creating another. Concerning Mark 13:32, Dunn points out:

> The earlier we postulate its origin the less need was there to attribute ignorance to Jesus, since Jesus' generation did not die out for decades (cf. Mk. 13.30); but the later we postulate its origin, to explain the delay of the parousia, the more exalted Jesus had become in the thought of the Christian communities and the less likely the ascription of ignorance to Jesus would be permitted. . . .[218]

This point is reinforced by examining the textual evidence. This text was seen by the church, even as early as Luke, as offensive and troublesome. This is why Taylor says: "Its offence seals its genuineness."[219] Barrett notes that this argument can only establish the authenticity of the substance of the saying, probably without the reference to "the Son."[220] I accept this critique, but Taylor's view is only one part of the argument for authenticity. Furthermore, it appears that Barrett finds the phrase "the Son" unlikely on Jesus' lips because it is "the most honorific title available."[221] Yet this is not the case, for even in the Fourth Gospel the language of sonship is regularly used in contexts where Jesus' subordination to the Father is stressed, as it is here. Surely the most honorific title, and the one that most clearly indicates Jesus' divinity, would be Lord, not Son, as the earliest Christian confession "Jesus is Lord" demonstrates. Further, there are other texts than Mark 13:32 that suggest a limitation in Jesus' knowledge about eschatological matters. As van Iersel points out, Mark 10:40 (and par.) may be pointed to, and probably from a different source Acts 1:7 suggests that only the Father knows such matters.[222]

There are structural problems with arguing that the phrase "not even the Son" is a later addition to this saying. Metzger puts it this way: "*'oude . . . oude'* belong together as a parenthesis, for *'ei me ho pater'* . . . *goes with 'oudeis oiden'*" (he goes on to urge that the whole cast of the saying suggests the originality of the phrase "not even the Son").[223] Furthermore, as Kümmel

---

[217] T. F. Glasson, *Jesus and the End.*
[218] Dunn, *Jesus and the Spirit,* 35.
[219] Taylor, *Mark,* 522.
[220] Barrett, *Gospel Tradition,* 25–26.
[221] Ibid.
[222] van Iersel, *'Der Sohn,'* 120; cf. Beare, *Matthew,* 473.
[223] Metzger, *TC,* 62.

recognizes there would be little or no point of mentioning the angels in the other *oude* clause if the "not even the Son" was not original.[224] Rather, the sentence would have most naturally read, "No one knows, except the Father." Van Iersel adds a further point. "The fact that Jesus does not know . . . is truly seriously problematical, if one thinks that he is the Son of the Father. . . ."[225] In short, this saying offers offense only to the extent that it is claiming ignorance in someone who is more than an ordinary mortal.[226] To put it another way, if one argues that the reference to the Son was inserted to compensate for the predication of ignorance to Jesus, then one is arguing at cross purposes with oneself. The insertion of "the Son" on this showing only makes this saying more difficult for the church to swallow. I conclude with van Iersel that this saying, essentially as we find it in Mark,[227] is authentic. This conclusion presents the exegete and historian with fewer problems than the denial of the authenticity of the saying.[228] However, even if we were to allow only two aspects of this saying to be authentic—the predication of ignorance to Jesus and his calling himself the Son—this saying would be very important indeed. It would show that in at least two different sources of the Synoptic material (here and Matt. 11:27/Luke 10:22) we have evidence that Jesus called himself "the Son," a conclusion further supported by the Fourth Gospel.

Mark 13:32 is best seen as an independent eschatological or apocalyptic saying of Jesus placed here by Mark with other sayings of a similar nature. Manson's conjecture that this verse is the answer to the question in 13:4 is plausible, but it is not necessary for our purposes to decide whether or not this is the case.[229] This saying was probably part of Jesus' private discussions with his inner circle of followers about esoteric matters. It is also unnecessary for us to determine whether "that day" refers to Jesus' Parousia (cf. Mark 13:26) or the final day of judgment.[230] As Beasley-Murray shows, in

---

[224] Kümmel, *Promise and Fulfilment*, 42.

[225] van Iersel, 'Der Sohn,' 118–19.

[226] Marshall "Divine Sonship," 94, puts it this way: "if a saying existed which made no reference to the ignorance of the Son, it is hard, if not impossible, to conceive of the early church's proceeding to transform an unexceptionable saying into a 'hard' one."

[227] Matthew has added *monos* for clarification and changed the words modifying angels from "in heaven" (Mark) to "of heaven."

[228] Cf. van Iersel, 'Der Sohn,' 119.

[229] Cf. Manson, *Teaching of Jesus*, 262 n.1. If this is the case it would, as van Iersel says, provide another argument for the authenticity of this saying. Jesus would be giving his views about the familiar early Jewish speculation about when the end would come or whether it would be preceded by signs. Cf. van Iersel, 'Der Sohn,' 122.

[230] On the development of the concept of the *Yom Yahweh* in the Old Testament and New Testament periods, cf. J. Gray, "Day of Yahweh." I do not agree with Gray that this concept likely derived from the autumn festival in early Israel, but he is quite right that in the New Testament when "the Day" is mentioned it refers to the time of *Mishpat*, in the narrower sense. Also, in texts like Luke 17:22–24 it is connected with the Parousia of the Son of man, developing ideas found in Dan. 7:13–14. (Cf. Gray, 35–36.)

the phrase "that day or hour," day and hour both refer to the same thing, being used like *kairos* in 13:33. "To say that no one knows 'that day or hour' is to affirm a universal ignorance of the time when 'the day' will break or 'the hour' will strike."[231] Thus, the saying has to do with Jesus' ignorance about some crucial future eschatological event—the phrase day or hour being a metaphorical way of referring to a specific eschatological event in time.[232]

This saying seems to present us with, if not a chain of being, at least an "ascending line" of closeness of knowledge or relationship to the Father.[233] No one knows, that is, no ordinary mortal, nor the angels in heaven, nor the Son, except the Father. Whether one takes *oudeis* to include all beings including the angels and the Son, in which case the *oude . . . oude* singles out two special examples from among everyone, or whether one takes the *oudeis* to refer to ordinary mortals not including angels or the son, in any case the son is placed closer to the Father than even the angels who are in heaven or at least as close to the Father. Since the subject is knowledge about an eschatological event one presumes that the ascending order refers to closeness in knowledge, and thus it would not necessarily be a statement about ontological matters. Nevertheless, the Son is singled out here, and the point of mentioning him last is that despite his closeness to *abba* not even he knows that sort of information. What seems implied is that Jesus thought either that he is in the same category of knowledge of God's will as the angels or that he knows even more than they do.

It takes an exceptional person even to imply this sort of thing, especially in a Jewish setting. But it should be noted that this saying, while probably ranking the son above ordinary mortals in knowledge of God's will and plan and even ranking him with or above the angels, nevertheless distinguishes the son from the Father in knowledge; thus, the former is subordinated to the latter in such matters. Yet in the wisdom literature this seems also to be the position of Wisdom—intimate with God and knowing a great deal more about God's will than do human beings, yet also subordinate to Yahweh. If

---

[231] Beasley-Murray, *Jesus and the Kingdom,* 335; cf. LXX Joshua 6:26; Zech. 1:12; Gen. 38:1; Jer. 3:17; Dan. 11:40; 12:1, 4.

[232] If authentic, then this saying must count strongly against the idea that Jesus necessarily expected the end of the world within a generation. One must not confuse either the coming of God's dominion, which in Jewish thought could be associated with a messianic age that preceded the end or sayings about the fall of Jerusalem or the demise of Israel's current world, with predictions of the end of the world. In terms of timing these three matters may have been distinguishable in Jesus' thought, even if they had some relationship to each other. When Jesus spoke of the final judgment (cf. Matt. 12:42/Luke 11:32; Luke 17:34–35 and par.), he did not attempt to indicate a date but simply used conventional metaphors to describe "that day" (cf. Witherington, *Women in the Ministry,* 44ff. on these passages). More difficult are the sayings about the Parousia, some of which may suggest that Jesus thought it would happen within a generation. It should be noted that the earlier form of the saying found in Mark 9:1/Matt. 16:28 refers to the coming of God's dominion with power, not the Son of man. Matt. 10:23 is not found in Mark or Luke.

[233] van Iersel, *'Der Sohn,'* 123.

Jesus saw himself as fulfilling the role of Wisdom on earth, a verse such as this should not surprise us. We are now in a position to sum up what we know of the term "the Son" on Jesus' lips.

Jesus was willing to allude to himself as God's son, the final eschatological messenger of God, and the heir of the vineyard (Mark 12). Jesus' use of *abba* implies that Jesus had a unique closeness and relationship with God, or a unique filial consciousness. More explicitly, in a wisdom saying found in Q (Matt. 11:27/Luke 10:22), Jesus affirms that he has been given an unparalleled amount of information from God about God's plan and will, so much so that only the Son can truly reveal the Father to others of his choice. The reason Jesus has such information is because of his unparalleled relationship of mutual intimacy with the Father. This saying suggests that Jesus saw himself as the unique mediator of the true knowledge of God and thus of God's salvation. Mark 13:32 simply gives further testimony to that intimacy of relationship, but here it becomes clear that this relationship between Father and son does not entail that the son knows all the things the Father knows. In short, although implying the superiority of the son in knowledge and relationship to the Father over ordinary mortals and even perhaps over angels, this saying nevertheless implies the inferiority of the son to the Father in knowledge of eschatological matters. This was surely no invention of the early church.

While I agree with Dunn that the idea of preexistence is not integral to or explicit in the thought of any of these three passages, nonetheless, if Jesus did present himself as the final embodiment of divine Wisdom, then in view of such texts as Proverbs 8, the idea was probably bound to arise.[234] After all, did not Mark 13:32 suggest that the son has at least equal if not greater knowledge than those who are in heaven—the angels? This would raise the question of the status of the son vis-à-vis heavenly beings.

THE SON OF MAN

One of the most complex problems in New Testament studies is how to understand the one label almost all scholars agree Jesus used of himself—the Son of man.[235] The problems are both linguistic and methodological. Should we interpret the phrase in light of the later Aramaic usage of *bar nash* and *bar nasha* or in light of the earlier biblical usage of *bar enash* and *bar enasha*? Was there a widespread, ancient *Ur-Mensch* myth upon which Jesus could

---

[234] Dunn, *Christology*, 47.

[235] That this title goes back to Jesus is evident even in Mark where it is neither used in confessions by disciples nor taken up by Jesus' adversaries. In fact, with the possible exception of a text like Mark 2:10 (which may be a parenthetical and editorial comment), there is little evidence that Mark added the title in his redactional work. Cf. de Jonge, *Christology in Context*, 59.

have drawn that would have been familiar to his audience, so that a mere allusion to "the (that) Son of man" would have conjured up a whole set of ideas? What bearing do the recent gains in the study of the apocryphal and pseudepigraphical literature by the SBL and SNTS Pseudepigrapha Seminars have on this whole discussion?

BACKGROUND ISSUES: ENOCH AND HIS KIN

Studying the extracanonical literature of early Judaism highlights the multiplicity of titles and functions used in discussions of messianic figures. Messiah and Son of man appear to be malleable concepts "frequently related and sometimes used interchangeably."[236] But many more terms were also used to express messianic thoughts. Of special relevance to our immediate focus is whether the *Similitudes of Enoch* existed in some form before or during the lifetime of Jesus because in this document, the phrase "Son of Man" is used in a manner not unlike what we find in the Gospels.

The consensus about the *Similitudes* in the early part of this century was that they were written about 105-64 B.C.[237] Recently, many scholars have been persuaded, largely in light of certain Qumran finds, that the *Similitudes* date as late as the end of the first century A.D. It is thus critical to assess the Qumran evidence itself.

The evidence can be listed as follows: (1) certain Aramaic fragments of the *Enoch* literature were found at Qumran, but they amount at most to five percent of the total corpus;[238] (2) five of the fragments (almost half) come from the *Book of the Watchers* (*Enoch* 1–36); (3) the other fragments (about one percent of the total corpus) come from the other portions of the *Enoch* literature, excluding the *Similitudes* (*Enoch* 37–71); (4) thus, we must be clear that the argument that the *Similitudes* could not be pre-Christian is an argument based mainly on only a few Qumran fragments of the *Enoch* literature – a miniscule percent of the whole corpus. It should also be recognized that this is an argument from silence. What one can conclude from the Aramaic fragments of *Enoch* found at Qumran is that *Enoch* was at least partially composed in Aramaic.[239] Furthermore, Knibb has provided evidence for a Semitic original behind all of *1 Enoch* 37–71.[240] We must stress the following conclusion of J. Charlesworth about the *Similitudes*:

> Repeatedly the specialists on *1 Enoch* have come out in favour of the *Jewish* nature of this section of *1 Enoch*, and its first-century C.E. origin and probable

---

[236] J. H. Charlesworth, *Pseudepigrapha*, 109.
[237] Cf. R. H. Charles, "The Book of Enoch," in *APOT* 2:170ff.
[238] Cf., for instance, M. Black, "Aramaic Barnasha."
[239] So, for instance, E. Isaac, "1 Enoch," in *OTP*, 6–7.
[240] Knibb, "The Date of the Parables of Enoch: a Critical Review" (paper presented at SNTS meeting, 1978).

pre-70 date. The list of specialists on *1 Enoch* arguing for this position has become overwhelmingly impressive: Isaac, Nickelsburg, Stone, Knibb, Andersen, Black, Vanderkam, Greenfield, and Suter . . . no specialist now argues that *1 Enoch* 37–71 is Christian and postdates the first century.[241]

In short, J. T. Milik's view of the late date and Christian origin of the *Similitudes* has been generally discredited. It was always difficult to make this into a Christian document in view of the fact that the text itself identified Enoch, not Jesus or some veiled representation of Jesus, as the Son of man (71.14).

G. Nickelsburg points out several pieces of evidence that suggest at least the traditions used to compose the *Similitudes* were known around the turn of the era: (1) the end of *1 Enoch* 56 may refer to the invasion of Judea by the Parthians and Medes in 40 B.C.; (2) *Similitudes* 67.8-13 may be an allusion to Herod's treatment at Callirrhoe; (3) the judgment scene in *Enoch* 62–63 seems to be a reworking of Wisdom 2, 4–5 (note also Wisdom 4:10-15 identifies Enoch as the prototype of the righteous one); and (4) various parallels with New Testament material itself can be also cited, for example, Matt. 25:31-46 seems to reflect *1 Enoch* 62–63.[242]

Thus, New Testament scholars should acknowledge the likelihood that the ideas that went into the composition of the *Similitudes* were already extant and probably familiar in Jesus' era. This is important for two reasons. First, there is a remarkable degree of correspondence between the reference to the Son of man in the *Similitudes* and certain sayings about the Son of man in the Gospels, for example, in both the *Similitudes* and the future sayings about the Son of man in the Gospels, the Son of man is depicted as a judge.[243] Second, the use of the demonstrative in various places in the *Similitudes* before the phrase Son of man, producing the translation "that Son of Man" seems to be a possible parallel to the Greek phrase in the Gospels *ho huios tou anthropou.* Thus, there seems to be a background in the *Similitudes of Enoch* for a possible semi-titular use of the phrase "the [well-known] Son of Man." This does not mean there was an elaborate, even pan-cultural, Son of man mythology in Jesus' day; the *religionsgeschichtliche* efforts to demonstrate the existence of such a myth are unpersuasive and now widely rejected. However, the material in Daniel coupled with what we find in the *Similitudes* could have provided an adequate stock of ideas and terms for Jesus to use the phrase Son of man and be understood to mean something more than just I, or I and those in the same class or position, or

[241] Charlesworth, *Pseudepigrapha*, 89; cf. n.82.

[242] G. Nickelsburg, *Jewish Literature*, 221–22.

[243] Cf. Nickelsburg, review of *"Books of Enoch,"* by Milik, *CBQ* 40 (1978): 411–18.

someone, or human beings.[244] In the *Similitudes* as in the New Testament, the phrase is used of an apocalyptic or eschatological individual.[245]

JESUS' LANGUAGE

Few scholars dispute that Jesus' main spoken language was Aramaic, although he probably used Hebrew when reading the scrolls in the synagogue and Greek when conversing with Gentiles.[246] The question then becomes, Was Jesus' Aramaic more like the Aramaic of the post-New Testament era, or more like middle Aramaic? First, the titular use in the New Testament cannot be derived from a Hebrew vocative *ben adam*, such as we find in Ezekiel.[247] The case seems to be otherwise when we consider the middle Aramaic phrase *bar enas* or its hebraized form *bar enos*. This phrase is attested in various pre-Christian Palestinian and Syrian texts (cf. *Sefire* III 16; 1Qap-Gen 21.13; 11QTg.Job 9.9; 26.3) where it has either a generic sense (a human being, a mortal) or an indefinite sense (someone or no one).[248] It is not found in pre-Christian or early Jewish literature used simply as a circumlocution, that is, Son of man equals I. There is evidence for such a usage in some of the Targumic material from a later period, but it is an argument from silence to predicate such usage in the earlier period when there is no evidence to support the claim (unless the Gospels provide such evidence).[249]

---

[244] Those familiar with the Son of man debate will recognize the various positions that have been taken on this issue among these scholars. Vermes, *World of Judaism*, 89–99, continues to advocate the circumlocution theory. Bauckham, "Son of Man," 25–33, urges the indefinite use ("someone") as the meaning of the phrase. Compare B. Lindar's rebuttal, "Response," and *Jesus Son of Man*, who champions the view that what is meant is "a man in my position," or class, appealing to the idiomatic use of the definite article in basically indefinite statements. Casey, "The Jackals," and "General, Generic and the Indefinite," continues to uphold the view that what we have is a simple generic usage in the Gospel, i.e., that Son of man means human beings in general. Against Lindars, Vermes cites very few examples from the Gospels in which his view is even plausible, and Bauckham shows that even some of these critically limited select texts may not support his view. Against Casey, he is hard pressed to explain why some of these sayings were even preserved in a christologically oriented community if, for instance, they mean no more than say "the Sabbath was made for human beings," or "human beings do not come to be served but to serve," or "a human being will die and after three days he will rise." On this showing Jesus was a frequent purveyor of clichés that if not banal or obvious, were in some cases not even true of all Israelites, much less all human beings. For general surveys of the recent proposals of these and other scholars, see Coppens, "Probleme de Jesus," and Goergen, *Ministry of Jesus*, 177–92.

[245] Charlesworth, *Jesus within Judaism*, 42, reaches the same conclusion independently: "I am persuaded that he knew and was influenced by Daniel and 1 Enoch 37–71, even if it was via the traditions that flowed to, or through, or from these apocalypses."

[246] For example, the survey by P. Lapide, "Insights from Qumran," esp. 491.

[247] Cf. Fitzmyer, *Luke 1–9*, 208.

[248] Ibid.

[249] For this reason it is wiser not to accept Vermes's circumlocution theory about the phrase Son of man as espoused in *Jesus the Jew*, 163–68. All his evidence comes from a late date.

Now, it is crucial to note that in later Aramaic there was a tendency to drop the initial consonant *aleph* on words. Fitzmyer stresses that

> *enas* (or the hebraized form *enos*) . . . never seems to occur in any pre-Christian texts or in any Palestinian Aramaic texts of the first century A.D. or of the early second century A.D. without the initial consonant *'aleph*. . . . Consequently, the form *bar nasha* or *bar nash* immediately reveals its late provenience, and one should be wary of citing texts in which this form of the expression occurs as if they were contemporary with the New Testament material.[250]

This warning seems to have gone unheeded by various scholars. Also unheeded by those who have focused on the Son of man issue is the probability that both the Qumran Aramaic and the Aramaic words and substratum in the New Testament fit into the grammar and style of middle Aramaic (200 B.C. to A.D. 200), not late Aramaic (post-A.D. 200). Fitzmyer insists that "Qumran Aramaic, either slightly prior to the New Testament period or contemporary with at least part of it—and other first-century Aramaic, such as tomb and ossuary inscriptions—must be the latest Aramaic that should be used for philological comparisons of the Aramaic substratum of the Gospels and Acts."[251]

This is especially germane because the forms *bar nash* and *bar nasha* are witnessed only in texts reflecting late Aramaic. Texts reflecting the later Aramaic usage cannot be determinative in discussions of any Gospel material that has the phrase Son of man. The phrase *bar enash* or *bar enasha* seems to have been used three ways in the time of Jesus: (1) in the indefinite sense; (2) in the generic sense; and (3) in a titular or semi-titular sense, probably drawing on Daniel and *Enoch*. What would have signaled the third sort of usage would be either when the phrase had the form *bar enasha* or when the larger context suggested an allusion to Daniel or the *Similitudes of Enoch*.

The distinction between the definite and the indefinite in the middle and older Aramaic seems to have been as firm as it is in Hebrew and

> is one of the main distinctive features of the old West Aramaic dialect as distinct from East Aramaic, Syriac, or later rabbinic and Targumic Aramaic. . . . [It is thus] . . . a capital error to assume that . . . *bar enasha* "the Son of Man" cannot be used as a designation or with titular force for a particular individual. The designation or title Barnasha for the "Son of Man" has the same force in the Old Aramaic as does Greek *ho huios tou anthropou*.[252]

These observations have direct bearing on the views of Casey, Lindars, Vermes, and others who seem to have followed Lietzmann's errors both in regard to the nature of the force of the definite article in middle Aramaic (for

---

[250] Fitzmyer, "Aramaic Substratum of Jesus' Sayings," 92–93.

[251] Ibid., 84–85.

[252] Black, "Aramaic Barnasha," 202. Note also that in the Syriac version of 2 Esdras 13:1 the expression "the Son of Man" as a title actually occurs for the messiah—"the man from the sea."

example, the Aramaic emphatic state) and in regard to the usefulness of citing examples from late Aramaic where it is true that the emphatic state was weak.[253] Qumran Aramaic makes clear that the emphatic state had not yet become weak during and before the New Testament period.[254] Thus, attempts to dismiss the possible titular or definite use of *bar enasha* by Jesus, and arguments that there was probably no conceptual background for such a usage—both fail to convince.

BAR ENASH *IN DANIEL 7 AND* 1 ENOCH

Any study of the use of the phrase Son of man in the Gospels must deal with previous uses of the phrase and ask whether and how they are similar or different. This is important because there are clear allusions to Daniel 7, notably in Mark 13:26 (and par.) and 14:62 (and par.).

The identity of the human figure in Daniel 7 can be gathered into basically three views: (1) the figure refers to one or more angels; (2) it is a symbol for Israel, or at least for faithful Israel—the "Saints of the most High" who endure persecution; and (3) *bar enash* in Daniel 7 does not so much represent Israel as present a representative of and for Israel in the presence of the Almighty.

All three views have a certain plausibility. For instance, in regard to the first, elsewhere in the Old Testament "holy ones" is a phrase applied to angels. Furthermore, Gabriel is described in Daniel (1) as having a human appearance and human voice (8:15–16); (2) as being "like the appearance of the sons of humanity" (10:16); (3) as a man (9:21; cf. 10:5; 12:6, 7). One could also urge that Daniel 7 does not identify the figure in question as a man but *kebar enas*—one like a son of humanity. The same applies to what we find in Rev. 1:13, which draws on Daniel 7.[255]

Against this view the following points can be made: (1) *qedosim* or *hagioi* can also refer to human beings (cf. Ps. 34:10; Wis. 18:9; 1 Mac. 1:46), meaning that one would have to prove the reference was to angels in the context of Daniel 7, which is difficult to do; (2) Dan. 7:27 states that the people of the saints of the Most High will be given the kingdom;[256] (3) if angels are meant by the saints of the Most High and the *bar enas* is one of them or their representative, it is difficult to see how this would be a comfort to Jews

---

[253] Moule, "Neglected Features," 420–21, rightly affirms Fitzmyer's insights and rejects the view that what is meant in the Gospels is simply someone, or a human being, or I. While disagreeing with his corporate symbol interpretation of "the one like a son of man" in Daniel, I think he is right that the major matrix in which the Gospel usage should be interpreted is Daniel.

[254] Cf. Fitzmyer, *Genesis Apocryphon*, 220.

[255] This view is persuasively argued by J. J. Collins, "Book of Daniel." See also his *Apocalyptic Imagination*, 68–92.

[256] Cf. Casey, *Son of Man*, 30–32.

under pressure. How much real comfort is there in being told that the angels will receive the kingdom and possess it forever (7:18, 22, 27)? Furthermore, in what sense had that horn (perhaps Antiochus) been waging war against the angels, and even more difficult in what sense could he be said to devastate them by changing feast days and the law?[257] This interpretation has considerable difficulties to overcome not only in the immediate context of Daniel 7 but also in view of the nature and purpose of this apocalyptic work.

The second view is more plausible. It can be urged in its favor that the author has used individual beasts to symbolize earthly kingdoms in Daniel 2–7 and that an individual human being could be used to symbolize Israel. The symbolism would indicate the inhumanity or "unhumanity" of the pagan empires in comparison with the people of God. This view makes sense in terms of the nature of the document and the immediate context of Daniel 7. Here then, we would be told that Israel, or at least faithful Israel, will triumph despite its present suffering.

Better yet is the third view, which takes into account the oscillation between the one and the many in our text. Thus, for instance, we are told that the four beasts represent four kings at Dan. 7:17. The king is the representative of his kingdom, and the two would not have been radically separated in ancient thinking.[258] Notice also that at Dan. 8:21 the he-goat is identified as the king of Greece. There are, however, further difficulties with arguing that *bar enas* is a pure symbol, that is, it is not a cipher for any real person or thing. On the one hand, Casey must admit that to *bar enas* is given dominion and glory, so that all will serve him because this is what 7:14 says. On Casey's interpretation, this means that Israel will be given these things in the future. On the other hand, Casey urges against Moule and M. D. Hooker that we detach *bar enas* from the saints of the Most High when it comes to the matter of suffering.[259] Casey says, "It is not that the man-like figure has independent experiences; he is a pure symbol with no experiences at all, other than the symbolic ones in vv. 13–14. To that extent he is a separate figure and he is to be disassociated from the suffering of the Saints."[260]

But it is doubtful that our author meant us to see the experiences mentioned in 7:13-14 as purely symbolic. They were meant to figure forth a real hope of future triumph for God's people. One suspects that Casey concludes as he does because he has already decided that the human figure is a symbol not merely of Israel but of Israel triumphant.[261] Yet it is crucial to

---

[257] Cf. A. A. Di Lella, "Daniel 7."
[258] Cf. Casey, *Son of Man*, 30.
[259] Cf. Moule, *Origins of Christology*, 11ff.; Hooker, *Son of Man in Mark*, 11–32.
[260] Casey, *Son of Man*, 39.
[261] Ibid., 26.

the concepts being conveyed here that the one who receives the kingdom may also be identified as one who has gone through what Israel was now experiencing, otherwise the attempted effort to comfort God's people is not effective because they could not fully identify with this figure. It is no accident that a human figure, who would be subject to suffering, is portrayed as ultimately triumphing. There is one further reason for not accepting Casey's view: the interpreters of this material before and during the New Testament era did not understand it in this way.

Not only in the Gospels but also in the *Similitudes of Enoch* as well as in the Book of Revelation (cf. Rev. 1:13–20), the human figure of Daniel 7 seems to refer to an individual. Note that the imagery of Daniel 7 is used to describe the experience of the individual Enoch, in what most scholars believe is a separate piece of Enochian literature—the *Book of the Watchers*. Here in *1 Enoch* 14.8 we see Enoch having a visionary experience described in terms of the imagery used of the *bar enas*' experience in Daniel 7.[262] This is important because in *1 Enoch* 1–36, we have one of the earliest interpretations of Daniel 7,[263] or possibly even a source for Daniel 7. In either case, *1 Enoch* 14 refers to an individual's experience.

This leads us to the third view, that Daniel 7 describes in apocalyptic language the experience of an individual who is a representative of and for Israel. Immediately in favor of this view is the fact that the kingdoms previously mentioned are associated with kings, and we are told that *bar enas* is to be given a kingdom. The Jewish reader would naturally assume that 7:14 meant that one individual would be given kingship and glory and would rule over all nations (notice the distinction here between the one like a *bar enas*, and the peoples and nations [plural] who would become his servants). The reign of the *bar enas* meant the reign of the saints since he was their ruler and representative (7:27). "A people is always drawn up in its head (King)."[264] We do not need to resort to any theory of corporate personality to come to this conclusion.[265] Rather, we can conclude about the

---

[262] Cf. Glasson, "Son of Man Imagery," argues that Daniel 7 borrows from 1 Enoch 14, a view that neither the majority of scholars nor I hold.

[263] Cf. Nickelsburg, *Jewish Literature*, 48–49.

[264] A. Deissler, "Der 'Menschensohn,'" 91. Deissler, however, wants to have it both ways— *bar enasha* is both a representation of Israel and their representative in Daniel 7.

[265] Cf. J. Rogerson, "Corporate Personality." Lindars, "Jesus as Advocate," 478ff., shows how tenuous the theory of Jesus proclaiming a corporate Son of man is, i.e., involving Jesus and his followers, especially if it is based on a saying like Mark 8:38 (and par.) and its variant reading "me and mine" which has poorer support than "me and my words." Cf. Metzger, *TC*, 99–100. Barrett, "I am not Ashamed," plausibly argues that Rom. 1:16 reflects a knowledge of the saying found in Mark 8:38 (and par.) in some form, and if so then *logous* must have been part of the original saying. Lindars stretches credulity when he argues that the Danielic associations with *bar enasha* were all inserted into the Son of man material at a time after Jesus' death (cf. 491ff.). He does rightly entertain the possibility "that Jesus actually saw his role in the light of contemporary speculation concerning Enoch" (491).

figure in Daniel 7 what Lindars concludes about the parallel figure in the *Similitudes of Enoch:*

> [The] figure of the *Similitudes,* variously termed, as we have seen, the Righteous One, the Chosen One, or "that Son of Man," is a leader of the righteous and chosen ones, i.e., the faithful Jews. Consequently he must be seen as a representative figure, embodying the expectation of the Jews that their righteousness before God will be vindicated, their enemies will be liquidated, and they will reign with God. . . . It would be a mistake to suggest that he is in some way a corporate figure, i.e., identical with the faithful Jews. But he represents their aspirations and expectations, and so is the head of them as a group. . . .[266]

This raises the question of whether *bar enas* is depicted as a messianic figure in Daniel 7. Several factors favor this conclusion: (1) the clear sequence of *bar enas* following the previous kings who are described in nonhuman terms; (2) the fact that Dan. 7:14 appears to present an investiture scene; (3) the fact that the one like *bar enas* will rule over people and that he is given a kingdom ("his kingdom"; 7:14d); (4) the fact that this material was interpreted in messianic terms in one of its earliest uses—the *Similitudes of Enoch;*[267] and (5) it is also possible, although not probable, that 4QpsDanAᵃ indicates that Daniel 7 was interpreted in a messianic sense.[268]

Daniel was a popular book in the first century A.D. as is amply attested by allusions to it not only in the New Testament but also in Josephus (cf. *Ant.* 10.275ff.; 12.321ff.). Indeed, Josephus tells us that Daniel's book(s) "are still read by us even now" (*Ant.* 10.267) and that Daniel remained popular because he was a prophet of good tidings and thus "he attracted the goodwill of all" (*Ant.* 10.268).

Moule draws our attention to another interesting point: in the *Similitudes of Enoch* 46.1, the Son of man is referred to simply as "another being whose countenance had the appearance of a man." But thereafter he is always called "that" or "the" (previously referred to) Son of man (cf. 46.2, 3, 4; 48.2; 62.5, 7, 9, 14; 63.11; 69.26, 7; 70.1; 71.14).[269] Moule concludes that this could explain the continual presence of the definite article in Greek when the phrase "the Son of Man" is used. Jesus, Moule argues, uses the phrase *bar enasha* to allude back to the well-known Son of man figure in Daniel but in such a way that it became clear that Jesus saw it as his vocation to fulfill what Daniel spoke of as the *bar enas.*[270] Moule then urges that we

---

[266] B. Lindars, "Enoch and Christology," 297. Cf. what Bruce, "Background," 55, says about the use of *bar enash* in Daniel 7: "Since Daniel's 'one like a son of man' is not explicitly identified with the 'saints of the Most High,' it might be wiser to say that he represents them than that he symbolizes them." So also Marshall, *New Testament Christology,* 66.

[267] Cf. Rowe, "Daniel's 'Son of Man,'" 71–96.

[268] Kim, *Son of God,* 20–25.

[269] Moule, *Origins of Christology,* 15.

[270] Ibid., 16. I do not share Moule's view that it could also have a corporate sense so that

take the allusion to Daniel as our starting point for understanding the use of Son of man in the Gospels, even when that text is not referred to or alluded to in the larger context of the passage. F. F. Bruce supports this conclusion:

> Jesus' special use of the expression (as distinct from its general Aramaic use in the sense of "man," "the man," or a possible use to replace the pronoun "I") was derived from the "one like a son of man" who is divinely invested with authority in Daniel 7:13f. Because it was not a current title, it was not liable to be misunderstood, as current titles were, and Jesus was free to take up the expression and give it what meaning he chose.[271]

Only in Daniel 7 do we find the two major leitmotifs of the sayings material in the Gospels that almost all scholars agree go back to Jesus: the reference to the *malkut* and *bar enash*. This fact cannot be ignored when positing a plausible background for Jesus' use of *bar enasha*. Nevertheless, it is odd that Jesus never seems to refer to *malkut* and *bar enasha* in the same breath. It could be objected that one should not use external data to control the semantic force of the Gospel usages of Son of man.[272] But when one is dealing with such an enigmatic phrase that may be drawn from apocalyptic literature and seems to allude to some prior shared context of usage or shared realm of ideas, a proper understanding of the appropriate background material is crucial in determining whether we will understand the phrase at all. Words and phrases have meaning only in specific matrices or contexts, so understanding the proper larger semantic field and context of the phrase is crucial to grasping the meaning of the Son of man. Such elliptical phrases, much like idiomatic English sentences ("he has an ax to grind"), can be understood only if one studies both the literal meaning and allusions to the larger and sometimes different set of ideas.

It could also be objected that if one demonstrates that Jesus used the phrase Son of man to refer uniquely to himself, he was abandoning the indirect means of self-revelation that seems to have characterized his approach. Against this it must be urged that (1) the phrase itself was enigmatic and required thought, as well as a knowledge of Jewish ideas and literature, to be fully comprehended because its significance was not immediately apparent to the listener so that the lack of use of this phrase by the early church points to its enigmatic and uniquely Jewish character; (2) that Jesus did occasionally indicate who he thought he was. However,

---

Jesus' friends are also to fulfill this destiny because this is having Daniel 7 both ways.

[271] Bruce, "Background," 70.

[272] The term "control" here is too strong a word. The Danielic context does not control the usage, but it does provide a primary basis and, to some extent, parameters for the range of meaning of the phrase in the Synoptics in *most* cases. There are perhaps some texts where the Danielic material is not immediately in the background, but they seem to be logia where the phrase is being used in a more extended sense.

one should not categorize the Son of man material as an example of direct self-revelation, at least not for most of Jesus' listeners.

POSSIBLE GOSPEL ALLUSIONS TO THE
SIMILITUDES *AND DANIEL*

If the *Similitudes* in some form stand behind Jesus' sayings, particularly the Son of man material, and if Daniel 7 does so, then an effort should be made to examine possible parallels. It is surprising how seldom this has been attempted in any systematic way. Here we will be able to examine only a few possible parallels. To anticipate our conclusions, what the evidence shows is that there are various parallels between the *Similitudes* and Gospel sayings tradition in general, but only a few direct parallels to the synoptic Son of man material. However, there are more specific parallels in the Gospels to the Son of man material in Daniel 7 and its surrounding context. This suggests, as Moule, Bruce, and Marshall among others have concluded,[273] that Daniel is the primary background for interpreting the synoptic Son of man material.

In both the *Similitudes* and in the authentic Jesus tradition, the dominant form of utterance is the parable, a form of wisdom utterance. In fact, almost all of the *Similitudes*, like most of Jesus' utterances, manifest one form or another of wisdom speech. For example, the beatitude in *1 Enoch* 58.1–2 "Blessed are you, righteous and elect ones, for glorious is your portion," is similar in form to the Lukan Beatitudes with their direct address (cf. esp. Luke 6:21), but the content has parallels to the fourth Matthean beatitude, "Blessed are those who hunger and thirst for what is right: they shall be satisfied."

A second feature found in the *Similitudes* and synoptic sayings material, including the Son of man passages, is the mixture of wisdom and apocalyptic or eschatological sayings. As A. Y. Collins shows, both wisdom and apocalyptic sayings seem to be found in the earliest stages of the Q Son of man material.[274] Third, the idea of a hidden or revealed Wisdom or wise one is found, for instance, in the primitive Son of man sayings in Luke 17:22–30, which concerns the disappearance of the Son of man, and then in 17:30, which tells about the day he will be revealed. Another wisdom motif—the

---

[273] One may also compare Deissler, "Der 'Menschensohn,'" 81–91. He argues that in the "magnetic field" of messianic expectation the figure in Daniel 7 came to be seen as the messianic representative of Israel, although this idea is perhaps not part of the author's original intentions (91). Black, "Die Apotheose Israels," offers the new suggestion that Daniel envisions the apotheosis of Israel in the endtime in Daniel 7. By this he means that *bar enasha* here is a deification of the "holy ones of the Most High" in Daniel (cf. *Assumption of Moses* 10). This suggestion amounts to rejecting Casey's sound arguments about where the court scene takes place, and it resolves the-one-and-the-many tension in Daniel 7 on the side of the many, ignoring the references to individual kings.

[274] A. Y. Collins, "Son of Man Sayings," 15ff.

rejection of wisdom on earth—is found in 17:25 of this passage. In *1 Enoch* 48.6-7 we read of the Son of man who "was concealed in His own presence prior to the creation of the world . . . and he has revealed the wisdom of the Lord of the Spirits to the righteous and holy ones." One may argue that the major role of the Son of man in *Enoch*, other than as judge, is to be a revealer of wisdom. Thus, for instance, we read in *1 Enoch* 51.3, "In those days the Elect One shall sit on my throne, and from the conscience of his mouth shall come out all the secrets of wisdom. . . ."[275] Or again, in *1 Enoch* 49.3 we hear of the Son of man that "in him dwells the spirit of wisdom . . . the spirit of knowledge and strength." A more striking parallel to the material in Luke 17 is found in *1 Enoch* 62.7, "For the Son of Man was concealed from the beginning, and the Most High One preserved him in the presence of his power; then he revealed him to the holy and elect ones."

Fourth, the motif of the Son of man as a judge is prevalent throughout *1 Enoch* 46–62. Thus, when he is first mentioned in *1 Enoch* 46.1ff. in a passage that draws on Daniel 7, it is said that the Son of man will open the hidden storerooms (of wisdom?) and will depose kings from their thrones and kingdoms. If one compares *1 Enoch* 46.6 to 48.10, it becomes clear that the Son of man is viewed as a bestower of kingship or kingdom and as the messiah of the Lord of Spirits. At *1 Enoch* 51.3 we hear, "In those days the Elect One shall sit on my throne," and a little later from that throne he judges Azaz'el and the fallen angels (55.4). All of this material should be compared to the future and forensic sayings about the Son of man, especially Matt. 19:28, which speaks of "when the Son of Man will sit on his glorious throne, you who have followed me will also sit on twelve thrones, judging the twelve tribes of Israel." Bear in mind that in Daniel 7 the Son of man is never said to sit on a throne or to pass judgment; he is given only dominion and glory. Daniel 7:9 speaks of God sitting on God's throne and mentions the thrones of the heavenly court who sit in judgment (7:10), but the Son of man receives only the benefit of the judgment. Thus, the future and forensic Son of man sayings in the Gospels seem closer to *Enoch* than to Daniel at this point.

Fifth, there are a couple of other interesting sayings in *Enoch* that have counterparts in the synoptic sayings tradition. Referring to a time of turmoil and tribulation in the Holy Land and an attack by heathen armies upon Jerusalem, *1 Enoch* 56.7 mentions, "A man shall not recognize his brother nor a son his mother." This is similar to a saying in Luke 12:53 found in the midst of a passage explaining the result of Jesus coming to cast fire upon the earth, "They will be divided father against son, and son against father, mother against daughter and daughter against mother" (Luke 12:53). But even more strikingly, "And brother will deliver up brother to death, and the father his

---

[275] Here and elsewhere I basically follow Isaac's translation in *OTP*.

child, and children will rise against their parents and have them put to death" (Mark 13:12 and par.). Finally, *1 Enoch* 62.5, in speaking of the day of judgment, says, "Then pain shall come upon them as on a woman in travail with birth pangs . . . pain shall seize them when they see that Son of man sitting on the throne of his glory." This may be compared to the apocalyptic material in Mark 13:8, which also uses the imagery of birth pangs to describe that tribulation and explains how horrible it will be for the pregnant in that day (13:17, cf. Luke 23:29). These images may be drawn from a conventional stock of such images and thus not reflect any relationship between *1 Enoch* and the Gospels, but one does get the feeling that in both places we are dealing with the same sort of literature and material.

For our purposes the crucial parallels are those discussed in the second and third points above. They are sufficient to raise the possibility of a relationship between the Son of man material in the Gospels and in the *Similitudes of Enoch*. Recent confirmation of this conclusion has come from the helpful study of Margaret Barker. She argues that the ideas about the Son of man found in the parables of *Enoch* provide some of the crucial background to and explanation of the synoptic Son of man material. In addition she stresses that the larger field of ideas conjured up by the term Son of man includes the idea of the Son of man as a messianic and possibly even a divine or angelic figure.[276]

It has become conventional to divide the Son of man material in the Gospels into three categories of sayings: (1) about the ministry of Jesus; (2) about the suffering, death, and resurrection of the Son of man; and (3) about the future coming and forensic activity of the Son of man. On the basis of this division, some scholars are willing to assert that one or another whole group of these sayings is likely inauthentic.[277] Yet Hooker has cautioned us about overpressing the threefold categorization and drawing conclusions about authenticity on the basis of it.[278] Even if we do categorize the synoptic Son of man sayings, the Daniel material involves the essential ideas entailed in all three types of sayings: the frailties of earthly existence, suffering, and ultimate vindication and bestowal of authority.[279]

---

[276] Barker, *Lost Prophet*, 91–113.

[277] Some sayings such as Mark 8:38 suggest these sharp distinctions may have come in the later passing on and collection of the material (cf. also the primitive material in Luke 17:22–30).

[278] Hooker, *Son of Man*, 80; but cf. esp. her "Is the Son of Man Problem Really Insoluble?" *Text and Interpretation: Studies in the New Testament Presented to Matthew Black*, ed. E. Best and R. McL. Wilson (Cambridge: Cambridge University Press, 1979), 155–68, esp. 150–60, noting that a saying like Mark 8:31 is actually not merely a passion saying but a prediction of death and resurrection in its present form. She also notes how all the eschatological sayings in Mark occur in contexts that refer to suffering and, thus, should be seen as promises of vindication.

[279] Moule, "Neglected Features," 421ff., argues that some sayings from all three groups may be authentic. M. Muller, "'Menschensohn' in den Evangelien," concludes after studying the various sorts of sayings, "The connecting Moment for all Son of Man Words of the Gospels is *Jesus himself* as Messiah" (82). He urges that the proper context for understanding the phrase *bar*

A. J. B. Higgins would rule out all sayings concerning the activity of the Son of man during Jesus' ministry, "The kernel sayings refer only to the future activity of the Son of man."[280] But Higgins, like others before him, must assume that Jesus did not identify himself as the Son of man during his earthly ministry, but either referred to someone else (Bornkamm's view) or, as Higgins would have it, only to himself in some future eschatological role he would assume.[281] Lindars, using a different sort of razor, would eliminate all sayings that do not fit the idiomatic use of the generic article attached to *bar enash* in which the speaker refers to a group of people with whom he identifies himself.[282] Lindars's approach leaves him with too small a base of authentic sayings from which to draw any firm conclusions. Equally unconvincing is Vermes who accepts only sayings that can be seen to be a circumlocution for "I" and that have no allusions to Dan. 7:13.[283]

The problem with all of these approaches is that they assume people use words or phrases only in one way. As Casey protests, in another context "variation within the normal semantic area of any word [or phrase] is normal in any author."[284] A more balanced approach is found in the works of Morna Hooker and F. H. Borsch who find that some sayings in all three categories of Son of man material may be authentic.[285] It can be argued that some sayings in all three categories reflect the influence of Daniel (esp. Daniel 7).

In Mark 2:10, which may be a Markan parenthesis and thus redactional, we are told of the Son of man having authority to forgive sins. Daniel 7:13–14 is probably an investiture scene in which the one like a son of man is given power and authority over all peoples and nations. The essential thrust of having authority or power is the same in both texts. In Mark 2:28 we hear of the Son of man being lord even over the Sabbath. This is a significant claim in light of Dan. 7:25 where the enemy of God's people (Antiochus?) is said to change the times and the law. If this is a reference to Antiochus Epiphanes, as even Josephus holds (*Ant.* 10.276), then it is significant that he attempted to place a ban on observance of the Sabbath and other feast days. Jesus, in contrast to such a despot, would be claiming (or the evangelist on his behalf) that he is ruler over the Sabbath and that it may continue to be observed in a way that benefits human beings. Daniel

---

enasha in the Gospels is not any sort of *Ur Mensch* mythology, which it is difficult to show even existed in Jesus' age and setting, but rather the material in the Gospels that deals with Jesus' call and sense of destiny and personal future (67–68). In short, he argues that Jesus' use of the term was personalized by Jesus to fit his own conception of his ministry and destiny.

280. Higgins, *Teaching of Jesus*, 123.
281. Cf. Bornkamm, *Jesus of Nazareth*, 228ff.
282. Lindars, *Jesus Son of Man*, 24.
283. Cf. Vermes, *Jesus the Jew*, 186ff.
284. Casey, *Son of Man*, 28.
285. Cf. Hooker, *Son of Man in Mark*, 25ff.; and Borsch, *Son of Man*.

4:16–23 is a remote but possible parallel to Luke 9:58 which speaks of birds having nests but the Son of man having nowhere to rest his head.[286] Is it accidental that in Dan. 4:15, another kingly figure is described with the words, "Let him be wet with the dew of heaven; let his lot be with the beasts in the grass of the earth"? There is also a reference to the birds of the air nesting (4:21). In both texts the focus is on an important figure who is experiencing something less than royal treatment.

There are substantive parallels with Daniel 7 and its surrounding context in the case of the second category (passion and resurrection) and the third category (future activity) of Son of man sayings. Because Hooker has taken pains to draw out the allusions to Daniel 7 in some of the less obvious cases from the second category,[287] we will not pause to reiterate her arguments here. One point about the future sayings is worth exploring. Casey argues that the location of the judgment scene in Daniel 7 is not heaven but earth, in particular, the promised land where the fourth beast, which had come forth from the (Mediterranean) Sea onto the (promised) land, is confronted. If so, then we have not only various parallels to numerous texts that speak of God coming forth to judge the earth (cf. Zech. 14:5; Ps. 96:13; Joel 3:12), but also a clarification about the future Son of man sayings. "Daniel saw the man-like figure coming down 'with the clouds of heaven.'"[288] We thus have a clear backdrop for sayings such as Mark 13:26, "And then they will see the Son of man coming in clouds with great power and glory"; and Mark 14:62, "I am, and you will see the Son of Man seated at the right hand of Power, and coming with the clouds of heaven." Again, Luke 18:8, which also speaks of a future coming of the Son of man, has as its background Daniel 7.

Thus, the case for Daniel 7 lying in the background of a good many of the Son of man sayings, and at least some from all three categories or types of sayings, is a strong one. The case is stronger than the possible allusions to the *Similitudes of Enoch*, which nonetheless should be considered.[289] We

---

[286] I agree with Casey, *Son of Man*, 7ff., that Daniel 2−7 should be looked at as a unit.

[287] Hooker, *Son of Man in Mark*, 27ff.

[288] Casey, *Son of Man*, 28. "With the clouds" here may mean "upon." Manson, *Son of Man*, 174ff., although he takes basically the same position as Casey on most of these matters, disagrees strongly on the point of whether *bar enas* goes up to heaven or comes down to earth with the clouds. Manson relies on the dubious theory of corporate personality even to the extent of interpreting the Son of man sayings in the Synoptics in that light (191ff.). For support of Casey's view as to whether the Son of Man ascends or descends, cf. K. Müller, "Der Menschensohn im Danielzyklus," 45: We are "to understand [that the] participial construction expresses in a pointed way the Coming of the Son of Man as *descent* from heaven to earth."

[289] One needs always to be cautious about taking a history-of-ideas approach to concepts such as *bar enasha*. Ideas do not often develop in a simple linear or evolutionary progression. Different individuals of the same era may use a phrase or concept in various ways. More importantly, room must be granted for new uses of familiar phrases. The chief problem with a history-of-ideas approach is not merely its developmental assumptions but also the assumption that there must be a precedent for a certain sort of usage for a phrase. This, however, is not always the way language works. Jesus, for instance, could have used the phrase *bar enasha* in

need to now examine some of the sayings about the Son of man that may be primitive, going back in some form to Jesus, and see what they tell us about Jesus' self-understanding.

THE SON OF MAN AND HIS ITINERANT LIFESTYLE (LUKE 9:58/MATT. 8:20)

Luke 9:58/Matt. 8:20 is a Q saying clustered together with other sayings about the cost of discipleship.[290] That this is the original and correct context for understanding this saying is probable in view of the fact that:

> Jesus went around in Galilee and the adjacent regions more like a wandering Cynic preacher than a rabbi. . . . He and his disciples quite likely lived on the strength of donations (Luke 8:3), and he rejected the making of any provision for the future. Consequently "following after" has primarily the very concrete sense of following him in his wanderings and sharing with him his uncertain and indeed perilous destiny.[291]

Bultmann, however, argues that this was originally just a well-known "proverb" (Plut., *Tib. Grac.* 9.4–5) about human homelessness that was turned into a Son of man saying by the addition of that phrase.[292] Against this, as Marshall points out, the parallels usually cited to prove this are not sufficiently close or convincing, especially in regard to the point of such passages compared to the point of this saying.[293] The problem with arguing that this was a general maxim is that it is not true of all human beings.[294]

More convincing are the arguments that here we have another example of Jesus alluding to himself as Wisdom who could find no home amongst human beings.[295] We have also reckoned with the possibility of an allusion to Daniel 4. On balance, it seems that the saying originally belongs in the setting in which we find it and that the allusions to Wisdom are a secondary implication.

Theissen builds a great deal on the idea that Jesus proclaimed a radical ethic suitable only for his itinerant followers. He argues, "The Word of Jesus represents an ethos of homelessness."[296] As exhibit A he cites the text we are presently examining, and the fact that *Didache* 11.8 shows that this

---

a new way and still be understood, because the larger context and style in which he used it gave clear clues to what this new meaning might be.

[290] On the Son of man material in Q, see Vögtle, "Logienquelle," although the author's conclusions are largely negative.

[291] Hengel, *The Charismatic Leader*, 54.

[292] Cf. Bultmann, *Synoptic Tradition*, 28–29.

[293] Marshall, *Luke*, 410. Plut., *Tib. Grac.* 9.4–5 is not a general proverb but a statement about poor Italians who fight for their country.

[294] Cf. Creed, *Luke*, 142.

[295] Cf. Christ, *Jesus Sophia*, 70 and esp. 1 Enoch 42.1ff. in light of the previous discussion.

[296] Theissen, "Wanderradikalismus," 249.

itinerant philosophy and the ethic that accompanied it were continued even after Jesus' death. If he is correct, then this supports the view that this saying is about the cost of discipleship, the point being made by showing what it cost Jesus to pursue the course he had chosen. Theissen's case however, has of late been subject to trenchant criticism by R. A. Horsley and it is doubtful that Theissen's strong distinction between teaching for itinerant followers and teaching for less mobile followers can be maintained.[297]

Luke 9:58/Matt. 8:20 is another saying Lindars uses to support his theory about *bar enasha* and here he has a case. His view is that *bar enasha* means a person in my position.[298] But the question has to be asked whether Jesus intended this saying as a comment on a group of people and thus on himself, or on himself and thus by implication on those who followed him. My point is that this is a saying with implications for disciples by the nature of the saying and its probable original *Sitz im Leben*. One does not need to find the reference to the larger group in the use of *bar enasha* itself. Furthermore, if the view that this was once a general maxim fails, then so does the view that the Son of man phrase was added to a general maxim. This saying is not a comment on all lives but on Jesus' life and by implication on those who follow him. Lindars is correct that this saying has christological implications:

> Jesus refers to the conditions in which his mission is undertaken. It is implied that such conditions are unavoidable. Jesus has accepted for himself the vocation to work which requires some measure of hardship. Obedience to a divine call is an indispensable feature of Christology.[299]

Here, then, we have a saying reflecting Jesus' sense that he was called to a unique mission in life that would entail various sacrifices and hardships.

Buchanan has pointed out the *kataskenoseis* means "encampments" and is usually applied to soldiers engaged in battle.[300] He concludes that the saying means: Birds were equipped for their outdoor dwelling, but Jesus had neither a cot nor a military tent. The Maccabean guerrillas had found cover and protection in the caves in the mountains—the same kind of protection as foxes found in their holes—but the Son of man still did not have caves at his disposal. Those interested in the movement Jesus was leading were put under extreme pressure. They had either to sacrifice a great deal or withdraw.[301] This may suggest that Jesus is distinguishing himself and by implication his followers from those of a more revolutionary orientation.

Luke 9:58/Matt. 8:20 may also imply that Jesus has been rejected.[302] If so, then there is a certain overlap between this saying, which is a comment on

---

[297] Cf. Horsley, *Sociology*, 43ff.
[298] Cf. Lindars, *Jesus Son of Man*, 29–31.
[299] Ibid., 31.
[300] Buchanan, *Jesus the King*, 83.
[301] Ibid., 84.
[302] Marshall, "Synoptic Son of Man," 335.

the present ministry, and some of the sayings that deal with Jesus' coming passion (cf. Mark 8:31). Thus, the authenticity of this saying cannot be decided by too rigid an application of the threefold division of synoptic Son of man sayings. Some of the sayings seem to fit in more than one category. If we ask why Jesus chose to use *bar enasha* to make such a remark, it may be because he had a sense of special mission like Daniel's *bar enash* or because Jesus' human frailty is being emphasized. There is also a possible allusion to Wisdom, and Jesus may have held the view that he was (or was taking on the role of) Wisdom incarnate.[303]

THE SON OF MAN MANHANDLED (LUKE 9:44b)

That there was a great deal of reflection by early Christians on the death of Jesus, and that some of this post-Easter reflection may be seen in the Gospels – this is a thesis few scholars would dispute. Most scholars, however, have not been led to the radical conclusion that we can know nothing from the Gospels about how Jesus viewed his coming demise, despite Bultmann's typically radical remark: "The great difficulty for the attempt to reconstruct a character sketch of Jesus, is the fact that we do not know how Jesus understood his end, his death."[304]

The usual approach to our problem is to argue that in Mark 8:31/9:31/ 10:33–34 (and par.) we have three forms of one original saying. Normally it is concluded that Mark 9:31 is the simplest and thus the most primitive form of the logion.[305] However, if Jesus spoke in Aramaic, then it is well to ask which form of the saying found in Mark 9:31 represents an underlying Aramaic original, and here Luke 9:44b has a decided edge. Not only does the *mellei paradidosthai* point to an underlying Aramaic participle, but *eis cheiras* is a non-Greek expression and represents Aramaic *lide*. Most striking of all we have a word play: "The Son of Man will be delivered up into the hands of the sons of humanity" (*bar enasha . . . bene enasha*).[306] Jeremias stresses that this saying has three features characteristic of the authentic sayings of Jesus: (1) a *mashal* character; (2) use of the divine passive; and (3) *paronomasia*.[307] The original saying in the Aramaic would have read: '*mitmesar bar enasha lide bene enasha.*'[308]

The saying implies that Jesus expected a violent end, but that God would be involved in this demise: Jesus was to be delivered up by God into the

---

[303] We explored this possibility when we studied such sayings as Luke 7:34 in the context of our discussion of the Baptist material.

[304] Bultmann, *Das Verhaltnis*, 11–12.

[305] Cf., for instance, Lindars, *Jesus Son of Man*, 63ff.

[306] Cf. Jeremias, *New Testament Theology*, 281–82; Marshall, *Luke*, 394.

[307] Jeremias, *New Testament Theology*, 282.

[308] Cf. Lindars, *Jesus Son of Man*, 68, for a slightly different reconstruction in order to suit his particular theory.

hands of human beings. Here we should compare such texts as Rom. 4:25; 8:31–32, rather than the texts that speak of Judas handing over Jesus (Luke 22:3). The fact that Luke leaves out any reference to the resurrection speaks for the authenticity of this saying and also argues for his using an independent version of the saying found in Mark 9:31 (as does the first evangelist at Matt. 17:22b). This may raise the possibility of a Q passion prediction.

If Jesus did receive a significant amount of resistance and rejection during his ministry, then we would expect him to entertain the possibility of a premature death, especially if he considered himself on some sort of divine mission. Even if Jesus had seen himself only as a prophet, still there was a considerable martyrology developing around certain prophets that included building great tombs for the murdered prophets. It appears that Jesus saw martyrdom in Jerusalem as part of the prophetic office, if Luke 13:33 in some form goes back to a saying of Jesus. Thus there is nothing improbable at all in Jesus foretelling his demise late in the ministry when things became more ominous, especially when he chose to go to Jerusalem. One may also compare Luke 11:49–51/Matt. 23:34–36.[309] What is important for our purposes is that Jesus saw God's hand in this coming demise. It was neither an accident nor an inevitable consequence of his rejection, but God's plan for him.

If this is the case, then we must note that the figure of *bar enash* in Daniel is one who is given glory and dominion after a period of suffering by God's people. If *bar enash* is a representative of those people, then it may be implied that he also suffered at the hands of the beasts but triumphed beyond that period of suffering. Thus, it is believable that Jesus, who saw himself as fulfilling the roles indicated for Daniel's *bar enash*, may have spoken of his vindication beyond death, which was made more specific in the hands of early Christians, taking on the form we find in Mark 9:31. There is no doubt, as the early tradition in 1 Cor. 15:3 shows, that this idea of Jesus' death according to God's word or plan, followed by his triumph beyond the grave, was well known, indeed considered authoritative teaching only twenty years or less after Jesus' death. Because it is doubtful that the early church would have invented the idea that God planned to have Jesus killed, our saying in Luke 9:44b (and par.), perhaps with an added comment about the Son of man being vindicated (cf. Mark 9:31), becomes very plausible on Jesus' lips.

A RANSOM FOR MANY (MARK 10:45)

This raises the major question of why Jesus thought God sent him to his death. Thus, we cannot avoid exploring the difficult saying found in Mark 10:45 (and par.). Whatever one decides about Mark 10:45, the conclusions

---

[309] Cf. O'Neill, *Messiah*, 50, on the authenticity of this saying.

drawn thus far will stand even if Mark 10:45 is a later church creation.

The idea of a human sacrificial death atoning for sin seems to have been very much alive in Judaism during Jesus' era. For instance, in 4 Macc. 6:27–29 Eleazar says, "You know, God, that although I might save myself from fiery torments, I am dying for the Law. Be merciful to your people (who broke the Law) and be satisfied by our sacrifice for them. Make our blood their cleansing, and receive my life as their ransom" (*antipsuchon;* cf. 17:21–22 and 2 Macc. 7:37–38). This text should not be ignored because 4 Macc. probably originated in the period A.D. 19–54, as the allusion in the text to the temple being still standing suggests (4:11–12).[310] In *J.T.Yoma* 38b,[311] *T.Ben.* 3.8, and in 1QS 5.6, 8.3–10, and 9.4 we also find the idea that the death of the righteous atoned vicariously for the sins of others. These texts indicate that the idea was "in the air" during Jesus' day.[312] Thus, whether or not Jesus viewed his death in terms like those found in Mark 10:45 (and par.) can be decided only by an examination of the text. The idea cannot be ruled out either as a later Christian notion or as something that would have been unthinkable on Jesus' lips.

The objections to the authenticity of this saying are summed up by C. E. B. Cranfield: (1) this saying is out of harmony with its context, which focuses on service; (2) the use of *elthen* suggests a date after the lifetime of Jesus looking back on it as a whole; (3) *lutron* and the ideas associated with it are found nowhere else in Jesus' teaching; and (4) the original form of the saying is found in Luke 22:27, and Mark 10:45 is a dogmatic recasting of it, perhaps under Pauline influence.[313] We will deal with each objection in some detail and present reasons for accepting this saying as authentic. We also need to deal with the contention that this was originally not a Son of man saying but an "I" saying.

The first objection mentioned above is the weakest. The literature dealing with the Maccabees makes it clear that some Jews believed the ultimate form of service to and for one's people was to give one's life for them. The saying is cast in this form for two reasons. First, as Barrett notes, the mention of *bar enasha* sets up a certain expectation of a figure associated with glory and dominion, not service, in view of what is said in Dan. 7:14. Jesus then would be qualifying such ideas about *bar enasha* in light of his own concept of his mission and future. Second, the *ou . . . alla* intends to bring out the contrast—the Son of man has come "not as *you might think,* or *do think,* to

---

[310] Cf. Anderson, "4 Maccabees."

[311] Cf. J. Roloff, "Deutung des Todes Jesu," 48–49, for analysis of some of these texts and their possible relevance. Some of this evidence, such as *J.T. Yoma* 38b, probably comes from a later period.

[312] Note Anderson's remark, "4 Maccabees," about the relevant passages not being Christian interpolations and about the fact that the idea has deep roots in the Old Testament (Lev. 16–17, Isa. 53). Cf. *OTP,* 2:539.

[313] Cranfield, *Mark,* 343.

be served, but to serve."[314] Yet Jesus would not be really departing from the larger context of Daniel in this saying because, as Barrett says, "Daniel as a whole is a book of martyrdom. This is evident in the narrative sections, but it is true of the rest of the book too."[315]

The argument based on *elthen* is also a weak one. First, some *elthen* sayings are authentic (cf. Luke 12:49). Second, as Dodd has noted, *elthen* with the infinitive of purpose or equivalent *hina* clause "is one of the most widely established forms in which the sayings of Jesus are transmitted."[316] Furthermore, although *elthen* can be used retrospectively as in Matt. 11:18, it can also explain one's sense of purpose or mission without having the sense of providing an overview after the fact (cf. Mark 2:17).[317]

Even though *lutron* is used only here in the Gospels, some of the ideas associated with it seem to be present in the so-called cup saying in Mark 14:24. The idea of a ransom is a familiar Old Testament concept, as is the idea of ransoming life back (cf. Exod. 30:12; 31:30; Num. 18:15; Lev. 25:51–52). Furthermore, it is not true that *lutron* is a Pauline word. The only place where we have a cognate term, *antilutron*, is 1 Tim. 2:6, and many scholars would call this material deutero-Pauline. This word and indeed the whole sentence in Mark 10:45 is thoroughly Semitic and can be translated as a whole back into Aramaic.[318] Beside *bar enasha,* one may point to the epexegetical use of *kai,* the phrase *dounai ten psuchen* (which can be compared to 1 Macc. 2:50; 6:44), *psuchen* used instead of the reflexive pronoun, the use of "many" here, as well as the way *lutron* is used, as Semitic features of this saying.[319] By comparison, 1 Tim. 2:6 seems to be a later Greek form of the saying.

Several other objections to the authenticity of this saying will not stand close scrutiny. As Stuhlmacher shows, it is not convincing to argue that this material derives from the church's Last Supper theology.[320] Those traditions do not use the key word *lutron,* nor do we find in them *anti pollon,* but rather *hyper* or *peri pollon.* Also missing in such material is any use of the phrase "Son of man." Thus, Stuhlmacher is right to conclude, "There is no real foundation for a derivation of Mark 10:45 from the Last Supper connection."[321]

---

[314] Barrett, "Background," 8. This whole argument depends upon this originally being a Son of man saying. The fact that this argument makes sense and helps fit the saying into a plausible context for its understanding may be taken as an argument in favor of this originally being a Son of man saying.

[315] Ibid., 13.

[316] Dodd, *Fourth Gospel,* 355.

[317] So Arens, *The ELTHON-Sayings,* 87.

[318] Cf. Kim, *Son of God,* 39.

[319] Cf. Page, "Ransom Logion," 148.

[320] Stuhlmacher, "Existenzstellvertretung," 415ff.

[321] Ibid., 416.

Nor is Mark 10:45 (and par.) a product of the early church's use of Isaiah 53. For one thing Mark 10:45 more closely parallels Isa. 43:3–4 than Isaiah 53. In Isaiah 43 we find (1) *kofer*, the Hebrew word that probably stands behind *lutron* (the Aramaic would be *purkan*); (2) the SMS root that stands behind the use of *diakonein*; and (3) *tahat*, which lies behind the use of *anti* (*pollon*). Strikingly, there is also a reference in Isaiah 43 to Yahweh giving "a man" for Israel.[322]

All of this is important in view of the fact that we have no evidence the early church used Isaiah 43 to reflect on Jesus. By contrast, the servant in the Septuagint of Isaiah 53 is called *ho pais mou,* and the word used for service is *douleuein,* not *diakonein.* Likewise absent from this text in the Septuagint is *lutron.* Thus, the case that our saying was created by Hellenistic Jewish Christians out of the Septuagint of Isaiah 53 is weak. I conclude that the objections to the authenticity of this saying fail.

Has Luke or Mark provided us with the more primitive form of this saying? Some scholars who are normally strong advocates of some form of Markan priority insist that the Markan form of the saying is later dogmatic recasting of the Lukan saying.[323] On the contrary, the absence of the *lutron* clause and the reference to *bar enasha* can be accounted for as Luke's attempt to make the saying comprehensible to a Gentile Christian audience. As Marshall points out, Luke 22:27b alone seems to correspond to Mark 10:45a, whereas we do not find any form of 10:45b in the Lukan saying. In short, it is doubtful that Mark 10:45b is a *recasting* of Luke's saying.[324] The balance of probabilities supports the view that Mark's version is more primitive. He, unlike the first evangelist, does not seem to be in the business of re-Semitizing non-Semitic sayings.

It has also been argued that this saying reflects the early church's later attempt to cast Jesus in the light of the Suffering Servant, with Isaiah 53 in view. Yet Barrett shows that our saying owes less to Isaiah 53 than Jeremias and Cullman among others would have us believe and can more profitably be seen in the light of Daniel, the *Similitudes of Enoch,* and the Maccabean literature.[325] To some extent the saying is a deliberate contrast with Daniel, but it presupposes Daniel as its frame of reference, and it does draw on some of the same ideas found in martyrological material in the Maccabean corpus.

In addition, note the extensive defense of the authenticity of Mark 10:45 by Stuhlmacher.[326] Among his arguments he stresses that *bar enasha* in the definite state appears only on the lips of Jesus, with the exception of Acts 7:56. In Rev. 1:13; 14:14; and Heb. 2:6, we have quotations of Daniel 7

---

[322] Cf. ibid., 422, where he concludes, "The connection between Isa. 43:3f. and Mark 10:45 . . . is fundamental."

[323] Cf. Bultmann, *Die Geschichte,* 154; and Schürmann, "Wie hat Jesus."

[324] Marshall, *Luke,* 813–14.

[325] Barrett, "Background," 1–7, 12–14.

[326] Stuhlmacher, "Existenzstellvertretung," 412–27.

where the Aramaic is *bar enash,* and thus the Greek follows suit with no definite article. The burden of proof is on those who think this saying was originally an "I" saying turned into a Son of man saying by the early church.[327]

Finally, reference should be made to Schürmann and Meyer's arguments that the "for or on behalf of you" or "for many" motif is an important one in the synoptic Gospel material and goes back to Jesus (cf. Mark 10:45; 14:24; Luke 22:20; 1 Cor. 11:24–25).[328] There is nothing in Mark 10:45 that could not go back to Jesus, especially in light of the Maccabean literature. Schürmann may be right that Mark 10:45, if it is authentic, comes from a time late in the ministry when Jesus seemed to have been rebuffed. Since the work of Jesus and the disciples was not fully accomplished, Jesus resolves to complete it by means of his death for his people.

Mark 10:45a is in the form of antithetical parallelism, which points to its Semitic origin. This half of the verse stresses that Jesus' purpose, his divine mission, is to serve human beings, not to be served by them. The implication of the saying may be that the disciples must revise their understanding of true leadership. The Lukan form of the saying may point us to a discussion around the table as to who gets the choice seats and who serves whom. Some would connect this saying with the Last Supper,[329] but this is uncertain. The tradition found in John 13:1–20 might support such a conclusion, but we will build nothing on this conjecture.

The crucial word in the second half of the verse is *lutron.* The basic idea of this word is "deliverance by purchase,"[330] and it is used to describe an act of redemption, the buying back of human beings. The price of this ransom is not money, but the life of *bar enasha.* In view of the word's Old Testament background and its connection with the preposition *anti,* a substitutionary suffering or giving of a life that frees others is in view.[331]

Barrett stresses that the basic idea is one of equivalence or substitution of something of equivalent value.[332] This view is supported by the famous quote from Josephus (*Ant.* 14.107) where the priest Eleazar tries to buy off

---

[327] On the issue of I vs. Son of man as more original in various sayings, cf. Higgins, *Jesus,* 115–16. Although Higgins finds the evidence ambivalent, nonetheless in an article like his "'Menschensohn,'" he is willing to argue that in Q, at least in various sayings like Luke 12:8–9 (and par.), "Q had Son of Man, not 'I'" (123).

[328] Meyer, *Aims of Jesus,* 218–19; Schürmann, "Wie hat Jesus," 328ff.

[329] Cf. Kim, *Son of God,* 43.

[330] Taylor, *Mark,* 444.

[331] Kim, *Son of God,* 58; cf. Isa. 43:3ff.

[332] Barrett, "Background," 6. In his later essay, "Mark 10:45," 22–23, he seems to suggest that Mark 10:45 may mean no more than a saying like *B.T.Kid.* 31b, which uses the language of expiation to indicate sympathy or attachment to a living or deceased person, or to express devotion to one's people as a whole. It is in the latter sense of devotion to Israel, the willingness to do all for her, that Barrett interprets the original sense of Mark 10:45. This under-interprets *lutron/ koper* here or requires that we argue that the key word was not a part of the original saying— something 1 Tim. 2:6 would argue against.

Crassus (*ten dokon auto ten chrusen lutron anti panton edoken*). We are not told in Mark 10:45b what the many are freed from, although it is not unreasonable to conjecture, in view of Jesus' exorcisms, that he was thinking of freeing them from Satan's grasp; freeing God's people from sin may be in view. In any event, the phrase *anti pollon* when contrasted with *bar enasha* indicates one life given in place of all, the contrast being between the one and the many.[333] This is why the later form of this saying in 1 Tim. 2:6 uses the word "all," thus rightly interpreting the original meaning of the saying. Barrett, however, suggests that in its original setting the reference to "many" could have referred to Jesus' concern for the *am ha 'aretz*, that is, the neglected masses, as opposed to the pious groups.[334] We have shown, however, that *am ha 'aretz* is not a technical term for sinners or the wicked but has a broad general sense of people who are not strictly observant of all the stipulations of Torah. I would not rule out Barrett's view, but because he admits that Jesus' ministry was directed to all of Israel, this limitation of the meaning of "many" probably was not intended in the original form of the saying. If this is an authentic logion, it implies an exalted sense of self-worth or value on Jesus' part—the life of *bar enasha* is equivalent to that of many.

Taking Luke 9:44b (and par.) and Mark 10:45 together, we learn that it is God's plan that Jesus die and that out of that death a great good will come—the redemption of many. Thus, even if things seem to be turning out all wrong, it will still be all right because *bar enasha* will provide the ultimate example of serving—giving his life in place of "the many." Now we understand why Jesus went to Jerusalem. His mission to the lost sheep of Israel was not completely fulfilled by what he did in life; he had to give up his life to complete the task. Doubtless this was not the sort of *bar enasha* people might ordinarily have conceived of when they thought of Daniel 7, but it was the sort that Jesus felt called to be. As R. Pesch concludes, "The passion of the Son of Man was announced by Jesus himself."[335]

"TRAILING CLOUDS OF GLORY" (MARK 14:62)

We will conclude our investigation of Son of man sayings by looking at one example of a saying from category 3—Mark 14:62 and par. Some future sayings in the Son of man corpus have led scholars such as Bultmann and Bornkamm to conclude that Jesus did speak of *bar enasha* who would come

---

[333] Cf. Hill, *Matthew*, 289; Cranfield, *Mark*, 343.

[334] Barrett, "Mark 10:45," 24. I agree with his assessment that "the mission of Jesus was to Israel as a whole, but in the circumstances of the time this meant a special emphasis upon those who otherwise were neglected."

[335] Although Pesch draws this conclusion based mainly on several other texts, in the end his conclusion is the same as ours. Cf. Pesch, "Die Passion," 195.

in the future, but that he was referring to someone other than himself.[336] Only four sayings could possibly support such a theory: Luke 12:8–9 (Mark 8:38 may be a variant of this); Mark 13:26; 14:62; and Matt. 19:28 (thought to be a church formulation). In view of the numerous Son of man sayings, including some future sayings that identify Jesus as Son of man, this is a radical theory indeed that requires us to deny the authenticity of the vast majority of Son of man sayings in favor of these four (or three if Matt. 19:28 is a community formulation). If just one saying where Jesus identifies himself as the Son of man is authentic, this radical approach is a failure, for surely neither Jesus nor the church spoke of two Sons of man. We have already shown that more than one such saying is authentic, and the majority of scholars accept a Q saying like Luke 9:58 (and par.) as authentic.

There are several other reasons for rejecting this theory. First, nowhere else in the Gospel tradition is there so much as a hint that Jesus expected a successor.[337] Second, in passing along the Gospel tradition the early church apparently saw no difference between sayings like Mark 14:62 and Luke 18:8. They were preserved because they were both thought to be about Jesus. Third, as Marshall points out, this theory leads to a peculiar conclusion—that a proper response to Jesus now will lead to some favored status with a hitherto unknown Son of man. But why should this be the case if Jesus and the Son of man are not one and the same, or if their connection is never made clear? In short, this theory raises more problems than it solves and is based on too little evidence.[338]

One suspects that this theory arose because certain scholars had difficulties believing that Jesus conceived of himself having a role beyond death or in the future like that described in some of the future sayings.[339] Yet is this role more difficult to conceive of than the early belief that Christians would arise from the grave and be involved in judging the world and angels (cf. 1 Corinthians 15; also 6:2, 3)? In short, modern skepticism should not be a factor in deciding what Jesus could and could not believe about himself. Of course, if Jesus uttered a saying like Mark 14:62 (and par.) about himself, then he did not have an ordinary self-understanding. However, all the evidence about Jesus that we have been examining in this study suggests that he did not view himself as simply an ordinary mortal.

The question of authenticity of Mark 14:62 is partly bound up with whether the trial narrative is plausible. We will not deal with that issue except to say that Jesus' appearance before the high priest may have amounted to a pretrial hearing to discern whether Jesus could be charged

---

[336] Cf. Bultmann, *Synoptic Tradition*, 152; Bornkamm, *Jesus of Nazareth*, 161ff.

[337] Cf. Cranfield, *Mark*, 274.

[338] Marshall, "Synoptic Son of Man," 338–39.

[339] Cf. Fuller, *Foundations*, 123.

with some crime and turned over to the Roman authorities.[340]

O. Betz has explored messianic expectation in early Judaism in relationship to the discussion in Mark 14:53–65. His examination of 2 Samuel 7 and how it was interpreted eschatologically at Qumran (cf. 4QFlor. 1–13) and perhaps elsewhere, is especially illuminating.[341] The oracle in 2 Samuel 7 speaks of: (1) David's offspring; (2) whose reign will be established; (3) who will build God's house; (4) "I will be his Father and he shall be my Son." In the Markan sequence the relevant motifs occur as follows: (1) (destruction and) construction of the temple (Mark 14:58; 2 Sam. 7:13); (2) "the Messiah, the Son of the Blessed One" (Mark 14:61; 2 Sam. 7:14); and (3) definitive enthronement (Mark 14:62; Luke 22:69; 2 Sam. 7:13). "As the root of the thematic complex 'temple, Messiah, Son of God, enthronement,' the oracle of Nathan has thus contributed directly to the Markan scene's intelligibility and indirectly . . . to the issue of its historicity."[342]

In short, the contemporary interpretation of this text, especially at Qumran, makes plausible the sequence of questions and some of Jesus' response in the Markan account, except for one point—Jesus responds not only in terms of Ps. 110:1, which has an obvious connection to Davidic speculation, but also in terms of Dan. 7:13–14. To anticipate our conclusions, it appears that Jesus is depicted as partially correcting Messianic expectation based on 2 Samuel 7 by interjecting *bar enasha* from Daniel 7 and the complex of ideas associated with that text. This comports with what we find in texts like Mark 12:35–37 (and par.) where again Jesus seems to be determined to question, if not refute, traditional understanding and Davidic messianic expectation based on texts such as Ps. 110:1 or 2 Samuel 7.

Kümmel argues that Christians could have obtained information from a Sanhedrin member about these events, which were so crucial for them (especially if there is any historical basis to a text like John 18:15–16). He agrees that this scene need not be understood as a formal legal proceeding or trial. He points out that Jesus' reply has no later analogy (where else does one find Ps. 110:1 and Dan. 7:13–14 combined?) and is a prediction that went unfulfilled. The high priest and the members of the Sanhedrin did not in fact during their earthly lifetimes see *bar enasha* sitting at the right hand or coming with the clouds.[343] Thus, Mark 14:62 has good claims to authenticity, for the church would not make up what appeared to be an unfulfilled prophecy.

---

[340] On the general authenticity and historicity of the so-called trial before the Sanhedrin, cf. J. Blinzler, *Trial of Jesus*; and Catchpole, *Trial*, 153–220. Catchpole may be right that the course of events was as follows: (1) pre-trial hearing at Annas's house; (2) meeting before the Sanhedrin the next morning; and (3) case passed on to the Romans in view of the lack of power of capital punishment amongst the Jews at the time (271).

[341] Betz, "Die Frage," 34ff.

[342] Meyer, *Aims of Jesus*, 180.

[343] Cf. Kümmel, *Promise and Fulfilment*, 50.

Although it is later material and can be taken as an attack on Christian views of Jesus, *J.T.Ta'an.* 65B.1.68ff., which records the words of the Amorean Abbahu, may reflect our scene and provide an independent witness to it. There we read: "If a man says to you 'I am God,' he lies; 'I am the Son of Man' he will regret it; 'I will ascend into heaven,' he speaks but will not achieve it."[344] Kim also urges that John 1:51 is an independent variant of our saying.[345]

Norman Perrin suggests that the original trial scene had only *ego eimi*, and that Mark 14:62 was added later as a Christian *pesher* on the Old Testament texts cited.[346] But insofar as the contemporizing interpretation of the texts of Ps. 110:1 and Dan. 7:13–14 are concerned, we have seen that Jesus did discuss or allude to these texts in another context, and there is no reason why he could not have provided the creative *pesher* here. As Chilton shows, Jesus was creative in his handling of Scripture, and can be shown to have proclaimed Scripture fulfilled in his actions.[347]

As Marshall points out,[348] some of the difficulty in seeing Mark 14:62 as an authentic utterance of Jesus is based on the assumption that this text refers to an act of exaltation. No act of exaltation is described, however; rather, the Son of man is already seated at the right hand and coming on the clouds (for judgment).[349] Furthermore, there is no difficulty in understanding the transition from discussing messiah to Son of man if the *Similitudes of Enoch* are, at least in their oral formulation, from Jesus' era. Clearly, the Son of man is viewed as messiah in *1 Enoch* 37ff., and this may also be the case in Daniel 7.

Additional support for the authenticity of this trial narrative can be found. K. Berger provides us with evidence that the messiah could be described as the future coming judge.[350] Hengel, after examining the early Jewish evidence, is not hesitant to conclude that "in the few Jewish witnesses about the Son of Man, this can be always identified with the Messiah."[351] On the basis of the work of Berger and Hengel among others,

---

[344] Ibid., 51 n.102.

[345] Cf. Kim, *Son of God*, 86.

[346] Perrin, "Mark 14:62." For a helpful critique of Perrin, see Higgins, *Teaching of Jesus*, 97–99.

[347] Cf. Chilton, *Galilean Rabbi*, 57ff., and 148ff.; cf. esp. our discussion on Jesus' response to John's question from prison (pp. 42–44).

[348] Marshall, "Synoptic Son of Man," 346–47.

[349] It is interesting as R. B. Y. Scott, "Behold, He Cometh with Clouds," *NTS* 5 (1955–56): 127–32, points out that wherever Dan. 7:13 is cited in the New Testament, the word order of the original Aramaic is reversed so that "with the clouds of heaven" immediately follows the word "coming." This alteration is not found in any of the Greek versions and suggests a creative handling of the text of Daniel, which may go back to Jesus. The point of this alteration is, no doubt, to make clear that this is a coming from heaven.

[350] Berger, "Problem der Messianität," esp. 20ff. One may compare *Ps. Sol.* 17:33ff., for example, but also intriguing is the material in Justin *Dialogue* 32:1ff.

[351] Hengel, "Christologie," 53.

Pesch concludes that the substance of this narrative about Jesus' appearance before the high priest is not problematical.[352]

There are some textual difficulties to resolve before we proceed to analyze the text.[353] In some manuscripts Jesus' reply to the High Priest reads as follows: *su eipas hoti ego eimi* (theta, fam. 13, 472, 543, 565, 700, 1071, geo, arm, Or). This has led scholars to conjecture that this may have been the original reading.[354] Cranfield also points out that this reading is just different enough from what we find in Matthew and Luke to hint that it is not a product of assimilation. If it is original, then (1) we avoid the anomaly of the first evangelist making more opaque Jesus' christological affirmation; and (2) we have a form of the saying that comports with the veiled or indirect way Jesus speaks of himself in public in Mark. Yet the weight of the manuscript evidence strongly supports the shorter text, *ego eimi*,[355] and in view of the popularity of Matthew in the early church, it is easy to see how Mark 14:62, if it originally read *ego eimi*, could have been combined with the Matthean text to form the variant text cited above. Furthermore, in Mark's outline the time for keeping the messianic secret is over. The Son of man must go as God intended. It is also the case that Matthew's form of the response, *su eipas*, is a change to a more Semitic idiom characteristic of that Gospel, and even in Matthew the response is "affirmative in content, and reluctant or circumlocutory in formulation."[356] I conclude that Jesus' original response was affirmative in some sense,[357] but that he went on to qualify that affirmation by what he says about *bar enasha*.

Note that Jesus seems to be deliberately taking Ps. 110:1, a Davidic text, and applying it to *bar enasha*.[358] We find the Son of man in a similar position in *1 Enoch* 45.3; 55.4; and 62.5. Although in the *Similitudes* there is no

---

[352] Pesch, "Die Passion," 186–88, thinks that the historical starting point for discussing the basis of Jesus' condemnation to death must be the Temple saying, the High Priest's question about Messiah, and Jesus' response in 14:62: "14:62 can also go back to Jesus" (187). He adds that perhaps the *religionsgeschichtliche* search for precise parallels to what we find in Mark 14:62 founders because Jesus assumes his own special interpretation of these texts.

[353] One of the more interesting features of the Trial narratives in general is Jesus' silence at various points. It may be of relevance to point out that "silence is a prominent theme in Israelite wisdom . . . [as] . . . a means of combating slander and gossip, and depicts the proper reverence before the Holy One (Job 4:12-21; 40:4f.; Hab. 2:20, *Kohel.* 5.2)'"; Crenshaw, "Determining," 133.

[354] Cf. Taylor, *Mark*, 568; Cranfield, *Mark*, 443–44.

[355] So much so that Metzger's textual committee does not even discuss the variants at Mark 14:62.

[356] Catchpole, "Answer of Jesus to Caiaphas" 221; quote, 226.

[357] In regard to the use of "I am" here, if it was Jesus' original response, then it does not seem to have been an *Offenbarungsformel* and certainly the later Synoptics do not interpret it as such. In any event, I am basing none of my argument on such a conclusion, except that I take it that Jesus in some manner responded in the positive to the questions. Cf. Howard, *Das Ego Jesu*, 146–47.

[358] As Howard notes, *Das Ego Jesu*, 144–45, the citation of Psalm 110 and Daniel 7 here cannot be judged on literary grounds to be a later addition to the text.

reference to the right hand, *bar enasha* is clearly said to be sitting on his throne of glory (and judgment ensues from such enthronement; cf. *1 Enoch* 45.3; 55.4). It is also noteworthy that the basis for the response of Jesus is (at least in part) a text like Ps. 80:17, "But let thy hand be upon the man of thy right hand, the son of man (*ben adam*) whom thou hast made strong for thyself."[359] This is a distinct possibility, but the wording is so close to Ps. 110:1 that it may also be in view. We may reckon, then, with a creative conglomerate reference involving at least Ps. 110:1 and Dan. 7:13–14, but possibly also Ps. 80:17.

The allusion to Ps. 110:1 suggests that Jesus sees himself as one who will assume a position of divine power and authority as God's right-hand man, his *mashiach*. This, however, is not yet his position. There may be some force in the view that Jesus saw himself as messiah-designate, one who could not or would not personally claim the title until he had first fulfilled the responsibility of *mashiach*.[360] Although the second half of Mark 14:62 does not specifically mention judgment, this is probably in view considering the background in Daniel 7 and *1 Enoch* 37–71, and in light of such sayings as Mark 8:38. Here we do have a prediction of what later came to be called the Parousia. The implication of this text is not only that Jesus is to be identified with this coming Son of man but also that those who judge him now will be judged by him later—the kind of reversal of which Jesus apparently spoke on more than one occasion (cf. Luke 12:8–9).[361] How one reacts to the Son of man now will determine how he reacts to them later. One's reaction to him is decisive for one's ultimate destiny.

CONCLUSIONS

Barrett believes that "the title Son of Man . . . does more than any other to cement the unity of the Gospel tradition. We have seen that in the background of this expression both suffering and glory play their part."[362] In our investigation of the Son of man material we have found the motifs of suffering and glory brought to the foreground. The proper matrix in which to interpret the Son of man material, that which provides the clue as to how Jesus himself viewed the material, is Dan. 7:13–14 and probably also the *Similitudes of Enoch*.

The evidence seems sufficient to conclude that because Jesus used *bar enasha* implies a certain form of messianic self-understanding on his part, although it does not take the form of the popular Davidic expectation. Indeed, Mark 14:62 suggests that Jesus corrected such an interpretation of

---

[359] On this possibility, cf. Moule, *Origins of Christology*, 24–26.
[360] Cf. Fuller, *Foundations*, 102ff.
[361] Cf. Marshall, "Son of Man," 346.
[362] Barrett, *Gospel Tradition*, 67.

himself by referring to the Danielic Son of man. Only later when he comes upon the clouds will he assume the role of world judge and, indeed, judge of the people of God.

Jesus saw it as God's will that he die in Jerusalem to provide a ransom for many. This conclusion may have come to Jesus only late in the campaign after it became apparent that the ministry was not fully accomplishing the task of calling the lost sheep of Israel back to God. In Mark 10:45 we find Jesus correcting the impression that Daniel 7 may have left in many minds — that when *bar enasha* came he would come to be served. Mark 14:62 suggests Jesus did not think his death would be the end of his story or work. Whether Jesus predicted his resurrection, he did expect vindication of his cause beyond the grave. That vindication was spoken of both in terms of his assuming divine power and authority as world judge and in terms of his coming to earth to perform that final judgment. Here we see a rather full-orbed picture of how Jesus viewed his life, death, and its sequel.

Barrett is right that the key to seeing the coherence in the story is found in the Danielic Son of man concept and various of the Son of man sayings that draw on that concept. Even if we leave out of consideration a text like Mark 10:45, which is so controversial, we still have evidence that Jesus experienced rejection and expected vindication as Son of man. Jesus' self-understanding may not have been messianic in the conventional sense, but it was messianic in the Danielic sense, especially as seen through the later interpretation of Daniel found in the *Similitudes of Enoch*, among other places. The conclusions of de Jonge may be endorsed:

> There seems to be no reason to deny that Jesus himself did claim a particular authority, there and then and in the future; thought of himself in terms of suffering and vindication; and expressed this in the term *"the* Son of Man" — covertly referring to the destiny of the "one like a son of man" in Daniel.[363]

Our purpose was to examine selected biblical examples that reveal to us something about Jesus' self-understanding insofar as it went beyond a normal human self-concept. It is significant that even with the few examples we have investigated, we can conclude that not one of the three major categories of Son of man sayings seems to be entirely devoid of allusions to the Danielic material. More importantly, some material from all three categories seems to suggest that Jesus had a messianic or transcendent self-understanding.

---

[363] de Jonge, *Christology in Context*, 172.

5

Afterword and Conclusions

THE MESSIANIC SECRET theory of W. Wrede has received to this point only passing mention. Many scholars since Wrede have pursued Wrede's trajectory and credited the messianic secret motif to Mark's redactional activity. We have looked at the most primitive source material in and behind Mark and Q rather than focus on the evangelist's or Q's redactional activity. Furthermore, our conclusions are not based on texts that are at the heart of the debate (such as Peter's confession in Mark 8:27–30 or the acclamations of the demons in Mark 1:24) as to whether or not Wrede was right. The exorcism narratives were taken as one if not the key to Wrede's case.[1] What we have seen is that in Mark, quite apart from texts that purportedly manifest the messianic secret, much material should be seen in a messianic light. How, then, are we to analyze Wrede's argument, especially in regard to the claim that the ministry of Jesus and perhaps the earliest gospel traditions were non-messianic?[2]

WREDE'S "MESSIANIC SECRET" MOTIF

Since 1901, when Wrede published *Das Messiasgeheimnis in den Evangelien*,[3] passages suggesting a messianic Jesus have been taken by scholars to be the later church's theologizing on the non-messianic ministry of Jesus. Wrede

---

[1] The English translation is *The Messianic Secret*, but the German title uses the word *Geheimnis*, which can have the sense of secret or mystery.

[2] W. C. Robinson, "Wrede's Secret Messiah."

[3] See n. 1 above. When we dealt with the exorcisms, we deliberately made nothing out of those exclamations, but only out of the probability that Jesus did perform exorcisms and that he interpreted these as signs of the in-breaking dominion of God.

assumed that Mark himself redacted his material so as to introduce the idea of the messianic secret into the tradition, prompting his reputation as the progenitor of redaction criticism of the Gospels. But, at the end of his book, Wrede suggests that the messianic secret motif may have been present in Mark's source.[4]

Close scrutiny shows no unified messianic secret motif in Mark. The secrecy material is not of one piece, and it might be better to talk about a dominion secret (4:10-12), or a miracle secret (5:43), or a messianic secret (1:24), or a sonship secret (3:11).[5] Awkward for Wrede's theory is that in the one Markan story where Jesus is called by a Davidic *messianic* label—Son of David (10:46ff.)—the one who cries out is not silenced. Was this because Mark was a careless editor of his source material, or is it evidence that he was not imposing a messianic secrecy motif on his source material? Several recent studies of Mark in general and the messianic secret theory in particular have concluded that Mark was a conservative editor of his source material, not the creative author many redaction critics claim.[6] Räisänen, for instance, agrees with my division of the secrecy material. His conclusion is that no analysis of the secrecy motif, which is present in some Markan texts, can remove the tension that exists between secrecy and openness in the Gospel. Thus, we should not stress the idea that Mark is a creative writer; he is often more a collector of diverse traditions.[7]

Let us consider the Markan texts at the heart of Wrede's case. Examining the exorcism narratives, the command to silence is not found in all of them (cf. 5:1-20; 7:24-30; 9:14-29), even though Wrede singles out the exorcisms as the key to understanding Mark's secrecy theme.[8] Instead, Dunn points out what could be called a publicity theme in Mark, even in an exorcism story (5:20) where the Gerasene demoniac is commanded to go and tell "what the Lord in his mercy has done for you" (5:19f.). Thus, it is difficult to argue for a pre-Markan collection of exorcism tales with the secrecy motif as a major theme.

---

[4] I am not the first to object to this conclusion. Cf. Hoskyns and Davey, *Riddle,* 145: "The Christology lies behind the aphorisms, not ahead of them; this means that at no point is the literary or historical critic able to detect in any stratum of the synoptic material evidence that a Christological interpretation has been imposed upon an un-Christological history."

[5] I agree with U. Luz, "The Secrecy Motif," that there is more than one sort of secrecy material to be found in Mark. He thinks it can all be placed under two headings—messianic secret and miracle secret. I am not sure we can stop there.

[6] R. Pesch, *Das Markusevangelium II* (Freiburg: Herder, 1977), 36-45; and esp. H. Räisänen, '*Messiasgeheimnis,*' 159-68.

[7] In some respects Mark is not simply a compiler of traditions, e.g., in the use of his famous sandwich technique in Mark 3 and 5, he shows creativity. My concern is to talk about the dominant tendency that characterizes his editing, so far as it affects christological matters. He did not, by and large, give free reign to his imagination in his handling of this source material.

[8] J. D. G. Dunn, "Messianic Secret," 116-31.

This publicity theme can also be discerned in healing stories (2:12; 3:3ff). In contrast, other healing stories employ a privacy motif because Jesus is showing compassion and trying to protect the family or individual from unnecessary attention (5:43). Further, why is it, after Jesus gives a command to silence, that Mark records the disobedience to the command (1:25–28; 43–45; 7:36f.)? I think it could be because he is not concerned to impose or even consistently stress a secrecy motif. As Dunn says, "If the messianic secret motif was added to explain why Jesus was not recognized as Messiah, and part of that motif is the command to demons and men not to tell of their cures, I am at a loss to understand what Mark was trying to achieve by adding or at least retaining the publicity sequel."[9]

This short survey of Wrede's key texts makes clear that the messianic secret theory both fails to explain all the Markan texts that deal with messianism, and is a conceptual umbrella under which too many of the secrecy or privacy texts do not fit. Neither the healing texts that call for privacy nor the kingdom secret material fit. Furthermore, when the disciples are instructed in private, sometimes it has nothing to do with a messianic secret (cf. 10:10–12, where the subject is divorce and marriage, not messianism). Stuhlmacher concludes:

> The so-called Messianic secret is not simply . . . a post-Easter theological construction, and in general it had nothing to do with the attempt after Easter to hide the fact that Jesus' life had proceeded unmessianically and beginning at Easter had first been put in the light of Messianism. It is a question much more of a characteristic of the work of Jesus himself![10]

He goes on to urge against Wrede that Jesus used parables in order to accomplish the veiling of various aspects of his work and self-conception. He also points to such sayings as Matt. 11:25ff. that indicate a veiling of the proclamation to a part of the audience. He finally concludes that Jesus at times deliberately spoke in elliptical fashion so as not to be misunderstood as the messiah of popular and political expectation along the lines of *Psalms of Solomon* 17.

The Markan secrecy material can be explained by the alternative theory of Stuhlmacher and others that there was a certain indirectness or veiledness to Jesus' self-expression in his words, deeds, and relationships, and that Mark emphasized this fact in certain passages. Furthermore, the command to silence when Jesus' identity is at issue results from an environment

---

[9] Ibid., 121.

[10] P. Stuhlmacher, *Jesus von Nazareth*, 30–31. Cf. similarly M. Hengel, "Jesus und die Tora," 157: "The much-disputed Messianic Secret is neither a Markan theologoumena nor an apologetical invention of the post-Easter Community, which thereby will account for the alleged unmessianic preaching of Jesus, but finally it goes back to Jesus' own situation. The Messiah could not reveal himself; this was rather God's duty."

where there was a variety of misconceptions about God's *mashiach*, often including the idea of messiah as some sort of political liberator. Jesus did not wish to fit into these preconceptions of what the messiah must be like; rather, by creating his own speech event (his own conceptual world by word, deed, and relationship) he wanted people to judge him on his own basis. Even at the most primitive stage of the synoptic tradition, no basis for a completely non-messianic interpretation of Jesus' self-understanding could be found.

This conclusion could be strengthened by a detailed study of the passion narratives in the Synoptics. Because this material has been subjected to a great deal of christological expansion by its Christian handlers, we have by and large eschewed basing our argument on the passion narratives or on the passion predictions. It is, however, crucial to point out, as H. Boers does, that "attempts to interpret Jesus' messiahship in the light of his passion and death presuppose that he was understood as the messiah in some sense already before his passion. The most obvious prepassion conception of his messiahship would have been as a political pretender."[11] That Jesus rejected the role of political pretender does not mean, however, that he rejected all messianic ideas when applied to him.

Jesus' way of expressing his transcendent self-understanding was by using metaphorical language, symbolic gestures, and actions that, in the light of the Old Testament, had messianic overtones. The indirectness was necessary not only because Jesus was suggesting something that went beyond ordinary and popular understandings of what *mashiach* would be like but also because Jesus sought to provoke a mental effort on the part of his listeners to grasp the truth for themselves. Jesus believed that keen searching with the eyes of faith leads to seeing and not that seeing leads to the right and sufficient sort of believing. This means that Jesus' implicit claim to be someone of messianic significance would not have been obvious to all his contemporaries. Only those willing to see with the eyes of faith could grasp the meaning of God's great parable of redemption—Jesus himself. The messianic secret motif in Mark is neither a literary device to keep something hidden from the reader[12] nor a piece of Christian apologetics;[13] it derives from Jesus' attempts, however unsuccessful, to avoid misunderstanding.

In the end, Wrede was right: The secrecy motif was likely in Mark's source. But this is because it accurately reflected the character of Jesus' ministry. I find support for this conclusion in Longenecker's presentation of the following parallels between the synoptic Jesus and both the Qumran teacher and Simeon ben Koseba: (1) external acclamation; (2) reticence on

---

[11] Boers, *Who was Jesus?* 64.

[12] N. A. Dahl, *Jesus*, 52.

[13] Mark may have stressed this theme in some texts in order to make clear that only with the eyes of *Easter* faith could the mystery of Jesus' being and revelation be fully understood.

the part of the individual to speak of himself in terms used by others; and (3) awareness on the individual's part that the titles employed are at least partially valid. Longenecker associates the reticence of Jesus with the Jewish view that no one can fully accept messianic acclamation until he has fully accomplished the messianic tasks.[14] The reason Jesus is more open about the matter both visibly and verbally during the last week of his life is that it is no longer in order to keep the messianic secret because the messianic tasks are nearly fulfilled.

JESUS' SELF-PERCEPTION

Because our study of Jesus' self-understanding has led us in many directions, we need to gather the pieces together and produce a coherent whole. One major conclusion is that Jesus was a rather unique teacher not only in the manner of his speaking (e.g., "amen," speaking on his own authority, his hermeneutic) but also in the matter of his teaching (e.g., his unique exegesis of Ps. 110:1). Attempts to fit Jesus *wholly* into one category such as teacher, prophet, *hasid*, or magician, so far as how Jesus seems to have viewed himself, fail, however, because they are inadequate rather than inaccurate. In particular, these categories require that one dismiss, ignore, or deny the authenticity of too much of the data that comes from our earliest sources in order to make these various portraits of Jesus appear adequate.

Furthermore, these reconstructions founder especially on the material dealing with the last week or so of Jesus' life. The action in the temple, the trial of Jesus, and his crucifixion as king of the Jews all are more adequately interpreted as evidence that Jesus did not simply see himself as yet another prophet or teacher. Teachers and prophets were martyred before Jesus, but they did not spawn movements that lasted centuries after such a humiliating form of death. It is striking not only that the Jesus movement continued but also that it continued to focus on its crucified leader and his crucifixion. Thus, we must agree with E. Schweizer when he calls Jesus "the man who fits no formula."[15] This is not to say that Jesus is in all respects without analogy in early Judaism. It is rather to insist that although he is similar in various respects to various other early Jews, he cannot be categorized as simply a *hasid*, or a prophet, or any other label one might choose. Even the term messiah is not fully adequate to encompass the many-faceted impression Jesus left on his contemporaries.

---

[14] R. N. Longenecker, "Messianic Secret."

[15] Cf. his *Jesus Christ: The Man from Nazareth and Exalted Lord*, 86. Our conclusion that there is no non-messianic historical Jesus to be found also comports with Schweizer's view that "a Jesus of Nazareth who is not seen in the sense of the post-Easter kerygma as the Christ of God is not Jesus of Nazareth at all" (56).

Whatever theory one espouses of Jesus' view of himself, it must also be adequate to explain: (1) Jesus' independent approach to the law; (2) his feeding of the 5000; (3) his interpretation of his miracles; (4) his proclamation of the dominion of God as present and inbreaking in his ministry, and his action based on the conviction of the inbreaking dominion;[16] (5) his choosing of twelve disciples; (6) his use of *bar enasha*; (7) his use of Amen; (8) his use of *abba*; (9) the way he distinguished himself from all his close contemporaries to one degree or another, including the Baptist, the Pharisees, the revolutionaries, and even the disciples; (10) his belief that one's future standing with Yahweh hinged on how one reacted to his ministry; (11) his understanding that it was necessary for him to die, to undergo a baptism to rectify matters between God and God's people; (12) Jesus' sense of mission to the whole of Israel, but especially to the least, lost, and last, the sinners and outcasts, which led to table fellowship with such people; and (13) his raising messianic expectations with a repeated pattern of controversy between Jesus and various of his contemporaries even at the earliest stages of the Gospel material.

It appears to me that these factors are fully accounted for only if Jesus saw himself as God's *mashiach*,[17] God's royal Son (at least as early as his baptism) that he acted throughout his ministry in the light of his belief that he was called to a messianic mission, and that he had been endowed with the necessary divine knowledge, power, and authority by God's Spirit to carry out that mission to Israel. In Jesus' view, Israel as a whole was lost, and it was his task to call his fellow Jews to repentance because judgment would soon befall the nation. Unlike the Baptist, Jesus offered both preparation for and a positive alternative to the wrath to come.

Our study of the *abba* material suggests that Jesus thought of himself as having a unique relationship with God. He believed he had an unusual degree of intimacy with God, and he had an unusual self-understanding that involved what may be called a filial consciousness. It may be true that Jesus chiefly understood himself as God's special or royal Son, an idea that expresses a certain kind of messianic thinking. This special relationship that Jesus had with God, and the roles and status that accompanied it, were confirmed to Jesus in an ecstatic visionary experience when he submitted to John's baptism. Although Jesus' belief in his sonship status was implicit in his use of *abba*, it becomes more explicit in contexts where the subject of knowledge comes up—Jesus' intimate, and in some sense exclusive, knowledge of the Father (Matt. 11:27//Luke10:22), and also paradoxically his

---

[16] de Jonge, *Christology in Context*, 206.

[17] Ibid., 211. de Jonge concludes on the term Messiah/Christ: "In view of the central position of the designation in early Christian Christology, however, it remains likely that the term was not chosen by overenthusiastic admirers or by his opponents, but was regarded as suitable by Jesus himself."

lack of knowledge of the timing of some events in God's future plans for his people (Mark 13:32). By the term Son, Jesus made clear at least to his circle of intimates how he was to be distinguished from all other human beings with regard to the knowledge of God and from the Father with respect to his lack of knowledge of divine future plans. Jesus saw himself as above other humans, perhaps even above the angels, in his knowledge of God and God's will, but below the Father because ignorance of the timing of the Parousia could be predicated of the Son. Because of this knowledge theme and the way it is formulated (especially in Matt. 11:27 and par.), Jesus casts himself in a role that elsewhere in Jewish literature is given to personified Wisdom—the one who knows the mind of God and shares that knowledge.

Jesus chiefly expressed his identity to the general public by the use of the phrase *bar enasha*. In our investigation of the "Son of man" material, we discovered that Jesus' use of *bar enasha* often reflects his understanding of himself in light of Daniel 7, but supplemented by the sort of ideas expressed in the *Similitudes* of Enoch. If the latter does lie in the background of Jesus' use of *bar enasha*, then that phrase may be Jesus' way of expressing his messianic self-understanding to his wider audience. It is not necessary to affirm the existence of any mythological *Ur-Mensch* idea in Jesus' era to draw this conclusion because the idea is clearly expressed in the *Similitudes*. More clearly, Jesus used the term *bar enasha* to indicate that he saw himself taking on the role of Israel's representative, both at the last judgment before God and presently as the representative of suffering Israel on earth. Mark 10:45 should be understood in light of the wider context of suffering expressed in Daniel and may also owe something to Maccabean martyr theology.[18] Jesus would be the representative of Israel during his life, in his death, and at the judgment that was to come. At the end of Jesus' life, as all through the ministry, Jesus was still using the phrase *bar enasha* to express his self-understanding. Jesus did not refuse the suggestion by the high priest that he saw himself as the *mashiach*, but he immediately qualified that assent by referring to the future coming of *bar enasha* for judgment (Mark 14:62). I agree with Barrett that "the title Son of Man . . . does more than any other to cement the unity of the gospel tradition. We have seen that in the background of this expression both suffering and glory play their part."[19]

---

[18] One must, however, use the parallels with the Maccabean movement with caution. Boers, *Who Was Jesus?* 89ff., suggests for instance that the parallels between Jesus' action in the temple and that of Simon Maccabeus as recorded in 1 Macc. 13:49–53 and 2 Macc. 10:1–9 suggest Jesus was a political pretender. But this is precisely where the parallels break down. Simon both literally cleansed the whole temple and accepted accolades with palm branch waving thereafter. Jesus in fact only undertook a symbolic act and then immediately withdrew; the accolades, if they were offered at all to Jesus, and that is uncertain from the entrance narratives, came before Jesus' temple cleansing.

[19] Barrett, *Gospel Tradition*, 127.

Frequently, we observed that Jesus directed his ministry to God's chosen people – to Israel. This factor comes to light even in the First Gospel, which seems clear about the church's mission to the Gentiles. The Jews were the people Jesus came to ransom; even his choice of the Twelve indicates that was the focus of his attention. This evidence led us to conclude that Jesus saw himself as the Messiah – the *Jewish mashiach.* A focus purely on Jews is something the later church would hardly have invented.

Not to be neglected is Jesus' teaching on God's dominion. Jesus expressed himself not only in apocalyptic images (*bar enasha*), which is one form of metaphorical speech, but also in *meshalim,* which is metaphorical wisdom speech. Jesus believed this dominion, as God's liberating reign in human lives, was breaking in during and through his ministry. Nevertheless, he also saw the dominion as a realm that could be entered only if one responded positively to the message of Jesus (and perhaps also of John). The already/not yet aspects of Jesus' eschatological teaching about God's dominion need to be held in tension, with neither side being dismissed or ignored. Luke 11:20 (and par.) strongly suggests that Jesus saw himself as the agent or *shaliach* of God, endowed with God's authority, power, and God's knowledge. As a result of this self-understanding, Jesus sent out his inner circle as his own agents (*apostoloi*), even during his ministry. Just as he made possible their sharing in a sonship status so also he made possible a sharing in God's mission on earth, as agents of God's agent.

In our discussion of Jesus' deeds we noted that: (1) he interpreted his exorcisms as the inbreaking of God's final dominion; and (2) he interpreted his other healings in light of the Isaianic vision of future eschatological restoration. It is in Jesus' interpretation of these deeds that we found at least an implicit christological claim. The deeds themselves were not unprecedented. In a Jewish setting, however, there may have been a special messianic significance to the healing of the blind, and possibly also to the exorcisms (neither of which are predicated of Old Testament figures). We argued that these interpretations of Jesus' deeds go back to Jesus, at least in substance, because the christological overtones are latent and without elaboration. Indeed, Jesus, in his exorcisms and other acts of compassion, believed he was doing battle with the powers of darkness – and winning! This suggests a great sense of supernatural power and authority on his part.

Comparing and contrasting Jesus with his closest contemporaries further clarifies our understanding. Jesus, like John the Baptist, was initially a preacher of repentance in view of the coming action of God. But unlike John, Jesus not only focused on such coming judgment but also stressed good news about the inbreaking of God's acts of compassion and help for God's people. Jesus saw such action as already here, but in regard to the judgment he saw it as hovering on the near horizon, as had John. Hence, a crisis was upon Israel and the nation must respond decisively to it – time could not be wasted. Perhaps most striking was that Jesus, unlike John, did not expect any successors. Jesus' style of ministry, which included his sharing table fellowship with sinners and tax collectors, contrasted sharply with John's more ascetical approach to the coming crisis.

Perhaps the group in early Judaism with whom Jesus had most in common was the Pharisees. Both were concerned about the moral condition of God's people. Neither advocated a violent political remedy to the oppression that God's people were enduring; both called the people to spiritual rejuvenation. Jesus and the Pharisees acted in public, and neither had written off the mass of Israel, in contrast to more sectarian groups such as the Qumranites. Both had hopes of bringing the whole nation back to God. But they radically disagreed about how to recover the lost sheep of Israel. Rather than spreading the standards of priestly holiness throughout the land, Jesus went on a rehabilitation and reclamation campaign, performing acts of compassion and breaking bread even with outcasts, toll collectors, and sinners.

Jesus both identified himself with and distinguished himself from his disciples. The identification is clearest: (1) in the sending out of the Twelve to perform the very same deeds and preaching as Jesus had engaged in, (2) in the promise that they too, like the Son of man, would have a role in the future judging of Israel, and (3) in sayings that implied that the rejection of Jesus' *shalihim* implied the rejection of God's *shaliach* and thus of God himself. Yet clearly Jesus distinguished himself from the Twelve in the following ways: (1) Jesus never identified himself as one of the Twelve; (2) he saw it as his unique task to provide a ransom for many (the disciples might also die, but there is no hint that Jesus ever saw their sufferings as redemptive); (3) Jesus alone was the one who could initiate a person into that special filial relationship with God; and (4) he alone was *bar enasha*, a term which never became a designation for any of his followers.

In all of Jesus' key relationships we see both elements of identification and distinction. No doubt this is the reason that people had such a hard time categorizing Jesus, and still do. We find the Christology of Jesus chiefly in the way he distinguished himself from his close contemporaries because here we see the ways he stood out from the crowd, the ways in which he was unique. Fortunately, it is here that the most widely accepted criterion for authenticity comes into play—the criterion of *dissimilarity*.

Apparently, it was not unique in Jesus' era to perceive of oneself as Israel's messiah. There were various messianic movements in Jesus day, led by persons who, like Jesus, saw themselves in a messianic light. Messianic expectation in the early first century took various forms as to what *mashiach* might be like and might do. Probably the most popular form of expectation in Jesus' day involved the hope of a descendant of David who would come and throw off the yoke of foreign rule.

Jesus, however, deliberately distanced himself from that form of expectation. Instead, he expressed his self-understanding using the Danielic *bar enasha*. Apparently, his self-concept was shaped by some of the shepherd king material in Zechariah and, to a lesser extent, by some royal psalms. In Jesus' response to the Baptist, it appears he also saw some of the Isaianic material as being fulfilled in his life and ministry. Jesus' self-concept was shaped chiefly by the prophecies in the later prophetical books of the Old Testament and, in view of the prevalence of both *bar enasha* and *basileia* in the authentic Jesus material, by the apocalyptic material in Daniel.

Study of messianic movements revealed that Jesus by his words and deeds—even if he never made a single public claim about his messianic status—meets the criteria so that he can be called the intentional founder of a messianic movement. He not only served as the catalyst for the criticism of the existing order but also raised the positive hopes of many that God's promises to God's people about Torah, temple, and territory were now finally coming to pass. Further, Jesus offered an interpretative schema that gave the people a vision of God's ways, a schema distinct from that of the Pharisees and other major groups in his society; hence, their hostile reaction. The Pharisees and probably others rightly took Jesus' message as a critique of theirs.

Jesus critiqued not only the "traditions of the elders," which were so important to the Pharisaic approach to life, but also the interpretation of Torah and even Torah itself. God was doing a new thing in Jesus' ministry; those who witnessed his ministry witnessed the inbreaking of the eschatological era, the very *malkut* of God. This being so, new wine could not always be poured into old wineskins—the law had to be and was transcended in the ministry of Jesus. He made a radical demand on those who would follow him, insisting that the priorities of the family of faith supersede those of the physical family. Even more radical is Jesus' approach to persons who were physically or morally unclean. In his association with the diseased and sinners, Jesus not only disregarded the rules of clean and unclean in the Old Testament, he also indicated that they no longer applied in the new situation God was initiating through Jesus' ministry. Especially striking is how Jesus, following John, believed that forgiveness could be had by repentance and reception of the inbreaking work of God, apart from the temple cultus. This characterizes one who believed he was God's final and eschatological messenger, doing a new thing, and not merely someone interested in the restoration of Israel's former glories.

The conditions in Israel as a whole, including Galilee, were ripe for a messianic movement. Horsley noted how difficult the social and economic situation was becoming in Jesus' day with farmers increasingly losing their land to absentee landlords.[20] A growing underclass of day laborers or indentured servants was emerging just to survive. In such an environment, a

---

[20] Horsley, *Spiral of Violence*, 3ff.

person who went about proclaiming God's inbreaking *malkut,* and saying things like "the meek would inherit the land," would be understood as a messianic figure. More importantly, in such an environment Jesus had to know that he would be interpreted in that fashion, for surely he was aware of the Old Testament promises.

If Jesus intentionally performed an act such as the feeding of the 5000 in a remote area of Galilee, it is hardly surprising that some sought to proclaim or even make him their king. Jesus' withdrawing from the crowd could be interpreted either as a rejection of messianic acclaim or, because Jesus seems to have deliberately provoked such an idea in the first place, as a rejection of a particular interpretation of messianism. In view of the sequel to the feeding miracle—Jesus going to Jerusalem, riding a donkey, and performing a symbolic action in the temple—his reaction to the crowd at the feeding should not be interpreted as his outright rejection of being the *mashiach.*

What Jesus rejected is being a Davidic conqueror and not his bringing significant social and religious change as a messianic figure. Because a variety of messianic ideas circulated in early Judaism, Jesus' rejection of one model of what the messiah must look like does not lead to the conclusion that he rejected all such models.[21] Rather, he saw himself in the light of the shepherd king of Zechariah, the *bar enasha* of Daniel, and certain royal psalms. He also interpreted his healing activities in light of the vision of the eschatological age found in the Isaianic literature. The evidence suggests that at the end of his ministry Jesus became more vocal and visible about who he thought he was—as the temple action and dialogue with the high priest show.

How Jesus reacted to the three pillars of early Judaism—Torah, temple, and territory—offers a different way to view the data. S. Freyne reminds us that "any shift in emphasis in regard to one of those symbols inevitably meant a change of focus on all three, thereby giving rise to a new Judaism."[22] Surprisingly, Jesus said little about the territorial doctrine. The significance is that it shows he was not an advocate of inaugurating the final age by a retaking of the land. Jesus was no political revolutionary, even though certain of his actions were socially and religiously radical. God's *malkut* was breaking into human lives and changing them, but the call to throw off the yoke of Roman rule and retake the land is missing in Jesus' message. He did not use (as far as we can tell) the ancient Near Eastern myth of the divine warrior to articulate his vision of the coming dominion of God.[23]

In regard to Torah, Jesus sometimes endorsed, sometimes intensified, sometimes abrogated or transcended the Torah. This approach to Scripture,

---

[21] Cf. Charlesworth's summary of probable authentic aspects of Jesus' ministry that have christological weight, in *Jesus within Judaism,* 169.

[22] S. Freyne, *Galilee,* 261, following J. Neusner among others.

[23] Rightly noted by Freyne, *Galilee,* 267.

coupled with his hermeneutic of seeing Scripture fulfilled in his ministry, surely points to a self-conception that goes beyond that of the Old Testament prophets or the teachers of Jesus' day.

In regard to the temple, if Jesus' prophetic action in the outer court were either a symbol of God's coming to cleanse out the corruption or a prophetic sign of God's coming judgment on the temple, then we have an action with messianic overtones. This is even more the case if Jesus also made a claim to build the (final) temple of God, especially if it were coupled with a prophecy of the fall of the present temple. If we add to this Jesus' offer of forgiveness apart from the temple cultus, then it becomes hard to deny that Jesus saw himself in a transcendent category. Surely, Jesus' critique of Torah, temple, and territory went beyond previous prophetic critiques of these key pillars of Judaism.[24]

Thus, we are on firm ground when talking about Jesus' messianic, filial, or *bar enasha* self-conception. At this point, however, we should consider whether there is authentic material that goes even beyond such categories. In some parables, Jesus alluded to himself as taking on roles predicated of Yahweh in the Old Testament. Jesus may have seen himself as God's agent or *shaliach*, although the case for such a conclusion is less strong than for Jesus' messianic self-understanding. The church's later high Christology seems to build on the observations: (1) that Jesus operated with divine power and authority; (2) that he was able to bestow such divine power and authority on some of his followers during the ministry; (3) that he believed a rejection of his ministry meant a judgment of that person at the eschaton; and (4) by contrast, that an acceptance of Jesus and his mission got one into God's *malkut* and secured a reservation at the messianic banquet.

More speculative was whether Jesus saw himself also as Wisdom incarnate, the very embodiment of the mind and plan of God for God's people. There seems to be some evidence for this in Q. Because Q cannot simply be classified as *Logoi Sophoi*, the question arises whether or not this depiction of Jesus as divine Wisdom may be more than merely a redactional agenda of early Jewish Christians and, in fact, go back to Jesus himself. Three things support the view that the Wisdom persona goes back to Jesus himself. First, there is evidence of Jesus being depicted as Wisdom or at least as a teacher of wisdom in early material that was not only in Q (cf. Mark 6:2ff. and par.;

---

[24] The summary statement of P. Fredricksen is judicious and in some important ways parallels our own. Cf. her *Jesus to Christ*, 125: "His calling twelve disciples to represent all the eschatological tribes of Israel; his intensification of the ethical norms embodied in Torah; his journey to Jerusalem to greet the coming Kingdom; his prophetic gesture at the temple, in anticipation of a Temple not made by hands; his prophecy of the imminent fulfillment of God's promises to Israel revealed in Torah . . . [explain] in the tinderbox of early first century Palestine, [why] crucifixion of such a prophet would be a prudent Roman response." She refuses, however, to draw the conclusion that all this suggests Jesus saw himself in messianic categories; cf. 129.

Luke 2:40–52; esp. Matt. 11:28–30). Second, casting Jesus as Wisdom is not part of the first evangelist's christological agenda. Third, and perhaps most important, Jesus chose as his major vehicle of public self-expression the *mashal*, a form of wisdom utterance. These seem to be strong hints that Jesus assumed the persona of Wisdom.

The recent detailed study by R. Piper on *Wisdom in the Q-tradition*[25] provides evidence that Jesus may have seen himself as an envoy of Sophia and perhaps a good deal more. He concludes his study by saying, "the agenda is therefore set for recognizing in Jesus that not only 'something greater than Jonah,' but also 'something greater than Solomon is here.'"[26] If so, then it is possible that the composers of the early christological hymns developed the idea of the preexistence of the Son from these hints in the Gospel wisdom material.

Based on the same material, J. Ernst concludes his study of Christology:

> Easter is nevertheless not in an absolute sense the Beginning. Easter has much more released what was already implicit beforehand. Such a Christological foundation stone is tangible for all in the words of Jesus, which have been collected from the earliest days of the Christian Community, but which let us recognize a pre-Easter *Sitz im Leben*. The words of Jesus, in particular any of the hard, scandalous demands to follow and the rigor of the ethical preaching, make the way free for an in-depth understanding of the person that Jesus was.[27]

In addition, Hoskyns insists:

> Only when the Christology is taken seriously and when its fundamental importance is fully recognized does Jesus emerge as a concrete figure in history. Only upon the background of the Christology do the great *Logia* which lie scattered about in the various literary strata of the Gospels cease to be disconnected fragments and come together as component parts of one messianic whole.[28]

One final question: Did Jesus think himself to be divine? In early Judaism it appears the *mashiach* was usually expected to be just another human being, although one with God-given role, power, and authority. It is not

---

[25] Subtitled *The Aphoristic Teaching of Jesus* SNTS Mono. 61 (Cambridge: Cambridge University Press, 1989), 193–96.

[26] Piper, *Wisdom*, 196; cf. esp. 161–92.

[27] J. Ernst, *Anfänge der Christologie*, 160.

[28] E. Hoskyns, "Jesus the Messiah," *Mysterium Christi*, 69–89, here p. 88, cf. p. 82. Along the same lines as our conclusions are those of Moule, *Origins of Christology*, 80–81: "When one asks, Who could Jesus have been, to affect his disciples and their successors in the ways in which he did? the 'evolutionary' type of answer, plausible though it may seem at first, seems less than adequate. More adequate is the answer which finds, from the beginning, a Person of such magnitude that, so far from pious imagination's embroidering and enlarging him, the perennial problem was, rather, how to reach any insight that would come near to fathoming him, or any description that was not pitifully inadequate."

possible to be unequivocal about the shape of early Jewish expectation, for some material (e.g., the *Similitudes* of Enoch) seems to suggest that the *mashiach* would have a transfigured if not transformed humanity, and thus would not be just a normal or ordinary human being with an extraordinary God-consciousness.

Material in the Synoptics hints that Jesus had a transcendent self-image amounting to more than a unique awareness of the Divine. If, however, one means by divine awareness something that suggests either that Jesus saw himself as the whole or exclusive representation of the Godhead or that he considered himself in a way that amounted to the rejection of the central tenet of Judaism, (i.e., monotheism), then the answer must be no. Jesus clearly prayed to a God he called *abba*, which excludes the idea that Jesus thought he was *abba*. Jesus' affirmation of monotheism seems clear (e.g., Mark 10:17–18; Matt. 23:9).

Yet, as Raymond Brown points out, if the question, 'Are you God?', had been asked of Jesus during his lifetime, the question would have meant "Are you the Father in heaven?" not "Are you the second person of the Trinity?"[29] Later trinitarian thinking cannot be read back into early Judaism. Put in those terms, Jesus' answer to the question would have been no. In fact, it is almost impossible to believe that the question would have been raised in those terms. On the one hand, what sense does it make to ask of a human being dwelling on earth if he is the Father in heaven? On the other hand, "to say that the enormous impact of Jesus changed the meaning of 'God' is no exaggeration."[30] It is also true that what one publicly claims or hints about oneself and what one believes about oneself can be two different things. We have sought in this study to go beyond the so-called titles and public claims of Jesus to his self-concept. One must then ask questions like, What did Jesus imply when he left the suggestion that he should be seen as David's Lord? I think he implied that he should be seen not merely as a greater king than David but in a higher and more transcendent category. What Jesus implied about his self-conception is as important as what he publicly claimed.

In conclusion, I can do no better than quote Raymond Brown:

> Jesus knew his own identity which involved a unique relationship to God that we call the divinity of the Son. Christians of a later period were able to formulate Jesus' identity as "true God and true man," a formulation better than any other that had been attempted but certainly not exhaustive of the mystery. . . . The idea that he was divine I find on most Gospel pages. An attempt to lessen the self-evaluation of Jesus to something like "he thought only that he was a prophet" would, in my judgment, involve proving the

---

[29] R. E. Brown, "Did Jesus Know," 77.
[30] Ibid.

Gospels misunderstood Jesus. No Old Testament prophet acted in such independence of the Mosaic Law; and it is remarkable that one never finds in reference to Jesus a prophetic formula such as, "The word of God came to Jesus of Nazareth." . . . Jesus' intuitive knowledge of his self-identity would have been a knowledge of what we call in faith being God and being man, and certainly such self-knowledge can have been no less difficult to express than our knowledge of being human. I regard the term "God" applied to Jesus to be a formulation of Christians in the second half of the first century seeking to express an identity that Jesus knew better than they and which is scarcely exhausted by the term "God" . . . *It is not evident that Jesus formulated . . . his self-identity* in the terms of later New Testament Christianity, such as . . . God. [Nonetheless] I have no difficulty with the thesis that if Jesus . . . could have read John, he would have found that Gospel a suitable expression of his identity . . . The affirmation that Jesus had knowledge of his self-identity . . . is not meant to exclude *a development in his existential knowledge of what that identity implied for his life.*[31]

Nor does it exclude Jesus from partaking of some of the limitations in knowledge that humans experience about life, especially in regard to the future (Mark 13:32). But one sort of knowledge—of himself—Jesus did seem to have with clarity. There is no evidence in the Gospel material that Jesus ever had an identity crisis, although there appear to have been some ongoing uncertainties about how he should fulfill the mission God had given him, especially in regard to the temptation to be a messianic figure in the popular political mold, and to avoid the cross.

In this study we have seen that the seeds of later christological development are found in the relationships, deeds, and words of Jesus, and that in these three ways Jesus indirectly expressed some of his self-understanding. In short, he may have been mysterious and elusive at times, but this was because he intended to tease his listeners into thought and ultimately into a response of faith or trust. As F. Buechner says, he had a face that was "not a front for him to live his life behind but a frontier, the outermost visible edge of his life itself in all its richness and multiplicity. . . . So once again, for the last time or the first time, we face that face."[32]

---

[31] Ibid., 77–78.
[32] Buechner, *Life of Jesus*, 9, 14, 10.

Abbreviations

AER	*American Ecclesiastical Review*
AJA	*American Journal of Archaeology*
AJP	*American Journal of Philology*
AJT	*American Journal of Theology*
APOT	Charles, R. H., ed. *The Apocrypha and Pseudepigrapha of the Old Testament in English.* 2 vols. Oxford: Clarendon Press, 1913.
A-S	Abbott-Smith, G. *A Manual Greek Lexicon of the New Testament.* Edinburgh: T. & T. Clark, 1937.
BA	*Biblical Archaeologist*
BAG	Bauer, W., Arndt, W., and Gingrich, F. W. *A Greek-English Lexicon of the New Testament.* Chicago: University of Chicago Press, 1952.
BAR	*Biblical Archaelogy Review*
BASOR	*Bulletin of the American Schools of Oriental Research*
Barrett, *John*	Barrett, C. K. *The Gospel according to John.* London: SPCK, 1955.
BDF	Blass, F. and Debrunner, A. *A Greek Grammar of the New Testament.* Trans. R. W. Funk. Chicago, 1961.
Beare, *Matthew*	Beare, F. W. *The Gospel according to Matthew.* Peabody, Mass.: Hendrikson, 1981.
BeO	*Biblia E Oriente*
Bib	*Biblica*
BibLeb	*Bibel und Leben*
BJRL	*Bulletin of the John Rylands University Library of Manchester*
BNTC	Black's New Testament Commentary
BR	*Biblical Research*
Brown, *John*	Brown, R. E. *John 1–20.* New York: Doubleday, 1966.
BSac	*Bibliotheca Sacra*

BT	*Bible Translator*
BTB	*Biblical Theology Bulletin*
Budé	Paris: Société d'Editions "Les Belles Lettres"
BW	*Biblical World*
BZ	*Biblische Zeitschrift*
BZNW	Beihefte zur Zeitschrift für die neutestamentliche Wissenschaft und die Kunde der älteren Kirche
CBQ	*Catholic Biblical Quarterly*
CBR	*Christian Brethren Review*
CGTC	Cambridge Greek Testament Commentary
Cranfield, *Mark*	Cranfield, C. E. B. *The Gospel according to Mark.* Cambridge: Cambridge University Press, 1963.
Creed, *Luke*	Creed, J. M. *The Gospel according to St. Luke.* London: Macmillan, 1930.
CTJ	*Calvin Theological Journal*
CTM	*Concordia Theological Monthly*
Danby	Herbert Danby, trans. *The Mishnah.* London: Oxford University Press, 1933.
DNTT	*Dictionary of New Testament Theology.* Edited by Colin Brown. Grand Rapids: Zondervan, 1976–78.
Ellis, *Luke*	Ellis, E. E. *The Gospel of Luke.* London: Oliphants, 1974.
EspV	*Esprit et Vie*
ET	*Expository Times*
ETh	*Église et Théologie*
ETL	*Ephemerides Theologicae Lovanienses*
EvQ	*Evangelical Quarterly*
Fitzmyer, *Luke 1–9*	Fitzmyer, J. *The Gospel according to Luke 1–9.* Garden City, NY: Doubleday, 1981.
Fitzmyer, *Luke 10–24*	Fitzmyer, J. *The Gospel according to Luke 10–24.* Garden City, NY: Doubleday, 1985.
FRLANT	Forschungen zur Religion und Literatur des Alten und Neuen Testaments
Greg	*Gregorianum*
HGNT	Handbuch zum Griechen Neuen Testament
Hill, *Matthew*	Hill, D. H. *The Gospel of Matthew.* London: Oliphant, 1972.
HNT	Handbuch zum Neuen Testament
HNTC	Harper's New Testament Commentary
HR	*History of Religions*
HTKNT	Herder's Theologischer Kommentar zum Neuen Testament
HTR	*Harvard Theological Review*
ICC	International Critical Commentary
IDB	*Interpreter's Dictionary of the Bible.* Nashville: Abingdon, 1962.
IDB Suppl.	*Interpreter's Dictionary of the Bible. Supplement.* Nashville: Abingdon, 1976.
IEJ	*Israel Exploration Journal*

Int	*Interpretation*
JAAR	*Journal of the American Academy of Religion*
JBL	*Journal of Biblical Literature*
JETS	*Journal of the Evangelical Theological Society*
JHS	*Journal of Hellenic Studies*
JJS	*Journal of Jewish Studies*
JR	*Juridical Review*
JSemS	*Sournal of Semitic Studies*
JSNT	*Journal for the Study of the New Testament*
JSOT	*Journal for the Study of the Old Testament*
JTNT	*Journal of the Theology of the New Testament*
JTS	*Journal of Theological Studies*
JTSA	*Journal of Theology for South Africa*
KEK	Kritisch-exegetischer Kommentar über das Neue Testament
KG	*Kathologische Gedänke*
Lane, *Mark*	Lane, W. *The Gospel according to Mark.* Grand Rapids: Eerdmans, 1974.
LCL	Loeb Classical Library
LTQ	*Lexington Theological Quarterly*
LV	*Lumen Vitae*
Marshall, *Luke*	Marshall, I. H. *Historian and Theologian.* Exeter: Paternoster, 1970.
Metzger, *TC*	Metzger, Bruce M. *A Textual Commentary on the Greek New Testament.* London: United Bible Societies, 1971.
MHT	Moulton, J. H., Howard, W. F., and Turner, N. *A Grammar of New Testament Greek.* 4 vols. Edinburgh: T. & T. Clark, 1908–76.
MM	Moulton, J. H., and Milligan, G. *The Vocabulary of the Greek New Testament.* Grand Rapids: Eerdmans, 1930.
M'Neile, *Matthew*	M'Neile, A. H. *The Gospel according to St. Matthew.* London: Macmillan, 1965.
MNTC	Moffatt New Testament Commentary
Moule, *I-B*	Moule, C. F. D. *An Idiom-Book of New Testament Greek.* Cambridge: Cambridge University Press, 1953.
MS	*Marian Studies*
NCB	New Century Bible
NICNT	New International Commentary on the New Testament
NIGTC	New International Greek Testament Commentary
NovTest	*Novum Testamentum*
NPNF	Nicene and Post-Nicene Fathers
NRT	*Nouvelle Revue Théologique*
NTA	*New Testament Abstracts*
NTAp	Edgar Hennecke. *New Testament Apocrypha.* 2 vols. Philadelphia: Westminster Press, 1963–65.
NTD	*Das Neue Testament Deutsch*
NTGNA	*Novum Testamentum Graece.* Edited by E. Nestle and K. Aland. London: United Bible Societies, 1971.
NTS	*New Testament Studies*

NVet	*Nova et Vetera*
OTP	*Old Testament Pseudepigrapha*. Edited by J. H. Charlesworth. 2 vols. Garden City, N.Y.: Doubleday, 1983.
PalCler	*Palestra del Clero*
Philo *Q.R.D.H.*	*Quis Rerum Divinarium Heres*
Plut. *Tib. Grac.*	Plutarch *Tiberius Graecus*
PNTC	Pelican New Testament Commentary
RB	*Revue Biblique*
RevExp	*Review and Expositor*
ResQ	*Restoration Quarterly*
RHE	*Revue d'Histoire Ecclésiastique*
RHPR	*Revue d'Histoire et de Philosophie Religieuses*
RJ	*Reformed Journal*
Robertson	A. T. Robertson. *A Grammar of the Greek New Testament in Light of Historical Research*. Nashville: Broadman Press, 1934.
RSPT	*Revue des sciences philosophiques et théologiques*
RUO	*Revue de l'Université d'Ottawa*
SBL	*Society of Biblical Literature*
SBLDS	*Society of Biblical Literature Dissertation Series*
SBLMS	*Society of Biblical Literature Monograph Series*
Schweizer, *Matthew*	Schweizer, E. *The Good News according to Matthew*. Atlanta: John Knox Press, 1975.
SJT	Scottish Journal of Theology
SNTSMS	Society of New Testament Studies Monograph Series
Str-B	Strack, Hermann L., and Billerbeck, Paul. *Kommentar zum Neuen Testament aus Talmud und Midrasch*. Munich, 1974–75.
Tacitus *Hist.*	Tacitus *Histories*. Loeb Classical Library.
Taylor, *Mark*	Taylor, V. *The Gospel according to Mark*. New York: St. Martin's Press, 1966.
TDNT	*Theological Dictionary of the New Testament*. Edited by Gerhard Kittel and G. Friedrich. 10 vols. Grand Rapids, 1964–76.
TGL	*Theologie und Glaube*
ThHk	Theologischer Handkommentar
THKNT	Theologischer Handkommentar zum Neuen Testament
ThR	*Theological Review*
TNTC	Tyndale New Testament Commentary
TQ	*Theologische Quartalschrift*
TS	*Theologische Studien*
TSK	*Theologische Studien und Kritiken*
TynB	*Tyndale Bulletin*
TZ	*Theologische Zeitschrift*
UBSGNT	*The Greek New Testament* (United Bible Society). Edited by Kurt Aland et al. 3 ed. London, 1975.
UNT	Untersuchungen zum Neuen Testament
USQR	*Union Seminary Quarterly Review*
VD	*Verbum Domini*

WTJ	*Westminster Theological Journal*
Zerwick	Zerwick, Maximilian. *Biblical Greek.* Rome, 1963.
ZNW	*Zeitschrift für die neutestamentliche Wissenschaft*
ZTK	*Zeitschrift für Theologie und Kirche*

PSEUDEPIGRAPHICAL BOOKS

2 Bar.	*Syriac, Apocalypse of Baruch*
Assum. of Moses	*Assumption of Moses*
1 Enoch	Ethiopic *Enoch*
Gos. Thom.	*Gospel of Thomas*
Jub.	*Jubilees*
Pss. Sol.	*Psalms of Solomon*
Reuben	*Reuben*
Test. Levi	*Testament of Levi*

DEAD SEA SCROLLS AND RELATED TEXTS

1QH	*Thanksgiving Hymns*
1QM	*War Scroll*
1QS	*Rule of the Community*
1QSa	Appendix A to 1QS
1QSam	Samuel
4QFlor.	*Florilegium*
4QTestim	*Testimonia*
11QMelch	*Melchizedek*
11QPs-a	Psalms manuscript a

TARGUMIC MATERIAL

Targ.Isa.	*Targum of Isaiah*
Targ.Mal.	*Targum of Malachi*
Targ.Ps.	*Targum of Psalms*
Targ.Song	*Targum of Song of Songs*
Targ. Yer.	*Targum Yerushalmi*

MISHNAIC AND RELATED LITERATURE

Aboda Zar.	*'Aboda Zara*
B.T.Bab.Hag.	*Babylonian Talmud Hagigah*
B.T.Ber.	*Babylonian Talmud Berakot*
B.T.Kid.	*Babylonian Talmud Kiddushin*
B.T.Men.	*Babylonian Talmud Menahot*

B.T.Niddah	Babylonian Talmud Niddah
B.T.S(h)ab(b).	Babylonian Talmud S(h)abbat
B.T.San.	Babylonian Talmud Sanhedrin
B.T.Seb.	Babylonian Talmud Sebi'it
B.T.Taan.	Babylonian Talmud Taanith
B.T.Ta'an.	Babylonian Talmud Ta'anit
B.T.Yom.	Babylonian Talmud Yoma
Eduyoth	'Eduyyot
J.T.Av Zarah	Jerusalem Talmud
J.T.Erub.	Jerusalem Talmud 'Erubin
J.T.S(h)ab(b).	Jerusalem Talmud Shabbat
J.T.Ta'an.	Jerusalem Talmud Ta'anit
J.T.Ter.	Jerusalem Talmud Termot
M.Benj.	Mishna Benjamin
M.Berak.	Mishna Berakot
M.Demai	Mishna Demai
M.Rosh Ha-Shanah	Mishna Rosh Ha-Shanah
M.San.	Mishna Sanhedrin
M.Shek.	Mishna Shekalim
M.Sotah	Mishna Sotah
M.Suk.	Mishan Sukka
M. Taan.	Mishna Taanith
M.Yoma	Mishna Yoma (= Kippurim)
T.Ash.	Tosepta Asheret
T.Dan.	Tosepta Daniel
T.Jud.	Tosepta Judiah
T.S(h)ab(b).	Tosepta Sabbat
T.Suk.	Tosepta Sukka

OTHER RABBINIC WORKS

C.D.	Community Document
Lev.R.	Leviticus Rabbah
Mekil.Exod.	Mekilta to Exodus
S.Lev.	Sifre Leviticus
S.Num.	Sifre Numbers

Bibliography

For a fuller, annotated bibliograpy, consult: Evans, Craig A., *Life of Jesus Research: An Annotated Bibliography*. Leiden: E. J. Brill, 1989.

Abbott, M. "Wisdom and Christology in Q." Paper presented December 1984 at John Wesley Fellows Meeting, Shakertown, Ky.

Achtemeier, P. J. "He Taught Them Many Things: Reflections on Marcan Christology." *CBQ* 42 (1980): 465–81.

------. "The Origin and Function of the Pre-Markan Miracle Catenae." *JBL* 80 (1972): 198–221.

------. "Toward the Isolation of pre-Markan Miracle Catenae." *JBL* 79 (1971): 265–291.

Allison, D. C. *The End of the Ages Has Come: An Early Interpretation of the Passion and Resurrection of Jesus*. Philadelphia: Fortress Press, 1985.

------. "Jesus and the Covenant: A Response to E. P. Sanders." *JSNT* 29 (1987): 57–78.

Anderson, H. "4 Maccabees." *OTP* 2:534.

Arens, E. *The ELTHON-Sayings in the Synoptic Tradition: A Historico-critical Investigation*. Göttingen: Vandenhoeck and Ruprecht, 1976.

Aune, D. E. "A Note on Jesus' Messianic Consciousness and 11Q Melchizedek." *EvQ* 45 (1973): 161–65.

Avi-Jonah, M., ed. *The World History of the Jewish People*. Vol. 7, *The Herodian Period*. New Brunswick: Rutgers University Press, 1975.

Bammel, E. "The Feeding of the Multitude." In *Jesus and the Politics of His Day*, 211–40. Cambridge: Cambridge University Press, 1984.

------. "Is Luke 16:16-18 of Baptist's Provenience?" *HTR* 51 (1958): 101–6.

------. "The Poor and the Zealots." In *Jesus and the Politics of His Day*, 109–28. Cambridge: Cambridge University Press, 1984.

------. "Titulus." In *Jesus and the Politics of His Day*, 353–364. Cambridge: Cambridge University Press, 1984.

Bammel, E., and Moule, C. F. D., eds. *Jesus and the Politics of His Day*. Cambridge: Cambridge University Press, 1984.

Banks, R. *Jesus and the Law in the Synoptic Tradition*. London: Cambridge University Press, 1975.

Barbour, R. S. "Uncomfortable Words. 8: Status and Titles." *ET* 82 (1970–71): 137–42.

Barker, M. *The Lost Prophet: The Book of Enoch and its Influence on Christianity*. Nashville: Abingdon, 1989.

Barnett, P. W. "The Jewish Eschatological Prophets." Ph.D. Diss., University of London, 1977.

Barr, J. "'Abba, Father' and the Familiarity of Jesus' Speech." *Theology* 91 (1988): 173–79.

------. "Abba Isn't Daddy." *JTS* 39 (1988): 28–47.

Barrett, C. K. "The Background of Mark 10:45." In *New Testament Essays: Studies in Memory of T. W. Manson, 1893–1958*, 1–18. Manchester: Manchester University Press, 1959.

------. *The Holy Spirit and the Gospel Tradition*. Philadelphia: Fortress Press, 1947.

------. "I am not Ashamed of the Gospel." In *New Testament Essays*, 116–43. London: SPCK, 1972.

------. *Jesus and the Gospel Tradition*. Philadelphia: Fortress Press, 1968.

------. "Mark 10:45: a Ransom for Many." In *New Testament Essays*, 22–33. London: SPCK, 1972.

------. "Shaliah and Apostle." In *Donum Gentilicium: New Testament Studies in Honour of David Daube*, 88–102. Oxford: Oxford University Press, 1978.

------. *The Signs of an Apostle*. London: Epworth Press, 1970.

Bartsch, H. W. *Jesus, Prophet und Messias aus Galilaa*. Frankfurt am Main: Stimme Verlag, 1970.

Bauckham, R. "The Son of Man: 'A Man in my Position' or 'Someone'." *JSNT* 23 (1985): 35–41.

------. "The Sonship of the Historical Jesus in Christology." *SJT* 31 (1978): 245–60.

Beasley-Murray, R. *Jesus and the Kingdom of God*. Grand Rapids: Eerdmans, 1986.

Becker, J. *Johannes der Taufer und Jesus von Nazareth*. Neukirchener-Vluyn: Neukirchener Verlag, 1972.

Benoit, P. "Reflexions sur la Formgeschichtliche Methode." *RB* 53 (1946): 481–512.

Berger, K. *Die Amen-Worte Jesu*. BZNW 39. Berlin: De Gruyter, 1970.

------. *Die Gesetzesauslegung Jesu: Ihr historischer Hintergrund im Judentum und im Alten Testament. Teil I: Markus und Parallelen*. Neukirchen-Vluyn: Neukirchener Verlag, 1972.

------. "Die Koniglichen Messiastraditionen des Neuen Testaments." *NTS* 20 (1973): 79–87.

------. "Zum Problem der Messianitat Jesus." *ZTK* 71 (1974): 1–30.

Best, E. *Disciples and Discipleship: Studies in the Gospel according to Mark*. Edinburgh: T. & T. Clark, 1986.

Betz, O. "Die Frage nach dem Messianischen Bewusstsein Jesu." *NovTest* 6 (1963): 20–48.

Black, M. *An Aramaic Approach to the Gospels and Acts*. 3d ed. Oxford: Clarendon Press, 1967.

------. "Aramaic Barnasha and the Son of Man." *ET* 95 (1983–84): 200–6.

------. "Die Apotheose Israels: eine neue Interpretation des danielischen 'Menschensohn.'" *Jesus und der Menschensohn*. Ed. R. Pesch et al., 92–99. Freiburg: Herder, 1975.

------. "Judas of Galilee and Josephus's 'Fourth Philosophy.'" In *Josephus Studien*. Ed. O. Betz, L. Haacker, and M. Hengel, 45–54. Göttingen: Vandenhoeck and Ruprecht, 1974.

Blackburn, B. L. "THEIOI ANDRES." *Gospel Perspectives*. Vol. 6, The Miracles of Jesus. Ed. D. Wenham and C. Blomberg, 185–218. Sheffield: JSOT Press, 1986.

Blinzler, J. *The Trial of Jesus: The Jewish and Roman Proceedings against Jesus Christ Described and Assessed from the Oldest Accounts*. Westminister: Newman, 1959.

Boers, H. *Who Was Jesus? The Historical Jesus and the Synoptic Gospels*. San Francisco: Harper & Row, 1989.

Booth, R. *Jesus and the Laws of Purity: Tradition, History, and Legal History in Mark 7*. Sheffield: JSOT Press, 1986.

Borg, M. *Conflict, Holiness, and Politics in the Teaching of Jesus*. New York: Edwin Mellen Press, 1984.

------. *Jesus: A New Vision Spirit: Culture, and the Life of Discipleship*. San Francisco: Harper & Row, 1987.

------. "An Orthodoxy Reconsidered: The End of the World Jesus'." In *The Glory of Christ in the New Testament*. Ed. L. D. Hurst et al., 207–17. Oxford: Clarendon Press, 1987.

------. "A Temperate Case for a Non-Eschatological Jesus." *SBL Seminar Papers* 25 (1986): 521–35.

Boring, M. E. "How May We Identify Oracles of Christian Prophets in the Synoptic Tradition? Mark 3:28–29 as a Test Case." *JBL* 91 (1972): 501–21.

------. *Sayings of the Risen Jesus: Christian Prophecy in the Synoptic Tradition*. Cambridge: Cambridge University Press, 1982.

Bornkamm, G. *Jesus of Nazareth*. New York: Harper & Row, 1960.

Borsch, F. H. *The Son of Man in Myth and History*. London: SCM Press, 1967.

Bowker, J. *Jesus and the Pharisees*. Cambridge: Cambridge University Press, 1973.

Brandon, S. G. F. *Jesus and the Zealots*. Manchester: Manchester University Press, 1967.

------. "Jesus and the Zealots: A Correction." *NTS* 17 (1970–71): 453.

Braun, H. *Spätjudisch-Haretischer und fruhchristlicher Radikalismus*. Vol. 2. Tübingen: J. C. B. Mohr, 1956.

Breech, J. *The Silence of Jesus: The Authentic Voice of the Historical Man*. Philadelphia: Fortress Press, 1983.

Brown, R. E. "After Bultmann, What? An Introduction to the Post-Bultmannians." *CBQ* 26 (1964): 1–30.

------. "Did Jesus Know He was God?" *BTB* 15 (1985): 74–79.

------. *New Testament Essays*. Garden City: Image Books, 1968.

Bruce, F. F. "The Background to the Son of Man Sayings." In *Christ the Lord: Studies in Christology Presented to D. Guthrie*, 50–70. London: InterVarsity Press, 1982.

------. "The Book of Zechariah and the Passion Narrative." *BJRL* 43 (1961): 336–53.

------. "Render to Caesar." In *Jesus and the Politics of His Day*. Ed. E. Bammel and C. F. D. Moule, 249–63. Cambridge: Cambridge University Press, 1984.

Buchanan, G. W. *The Consequences of the Covenant*. Leiden: E. J. Brill, 1970.

------. *Jesus the King and His Kingdom*. Macon: Mercer, 1984.

Buechner, F. *The Life of Jesus*. New York: Weathervane Books, 1974.

Bultmann, R. *Die Geschichte der synoptischen Tradition*. 2d ed. Göttingen: Vandenhoeck and Ruprecht, 1931.

------. *The History of the Synoptic Tradition.* Trans. J. Marsh. Oxford: B. Blackwell, 1963.

------. *Das Verhaltnis der urchristlichen Christenbotschaft zum historischen Jesus.* Heidelberg: Kerle, 1960.

Burney, C. F. *The Poetry of Our Lord—An Examination of the Formal Elements of Hebrew Poetry in the Discourses of Jesus Christ.* Oxford: Clarendon Press, 1925.

Caird, G. B. *Jesus and the Jewish Nation.* London: Athlone Press, 1965.

------. "Uncomfortable Words. 2: Shake off the Dust from Your Feet (Mk. 6:11)." *ET* 81 (1969–70): 40–43.

Carlston, C. E. "Wisdom and Eschatology." In *Logia: Les Paroles de Jesus—The Sayings of Jesus: Memorial Joseph Coppens.* Ed. J. Delobel, 101–19. Leuven: Leuven University Press, 1982.

Carmignac, J. *Christ and the Teacher of Righteousness: The Evidence of the Dead Sea Scrolls.* Baltimore: Helicon Press, 1962.

Casey, M. "General, Generic and the Indefinite: The Use of the Term 'Son of Man' in Aramaic Sources and in the Teaching of Jesus." *JSNT* 29 (1987): 21–56.

------. "The Jackals and the Son of Man (Matt. 8:20/Luke 9:58)." *JSNT* 23 (1985): 3–22.

------. *Son of Man: The Interpretation and Influence of Daniel 7.* London: SPCK, 1979.

Catchpole, D. "The Answer of Jesus to Caiaphas (Matt. 26:64)." *NTS* 17 (1970–71): 213–26.

------. "John the Baptist, Jesus and the Parable of the Tares." *SJT* 31 (1978): 557–70.

------. *The Trial of Jesus.* SPB 18. Leiden: E. J. Brill, 1971.

------. "The 'Triumphal' Entry." In *Jesus and the Politics of His Day*, 319–24. Cambridge: Cambridge University Press, 1984.

Charles, R. H. *Apocrypha and Pseudepigrapha of the Old Testament.* 2 vols. Oxford: Oxford University Press, 1913.

Charlesworth, J. H. "From Jewish Messianology to Christian Christology: Some Caveats and Perspectives." In *Judaisms and Their Messiahs at the Turn of the Christian Era.* Ed. J. Neusner et al., 225–64. Cambridge: Cambridge University Press, 1987.

------. *Jesus within Judaism: New Light from Exciting Archaeological Discoveries.* New York: Doubleday, 1988.

------. *The Old Testament Pseudepigrapha and the New Testament.* Cambridge: Cambridge University Press, 1985.

Charlesworth, J. H., ed. *The Old Testament Pseudepigrapha.* 2 vols. Garden City: Doubleday, 1983–85.

Childs, B. S. *Introduction to the Old Testament as Scripture.* Philadelphia: Fortress Press, 1979.

Chilton, B. D. *A Galilean Rabbi and his Bible: Jesus' Use of the Interpreted Scripture of His Day.* Wilmington: Michael Glazier, 1984.

------. "Exorcism and History: Mark 1:21–28." In *Gospel Perspectives.* Vol. 6, *The Miracles of Jesus.* Ed. D. Wenham and C. Blomberg, 253–71. Sheffield: JSOT Press, 1986.

------. *God in Strength: Jesus' Announcement of the Kingdom.* Freistadt: Verlag F. Plochl, 1979.

------. "Jesus and Judaism." *JBL* 106 (1987): 537–39.

Chilton, B. D., and McDonald, J. I. H. *Jesus and the Ethics of the Kingdom.* Grand Rapids: Eerdmans, 1987.

Christ, F. *Jesus Sophia: Die Sophia-Christologie bei den Synoptikern.* Zurich: Zwingli Verlag, 1970.

Collins, A. Y. "The Son of Man Sayings in the Sayings Source." Paper presented at SBL, December 1986.

Collins, J. J. *The Apocalyptic Imagination.* New York: Crossroad, 1984.

------. "The Son of Man and the Saints of the Most High in the Book of Daniel." *JBL* 93 (1974): 50–66.

Comber, J. A. "The Composition and Literary Characteristics of Matt 11:20–24." *CBQ* 39 (1977): 497–504.

Conzelmann, H. *Jesus.* Trans. J. R. Lord; ed. J. Reumann. Philadelphia: Fortress Press, 1973.

Cook, M. J. "Jesus and the Pharisees—the Problem as It Stands Today." *Journal of Ecumenical Studies* 15 (1978): 441–60.

Coppens, J. "Où en est le problème de Jésus 'fils de l'homme'." *ETL* 56 (1980): 282–302.

Cothenet, D. "Prophetisme dans le Nouveau Testament." In *Supplement au Dictionnaire de la Bible*, 8:1285–86. Paris: Ceffonds, 1972.

Cranfield, C. E. B. "The Baptism of Our Lord—A Study of Mark 1.9–11" *SJT* 8 (1955): 53–63.

Crenshaw, J. L. "Method in Determining Wisdom Influence upon 'Historical' Literature." *JBL* 88 (1969): 129–42.

Crossan, J. D. *In Parables: The Challenge of the Historical Jesus.* New York: Harper & Row, 1973.

Cullmann, O. *Christology of the New Testament.* Rev. ed. Philadelphia: Westminster Press, 1963.

------. *Jesus and the Revolutionaries.* New York: Harper & Row, 1970.

Dahl, N. A. *Jesus in the Memory of the Early Church.* Minneapolis: Augsburg Publishing House, 1976.

Dalman, G. *The Words of Jesus.* Edinburgh: T. & T. Clark, 1902.

Daly, R. J. "The Soteriological Significance of the Sacrifice of Isaac." *CBQ* 39 (1977): 45–75.

Danby, H., ed. *The Mishnah.* London: Oxford University Press, 1933.

Daube, D. *Ancient Jewish Law.* Leiden: E. J. Brill, 1981.

------. *The New Testament and Rabbinic Judaism.* London: Athlone Press, 1956.

------. "Responsibilities of Master and Disciples in the Gospels." *NTS* 19 (1972): 1–15.

Davids, P. H. "The Gospels and Jewish Tradition: Twenty Years after Gerhardsson." In *Gospel Perspectives: Studies of History and Tradition in the Four Gospels.* Vol. 1. Ed. R. T. France and D. Wenham, 75–100. Sheffield: JSOT Press, 1980.

Davies, W. D. "From Schweitzer to Scholem: Reflections on Sabbatai Svi." *JBL* 95 (1976): 529–58.

------. *The Gospel and the Land: Early Christianity and Jewish Territorial Doctrine.* Berkeley: University of California Press, 1974.

------. "Reflexions on Tradition: The Aboth Revisited." In *Christian History and Interpretation: Studies Presented to John Knox.* Ed. W. R. Farmer et al., 127–59. Cambridge: Cambridge University Press, 1967.

------. *The Setting of the Sermon on the Mount.* Cambridge: Cambridge University Press, 1976.

------. *Torah in the Messianic Age and/or Age to Come.* Philadelphia: SBL Literature, 1957.

Davis, J. A. *Wisdom and Spirit: An Investigation of 1 Corinthians 1:13—3:20 against the Background of Jewish Sapiential Traditions in the Greco-Roman Period.* New York: University Press of America, 1984.

Deissler, A. "Der 'Menschensohn' und 'das Volk der Heiligen des Hochsten' in Daniel 7." In *Jesus und der Menschensohn.* Ed. R. Pesch et al., 81–91. Freiburg: Herder, 1975.

Deissmann, A. *Light from the Ancient East.* Trans. L. R. M. Strachan. Reprint. Grand Rapids: Baker, 1978.

de Jonge, M. *Christology in Context: The Earliest Christian Response to Jesus.* Philadelphia: Westminster, 1988.

------. "The Earliest Christian Use of *Christos.*" *NTS* 32 (1986): 321–43.

------. "The Use of the Word 'Anointed' in the Time of Jesus." *NovTest* 8 (1966): 132–48.

Delling, G. "Gepragte Jesus-Tradition im Urchristentum." *Communio Viatorum* 4 (1961): 59–71.

Derrett, J. D. M. "Law in the New Testament: The Palm Sunday Colt." *NovTest* 13 (1971): 241–58.

------. "The Zeal of the House and the Cleansing of the Temple." *Downside Review* 95 (1977): 55–86.

Dibelius, M. *Die Formgeschichte der Evangelien.* Tübingen: J. C. B. Mohr, 1971.

------. *From Tradition to Gospel.* 2d ed. Trans. B. L. Wolf. London: Ivor Nicholson and Watson, 1934.

Di Lella, A. A. "The One in Human Likeness and the Holy One of the Most High in Daniel 7." *CBQ* 39 (1977): 1–19.

Dodd, C. H. *Historical Tradition in the Fourth Gospel.* Cambridge: Cambridge University Press, 1963.

------. "Jesus as Teacher and Prophet." *Mysterium Christi: Christological Studies by British and German Theologians,* 53–66. London: Longmans, Green & Co., 1930.

------. "The Kingdom of God Has Come." *ET* 48 (1936–37): 138–42.

------. *More New Testament Studies.* Manchester: Manchester University Press, 1968.

------. *The Parables of the Kingdom.* New York: Scribners, 1961.

Downing, G. "The Social Contexts of Jesus the Teacher: Construction or Reconstruction." *NTS* 33 (1987): 439–51.

Duling, D. C. "Solomon, Exorcism, and the Son of David." *HTR* 68 (1975): 235–52.

Dunn, J. D. G. *Baptism in the Holy Spirit.* Philadelphia: Westminster Press, 1970.

------. *Christology in the Making: A New Testament Inquiry into the Origins of the Doctrine of the Incarnation.* Philadelphia: Westminster Press, 1980.

------. *Jesus and the Spirit: A Study of the Religious and Charismatic Experience of Jesus and the First Century Christians as Reflected in the New Testament.* Philadelphia: Westminster Press, 1975.

------. "Matthew 12:28/Luke 11:20—A Word of Jesus?" In *Eschatology and the New Testament: Essays in Honor of G. R. Beasley-Murray.* Ed. W. H. Gloer, 29–49. Peabody, Mass.: Hendrickson, 1988.

------. "The Messianic Secret in Mark." In *The Messianic Secret.* Ed. C. Tuckett, 116–31. Philadelphia: Fortress Press, 1983.

------. "Pharisees, Sinners and Jesus." Lecture at Duke University, 1986.

------. "Prophetic 'I'-Sayings and the Jesus Tradition: The Importance of Testing Prophetic Utterances within Early Christianity." *NTS* 24 (1977–78): 175–98.

Eisler, R. *The Messiah Jesus and John the Baptist.* Trans. A. H. Krappee. New York: Dial Press, 1931.

Ellis, E. E. "New Directions in Form Criticism." In *Jesus Christus in Historie und Theologie, Neutestamentliche Festschrift fur Hans Conzelmann zum 60. Geburtstag.* Ed. G. Strecker, 299–315. Tübingen: J. C. B. Mohr, 1975.

Eppstein, V. "The Historicity of the Gospel Account of the Cleansing of the Temple." *ZNW* 55 (1964): 42–58.

Ernst, J. *Anfange der Christologie.* Stuttgart: KBW Verlag, 1972.

Farmer, W. R. *Jesus and the Gospel: Tradition, Canon, and Scripture.* Philadelphia: Fortress Press, 1982.

------. "The Palm Branches in John 12, 13." *JTS* n.s. 3.1 (1952): 62–66.

Ferguson, E. *Backgrounds of Early Christianity.* Grand Rapids: Eerdmans, 1987.

Fitzmyer, J. A. *The Genesis Apocryphon of Cave 1: A Commentary.* Rome: Biblical Institute Press, 1971.

------. "Methodology in the Study of the Aramaic Substratum of Jesus' Sayings in the New Testament." In *Jesus aux origines de la Christologie.* Ed. J. Dupont, 73–102. Gembloux: Leuven University Press, 1975.

------. "Son of David and Mt. 22:41–46." *Essays on the Semitic Background of the New Testament,* 113–26. Missoula: Scholars Press, 1974.

Flusser, D. *Jesus.* New York: Herder and Herder, 1969.

------. "Two Notes on the Midrash on 2 Sam. 7:1." *Israel Exploration Journal* 9 (1959): 99–109.

France, R. T. *Jesus and the Old Testament.* London: Tyndale Press, 1970.

------. "Old Testament Prophecy and the Future of Israel: a Study of the Teaching of Jesus." *TynB* 26 (1975): 53–78.

Fredricksen, P. *From Jesus to Christ: The Origins of the New Testament Images of Jesus.* New Haven: Yale University Press, 1988.

Freyne, S. *Galilee from Alexander the Great to Hadrian (323 B.C.E. to 135 C.E.).* Notre Dame: University of Notre Dame Press/Michael Glazier, 1980.

------. *Galilee, Jesus, and the Gospels: Literary Approaches and Historical Investigations.* Philadelphia: Fortress Press, 1988.

Fuller, R. H. *The Foundations of New Testament Christology.* New York: Scribners, 1965.

------. *Interpreting the Miracles.* London: SCM Press, 1963.

------. *The Mission and Achievement of Jesus.* London: SCM Press, 1954.

Funk, R. "Beyond Criticism in Quest of Literacy: The Parable of the Leaven." *Int* 25 (1971): 149–70.

------. *Language, Hermeneutic, and the Word of God.* New York: Harper & Row, 1966.

Gardner, R. B. *Jesus' Appraisal of John the Baptist: An Analysis of the Sayings of Jesus Concerning John the Baptist in the Synoptic Tradition.* Bamberg: Theol. Fak., 1973.

George, A. "Paroles de Jesus sur ses miracles (Mt. 11:5–21; 12:27–28 et par)." In *Jesus aux origines de la Christologie.* Ed. J. Dupont, 283–301. Gembloux: Leuven University Press, 1975.

Gerhardsson, B. *Memory and Manuscript—Oral Tradition and Written Transmission in Rabbinic Judaism and Early Christianity.* Lund: C. W. K. Gleerup, 1964.

------. *The Origins of the Gospel Tradition.* Philadelphia: Fortress Press, 1979.

------. *Tradition and Transmission in Early Christianity.* Lund: C. W. K. Gleerup, 1961.

------. "Der Weg der Evangelientradition." In *Das Evangelium und die Evangelien: Vortrage vom Tubinger Symposium 1982*. WUNT 28. Ed. P. Stuhlmacher, 79–102. Tübingen: J. C. B. Mohr, 1983.

Gill, J. H. "Jesus, Irony and the New Quest." *Encounter* 41 (1980): 139–51.

Glasson, T. F. *Jesus and the End of the World*. Edinburgh: Saint Andrew Press, 1980.

------. "The Son of Man Imagery: Enoch 14 and Daniel 7." *NTS* 23 (1977): 82–90.

Goergen, D. J. *The Mission and Ministry of Jesus*. Wilmington: Michael Glazier, 1986.

Grant, F. C. "The Economic Significance of Messianism." *Anglican Theological Review* 6 (1924): 196–213; 7 (1925): 281–89.

Gray, J. "The Day of Yahweh in Cultic Experience and Eschatological Prospect." *Svensk Exegetisk Arsbok* 39 (1974): 5–37.

Grudem, W. "The Gift of Prophecy in 1 Corinthians." Ph.D. Diss., University of Cambridge, 1978.

Guelich, R. *Sermon on the Mount: A Foundation for Understanding*. Waco, Tex.: Word Publishing, 1982.

Gundry, R. H. *The Use of the Old Testament in St. Matthew's Gospel—with Special Reference to Messianic Hope*. Leiden: E. J. Brill, 1967.

Güttgemanns, E. *Candid Questions Concerning Form Criticism: A Methodological Sketch of the Fundamental Problematics of Form and Redaction Criticism*. Trans. W. G. Doty. Pittsburgh: Pickwick Press, 1979.

Hahn, F. *The Titles of Jesus in Christology: Their History in Early Christianity*. Trans. H. Knight and G. Ogg. New York: World Publishing Co., 1969.

Hamilton, N. Q. "Temple Cleansing and Temple Bank." *JBL* 83 (1964): 365–72.

Harnack, A. von "'Ich bin gekommen': Die ausdrucklichen Selbstzeugnisse Jesu über den Zweck seiner Sendung and seines Kommens." *ZTK* 22 (1912): 1–30.

Harvey, A. E. *Jesus and the Constraints of History*. Philadelphia: Westminster Press, 1982.

Hase, K. A. von. *Die Geschichte Jesu*. 2d ed. Leipzig: Breitkopf and Hartel, 1876.

Hasler, V. *Amen*. Zurich: Gotthelf, 1969.

Havener, I. *Q—The Sayings of Jesus, With a Reconstruction of Q by A. Polag*. Wilmington: Michael Glazier, 1987.

Hempel, J. "Amen." *IDB* 1:105.

Hengel, M. *Acts and the History of Earliest Christianity*. Trans. J. Bowden. London: SCM, 1979.

------. *The Charismatic Leader and His Followers*. Trans. J. Grieg. New York: Crossroad, 1981.

------. "Christologie und neutestamentliche Chronologie." In *Neues Testament und Geschichte. Festschrift für O. Cullmann*, 43–67. Tübingen: J. C. B. Mohr [Siebeck], 1972.

------. "Jesus als messianischer Lehrer der Weisheit und die Anfange der Christologie." *Sagesse et Religion* (1979): 148–88.

------. "Jesus und die Tora." *Theologische Beitrage* 9 (1978): 152–72.

------. *Judaism and Hellenism*. 2 vols. Philadelphia: Fortress Press, 1974.

------. "Reviews." *JSemS* 14 (1969): 231–40.

------. *The Son of God: The Origin of Christology and the History of Jewish-Hellenistic Religion*. Trans. J. Bowden. Philadelphia: Fortress Press, 1976.

------. *Was Jesus a Revolutionist?* Philadelphia: Fortress Press, 1971.

------. *Die Zeloten*. 2d ed. Leiden/Koln: E. J. Brill, 1976.

Higgins, A. J. B. *Jesus and the Son of Man*. Philadelphia: Fortress Press, 1964.

------. "Menschensohn oder 'ich' in Q Lk.12,8-9/Mt. 10,32-33." In *Jesus und der Menschensohn*. Ed. R. Pesch et al., 117-23. Freiburg: Herder, 1975.

------. *The Son of Man in the Teaching of Jesus*. Cambridge: Cambridge University Press, 1980.

Hill, D. H. *New Testament Prophecy*. London: Marshall, Morgan and Scott, 1979.

------. "Toward an Understanding of the 'Kingdom of God.'" *Irish Biblical Studies* 3 (1981): 62-76.

Holladay, C. H. *Theios Aner in Hellenistic Judaism*. Missoula: Scholars Press, 1977.

Hooker, M. D. "Is the Son of Man Problem Really Insoluble?" In *Text and Interpretation: Studies in the New Testament presented to Matthew Black*. Ed. E. Best and R. McL. Wilson, 155-68. Cambridge: Cambridge University Press, 1979.

------. *The Son of Man in Mark*. London: SPCK, 1967.

Horbury, W. "The Temple Tax." In *Jesus and the Politics of His Day*, 265-86. Cambridge: Cambridge University Press, 1984.

Horsley, R. A. *Jesus and the Spiral of Violence: Popular Jewish Resistance in Roman Palestine*. San Francisco: Harper and Row, 1987.

------. *The Sociology of the Jesus Movement*. New York: Crossroad, 1989.

Horsley, R. A., and Hanson, J. S. *Bandits, Prophets, and Messiahs: Popular Movements at the Time of Jesus*. Minneapolis: Winston Press, 1985.

Hoskyns, E., and Davey, N. *The Riddle of the New Testament*. London: Faber & Faber, 1958.

Howard, V. *Das Ego Jesu in den Synoptischen Evangelien: Unterschungen zum Sprachgebrauch Jesu*. Marburg: N. G. Elwert Verlag, 1975.

Hull, J. M. *Hellenistic Magic and the Synoptic Tradition*. Naperville: Allenson, 1974.

Hunter, A. M. "Crux Criticorum—Matt. 11:25-30—A Reappraisal." *NTS* 3 (1961-62): 241-49.

Hurtado, L. W. *One God, One Lord: Early Christian Devotion and Ancient Jewish Monotheism*. Philadelphia: Fortress Press, 1988.

Isaac, E. "1 (Ethiopic Apocalypse of) Enoch." *OTP* 1:6-7.

Jeremias, J. *Jerusalem in the Time of Jesus*. Philadelphia: Fortress Press, 1969.

------. *Jesus als Weltvollender*. Gütersloh: E. Bertelsmann Verlag, 1930.

------. *Jesus' Promise to the Nations*. London: SCM, 1958.

------. *New Testament Theology: The Proclamation of Jesus*. New York: Scribner's, 1971.

------. "Paarweise Sendung im Neuen Testament." In *New Testament Essays: Studies in Memory of T. W. Manson, 1893-1958*. Ed. A. J. B. Higgins, 136-43. Manchester: Manchester University Press, 1959.

------. *The Parables of Jesus*. 2d ed. New York: Scribners, 1963.

------. *The Prayers of Jesus*. Trans C. Burchard et al. Naperville: Allenson, 1967.

------. *Die Sprache des Lukasevangeliums*. Göttingen: Vandenhoeck and Ruprecht, 1980.

Johnson, M. D. "Reflections on a Wisdom Approach to Matthew's Christology." *CBQ* 36 (1974): 44-64.

Juel, D. *Messiah and Temple: The Trial of Jesus in the Gospel of Mark*. Missoula: Scholars Press, 1977.

Juster, J. *Les juifs dans l'Empire Romain: Leur condition juridique, économique, et sociale I*. Paris: Geuthner, 1914.

Käsemann, E. *The Testament of Jesus according to John 17.* Translated by G. Krodel. Philadelphia: Fortress Press, 1968.

Keck, L. E. *A Future for the Historical Jesus: The Place of Jesus in Preaching and Theology.* Philadelphia: Fortress Press, 1981.

------. "Mark 3:7-12 and Mark's Christology." *JBL* 84 (1965): 341-58.

Kee, H. C. *Miracle in the Early Christian World.* New Haven: Yale University Press, 1983.

Kelber, W. *The Oral and the Written Gospel: The Hermeneutics of Speaking and Writing in the Synoptic Tradition, Mark, Paul, and Q.* Philadelphia: Fortress Press, 1983.

Kim, S. "Jesus – The Son of God, the Stone, the Son of Man, and the Servant: The Role of Zechariah in the Self-Identification of Jesus" In *Tradition and Interpretation in the New Testament: Essays in Honor of E. Earle Ellis.* Ed. G. F. Hawthorne with O. Betz, 134-48. Grand Rapids: Eerdmans, 1987.

------. *The Son of Man as the Son of God.* Grand Rapids: Eerdmans, 1985.

Kingdon, H. P. "Who were the Zealots and their Leaders in A.D. 66?" *NTS* 17 (1970-71): 68-72.

Klappert, B. "King, Kingdom." *DNTT* 2:373.

Klassen, W. "Jesus and Phineas: a Rejected Role Model." *SBL Seminar Papers,* 490-500. Atlanta: Scholars Press, 1986.

Klausner, J. *The Messianic Idea in Israel: From its Beginning to the Completion of the Mishnah.* Trans. W. F. Stinespring. New York: Macmillan, 1955.

Kuhn, K. H. "Basileus." *TDNT* 1:570-73.

Kümmel, W. G. *Promise and Fulfilment: The Eschatological Message of Jesus.* London: SCM Press, 1957.

Ladd, G. E. *The Presence of the Future.* Grand Rapids: Eerdmans, 1974.

Lane, *Mark.* Grand Rapids: Eerdmans, 1974.

Lapide, P. "Insights from Qumran into the Languages of Jesus." *Revue de Qumran* 8.4 (1975): 483-501.

Lapide, P., and Luz, U. *Jesus in Two Perspectives: A Jewish-Christian Dialog.* Trans. L. W. Denef. Minneapolis: Augsburg Publishing House, 1985.

Latourelle, R. "Authenticité historique des miracles de Jésus: Essai de critériologie." *Gregorianum* 54 (1973): 225-62.

Lattke, M. "On the Jewish Background of the Synoptic Concept." In *The Kingdom of God.* Ed. B. D. Chilton, 72-91. Philadelphia: Fortress Press, 1984.

Leivestad, R. *Jesus in His Own Perspective: An Examination of His Sayings, Actions, and Eschatological Titles.* Trans. D. E. Aune. Minneapolis: Augsburg Publishing House, 1987.

Le Moyne, J. *Les Sadducéens.* Paris: Gabalda Press, 1972.

Lindars, B. "Enoch and Christology." *ET* 92 (1980-81): 295-99.

------. "Jesus and the Pharisees." *Donum Gentilicium.* Ed. C. K. Barrett et al., 51-63. Oxford: Oxford University Press, 1978.

------. "Jesus as Advocate: A Contribution to the Christology Debate" *BJRL* 62 (1980): 476-97.

------. *Jesus – Son of Man: A Fresh Examination of the Son of Man Sayings in the Gospels.* Grand Rapids: Eerdmans, 1981.

------. "Response to Richard Bauckham: The Idiomatic Use of *Bar Enasha.*" *JSNT* 23 (1985): 35-41.

Linnemann, E. "Jesus und der Taufer." *Festschrift für Ernst Fuchs.* Ed. G. Ebeling et al., 219–36. Tübingen: J. C. B. Mohr, 1973.

Lohfink, G. *Jesus and Community: The Social Dimension of Christian Faith.* Trans. J. P. Galvin. Philadelphia: Fortress Press, 1984.

Lohse, E., ed. *Die Texte aus Qumran: Hebraisch und Deutsch.* Munchen: Kosel-Verlag, 1971.

Longenecker, R. N. "The Messianic Secret in the Light of Recent Discoveries." *EvQ* 41 (1969): 207–15.

Lord, A. B. "The Gospels as Oral Traditional Literature." In *The Relationships among the Gospels.* Ed. W. O. Walker, 33–91. San Antonio: Trinity University Press, 1978.

------. *The Singer of Tales.* HSCL 24. Cambridge, Mass.: Harvard University Press, 1960.

------. *Slavic Folklore: A Symposium.* Philadelphia: American Folklore Society, 1956.

Lührmann, D. *Die Redaktion der Logienquelle.* WANT Monograph 33. Neukirchen-Vluyn: Neukircher Verlag, 1969.

Luz, U. "The Secrecy Motif and the Marcan Christology." In *The Messianic Secret.* Ed. C. Tuckett, 75–96. Philadelphia: Fortress Press, 1983.

Maag, V. "Malkut JHWH." In *Congress Volume, Oxford 1959: Supplements to Vetus Testamentum VII.* Ed. G. W. Anderson et al., 129–53. Leiden: E. J. Brill, 1960.

McEleney, N. J. "Authenticating Criteria and Mark 7:1-23." *CBQ* 34 (1972): 431–60.

Malina, B. J. "Jesus as Charismatic Leader." *BTB* 13 (1983): 55–62.

------. *The New Testament World: Insights from Cultural Anthropology.* Atlanta: John Knox, 1981.

Manek, J. "Fishers of Men." *NovTest* 2 (1958): 138–41.

Manson, T. W. *The Sayings of Jesus.* London: SCM Press, 1957.

------. *The Son of Man in Daniel, Enoch and the Gospels.* Manchester: Manchester University Press, 1950.

------. *Studies in the Gospels and Epistles.* London: SCM, 1962.

------. *The Teaching of Jesus.* Cambridge: Cambridge University Press, 1935.

Marshall, I. H. "The Divine Sonship of Jesus." *Int* 21 (1967): 87–103.

------. *The Origins of New Testament Christology.* Downer's Grove: InterVarsity Press, n.d.

------. "The Synoptic Son of Man Sayings in Recent Discussion." *NTS* 12 (1965–66): 327–51.

Merkel, H. "Zealots." *IDB Supp.* 979–82.

Merklein, H. "Die Umkehrpredigt bei Johannes dem Taufer und Jesus." *BZ* 25 (1981): 129–46.

Meye, R. P. *Jesus and the Twelve: Discipleship and Revelation in Mark's Gospel.* Grand Rapids: Eerdmans, 1968.

Meyer, B. F. *The Aims of Jesus.* London: SCM, 1979.

Meyers, E. M. "Galilean Regionalism as a Factor in Historical Reconstruction." *BASOR* 221 (1976): 93–101.

Meyers, E. M., and Strange, J. F. *Archaeology, the Rabbis, and Early Christianity.* Nashville: Abingdon, 1981.

Michaels, J. R. *Servant and Son: Jesus in Parable and Gospel.* Atlanta: John Knox Press, 1981.

Moore, E. "BIADZO, HARPADZO and Cognates in Josephus." *NTS* 21 (1974–75): 519–43.

Morgan, R. "The Historical Jesus and the Theology of the New Testament." In *The Glory of Christ in the New Testament*. Ed. L. D. Hurst and N. T. Wright, 187–206. Oxford: Clarendon Press, 1987.

Moule, C. F. D. "The Gravamen against Jesus." In *Jesus, the Gospels, and the Church: Essays in Honor of William R. Farmer*. Ed. E. P. Sanders, 177–95. Macon: Mercer University Press, 1988.

------. "Neglected Features in the Problem of 'the Son of Man.'" In *Neues Testament und Kirche: Für Rudolf Schnackenburg*. Ed. J. Gnilka, 413–28. Freiburg: Herder, 1974.

------. *The Origins of Christology*. Cambridge: Cambridge University Press, 1977.

------. *The Phenomenon of the New Testament*. London: SCM, 1967.

Mowinckel, S. *He That Cometh*. Trans. G. W. Anderson. Nashville: Abingdon, 1954.

Müller, K. "Der Menschensohn im Danielzyklus." In *Jesus und der Menschensohn*. Ed. R. Pesch et al., 37–80. Freiburg: Herder, 1975.

Müller, M. "Über den Ausdruck 'Menschensohn' in den Evangelien." *Studia Theologica* 31 (1977): 65–82.

Müller, P. *Der Traditionsprozess im Neuen Testament: Kommunikationsanalytische Studien zur Versprachlichung des Jesusphanomens*. Freiburg: Herder, 1982.

Mussner, F. "Gottesherrschaft und Sendung Jesu nach Mk. 1:14 f." In *Praesentia Salutis: Gesammelte Studien zu Fragen und Themen des Neuen Testamentes*. Düsseldorf: Patmos Verlag, 1967.

Naveh, J. "A Hebrew Letter from the Seventh Century B.C." *IEJ* 10 (1960): 129–39.

Neirynck, J. "The Miracle Stories in the Acts of the Apostles." In *Evangelica: Gospel Studies – Etudes D'Evangile*, 835–80. Leuven: Leuven University Press, 1982.

Neugebauer, F. "Die Davidssohnfrage (Mark 12:35-37 parr.) und der Menschensohn." *NTS* 21 (1974–75): 81–104.

Neusner, J. *Judaism in the Beginning of Christianity*. Philadelphia: Fortress Press, 1984.

------. *The Rabbinic Traditions about the Pharisees before 70*. Vol. 3. Leiden: E. J. Brill, 1971.

Nicholson, E. W. "The Meaning of the Expression *Am Ha Aretz* in the Old Testament." *JSemS* 10 (1965): 59–65.

Nickelsburg, G. *Jewish Literature between the Bible and the Mishnah*. Philadelphia: Fortress Press, 1981.

------. "Books of Enoch." *CBQ* 40 (1978): 411–18.

Oepke, A. "Bapto." *TDNT* 1:530, 538.

O'Neill, J. C. *Messiah: Six Lectures on the Ministry of Jesus*. Cambridge: Cochrane Press, 1980.

Oppenheimer, A. *The 'Am Ha-Aretz: A Study in the Social History of the Jewish People in the Hellenistic-Roman Period*. Leiden: E. J. Brill, 1977.

Overman, J. A. "Who were the First Urban Christians? Urbanization in Galilee in the First Century." In *SBL 1988 Seminar Papers*. Ed. D. J. Lull, 160–68. Atlanta: Scholars Press, 1988.

Page, S. H. T. "The Authenticity of the Ransom Logion (Mark 10:45b)." In *Gospel Perspectives: Studies of History and Tradition in the Four Gospels I*. Ed. R. T. France and D. Wenham, 137–61. Sheffield: JSOT Press, 1980.

Payne, P. B. "The Authenticity of the Parable of the Sower and its Application." In *Gospel Perspectives*. Ed. R. T. France, 163–207. Sheffield; JSOT Press, 1980.

------. "Jesus' Implicit Claim to Deity in His Parables." *Trinity Journal* 2 n.s. (1981): 3–23.

------. "Metaphor as a Model for Interpreting the Parables of Jesus." Ph.D. Diss., Cambridge University, 1975.

Pelikan, J. *Jesus through the Centuries: His Place in the History of Culture.* New Haven: Yale University Press, 1985.

Perrin, N. *Jesus and the Language of the Kingdom: Symbol and Metaphor in New Testament Interpretation.* Philadelphia: Fortress Press, 1983.

------. "Mark 14:62: The End Product of a Christian Pesher Tradition?" *NTS* 13 (1965-66): 150-55.

Perspectives on Christology. Symposium Papers, Florida Southern College, March 1988, Nashville: Exodus Press, 1989.

Pesch, R. *Anfang des Evangeliums Jesu Christi: Eine Studie zum Prolog des Markusevangeliums (Mk. 1:1-15), Die Zeit Jesu.* Ed. G. Bornkamm and K. Rahner. Freiburg-Basel: Herder, 1970.

------. "Der Anspruch Jesu." *Orienterung* 35 (1971): 53-56.

------. "Die Passion des Menschensohnes: Eine Studie zu den Menschensohnworten der vormarkinischen Passionsgeschichte." In *Jesus und der Menschensohn,* 166-95. Freiburg: Herder, 1975.

Piper, R. *Wisdom in the Q-tradition: The Aphoristic Teaching of Jesus.* Cambridge: Cambridge University Press, 1989.

Polkow, D. "Method and Criteria for Historical Jesus Research." In *Society of Biblical Literature 1987 Seminar Papers 26.* Ed. K. H. Richards, 336-56. Atlanta: Scholars Press, 1987.

Pokorny, P. *The Genesis of Christology: Foundations for a Theology of the New Testament.* Edinburgh: T. & T. Clark, 1987.

Pusey, K. "Jewish Proselyte Baptism." *ET* 95 (1984): 141-45.

Räisänen, H. *Das 'Messiasgeheimnis' im Markusevangelium.* Helsinki: Lansi Suomi, 1976.

Reese, J. M. "Christ as Wisdom Incarnate: Wiser than Solomon, Loftier than Lady Wisdom." *BTB* 11 (1981): 44-47.

Reicke, B. "The Historical Setting of John's Baptism." In *Jesus, the Gospels, and the Church: Essays in Honor of William R. Farmer.* Ed. E. P. Sanders, 209-24. Macon: Mercer University Press, 1988.

Rengstorf, K. "*apostolos.*" *TDNT* 1:414ff.

------. "*lestes.*" *TDNT* 4:259.

Riches, J. *Jesus and the Transformation of Judaism.* New York: Seabury Press, 1982.

Riesenfeld, H. *The Gospel Tradition and Its Beginnings: A Study in the Limits of "Formgeschichte."* London: A. R. Mowbray, 1957.

Riesner, R. *Jesus als Lehrer: Eine Untersuchung zum Ursprung der Evangelien-Überlieferung,* WUNT 2.7. Tübingen: J. C. B. Mohr, 1981.

------. "Der Ursprung der Jesus-Überlieferung." *TZ* 38.6 (1982): 493-513.

Rivkin, E. "Defining the Pharisees: The Tannaitic Source." *Hebrew Union College Annual* 40 (1969): 205-49.

------. "Pharisees." *IDB Suppl.* 657-63.

Robbins, V. *Jesus the Teacher.* Philadelphia: Fortress Press, 1984.

Robinson, J. M. "'Logoi Sophon': On the Gattung of Q." In *Trajectories through Early Christianity.* Ed. J. M. Robinson and H. Koester, 71-113. Philadelphia: Fortress Press, 1971.

Robinson, W. C. "The Quest for Wrede's Secret Messiah." In *The Messianic Secret*. Ed. C. Tuckett, 97–115. Philadelphia: Fortress Press, 1983.

Rogerson, J. "The Hebrew Conception of Corporate Personality: A Re-examination." *JTS* n.s. 21 (1970): 1–16.

Roloff, J. "Die Anfange der Soteriologischen Deutung des Todes Jesus (Mk. 10:45 und Lk. 22:27)." *NTS* 19 (1972–73): 38–64.

------. *Das Kerygma und der irdische Jesus: Historische Motive in den Jesus-Erzahlungen der Evangelien*. Göttingen: Vandenhoeck and Ruprecht, 1970.

Roth, C. "The Cleansing of the Temple and Zechariah." *NovTest* 4 (1960): 174–81.

Rowe, R. D. "Is Daniel's Son of Man' Messianic?" In *Christ the Lord: Studies in Christology Presented to D. Guthrie*, 71–96. London: InterVarsity Press, 1982.

Rowland, C. *Christian Origins: From Messianic Movement to Christian Religion*. Minneapolis: Augsburg Publishing House, 1985.

------. "Sander's Jesus." *New Blackfriar's* 66 (1985): 412–17.

Safrai, S. "The Teaching of the Pietists in Mishnaic Literature." *JJS* 16 (1965): 15–33.

St. J. Hart, H. "The Coin of 'Render unto Caesar . . .' (A note on some aspects of Mark 12:13–17; Matt. 22:15–22; Luke 20:20–26)." In *Jesus and the Politics of His Day*, 241–48. Cambridge: Cambridge University Press, 1984.

Saldarini, A. J. "Political and Social Roles of the Pharisees and the Scribes in Galilee." *SBL 1988 Seminar Papers*. Ed. D. J. Lull, 200–9. Atlanta: Scholars Press, 1988.

Salomonsen, B. "Some Remarks on the Zealots with Special Regard to the Term 'Qannaim' in Rabbinic Literature." *NTS* 13 (1965–66): 164–76.

Sanders, E. P. *Jesus and Judaism*. Philadelphia: Fortress Press, 1985.

------. "Jesus and the Kingdom: the Restoration of Israel and the New People of God." In *Jesus, the Gospels, and the Church: Essays in Honor of William R. Farmer*. Ed. E. P. Sanders, 225–39. Macon: Mercer University Press, 1988.

------. *Paul and Palestinian Judaism: A Comparison of Patterns of Religion*. London: SCM, 1977.

------. *The Tendencies of the Synoptic Tradition*. SNTS Monograph 9. Cambridge: Cambridge University Press, 1969.

Schafer, P. *Studien zur Geschichte und Theologie der Rabbinischen Judentums*. Leiden: E. J. Brill, 1978.

Schillebeeckx, E. *Jesus: An Experiment in Christology*. New York: Vintage Press, 1981.

Schlosser, J. *Le Règne de Dieu dans les Dits de Jésus*. Paris: Gabalda Press, 1980.

Schnackenburg, R. *Gottes Herrschaft und Reich: Eine biblische theologische Studie*. Freiburg: Herder, 1959.

------. *God's Rule and Kingdom*. Trans. J. Murray. Edinburgh: Nelson, 1963.

Scholem, G. *The Messianic Idea in Judaism and Other Essays on Jewish Spirituality*. New York: Schocken Books, 1971.

Schürer, E. *The History of the Jewish People in the Age of Jesus Christ*. Vol. 2. Revised by G. Vermes et al. Edinburgh: T. & T. Clark, 1979.

Schürmann, H. *Das Geheimnis Jesu*. Leipzig: St. Benno Verlag GMBH, 1972.

------. "Mt. 10:5b–6 und die Vorgeschichte des synoptischen Aussendungberichtes." In *Neutestamentliche Aufsätze*. Ed. J. Blinzler, 270–82. Regensburg: Pustet, 1963.

------. "Die Symbolhandlung Jesu als Eschatologische Erfullungszeichen: Eine Ruckfrage nach dem irdischen Jesus." In *Das Geheimnis Jesu*, 270–82. Leipzig: St. Benno, 1972.

------. *Ursprung und Gestalt: Eroterungen und Besinnungen zum Neuen Testament.* Düsseldorf: Patmos Verlag, 1970.

------. "Die Vorosterlichen Anfange der Logientradition-Versuch eines Formgeschichtlichen Zugangs zum Leben Jesu." In *Traditions-geschichtliche Untersuchungen zu den Synoptischen Evangelien,* 39–65. Düsseldorf: Patmos Verlag, 1968.

------. "Wie hat Jesus seinen Tod bestanden und verstanden? Eine methodenkritische Besinnung." In *Orientierung an Jesus: Zur Theologie der Synoptiker.* Ed. P. Hoffmann, 325–63. Freiburg: Herder, 1973.

Schweitzer, A. *The Quest for the Historical Jesus.* Trans. W. Montgomery. New York: Macmillan, 1961.

Schweizer, E. *Jesus Christ: The Man from Nazareth and the Exalted Lord.* Ed. by H. Gloer. Macon: Mercer University Press, 1987.

Scott, R. B. Y. "Behold, He Cometh with Clouds." *NTS* 5 (1955–56): 127–32.

Segal, A. F. "The Cost of Proselytism and Conversion." In *SBL 1988 Seminar Papers.* Ed. D. J. Lull, 336–69. Atlanta: Scholars Press, 1988.

Segundo, J. Luis. *The Historical Jesus of the Synoptics.* Trans. J. Drury. Maryknoll, N.Y.: Orbis, 1985.

Senior, D. "Jesus and Judaism." *CBQ* 48 (1986): 569–71.

Sevenster, J. N. *Do You Know Greek? How Much Greek Could the First Jewish Christians Have Known?* Leiden: E. J. Brill, 1968.

Sherwin-White, A. N. *Roman Society and Roman Law in the New Testament.* Oxford: Oxford University Press, 1963.

Sjöberg, E. *Der verborgene Menschensohn in den Evangelien.* Lund: C. W. K. Gleerup, 1955.

Smallwood, E. M. *The Jews under Roman Rule from Pompey to Diocletian.* Leiden: E. J. Brill, 1976.

Smith, C. E. F. "Fishers of Men: Footnotes on a Gospel Figure." *HTR* 52 (1959): 187–203.

Smith, D. "Jesus and the Pharisees in Socio-Anthropological Perspective." *Trinity Journal* 6 n.s. (1985): 151–56.

------. "Jewish Proselyte Baptism and the Baptism of John." *ResQ* 25 (1982): 13–32.

Smith, M. "Jesus and the Zealots: a Correction." *NTS* 17 (1970–71): 453.

------. *Jesus the Magician.* New York: Harper & Row, 1978.

------. "The Origins of the Zealots." *NTS* 19 (1972–73): 74–81.

------. "Palestinian Judaism in the First Century." In *Israel: Its Role in Civilization.* Ed. M. David, 67–81. New York: Harper & Row, 1956.

------. "Review of Dunn's Jesus and the Spirit." *JAAR* 44 (1976): 726.

------. "Zealots and Sicarii, Their Origins and Relation." *HTR* 64 (1971): 1–19.

Stanton, G. N. "On the Christology of Q." In *Christ and the Spirit in the New Testament: Studies in Honour of C. F. D. Moule.* Ed. B. Lindars and S. Smalley, 27–42. Cambridge: Cambridge University Press, 1973.

Stone, M. E. "Judaism at the Time of Christ." *Scientific American* 115 (1973): 79–87.

Stuhlmacher, P. "Existenzstellvertretung für die Vielen: Mk. 10:45 (Mt. 20:28)." In *Werden und Wirken des AT. Claus Westermann Festschrift,* 412–27. Göttingen: Vandenhoeck and Ruprecht, 1980.

------. *Jesus von Nazareth–Christus des Glaubens.* Stuttgart: Calwer Verlag, 1988.

Suggs, M. J. *Wisdom, Christology, and Law in Matthew's Gospel.* Cambridge: Harvard University Press, 1970.

Suter, D. W. "Ecclesiasticus." In *Harper's Bible Dictionary*. Edited by P. J. Achtemeier, 237–38. San Francisco: Harper & Row, 1985.

Taylor, V. *The Formation of the Gospel Tradition*. London: Macmillan, 1933.

Theissen, G. *The First Followers of Jesus: A Sociological Analysis of the Earliest Christianity*. London: SCM, 1979.

------. *The Miracle Stories of the Early Christian Tradition*. Trans. F. McDonagh. Philadelphia: Fortress Press, 1983.

------. *The Shadow of the Galilean*. Philadelphia: Fortress Press, 1987.

------. "Die Tempelweissagung Jesu: Prophetie im Spannungsfeld von Stadt und Land." *TZ* 32 (1976): 144–58.

------. "Wanderradikalismus: Literatursoziologische Aspekte der Überlieferung von Worten Jesu in Urchristientum." *ZTK* 70 (1973): 245–71.

Tiede, D. L. *The Charismatic Figure as Miracle Worker*. Missoula: Scholars Press, 1972.

Twelftree, G. H. "Ekballo ta Daimonia." In *Gospel Perspectives* 6. Ed. D. Wenham and C. Blomberg, 361–400. Sheffield: JSOT Press, 1986.

van Iersel, B. M. F. *'Der Sohn' in den synoptischen Jesusworten*. Leiden: E. J. Brill, 1964.

Van Tilberg, S. *The Jewish Leaders in Matthew*. Leiden: E. J. Brill, 1972.

Vermes, G. *The Dead Sea Scrolls in English*. Rev. ed. Middlesex: Penguin, 1965.

------. *Jesus and the World of Judaism*. Philadelphia: Fortress Press, 1983.

------. *Jesus the Jew: A Historian's Reading of the Gospels*. London: Collins, 1973.

------. *Scripture and Tradition in Judaism: Haggadic Studies*. Leiden: E. J. Brill, 1961.

Vögtle, A. "Bezeugt die Logienquelle die Authentische Redeweise Jesu vom 'Menschensohn'?" In *Logia: Les Paroles de Jesus—The Sayings of Jesus, Memorial to Joseph Coppens*. Ed. J. Delobel, 77–99. Leuven: Leuven University Press, 1982.

Wachter, L. "Judische und christlicher Messianismus." *Kairos* 18 (1976): 119–34.

Wallace, A. F. C. "Revitalization Movements." In *Reader in Comparative Religion: An Anthropological Approach*. 3d ed. Ed. W. A. Lessa and E. Z. Vogt, 503–12. New York: Harper & Row, 1972.

Weber, M. *Economy and Society*. Trans. G. Roth and C. Wittich. Berkeley: University of California Press, 1968.

Wells, D. F. *The Person of Christ: A Biblical and Historical Analysis of the Incarnation*. Westchester: Crossway Book, 1984.

Westerholm, S. *Jesus and Scribal Authority*. Lund: C. W. K. Gleerup, 1978.

Wilken, R. L. *John Chrysostom and the Jews*. Berkeley and Los Angeles: University of California Press, 1983.

Windisch, H. *Imperium and Evangelium*. Kiel: Lipsius and Tischer, 1931.

Wink, W. "Jesus and the Revolution: Reflections on S. G. F. Brandon's *Jesus and the Zealots*." *USQR* 25 (1969): 37–59.

------. *John the Baptist in the Gospel Tradition*. London: Cambridge University Press, 1968.

Witherington, B. "On the Road with Mary Magdalene, Joanna, Susanna, and Other Disciples: Luke 8:1–3." *ZNW* 70 (1979): 242–48.

------. "Principles for Interpreting the Gospels and Acts." *Ashland Theological Journal* 19 (1987): 35–70.

------. "Women and Their Roles in the Gospels and Acts." Ph.D. Diss., University of Durham, 1981.

------. *Women in the Earliest Churches.* Cambridge: Cambridge University Press, 1988.
------. *Women in the Ministry of Jesus.* Cambridge: Cambridge University Press, 1984.
Woods, H. G. "Interpreting This Time." *NTS* 2 (1956): 262–66.
Wrede, W. *The Messianic Secret.* Greenwood, S.C.: Attic Press, 1971.
Wright, N. T. "'Constraints' and the Jesus of History." *SJT* 39 (1986): 189–210.
Wuellner, W. H. *The Meaning of "Fishers of Men."* Philadelphia: Westminster Press, 1967.
Yamauchi, E. "Magic or Miracle? Disease, Demons, and Exorcisms." In *Gospel Perspectives.* Vol. 6, *The Miracles of Jesus.* Ed. D. Wenham and C. Blomberg, 89–183. Sheffield: JSOT Press, 1986.

Index

SCRIPTURE

OLD TESTAMENT

GENESIS
1:2	155
22:2 LXX	151 n.22
38:1 LXX	232 n.231
49:10	153

EXODUS
8:15	202
13:14	68
15:17	112, 212
16:25-26	68
19:6	197
23:20	45
23:20a	36
30:12	253
31:18	202
31:30	253
34:23	212

LEVITICUS
11	64
16–17	252 n.312
19:9-10	67
21:11	139
23:22	67
25:51-52	253

NUMBERS
6:6-7	139
18:15	253
27:17	100

DEUTERONOMY
4:7	199
9:10	202
14	64
18:15	100
23:24-25	67
24:19ff.	67
32:5	49
32:20	49

JOSHUA
6:26 LXX	232 n.231

JUDGES
2:10	49

2 SAMUEL
5:2	212
7	153, 189, 229, 258
7:1	189
7:12-14	213
7:13	111–12, 258

1 KINGS
14:6	133
19:19-21	130
19:20	139

2 KINGS
1:8	37
5	44

1 CHRONICLES
7:11	189
7:14	189, 197
28:5	197

NEHEMIAH
13:4-9	115
13:12-13	115

JOB
1	51
1:6-12	147
2:1-7	147
4:12-21	260 n.353
28	51
28:1-27	227
40:4ff.	260 n.353

PSALMS
2:1-2	153
2:7	151–152, 154, 213, 229
8:3	202
10:15	77
23	125, 212
34:10	238
42:7	123
51:11	42
69:1-2	123
74:13	131
78:8	49

PROVERBS
80:17	261
89:19-37	217
95:10	49
96:13	247
110	260 n.358
110:1	186, 190, 258–61, 267
118:26ff.	105
141:5	77

PROVERBS
1	51
2:22	77
8	51–52, 53, 233
8:12	227
8:14ff.	222
10:30	77
14:9	77

ISAIAH
5	213
6:1-13	154
9:2-7	189
11:1-9	189
11:1-5	153
14:12	146 n.4
20:1-6	173
24:21-22	204
26:19	44
29:13	62
29:18-19	44
29:18	171
29:20	44
32:15	42
34:4	173
34:5	122
35	170–71
35:4-6	166
35:5-6	44
35:5	156, 171, 165
40:1ff.	200
40:3 LXX	36
41:21	199
42:1	151 n.22
42:7	171
42:18ff.	171
43	254

ISAIAH (*cont.*)
43:3-4   254
44:3   42
48:16   199
49:14-26 212
51:1-2   41
51:5   199
53   252 n.312; 254
53:8 LXX 72
53:12   211
54:4-8   212
56:1   198, 199
56:7   111
60:22   199
61   170-71
61:1ff.   165
61:1   44, 166
61:2   44
61:11   212
63:10ff. 42
66:16   122

JEREMIAH
1:5-19   154
2:2   212
3:17 LXX 232 n.231
7:11   111
7:29   49
8:13   173
13:1-11   173
16:16   130
19:1-13   173
23:5f.   189
23:23   199
26:20   112
29:17   173
30:9   189
31:27ff. 212
33:15   189
33:22   189
50:6   125, 143

EZEKIEL
1-2   154
4:1-15   173

7:3   198
7:7   199
7:12   198
9:1   199
16:8-14   212
18:31   42
21   122
29:4ff.   130
34   125-26
34:23-24 189
36:25-27 42
37:24   189
38:4   130

DANIEL
2-7   239
2:20-23   221
2:44   197
3:10   202
4:15   247
4:16-23   247
4:21   247
4:22   197
7   238-48, 254-56,
          259, 260 n.358,
          262, 269
7:9   244
7:10   244
7:13-14   185-86, 231 n.230,
          239-40, 246,
          258-59, 261
7:13   246, 259 n.349
7:14   239-41, 252
7:17   239
7:22   142
7:25   246
7:27   197, 238-39, 240
8:15-16   238
9:21   238
10:5   238
10:16   238
11:40 LXX 232 n.231
12:1 LXX 232 n.231
12:4 LXX 232 n.231
12:6-7   238

HOSEA
2:16-23   212
3:5   189
9:10   173
9:16   173

JOEL
1:7   173
2:28-30   42
3:12   247

AMOS
4:2   130
6:4-7   166
9:11   189

MICAH
2:1   166
2:12   173
7:1-6   173

HABAKKUK
1:14-17   130
2:6-7   166
2:20   260 n.353

ZEPHANIAH
2:5   166

ZECHARIAH
1:12 LXX 232 n.231
6:12   112, 114 n.314
7:5   71
8:19   71
9:1ff.   104
9:9 LXX   43
9:9   104-7
9:10   104
10:2   212
14:5   247
14:21   111, 114

MALACHI
3:1   36, 43, 45

NEW TESTAMENT

MATTHEW
2:1ff.   124
2:7-9   217
3   36, 39-42
3:9   40
3:10   174
3:11   38
3:17   150
4:15   124
5:3   165
5:9   107
5:17-18   59
5:20   59, 78, 205
5:23-24   113
5:38-48   107
6:8   132

6:9   218, 220 n.170
6:10   204-6
6:24   102
7:13-14   205
7:21   205
8:5-13   163
8:11ff.   124
8:11-12   79, 206
8:19   57
8:20   52-53, 248-50
8:21-22   118, 137-40
8:21   138
8:22   138
9:9-13   97
9:14   57
9:20   183

9:32-34   158
9:36   125
10:1   127
10:2ff.   134-37
10:2-4   127, 132, 134
10:2   133
10:4   97
10:5-6   132, 141
10:5   127
10:6   124-26
10:7   135, 199
10:10   132
10:11-14 136
10:15ff. 132
10:15   136
10:23   232 n.232

MATTHEW (cont.)
10:24   180
10:32-33   122
10:32   206
10:34   121–24
10:39-40   122
10:40   136, 143
11   42
11:1-19   221
11:2-19   36, 42–53, 165–66
11:2-6   42, 185
11:2   43, 49
11:4-6   165
11:5   170
11:7-11   42, 45–46
11:9   45
11:11ff.   45
11:11   45, 46
11:12-13   42, 46–48
11:12   47
11:13   47
11:14   47
11:16-19   42, 49–53, 180 n.5,
               221, 223
11:18-19   50
11:18   253
11:19   52, 73, 76
11:19b   51, 53
11:20-24   222
11:21-24   163
11:21-23a   166–67
11:21   136, 165
11:23b-24   166
11:25ff.   265
11:25-27   52 n.84, 209, 222
11:25-26   222, 226
11:25   222
11:27   221–28, 229, 231,
               233, 268, 269
11:27a   227
11:27b   227
11:28-30   52 n.84, 275
12:18-21   124
12:22   158 n.53
12:23   189
12:27-28   158, 163
12:27   164
12:28   164, 175, 214, 201–4
12:29   211
12:38   168
12:40   168
12:42   52, 180, 223, 232
               n.232
13:11   5
13:24b   40
13:26b   40
13:30   122
13:30b   40
13:41   40
13:52   57
15:2   220
15:21ff.   124
15:24   124–26
15:30   170
16:1   39, 168

16:6   39
16:11ff.   39
16:28   232 n.232
17:22b   251
17:24-27   103 n.263
17:34-35   232 n.232
18:8   257
18:9-14   208
18:12-14   212
18:15   131
19:3-9   65
19:28   122 n.339, 127, 134,
               140–42, 244, 257
19:29   134
20:29-34   170
21:1   134
21:28-32   212
21:31-32   38
21:31   209, 212, 205
22:1-10   208
22:37   124
23   60
23:1-7   78
23:2   78
23:3   59
23:5-7   180
23:9   220, 276
23:13   205
23:15   61, 124
23:34-36   223, 251
23:37-39   223
23:37   100
24:36   228–33
25:1-13   212
25:10   205
25:21   205
25:23   205
25:30   205
25:31ff.   142
25:32   126
26:39   218
26:42   218
26:52   48, 121
28:18   214, 227
28:19   124

MARK
1:1—3:6   198
1   45, 175
1:1-11   36–39
1:1-4   39
1:1   38
1:2-3   38
1:4-5   150
1:5-6   37
1:5   36, 37
1:7-8   38
1:9-11   148–55
1:10   150
1:11   152, 224
1:14-15   36, 198–201
1:14   199
1:15   198–201, 203
1:16-20   130
1:17   129–31

1:21-28   162, 201
1:24   263, 264
1:25-28   265
1:32-34   162
1:43-45   265
2:10   233 n.235, 246
2:12   265
2:13-17   97
2:13-14   76
2:15-17   74–79, 208
2:15   76
2:16   57, 76
2:17   253
2:17a   77–78
2:17b   76, 78, 79, 125
2:18-22   71–72, 80
2:19ff.   212
2:19a   71
2:19b-20   71
2:21-22   71
2:23ff.   70
2:23-28   66–71, 80
2:24   67
2:27   67–68
2:28   67, 246
3   157, 189, 264 n.7
3:1ff.   66
3:3ff.   265
3:4   102
3:6   163
3:11   264
3:7-12   162
3:14-19   126
3:14   133
3:16   127
3:17   97
3:18   97
3:20ff.   204
3:20-30   201
3:21   146
3:22   57, 62, 163
3:22b   201
3:23–27   148
3:27   211
3:31-35   127–28
4   210
4:3ff,   212
4:10-12   264
4:10   127–28
4:11   5
4:14-20   210
4:17   44
4:34   183
4:35-43   162
5   264 n.7
5:1-20   264
5:19ff.   264
5:20   264
5:30   158 n.54
5:34   172
5:35   180
5:41   158
5:43   159, 264
6:2ff   274
6:2-3   163

MARK (*cont.*)
6:3	44
6:4	46, 100
6:5-6	172
6:8	184
6:11	136
6:12	135
6:14-29	51
6:14-16	163
6:15	97
6:30	127, 133, 135
6:31-52	162
6:34	125, 126
6:37	99
6:52	163
6:53-56	162
7	60, 239
7:1	62
7:1-8	62, 63
7:4-15	63
7:5	61, 220 n.169
7:7-8	62
7:8	62, 220 n.169
7:15ff.	61
7:15	63–65, 68, 70, 75, 80
7:18	239
7:19a	64
7:19b	61, 64
7:21-22	64
7:22	239
7:24-30	264
7:27-28	68
7:32-37	171
7:33	158
7:36ff.	265
8:6-8	99
8:11ff.	159
8:11	168–70
8:12	49
8:14-21	162
8:17-21	163
8:21	239
8:22-26	170–73
8:23	158
8:24	172
8:26	172
8:27ff.	191
8:27-30	263
8:31	245 n.278, 250
8:38	15, 49, 133 n.392, 240 n.265, 213–14
9:1	232 n.232
9:14-29	264
9:29	183 n.19
9:31	250, 251
9:32-34	158 n.53
9:42-47	44
9:43-47	205
9:43	196
10:1-12	65
10:6	103
10:10-12	265
10:15	205
10:17-18	276

10:23	205
10:25	102
10:32	128
10:33-34	250
10:45	183, 251–56, 262, 269
10:45a	254–55
10:45b	254–56
10:46ff.	264
10:46-52	170
11:1-11	104–5
11:1	134
11:8	45
11:12-14	173–75
11:15-17	110–111
11:16	111
11:17	111, 114
11:20-25	173–75
11:20	175
11:21	174
11:27-33	49, 54–55, 148, 149, 150 n.16
11:28ff.	214
11:34	183 n.19
12	233
12:1-9	213–14, 224–25
12:6	224
12:13-17	101–4
12:18ff.	60
12:18-27	15
12:35-37	188–91, 258
12:38-40	78
13	175 n.123, 181
13:1-2	111
13:4	231
13:8	245
13:12	244–45
13:17	245
13:26	231, 238, 257
13:30	230
13:32	224, 225 n.195, 228–33, 269, 277
13:33	232
14:13	134
14:22-24	99
14:24	253, 255
14:25	206
14:27-31	212
14:27	44, 114 n.314, 126
14:29	44
14:36	218–19
14:41	74
14:53-65	258
14:57-58	111–12
14:58	258
14:58b	114
14:62	190–91, 238, 247, 256–61
15:40-41	128

LUKE
1:1ff.	13
1:1-4	ix, 20
1:32	95
1:34-35	152 n.23
2:40-52	275

2:49-52	152 n.23
2:52	33
3:1-22	36, 39–42
3:1	36
3:9	174
3:12-14	38
3:15-17	43
3:16-17	122
3:16	38
3:21	150
3:22	150
4:16ff.	165
4:16-30	16
4:18ff.	208
4:23	78
4:43	47
5:10	130
5:27-32	97
6:13-17	127
6:13-16	126
6:13	133 n.394
6:19	158
6:20	165
6:21	243
6:40	180
7	42
7:1-10	163
7:18-35	36, 42–53, 165–66
7:18-23	42–44, 185
7:18	134
7:22ff.	191
7:22-23	165
7:22	170
7:24-28	45–46
7:28	46
7:29-30	38, 39
7:31-35	49–53, 180 n.5, 221, 223
7:34	73
7:35	49, 52
7:36-50	73
8:1-3	125, 127
8:1	47
8:10	5
8:46	158
9–10	132
9:3	132
9:11	132
9:44b	250–51, 256
9:54	122
9:58	52–53, 247, 248–50, 257
9:59-60	118, 137–40
10	201
10:1-12	132, 221
10:4	184
10:9	199
10:11	135
10:12	136
10:13-15	163, 166–67, 222
10:13	136, 165
10:17	147
10:18	133 n.392, 146–48, 175
10:19ff.	214

LUKE (*cont.*)
10:20 147, 201
10:21-22 209
10:21b 222
10:22 221–28, 229, 231,
233, 268
10:38-42 125
11:2 204–6, 219–20
11:14-19 202
11:19-20 158, 163
11:19 164, 201
11:20 147, 164, 201–4,
214, 270
11:21 211
11:29-32 49
11:29 168–70
11:29b 168
11:31-32 201
11:31 52, 180 n.5, 223
11:32 232 n.232
11:49-51 223, 251
11:50 49
11:52 205
12:8-9 255 n.327, 257, 261
12:8 206
12:32 196, 205
12:49-50 121–24
12:49 121
12:49 123, 253
12:50 41, 121, 123–24
12:50a 121
12:53 244
13 201
13:1-3 74
13:1 108
13:6-9 173–74
13:10-17 66
13:28-30 208
13:29 79
13:32 124
13:33–34 46
13:33 251
13:34-35 223
14:7-14 208
15 201
15:2 76
15:4-7 212
15:11-32 212
16:9 102
16:16-18 201
16:16 42, 46–48
16:17 59
16:19-31 102
17:2 44
17:22-30 243–44
17:22-24 231 n.230
17:25 49, 244
17:22-30 245 n.277
17:30 243–44
18:8 247
18:12 71
18:35-43 170
19:1-10 73
19:9-10 125
19:10 126

21:15 52
22:3 251
22:20 255
22:27 252
22:27b 254
22:30 127, 133 n.392,
140–42
22:35-38 132
22:49-51 48
22:49-50 97
22:69
23:2 116
23:29 245
23:43 206
24:19-21 100

JOHN
1 42
1:4 198
1:29-34 150
1:31 94
1:51 259
2:16 114
2:16b 115
2:19 111, 115
2:19b 114, 115
3:5 205
3:22—4:3 36, 37, 53–54
3:22-23 54
3:26 180
4:2 53
5:27 214
6:14-15 99
6:67 127
6:71 98
7:27 224
9 170, 172
9:6 158
10:15-27 126
12:4 98
12:16 106
12:31 146 n.4
13:1-20 255
13:2 98
13:26 98
14:22 98
16:4 15
18:15-16 258
20:16 180
20:30 13
21 129

ACTS
1:7 230
1:13 134
2:46 113, 109
5:34-35 84
6:14 94
7:2 220
7:56 254
8:7 201
8:12 196
10:37-38 151–52
10:38 201
11:27-29 6
11:27-28 4

13:1-2 4
13:50 137
14:22 205
16:16-18 201
16:25ff. 159
21:10-11 6
21:10 4
21:28-29 109
22:1 220
22:3 130
23:9 77

ROMANS
4:25 251
8:15-16 218
8:15 218
8:31-32 251
11:25-27 5
13:12 200
14:14 63
14:17 196

1 CORINTHIANS
1:22 169
3:13 122
6:2-3 257
6:3 141–42
6:9 196
6:10 205
7 5
7:10-11 12
7:10 3
7:12 3
7:25 3
7:40 3
11:2 12
11:23 12
11:23ff. 12
11:23-25 99
11:24-25 255
14:15 187
14:29 3
14:34 102
15 257
15:1 12
15:3 12, 251
15:4 12
15:5 126
15:24 196
15:51-52 5

2 CORINTHIANS
1:20 187
11:2 72
12:1ff. 146

GALATIANS
1:9 12
4:6 218, 225 n.195
5:21 205

EPHESIANS
5:5 205
5:22-32 72

PHILIPPIANS
2 53

1 THESSALONIANS
2:13   12
4:1-2   12
4:1   12
4:15-17   5

2 THESSALONIANS
1:5   205
2:15   12
3:6   12
2:15   12
3:6   12

1 TIMOTHY
1:15   126
2:6   253, 255 n.332, 256

HEBREWS
2:6   254

JAMES
5:8   200

1 PETER
4:7   200

2 PETER
1:11   205

1 JOHN
4:14–15   225 n.195

REVELATION
1:10   149
1:13-20   240

1:13   238, 254
2:18   225 n.195
2:27   225 n.195
4:1-2   149
5:14   187
7:12   187
10:1   149
11:15   205
12:9-12   146
14:14   254
19:7   72
19:9   72
20:1-3   146 n.4
20:2-3   204
21:2-3   149
21:2   72
21:9   72
22:17   72

MODERN AUTHORS

Abbott, M., 223
Achtemeier, P. J., 19, 162–63
Albright, W. F., and Mann, C. S., 121
Allison, D. C., 41, 194
Anderson, H., 252
Arens, E., 121, 122–23, 253
Aune, D. E., 200
Avi-Jonah, M., 82

Bammel, E., 47, 99, 100, 101, 108, 116, 118
Bammel, E., and Moule, C. F. D., 96
Banks, R., 68, 69, 138, 139
Barbour, R. S., 220
Barker, M., 245
Barnett, P. W., 48, 82, 85, 88, 89, 91, 100
Barr, J., 217, 218
Barrett, C. K., x, 100, 134, 137, 142,151, 157, 158, 167,159, 163, 167, 169, 171, 230, 253, 254, 255, 256, 261, 269
Bartsch, H. W., 140
Bauckham, R., 221, 228, 236
Beare, F. W., 124, 139, 140, 141, 174, 230
Beasley-Murray, R., 204, 229, 232
Becker, J., 35, 40
Benoit, P., 8
Berger, K., 69, 181, 186, 259
Best, E., 127, 129, 160, 162
Betz, O., 258
Black, M., 10–11, 82, 84, 87, 172, 200, 234, 237
Blackburn, B. L., 160, 161
Blinzler, J., 258
Boers, H., ix, 2, 37, 46, 48, 266, 269
Booth, R., 61, 64

Borg, M., ix, 24, 27, 30, 46–47, 60, 77, 106, 113, 145, 146, 153, 156, 180, 181, 192, 194
Boring, M. E., 4–7
Bornkamm, G., 35, 38, 103, 229, 246
Borsch, F. H.
Bowker, J., 57, 58
Brandon, S. G. F., 82, 96, 98, 107
Braun, H., 68
Breech, J., 49, 51–52, 192, 208
Brown, R. E., 8, 53, 99, 110, 210, 276–77
Bruce, F. F., 102, 103, 106, 107, 241, 242
Buchanan, G. W., 129, 192, 249
Buechner, F., vi, 276
Bultmann, R., 3, 7–8, 11, 38, 39, 42, 63, 99, 101, 104, 120, 138, 110, 120, 130, 138, 141, 147, 168, 180, 181, 190, 222, 229, 248, 250, 254, 257
Burney, C. F., 9

Caird, G. B., 30, 131, 137, 136, 137
Carlston, C. E., 52, 223
Carmignac, J., 184
Casey, M., 236, 238, 246, 247
Catchpole, D., 40, 104–5, 118, 258, 260
Charles, R. H., 234
Charlesworth, J. H., ix, 30, 62, 65, 95, 113, 193, 197, 214, 221, 234, 235, 236, 273
Childs, B. S., 190
Chilton, B. D., 22, 27, 48, 60, 170, 185, 187, 195, 198, 199, 259
Chilton, B. D., and McDonald, J. I. H., 207
Christ, F., 248

Collins, A. Y., 223, 243
Collins, J. J., 193, 238
Comber, J. A., 166
Conzelmann, H., 2, 118, 126, 127
Cook, M. J., 58
Coppens, J., 236
Cothenet, D., 6
Craigie, P., 152
Cranfield, C. E. B., 39, 49, 67, 72, 149, 172, 174, 219, 252, 256, 257, 260
Creed, J. M., 147, 148, 248
Crenshaw, J. L., 207, 260
Crossan, J. D., 207, 209
Cullmann, O., 46, 96, 97, 102, 229

Dahl, N. A., 266
Dahood, M., 152
Dalman, G., 228
Daly, R. J., 151
Danby, H., 57
Daube, D., 41, 187–88, 189–90, 63, 67, 131, 187, 190
Davids, P. H., 16
Davies, W. D., 8, 13, 70, 94, 70, 77, 91, 94, 113, 122
Davis, J. A., 154
Deissler, A., 240, 243
Deissmann, A., 170
de Jonge, M., ix, 1–2, 35, 123, 152–53, 156, 223, 227, 233, 262, 268
Delling, G., 6
Derrett, J. D. M., 105, 110, 115
Dibelius, M., 3, 7–8, 11, 104
Di Lella, A. A., 239
Dodd, C. H., 10, 13, 44, 78, 99, 179, 180, 199, 202, 208, 211, 225, 253
Downing, G., 160, 182, 184
Duling, D. C., 156, 188

Dunn, J. D. G., 3–4, 13, 43, 74, 82, 145, 148, 150, 154, 155, 157, 159, 167, 171, 188, 201, 202, 204, 216, 217, 224, 225, 226, 227, 230, 233, 264, 265

Eisler, R., 97
Ellis, E. E., 8
Eppstein, V., 110
Ernst, J., 275
Evans, C. A., 113

Farmer, W. R., 50, 61, 106
Ferguson, E., 195
Fitzmyer, J. A., 40, 43, 44, 47, 48, 95, 106, 120, 126, 128, 130, 132, 137, 141, 147, 154, 164, 169, 186, 187, 189, 191, 202, 203, 222, 225, 236, 237, 238
Flussner, D., 44, 105, 189
France, R. T., 44, 135, 186
Fredricksen, P., 175, 274
Freyne, S., 24, 89–90, 108, 62, 66, 88, 90, 107, 127, 273
Fuller, R. H., 171, 200, 203, 227, 228, 257, 261
Funk, R., 22, 209

Gardner, R. B., 54–55
George, A., 165, 166
Gerhardsson, B., 8, 12, 13, 16–17, 18
Gill, J. H., 74, 176
Glasson, T. F., 192, 230, 240
Goergen, D. J., 202, 203, 206, 236
Grant, F. C., 93, 107
Gray, J., 231
Grudem, W., 3, 4
Guelich, R., 107, 181
Gundry, R. H., 9
Güttgemanns, E., 20–21

Hahn, F., 190, 227
Hamilton, N. Q., 109, 113
Harnack, A. von, 121
Harvey, A. E., 63, 70, 114
Hase, K. A. von, 221
Hasler, V.
Havener, I., 38, 39, 132, 138, 150, 163, 204
Helmholm, D., 193
Hempel, J., 187
Hengel, M., ix, 9, 61, 82, 83–84, 86, 97, 98, 109, 118, 129, 130, 138, 139, 140, 181, 217, 248, 259, 265
Higgins, A. J. B., 49, 246, 255, 259
Hill, D. H., 40, 45, 49, 136, 139, 168, 174, 188, 195, 205, 256
Holladay, C. H., 160

Hooker, M. D., 239, 245, 246, 247
Horbury, W., 103
Horsley, R. A., ix, 30, 74, 75, 83, 86–87, 152, 184, 159, 184, 249,272
Hoskyns, E., 171, 275
Hoskyns, E., and Davey, N., 15–16, 264
Howard, V., 260
Hughes, G., 9
Hull, J. M., 157, 158, 159, 160, 170, 172
Hunter, A. M., 224
Hurtado, L. W., 2, 18, 51

Isaac, E., 234

Foakes Jackson, F. J., and Lake, K., 137

Jeremias, J., 10, 43, 50, 61, 63, 107, 108, 109, 110, 125, 134, 148, 166, 180, 186, 187, 204, 210, 211, 213, 216, 219, 220, 224, 225, 226, 229, 250
Johnson, M. D., 52, 222
Juel, D., 107, 110, 112
Juster, J., 109
Justin, 259
Josephus, 36–37, 81–88
    Jewish Antiquities, 36, 37, 81–84, 86, 87, 88, 89, 100, 108, 109, 124, 130, 151, 153, 156, 241, 255
    Jewish Wars, 81–88, 90, 100, 109
    Life, 83

Käsemann, E., ix, 6, 161
Keck, L. E., 31, 160, 162
Kee, H. C., 10, 151, 157, 159, 211
Kelber, W., 17–20
Kim, S., 215, 228, 253, 255, 259
Kingdon, H. P., 82, 85, 86
Klappert, B., 197
Klassen, W., 87
Klausner, J.
Kuhn, K. H., 147, 197
Kümmel, W. G., 31, 42, 48, 106, 121, 141, 202, 229, 231, 258, 259

Ladd, G. E., 195
Lane, W., 39, 72, 172, 173, 190
Lapide, P., 236
Lapide, P., and Luz, U., 80
Latourelle, R., 167
Lattke, M., 197
Leivestad, R., ix, 123, 200, 213
Le Moyne, J., 57
Lindars, B., 79, 133, 236, 240, 241, 246, 249, 250
Linnemann, E., 36, 37, 40, 53

Lohfink, G., 128, 129, 136
Lohse, E., 76
Longenecker, R. N., 267
Lord, A. B., 17, 20
Luhrmann, D., 43
Luz, U., 264

Maag, V., 197
Malina, B., 24–25, 65, 119–20
Manek, J., 131
Manson, T. W., 4, 121, 133, 132, 133, 135, 137, 141, 142, 225, 228, 231, 247
Marshall, I. H., 13–14, 39–40, 42, 44, 45, 46, 51, 105, 107, 121, 123, 124, 126, 130, 132, 137, 138, 146, 147, 164, 191, 221, 225, 231,231, 241, 249, 254, 257, 259, 261
McEleney, N. J., 27
Merkel, H., 82
Merklein, H., 200, 201
Metzger, B., 191, 224, 229, 230, 240, 260
Meye, R. P., 127
Meyer B. F., 23–24, 28, 30, 36, 124, 128, 255, 258
Meyers, E. M., 16, 88–89
Meyers, E. M., and Strange, J. F., 89
Michaels, J. R., 198, 207, 210
M'Neile, A. H., 173, 205
Montefiore, H., 100
Moore, E., 47, 106
Morgan, R., 2, 15, 30
Moule, C. F. D., 4, 26, 147, 174, 238, 239, 241–42, 245–46, 261, 275
Mowinckel, S., 95
Müller, K., 247
Müller, M.
Müller, P., 14–15
Mussner, F., 31, 198

Naveh, J., 186
Neugebauer, F., 191
Neusner, J., 57, 58, 59
Nicholson, E. W., 73, 134
Nickelsburg, G., 235, 240

Oepke, A., 123
O'Neill, J. C., 30, 38, 107, 114, 251
Oppenheimer, A., 75–76, 135
Overman, J. A.,62

Page, S. H. T., 253
Payne, P. B., 210, 212
Pelikan, J., 180
Perrin, N., 49, 194, 198, 204, 208, 259
Pesch, R., 115, 198, 256, 260, 264
Piper, R., 275
Plummer, A., 138

Polkow, D., 28
Polag, A., 39
Pokorny, P., 197
Pusey, K.

Räisänen, H., 37
Reese, J. M., 222
Reicke, B., 36, 37, 50
Rengsdorf, K., 85, 134
Riches, J., 30, 63, 64
Riesenfeld, H., 8, 13
Riesner, R., 13, 16–17, 180, 181, 182
Rivkin, E., 56–58, 59
Robertson, A. T., 147
Robbins, V., 184
Robinson, J. M., 222, 223
Robinson, W. C., 263
Rogerson, J., 240
Roloff, J., 113, 159, 252
Roth, C., 114
Rowe, R. D., 241
Rowland, C., 23, 94, 192, 193

Safrai, S., 182, 183
St. J. Hart, H., 102
St. J. Thackeray, H., 82
Saldarini, A. J., 61, 62
Salomonsen, B., 97
Sanders, E. P., x, 7–8, 14, 22, 30, 58, 61, 63, 65, 66, 73, 118, 122, 140, 206, 209
Schafer, P., 92
Schillebeeckx, E., 157, 168, 193, 208

Schlosser, J., 47, 195, 198, 200, 201, 203
Schnackenburg, R., 54, 128, 196, 203, 229
Scholem, G., 92, 93
Schuller, E. H., 217
Schürer, E., 58
Schürmann, H., 9, 11, 12, 13, 29, 79, 105, 125, 128, 182, 255
Schweitzer, A., 29, 145
Schweizer, E., 45, 49, 124, 136, 138, 168, 169, 187, 226, 267
Scott, R. B. Y., 259
Segal, A. F., 61
Segundo, J. Luis, 96
Senior, D., 23
Sevenster, J. N., 9–10
Sherwin-White, A. N., 90, 102, 109
Sjöberg, E., 27
Smallwood, E. M., 82, 85, 109
Smith, C. E. F., 131
Smith, D., 37, 58
Smith, M., 59,61, 82, 86, 158, 202, 217
Stanton, G. N., 10, 13
Stenning, J. F., 199
Stone, M. E., 95
Strack, H. L., 70
Strecker, G., 127
Stuhlmacher, P., 253, 254, 265
Suggs, M. J., 52, 222, 223
Suter, D. W., 217
Swete, H. B. 37

Taylor, V., 11, 38, 49, 62, 71, 98, 99, 100, 105, 106, 130, 150, 171, 172, 174, 191, 198, 219, 230, 255, 260
Theissen, G., 23, 88, 90–91, 112, 164–65, 94, 112, 136, 165, 248
Tiede, D. L., 160
Twelftree, G. H., 201, 202

Iersel, B. M. F. van, 190, 221, 226 , 230, 231, 232
Van Tilberg, S., 127
Vermes, G., 76, 145, 151, 153, 216, 236, 246
Vögtle, A., 248

Wachter, L., 91
Wallace, A. F. C., 155
Weber, M., 119
Weiser, A., 152
Wells, D. F., 29
Westerholm, S., 63, 65, 66
Wilken R. L., 29
Windisch, H., 118
Wink, W., 34–35,38, 42–43, 98
Witherington, B., 2, 13, 52, 60, 65, 68, 69, 78, 95, 98, 103, 125, 127, 128, 138, 139, 146, 172, 194, 209, 224
Woods, H. G., 84, 101
Wrede, W., 263
Wright, N. T., x
Wuellner, W. H., 131

Yamauchi, E., 157

Zerwick, M., 122, 147

SUBJECT INDEX

Abba, 216–21
Agent. *See* Shaliach
Amen sayings, 186–189
Am ha'aretz, 73–75
Apocalypse, Features of, 149
Apocalyptic Literature, 193
Ascended Christ. *See* Christian prophets, and sayings of ascended Christ

Christ. See Jesus, as Messiah; Messianism
Christian prophets, and sayings of Ascended Christ, 3–7, 20

Disciples, 96–98, 117, 120, 125–43
as shalihim, 126, 133–37, 143, 270
Discipleship, demands of, 137–40
Dominion of God, 164–65, 167, 172, 185, 191–215, 270

Eschatology, 185, 193

Exorcism, 161,170
See also Solomon, as exorcist; Jesus, as exorcist
Exorcism Sayings, 148, 201–4, 211

Fasting. *See* Jesus, and fasting
Form criticism, 3ff.
Folk literature, and gospel formation, 7–8

Hasid, 182

Jesus,
and fasting, 71–73
and sabbath, 66–71
and Torah 59, 61, 64–65, 69–71, 77–78, 80–81, 139–140, 272–74
and ritual purity, 59–65
and the temple, 274
as apocalyptic seer, 194
as charismatic leader, 118–120, 142
as coming One, 186

as exorcist, 156, 163–164, 201
as *hasid*, 182–183
as Messiah, 101, 107, 115–116, 118, 123, 139–140, 172, 215
as miracle worker, 157–160, 164–167
as Preacher, 184
as ransom, 251–56
as *shaliach*, 51, 55, 80–81, 123, 136, 142–43, 213–15, 270
as Shepherd, 107, 143, 125–26, 186
as Son of David, 189–91
as Son of God, 183, 213–14, 221, 224–28, 233
as Son of man, 269
as Teacher, 179–85
as wisdom, 222-3, 227, 232–33, 248, 269, 274–75
baptism of, 148–55
doctrine of the land, 122 n.339, 273
hermeneutics of, 185–86
John the Baptist, 34–56, 150–51

Kingdom of God. *See* Dominion of God

Land. *See* Jesus, doctrine of the
   land
Law. *See* Jesus, and Torah

Magic. *See* Miracles
Meshalim, 206–15
Messianic secret, 263–67
Messianic woes, 123–24
Messianism, 90–96, 117, 128,
   143
   and Son of David, 189–90
Miracles, 156–58

Parables. *See* Meshalim
Pharisaism, 56–66, 81–83

Ransom, 252
   See also Jesus, as ransom

Ritual purity. *See* Jesus, and
   ritual purity

Sabbath. *See* Jesus, and sab-
   bath, 66–71
Sacrifice, substitutionary. *See*
   Ransom
Satan, 147–48
Shaliach, 133–34
   Wisdom as, 51
   See also Disciples, as *shalihim;*
      Jesus, as *shaliach*
Simon bar Jona, 97–98
Simon the Zealot, 97–98, 117
Solomon, as exorcist, 156, 189
Son of David. *See* Messianism,
   Son of David
Son of man, 233–61
   and wisdom, 243–44

   as judge, 244
   See also Jesus, as Son of man
Son of God, 123
   See also Jesus, as Son of God

Taxes. *See* Tribute to Rome
Temple, cleansing of, 108–116
   See also Jesus, and the
      temple, 274
Theios aner, 160–161
Torah. *See* Jesus, and Torah
Tribute to Rome, 101–3, 117
Triumphal Entry, 104–7

Wisdom, 51–53, 55
   See also Jesus, as wisdom;
      Shaliach, wisdom as; Son of
      man, and wisdom

The County Books Series

GENERAL EDITOR: BRIAN VESEY-FITZGERALD

GLOUCESTERSHIRE

THE COUNTY BOOKS SERIES

FOLLOWING ARE THE FIRST TWENTY
VOLUMES IN ORDER OF PUBLICATION

Sussex	. Esther Meynell
Surrey	. Eric Parker
Kent . . .	Richard Church
Herefordshire . .	H. L. V. Fletcher
Staffordshire . . .	. Phil Drabble
Shropshire	. Edmund Vale
Worcestershire . . .	. L. T. C. Rolt
Hampshire and Isle of Wight	
	Brian Vesey-FitzGerald
Gloucestershire . . .	. Kenneth Hare
Cheshire	. F. H. Crossley
Cornwall	. Claude Berry
Somerset . . .	M. Lovett Turner
Lowlands of Scotland . .	. George Blake
Devonshire . . .	. D. St. Leger Gordon
Dorset	. Eric Benfield
Derbyshire . . .	Crichton Porteous
Yorkshire—East Riding	
	John Fairfax-Blakeborough
Cambridgeshire and Huntingdonshire	
	E. A. R. Ennion
Isle of Man . . .	. Canon E. H. Stenning
Essex . . .	C. Henry Warren

PLEASE WRITE TO THE PUBLISHERS
FOR FULL DESCRIPTIVE PROSPECTUS

GLOUCESTERSHIRE

by

KENNETH HARE

Illustrated and with a Map

London
Robert Hale Limited
18 Bedford Square WC1

I desire to thank Jonathan Cape Ltd for their courtesy in giving me permission to print extracts from the following: The Autobiography of a Super Tramp *by W. H. Davies, and* The Collected Poems of W. H. Davies, *both published by them. I also take this opportunity of thanking Mrs W. H. Davies for very kindly allowing me to make use of the same passages from her late husband's works.*

I have pleasure in expressing my thanks to Martin Secker & Warburg for their kind permission to reprint extracts from The Collected Poems of James Elroy Flecker.

THIS BOOK IS PRODUCED IN
COMPLETE CONFORMITY WITH THE
AUTHORIZED ECONOMY STANDARDS

PRINTED IN GREAT BRITAIN
BY WESTERN PRINTING SERVICES LTD., BRISTOL

To the learned and genial
Historian of the wine trade in England
ANDRÉ L. SIMON
whose style is as clear and invigorating
as the commodity of which he treats

CONTENTS

Chapter   *page*

I   THE EARLIEST GLOUCESTRIANS   1

II   ROMAN GLOUCESTERSHIRE   11

III   ROMANS AND AFTER   20
         Gloucestershire in the Middle Ages—The Normans—
         Wars of the Roses

IV   THE BATTLE OF TEWKESBURY   32

V   THE CIVIL WAR IN GLOUCESTERSHIRE   44
         Siege of Bristol—Siege of Gloucester—Gloucester
         relieved

VI   THE BATTLE OF STOW-ON-THE-WOLD   58
         Origin of the Gloucestershire Regiment

VII   GLOUCESTERSHIRE REGIMENT   69
         Napoleonic War—The Great War

VIII   RUDE TONGUES OF SHEPHERDS   81

IX   FOLKLORE   93

X   POPULAR SAYINGS AND A POPULAR SPORT   109

XI   THE COTSWOLD BACCHUS   121

XII   COTSWOLD FARE   133

XIII   SCHOOLS—BRISTOL GLASS   144

XIV   HISTORIC HOUSES   156

XV   GREAT GLOUCESTRIANS   170

XVI   COTSWOLD VILLAGES (I)   197
         Cobberley—Miserden—Bourton-on-the-Water

XVII   COTSWOLD VILLAGES (II)   208
         Minchinhampton—Lower Slaughter

         BIBLIOGRAPHY   220

         INDEX   222

ILLUSTRATIONS

1	A Cotswold stream at Upper Slaughter	*frontispiece*
		facing page
2	The Roman Villa, Chedworth	16
3	Looking through the Chapter House arches of Hailes Abbey	17
4	The Norman Arch of the West Front of Tewkesbury Cathedral	32
5	Tewkesbury—Old Abbey Mill, Abbey Tower and timbered houses	32
6	Chipping Campden—fourteenth-century house	33
7	Cotswold escarpment over Broadway	33
8	Black and white gabled house at Forthampton	48
9	Spring at Hilcot	48
10	St Briavels in the Forest of Dean	49
11	The River Wye between Chepstow and Tintern	49
12	Portion of front of *St Edwards*, a house in the Market Square, Stow-on-the-Wold	64
13	A Gloucestershire farm at Cowley	64
14	A sunlit glade—Forest of Dean	65
15	View over the Cotswolds from Stow-on-the-Wold	65
16	Natives of Deerhurst with their quaint elver nets	80
17	Naunton	80
18	The River Avon at Shirehampton	81
19	Avonmouth Docks	81
20	The Severn Bore	96
21	Looking across country towards the hills above the Severn Valley	96
22	Wool Market Hall, Chipping Campden	97
23	Ancient Dovecote, Naunton	97
24	Snowshill village	112
25	Cranham	112
26	Berkeley Castle	113
27	Detached tower of Berkeley Church	113
28	View from the Cotswold Escarpment at Frocester	128
29	Duntisbourne Rous, a farm	128
30	Cottages at Bibury	129
31	Broadway Church	129
32	Avon Gorge	144
33	Parish Church, Cirencester	144

ILLUSTRATIONS

facing page

34 The ninety-nine Yew Trees in Painswick Church-
    yard   145
35 Painswick   145
36 Sapperton   160
37 Near Sapperton   160
38 Painswick   161
39 Stanway House   161
40 River Avon at Twyning Ferry   176
41 Elkstone   176
42 The old steps, Tetbury   177
43 The stone footbridge, Eastleach   177
44 Gloucester Cathedral   192
45 Cotswold Landscape   192
46 Ozleworth Valley   193
47 Tetbury   193
48 Chipping Sodbury   208
49 Lower Slaughter   209

ACKNOWLEDGMENTS

The illustrations above, numbered 3, 7, 18, 25, 29, 30, 38, 40, 46, 49 are reproduced from photographs by Mr Will F. Taylor of Reigate; 4, 5, 8, 10, 21, 33, 39 by Mr Staniland Pugh of Amersham; 12, 15, 23, 34, 43 by Mr T. Edmondson of Folkestone; 19, 27, 42, 47 by Mr E. Orchard of Bristol; 32, 48 by the Bristol Evening Post; 24, 17 by Mr Alec Davis of London; 11, 26 by Mr H. A. Summers of Keynsham; 14, 45 by Mr Reece Winstone, A.R.P.S., of Bristol; 2, 6 by Humphrey & Vera Joel of Radlett; 20 by the late Mr W. F. Chubb; 44 by Mr Sydney Pitcher of Gloucester; 16 by Fox Photos Ltd. The remaining 10 are reproduced from photographs supplied by Mr E. W. Tattersall of St Albans.

GLOUCESTER

Gloucester, of lovely counties loveliest one,
   To thee the train returns me homeward bent
   After brief absence, with what huge content
To tread thy bird-loved woods, in shade or sun,
Most musical : to watch your rivulets run
   By coverts thick which Faunus might frequent
   Worn by the chase or love, on rest intent,
To sleep and all the wild wood voices shun.
   Your cots compact which fear no tempest's dart,
    Crown your dusk hills beneath their fir trees tall :
To their rough walls Propertius' ivy clings—
   The plant which grew without recourse to art—
And thence the dapper cock his challenge flings :
   The homeliness, the beauty of it all !

A GLOUCESTERSHIRE LANE

Herb Robert, Jack-beside-the-Hedge,
Fringe my deep lane, with rill and sedge,
And nettles with their knife-blade edge

From out whose cruel shade and tall,
A hardy band of whitethroats call,
As safe as from a castle wall.

From holm-oak, elm, and hedgerow lush,
Sing cuckoo, linnet, wren and thrush
Till fierce noon puts them to the hush.

In good companionable way,
The rose-cheeked farm-girls bid "Good-day,"
Bare legged, short-skirted, fresh as May,

Oft pausing on their homeward track,
To see and be seen never slack,
And curious, glancing back, and back.

Here Faunus or Sylvanus might
Return to look upon the light,
Nor deem their day had vanished quite,

And sure that bless'd Elysian sphere
Unto their rapt eyes might appear
Less worth than May in Gloucestershire.

CHAPTER I

THE EARLIEST GLOUCESTRIANS

S I N C E the history of Gloucestershire is, for the most part, intimately bound up with that of England itself, it can only in some rare cases be considered as detached from it. The earliest men of whom we find traces in this county are those of the First Stone Age. It has been maintained that they spoke Iberian, an extinct tongue which was the ancestor of modern Basque. When, however, one reflects that these men inhabited an England so different from ours, that a hardy Cotswolder travelling south might have built himself a hut midway between what are to-day Dover and Calais—for the Titanic axe of the Atlantic had not then cleft the passage of the Straits—and when we further call to mind that he might have encountered on the way at least twenty examples of extinct animals—including the mammoth, Irish elk, and sabre-toothed tiger—it will dawn upon us that to dispute about the idiom in which he expressed his ideas must remain a parlour-game for professors upon a very wet day. For these men have left no inscriptions; and it is the written word that conveys immortality.

There is a Greek epic poet, Nonnos of Panopolis—the City of Pan—whose *Dionysiaca,* or "Life of Bacchus," is not a great poem, though it contains much superb poetry. Well, where is Panopolis? Nobody has the remotest notion! We deduce the city from the citizen. The hexameters of Nonnos have outlived the deep-dug foundations of his city and the towers and walls of its master-carpenters and masons.

These First Stone Age men belonged, it is believed, to two successive races. The remains of the first are discovered in gravels deposited by rivers which have ceased to exist. The later men were cave-dwellers. In King Arthur's Cave, between Monmouth and Symonds Yat, man-made tools have been found buried with the bones of cave-lion, mammoth, and other extinct creatures. This proximity argues, but it by no means proves incontestably, simultaneous coexistence. The

B   I

highwaymen Turpin and Tom King inhabited for a time a cave in Essex. Had those anti-social geniuses chanced to die in their hide-out, and had their bones been exhumed later, with those of a sabre-toothed tiger, it might be argued on presumptive evidence that the three beasts of prey were contemporaneous. From their skeletons, we get an idea of the height of the First Stone Age men. This rarely exceeded five foot, six inches. They were what is called "long-headed," a word which must not be allowed to convey the idea of anything freakish. On the contrary, craniologists concur in thinking that they must have been good-looking. It is believed that they had dark hair and eyes.

Their burial-places were long mounds, erected on the high-points of high-lying lands. "Tumuli," the Romans called them; and we "barrows," from the Old-English word "bearw," a sepulchre.

In his monumental work *The Story of Gloucestershire*, Mr John Sawyer gives a detailed description of the long barrow at Uley, and a list of the principal places in Gloucestershire where sepulchres of this type are to be found. Uley Barrow is "120 feet long and 85 feet broad in its widest part. A dry wall surrounds the whole mound, and, at one end, curves inwards like the mouth of a cave and leads to the entrance, which is formed of two upright stones and a huge stone laid across them. From the entrance there is a straight, narrow passage 24 feet long and 5 feet high, and at its end are four small rooms, made of stone, in which about thirty skeletons were found. The bodies were usually buried in a squatting or 'nose-to-knees' posture, which probably was the resting posture during life."

These men of the First Stone Age were handy workmen, if we can judge by their tools. The materials of which these are fashioned are, besides flint, chert and quartzite. They include scrapers, presumably for dressing hides, spear-heads now and again, and arrow-heads in quantity. The British Museum possesses a spear-head of this period (though this may not be English) on which a reindeer's head is portrayed with great spontaneity and spirit. If we can view the art of these men with pleasure, it is scarcely to be doubted that we should be able likewise to understand their emotions and passions, could a "Time Machine" bring us together and the barrier of language be broken down.

And here is Mr Sawyer's list of places where long barrows are to be found in the county. It is not exhaustive. My friend Dr Mulligan, of the Gloucester Field Club, drew my attention to a long barrow in Cranham Woods, at a distance of about a quarter of a mile from the Cotswold Sanatorium, if, keeping the road to your left, you set out in the direction of Birdlip. Yet the man must be an archæological glutton if, having examined all Mr Sawyer's long barrows, he can still emulate Oliver Twist. Ablington, Amberley, Aston, Avening, Birdlip, Charlton Abbots, Cirencester, Duntisbourne, Eastington, Edgeworth, Eyeford, Farmington, Hasleton, Leighterton, Notgrove, Nymphsfield, Randwick, Selsley, Shurdington, Swell, Uley, Willersey, and Withington. At the last-mentioned village stands that most picturesque of inns, the Bell, with its Tudor fireplaces where the logs roar in winter, and here—having solaced his soul with the remnants of oldest Gloucestershire—the antiquary may call for a pint and refresh his inner man, after the traditional fashion of heroic Beowulf, and our Anglo-Saxon kings.

Ornaments of dress have been recovered from the long barrows; jet or lignite buttons, decorated rings, armlets, pendants, necklaces, and beads. But the only ornament of this First Stone Age found in our Cotswolds was that discovered in the long barrow at Eyeford near Stow-on-the-Wold. This was a bead—perhaps an amulet?—found upon a woman's breast. Does not this insignificant yet pathetic fact help to bring the past alive? The lady was superstitious—how human!—or possessed of coquetry. And she bore her trinket with her into the shadow land, when she came at last to inhabit this barrow of stone upon a windy upland of the Cotswolds.

Next, after how long an interval of time is unknown, came the Neolithic men, those of the New Stone Age. Their advance in the art of tool-making is remarkable. Sometimes indeed, like their predecessors, they fashion tools by chipping only, but more often now they both grind and polish them. They possess long flint knives, some scimitar-shaped, some rounded to a point. Pencil-shaped flints begin now to be found, for use as borers; and pieces with serrated edges which can only, one fancies, have done duty for saws. Hammers and hatchets have been found, though these are far from numerous in the Cotswolds; and worked balls of flint for use as slinging-stones. Their bowmen must have taken pride in their tackle; their beautifully worked and polished arrow-heads are barbed, leaf-shaped, or triangular.

Many of these New Stone Age relics are brought to light in newly ploughed land, and in potato fields. Potatoes need earthing up, or the sunlight will turn them green, and it is whilst this hoeing is in progress that a find may be made. A farmer at Eastcombe once called me in to view a most presentable private museum of New Stone Age relics which he had recovered from his high-lying fields. Whilst I was examining them, he filled me a tumbler of home-brewed dandelion wine so that, in case I found the subject dry, I should at least not feel dry myself. But the precaution, although I appreciated it, was unnecessary, for I found his exhibits fascinating. Most of his arrow-heads were of exquisite finish : worked so patiently, and with such inadequate tools! By way of contrast with these, he had hung above the small cabinet which contained them a "Jerry bayonet"; presumably to display the continuity of slaughter characteristic of the rise to civilization, or whatever it is, of that exceedingly odd individual *homo sapiens*! These Stone Age tools and weapons were anything but toys. The friend of an old Oxford friend of mine chanced to unearth a flint axe-head in his garden. Before presenting it to a museum, curiosity impelled him to put it to the test of actual use. Binding it to a haft with strong cord, he successfully hewed down with it an old apple tree which he desired to remove.

Relics of this New Stone Age are in sufficient plenty for us to be able to form a stimulating picture of the sort of life which the craftsmen who produced these tools and weapons lived. With their bows and arrows, spears and slinging-stones, they would hunt bear, wolf and fox. That they wore their skins for clothes is, at least, exceedingly probable, for, whilst there is nothing to suggest the existence of any other suitable material, bone needles of many sizes have been discovered. Their homes were assuredly primitive. In the

4

vicinity of Cheltenham and Stroud, savants have found remains of dwellings which were little more than pits dug in the ground. These would be roughly roofed, or protected lean-to fashion, with brushwood bound to poles.

These New Stone Age men farmed as well as hunted. They reared pigs, goats, sheep—yes, the famous Cotswold sheep have a prodigious pedigree!—oxen, fowls, and horses. They treated the noble steed cavalierly, eating him with the plebeian ox and pig, and they broke the bones for marrow. Well, even to-day one may come upon Stone Age fare, and dine economically in the poorer quarters of France and Belgium upon *bifteck de cheval*! The New Stone Age men grew wheat. Did they pay with toothache for their primitive method of hand-grinding it? It seems probable. The teeth of adult skeletons are found worn down to the gums as a result of the grit which got mixed in with the flour. The British Museum contains an example of a quern of this period for grinding. It consists of two pieces, a saddle-shaped stone to serve as mortar, and a grinder something after the shape of a fowl's egg but longer. Grit from stone and roller must have found its way into the flour, nor is it easy to see how this defect was to be avoided. These men had no acquaintance with anything in the nature of such earthenware as is made use of in the making of a modern kitchen pestle and mortar. Flints would have served their turn, but flints of adequate size were doubtless next to impossible to procure.

These men formed themselves into communities and built primitive camps, which they surrounded with mounds of earth and surmounted with timber stockades : castles adequate to resist besiegers whose nearest approach to artillery was bow or sling.

As in a perpetually shifting pageant, wave after wave of invaders cross over into England. "The tree of man was never quiet." After the two races of the First Stone Age men came those of the New Stone Age whom we have just been discussing. After these come the tall, pale, and light-haired Celts : restless wanderers, whose raids are the terror of the ancient world. Galatia, Thrace, the Alps, North Italy, Spain, Belgium, France, in all these countries men decamp before the invaders or remain to bow before their will. The heads of the newcomers are not "long," but "round"; and round too are the barrows in which they bury their dead. These round barrows of the Celts have less of art than have those of the Stone Age men. The interior of a Celtic round barrow is a mere stone box (kist), in which the dead are found disposed in the customary sitting posture.

Fighting doubtless many a losing battle, the Iberian Stone Age men retreated before the invaders towards the Scottish highlands. Or, taking boat, they put the sea between themselves and their foes and reaching Ireland and the Isle of Man, became the ancestors of the Gaelic-speaking inhabitants of those localities to-day.

How are we to account for the success of the newcomers? How did they contrive to eject the Iberians from their stockaded forts upon the heights of the Cotswold hills? And that in the teeth of thrown spears and slung stones and feathery sleet of arrows? The answer lies not only in the superior height of the Celts. These invaders had discovered *bronze*. Of this metal their weapons were made; and those of flint cannot be compared with them.

Scattered about the Cotswolds are some 150 Celtic burial mounds, whilst in the neighbourhood of Cheltenham and Stroud pit dwellings have been brought to light which, after careful sifting of the findings by savants, reveal something of the life of their inhabitants. They farmed as well as hunted. They had domesticated the horse, pig, ox, sheep, and they kept fowls. They ate all these creatures. The Celts who conquered the Iberian New Stone Age men were of the race known as "Goidels."

At a later period, how much later cannot be determined with precision, these "Goidels" were, in their turn, driven into the extremities of the country : to Cumberland, to Wales and to Cornwall. There the Cornish variant of the Celtic tongue long survived. The last woman to speak it was Dolly Pentreath, who was still alive in the eighteenth century. She outlived all those who could converse with her, and died, at last, as might the ultimate Dodo : a prodigy of Nature!

The new invaders were Celts likewise, but of the race known as Brythons (Britons). We must, however, guard against supposing that the invading hordes exterminated the men of the earlier races. Some fusion there would always be. Fighting men of the earlier race would hold out long in marsh and primeval forest. The aged, whether men or women, would be unable or unwilling to fly. Prisoners of war would remain as slaves, and, on the arrival of the invaders, attractive women captives would be treated with less acerbity than their brothers and fathers.

As the Ancient Britons came into conflict with the Romans, the latter as civilized and lettered men were in a position to give us many particulars about them. The legions confronted for the most part a fair-haired, tall, and comparatively pale race, though they find, in the Silures of South Wales and the Forest of Dean, the earlier Iberians. The British costume was curious. It consisted of (the Romans tell us) a sleeved blouse, often belted, with trousers fitting close to the ankle— the "trews," in fact, of Highland tradition. The Celts were a trousered race and this impressed the Romans, a toga-wearing people. It was not only in England that the out-landish garb was to be seen. Far from it. It was so general a Celtic characteristic that "Trans-alpine" (beyond the Alps) and "Braccatus" (breeches-wearing) were interchangeable terms.

To the Goidel bill of fare the British would seem to have added an admirable item in Honey Beer—"Metheglin" or "Mead"—a beverage which may, for all I know, be drunk in Wales to-day, for it certainly survived there into Queen Victoria's time. This was the drink—dictation speed here, please, for teetotallers!—regularly consumed by "Old" Parr who, born in 1483, died only in 1635, when dissecting autopsists could detect no manner of disease! Parr is the oldest man serious history finds to chronicle. His son, that decadent seedling, disgraced his old mead-drinking father by dying, a mere chicken, at the premature age of a hundred and thirteen.

The British of the first century were conspicuous by their tartan clothing, their favourite colours being crimson and red. They wore plated armour of bronze and iron, or at other times chain-mail coats. Their weapons were swords, daggers, pikes, bows, javelins, slings, and—what sounds curious, but may well have been effective—lassos! They employed the two-wheeled fighting chariot with its projecting scythes of bronze. In a casual simile, the poet Lucretius throws out that the shock of having your leg cut off in a British chariot-charge was such that, for the moment, your system didn't register the pain. That—alas!—was only deferred.

The Ancient Britons understood the working of gold, bronze, iron, and tin. Their religion was Druidism, and England, and more particularly the island of Anglesea, was the centre of the cult. To Britain, as to a university, continental aspirants to Druidical honours would flock, to study the *arcana* at the fountain-head. The Druids believed in metempsychosis, practised hypnotism, and divined future events by studying the flight of birds. Much has been written of their love of liberty, and of their belief in individual survival after death. But foul cruelties were an integral part of the cult. Their quinquennial festivals never lacked their quota of human sacrifices, victims being shot with arrows, impaled, or burned alive in wickerwork cages. Captives were also shot in order that the priests might practise divination by the cold-blooded observation of their dying convulsions. The Celtic craftsman stands higher in the category of human beings than the Druid, for his blood-sacrifices lower the latter to the level of the native Ju-ju man of equatorial Africa. The invading Romans stamped out Druidism, and none but an arrant sentimentalist will lament the disappearance from the Forest of Dean of the Druidesses (for they had their priestesses too, who graced their festivals naked, with their bodies dyed black), or the white-bearded, white-robed old sadist cutting with his golden sickle the mistletoe from the oak.

Julius Cæsar's landing in the South proved little more than a raiding and reconnaissance expedition. Aulus Plautius was the first Governor of Britain and he held consular rank. His army numbered about forty thousand. Landing in A.D. 43 he marched north and soon found himself in conflict with the Boduni, a British word meaning "hill dwellers." He had come to the Cotswolds. Some tribes of these Boduni submitted without serious fighting. Aulus Plautius built a camp at Corinium, our modern Cirencester. His next objective was Gloucester (Glevum). Colchester (Camulodunum) had been conquered by another detachment. The object was to draw a line right across England from west to east with a view to mastering and consolidating all that lay south of it. The invaders, however, were to discover that they had reckoned without their hosts.

The Silures were a warlike tribe who inhabited the Forest of Dean and South Wales. Hardy hill-men and foresters, they would seem to have been the later Stone Age men whom the Celts had driven west, rather than the Britons proper. Tacitus thus describes them : "Their dark complexion, their usually curly hair, and the fact that Spain is opposite them [an error : accurate maps of Europe were yet to be made] are evidence that Iberians of a former date crossed over and occupied these parts."

Again and again these men attacked the Romans, and were as often defeated, but these defeats were no routs. After every reverse, the hill-men and foresters retired to their native haunts in wood and mountain, where the Romans feared to follow as all the advantages of terrain lay with their enemies. For three years the Silures maintained the struggle with a tenacity which can never be sufficiently admired. Then Aulus Plautius was recalled to Rome, and Ostorius Scapula took his place. To isolate the Silures and prevent their incursions into the parts which were already conquered, Scapula entered upon the construction of an extensive chain of forts, which must have entailed a prodigious amount of labour. Almost every outstanding height between the Avon of Warwickshire, passing through Gloucestershire, and this same river at Bath (Somerset) had its fort, and these forts were of such strength as to be immediately recognizable to-day, after close upon two thousand years of human existence, for what they then were. Mr Sawyer enumerates the most important of these, and I cannot do better than reproduce his list. A glance at the map will show the reader the general disposition of the Roman front line of defence : Willersley, Stanton, Charlton Abbots, Nottingham Hill, Cleeve Hill, Leckhampton, Crickley, Birdlip, Cooper's Hill —where the sport of rolling the cheese takes place every Whit-Monday, as will be elsewhere described—Painswick

Beacon—where, in the days of the Great Civil War, the Cavaliers made a stand, expecting attack by Fairfax, who, however, having relieved Gloucester, returned straightway to London. Haresfield Beacon—a beauty spot of unexampled loveliness, saved when the streets which were to cover it had been already plotted out and preserved for the beauty-lover by the National Trust. Uley Bury, Stinchcombe Hill, Westridge, Sodbury, Dyrham, and Lansdown, these high places with many more of lesser note the Romans fortified. The garrison upon each of these vantage points could keep in touch with its neighbouring garrisons to left and right, and summon assistance in case of assault. It was obvious that Scapula meant business!

The King of the Silures had for a long while past been harassing the invaders. His name was Caradoc, better known under its latinized form Caractacus. He is universally allowed to have possessed not only courage of the highest quality, but considerable gifts as a strategist. He now summoned his Hill and Forest of Dean men together, for what he believed was to prove the final struggle. He was defeated by the better-armed and better-disciplined Romans (A.D. 50) and, flying for refuge to a native princess, was betrayed by her, cast into chains, and delivered bound to the Romans. Well might Tacitus declare that the British were not conquered save by their own dissentions!

Men did not willingly suffer his fame to die and over eleven hundred years after his death the superb Elizabethan dramatist, Fletcher, may be said to have given Caradoc his epitaph by making him the hero of the admirable historical play *Bonduca*. Caradoc was sent to Italy, to grace the triumph of Claudius Cæsar, whom he impressed by the nobility of his bearing. The prisoner is said to have expressed astonishment that, possessed of such luxury as he saw displayed everywhere about him, the Romans could envy him his thatched cottage in Britain! Claudius granted him his life, but Caradoc was too dangerous to be allowed to return to Britain. He remained in Italy, and the date and manner of his death are alike unknown.

CHAPTER II

ROMAN GLOUCESTERSHIRE

COLONIZATION by the Romans proceeded slowly, but with prodigious thoroughness. The British were ready for a type of civilization higher than that to which they had hitherto been accustomed. That they were far from barbarous is proved, if proof be necessary, by the so-called Birdlip Mirror, and the objects found with it.

In 1879, by the roadside between Birdlip and Crickley on the edge of the Cotswold Hills, a workman came upon three skeletons in a line, in graves boxed and lidded with slabs of whitewashed limestone. The two at the extremes were men's, that in the centre a woman's. And this last contained grave furniture. There were two bronze bowls, one large, one small; a bronze bracelet, four plain bronze rings, and a necklace of ring-beads of jet, amber, and grey marble. The haft of a small knife was found; and a silver brooch plated with gold. It is worth noting, parenthetically, that after a lapse of two thousand-odd years the spring of this brooch still retains its elasticity. It terminates in the head of some beast unknown to zoologists. So likewise does the knife-haft, horned this time, and with empty eye-sockets which doubtless once contained eyes made of gems or glass.

Before that order and proportion which characterizes classical art became known here, Ancient British art—like that which was to follow in the later Middle Ages—had a bias towards the fantastic and grotesque. The outstanding piece of treasure-trove was the famous Birdlip Mirror, which would not disgrace Goldsmiths' Hall at the present day. That it is of native British workmanship is proved by the craftsman's use of red enamel only, for Roman work displays more colours. The material, furthermore, is British bronze, not the white bronze of the mirrors in which the Roman ladies—the Lesbia of Catullus and the Cynthia of Propertius—studied their reflections. This Birdlip Mirror is oblong, and ten and five-eighths inches wide by nine and three-quarters long. The handle, a highly decorative one, is attached to the longer side. The effect would have been prettier had it been fixed, in modern style, to the shorter. I will not describe the mirror further, as this would involve technical terms which might prove boring to the reader who may not happen to be an expert, and perhaps give no very clear picture to the mind either. Those who are curious may view it at their leisure in Gloucester Museum.

The face which the Birdlip Mirror reflected was that of a blonde, which experts agree to have been the British type. Of what colour were the robes she would have fixed with her safety-pin? Red probably or crimson; those were the favourite colours. Who were the men buried with her? Who shall say? Were they successive husbands? Or slaves who might come in handy for carrying her litter in the under-world? I suspect they were only relations : those people who expect so much from us and give so little ! Who was she? Where does she wander? Perhaps she is even now smiling at this archæologically minded Peeping Tom, whose curiosity impels him to take such unashamed interest in what were once her most treasured possessions !

When we think of the Romans in Britain, we think first of their roads : Irmin Street, Foss-way, White-way.

> Greek busts, Italian painting, Roman roads,
> And English books.

But these roads presented a different aspect to the British Gloucestrian of those days from that of a modern road, however straight it may run. Woodlands now, and inns and farmhouses, abut upon them. They did not *then*. These roads were military, and so contrived as to be immune from the possibility of hostile ambuscade and, therefore, neither house nor forest was permitted near them. If the roads appeared lonely, they nevertheless looked *secure*. No boar nor prowling wolf could stalk the traveller unseen as in the days of the older tracks : no bowman speed his flint-headed arrow against the wealthy traveller ! For neither beast nor man had the means of taking cover. The Roman-Gloucestrian merchant, King Cymbeline or one of his senators, could roll forwards mile after mile asleep in his carriage. Which is more than our Georgian great-grandfathers could, when a visit to the Bath or pretty Cheltenham or Bristol Hot Wells might entail an encounter with that distinguished Gloucestrian highwayman, the Golden Farmer!

One may tread the Roman roads to-day and pause at the very spots where the Legions halted, which seems to bring them very close to us indeed. Many's the glass I have drunk with friends at the Golden Heart, a mile or so on from Birdlip village, "where," says mine host, "there was a tavern in Roman days"—Gloucestershire is the county of traditions *par excellence*!—"if you care to bring a ladder with you and explore, you'll see the old tiles in the cellar!" But a ladder is a thing I rarely carry with me, and the prospect of ranging sparsely populated country, begging the loan of one at this or the other isolated farm, and then of carrying it away *and* back again, does not appeal to me. Besides, one might be gassed! Conceivably there may never have been a throughdraught of air since the days when Probus, best of Emperors, conferred upon the British the right to grow their own vines and make wine.

Whilst mine host and I are talking, a young ruddy-faced farmer comes in and joins our group.

"Now what was a chap telling me about their cellar," says he, "only the other day in Glaaster Market?"

The landlady, who has been listening unseen, now enters.

"Not that it was *haunted*, I hope?"

"Oh, *no*! Not *that*!" says the farmer kindly, and then, turning to me with a whisper which seems to fill all space, "Now *that*," says he, "were just what I *were* told; that their cellar *were* haunted!"

The landlady turns pale.

Vague traditions of the luxury of the old days die hard with us. "In that wood," a roadmender tells me, as he jerks his head towards Cranham, with its splendid greenery and russet carpet of fallen beech-leaves, "a king lies buried with his golden throne. But no map were left. And no one doan't know where to dig!"

They will tell you at Birdlip that the Royal George inn stands upon the site of a Roman posting-house where travellers changed horses. It may be so. In 1919, the heating tiles

13

of a Roman hypocaust were unearthed, installed—the savants declare—to warm the Guard House (*Castellum*). If so, there may well have been stables hereabouts also; from either way of approach, horses would have had a stiff climb.

Unlike the invaders of the Stone Age—and those of our own day, the Huns no whit less barbarous—the Romans neither slaughtered, starved nor drove off, but *civilized*. They did not extirpate; they colonized. Many a Roman veteran settled in Gloucestershire with his fair-headed British wife to live, a good farmer, upon a small estate. There was no such thing as religious persecution. The Druids were suppressed, not for their tenets but as hostile agents inciting to revolt. No race ever surpassed the Romans in the practice of the masculine and philosophic virtue of tolerance. They had nothing of the bigoted proselytizing of the Middle Ages and of the Renaissance. They were strangers to the passions that caused the extermination of the Incas of Peru, the massacre of St Bartholomew, the Holy Wars, the romantic imbecilities of the Crusades, the witch persecutions with their demented ferocity! The Romans sought to discover *similarities* between their cults and those of subject races. Native gods were not vilified and cast out. Did the Britons worship, under the name of Sul, a goddess of wisdom and health? The new invaders identified her with their own Minerva, and Bath—*Aquae Solis* : Waters of the Sun—emerges in her beauty under the patronage of this Romano-British goddess.

Neither did the Romans reserve all the privileges of control to themselves. With a minimum of restraint the British managed their own affairs. Corinium, a larger and livelier city than the Cirencester of to-day, possessed its native Senate (*Ordo*), its native magistrates, its citizen electors. In common with all the other British-Roman cities it had its grammar school where boys of all classes received instruction in one of the noblest mediums of expression which the mind of man has forged, the flexible, lucid, concise and epigrammatic Latin tongue. So thoroughly was this acquired that, as Mr St Clair Baddeley reminds us, even the fragmentary inscriptions which the pottery-hands scribbled upon their bricks and tiles they scratched in *Latin*.

All education is futile where the will to be benefited by it is lacking. In Britain there must have been abundant desire to learn. The Roman historian Tacitus tells us : "The sons of the princes began now to be proficient in liberal arts, and he" (Agricola, Roman Governor of Britain A.D. 78–85) "preferred the natural wits of the Britons to the laboured arts of the Gauls." He tells us further : "Those who at first refused Latin began now to be ambitious of acquiring eloquence in it." The poet Martial writes : "*Dicitur et nostros cantare Britannia versus:* They tell me that Britannia sings my verses." Martial has another epigram, which though not strictly to the point, may perhaps be mentioned here. It is upon a basket. "I came a foreign basket from the painted Britons; but now Rome prefers to call me hers!" From this epigram it has been argued that British-made baskets were imitated at Rome, and sold as genuine importations. It is possible. Chinese vases of the Ming dynasty have sometimes spoken with a Birmingham accent!

Let us study the layout of a Roman-British town. This is more immediately apparent in Gloucester than elsewhere in this county. Glevum, as the Romans called it, is still recalled by the four main thoroughfares which meet at a central point, The Cross. Their names—Northgate, Southgate, Eastgate, and Westgate—tell us something of their history. Glevum was square-walled and moated with a gate at the centre of each of the four straight walls. These four streets to-day are essentially the Roman streets unchanged. They led directly to, or from, the four gates, according to the direction in which one was travelling. Northgate Street and those others were the main arteries from which, as to-day, lesser streets opened off. It need hardly be said that the houses along these main streets would be handsomely furnished, with painted walls, tessellated pavements, and the usual elaborate system for heating by hot air.

Corinium (Cirencester) was latinized as *Cissiterus* by the monks of the Middle Ages, and following the centuries-old tradition it is still pronounced Cissiter by the natives. This will not prevent the bus conductorette from kindly correcting you, in your ignorance, should you not ask for a ticket to Ci-ren-ces-ter. The pedant is not always a bespectacled professor! Unlike Gloucester, modern Cirencester has totally lost its Roman layout, which is more the pity as Corinium was to become the second city after Londinium (London) in Roman Britain. Corinium covered some 420 acres of ground and in the fourth century A.D. is believed to have numbered about five thousand inhabitants. If these figures do not sound impressive to-day, it must be borne in mind that no city of the ancient world harboured the swarming millions which the modern industrial system has called into existence.

Amongst other splendid buildings, Corinium contained a basilica—discovered and measured by Mr William Cripps— of no less than 320 feet in length. It was terminated by an apse of eighty feet at the west—which contained, it is surmized, a court of justice—and decorated at its eastern approach with a handsome portico of Roman-Corinthian columns. At a distance of 220 yards from the West Gate, outside the walls, was the Amphitheatre, the so-called Bull-ring of to-day. It is conjectured that the baiting would be of native beasts, as more accessible; bulls, wolves, and that rarer fellow the wild boar, which was still hunted many centuries later in this country, as we can read in that jewel of English medieval poetry, *Sir Gawayne and the Green Knight*. No trace of the old seats nor even of shelfing in the rocks has survived.

The walls of Corinium, standing reflected in their double moat, must have been exceedingly impressive, built, as presumably they were, of our honey-coloured Cotswold stone which seems with the flight of time to store up sunlight, and to acquire in consequence something of luminosity. Their thickness was from ten to eight feet from base to top. They rose above the water to the height of thirty feet. Their circuit measured two miles, three furlongs. And there were, of course, the usual gates and towers. Some of these latter were yet standing in King Henry VIII's day, for Leland the antiquary, who was a guest of the Abbey of Cirencester from 1540 to 1541, speaks of a ruinous tower being pulled down that the stones might be employed in the making of Mylle Walls.

So long as the monuments of antiquity are used as quarries from which new buildings are to arise, destruction is to some

extent balanced by construction. But too often one hears of demolitions which reveal an almost criminal lack of civic sense. In a village just beyond our boundaries I know of a newly discovered Roman pavement having been deliberately dug up and the *tesserae* given to a commercial traveller that they might be used for ornamental layouts before his gas-stoves! I have been told of a builder in this county who gave a tessellated pavement to two of his hands who, in their inexpert attempts to get it out entire, shattered it to pieces!

We have many Roman remains in this county which are either unexplored or at all events still concealed from the public from lack of adequate funds to protect them from the weather. Is it Utopian to suggest that a Government which flings away public money with shovels, in the education even of mental defectives, should contribute to the upkeep of monuments which are of interest to rational creatures the world over?

The villas in and about Corinium were no slavish copies of those in Italy. The builders of our British houses aimed at achieving *warmth*, which the coolness of our humid northern air made a prime desideratum. Nowhere was the heating apparatus carried to greater perfection. In Italy, however, the workmen aimed at *coolness*, for with them the sun—so dear to us!—is not wholly a friend. Tessellated pavements do not perhaps suggest comfort to us to-day. We instinctively tend to think of them as cold. In this, of course, we are absurdly mistaken. We still have tessellated pavement of sorts in our Turkish baths, and do not think of *them* as cold! In the dining-room of the British merchant's villa at Corinium the heat was evenly diffused beneath the handsome floor. The material with which these colourful pavements were constructed was British—white and blue lias, and red sandstone from beyond the Severn. The walls of these villas were gay with colour. The method of their artificers was briefly this: The builders first treated the walls with stucco, which, after finely smoothing, they allowed to dry and harden. Then, when the ground permitted, those who specialized in this work proceeded to paint upon this prepared surface their rich colour-patterns in various combinations of bands, scrolls, circles, squares, leaves and wheat-in-the-ear.

Looking through the Chapter House arches of Hailes Abbey

Let us leave the house and come out again into the open. At the back of the Bathurst Museum, Cirencester, you can see paving-stones which still bear the imprint of Roman wheeled traffic. What sort of vehicles should we meet with in the busy streets? Corinium was, it is known, a market town, and as such would have in quantity the broad-wheeled ox-drawn country carts transporting all manner of agricultural produce : fruit, if it were the season, and corn (we exported this to the Rhineland), and the famous Cotswold fleeces. If the twice-weekly market were in full swing we should see droves of sheep and oxen. There would also be wine, which—alas ! —we should not see to-day, brought overseas from Gaul via the Thames to Lechlade and then overland, or down from our own Severn's mouth.

And there would be folk borne in litters : *hack* litters for those who could not afford the real thing. The Roman poet Catullus has left us a humorous sketch in verse of a talk with the girl friend of his old companion Varus. Back from Bithynia, where the poet has been serving as lieutenant, the girl asks him the inevitable feminine question : "Did you make any money?"

"No," says Catullus, "no. None of us came back any fatter than he went. And the Praetor was a beast too. He didn't give a hoot for the welfare of his subs !"

"But," the girl insists, "I suppose you *did* at least get a few chair-men to carry you? I'm told it's in Bithynia that they are bred."

"M'yes," says he, anxious to impress the young "lovely," "things didn't go all that badly with us. I certainly *did* manage to get hold of eight tough scoundrels to carry my chair."

(Now this, he tells us, was bluff ! Catullus had not acquired, upon this starvation campaign, so much as one poor creature who could have carried for him the leg of his old broken camp-bedstead !)

The girl's answer was a knockout !

"*Dear* Catullus, *do* lend me those eight fellows ! You come just in the nick of time ! I want them to take me to the Temple of Serapis !"

"Stop !" gasps the poet, "that about the slaves was a slip

of the tongue! In point of fact, they belong to my friend
Gaius—Gaius Cinna, you know—though . . . dash it! . . . I
use them exactly as though they were actually mine. . . . But
what a dreadful girl you are not to let a fellow talk easily
and naturally!"

Such a light comedy scene might have had Corinium for its
setting as easily as Rome itself. There would not be many
litters of the type the girl was on the look-out for. The poet,
remember, was trying to make an *impression*! A litter with
eight *lecticarii* to carry it was on a par with a Rolls-Royce
to-day. Some of these machines were borne by six, some by
four, but the greatest number by two only, like our own
eighteenth-century sedans. Not indeed that they resembled
the sedans except in the matter of their being carried, for
most of these litters were constructed to take passengers
not sitting but lying. They were built with a framework
spanned with girths and contained a bolster and a pillow.
For greater privacy they had windows of transparent talc,
which could be closed at will, when the occupier could see
out without being recognized by the passers-by.

I can best compare the litter with the awning of a modern
Venetian gondola plus the central portion of the boat which
that awning covers, but minus the prow and stern. The
contraption would be supported upon the shoulders with
poles, or swung from these same poles with straps. In later
Imperial times, the *basterna* enjoyed a vogue. This was a
litter attached to shafts and mounted between a fore and
aft mule to which it was harnessed.

CHAPTER III

ROMANS AND AFTER

B E Y O N D the walls of Corinium, Glevum, and Bristollium (Bristol), handsome villas sprang up, of which that at Chedworth amply repays a visit. The men who lived in these sumptuous residences were probably the merchant princes of agriculture, the sheep-farmers, fruit-growers and dyers. Deposits of fuller's-earth have been found in the immediate vicinity of Chedworth and of four villas which are believed to have existed formerly in the neighbourhood of the Great Western Railway tunnel at Sapperton. This lends support to the theory that dyeing was practised, as fuller's-earth is of use in scouring and cleansing cloth and it absorbs the grease and oil which are employed in preparing wool.

Another villa of outstanding interest is that at Woodchester near Stroud. Though this is only shown to the public every three years, an excellent general idea of it can be gleaned from an illustrated booklet with scholarly reproductions of the mosaics in colour. So late as the eighteenth century this now world-famous pavement lay unsuspected and unguessed-at beneath a churchyard, and its multicoloured surface was rudely shattered by many an inadvertent blow of the pick. Much of the villa lies under the foundations of modern houses, so only a fragment of its whole extent can be viewed.

The pavement is designed—dinner-plate fashion—with a band of colour around it, by way of margin. About this band, as though in procession, proceed the beasts which Orpheus charms, sitting in their midst and playing his lyre. It is thought that the sketches from which this pavement was worked up were taken from the life, as the animals with one exception are known to have been exhibited in the circus shows at

Rome. But this exception? Well may you ask! This singular creature has a panther's tail and hindquarters, but the head, horns and forequarters of an English red deer! A cupola, it is supposed, once surmounted this pavement from which, it has been ingeniously conjectured, a stone may have fallen, crushing the panther's head and forefeet. What was our British householder to do? Send an artist all the way to Rome to sketch another panther from a new model? The Legions had been recalled. The world was full of wars and rumours of wars. The scheme was impracticable. So our friend despatched his artificer into the Gloucestershire woods —or perhaps took a walk there himself, tablets in hand— and this "pantho-deer" was the result! The creature's hind-legs slink, the forefeet prance. And his horns, overlong for the original design, pierce that band of colour within the limits of which the other animals are confined. This unique pavement is further enriched by the head of a River God, who is believed to be none other than the tutelary deity of our little local stream, the Frome, where schoolboys fish for dace with bent pins! Yes, here at Woodchester you may behold the image of Frome the God, with his bushy beard and those slight horns which some have supposed symbolic of a river's windings! Could anything be more delightful?

We are to look our last now upon Roman Gloucestershire. From henceforth, and for long ages, all is to be a tale of destruction. Can it be that when—with how slow growth!— man achieves civilization and is at his farthest from the beast, he is *ipso facto* in danger of dissolution; as the rose has but to attain perfection for her petals to fall? One would like not to think so.

Savage hordes begin now to threaten the Empire. And from many quarters. An avalanche of destruction is unloosed. To the Goths—people, as we should suppose, of Germanic origin—belongs the deplorable glory of plundering Athens, and the burning of the famous Temple of Diana at Ephesus. These Goths defeated and slew the Emperor of the Eastern Roman Empire, Valens. Stillicho, of the Western Roman Empire, twice defeated them, at Pollentia and at Verona. But when Stillicho was dead, their King Alaric invaded Italy, drove all before him and thrice besieged Rome itself. Upon the third occasion—A.D. 410—he was successful. He plundered and sacked it.

In A.D. 441, Attila and his Huns laid waste Thrace and Illyria. In A.D. 451, he ravaged Belgic Gaul, destroying the cities there also. He was defeated at Chalons, but not, unfortunately, killed. The Romans, however, made the mistake of not following up their victory, and in A.D. 452, this same Attila invaded Northern Italy, plundered the cities of that garden in nature Western Lombardy and utterly destroyed those at the head of the Adriatic, together with Aquileia the capital of Venetia. He was now threatening Rome. He made no secret of his desire to conquer the whole world. He insulted prisoners of war and dragged conquered kings in his train. With the sentimental-sadistic German people, this aggressive monster became a star of romance. They cherish his memory. In the war of 1914–18, the posturing Paladin Wilhelm II, called upon *his* hordes to "emulate Attila and his Huns." The incitement was unnecessary. Having constructed a siege gun of hitherto undreamed-of proportions, the *Grosse Bertha*, they sent a shell into Paris every quarter of an hour, being the first men of modern Europe to make war not upon those working on munitions, who must rank as soldiers, but upon defenceless civilians; old men, women, and children. Attila must have smiled in his grave! One of the first of the *Grosse Bertha*'s shells—so a Parisienne of that day informed me—struck a maternity hospital and blew it to pieces! In A.D. 453 Wilhelm's spiritual ancestor, Attila, gave a banquet on the night of his marriage with Ildiko, a Burgundian princess. Before morning he was dead! Whether from poison, indigestion, or exhaustion after the wrecking of so many of the flourishing works of peace, is not recorded. The event was doubly fortunate both as preserving Civilization from her assassin and preventing him from begetting his like.

But the world of arts and ordered life was doomed. Landing at Tiber's mouth in the June of A.D. 455, the Vandals indulged themselves in those orgies of senseless destruction which have made their name—equally with that of the Huns—odious throughout all succeeding ages. From the 15th to the 29th of the June of that year, they plundered Rome and bore away with them at their departure whatsoever things of price the earlier wolves and locusts had left.

In the same year that Alaric conquered Rome, the Emperor Honorius despatched letters to the British cities, absolving them from their allegiance to the Empire. We cannot blame the Romans, who were no longer themselves in a position to beat back the spoilers, and yet this was terrible for the British who had served them nobly. As the cities of Gloucestershire looked to foreign markets for their livelihood—the export more especially of Cotswold fleeces— those must have been days of short commons, of a sinking into shabbiness. A Nemesis of war and dissolution hovered over us. Irish pirates sailed up the Severn. Northern Picts came swarming over the walls which—with what sweat of human toil!—the Romans had raised to ward them off. These invaders—these also—laid waste with fire and sword wherever they prevailed. Foes from the West, foes from the North, and now foes from the South also. Saxons were marching up from their conquests of the south, not yet the Anglo-Saxons of the Christian Alfred who was to revive with his ministers the Roman letters but the unalloyed, perennial, destroying Teutons.

Between 500 and 550, the Saxons had established a settlement at Fairford, perilously near Corinium. There is no reason to assume, as is constantly done, that the British were sapped by luxury and had become an unwarlike people. They were probably hopelessly outnumbered. In 577, at the head of their levies, the three Kings, or chief men, of Corinium, Glevum, and Aquae Solis (Bath) met the Saxon invaders at Dyrham. The day proved disastrous. All three fell on the field. After this battle, the populations of the three cities were massacred. In modern Gloucester, in modern times, bones of men, women and children have been discovered lying in disorderly confusion a few feet below the surface of the ground. In one place the skeletons of two women and forty men were unearthed lying scattered pell-mell, amidst a litter of broken Roman tiles, shards of Samian-ware and Roman-British pottery. Eloquent witnesses to the Saxon reign of terror!

Corinium and Bath were given back to the floods. Through

the banks of the canalized Daglinworth stream and Churn
—wrecked by the invaders of set purpose, or perishing from
neglect—the waters seep, well, wash out, meander at will.
Slaves of men, they had supplied his domestic uses, his
lavatories and public baths. His masters now, they sub-
merge the very heart of the town for centuries. The noble
basilica, with its law courts and market and the fallen
columns of its gracious portico, lie under the waves. Where
the citizens had gathered for social converse or for traffic,
where the merchants' clerks had checked the tally of the
Cotswold fleeces, where the barristers had pleaded their
clients' causes, in that Latin tongue in which they were
"ambitious of eloquence," osier-beds increase, stork and
heron fish, and from the thickest of the reeds the breeding
bittern utters its bull-like cry.

In the mild climate of England, and influenced at last by
that tradition of Roman culture the gold of which their dross
had debased but not totally destroyed, the Saxon English
civilized apace, and excelled alike in verse and prose. The
device of alliteration which they employed in their verses

> The world's candle shone
> The southward sloping sun

survives to this day, and was made use of with consummate
mastery by Algernon Charles Swinburne. The "Venerable
Bede" translated the Gospel of St John into the English
tongue. The *Anglo-Saxon Chronicle*—traditionally said to
have been begun by King Alfred—is a vital document, a
thing of vivid phrasing and high imagination.

Neither are we to suppose that the daily way of life of the
pre-Norman Englishman was any longer barbarous. That a
standard of decency existed is manifest from the legend of
Caedmon. The supper of those days concluded with harp-
playing and improvisations in verse. Caedmon, who felt himself to possess no talent for such exercises, stole out before it
fell to his turn to play and sing his improvisation, threw
himself upon the bare ground and wept bitterly. Whilst thus
abandoning himself to grief, an angel stood beside him saying, "Caedmon, sing!" "I have no skill!" cried the weeping
man. "Nevertheless thou shalt sing!" declared the angel.

And from that hour Caedmon became the father of English sacred song, the forerunner of John Milton.

Though formed of the nobles and higher clergy, the parliament of Saxon England (Witan) was essentially popular. It met regularly at Easter, Whitsuntide and Christmas, although it might always be especially summoned upon any occasion of urgency. The Witan's most important prerogative was that of electing the king. Harold's absence in the North of England where he resisted and killed the invading Norwegian king, Hardrada, gave William the Norman the opportunity which he would not otherwise have enjoyed, of landing unopposed. We hear much of the Normans giving us abbeys, statesmen and knights, but there is a reverse to this picture. He also gave a now civilized and peace-loving nation a purely military government in his absurd feudal system. This system abolished liberty, for with the exception of the King, everybody was somebody's man. By abolishing the Witan, with its right of electing a king, he opened the way for disputed successions and gave us—amongst other things— the Wars of the Roses. Knights we could dispense with, for leaders we never lacked.

What sort of a man was William? To avenge the massacre of his garrison at York—aggressors whose home was Normandy—he devastated—like another Hun—all the land between the Humber and Tyne, destroyed houses, harvest and agricultural instruments, and left thousands of men, women and children to die of famine. Ninety thousand good acres of English ground and of populous villages the greedy Norman laid waste, to create for himself an artificial park wherein to indulge his hobby of chasing the deer! And what of his "forest laws"? In place of a freely elected Government which enjoyed the right of electing its King, we now had a King who, abetted by a band of foreign adventurers, could put out an Englishman's eyes for shooting his own deer!

Upon the Continent, I have always found, William is belauded not by those who love William, or know anything whatsoever about him, but by such as detest England. He is also highly rated, and always will be, by the tribe of flabby sentimentalists who praise

The keen, unscrupulous course,
Which knows no doubt, which feels no fear.

His advent marks a relapse into barbarism. His attempt
to extirpate English by teaching only French in English
schools failed so totally that to-day French is a traditional
elegance of the public schools, and like that of "Stratford-
atte-Bow," with which Chaucer was familiar, is not to be met
with upon the Continent.

The position of Gloucester after the Conquest was not
much changed, although so totally were the great Gloucestrian landlords plundered that within twenty years of
William's landing only eight of the whole number retained
lands which they had then possessed. A native Englishman,
a certain Brictric, Lord of Tewkesbury, had owned 20,000
good acres of Gloucestershire soil. The rapacious Norman
seized upon every square foot of it. But this was a case of
cherchez la femme. It is averred that before her marriage
with William, his future Queen, Matilda, had met Brictric
in Flanders, but, though she laboured at the task with intense
earnestness, she failed to induce him to fall in love with her.
Despite Matilda's metaphorical sweat and toil, phlegmatic
Brictric's emotional calm remained unruffled! Now that
Matilda had a King's ear to whisper into she proved his
Juno!

Under the pious but futile Confessor, Gloucester had been
the foremost town after London for royal councils and
assemblies. This tradition remained unbroken. William held
his Christmas here in state in 1085. A detailed history of
Gloucestershire throughout the Middle Ages is manifestly
beyond the scope of this book. Those who are interested
should consult the monumental folio volume of Sir Robert
Atkyns of Sapperton, or the yet more monumental work of
Samuel Rudder : mighty tomes and learned, by Hercules!
But exhaustive, not exhausting, for both are eminently read-
able. Or there is Fosbrooke's *Gloucestershire*, which I recom-
mend as a bed-time book to all who happen to be afflicted
with insomnia.

Brief mention, however, must be made of the atrocious
murder of Edward II in Berkeley Castle, which sent a wave

of horror through the county, for he was well known here and had been a frequent visitor. Apprehensive lest they should incur the resentment of his hypocritical Queen Isabella, who whilst lamenting her husband's murder with public tears was manifestly privy to it if not its instigator, the monks of the three Abbeys of Kingswood, Malmesbury and Bristol refused to have the burial within their walls.

John Thokey, Abbot of Gloucester, however, played the man. Providing himself with a hearse adorned with the arms of his Abbey he proceeded to Berkeley Castle, requested the body, and conducted it with procession to Gloucester. At the gate he was met by the monks who reinforced the funeral train, and thus through hushed but crowded streets they bore King Edward's body to the Abbey, which is to-day Gloucester Cathedral. So great was the concourse of those who desired to view the tomb that with part of the money-gifts which they presented, John Thokey was enabled to build the New Inn for the better accommodation of pilgrims. (No visitor to Gloucester should leave the town without viewing this superb half-timbered hostelry with its galleried courtyard, as also the "Monks' Retreat" beneath the Fleece.) Seven years after his death, the monument, which is one of the most beautiful in England, was erected. It marks the spot where the weak, inoffensive, ill-starred man lies buried.

Gloucestershire was the scene of the conflict which closes that bloodiest chapter in English history, the Wars of the Roses. The famous Battle of Tewkesbury was fought within sight of the loveliest of English provincial towns. Let us trace briefly the events which led up to it.

On 14th April 1471 the Battle of Barnet, which has been tersely described as a "medley of mistake, carnage and treachery," had been fought. The treachery was occasioned by the brother of the Yorkist Edward IV (Shakespeare's "false, fleeting, perjured Clarence"), who had been fighting against him with the Lancastrians, deserting the latter by night, and bringing over with him to Edward 12,000 men. The lateness of the hour and the proximity of the Yorkists made it impossible for the Lancastrian leader, the renowned Warwick the King-maker, either to retreat or make any alterations in the dispositions of his followers to meet the emergency. The mistake was this : Edward's cognizance was a Sun; Warwick's, a Star with rays. A dense fog coming on, and visibility being consequently impaired, a party of Lancastrians themselves attacked the Lancastrian Earl of Oxford who wore Warwick's Star for badge, mistaking it for Edward's Sun, and succeeded in driving him and his adherents from the field! A further mistake was that when the Yorkist left wing was routed and fled, no messenger was sent to acquaint Edward with this fact, and such was the obscurity that from where he stood he could not witness the disaster with his own eyes. He knew nothing therefore of the possibility thus opened up of a surprise attack upon the now unprotected left flank of his centre. But for six long hours Edward fought on, keeping up the struggle with his dogged constancy which was as notable in war as was his lack of it in love. Then the Lancastrians broke, and there was a wholesale slaughter of the remnants of their army. So much for carnage. Amongst the slain were most of their men of mark, and—for crowning triumph!—the most powerful baron in England, the Lancastrian Warwick, the dreaded King-maker.

The body of mighty Warwick was borne to London and exposed naked for three days in Old St Paul's, less to inflict an indignity upon the fallen, than in order that all might recognize him. For it sometimes happens, when a man of dominating personality is taken off, the rumour runs he is not dead, but escaped and in hiding.

Meanwhile Margaret, the Lancastrian Queen, was with a handful of French followers in Normandy, attempting to cross over to England and join Warwick. Time and again she took ship, but science not having yet tamed the waves with steam, she was as often hurled back by the force of the winds. At long last her mariners were successful and she landed at Weymouth on the very day of the battle. When the news of Barnet Field and its upshot was brought her, "she, like a woman all dismayed, for fear fell to the ground." We can pardon the virago for revealing this one recorded symptom of feminine sensibility. Resolution she had; but the winds had fought against her. A landing more inauspicious could hardly be conceived. The host of friends who should have flocked about her, kissed her hand, bade her welcome to England and put their lives and fortunes at her disposal, were scattered throughout the land or in their graves. She took sanctuary at Beaulieu Abbey.

In this state of mortal depression, Margaret was joined by two pillars of her cause in the West, Edmond, Duke of Somerset, and Thomas Courtney, Earl of Devonshire. They revived in her again her old indomitable spirit. The men of Cornwall and Devon began to flock in, followed fast by Lancastrians from the more outlying parts. The objective of the Lancastrians was Wales, where they hoped to join forces with the Welshmen, always loyal to their party, under the leadership of Jasper, Earl of Pembroke. A glance at the map will enable the reader to follow Margaret's moves and Edward's counter-moves.

The order now was, "March!" The Lancastrians left Weymouth and proceeded along a route—Exeter, Glastonbury, Bath. A circuitous way if you will, but it had two objects : (1) To gather recruits. (Both Hall and Holinshed agree that within ten days Margaret's generals had assembled an army of no fewer than 40,000 men.) (2) To bluff Edward, whose intelligence service was of the highest order, as to their true destination. No use for him to march direct on Wales if his opponents, by a circuitous counter-march, were to by-pass him and attack London in his absence !

Edward meanwhile was in the capital supervising arrangements for the relief of the Yorkist victims of Barnet, a staggering list of wounded and sick. He too had endured the hazards and fatigues of that bloody field, with the additional cares inseparable from the rank of commander-in-chief. But he was not "sycke." His physique was indestructible. Eating, drinking, hunting and love-making (as though he would replace in the bed-chamber the souls he had sent packing in the field) made up his days. The approach of Edward IV to life was not academic !

Now he increased his activities. To every corner of England where he had adherents, he despatched gallopers to bring in fresh men. His scouts and spies were instructed to maintain constant watch upon his adversaries and keep him supplied with ever-fresh reports of their movements. And—

alert as ever to the forward march of science—he made mighty provision of "artilary and ordinaunce, gonns and othar . . . gret plentye." On 19th April 1471 he shifted his headquarters to Windsor, where he appointed a general muster of his newly raised levies. Here he honoured "God and Seint George" and so far relaxed as to keep the "feaste of Seint George"; doubtless with the royal accessories of overflowing cups of malmsey and roosts of peacocks served up with their plumes.

The game of bluff meanwhile was kept up without intermission. To trick Edward into the belief that their true objective was London, the Lancastrians sent armed parties as far as Yeovil and Bruton. They spread it abroad that by way of Berkshire or Oxford they were marching on Reading! (To the efficacy of wars of rumour, the French of 1940 were no strangers!)

But Edward's scouts—and his own horsesense, of which he had enough and to spare—convinced him that despite specious appearances the true goal of the Lancastrians was Wales, where Lancastrian Jasper, Earl of Pembroke, was hastily raising levies. In the North too the Red Rose had sympathizers. And what had the Lancastrians to gain by risking a pitched battle with but a fraction of the numbers of men they could obtain by crossing the Severn? And so began the race to reach that river first, the race by which, if he won it, Edward would be able to fight the Lancastrians before their numbers became overwhelming. And in this expedition English tenacity would, in both parties, be pushed to the limit of human endurance. As mounted men, the knights gained no advantage, for the main strength of both factions was in its foot-soldiers, whom it would be folly to outstrip; but these footmen had to travel and toil as never men toiled or travelled before.

Picture the appalling condition of the roads of that day! Watch the lumbering victualling-wagons, their broad-built wheels now striking ridges, now sinking into ruts! Mark the cruel load borne by the horses which the knights—in steel from top to toe—urge on, on! And now, things of wrought-iron bars, hooped with wrought-iron bands, the bombards go forward, under the unquiet eyes of the engineers. Carters now cheer and halloo, now curse and strike the beasts of burden as these stumble in dragging the munition-wagons freighted with barrels of gunpowder and cannon-balls of stone of a hundred and sixty pounds' weight apiece! To add to the misery of man and beast, out comes the sun and shines down on them as relentlessly as though it were not April but July! Where is this Severn? The Londoners have never set eyes on the fabled stream : but they look as though they could drink the whole of it.

By 17th April Edward was at Abingdon in Berkshire. On the 29th—suspecting them no doubt of Lancastrian sympathies—he ejected its inhabitants from Cirencester. But he himself encamped, with his host, three miles from the town.

CHAPTER IV

THE BATTLE OF TEWKESBURY

RISE OF PURITANISM—PURITANS AT SUDELY CASTLE

IN this fashion the Lancastrians continued their delaying tactics which made any decisive measure upon Edward's part impossible. On Tuesday he was informed that his opponents were making for Bath and this was confirmed by events, for Wednesday found them there. They left Bath. Seeking them all the way, Edward marched from Cirencester to Malmesbury, in Wiltshire, only to learn that they had sidetracked him and were now at Bristol.

The Bristolians afforded them a royal welcome; either from profoundly Lancastrian convictions or respect for that learned aphorism, "possession is nine parts of the law." Behind the stout walls and towers of Bristol city, the men, who but now bivouacked upon the wet ground, after ample refreshment of food and drink slept warm and dry in beds, whilst their leaders not only dined and supped as trencher-men but received welcome contributions in men, money and artillery.

Refreshed and in better heart the Lancastrians now sent outriders to Sodbury, nine miles from the town. These came into conflict with a small party of Edward's purveyors who had been sent in advance of the main body to provide lodging. This petty skirmish added weight to a rumour which that party were now sedulously propagating, that Sodbury was their objective and that they intended to adopt a defensive position upon the strong height of Sodbury Hill. Accordingly Edward advanced in person, with all his host, baggage-wagons and artillery, arrived at Sodbury : and found nobody. Nothing remained to do but cultivate patience, send out scouts in all directions and await their reports. At three in the morning news was brought that after the clever feint towards Sodbury the party of Queen Margaret, having travelled all night, were leaving Berkeley behind them in

The Norman Arch of the West Front of Tewkesbury Cathedral
Tewkesbury—Old Abbey Mill, Abbey Tower and timbered houses

their advance upon Gloucester, with its bridge across the Severn.

Edward summoned a council of war. As a result of its feverish deliberations, messengers of approved worth were sent in hot haste to outstrip the Lancastrians, reach Gloucester first, and call upon Richard Beauchamp—son of the former Yorkist governor—to hold the castle and town for King Edward at all hazards. Beauchamp was given to understand that Edward himself was fast approaching and would arrive in time to give aid, if the enemy attempted to carry the town by assault. A man of resolution, he made his dispositions. Many were the Lancastrians within the walls who were only too ready to throw open the gates to Edward's enemies; but they were given no chance of doing so.

Having travelled the night through and the morning following until ten o'clock, never doubting of help from its citizens and welcome within its walls, the Lancastrians found the gates shut against them. To feint now would avail them nothing. Their menaces fell upon deaf ears. Twice in our history has Gloucester been instrumental in changing the course of a dynasty. This was the first time. By frustrating the junction of Queen Margaret with Jasper and his Welshmen, that town prevented such an overwhelming increase in the number of her forces as must have established her imbecile husband firmly upon his throne and thus secured the succession of her spirited and resolute son.

The second occasion was when, during the Great Civil War, Gloucester shut her gates against Charles I, thus altering the whole course of events and proving herself the main instrument in delivering the country over to the butcher of Drogheda and Wexford, the man who rose to power in a flourishing England and left it shackled with debt.

With Edward at their heels, a general assault upon Gloucester was impracticable for, had he come up whilst it was in progress, the Lancastrians might have been caught with their Yorkist foes both in the town before them and advancing upon them from their rear. There was nothing for it then but to set forward once more, this time for Tewkesbury, the next town after Gloucester to possess a bridge across the Severn, that turbulent water which strikes so deep a wound in the

Chipping Campden—fourteenth-century house
Cotswold escarpment over Broadway

England of the West! The going was unspeakable, through "fowle contrye, all in lanes and stonny wayes, betwyxt woodes, without any good refreshynge." They were short of water and their journey had been not only "fowle" but long. In actual distance by the map they had marched thirty-six miles with hardly a halt that could be called such, and the horses of the heavily armed knights were as mortally wearied as the men. The leaders therefore accepting the inevitable called a halt, determined to abide, upon the south of the Severn, the upshot of the quarrel they had taken in hand.

Although such was the plight of the Lancastrians, that of the Yorkists was assuredly not to be envied. Along the crests of the hills in this April heatwave Edward hastened through the " contrye callyd Cotteswolde." His men had the advantage of slightly better going. But there was nothing with which to slake their thirst. The one small brook which they passed lay across their line of march, and by the passage of the heavy wagons was soon reduced to a mere trickle of mud.

Still, for a lap of the journey Edward was able to make use of the Irmin Street which—though very different from what it had been in the days of the Legions—had not been suffered utterly to go to decay. The exceedingly steep lane which, breaking abruptly from the old Roman way and skirting the gardens of the Royal George inn, drops down into the valley, I have had pointed out to me by the curious in local lore as that by which Edward descended the hill with his royal expedition to a "village callyd Chiltenham."

Here a halt was called, but for a few moments only, and the men were allowed to eat such scanty provision as had been carried in the wagons. And then, On! On! for Tewkesbury! That crossing of the river by Tewkesbury bridge, Edward has set his heart on frustrating! Let his foes cross it and they will double their numbers. Beyond it lies Hereford : and Wales! Upon thwarting that manœuvre all his hopes are centred!

He came up within full sight of the Lancastrians at last, and still on the hither side of the stream. Like Margaret's men, Edward's Yorkists were not only tortured with thirst and exhausted with forced marches, but almost literally starving. Throughout the last thirty miles of their heavy journey they had been unable to find—poor devils !—"horse-mete" nor "man's-mete" nor so "moche as drynke for theyr horses."

Jasper, Earl of Pembroke, was already on the march from Chepstow to reinforce the Lancastrians with his Welsh levies. It is said that Margaret's generals were all in favour, even now, of delaying tactics; of fighting a rearguard action which though it might cause the destruction of the unfortunates who were employed in it, would enable the bulk of the army to cross the river. The Duke of Somerset, however, a man too rash and impetuous to be a leader, opposed this manœuvre and his vehemence overruled the others.

The Lancastrians had at least every advantage which the choice of ground afforded. Let the contemporary whom I have quoted above describe their position in characteristically vivid terms. "In the front of theyr field were so evell lanes and depe dykes, so many hedges, trees and busshes, that it was right hard to approche them nere and come to hands." To their right, as Edward viewed it, spread a thickly wooded park. Into this he sent a reconnaissance party of two hundred spearmen, lest ground which afforded such excellent cover should conceal an ambush. The leader of this small contingent was under orders to hold himself on the alert against any surprise move from this quarter, but if the wood were clear of men he was to act as seemed best upon his own initiative.

King Edward now ordered the disposition of his army, drawing it up in two long lines. The first, the vanguard, he placed under the command of his younger brother, Richard, Duke of Gloucester, the future Richard III, King of England. He himself assumed command of the second line which constituted the mainguard. Before the van, at the most advantageous points, he placed his bowmen and artillery, including shooters with the new hand-gun, well to the fore where they could work most havoc upon the enemy. His own second-in-command was another brother, that Duke of Clarence who had turned the scales at Barnet by deserting the cause of Warwick and the Lancastrians and coming over to him.

Edward does things with a flourish which makes gay reading in these mechanized days when a soldier's first thought is not to be conspicuous, but invisible! As though for a wedding he has especially "appareiled himself" against this royal field; and if his body be recovered from amongst the slain the merest chaw-bacon will divine it to be that of a king, and a King of England too! The impression flashes upon the mental eye of damascened armour scoured till it shines like gold; of tossing plumes; of his shield painted with his cognizance of the Sun. No horse, I think. It was the custom of this six-foot-odd soldier to fight on foot amongst his men.

With ritual piety he commits "his caws and qwarrell to Almyghty God, to owr most blessyd lady his mother, Vyrgyn Mary, the glorious martyr Seint George, and all the saynts"; which done, he "advaunced directly upon his enemyes"; whilst with a sudden blast his trumpeters shrill defiance as though ten thousand fighting-cocks were challenging to battle!

Bowmen upon both sides shower feathery sleet of deadly shafts. Gargantuan bombards, and petaras—with the general aspect of which monkish illuminators have rendered us familiar—vomit flames from blazing jaws and hurl stone cannon-balls of a hundred and sixty pounds in weight! The word "gonne" is sometimes used of the engine which throws; sometimes of the projectile thrown. As an old campaigner in the French wars, Geoffrey Chaucer, the poet, is familiar with the roar of these fantastic monsters:

> With grisly soun (*sound*) out goth (*goeth*) the greté gonne !

Strongly opposed to having their positions softened, the Lancastrians reply, and with spirit, to King Edward's greetings. One man, however, all unwittingly, betrays their cause. Whether unable to endure the galling fire of the Yorkists, or thinking to bring matters to a successful climax by a triumphant *coup de main* is unknown, Edmund, Duke of Somerset, brings down the vanguard which he commands from their entrenchments, sacrificing thereby every advantage of well-chosen cover. Some say that knowing the vehemence of Edmund's temperament, Edward ordered the Duke of Gloucester—the "Crookback"—to feign flight, lure the Lancastrians from their trenches by so doing, then immediately re-form and attack.

But whatever might be his motive, descending the incline by concealed lanes and by-paths, this Edmund, Lancastrian Duke of Somerset, brought his vanguard abreast of Edward's second line and impetuously attacked its left flank. The King stood his ground and something more, and Richard, who had command of the van, turned back and joined forces with him. Thus opportunely reinforced, Edward advancing upon his foes "full manly," with "great vyolence put them upe towards the hyll." Lord Wenlock, commander of the Lancastrian second line, from whom the Duke of Somerset expected support, stood his ground within the entrenchments, realizing, no doubt, that the duke's sally, when everything was to be gained by waiting, was mere madness.

And now that reconnaissance party, the two hundred spearmen whom Edward had despatched to clear the wood, burst forth from its shadows and fell upon the duke's flank. Thus harassed upon two sides, he withdrew his men and Edward and Richard improved their advantage to the uttermost. They pursued their enemies through those very gaps in their lines which they themselves had made use of for sallying out. Mad with mortification at his *coup* having failed and at Wenlock's not coming with the mainguard to his support, Edmund cleaves Wenlock's skull with a battle-axe! The steadier has been killed by the rasher leader!

The Lancastrian Prince of Wales was an inexperienced boy of eighteen. Had Edmund been a man of totally different temperament he might even now perhaps have succeeded in rallying the men. But at the moment he was of no more use to his party than a maniac. To slay the general at a moment of crisis rarely improves the morale of the troops. Main and rearguard broke in precipitate flight without dealing a blow! "Many rann towards the towne; many to the churche; to the abbey; and els where; as best they might." Many were drowned in the Severn; and a field hard by the town is called to this day the Bloody Meadow.

Queen Margaret was taken on the field, almost lifeless, in a wagon, and—pending ransom—was sent prisoner to the Tower. And now Edward's heralds make proclamation

bidding whosoever shall find him bring in the Lancastrian
Prince of Wales. If alive, his life will be spared. Upon the
faith of a King, Sir Richard Crofts—Yorkist captor of the
Prince—surrenders his prisoner, a "fair and well proportioned young gentleman."

What occurred and what was said exactly when the Lancastrian Prince of Wales *de jure* confronted the Yorkist King
of England *de facto* nobody can pretend to know with certainty. But the interview took place in a house in Tewkesbury
town; eavesdroppers there may well have been, and gossips,
and tradition dies hard in the country where men are avid
of every detail of any outstanding event, and where one so
unheard-of as the assassination of a prince would make an
ineffaceable impression. Shakespeare knew the people, their
traditions, and the county. Let him describe the scene :

KING EDWARD : Bring forth the gallant, let us hear him
        speak.
        What! can so young a thorn begin to prick?
        Edward, what satisfaction canst thou make
        For bearing arms, for stirring up my subjects,
        And all the trouble thou hast turn'd me to?

PRINCE : Speak like a subject, proud ambitious York!
        Suppose that I am now my father's mouth;
        Resign thy chair, and where I stand kneel thou,
        Whilst I propose the selfsame words to thee,
        Which, traitor, thou would'st have me answer to.

QUEEN MARGARET : Ah! that thy father had been so re-
        solved . . .

PRINCE : I know my duty; you are all undutiful :
        Lascivious Edward—and thou perjur'd George—
        And thou misshapen Dick—I tell ye all
        I am your better, traitors as ye are;
        And thou usurp'st my father's right and mine.

And then—so runs tradition—Edward struck the boy in
the face with his iron glove; when his attendants, Richard of
Gloucester, Clarence, Sir Thomas Grey and Lord Hastings,
stabbed him to death with their daggers! Faith has flown

back to Heaven! The bitterness of civil conflict has reduced men to the level of wild beasts!

And now what remains but to hold high celebration in Tewkesbury Abbey, and sing *Te Deums* of victory? I have read, in I know not what old chronicle, that as Edward was at his orisons before his Patron, St Anne, the wooden grill before her image opened, disclosing it at full, and as he made an end of his prayer, shut to again : a miracle witnessed by every soul present. *Now* let contentious heralds bicker about the legitimacy of Edward's claim to the throne of England! A little late in the day perhaps, yet by a most authentic miracle, Providence had sanctified the Yorkist claims and all but the most odious of sceptics must allow that Providence knew best.

In the follow-up, the Yorkists had chased a party of flying Lancastrians to the very threshold of Tewkesbury Abbey. They were confronted by a priest bearing the Host, who forbade them entry. At a more convenient season, however, Edmund, Duke of Somerset, the Grand Prior of St John's, and twenty more knights—says Polydore Vergil—were hailed from the altar to the block : a move morally infamous but of undoubted political expediency! The blissful company which Edward had invoked upon the morning of the battle, with the Christian virtues which they exemplified—the "Vyrgyn," all the "saynts" and the "glorious martyr Seint George," were already forgotten!

I spare you a spot of bother up North, and mopping-up operations. Jasper, Earl of Pembroke, wise man that he is, finding nothing at the moment which need detain him, is returning unostentatiously towards Wales. And now King Edward, "rejoysing immortally for the victory, which endyd intestine dyvysion . . . returnyd to London, where was wonderfull rejoysing of all sortes, with contynual prayer, the space of thre days."

How enchantingly medieval is that coupling of "immortal rejoysing" with "contynual prayer"!

In silks and velvets, young girls and buxom City wives flaunt it upon the cobbles of Chepe, beneath projecting stories and gargoyles and chimneystacks, and lattices now all a-flutter with arras and cloth-of-gold. The roar goes up as bowmen and spearmen with the rust of battle still upon them pour through the gates of the Queen of Cities!

Jongleurs, tumblers, taverners reap harvests of gold! Up climbs the slow moon, casts blue shadows from gables and pinnacles and fills winding lanes with shimmering magic. Bright eyes bid the soldiers welcome. Lovers meet and embrace. Monks chant. Swaggerers brawl. Church bells crash. Wine-fountains splash. And all is intoxication, vociferation, devotion and song!

The visitor to modern Tewkesbury who wishes to re-create in his mind the stirring and dreadful passages of its past, needs both a dash of antiquarianism and a vivid imagination. Civilized signposts indicate for the sightseer's benefit that "bloody meadow" where the bulk of the fighting took place, whilst centuries of reclaiming from waste have rendered the land ever more man's and less wild Nature's. Gone is the wild! Gone are the "fowle contrye," the "stonny wayes," the "evell lanes," the "depe dykes"!

And gone is the good greenwood through whose sun-dappled glades knight or baron galloped hot-foot after the flying deer : or fled themselves perhaps when, with sudden rush from his thicket—foam flying from his jaws!—that tank of mammals, the wild boar, crashed through the undergrowth upon his victim, intent on disembowelling him with knife-blade tusks!

But one mile out of Tewkesbury, off the Cheltenham–Gloucester road, is Gubshill Manor, a hotel "with every modern convenience" yet dating back to the days of Henry VI and here, according to a never-disputed tradition, Queen Margaret passed the night before the battle; I dare not say "slept"—I fancy sleep deserted her—so much she had to hope, so much to fear! And there the window through which she looked out on that fateful morning is still pointed out to you.

And in the noble Abbey—the stoutness of whose columns suggests to fancy that they were the work of giants—one may gaze up into the vaulting above the choir and view there fifteen Suns : Edward's cognizances, set there by his own orders to commemorate the most famous of his many victories, Tewkesbury.

Twice, as I have said, has the town of Gloucester deflected the course of a dynasty. Had its citizens thrown open their gates to Queen Margaret it is inconceivable that Edward, Duke of York, should have reigned long or undisputedly as Edward IV, King of England. And had this same city during the Great Civil War admitted Charles I within its walls, England would have been spared the tyranny of Cromwell, during whose singular protectorship more Englishmen were hanged, drawn and quartered than there were, in the like period of time, under any one of our legitimate kings! What turned Gloucestershire Puritan : that county which had been so pre-eminently civilized under the Roman rule, so gay under Elizabeth? One finds the answer in the Reformation.

During the Middle Ages, Gloucestershire had been pro-verbially rich in its houses of religion—"as sure as God's in Gloucestershire," so runs the proverb—but after their suppression under Henry VIII, the monk by temperament found himself cut off from his line of retreat upon the cloister. Every religion, and not Christianity alone, has had its hermits and ascetics who either alone or in company with others of like temperament have found their happiness in turning their backs upon the world of ordinary men and creating, in seclusion, one nearer their hearts' desire. And rarely has the world they forsook questioned their right to forsake it. Do the disciples of Pythagoras prefer beans and water to grouse and burgundy? Then so much the more burgundy and grouse will there be for those who have the palates to appreciate them! "As you make your bed, so you must lie!" Availing himself of the gracious permission, the Fakir woos slumber upon a bed of nails! That older monas-ticism had its uses. It followed its own bent and suffered others to follow theirs.

But the sublime idiocy of Puritanism lies in its endeavour to render all mankind ascetics : to square the circle : to render the world unworldly! Were this possible, which it is not, it would still be undesirable. No puritan has ever understood the humanistic wisdom of Horace, or learned that, "though you may expell human nature with a pitchfork yet it will come running back!" But though puritanism cannot create ascetics it can and does create hypocrites, as was observed in the seventeenth century by Ben Jonson and in the nineteenth by Charles Dickens.

But if fanaticism gave the new movement its driving force, we are not to suppose that all those who allied themselves with the Puritans were fanatics. Far from it. There were those who, inspired by the literature of Greece and Rome, desired an academic and possibly unattainable liberty and imagined that puritanism would give it them. Instead, it gave them only restrictions ! In this category we find John Milton, who loved poetry, music, and classical scholarship, which the more rigorous zealots detested; who drank wine, married three times and wore his hair long like a Cavalier.

Henry Marten also, as Bishop Burnet informs us, "drew all his principles from Ancient Greece and Rome." He profited strangely by his studies. Observing that there was "no further use for these toys and trifles," he seized upon the regalia at Westminster and made of it a present to a favourite mistress ! There was also an army of adventurers bent upon acquiring estates with as scant regard for their true owners as William the Conqueror displayed for the native English landowners. Many examples might be adduced but this is hardly the place for them. Let Bruno Ryves, no unscrupulous pamphleteer, sum up for us. In 1646, in *Mercurius Rusticus*, he writes of the Puritans : "To satisfy their Covetousness they have unmercifully robbed of their fortunes, and exposed to the extremest want, not only those who were their opposits and able to hurt them, but those whose sex, age and condition might have melted stones into pitty, women, children, the sicke, the aged, women in labour, and even those of their own party."

To-day the Puritan is represented in popular art as an eccentric but obviously benevolent old gentleman, with a blossoming wife or children in simple but attractive fancy dress ! That is not how he appeared to his contemporaries ! The beautiful church which stood within the walls of Sudely Castle, the fame of which extended far beyond the limits of Gloucestershire, the fanatics left "all covered with the blood and dung of beasts." They defiled "each corner both of church and chancell with their owne excrements." This is from *Mercurius Rusticus*, a contemporary news-sheet; and from certain particulars I am convinced the report is that of an eye-witness. Bruno Ryves, the editor, became Dean of Chichester after the Restoration.

The late Mr G. K. Chesterton remarks somewhere that although, as a system, Puritanism was impracticable, it will "remain its glory that it was fanatical." That is as may be. For my part I prefer reason and philosophy to the manners of a beast.

CHAPTER V

THE CIVIL WAR IN GLOUCESTERSHIRE

SIEGE OF BRISTOL—SIEGE OF GLOUCESTER—GLOUCESTER RELIEVED

THE Puritan lake—or marsh if you will; that depends upon the angle of thought!—was fed from many tributaries. Besides the genuine fanatics who shot bears, defaced statuary and hacked down maypoles, there were the politicians, with or without religious convictions, who made use of the zealots as their tools. Puritan demagogues possessed the arts for stirring up the rabble to frenzy, so often as they wished to render the roads unsafe for Royalist members desiring to attend a debate. The legal murder of Strafford would perhaps have been impossible had not many of his supporters stayed away during the trial, through fear of being lynched.

In another class were the soldiers of fortune, small numerically but of importance from the part they were to play in the Civil War. Colonel Massey is typical of the best of these. The Parliament appointed him Military Governor of Gloucester. But he had previously proffered his services to the King, and came to be fighting against him almost by accident! He had demanded a colonelcy as the price of his adherence to the royal cause, and with lamentable shortsightedness Charles had refused it him, thinking the price too high to pay.

There were also adventurers and land-grabbers innumerable, of whom, were this the place, a list might be drawn up with particulars of their ill-gained acquisitions. And there were the "old decayed serving-men and tapsters and such-kind of fellows," who must often have had few incentives to the struggle beyond class-hatred and envy of the breeding, culture, honesty or wealth of their superiors. The Bardolphs, Nyms and Pistols of Cromwell and Fairfax might win something; they had nothing to lose.

44

And below even the "decayed serving-men" was that sub-merged tenth-legion of seedy blackguardry of which every revolution in history—those of our own day not excepted—breeds plentiful examples : the "can't-works" and "won't-works," the professional agitators, the domestic spies in great men's houses : the motley horde of all who cannot build but *can* destroy! The French Revolution was to witness the emergence from obscurity of many such : the men-folk of the women who sat knitting at the foot of the guillotine! Bruno Ryves, Dean of Windsor, was acquainted with the type.

"Their malice [he writes in 1646] hath so farr transcended all bounds : that they have done mischief where they were not invited by any benefit to themselves, only for the delight they took in doing it, burning houses, spoyling goods . . . only to make themselves sport."

He himself, poor man, had some right to speak of parliamentary malice, for a preacher having been installed in his living over his head, "with his wife and four children and all his family he was taken out of doors, all his goods seized and all that night lay under a hedge in the wet and cold."

We might further illustrate the dean's strictures with an example from Minchinhampton, the little town with its Elizabethan market-house, which lies some four miles away from Stroud. One New Year's night, sent forward by their leader, a Captain Buck, a party of Puritan soldiers arrived at the house of Mr Fowler, Rector of Minchinhampton, a lame old man of sixty-three. They found him sitting with his family before the fire. He offered the intruders no resistance, yet they seized upon him as their prisoner. One took him by the throat with one hand and with the other threatened him with his sword's point at his breast! Two more ruffians held him covered with their pistols. A fourth brandished a pole-axe above his head. "Rogue! Rascal! Mass-priest!" they roared, and beat him with the poles of their weapons.

"Sirrah!" cries one of the rabble, "you can furnish the King with a musket, a corslet and a light horse; but, thou old knave, thou can'st not find anything at all for the Parliament!" (For it goes without saying that a rector of the

Established Church would not be forward in supporting the party which sought its overthrow.)

Fowler's wife and children—for all this took place in their presence—were upon their knees, begging and shrieking for mercy; but this moved the jeering intruders to clap their hands with joy! They redoubled their blows. They rendered the old man deaf. Their violence brought on a hæmorrhage which continued for six hours before the flow of blood could be stayed. They left him an incurable cripple. Then after stripping his house of everything of value he possessed, including the contents of his study, they decamped.

I am not one of those who is given to harping unduly upon the black side of things; far from it. But the Puritans have been the subject of such shameless panegyrics that it becomes an honest enquirer into the facts of history to present both sides of the case. The reign of Queen Victoria was to witness a revival of the Puritan spirit, so that it is only human if the historians of that day, embued themselves with puritanic principles, tend to forget what they find uncongenial to remember. The biographer of Cromwell in a popular encyclopædia I have by me, is clearly of this school. "Long execrated," says he, "as a regicide," Cromwell is "now revered as a hero, saint and demigod." Could adulation farther go? Macaulay terms him "the greatest prince that ever ruled England"; whilst Harrison speaks of his countenance breathing, amongst other fine qualities, "pity and sorrow."

Yet at Wexford and Drogheda this man of pity conducted himself after the fashion of Hitler's generals in conquered Poland. Both towns were taken by calculated treachery. The defendants of Drogheda were many of them English royalists raised by Charles's Lord Lieutenant, the Marquis of Ormond. These men twice beat back Cromwell's storming parties from the breach which his cannon had made in their walls. They surrendered and laid down their arms upon the promise that the lives of all within the town should be spared. So soon as the last of the defenders had been disarmed the massacre began.

"*Quinque diebus continuis*," writes the author of the *Propugnaculum*, "For five continuous days the butchery went on, without discrimination of place, sex, religion or age. Youths, young women suckling infants, men worn out with old age were brutally slaughtered." Drogheda was the Puritan St Bartholomew.

To return to Gloucestershire. Captain Buck's visit to the Rectory at Minchinhampton had afforded such exquisite sport that before long it was repeated. The rector's son was a doctor, who had fitted up one of the ground-floor rooms as his laboratory. Forcing a window, Buck climbed in with several of his men and amused himself and them by smashing the phials, some of which contained very costly drugs.

"You ought to be ashamed to spoil such things!" cried one of the daughters of the house.

Loosing a torrent of abuse upon her, Buck knocked her down with the weapon he was carrying : pole-axe or matchlock, we are not told which. As she struggled to regain her feet, he felled her a second time; and again a third, when she lay still.

"Do you think it possible," cried her mother, "for me to stand by and see my child murdered!"

Captain Buck now took the old lady by the throat, threw her upon the floor, kicked her with his heavy boots, and trampled on her! Then after ransacking the house once more, on the chance that it might yield some object which upon his previous visit he had neglected to steal, he departed with his rabble! Do you think my picture of this Gloucestershire scene too highly coloured? Every particular of it was deposed to upon oath, on 18th August 1643, before Sir Robert Heath, Lord Chief Justice of the King's Bench.

Much that was typical of Cromwell's England was but now characteristic of Hitler's Germany. Naturally, for the same leaven of phariseeism was at work. Hitler regarded non-Germans as inferiors; they were not Nordic, not Herrenvolk! In precisely the same pharisaical style the Puritans regarded non-Puritans. They were Popish, Babylonish and Profane! Well might a Cavalier disputing with a Puritan exclaim : "My men have the faults of men, women and wine; but yours the faults of devils : hypocrisy and spiritual pride!"

Despite the Eva Braun affair, there appears no evidence

of the Führer's having come early under the softening influence of women. Like Hitler, the Prynnes and Bastwicks
and Northbrooks abominate the fascination which the charm
of women exercises over normal men. Women cannot—*pace*
the feminists!—give us solidity. They *can* give us lustre and
humanity! Well might Otway exclaim, "We had been brutes
without you!"

Hitler forbade lipstick; and how these Puritans hated and
feared women in their hearts! How they sought to proscribe
every innocent artifice by which women increase their charm!
They must not be suffered to give the godly *ideas*!

". . . Those lascivious, Whorish, or ungodly Fashions and
attires, which metamorphize and Transforme our Light, and
Giddie Females of the Superior and Gentile [gentle] ranke,
into sundry Antique [antic], Horred [horrid] and Out-
landish shapes from day to day." So screams William
Prynne, Master of Tautology and Bathos. Despite their
ferocity, these Puritans are so unmanly as to evince a preference for ugliness in women over beauty! And as good
looks result from good health, without which no cheek will
glow, no eye will sparkle, it inevitably follows that these
fanatics most actively suppress, so far as that is possible,
health in women! Had the Puritan conquest of England ever
been complete, as it was all too successful; had they succeeded in engrafting their principles upon their dupes, they
must have affected with degeneracy the actual breed of Englishmen by reversing the laws of sexual selection and giving
coarseness and anaemia preference over beauty and health!
I have immersed myself in the Puritan pamphleteerists, and
think I know them: although, as the don said of the undergraduate who beat him at billiards, "It shows a misspent
youth."

"Those who have continent and chast [chaste] affections
. . . they deeme this corporall, and out-side Beautie a need-
less thing." William Prynne again!

In Chaucer's England men such as this would have been
flogging themselves in obscure monkish cells, not roaming the
sweet countryside and the warm towns, poisoning life at large
and endeavouring with pen or sword to foist their crazy
inhibitions upon healthful humankind! They would prohibit

Black and white gabled house at Forthampton
Spring at Hilcot

even any exercise which enables women to mix freely with men upon a footing of merry companionship!

"Why do not the men"—asks John Northbrook, Puritan divine—"daunce with men apart from the women, by themselves? And why not the Women and Maydes daunce by themselves?" And again of "dauncing" : "It is vain, fleshly, filthy and devilish."

And the inhibitions of these men engender an actual hatred of children also. In a sermon not pronounced before a handful of cretins in a barn but the House of Commons itself, it is in these terms that Marshall, a Puritan preacher, refers to the starving children of dispossessed Anglican divines : "If this work be to avenge God's church against Babylon he is a blessed man that takes and dashes the little ones against the stones!"

Vavasour Powell, Puritan Commissioner for the Propagation of the Gospel in Wales, gives similar advice : "Their heads should be dashed against the walls, as Babylonish brats, and so their portions should be paid!"

Nor were such ravings academic. Certain small Cockney children having demonstrated in favour of a free Parliament by playing football in the streets, Hewson—Parliamentary Colonel—formerly cobbler!—appeased the tumult by "wounding twenty of the players and killing either two or three." And one recalls that Cromwell's troopers, hunting down refugees in the cathedral at Drogheda, made use of living children as screens to ward off stones, should these be hurled down upon them from the clerestory!

With such men another Edward IV was required to deal! Charles's very virtues are his undoing. He is too humane : too much the gentleman! He is for ever offering honourable terms, when he should be following up his successes to the uttermost! He insists upon regarding rebels in arms as still, essentially, his loving subjects! His method is reason : theirs "total war"! When a philosopher encounters a homicidal lunatic it is not the lunatic who suffers! When war is *fait accompli* it is only as camouflage that the eagle should assume the mien of the dove! *Then*, when the sword has made the going safe for them, Pity, Peace and Sweet Reasonableness may enter and enquire after lodgings!

St Briavels in the Forest of Dean
The River Wye between Chepstow and Tintern

Gloucestershire was the scene of two outstanding sieges of the Civil War, Bristol and Gloucester. In Gloucestershire too the last battle of the conflict was fought; that of Stow-in-the-Wold. Bristol, being strongly Puritan, was given for military governor an outstanding Parliamentarian, Nathaniel Fiennes, his garrison consisting of two thousand five hundred infantry and two regiments, the one of cavalry proper the other of dragoons, which at this time signified mounted infantry who could, as occasion served, be employed either as horse or foot.

Prince Rupert, for the King, was almost destitute of siege engines and forced to rely wholly upon the dash and courage of his men. He assaulted the town with characteristically vehement impetuosity. His Cornishmen, in three divisions, attacked from the west. Those of the centre succeeded in mounting the wall, but such were the disadvantages of the ground and so withering was the fire of the defendants that after a bloody struggle they were beaten back. The leader of one division, Lord Grandison, fell mortally wounded and a like fate awaited Colonel Bellasis who was conducting another. But one of the royalists, a certain Washington, discovering a part of the curtain where it appeared less strong than elsewhere, succeeded in smashing his way through.

(A "curtain" was that part of a barricade or wall which lay between towers, bastions or gates, and from which therefore, by reason of its being inset, a murderous fire could be brought to bear upon those entering the enclosed space.)

Bursting through and driving the defendants before him, Washington made room for the cavalry to follow, and all assumed that Bristol was taken! But to the dismay of the attackers it now appeared that they had won only the suburbs. The town proper rose before their astonished eyes in all its majesty of walls and towers! But an unlooked-for turn of events was to convert dismay into triumph. Fiennes had the drums beaten for a parley.

A composition was agreed upon by which the garrison were to surrender the town and march out with arms and baggage. They were to leave their colours behind them in token of victory and, what the royalists needed above all things, their cannons and munitions. Although this victory was dearly won by the loss of five hundred picked men and many leaders of note, yet the lustre which it reflected upon all who had participated in it brought a welcome increase in the numbers of volunteers for the royal cause.

The only question now was whether it were better for Charles to march direct upon London whilst the Parliamentarians were still plunged into confusion by this setback to their schemes, or, as an alternative course, lay siege to Gloucester. It was decided that to march against London with Gloucester still unsubdued at their backs was too hazardous. And the advantages which the Royalists promised themselves if Gloucester should fall were considerable.

It would give Charles, now that he held Bristol, command of the whole course of the Severn, thus assuring him contact with loyal Wales. It would enable him to pay his garrisons at Worcester and Shrewsbury—without apprehensions lest his supplies should be intercepted from Gloucester—out of the subsidies levied upon the trade of Bristol. It would enable loyalists in Gloucestershire, who were now kept in check by the county's enemy-held capital city, to come out into the open and declare themselves. And more important perhaps than all else, it would enable Charles to unite into one compact body the whole north of England for combined action against the south. With these ends in view, Charles's Council of War gave their votes in favour of the siege.

On 10th August 1643, therefore, Charles ranged the whole of his army less the Welsh and those employed upon distant garrison duties, on a hill two miles distant from the town. He then sent forward a trumpeter with terms. These were typically magnanimous. "I do assure them [the citizens] in the word of a King, that they nor any of them shall receive the least damage or prejudice in their persons or estates; but that we will appoint such a governor and moderate garrison . . . as shall be both for the ease and security of that city and the whole county. . . ." He gave them two hours for their reply.

Within the time specified, the envoys from Gloucester were conducted to his presence. The pen-picture which Lord

Clarendon gives us of them is worthy of the brush of Hogarth or Rowlandson.

"With the trumpeter returned two citizens from the town, with lean, pale, sharp and bald visages, indeed faces so strange and unusual and in such a garb and posture that at once made the most severe countenances merry, and the most cheerful hearts sad; for it was impossible that such ambassadors could bring less than defiance. The men, without any circumstances of duty or good manners, in a pert, shrill, undismayed accent, said : 'They had brought an answer from the godly city of Gloucester to the King'; and were so ready to give insolent and seditious answers to any question, as if their business were chiefly to provoke the King to violate his own safe conduct." The paper refusing the King entrance bore the signatures of Wise, the Mayor; Massey, Military Governor for the Parliament; sundry Aldermen and substantial citizens; and eleven officers of the garrison. Having failed to win a crown of martyrdom by insulting a King in arms at the head of his general staff, this pair of grotesques returned, under safe escort, to the "godly city," when immediately the suburbs were fired, lest they should furnish the royalists with cover in the proximity of the walls. This move alone sufficiently testified to the resolution and promptitude of mind of the soldier of fortune whom the Parliamentarians had had the good sense to purchase for their cause. Massey was free from the "fumes" of religious "intoxication," but having given his word that he would fight for that cause or this he never went back upon it.

Whether it be ever justifiable to make war a branch of commerce, to fight not for principles but pay, may be disputed; but some degree of praise is assuredly due to the man who having, from what motives so ever, embraced a party, supports it with sustained courage, pre-eminent skill and absolute incorruptibility. Colonel Massey, Governor of Gloucester, would have made a fit captain for the Switzers of sheeplike *Louis Seize*. That bodyguard may have despised the monarch they served, but they had his gold pieces in their pockets and fought to the death for him!

If Massey's conduct of the defence was professional, that of the attackers revealed too much of amateurism.

Whilst the siege was actually in progress, Charles spent two days at Oxford to see the Queen whom he adored and to "compose some differences"! The works about the city progressed certainly, but so imperfectly did watchmen and patrols keep guard that time and again Massey's messengers slipped undetected through the net, bearing reports to Parliament of his increasingly necessitous state; of his steadily decreasing supplies of food; of the ever-diminishing numbers of his full barrels of gunpowder. Not content with passive defence, Massey sought to obtain the initiative.

He sent out fighter patrols. But not a few of these found their retreat cut, Charles's cavalry having contrived to interpose themselves between the Puritans on sortie and the city walls. Prisoners taken on such occasions were, Lord Clarendon informs us, "always drunk," and confessed when interrogated that Massey allowed the men engaged upon these operations "as much wine and strong waters as they desired to drink." And the thirst of those who are not called upon to put their hands in their pockets to satisfy it, can be prodigious. Not being subject himself to the "fumes of religious intoxication," the Governor seems to have been sceptical of their efficacy without some admixture of those more mundane fumes with which less visionary spirits are acquainted.

But Massey never lost control of his men or suffered discipline to relax. The King's party believed they numbered sympathizers within the walls, but if so only three men and one officer contrived to make their exit and join up with the besiegers. Amongst the royalists discipline was weak. How could it be otherwise? Country gentlemen for the most part, the officers had lived like petty kings upon their estates, giving not taking orders. And they lacked the driving force of fanaticism.

Instead of concentrating with heart and soul upon the business of prosecuting the siege, those blockaders who had suffered losses through the Puritan ascendancy in the county fell to such ill-timed reprisals as the slaughtering of thousands of sheep! Others, absenting themselves without the knowledge of their generals—or conceivably with their connivance—imprisoned Parliamentarians until these had redeemed their captivity with ransoms! The brilliant tactics of

Prince Rupert at Bristol were not, it seemed, to be repeated at Gloucester.

These might, of course, have failed. The defences of Gloucester were exceedingly strong and the King's forces were markedly deficient in all such engines as the prosecution of a siege required. The moat alone constituted a formidable barrier. A considerable length of the wall of Roman Glevum, besides that which the men of the Middle Ages had constructed, yet rose from its waters. And Massey lost not a moment in strengthening the existing defences and creating new ones, employing upon the works not men only, but women and every child strong enough to carry pails of earth.

Charles sent to Oxford for Lord Brentford to join him with his "pieces of battery" and such men as he judged might safely be spared from the garrison. This nobleman was put in charge of the general conduct of the siege and Prince Rupert invested with command of all the horse. Sir William Vavasour, who had been Charles's generalissimo in South Wales, was brought up to cover with his men the "forest side of the town."

From many quarters men came flocking to the Royal Standard. But the "sinews of war" are proverbially money. From the outset the Parliamentarians had seized upon the mint and the King's deficiencies in this most important particular were notorious. Batteries were posted. Grenades and red-hot cannon shot were projected over the walls, and showed at night like shooting stars. The King mined, and Massey countermined.

A breach was battered in the walls but, these having been further strengthened, the attackers were unable, in the teeth of a devastating fire, to press home their advantage. And all this while the extremists in London were howling down those who wished to embrace the very reasonable terms which Charles had offered. The Northbrooks and Burtons and Bastwicks were preaching up the raising of the siege as a sacred crusade!

All the gaols in and about London were crammed to suffocation with royalists. Ships at anchor on the Thames were requisitioned for additional incarcerations. Battened down beneath hatches, in the utter darkness of their noisome holds, the captives of the "Saints" lived by such air as they "took in from one anothers' mouths." Some indeed possessed of ready money contrived through the avarice of their tormenters to purchase short spells of air on deck.

A party of women brought to the House a petition, requesting the acceptance of Charles's terms. The fanatics dispersed them with such violence that many were injured and some were killed. Tomkins, Chaloner and Waller, London gentlemen who attempted a combination for opposing the illegal taxation to which men of all parties were now subjected, to raise funds for the ever-growing army of Fairfax, were betrayed to Pym by an eavesdropping servant. All were put under arrest, and Tomkins and Chaloner were gibbeted at their own doors.

Even now perhaps by an audacious concerted effort, Gloucester might have been carried by storm. But Charles was no Edward IV to put his enemies "up towards the hyll" with "great vyolence." Violence was no part of his make-up. Except in the matter of religion where his conscience was engaged he disliked coercion. And even in this field he attempted to please the million by keeping a mean between Catholicism and Calvinism. The attempt revealed the philosopher, but the world is not made up of philosophers!

Charles had many amiable qualities. He possessed a fine intelligence and was the most intellectually cultivated of our kings. He loved Shakespeare and the " Arcadia " of Sir Philip Sidney. He was the patron of Ben Jonson, Inigo Jones and Peter Paul Rubens when they were *the moderns*! And each and every one of Charles's excellences rendered him odious to the Puritans who would have preferred a Goth like one of themselves. The loneliness of the artist was his. He stands amidst Puritan neo-barbarity like an olive tree in the waste. Too humane for the turbulent role for which his fates had cast him, amongst foes who thought

"Fire, and sword, and desolation,
A godly, thorough reformation,"

he was for ever endeavouring to see what was best in his "loving subjects"! The fulminations of religious mania he would term the "workings of a tender conscience"! On more occasions than one, when he had actually won a battle, instead of pressing home his advantage he paused, proffered terms, and by so doing gave his enemies time to recover! Charles had a sincere aversion to shedding his subjects' blood though, as the upshot showed, they had no objection to shedding his.

The Royalists were convinced that for Fairfax to march from London to Gloucester, through country which war had "eaten bare," was impossible. They thought it would be courting starvation. They were deceived. Many a farmer who had pleaded bare cupboards when appealed to by the King's men came forward with hoarded food for the relief of the new army upon its line of march.

Many of Charles's advisers believed this expedition of Fairfax's to be an elaborate feint. They supposed Oxford to be the true objective; and the intention to draw them from their works about Gloucester by a ruse. To meet such a contingency, Lord Wilmot was despatched with a troop of horse to Banbury with orders to harass the enemy but not to close with them. Prince Rupert took up his station upon the hills about Gloucester.

At last Fairfax came into view upon the high ground overlooking Cheltenham. He was within eight miles of the blockaded city! Part of his army Fairfax billeted in Southam, Prestbury and the neighbouring villages. There was not lodging for all. His rearguard which had charge of some of the ordnance and ammunition were forced to bivouac in the open. Rain fell in torrents. They had neither fire nor food.

On 5th September 1643—a date ever memorable in the annals of Gloucester!—whilst such of the garrison as Massey could spare from the defences were indulging in the Puritan sport of fasting, watchmen at their look-outs viewed upon the sudden a ring of flames about the city! The besiegers had fired their huts and were breaking up the blockade!

They drew off, "in more disorder and distraction," says Lord Clarendon, "than might have been expected." And it is true that they had more dash than discipline. On the other hand, with Fairfax facing them and Massey at their backs, an immediate change of ground must have been necessary to avoid an encircling movement. Two centuries earlier, Queen Margaret's generals, finding themselves in a precisely similar predicament beneath the walls of this very town, had declined facing the issue! Fairfax had arrived not a moment too soon! One barrel of powder only was left to the defenders and foodstuffs were similarly depleted!

The royalists rallied and drew up, in excellent order, upon the heights about the town. Painswick Beacon—so runs local tradition—was one of those thus occupied. Alert, in good posture for defence, they awaited the onslaught. There was none! After some preliminary feinting, Fairfax—his mission accomplished—had drawn off his troops by night and was hastening back to London!

Charles's cavalry followed in hot haste, hovered about their line of march, harassed them unceasingly, fought a pitched battle with them at Newbury and retook Reading. By these belated activities the Royal party regained something of the reputation which they had forfeited by their failure at Gloucester. But that "tide in the affairs of men," which must be "taken at the flood," had been forsaken. From the fateful 5th of September, the fortunes of the Royal party declined. Charles's star was setting and would soon sink below the horizon.

CHAPTER VI

THE BATTLE OF STOW-ON-THE-WOLD

ORIGIN OF THE GLOUCESTERSHIRE REGIMENT

SIR JACOB ASTLEY—whom later, in recognition of his services, Charles created a baron—will always be remembered for his prayer before the Battle of Edgehill. Soldier-like and pithy, it deserves inclusion in a book of epigrams : "O Lord, Thou knowest how busy I must be this day. If I forget Thee, do not forget me. March on, boys !" His son, Sir Bernard, had been killed at the taking of Bristol. He himself had commanded one of the divisions at the ill-fated siege of Gloucester. Now, at Stow-on-the-Wold, he was destined to strike the last blow for the King, of the whole Civil War. This was the posture of affairs on the eve of that conflict.

Throughout the North of England the Royalists had been dispersed. Fairfax was master in the West; Cromwell in the South. At this moment both Waller and Fairfax were converging upon the King at Oxford. Thus menaced, Charles despatched Astley to collect the forces from the surrounding Royal garrisons. This he did and contrived to amass a force of some two thousand horse and foot with which he was now on the march from Worcester to Oxford. Charles, on his part, was to send a body of fifteen hundred horse and foot from Oxford to join with him. United, the two parties would have made a respectable force.

But despatches containing the orders relative to this manœuvre being intercepted, every detail became known to the enemy before there was any possibility of its being executed. The Parliamentarians withdrew their garrisons from the towns of Warwick, Coventry and Evesham; and Colonel Birch from Hereford, Sir William Brereton from the Midlands and Colonel Morgan from Gloucester, converged by separate routes upon the Royalists. Astley saw no

sign of Charles's detachment which was to have joined with
his, whilst they in their turn were no less nonplussed at Astley's leaving them in ignorance as to his whereabouts.

Birch and Morgan met, joined forces at Gloucester and
marched together to Evesham, the general rendezvous
where they were to meet Brereton.

Before Brereton could come up, however, hastening on by
forced marches, Astley had reached the Avon. Here Morgan disputed his passage, and valuable time was lost to
the Royalists and gained by the Parliamentarians. Then
Morgan retired to Chipping Campden and on 20th March
1646 Astley effected the passage of the river at Bidford. He
then crossed the vale and proceeded to climb Broadway Hill.
Morgan despatched light bodies of skirmishers to harass
them whilst upon this difficult ground, with orders not to join
battle. His main body he was holding back until he knew
Brereton to be close at hand. The King's party from Oxford
were at this time only seven miles distant : so narrowly the two
parties of Royalists missed effecting a junction ! It was to the
manifest interest of the Parliamentarians to force an engagement, of Astley to avoid one and bring his men into Oxford
intact. In this design, through the interception of his
despatches, he was frustrated.

Seeing at length that an action could not be delayed,
Astley drew up his forces, exhausted with intensive marches,
on unenclosed ground between Stow-on-the-Wold and Don-
nington. The battle began at daybreak and was maintained
for some while with varying success. Attacking with impetuosity, Astley's right drove back Birch's left, and when they
attempted to rally drove them back once more. But at last
Brereton's horse which formed the Parliamentary right wing,
charging the mixed horse and foot of Astley's left, succeeded
in breaking their ranks, when in one united effort Morgan,
Birch and Brereton attacking together made it impossible for
them to re-form ranks. The confusion became a rout.

A heavy slaughter was made in the follow-up and in Stow
itself, where an attempt appears to have been made to rally.
There were many wounded. The number of prisoners was
variously computed as one thousand six hundred or as two
thousand. Three hundred Royalists effected their escape, but

one-third of these were captured by the Parliamentary Colonel Fleetwood, now coming upon the scene for the first time.

A trifling tradition of the Gloucestershire countryside may raise a smile, and if so, is worth recording, since life is not wholly tragedy nor wholly comedy, but a patchwork of the two with a trifle of farce thrown in. It tells of a Royalist farmer and how he effected his escape. Concealing himself and his horse in a copse until nightfall, he was stealing away when he was detected and pursued. He was an old fox-hunter who could ride, and knowing his country well, he contrived to shake off his pursuers and reach his farm.

Slaughtering his beloved horse, which from the sweat he was in must needs betray his master's recent activities, he threw dung over the carcase. He had barely accomplished this gruesome task before a clatter of hooves warned him the enemy had picked up his traces and were at his heels again! Flinging himself up the broad stairs of the farmhouse, he almost fell into his bedchamber, where hauling on his night-dress over his leather coat and breeches and cramming a nightcap on his head, he fairly climbed into the four-poster beside his wife, mud, sweat, dung, spurs and all!

Bellowing "Malignant!" and "King's man!" the Puritans crashed up the stairs and into the room after him, but drew back, for they thought they saw a sleeping man, and did, in effect, see an uncommonly wideawake woman. She, the shrew of the neighbourhood, regaled the intruders with oaths, cursing them for a rabble of drunkards who couldn't carry their liquor! Breaking into folks' houses at midnight! Fine doings indeed! She cursed their fathers that begot them and their mothers that bore them, for not employing their time better than in bringing such a rout of cut-throats into the world! "Cut-throats, on my life! Every face shows, in the light of this candleflame, plain gibbet! How I pity the crows," cries she, "that must sup some nightfall on no better meat!"

And the native vinegar of her tongue took sharper edge as she thought of the havoc her good man's spurs had wrought amongst her finest sheets! The farmer meanwhile emitted an occasional snore, as though having supped well and partaken of a smacking pillow-drink he were now in a condition to sleep through thunder. Abashed by what they saw, and confounded by the acerbity of their reception, the intruders beat a precipitate retreat. No lingering to swill the ale! They forgot even to pocket the spoons!

Neither did the creak of an opening lattice induce them to reconsider the situation and come in again from the yard, for there stood the good wife framed in it, wishing them "God-speed in the devil's name!" with such sweetly expressed good wishes as that the foul fiend might "startle their horses and break their ribs and necks for them!" Relieved by these benedictions in reverse, the dame's liver ceased to boil and she became more like her buxom self of earlier years.

"Draw me a jack of ale, John," says she, "these bastards have flurried me. What's a few torn sheets after all in a righteous cause? Now sit to supper whilst I shift all this bedding."

During the meal, which was interspersed with kisses, she demanded an account of his doings. And John told her of the Battle of Stow-on-the-Wold, relating his personal exploits upon that immortal field with sympathy and enthusiasm.

"But the upshot was unfortunate."

"Neither rich nor poor can control Fortune," says the good wife, "so let all be as it will. To bed now, John, and there I'll show you, I warrant you, I think never the worse of you for this day's doings!"

After folklore, fact. Astley's words to his conquerors at Stow are as memorable as his soldierly prayer before Edgehill: "Gentlemen, you have done your work and may go to play, unless you fall out amongst yourselves." He was well inspired. They fell out amongst themselves. After the sometimes arbitrary rule of Charles, that of Cromwell, whatever might be his public professions, was one prolonged violation of English law. A thousand examples might be instanced, but one must suffice. He had laid an illegal tax upon the city. One Cony, a Puritan like himself, refused to pay Cromwell, precisely as, with ship-money, Hampden had refused to pay Charles. Of this tax Cony declared, "It was an imposition notoriously against the law and the property of the subject, which all honest men are bound to defend." But Cromwell having what Cony had not, to wit, an army, simply ordered him away to prison! With great spirit, this "metropolitan Hampden" brought his *Habeas Corpus,* and Maynard, Cony's counsel, demanded his client's release on the two unassailable grounds that the tax for which his client had been committed and the commitment itself were contrary to law!

Cromwell's reply was to commit Maynard, in his turn, to the Tower. The judges pleaded Magna Carta and the fundamental laws of the land. In a vocabulary reeking of the barracks the Protector assured them their "Magna f— should not control his actions!" He demanded of them "whether they had any authority to sit but what he gave them." And concluded by telling them that, were his authority once at an end, "they knew well enough what would become of themselves!"

Towards the end of his life the Protector wore armour beneath his clothes as a defence not only against his natural foes the Royalists, but his loving subjects of his own Left Wing! The Parliament offered him the Crown, but "several persons it is said had entered into an engagement to murder the Protector within a few hours after he should have accepted the offer of the Parliament."

In no circumstances was the King as tyrannical as the Protector. The "five members" whom Charles attempted to arrest were truly guilty of what he accused them, of attempting to make his government odious. But the ejection in April 1653 by military force of every member of a parliament—on the "Remove that bauble!" occasion—was what no King of England, not even authoritarian Henry VIII himself, had ever dreamed of doing before! The Puritans were to find that they had deposed King Log to establish King Stork!

But fanaticism was to run its course and common sense to reassert itself. After the anarchy of Richard Cromwell's brief interlude Charles II was recalled from exile. The vast majority of Englishmen discovered that they preferred the old order to the new. The Regicides were put on trial for their lives and one of the foremost of them, Henry Marten, declared with manifest sincerity : "If it were possible for the blood to be in the body again and every drop that was shed in the late wars, I could wish it with all my heart !" When extremists acquire moderation it is commonly too late !

Gloucestershire was no whit behind the other counties with bells, bonfires and such like manifestations of the public joy ! Of the two Royalist members elected to represent the "Godly City of Gloucester" in Parliament, one was the soldier of fortune, the ex-Governor, Colonel Massey, whose strenuous efforts during the siege had been the prime factor in turning the scales against the party he was now to represent ! Charles II bade him kneel, laid a sword upon his shoulder and he rose Sir Edwin Massey. Posterity has reproached the Merry Monarch with many failings, but not I think with a defective sense of humour !

So early as 16th February 1694 the Twenty-eighth Foot— later to receive its County title of the North Gloucestershire Regiment—was created for service in the French wars. Its first colonel was Sir John Gibson, Kt. The captains bore pikes or long-poled spears. Lieutenants were equipped with partisans. This latter was likewise a long-poled spear-pointed weapon, but the spear-head rose from between a double-axe, with diametrically opposed blades. Thus provided, an agile swashbuckler might stab a foe in front of him, strike down another to his left with the left-side blade and perhaps lay out a third to his right with a back-stroke ! With his partisan —Shakespeare-lovers will recall—Marcellus threatens the Ghost in the Platform Scene at Elsinore, and a moment after regrets his own irreverence :

> We do it wrong, being so majestical,
> To offer it the show of violence.

The ensign was the lowest-ranking commissioned officer, the equivalent of the modern second-lieutenant, with this difference, that the senior ensign bore, by right, the regimental colours. Ensigns bore half-pikes, a name which sufficiently explains the character of the weapon. Sergeants were equipped with halberts which did not differ essentially from the partisans; with the latter as with the former, the foot-soldier could either thrust or cut.

In 1697 the Peace of Ryswick terminated the war with the France of Louis XIV. William III, who had taken the field against Louis time and again, now made a triumphant entry into London. After the signing of the treaty the Twenty-eighth, which had been disbanded, was raised again, but unfortunately all records of its activities between 1697 and 1702—the year in which Queen Anne came to the throne —appear to have perished.

In 1706 the famous regiment fought with the utmost distinction at Ramillies, the name of which battle they bear to-day—with how many others!—upon their regimental colours. The great Duke of Marlborough—name to rank with that of Cæsar as a general!—being commander-in-chief, "the French, Spaniards and Bavarians, dismayed at the furious attacks of their opponents, rushed in wild disorder . . . and spread in every direction like a scattered swarm, while the British army pressing in the rear of the fugitives, and giving no respite from the pursuit, greatly increased the number of slain and prisoners.

"The pursuit was continued during the night and nearly all the enemy's cannon, with many standards, colours and kettle-drums, were captured. Thus was the magnificent allied army nearly destroyed, and Marshal Villeroy and the Elector of Bavaria, after narrowly escaping being made prisoners, fled to Lorraine, where a Council of War was held by torchlight in the market-place, and it was decided to abandon the forti-fied towns and take post with the wreck of the army behind the Brussels Canal. . . ."

The Sixty-first Foot were formed originally from a bat-talion of the East Kent Regiment—the "Buffs"—but in 1782 received the County title of the Sixty-first, or South Gloucestershire Regiment. This was the crisis with which this new body of Gloucestershires was called upon to cope. In the early eighteenth century, the British colonies in North America extended along the coast, but the trade with the Indians was extremely lucrative and this fact induced many Englishmen to enter the interior.

Portion of front of St Edwards, *a house in the Market Square, Stow-on-the-Wold A Gloucestershire farm at Cowley*

A company of merchants obtained a charter to a tract of land beyond the Alleghany Mountains, and began to establish a settlement. The French laid claim to this part of the country and proceeded to erect forts to command the entrance to what they considered their land on the Mississipi and Ohio rivers. The French regarded ourselves, and we regarded the French, as aggressors. The views of the scalping native nobody thought it worth his while to ask. It was as though a French *commis voyageur* and an English commercial traveller were to collide by the Grand Pyramid and each inform the other he was a scoundrel to be there !

The South Gloucestershires were embarked for the West Indies as part of an expedition under Major-General Hopson and Commodore Moore, and on 16th January 1759 the troops landed on the island of Martinique. They suffered many casualties in killed, wounded and sick. The climate and the mosquitos fought against both parties with the malignancy of natives who desired not to be disturbed. In the end, however, the English drove the French from the island.

In 1772 the American War of Independence broke out. The colonists flew to arms, when a patient diplomacy might perhaps have accomplished their ends. But they were active and adventurous and "Farmer" George the reverse of accommodating. France lost not a moment in uniting with the revolting provinces in their resistance to us, and whilst we were thus dually encumbered, Spain also commenced hostilities, besieging Gibraltar in 1779. The siege, insomuch as the Gloucestershires played no part in it, lies beyond the scope of this book. Not so that of Minorca.

In the middle of August 1781, a powerful combined Spanish and French force appeared before this island. The British troops upon it were withdrawn from detached stations and the whole assembled in the Citadel of St. Philip, the garrison of which place was offering resistance. The South Gloucestershire Regiment and the Fifty-first, two corps of Hanoverians and sundry minor detachments with some artillery constituted the defenders. All told they numbered some 2,500 men. They were commanded by the Hon James Murray and Lieutenant-General Sir William Draper, K.B. The Duke of Crillon, an officer of high reputation, was commander-in-

F   65

A sunlit glade—Forest of Dean
View over the Cotswolds from Stow-on-the-Wold

chief of the besieging force, which amounted to above five times our number, viz, sixteen thousand men.

For several months the British defended St Philip with the utmost gallantry. Manly courage is a virtue essential to the community, inasmuch as without it the community would soon cease to exist, but that of men well fed, well slept, and in robust physical health, does not belong to so high an order as that of men underfed, underslept and harassed by disease. The first is admirable, the second sublime. The garrison were attacked by scurvy and the "putrid fever." Dysentery broke out amongst all ranks with violence.

In the opening of February 1782, they could not muster sufficient men able to bear arms for the ordinary guards. Of the sixteen thousand men who constituted the garrison of St Philip there were not one hundred free from disease! In these circumstances the Hon James Murray capitulated. In his despatch to the British Government he stated :

"I flatter myself that all Europe will agree that the brave garrison showed uncommon heroism, and that thirst for glory which has ever distinguished the troops of my royal master. [George III.] Such was the uncommon spirit of the King's soldiers, that they concealed their diseases and inability rather than go into the hospital; several men died on guard, after having stood sentry : their fate was not discovered until called upon for relief, when it came to their turn to mount sentry again."

"Perhaps," James Murray's despatch continues, "a more noble, nor a more tragical scene was never exhibited than that of the march of the garrison through the Spanish and French lines. It consisted of no more than six hundred decrepit soldiers, two hundred seamen, one hundred and twenty artillery, twenty Corsicans and twenty-five Greeks. Such was the distressing appearance of our men that many of the Spanish and French soldiers are said to have shed tears."

The eighteenth century was, what all centuries should be, a hard, virile age. No alliance, no political manoeuvres, no Uno will ever make good deficiencies in morale. During a stay at the Cape of Good Hope, the South Gloucestershires were employed against the "hardy and warlike tribe of

Kaffirs," who were committing depredations upon the English colony. To support a detachment of the Eighth Light
Dragoons, the "light infantry company" of the South Gloucestershires marched on one occasion "upwards of forty miles
in one day"! An engagement was fought to the success of
which the timely appearance of the herculean foot-sloggers
materially contributed.

It was from the part they played in the Napoleonic wars
that the Gloucestershires won the right to wear the word
EGYPT, together with the Sphinx as a "distinguishing mark
of his Majesty's [George III] royal approbation of their
conduct." Heaven knows they deserved this signal honour!

Some companies of the South Gloucestershires marched in
nine days from Cossier to Kenna, enduring not merely the
physical exhaustion consequent upon long distance covered
and heavy going, but tropical heat and that terrible enemy,
thirst. On arrival and calling of the roll, it was discovered
that a drummer was missing. Private Andrew Connell, not-
withstanding the strain to which he had himself been exposed, asked permission to retrace his steps and assist the
drummer. His request was granted and back he trudged over
wastes of sand. He came at last upon the drummer's body.
He had "died of fatigue." It is good, however, to record that
for this humane act Private Connell was promoted to a commission in the regiment.

> Only the actions of the just
> Smell sweet and blossom in the dust.

A question frequently asked is why members of the Gloucestershire Regiment wear the cap badge at the back as well
as at the front of their caps. They owe this prized distinction to their conduct at the Battle of Alexandria—21st
March 1801—fought between the French of the Napoleonic
General Menou and the British Expeditionary Force under
Sir Ralph Abercrombie, near the ruins of Nicopolis. The
"Twenty-eighth"—North Gloucestershires—were drawn
up on the platform of the parapet of a redoubt. The French
attacked before daybreak and their first attack was repulsed.

The Gloucestershires were pouring a destructive fire into
the assaulting columns when a party of French, infiltrating in

the darkness between two British regiments, suddenly appeared to their rear. The "Twenty-eighth" found themselves completely surrounded and under fire from every quarter at once. Annihilation appeared imminent! Two things saved the situation—the unruffled coolness of the commander and the disciplined courage of his men.

As though upon his parade-ground, Colonel Paget gave the word of command : "Rear rank, right-about face!" The change in position was carried out with barrack-square orderliness. Where the enemy thought to find all in the utmost confusion, they were received with so vigorous and so well-directed a fire as effectively thwarted every effort of theirs to advance! Although the Gloucestershires thus engaged are described as a "mere handful," yet they maintained this extraordinary contest for a considerable time. Colonel Paget, however, fell, and being carried later, when occasion served, aboard ship for treatment, succumbed a short while after of his wounds. The Battle of Alexandria drove the armies of Napoleon out of Egypt.

CHAPTER VII

GLOUCESTERSHIRE REGIMENT

NAPOLEONIC WAR—THE GREAT WAR

IN the Battle of Maida, Italy, the South Gloucestershires played that outstanding part which earned them the right to bear the word MAIDA on their regimental colours. The French at this time, 1806, were intent upon dominating Sicily. To this end, General Régnier was amassing upon the coast of Calabria—for transportation to that island across the Straits of Messina—vast stores of every description. It was imperative to British interests to thwart this operation.

The "Light Company" of the South Gloucestershires formed at this time part of the troops commanded by Lieutenant-Colonel Kempt. They were confronted, says the author of the *Historical Records of the Sixty-first*, by the "celebrated French regiment, the Ier Leger." (Can Leger perhaps be a slip for Légion?—a word used formerly for regiments of the line, "La légion de la Corrèze," for example, or "La légion d'Indre-et-Loire.")

Both English and French fired a few rounds from about a hundred yards' distance. Then both simultaneously charged. Steadiness was preserved on both sides until the bayonets clashed, when British coolness and that alacrity for coming to hand-grips which had won the Gloucestershires their nickname of the "Slashers" gave us the victory. The French broke. "British valour," says the author of the *Historical Records*, was "triumphant in every part of the field, and the boasted invincible legions of Napoleon were proved inferior to the English in close combat with the bayonet."

By this engagement we obtained "every fort along the coast, all the stores, ammunition and artillery prepared for the attack upon Sicily." Hardly less important than the material success was the moral gain : the prestige which this spirited action won for us. It created "an indelible impression of the bravery and discipline of the British troops."

Human glory we know is brittle as glass : perishable as

the flowers of the field. In England it is yet more transient than elsewhere. We name few streets after our heroes, erect no statues.

> When the war's over and the trouble righted,
> God is forgotten and the soldier slighted.

And not the soldier only, but the giants of the creative arts.

Although it is hidden away in the grounds of St Mary Redcliffe, Bristol has indeed a monument to Chatterton. But Cheltenham can show no statue to honour the classically cultured poet, dramatist and translator, James Elroy Flecker, assured master of the singing quality, the colour and magic of words. Will straggling Nailsworth ever honour itself by honouring W. H. Davies, the nature poet, with a worthy and permanent memorial? For many years he made his home in that otherwise unknown little town, died there, and composed in its provincial greyness his lyrics fresh and sparkling as dew, a joy to beauty lovers on both sides of the Atlantic. But a truce to digression!

After Maida, medals were given to commanding officers, the first instance of this award being made in the annals of the British Army. The Lord Chancellor moved a vote of thanks to Major-General Stuart, commander-in-chief at Maida, which was committed to writing and despatched to him. I transcribe a passage :

"Reflecting upon the disasters which have befallen powerful princes and populous territories, under the pressure of the vast armies of France, I recollect at the same time that they were not defended by British soldiers, and that when the triumphant monuments of Paris shall record the victories of Austerlitz and Jena it shall appear upon the less ostentatious journals of a British Parliament that upon the plains of Maida her choicest battalions fell beneath the bayonets of half the number of our brave countrymen under your direction and that of the officers who were your glorious companions."

In the Peninsula, the Gloucestershires were to meet with adventures extensive and peculiar as was Mr Weller's knowledge of London. An incident at once ludicrous and macabre occurred at the monastery of Alenquer from which the British ejected the French who had been using it as a strong-point. A detachment of the South Gloucestershires were now its garrison and several officers and men were taken seriously ill. The only monk who had not made tracks suggested the water supply as a possible cause.

"Why so?"

The holy man observed that upon their precipitate departure the French to save trouble had thrown various dead bodies into the great well in the centre of the market-place. Investigation by British engineers revealed the penetrating genius of the monk's diagnosis! The softening hand of Time has smoothed out ancient animosities, converting the French from inveterate enemies into gallant allies : but a wayward genius still inspires their sanitary and plumbing arrangements!

To give more than an occasional indication, a note here and there as fancy directs, of the record of this splendid regiment would carry me far beyond the scope proposed for this book. At Talavera, Salamanca and Toulouse the Gloucestershires lived up to and added lustre to the highest traditions of the British Army. At Salamanca the regimental colours were saved from capture by two privates, W. Crawford and N. Coulson, who bore them to the very top of the hill under a murderous fire. At the close of the engagement only three officers and seventy-eight non-commissioned officers and privates remained standing in their ranks!

In his *History of the Peninsula War*, Sir William Napier writes : "The men of General Hulse's brigade which was on the left went down by hundreds, and the Sixty-first [South Gloucestershire] and the Eleventh [Devon] Regiments won their way desperately through such fire as only British soldiers can sustain."

After three years of fighting, Wellington drove Napoleon's armies out of Spain. Six days now of bloody struggle amongst the rocks and snows of the Pyrenees was to give the Gloucestershires amongst other British troops their first sight of France, which animated them extraordinarily! At the Battle of Toulouse, 10th April 1814, the French were broken. And here the Sixty-first, in recognition of the pre-eminence of their contribution to the success of the action, were rewarded with a regimental decoration which was to be exclusively theirs. Let the reader prepare himself for something rococo! They were to wear "Silver acorns on the tails of their coatees."

They had been known as the "Slashers," and also as "Old Bragg's" after one of their commanders, a Colonel Bragg who was a character. They were now jocosely nick-named the "Silver-tailed Dandies" and the "Flowers of Toulouse"! The Gloucestershires had "traversed kingdoms, fought battles and conquered powerful armies for the good of Europe; their valour had exalted the glory of the British arms and preserved their native country from the presence of war."

In 1849, the Gloucestershires served in the Second Sikh War and fought at all those places which our grandfathers loved to refer to when the decanter had passed; Chillian-wallah, for example, and Goojerat. At the former, a great body of enemy cavalry surrounded the regiment and it was threatened with annihilation. Colonel McLeod, the com-manding officer—consciously or unconsciously repeating the tactics of the Battle of Alexandria—ordered the men to stand back to back and by steady fire to drive off their oppo-nents. The manœuvre was so successful that they not only scattered them but, charging them afterwards, fell upon the Sikh gunners and captured seventeen guns!

Addressing the regiment, Sir Charles Napier said: "I have heard of your distinguished conduct at the Battle of Chillianwallah. Sir Colin Campbell tells me that in the heat of the action he ordered you to fire two rounds and then cease firing, and that you did so. A regiment that fires by order and ceases firing by order can do anything in action!" So pre-eminently successful in Europe, in Egypt and in India were those tactics of disciplined drill movements which proved so fatal to us in the American War of Inde-pendence when confronted with the new technique of the colonists!

The Sixty-first saw much hard fighting in the Indian Mutiny. They fought with desperate courage when assault-ing the Kashmir Gate during the Siege of Delhi. On this

occasion they attacked a rebel battery with such active resolution that they bayoneted the gunners before these had had
time to fire a single gun! In the year 1881 the Twenty-
eighth and the Sixty-first permanently linked up, when the
latter changed for white the buff facings upon their uniforms
which they had at first assumed as an additional battalion of
the "Buffs."

From considerations of space I shall continue speaking
only of the First Battalion of the Gloucestershires, with no
detriment to the Second or to the other battalions which were
gradually created. The First Battalion, then, was in India at
the outbreak of the South African War, but it was one of the
first units to reach the Cape. It took part in the first pitched
battles of the war. It fought at Rietfontein, at Lombards
Kop. It was beleaguered in Ladysmith.

Those where the halcyon days of the Volunteers who,
although they had at first to endure much ridicule, exemplified an admirable combination of active courage with the
civic sense. In an astonishingly short while the First, Second
and Third Volunteer were added to the First and Second
Regular battalions of the Gloucestershire Regiment. Chlori-
nated water was not yet thought of, and many were the cases
of typhus, typhoid and enteric.

A friend, an older man than I, told me as an excellent
joke that in the "Orders for the Day" issued to his detachment he had read: "The pool with the three dead mules in
it will, in future, only be used for watering horses." That
"in future" tells its own tale! Poor devil! He arrived back
in England half-crazy with toothache, having broken most of
his teeth in the course of a too-prolonged diet of ships'
biscuits.

At the outbreak of the Great War, the Gloucestershires
had had to their credit no less than two hundred and twenty
years of superb achievement as a fighting force. The fantastic yet beautiful uniforms of Queen Anne's individualistic
day had given place to the mud-coloured khaki of the
mechanized world. Firelock had been supplanted by flintlock; that again by the various types of breechloader which
now, in combination with the deadly bayonet, was pike,
halbert, partisan and musket in one! These things had

changed, but dogged courage in defeat, restraint in victory, and manly resolution at all times : these had undergone no change.

At the outbreak of the 1914–18 War the First Battalion Gloucestershire Regiment was at Aldershot, the Second was speeding home from Tientsin, North China, and the Third (Special Reserve) Battalion was at its depôt at Bristol. During that war prodigious numbers of men were trained at this depôt and drafted out to replace the cruel losses sustained by the ever-increasing numbers of battalions of the Gloucestershires on active service.

On 12th August 1914 the First Battalion, as a unit of the First Division, embarked with that division at Southampton and landed at Le Hâvre. On 20th August after a few days spent in a concentration area the battalion marched north to the Belgian frontier. The First Division—of which, as has just been said, the First Battalion of the Gloucestershire Regiment formed part—together with the Second Division, constituted the First Army Corps. This was under the command of the then Lieutenant-General Sir Douglas Haig. The British Expeditionary Force which began the advance consisted of four divisions and was commanded by General Sir John French. It was intended that these should form the left flank of the French Army and the right of the Belgian, with which contact was to be established near Brussels.

But when the British infantry reached Mons the cavalry brought news that vast masses of Germans were advancing, in consequence of which information Sir John French ordered a defensive line to be taken up along the Mons Canal. The First Division had the First Battalion Gloucestershires on its right, which gave it the responsible position of extreme right of the British Army in the field. Trenches were dug with speed and all awaited the German onslaught with confidence. Our numbers totalled approximately eighty-six thousand men with three hundred and twelve guns.

On 23rd August 1914 the Germans attacked in force, throwing their entire weight against the British left held by the Second Army Corps. The British repulsed every attack with heavy losses to the enemy. Late in the afternoon Sir

John French received two despatches. The first informed him that there were not, as had been estimated, two but four German Army Corps attacking his left, whilst a fifth was manœuvring to encircle his left flank. The second which arrived almost at the same moment stated that the French were already in rapid retreat!

With both left and right flanks exposed, Sir John French had now no alternative, if he were to avoid annihilation, but to retire also so as to conform with the French line. This he accordingly did. The famous Retreat from Mons had begun. The First Army Corps fell back upon Bavai; the Second upon Le Cateau. Here a delaying action was fought with the utmost heroism.

The First Division retired upon Landrecies, where they were ordered to entrench upon the outskirts of a village and cover the withdrawal of the rest of the brigade. On 26th August, about midday, they saw vast formations of the Germans advancing against them. They entered into long-range rifle fire and brought their two guns into action from their front line. Their superb marksmanship held up the German advance. The enemy countered by sending out a reconnaissance plane to observe the layout of the Gloucestershires' trenches and report back to the artillery, which enabled it to locate them. As the Huns had camouflaged their plane with French markings the British made no attempt to bring it down, a feat which could be sometimes performed in those days by one lucky shot from a rifle! When the ruse became known, it was universally regarded as infamous : a point of view difficult to appreciate to-day when German cunning is among the commonplaces of human existence. But in 1914 the tradition of chivalry in warfare was still very much alive. An English officer thought of himself as a gentleman *ipso facto*; and every man of his command, however humble his birth, was regarded as a man of honour whom his uniform ennobled. Now, of honour the Hun had no more conception than a camel; the Judas of every people but his own, he was already studying the manual of total war . . .

Into the country which the red squirrel had inhabited for centuries the grey was recently introduced. The newcomer frisked divertingly, but the red squirrel is now almost extinct. Whoever cannot apply the moral of this little fable is living in a dream.[1]

The pounding of the Gloucestershires' rapidly improvised trenches by heavy artillery began now in earnest. But the battalion had carried out orders and delayed the German advance long enough amply to justify a continuation of the withdrawal. History has no example of manly fortitude to record more lustrous than this of the Retreat from Mons. *Æquam memento rebus in arduis*—few men indeed fell out; march discipline was everywhere preserved. Having marched the fifty miles up to the Belgian frontier they now marched two hundred from it, and that within the compass of thirteen days, with occasional delaying actions and with the absolute minimum of food and sleep!

Mindful of the limits imposed upon me by a work of this nature, I must confine myself to a few incidents only of the long and bitterly contested struggle. The fight of the battalion for Beaulare Ridge—Battle of Chemin des Dames—held up by its success the dense German hordes which, with total disregard for human life, were being thrust between the First and Second Divisions. For days and nights on end the British held on to their precarious positions in the teeth of every effort the enemy could make. Without overcoats, drenched to the skin under the unceasing rain, and overmatched by artillery they could not be dislodged from their ground.

Later the French relieved the whole British Army, in order that the latter might move northwards and block the road to the Channel Ports. Whilst holding a position north of Langemark, three platoons of the battalion were attacked repeatedly, the German rushes carrying them to within a few yards of the trenches. Having been hastily dug, these were too shallow to admit of a man's standing upright in them. The Gloucestershires fired but little short of five hundred rounds per head. Bayonets were shot off the rifles.

Most of the non-commissioned officers, all the officers, and sixty per cent of the total strength were casualties, either

[1] Written in 1943. To-day it is obvious that every risk must be run to ensure a Europe united against Communist aggression.

killed or wounded. Captain R. E. Rising defended one point with such tenacity that when, some days later, the brigadier attempted to obtain the names of survivors for commendation not one could be found! In such circumstances was the position held until the order came through to retire.

The Gloucestershires took part in the fighting at the Menin Road where for a fortnight they were in the thick of continually launched German attacks, their improvised trenches affording no protection against continuous shelling. Time and again whole stretches of their line were blotted out, yet never once in this historical First Battle of Ypres were the men of the Gloucestershire Regiment blasted back.

At Kruiseck, Gheluvelt, Veldhoek, Heronthage, and later at Zillebeke and Polygon Wood, the Gloucestershires were in the thick of the most desperate fighting. Two D.S.O.s, two M.C.s and six D.C.M.s were awarded members for conspicuous gallantry. The road to the Channel Ports was barred. How could it be otherwise? It ran through the heart of England! It ran through Gloucestershire. But the cost had been fearful. On 20th October 1914 the First Battalion Gloucestershire Regiment had marched through Poperinghe to the Salient, at full war-strength, with twenty-six officers and one thousand other ranks. Four weeks elapsed. Then two officers and less than one hundred men marched back.

During January 1915 the battalion was called on for alternating spells of forty-eight hours in the line and forty-eight out. They held the first trench and so received the full fury of the attack. Once, advancing in six waves, the Germans were brought to a standstill some forty yards from the British position, nearly all the assailants being shot down. Some Stormtroopers, however, breaking through upon their left, the Gloucestershires were being attacked from front, flank and rear, yet they endured this murderous concentration of fire with superb discipline and steadiness.

On 25th September and again on 8th October 1915, during the Battle of Loos, the Gloucestershire Regiment won distinction in the fight for that tragic spot, the Chalk Pit, the scene of terrible casualties during the preceding days. Here they were subjected to four hours of continuous shelling which was followed by a mass attack of infantry. The

Germans went down in heaps before the rifle fire of the Gloucestershires, and at a cost of a hundred and fifty all ranks the enemy were driven off and the position saved.

Men of the Gloucestershire Regiment were in the thick of the fighting in High Wood during the Battle of the Somme, September 1916. They carried all their objectives, but inevitably at tragic cost. There remained only three officers and ninety-six other ranks when the battalion was withdrawn. By this time they had already suffered above a thousand casualties in the Somme fighting alone, losses which were to be yet further augmented when after a period of rest and reinforcement they returned to the Somme again in November 1917.

The 18th April 1918 found the Gloucestershires north-west of Festhubert where the Germans, advancing more rapidly than it was possible to shoot them down, poured through a gap in the line and reached the houses and gardens of Le Plantin held by a company under Captain Handford. This company was cut in two, but it re-formed. Lieutenant Gosling in command of the reserves attacked those of the enemy who had broken through and, when the assailants rushed up field guns and attempted to annihilate all opposition at point-blank range, the Gloucestershires shot down the gunners. Those of the attackers who had gained the shelter of the houses were now sniping down into the British trenches, but these same snipers were all eventually killed or taken prisoners. The Germans began to retreat, when the defenders took yet heavier toll of them than they had before in their first furious onrush! Here at Le Plantin—as formerly in the Salient—the Gloucestershires found themselves exposed to fire from an enemy to front, flank and rear, yet true to tradition they retained discipline. It is recorded that during this one day of fighting the fire was so fierce that the barrels of all the Lewis guns were worn smooth inside! But the end of the war was in sight when the Gloucestershires were to have ample revenge for Mons and their full share in the glory of driving the invaders back to the Hindenburg Line and to the Rhine.

I was serving with a battalion of the Durhams when—some days before we had even heard that the Armistice was

so much as under discussion—the Germans began to shower
leaflets over the countryside : fluttering strips of tissue-paper
which caught like seeds in every bush. They bore these words
in English, French and Flemish :

"Why are you still fighting? The Armistice is signed."

This fact alone would suffice to explode the myth of the
invincibility of the German Army when it caught at so slender a device to bring the struggle to a close !

I remember exploring a short stretch of the famous
Hindenburg Line in company with a sergeant-major not long
after the eviction of the tenants. We each examined different
dug-outs. Mine contained an upright piano and such litter of
empty wine bottles as would have taxed an auditor to count.

"There you are, sergeant-major," said I, when we came
to compare notes, "there you have the Hun : a true land
pirate ! It's not *his* country that's devastated, but his neighbour's. And not *his* wine that he guzzles ! Even the piano he
steals ! What did you find?"

"A dead woman; naked. Gassed as black as ——— !"

Once when in hospital for a war disability, a conscientious
objector—a fat and flabby man—threw out in my presence,
"Soldiers are good for nothing except to eat !" Were all of
like mind, that dug-out might have been erected upon English soil, and those charred remains of what had once been a
woman might have been those of this expostulating wise-
acre's sweetheart or wife !

From recalling scenes of military glory in the past this
fact seems to me to emerge. We had faith then in ourselves.
Upon whom but himself did Clive rely in India, or Wolfe at
Quebec? "We think highly of Englishmen in this country,"
said Dr Johnson, "yet Englishmen are not rare in it !" Have
we the same faith in ourselves to-day? Have our allies the
same faith in us? Has the individual Englishman the same
scope for his individuality? Or is he not rather, even proverbially, in leading-strings everywhere to a timid and passion-
less bureaucracy? How utterly did we suffer the national
temper to deteriorate in the years between 1918 and 1939 !
A treacherous and fanatical foe was arming. All knew it. It
was public talk. Our politicians disarmed, played ostrich and
hoped for the best ! It was as though the granting of uni-

versal suffrage and the throwing open to women of the universities and every department of public life—upon a theory of sex-equality not warranted by nature—had softened the national fibre and rendered Englishmen for the first time in their long history effeminate. Manliness went unregarded. The Quaker spirit spread. Man had surrendered his birthright!

Though one must regret the concomitant of war, destruction, yet resolute self-defence is always admirable. Unceasing effort is the condition of existence. The competitive struggle gave the greyhound its swiftness, the eagle its sharpsightedness and man his pre-eminence. All living is fighting. When you cease to fight you prepare to die!

Natives of Deerhurst with their quaint elver net
Naunton

CHAPTER VIII

RUDE TONGUES OF SHEPHERDS

"How does your fallow greyhound, sir?" asks Slender of Master Page, in the *Merry Wives*, "I heard he was outrun on Cotsall" (Cotswold). This dropping of the *w* in "Cotswold" is but one of several instances of Gloucestershire dialect to be found in Shakespeare. So to this day the beautiful town of Painswick is pronounced "Painsick," the *w* being dropped. "'Ooman" may still be heard : was one of Samuel Weller's parents not a Cockney after all, but Gloucestershire born? Who can say? But I have never heard of that dropping of the *w* as a typical London trick of speech. Some little while back I found an old labourer of seventy or thereabouts leaning over my garden gate. On asking if there were anything I could do for him, he answered with a laugh, "I was mistaking the sound of your typewriter for a 'oodpecker!" For in our county, if you wish to see a 'oodpecker, it is in the 'ood and not a house that you generally find one. Hence my old fellow's mystification.

I often think of that "Cotsall" of Shakespeare as a slip of the pen, due to hasty composition. The tradition is that *Merry Wives* was composed in record time, in order to satisfy the Virgin Queen, who was consumed with curiosity to see Falstaff in love. Even allowing for the fact that the famous "Dover's Games" were held in the Cotswolds, it is not easy to see why a Windsor gentleman should travel so far to see his greyhound race. Think of the condition of the roads at this time, and of the whole problem of transport. Even the coach was the possession of the privileged few and went slogging through the ruts, at best, at the pace of a soldier marching. Let savants say what they will, I am convinced that Shakespeare was rather hearkening to his boyhood's memories than studying the Windsor scene.

That our glorious poet knew Gloucestershire well does not admit of a doubt. The often-quoted

> These high wild hills and rough uneven ways
> Draws out our miles, and makes them wearisome

perfectly describes our hilly tracks—those "pitches" down the sides of our "banks"—which make such tough going to-day. The lines are so topographically correct, so vivid and true to Nature, one cannot doubt direct inspiration.

A frequent trick of speech of the Shakespearian low-life scenes is that of "'a" for "he" or "she." Mrs Quickly is a perfect example of the thing I have in mind. It is in these terms that she describes Sir John Falstaff's last moments: "'A made a finer end, and went away, an it had been any chrisom child; 'a parted even just between twelve and one . . . and 'a babbled of green fields." We have a Mrs Quickly amongst our neighbours. Of an impatient wooer joining his mistress after some enforced delay she said, "'A came out after she like a lion!"

Another local trick is the use of short *i* where standard speech demands double *e*; "strit," for instance, where we should expect "street." Whether Shakespeare did in fact hear this vowel variation in Gloucestershire, nobody at the present day can do more than hazard a guess; but certain it is that Speed, Valentine's servant of the *Two Gentlemen of Verona*, is punning in Cotswold when he says of his master's departure for Milan:

> Twenty to one, then, he is shipp'd already,
> And I have played the sheep in losing him.

If puns still raised a smile, a Gloucestershire farm-hand might relish this jest; a London clerk would be puzzled. The village of Sheepscombe—which I once played at darts with a Cranham team which defeated them; when the hospitable Sheepscombers regaled us with beer galore, and a mountain of cheese sandwiches—is still *Shipscombe* for its inhabitants, if they be either old or sticklers for tradition. In the *Midsummer Night's Dream*, Puck is sometimes made to sing of the "scritch-owl scritching loud"—a form which Spenser also uses—and this, for Gloucestrians, gives him an agreeably rustic tang which is eminently suitable to so lumpish a goblin. However, when I point out that something of Gloucestershire current dialect is to be found in Shakespeare, I am not definitely asserting that it was in this county that he learned it; I am only stating a coincidence from which I draw inferences with which others may disagree.

To continue : The use of "bin" for "been" is likewise of this county, doubly so since, in this little word two dialectical tricks meet, viz, the use of *i* where we should expect double *e*, and of subjunctive where indicative would be more customary. A little girl actress in a village pantomime, of whom I asked what part she was playing, replied excitedly, "I be a fairy!" Here is the Shakespearian variant of my little girl's "be," from the freshest, dewiest song ever poet composed, in any time or land. Were a redbreast miraculously endowed with human utterance thus he might express himself :

Hark! hark! the lark at heaven's gate sings,
  And Phœbus 'gins arise,
His steeds to water at those springs
  On chaliced flowers that lies;
And winking Mary-buds begin
  To ope their golden eyes;
With every thing that pretty bin :
  My lady sweet arise;
    Arise, arise!

—"How bist?" is the query when good friends meet; "thee bist a so-and-so," when they fall out.

Another peculiarity of Gloucestershire folk is their total elimination of the definite article before either *e* or *h*; not "the earth," "the house," but "thearth," "thouse."

H—the Cockney's dropping of this letter is thought to have been originally caused by the conscious or unconscious imitation of Norman French, or at least of the Norman inability to cope with it. These gallicized Danes were completely baffled by this tricky consonant, but they had seized upon all the money and all the lucrative posts, so that their broken English became a standard for the vulgar to imitate. A queer sort of jargon the King's English must have become, if Bastard William ever essayed to speak it! Ultimately, as

we all know, we refused to learn a foreign tongue and it may
be said with some degree of truth that we compelled them
to learn ours. And we were well advised to do so.

English literature could boast two native epic poems—the
Creation and *Beowulf*—and the popular, picturesque riddles
of Cædmon for the " man in the street." Neither was our
greatest deficient in classical culture. Alfred the Great and
his Archbishop of Canterbury, Alfric, were as well versed in
Latin as any French abbé was to be in the eighteenth century. Norman William, therefore, did *not*, as a kindly Hun-
garian refugee was so good as to inform me a short while
back, "put England on the map" ! The influence of Norman
French, in our popular literature at least, is slight. Were a
reader to turn from the prose of King Alfred by way of
fourteenth-century Langland's *Piers Plowman* to *Robinson
Crusoe*, or indeed to the immortal lyrics of Mother Goose,
he would be conscious of endless modifications, but of no
one abrupt break with the past of our native tongue.

But if the Norman gave the Cockney his *h*-lessness, he
favoured the Gloucestrians with no such indifferent gift. We
prefer to add them and, after dree *hegs* to our tea, like a
zound zleep in th' zun.

But, dialect apart, there is something racy and imaginative
about the idiom of our patriarchs. Listen, for instance, to
old Meadows strafing the landlady of one of the Rams or
Lambs.

"Zo I zaid to she, 'Damn thee bloody house,' I zaid, 'an'
may its walls bulge outward,' zaid I, 'an' may it vall over
into th' strit !'

"An' I haven't been there zince !"

The Cockney has wit, but the above is poetry ! (Not that
the Cotswolder lacks wit either, on occasion.) "How bist,
zur?" inquired one of the Nestors the other day, "Be 'ee
veeling good?" "Yes," said I, wondering what was coming.
"Good vor a *pint*?" was the next query !

Listen now to an old man's views on "walling," on the
craft, that is, of building a mortarless wall. This mode of
construction was favoured by the giant Polyphemus in
Homer's *Odyssey*, and was implanted in Gloucestershire, if
we may credit popular tradition, by the Romans.

"There be more art, look, goes to th' making of a dry wall than that there does to a wet 'un. I were *zo* high when they put they stwones [stones] up round o' Varmer's vield. An' there they be to-day: an' th' vires o' Hell won't vire they stwones down!"

The use of accusative for nominative—as in *"Them* were the days!"—is found in many localities, but Gloucestershire, like Devon and Cornwall, is remarkable for its transposition of accusative for nominative and vice versa. "'A told I what would happen to he, if he had aught to do wi' she!" And thus the narrator of a sporting incident:

"Her were a vighting bitch, her were; but when I shook that badger out o' that zack her didn't wait vor she!"
Or conversation in the bus. "Be your hens laying?"
"Oh, doan't talk o' they, th' lazy sluts!"

A few more jottings which seem to me to reveal that vein of poetry in the raw which I have ventured to claim for the older men amongst the Cotswold country labourers.

MYSELF: "But you're still strong?" HE: "I *were,* zur; strong as a helephant!"

DOG-LOVER: "I've bred the vinest dog that ever trod on England's earth!" ANOTHER: "A dog will vollow 'ee drough wet an' dry, shine an' shade; a woman may be out o' humour wi' 'ee, but not a dog."

A COMMON-SENSE CRITIC: "Virst thing ever a politician does when 'a be elected is to ask vor a million o' th' public's money! But if *I* were to ask *he* vor half a crown, '*Oh,* no!' 'a would zay, 'that's *mine!*'"

ENGLISHMAN'S HOME: "There I were born, an' my vather, an' his, an' his bevore 'un. None on us ever owned a rood o' land. Us lived sucking in th' sweet air. Brute health were our portion!"

GARDENER: "Ay, weeds will grow, though it were in th' middle o' hell!"

CHICKEN FARMER: "Of course, in th' spring you have th' comfort o' their laying; but they'm charging twenty shillings a pullet in Glaaster market an' though they were to lay eggs o' gold, that's dear!"

FIRST DARTS PLAYER (*after a near miss*): "How's *that*?"
SECOND: "No idea! Here to London!" (*Darts again*)—
Player's partner to obtrusive spectator: "Stand back!
Doan't hypnotize him! Give him air!" *Partner's turn*:
"Hand I they arrows! I'm just getting th' range."

GAY LOTHARIO: "You may kip all th' vat wenches. Give I
th' little flash greyhounds!"

OF A CIVIC DIGNATORY: "I zeed th' Mayor. I shouldn't
ha' recognized he, no more'n a pig!"

CARPENTER (*with perch for poultry-house*): "Will he do vor
'ee? Or be he too mighty?"

PHYLLIDA AND CORIDON: "Be your daughter engaged?"
"Not that." "Married then?" "No. Just having a little on
account like."

THE LOAFER IN WORK: "How be he going on, then?"
"He've zat down at present!"

NO INTELLECTUAL: "He be as zoft as bleeding dough!"

HOUSEWIFE AND CHURLISH BUTCHER: "I asked him for an
oxtail. You'd have thought I were asking for the Crown
Jewels!"

THE OLD WOODMAN'S PHILOSOPHY: "Logs warm 'ee
twice; when 'ee cuts them and when 'ee burns them up."

A STONECUTTER (*on being what you appear to be*): "'Fine
feathers make fine birds': but they *moult* damned
quick!"

MINE HOSTESS (*on Education*): "Women don't need education like men; they don't get the *fun* from it." *On
Teetotallers*: "How evil they look at you: as evil as the
grave." *And to an Objectionable Person*: "Go to the
devil," I said, "and don't take a *return ticket*!"

IN THE DAYS OF LONG HAIR: "Mine came down almost to
my knee when I were a girl. The boys did tease me. One
of them tied me by my hair to the village pump! But I
got even with him." "I expect you said something cutting?"
"'*Said*'? I threw a stone at him and broke his head!"

RAIN: "Doan't 'ee get wet now; run out between th' drops!"

TOPER'S TECHNIQUE (*or pumping the "vorreigner"*): "Just
one more then only—an' tell us o' thee relations!"

PATRIARCH MEETS PATRIARCH: "How's th' old man? Thee
woan't last out another o' these severe winters!"

THE REVELLER RETURNS : "No," zays I, "I haven't done no work and I bean't a-gwaine to! Not all th' bleeding salts that be in Epsom woan't make I work to-day!"

PARISHIONER DESCRIBES PARSON : "'A were a good old cock. I'd zay to 'un, 'Have a drink, Parson?' 'Ad zay, 'Now that *is* good of you!' An' if a old maid were to zay to 'un, 'Have a cup o' tea, Parson?' 'ad zay, 'Now that *is* good of you!' 'A were like a rainbow, a different colour to different men."

THE CHOICE OF A BRIDE : "Never marry a cousin, boy. Zooner than marry a cousin, I'd marry th' devil's daughter : an' live wi' th' old couple afterwards!"

Two little tales now, in *Double Gloucester*!

HANGMAN'S STONE

"That stone by the Irmin Street, Meadows, why do they call it Hangman's Stone?"

"Preston way? Ay? That be where th' ship-stealer met his death."

"What happened?"

"'A came vrom a dishonest vamily. 'A were a man, look, that would rather make ten shillings crooked than a guinea straight, an' work harder vor it too. To ask Jack to act different were asking tortoises to vly! One dark January afternoon, wi' th' night valling early, when 'a were planning vor to steal a ship, his nose valls a-bleeding—left nostril virst!—a bad sign.

"'Doan't 'ee go out after no ship to-night,' zays his wife, 'I've had a dream.'

"'What about, then?'

"'Thee! Just now; zitting by this vire; that a ship killed 'ee!'

"'*Thee'll* kill I : wi' *laughing*!'

"An' out 'a slips into th' dusk. Jack reached th' gap i' th' hedge he used vor to spy upon th' shepherd, when a voice cries clear i' th' night, 'Ship-stealing be hanging!'

"Jack were startled sure enough.

"'Nobody didn't speak,' zays he at last, ''t'were zomething in my head.'

"'Tweren't nothing in thee head,' comes th' voice again, 'ship-stealing be hanging!'

"Wi' that a hare crosses his path, leaping right over th' toes of his boots. 'Twere a witch giving he warning—a malefactor like herself—but 'a wouldn't hearken. His fate were upon him.

"Th' virst o' January were come an' past, an' th' rams had bin brought down vrom th' uplands vor better pasture. There were naught to reckon wi' but only th' shepherd an' his dog. Th' dog were quick, but Jack were quicker, an' stabbed he to th' heart wi' his knife. An' there th' creature lies a-bleeding on th' vrosty ground, a tangle o' long hair without a bark in' un. Jack were in th' shipvold, an' out again wi' his booty, bevore th' shepherd had done whistling up his dog, an' zearching vor 'un. Jack lashed th' ship's voorveet an' hindveet together wi' rope an' slung she over his shoulders like a soldier's bandolier, zo as her shouldn't be leaving no tracks.

"'If anybody zees I,' zays Jack, 'he'll only zay, "'A be carrying a sick ship; they works hard, shepherds!"'

"Zo 'a zits down on that stwone you asked me on an' takes a swig vrom a bottle o' smuggled brandy.

"'What about omens now?' zays he mocking, 'my nose bleeds, a hare crosses my path, a witch do warn I, an' my wife dreams a ship do murder I, but here I be! *Thee* wouldn't hurt a honest man would 'ee, woolly half-wit?'

"Wi' that, 'a gies th' ship's ear a twist which drives her crazy wi' pain, plunging, kicking an' dashing ov herzelf every road, till her had th' rope twisted clean about Jack's neck! Jack grabs vor his knife vor to cut hisself clear. 'Twere gone! Lost when 'a stabbed th' dog! Th' veins on his neck stood out; his eyes were bulging! 'A veels vor his pistol to shoot her, an' stop her capers : th' priming were all shook away! 'A tries to drag th' ship towards 'un to slacken th' rope, but wi' a heave her vlings herzelf clear ov th' stwone, valling all her weight an' drawing th' rope tight wi' a jerk!

"They vound Jack next maarning, *hanged*! Th' ship were alive. They returned she to th' shepherd."

"I'd ha' like to ha' lived in they days," says a burly farm-woman, "a man took his life in his hands but 'a were a *man*.

'A weren't a miserable controlled creature wi' forms to declare how much air his vamily took in wi' breathing or how many journeys they went daily wi' buckets to th' well!"

OLD-WIFE'S TALE

Mary's mother were dead, an' as her father were a soldier scrving in voreign parts, it vell to she to provide vor her younger brothers an' zisters. Zo early as midnight, her would rouse herzelf up an' load her pannier-donkey wi' vegetables vor Glaaster market; vor her had to be zetting out her stall, look, by th' virst light.

One moonlight night, young Mary zaw a hare running around in circles, vlinging up th' wet vrom th' grass behind 'un till it shone like sparks o' diamonds! Nigher th' hare drew to Mary, an' nigher yet, till it hops on to a dry-wall by th' roadside an' then, wi' one leap, it were in th' near-side pannier basket!

"Cover I wi' a napkin," zays th' hare, "an' zay nothing; an' doan't 'ee think o' zelling I at Glaaster market neither; that'd be too cruel vor words!"

"Do 'ee read thoughts, then? That *were* what I were thinking! But now I gie 'ee my word to protect 'ee; an' if I were to go back on myself, look, I'd veel just as small as a button on a shirt!"

An' Mary hid th' hare in th' pannier, an' covered she wi' th' napkin.

An' now a huntsman in scarlet, wi' a coal-black haarse, an' maartle queer boots an' haarns peaking up under his cap, hollas out,

"Maarning, my pretty! Thee hassn't zeen a hare hast thee hereabouts?"

"None haven't passed *this* way," zays Mary.

("It takes a woman," interjects old Meadows, "to deceive a devil!")

An' Mary zees a pack o' wish-hounds wi' vierce yellow eyes like bloodshot daffodils an' sweat dripping vrom their ribs in vlames!

"We'm off th' scent, boys!" cries th' devil, "We've lost th' game!"

Mary glances down at her basket an' there were th' little hare peeping vearfully out vrom beneath th' napkin.

A cock crows zomewheres near by, an'—Click!—huntsmen, hounds an' all were gone in a twinkling!

"When I were maartle," zays th' hare to Mary, "I were a lovely maid like thee; but vor th' crime o' witchcraft I were condemned to be coursed by th' spirits o' earth an' air until zuch time as I should zee th' tails o' all th' hounds! An' now I *have* zeen them vrom under your napkin! An' I be vree now to lead a happy life in a country more beautiful than any you can imagine!"

An' zudden as *that*, th' hare turned into a young maid in grass-green, standing there by th' wayside smiling, crowned wi' vlowers, an' beautiful as a dream!

"I'll zend 'ee good luck, Mary, vor helping I!"

Wi' they words, her ran to a copse in a meadow planted vor to shade cattle. Her hair were scented wi' th' fragrance ov a thousand vlowers an' vloated out behind she like a cloud o' gold; an' in th' copse, amindst o' th' brambles an' green branches, her were gone!

An' Mary's stall at Glaaster market zold out early now. It were more garden then: carts next: soon outbuildings. An' one day her zays:

"I be rich! I'll have a girt house like other rich girls. An' a coach and zix haarses!"

"And did she marry the Squire?"

"Her were too vly vor *that*! Squire were a roistering wretch who had bin th' death o' two wives already! But, of course"—Mrs Meadows adds reflectively—"'a had a *mighty* good *try* vor her wi' th' other gentlemen!"

That the dialects of England should disappear is sincerely to be regretted. Ours, here in Gloucestershire, will hardly survive another generation. Upon a recent visit to Devon I found the old imaginative idiom of my boyhood together with the distinctive accent of the county irretrievably lost. And what a world of imaginative diction has gone therewith! I recall a longshoreman's comment upon a handsome yacht in the estuary at Salcombe.

"Ah! She'm beautiful. Vlies through the air as light as vanity!"

And the East Anglian farmer whom I talked with early in the last war when on duty somewhere near Horsey Island. He had been put in charge of a dozen young land-girls.

"You must find them a handful?" said I, chaffing him.

He thought a brief while, then answered :

"They are good girls; they sing, and have rare voices." I doubt if he had ever heard of blank verse, and yet if this line of his—for such it was—were compared with those of a Beaumont and Fletcher or later Shakespeare play it would not strike false to the ear, but ring with the genuine gold of English. That style of speech we are not likely to hear again.

With the idioms of country labourers as raw material, Elizabethan poets revivified our tongue. When Hamlet laments that

> the native hue of resolution
> Is sicklied o'er with the pale cast of thought,

he is employing a term from the building trade. A cast is a coating of whitewash or the like, often applied particularly with old houses north of Severn, to keep out damp and generally to protect the walls. It survives to-day in the form of roughcast.

From the English dialects also came English slang. This may appear bathos after what has been said, but slang too was rich, vital and abundant in the past. So exuberant and so expressive was it in the days of the Regency that Pierce Egan, acquiring colloquial wealth in his Bohemian wanderings, found himself able to compose a novel almost wholly in it : *Life in London, or the Day and Night Scenes of Jerry Hawthorn and Corinthian Tom.* And if we go back further yet, think what happy use the Elizabethan pamphleteers made of slang, when they portrayed—with what zest and colour !—scenes and characters from low life !

To-day misguided educationalists have standardized the spoken word, and the influence of the B.B.C. has not always been happy. When broadcasting was new, the verb "listen in" arose spontaneously to express the action of a member of an audience who was attending to a radio programme. The B.B.C. itself, however, would have none of it. There must be no "listening in," only "listening." Now I happen to be one of those who prefer the concrete to the indeterminate, and to my mind "listening in" is the best word yet discovered to express the listening *within* a circuit. "Listening" without that "*in*" is vague as mist. You *may* "listen" to a lark above the hill-top, or to a clock in a submarine, but you can only "listen in" to a radio set.

The language of Farmer Hodge is becoming that of the professors, and *quis custodiet ipsos custodes?*

CHAPTER IX

FOLKLORE

"WHEN I was a small boy," says a neighbour, "I would be asked for Christmas and such grand occasions to the cottage of an old relation who had a real chimney-corner; for her house was eighteenth-century if not earlier. Here she would sit, and tell us children tales of ghosts and goblins. Sometimes, when more than usually awestruck, I would exclaim, 'But that isn't true, is it?' And to this she would reply, in very sinister accents, 'Oh-ho! It bean't true, bean't it?'"

That old sybil, not I, should be writing this chapter, but she has most regrettably passed on long since. Perhaps she now finds herself amongst the goblins, entertaining a select party of their children upon Hallowe'en with blood-curdling tales of humans and their ways : how revoltingly warm they are to the touch, and how, when the cock crows, instead of going straight home to bed they actually sally forth into the bright air, and are never more truly themselves than when the garish sun is shedding his brazen light!

Where are they now, these delectable old crones? With the good king Charlemagne? Progress, villainous progress, has been the spoil of them. Mass education has been over them like a steam-roller, and flattened them out. Oh, crablike march of Progress! What may not Michael Drayton, old classic Ben Jonson, and the sublime Shakespeare himself have learned of fairyland, as they sat, solemn children, quaking with delicious terror in the half-circle of ruddy light cast by the brands!

Yet, a short way past the duckpond, before the villa which is never referred to otherwise by our locals than as the Haunted House, I did come once upon a wizened old woman gathering sticks for her fire, her hair hanging in uncouth witch-locks, and walking with a stick cut from the hedge. And from this romantic and communicative crone I learned all that she had to tell of the legendary "Judge Coxe."

Attempts have been made by modern antiquaries to whitewash this man. When the Whig cause was triumphant, he was, forsooth, a Jacobite, and therefore suspect, and the victim of malevolent tongues. But so were eighty per cent of the country squires Jacobites, and so unashamedly that they were wont to refer to the newly established dynasty as the Hanover Rats. Politics alone never gave a man an ill name which endured above a couple of hundred years.

The Haunted House was formerly an old moated mansion. It was taken over by the Puritans as one of those strongpoints with which they designed to form a protective ring round what its sanctimonious Mayor preposterously styled the "godly town of Gloucester." Prince Rupert stormed the house and took it, for though he was miserably lacking in tenacity, he never wanted for dash. They tell me that when a modern drainage system was being introduced, a few years back, the workmen unearthed no fewer than six skeletons. So they gave over digging, and sought a less inauspicious corner for their labours. "Judge Coxe" acquired the ruinous old place, filled in the moat, and rebuilt it in the rather Frenchified William and Mary style that we see to-day.

I tackled the old folks about the Coxe legend, with all the zest of a Fleet Street reporter in hot haste after the very latest particulars of a murder for his crimes' column. One old fellow told me that, at some time prior to the siege of Gloucester, King Charles had made the house his headquarters, and that the gates of the forecourt were said to open every 28th of January, at midnight, in honour of the martyred king.

An old woman, not the crone but another, held a directly contrary view. "Doan't 'ee believe a word of it!" said she. "They gates doan't open in honour of no King Charles; neither be they opened by th' Blacksmith's ghost! It be th' devil who forces they gates open!" Doctors differ, you see.

I offered the old fellow who stood out for the legend of the "martyred King" the price of a pint: the least one can proffer for a tradition of King Charles. His mode of acceptance gratified but astonished me : "The Lord zend 'ee good luck," said he, "an' long life to enjoy it in !"

At last I felt that I had the situation well in hand. I wrote *The Gates* in the dining-room of an inn at Stroud, rebutting all the efforts of a socially disposed commercial gentleman who appeared intent upon forcing me into conversation. Baffled by my rock-like resistance, he next turned to my bull-terrier Johnnie, and finding him more conversible, set resolutely to work upon teaching him a new trick. Johnnie proved himself an apt pupil and, so often as he made progress, his new acquaintance would take a biscuit from a glass jar upon the table and toss it aloft. The "old bull," who was in the vigour of youth, would leap after it into the atmosphere. Unfortunately Johnnie never acquired the paratrooper's knack of deft landings. Upon his returns to this habitable globe he would collide with such objects as chairs, and throw them over. The air re-echoed with joyous bellowings : and that dog had a bark to bring the clock from the mantel-piece. But none of this disturbed me. I was as cavalier with the hotel notepaper as our friend was with its biscuits. I finished *The Gates* over my third pint. It took me just the hour and I have never retouched it.

THE GATES

Judge Coxe and Squire sat by the board :
   "This is a pleasant place, my lord,
This house you've built," exclaims the Squire,
   "What more could any man desire?
Your rooms are airy, light, and wide;
You've barns, and ricks, and all beside."
But Judge Coxe, frowning, hesitates :
   "My friend, I'd have some wrought-iron gates
To close my forecourt in, and 'Sblood !
No vulgar work, but choicely good."

With that, the Squire cleared his throttle,
And says, whilst emptying the third bottle,
   "You've jailed the best man in this kind,
Cunninger craftsman you'll not find
Though you should search all Gloucestershire !"

"What! Do you mean that blacksmith, Squire?"
"I do, the man who stole the goose;
But free the smith's neck from the noose :
He'll forge you gates worth a city's loot,
    That shall hang nobly in their place;
Strong as a regiment of foot,
    And cunning as maids' work in lace!"

Coxe brings his fist down with a thump :
A fork takes flight, and the glasses jump !
    "I'll have him out, by King William's leave,
And, zounds! I'll get him his reprieve.
And he his hammer shall stoutly swing,
The coal shall roar, and the anvil ring,
For be he lazy as a Turk,
When his neck's the stake, a man will work !
I'll hang him unless he do me right,
For Sessions come on to-day fortnight.
I have a way, friend, with such fellows,
You'll swear the devil blows the bellows !
He shall hang like a dog unless he do't,
    My gates shall hang then in their place,
Strong as a regiment of foot,
    And cunning as maids' work in lace!"

In truth, the blacksmith played his part,
He shaped the gates with cunning art,
A man of his neck may well be jealous;
They swore the devil blew the bellows !
From no stiff labour did he swerve,
But wrought them shapely with twist and curve,
Till they on their hinges swung,
Then no more his anvil rung.
    "Judge," says the smith, "I've done my part,
But I've shortened my life, for I've strained my heart;
A fortnight was too short a time
To forge those gates; but for my crime,
You've sworn my pardon I shall see,
So bring no shame on mine or me."
    "From my first sentence I'll not budge,"

The Severn Bore
Looking across country towards the hills above the Severn Valley

Declares this Jeffreys of a judge,
"I spoke no word of you at court,
But took a road a deal more short.
You've built the gates," says he, "indeed;
Yet shall you hang, the felons' meed,
But when you're dead and gone," says he,
"The gates shall your memorial be,
And water your fame both flower and root,
    For they shall hang yet in their place,
Strong as a regiment of foot,
    And cunning as maids' work in lace!"

But now befalls what's strange to state;
On January twenty-eight,
Of the year of sixteen-ninety-odd
Of William, King by Grace of God,
At stroke of twelve of a blowing night,
With twisted neck, all ghastly white,
The smith revisited the place,
On a great white horse with a great white face,
And the gates—his gates—they opened wide,
As though they bowed on either side.
The winds through the beech-wood bellow and
    shout,
He rides the court three times about.
The winds through the beech-wood shriek and moan;
He left : but he did not leave alone !
He beckoned the Judge through wind and rain,
And the gates—his gates—shut to again.

    "Vootman," says coachman, "if zo be
My lard be in danger, our place be wi' he;
Duty an' caanscience zay that plain,
Despite the devil, an' wind, an' rain!"
    Coachman and footman take lanterns and follow . . .
And they found Coxe dead, in Toadsmoor Hollow ! . . .
'Twas along o' the smith, and his gates to boot,
    That hang so nobly in their place,
Strong as a regiment of foot,
    And cunning as maids' work in lace !

Wool Market Hall, Chipping Campden
Ancient Dovecote, Naunton

There is nothing that the countryman of to-day hates more than to be suspected of superstition. He has, as we say to-day, a complex about it. And this he owes to the ridicule open or ill-concealed of the infiltrating urban population. Dreading the townsman's sarcasm, the countryman takes down the horseshoe which his grandfather nailed above the stable or barn door. He refrains from divining—at least aloud—the speedy arrival of a gentleman or lady unknown from the cockerel or pullet that has that moment entered his house by the open door.

It never occurs to rustic Hodge that Cockney Bill is a prey to fancies every whit as outlandish. Hodge has had no opportunity of seeing Bill upon a race-day helping to make the fortunes of the street-vendors of that curious "white heather" which was purple until it was metamorphosed white by a chemical process. He has not seen the lucky gems which add such variety to the display of the humblest no less than of the most fashionable of the jewellers' shop-windows! He has not seen Bill purchasing his girl that small horseshoe in silver or, if she fancy its efficacy to be greater, the minia-ture "lucky pig" of genuine "Irish bog-oak" made by the gross from snippets and chips of wood by the knowing carpenters of Whitechapel.

In the following sketch, I have altered the names of my characters, and sincerely hope that if those I portray recog-nize their portraits they will acquit me of the slightest desire to make fun of them.

Sleet outside. Inside the Fleece three old men sit roasting at the fire.

"What be you reading, Johnnie?"

Stocky, broad-shouldered John Ferrers puts down his Sunday paper.

"It be an article on what he calls Spiritism by a writer who signs hisself 'Scientist.' They be zo superstitious, they scientists, they do make a man blush vor 'un!"

"What do he zay, then?"

"It were at one o' these *séances*. A visitor rose dree voot off o' th' vloor, an' a 'spirit guide'—which be what my old granddad would ha' called a 'witch's vamiliar'—brought zome veathers vrom a lady's canary-bird through a brick wall!"

"An' didn't th' bird object?"

"'A weren't asked his opinion!"

"Queer things *do* happen, admitted," says James Black, white-haired, white-moustached, and thin as a greyhound, "but not zo out o' nature as they scientists do believe."

"Zartin they do," continues Ferrers, "like my grannie an' her vive-pound note."

"What were that then, Johnnie?"

"It were zavings that she'd put in a teapot. One day she opens th' lid, an' vinds 'un empty! Vive pounds took making in they days, an' she were nigh distracted. Round she went to Lucy Walters, th' wise woman: you know where th' cottage be that were hers? It bean't much changed.

"'Lucy,' zays my grannie, 'can thee tell I who've stolen my vive-pound note?'

"'I'll do more than that,' zays Lucy, 'I'll show her to you, if your nerves be strong! Look in that caarner!'

"'I doan't zee nothing,' zays my grannie.

"'Keep looking,' zays Lucy.

"'Why!' cries my grannie, zudden, 'I zee Bett Keteredge! What be that dress she'm wearing? I ha'an't ever zeen her in that dress bevore!'

"'That be th' dress she've bought wi' that vive-pound note o' yourn!'

"'Doan't touch her!' hollers Lucy, vor my grannie were hurling ov herzelf vorwards, 'her be all smoke like!'

"My grannie were away vrom Lucy's in a vlash, an' hammering at Bett's door.

"'Come out!'

"Bett comed out.

"'You low thief!' cries my grannie, 'you bought that dress you be wearing wi' my vive-pound note!'

"Her were zo surprised at my grannie's knowing, that her confessed everything."

"Did she pay your grannie back?"

"In kind she did: in vegetables an' vowls an' zuch. Her never had th' money." . . .

"There were a ghost on th' wireless," interjects Meadows, "that blew hot an' cold."

"I hope," says James Black, "they scientists doan't lay th' ghosts altogether, wi' their meddling ways. In my time, I ha' made money out o' they."

"Money vrom ghosts, man!"

"Ay. Virst job ever I had were 'prentice to a builder who made all his money vrom breaking open doors o' rooms which had been zealed up, in old times, vor haantings. I were builder's boy, an' carried his bag o' tools. It were thought unlucky to be virst across th' threshold, an' 'a were paid as much vor being 'virst over' as vor unscrewing hinges an' picking locks. I had my virst wages off o' he."

"Did you ever have anything to do with the Haunted House?" My reference was to the house already mentioned.

"It were my virst job!"

"When you broke into the room, did you *find* anything?"

"Nothing, zur," James Black makes answer, "except a birch broom in a caarner, an' a witch's circle wi' queer markings to it in chalk on th' vloor! Many's th' shilling I were given, ghosting, when I were a boy, an' by great ladies too! Had my head patted: slices o' cake, an' all!"

"In they var days," says Meadows, "thee must ha' bin good-looking, Jimmy. Lord! How times do change!" . . .

There is a curious tradition associated with Frith Wood, which was woodland even so short a time as a dozen years ago. Alas! the right every selfish tradesman appears to possess of buying a beauty spot and felling the trees which have given joy to thousands, with no sense of obligation to replant, has reduced this tract which was full of legends almost to a copse. Even when the Government take such a place over with a view to replanting, it is never again what it was, for pines and firs are alone of commercial value to-day. No shipwright demands heart of oak for the wooden walls; no miller elm for his water-mill; no bowman yew. And that enchanting variety of beech, thorn, ash, holly, oak, and sycamore which went to form the "good greenwood" of the Robin Hood tradition gives place to something disquietingly unEnglish in appearance—a miniature Black Forest.

There was, then, formerly in Frith Wood, a tree which possessed the supernatural quality of glowing whenever England was on the brink of a foreign war. Whether this tree took on the ominous lustre when the troubles flared up at Bunker's Hill and lost us America, I cannot find related. Did its foliage blush with conscious carmine when the younger Pitt decided it was time that somebody should do something about Napoleon? Nobody knows. But it is universally agreed that it glimmered prophetically—and for the last time!—at the opening of the fateful month of October 1899.

"There will be war!" cried my informant.

"Were there many watching the tree?"

"Quite a crowd!"

On the tenth of that month the Boers invaded the British colonies in South Africa. They shelled the camp of General Penn Symonds. Yet another war in the world's history had begun.

Rotten wood will sometimes glow in the dark, and this fact, arbitrarily interpreted by such as love to seek for omens, may yield the clue to the mystery. Or did the tree glow only to the mental eye? Let savants decide. For my part, I have only one comment to make. Were a tradition so extraordinary to reach us from Eire, or the Isle of Man, or the Outer Hebrides, some ass would unfailingly up and lecture us on the Celtic imagination. But Frith Wood— what they have left of it!—is in Gloucestershire. Some day perhaps a uniquely original philosopher of penetrating mental acuteness will give the world the paradoxical apophthegm that, in the land which produced Coleridge, Keats, and Shakespeare, men are not absolutely destitute of the imaginative faculty.

The following has an authentic element of folklore. I believe I have seen a ballad on this subject, but cannot recall where. I have given it my own atmosphere and colour, and have so far indulged poet's licence as to introduce a Gloucestrian Puck as, without some such *deus ex machina,* it seemed to me difficult to render the climax convincing, even to the eye of poetical faith.

A BALLAD OF A FAIR SHEPHERDESS AND A RICH
MERCHANT'S SON OF BRISTOL CITY

It fell in "Farmer" George's reign,
    Upon a lusty First of May,
When spring had come to Gloucestershire,
    In all her trim and fresh array.

The merry maids of Paganhill
    In many a wanton band advance,
With garlands green upon their heads,
    About their maypole for to dance.

And of the damsels dancing there,
    A shepherd's daughter did surpass,
For grace and comeliness of limb,
    All that had ever trodden grass!

Amongst the watchers standing by,
    Throughout the livelong day, was one
Who couldn't take his eyes from her,
    And he was a Bristol merchant's son.

He courted her with many a gift,
    And many a loving word he said,
But could not have his will of her,
    So naught would serve but they must wed.

"Then ask my father," said the maid,
    "If you may have me for your wife.
I'll love you with a single heart,
    My dearest, whilst I have my life!"

"Us be poor volk," the shepherd said,
    "Her beauty be her dowry, zur;
I'll give the wench wi' all my heart,
    But cannot give a groat wi' her."

"But I have wealth enough for two,
    Or count to have it certainly;
My father is a Bristol merchant,
    With trading vessels on the sea."

But when his father heard this news,
   His rage all measure did surpass!
His son, the heir to all his wealth,
   Had wed a penniless shepherd lass!

He razed his name from out the will,
   He cries, "You are son of mine no more.
Avoid me, or I'll be your plague!"
   And in his face he shuts the door.

The shepherd's daughter sobbed and cried
   For the ill fate of the merchant's son,
"Only," says she, "for loving me,
   My dearest, are you now undone!

"I'll be no clog to drag you down,
   But leave you for some distant place,
Then tell him I deserted you,
   And win again your father's grace!"

"Be comforted," says he, "my dear,
   I have a heart above his spite,
Return we to your father's cot,
   And spend therein our bridal night."

The merchant's son worked on the farm,
   To bed at twilight, up at morn,
In January at the plough,
   And at mid-June to cut the corn.

But coming through the haunted copse,
   One freezing January night,
From a late lambing on the hills,
   The Puck upstarted in his sight.

Says Puck to him, "Yoke up the plough,
   And drive her by the old dry wall,
Where the dead beech o'erhangs the field,
   And looks as though 'twere like to fall."

Says Puck to him, "Take spade and pick,
   And when the plough will drive no more
You'll find your luck within the ground,
   And dig what's worth the digging for!

"You've set the Puck his dish of cream,
  And luck and plenty shall you find;
But scoffing spies he tears in brakes,
  In ditches bogs, or strikes them blind!"

The merchant's son he rubs his eyes,
  In doubt if he has seen aright,
But he may rub and rub again,
  For now there's nothing but the night.

So home he trudged and yoked his bulls,
  And drove them by the old dry wall,
And when the share stuck fast, he led
  His smoking cattle back to stall.

The share was in an antique pot
  Of broad gold pieces, buried fast,
The treasure of some king of old,
  In troublous ages long gone past.

He bore it to the shepherd's cot,
  With more, and yet more, ere the day,
And hid it from the sight of man,
  With sacks and piled-up heaps of hay.

And now this youth in prudent wise
  Negotiates that great mass of gold,
For he to ledgers had been bred,
  And not at all to sheep in fold.

And he has built a gallant house,
  With fishponds, and with terraces,
A maze, and all such princely gear,
  And all his shepherdess to please.

With peacocks, and a bathing-pool
  Where she may keep her beauty bright;
And now to London will he fare,
  Of "Farmer" George to be made knight.

My lady's coach is at the door,
  With prancing horses well beseen,
The black boy he will bear her fan:
  What would she more though she were Queen?

And a world of folklore is bound up with the Rollright Stones. Strictly speaking, this Stonehenge in miniature is beyond the bounds of Gloucestershire, but it is within the limits of the Cotswolds, and is furthermore such a favourite goal for excursionists that I need make no apology for introducing it here. These megaliths are situated four-miles-odd north-west of Chipping Norton and under two miles from Long Compton. One of the singular things about them is that they stand almost, but not quite, at the top of a high hill. Why after the fabulous labour which it must have cost our strange ancestors to drag these monstrous stones nearly to the summit, they never did so completely remains a mystery which will probably never be solved.

How many stones are there? Nobody knows that either: except scientists who declare that there are fifty-eight. Dismissing their statement with caution, I proceed to explain why, in all probability, nobody will ever know. Stand at any point you choose within the circle and begin counting; you grow confused and begin counting all over again. And this for an excellent reason, the fairies do not want the number known! They haunt this circle—oh, yes, didn't you know?— and they abominate Nosey-Parkerdom in all its manifestations! For, as the Bishop of Oxford and Norwich very truly expresses it,

> A tell-tale in theyre company
> They never could endure,
> And whoeso kept not secretly
> Theyre mirth was punisht sure!

Although, to be sure, they never punished the baker, they only made game of him. What! My dear sir, you don't mean to assert that you never heard of the trick the fairies played the baker? And this when millions upon millions of public money are being lavished upon education! Sir, you astound me!

The baker tried again and again to count the stones, but could he reckon them up? Not on your life! He stood with his back against one stone, without shifting.

"That's one," said he, "well begun is half done!" And he began numbering the stones from right to left. He made it so much, but, just to check it, he began numbering them all again, this time from left to right. The total was different. Had he or had he not counted the stone against which he had so firmly set his back? Or had he perhaps counted it twice? His head was turning, so, like the sensible fellow he was, he retired to the inn, and meditated what stratagem he should adopt over a quart of the best ale. He had a veritable inspiration.

Back he tramped to his shop, although it was already owl-light, and filled his cart with loaves, and with these and a ladder he set out once more for the scene of his investigations. When he reached the circle, he got out, set his ladder against the stone he first came to, climbed up it, and placed a loaf on the top! He had made sure, before he set out on this expedition, of the exact number of the loaves he took with him.

"I have only to put one loaf on the top of each stone, and count what I have left over! What a clever fellow I am! I shall be somebody when I have counted the Rollright Stones."

But it was by no means so simple as he imagined. Loaf after loaf he put in position, but still the circle never seemed complete! At last, to his stupefaction, he discovered that he had used up all the loaves he had brought with him. He rested dumbfounded, his elbows on the top of a stone, and his heavy-soled shoes on the ladder. The round moon had risen by now, and the Stones were casting blue shadows. All of a sudden, a peal of laughter greeted his ears, so bewitching as to set him laughing also. It was like a rain of golden jewels, or the trill of the first skylark in April! It was clear; it was mocking; it was infinitely joyous.

The baker looked about him and was so astonished at what he saw that he almost fell from his ladder! A company of pretty maids, dignified but not above three fingers in height, were in merry converse upon the stone next to his, the perfection of their beauties now hidden, now flauntingly displayed by their robes, which were of some translucent stuff that glimmered like the moonshine. Some of the party, setting their white feet firmly in the soft moss on the top of the stone, put their shoulders to the loaf and thrust. Others fluttering delicately in the air on filmy wings pushed with their hands, the gems upon their slender fingers all a-glitter like dewdrops. And now all together in a concerted effort they succeeded in toppling the loaf over the edge of the stone !

Truth dawned on the baker. For every loaf that he had put on, the fairies had pushed one off ! So the poor man climbed down again, collected all his loaves which were strewn upon the ground except one, and packed them neatly in the cart. That one he left in the middle of the ring.

"For you, ladies," says he, "it is new baked; and my best respects, I'm sure."

Then, bowing, and sweeping the ground with the feather of his hat—bakers were more decorative then than now—he climbed back into the cart, and drove away. . . .

A solitary megalith, the King's Stone, is so placed as to point towards the rising sun. Hard by stand five others—the fabled Whispering Knights—in close conference together, and plotting mischief ! Old wives tell us that, before these Rollright Stones were here, a prophetess had informed a Danish invader that this hill was enchanted, and that if he climbed but to the top, by that symbolic rite he would make himself King of England.

But if one witch favoured him, a second was his enemy. Up he strode—up !—and up ! king already in his own conceit. His desperadoes follow close at heel—and the Crown of England seems to dance in the air before his eyes. They are now within a stone's-throw of the summit when suddenly that other witch, his enemy, starts up from the ground, barring his way ! Her bony forefinger menaces him, her tattered locks fly in the wind, as she half-chants, half-shrieks

> Rise up stick, and stand still stone,
> King of England thou shalt be none !
> Thou and thy men hoar stones shall be,
> And I myself an eldern tree !

And so it befell indeed. . . .

I cannot conclude this sketch of the Rollright Stones without relating what a very old man told me when, in company with a friend, I visited the inn at Long Compton, the best part of forty years ago. We three were alone in the tap-room, and the talk naturally turned upon the Stones as being the local object of outstanding interest.

"If one of our young married women," said he, "wishes to have a child, and can't, do you know what she does?"

"No idea!"

"She goes up to the Stones at midnight, and presses the tips of her breasts against any one of them!"

"But—does that have that effect?"

His reply was almost religious in its intensity: "It has *never* been known to *fail*!"

In my undergraduate days I had neither heard nor read of fertility cults or stones, so that his reply astonished me the more, and made a considerable impression on me. Since the far-off days of my visit to Long Compton, the Society for the Protection of Ancient Monuments has surrounded the megaliths with a protecting fence of iron rails which prevents close access to them. This was a well considered act; they will last the longer. But from this very circumstance it may be assumed that a rite which may well be coeval with this strange monument will never be practised again.

CHAPTER X

POPULAR SAYINGS AND A POPULAR SPORT

THE interest in proverbs is world-wide, and with reason : they are the epigrams of the poor. They possess a homely tang of the soil which produced them, and stand in the same relation to the *bon mot* of the wit by profession as a wild flower does to a gem. Proverbs are for the most part local in their appeal, but the author's apophthegm has this about it which the rustic proverb lacks; it is a traveller, a citizen of the world. Many a sparkling epigram of Wycherly or Dryden might raise a smile in Paris. The pregnant maxims of Lord Bacon owe much to that Latin in which it is obvious that, true child of the Renaissance that he was, he could think no less than write. The Baconian dictum is universal.

"Suspicions among thoughts are like bats among birds, they ever fly by twilight."

"In sickness respect health principally; and in health, action."

"To take a soldier without ambition, is to pull off his spurs."

Were it possible to confront Tacitus with these things, he would enjoy them as we do. Not so with proverbs. These, like certain "wines of the country," to be relished must be drunk on the spot. Let them travel and they become insipid.

I had asked a neighbour how his ploughing-up had progressed. "All shipshape," said he, "and Bristol fashion!" This saying was inspired, in ancient days, by the appearance of the ships of war in the old port, when "white wings" and gilded figureheads delighted the eye with the mixed impressions of beauty and efficiency. Such proverbs belong to history. This conjures up before the mental eye that city whence John Cabot, with his English crew and letters-patent from the English King, sailed forth in his diminutive galley *Mathew* to discover Newfoundland. Alas, for human dreams! Flushed with his first success, he embarked the following year with five ships for a second voyage, sailed away into the sunset, and was never heard of again.

Other counties claim some of our sayings, but they have yet to prove that they have not borrowed from us. That artless distich

> Apple-pie without cheese
> Is like a kiss without a squeeze!

is challenged for Yorkshire. I can only say it is thus that we Gloucestrians still make the dish. We grate the cheese—Double Gloster, naturally!—over the slices of apple before the pie goes into the oven. As the cheese melts it gives the fruit piquancy. "Apple-pie without cheese is insipid," a skilled cook of this county assures me; and she adds, "I wouldn't give a penny for one!"

One town has given us two proverbs: beautiful black-and-white Tewkesbury. These are "Thick as Tewkesbury mustard," and "Sharp" as it. With the former, Shakespeare shows his acquaintance. Doll Tearsheet is conversing with Sir John Falstaff at the Boar's Head in Eastcheap: "They say," she remarks, "that Poins has a good wit."

"He a good wit?" retorts Sir John, "hang him, baboon! his wit is as thick as Tewkesbury mustard!"

In the Virgin Queen's days, old Tewkesbury was famous for its mustard balls, which their manufacturers sent into other parts of England for sale. A learned commentator notes: "The peculiar slabbiness and heavy dampness of mustard, when made thick in consistency, renders the wit of Falstaff's simile lustrous."

"It's long a-coming as Cotswold barley." This crop matures slowly in the cool air and stony soil of our hills.

"That put the cat in the pigeon-house!" (The climax was reached.)

"Poorly sit, richly warm," counsels content in a cottage.

"Sleeping out of doors" is said euphemistically of the dead.

"The grey mare is the better horse," a nonsense expression of considerable antiquity. It is believed to originate in that banner of the White Horse under which King Alfred defeated the Danes, the same creature which cut in effigy in the chalk of the hillside decorates the Vale of the White Horse, Wiltshire.

"The bird whistles in the morning; the cat gets him before the night" expresses, less tersely, the Roman maxim, *Cavete, Felices.*

> The squirrel can hop from Swell to Stow,
> Without resting his foot, or wetting his toe!

A jolly thought from leafy country!

"As the goodman says, so it *should* be; as the goodwife says, so it *will* be!" An ultra-pacifist *cri de cœur* from the henpecked!

Topers' Proverbs: "It's a poor belly that can't warm a pint of beer!"—"He'll dine on tongue pie." (His wife will nag him for getting home late!)

> Beer on cider
> Is a very bad rider!

"At Painswick they never grow old."

"They're tough in the West."

A Sophisticated Proverb: "You must hunt at Cheltenham, fish at Cirencester, but talk blank verse at Painswick!"

> Be the counsel better or worse
> Follow him that bears the purse!

Peasant philosophy the world over!

"Beware the fox in the furze-bush!" As the fox's ruddy coat is indistinguishable to the human eye from the decaying fern amongst which he conceals himself, the proverb means: "Be not overreached by cunning": advice which it is exceedingly easy to give.

"The master's eye fats the horse," and "The master's foot fats the soil," throw doubt upon the disinterestedness of hostlers and gardeners.

"Smoke will to the snicker." "Snicker" is a colloquialism for a pretty girl, and is, so the philologists maintain, one of our Gloucestershire words of Danish origin, as are the place-names, Daneway, Dane Bottom, Birdlip, Lypiatt, Frith, Knapp, Hazelhanger, Wishanger, Brookthorpe, Colthrop, and Kingsholm. The saying commemorates a curious and pretty superstition. When maids cluster about the hearth on a windy day, the puffs of smoke which are blown down into the room instinctively seek out the prettiest face.

> The Tracies
> Have always the wind in their faces!

This variously quoted proverb recalls the divine punishment meted out to that owner of large estates in Gloucestershire, Sir William Tracy, one of the four knights who slaughtered that provoking cleric Thomas à Becket. The wind which was supposed to be hereditary in the family is unknown to modern meteorologists. Fuller, the Church historian, heretically suggests that in the summer the curse would prove a blessing and save the Tracy ladies the expense of fans!

"Like Punch's bellyache, worse and worse!"

In Gloucestershire dialect many inanimate objects are masculine which would, of course, be neuter in standard English. This was doubtless the case in Elizabethan English, if we may judge by the poets. Herrick, for example, in an exquisite fairy poem:

> If you will with Mab find grace,
> Set each platter in his place.

Not "its." From this survival in traditional speech comes the proverb, "Everything is 'he' in Gloucestershire except a tom-cat, and that's 'she'!"

An old man tells me that he went to the "local" away back in Victorian times with the village schoolmaster. There was some whispering and nudging, when one of the company, who seemed to be an oracle to the rest, spoke up. He quoted a rustic epitaph:

> Here lies Moore—
> This is not he!
> Moore is no more!—
> How can this be?

"There, schoolmaster," he concluded, "I bet thee cassn't turn that into Latin!"

In "next to no time" the schoolmaster answered:

Snowshill village
Cranham

Hic jacet Plus—
Plus non est hic :
Plus est *non plus!*
Quo modo sic?

Though the heckler knew no Latin, it was agreed that the intended victim had scored.

"As sure as God's in Gloucestershire," is explained by some as referring to the number and splendour of the religious houses before the Reformation. Others see in it a specific reference to Hailes Abbey, where the relic of the Holy Blood was preserved from 1270 to 1539.

Blest is the eye
'Twixt Severn and Wye,

praises, without overpraising, an enchanting stretch of country.

"To hold a candle to the devil" is to offer politic homage to a knave. In 1584 a rustic named Philimore was seen carrying a sugarloaf. Sugar was dear then. "Where are you going with that?" inquires a gossip. Now Philimore was taking it as a gift to placate Sir Thomas Throckmorton, a tyrannical squire. Sinking his voice to a whisper, Philimore smilingly answered : "To hold a candle to the devil!" Rash confession! Ill-timed jest! The gossip told the County, and a bevy of mischief-makers told Sir Thomas Throckmorton. "At the next muster, hee sent two of ffilimores sonnes soldiers into the Low Countries, where the one was slayne, and the other at a deere rate redeemed his returne."

The four following sayings I owe to an old servant who, when I had asked her once to give the dog a run as my wife and I were to be out that afternoon, regaled that tough bull-terrier with a specially cooked milk pudding and a hot-water bottle! Some readers may think that an anecdote so trivial should find no place in this book. I disagree. If Hamlet thought it worth noting that "one may smile, and smile, and be a villain," let *me* note as an offset that not even a world war will harden a heart that is naturally kind.

"Sprack as a banty-cock" was one of her sayings. "Sprack" is a frequent word with us. We apply it to a woman who dresses "flash," or to a man who swaggers. "Sprack" is the

Berkeley Castle
Detached tower of Berkeley Church

exact counterpart of the Scotch "sprush." Burns makes use of this word :

> Cock up your beaver,
> And cock it fu' sprush,
> We'll over the border
> And gie them a brush!

"Black as the devil's nutting-bag" was one of her vivid similes; and "The black crow haven't trod on her foot yet" was her proverbial way of saying that a child was happy.

> A whistling maid, and a crowing hen,
> Frighten the devil out of his den!

Our old friend would apply this to any ultra-masculine type of woman. If indeed the proverb originated in Gloucestershire, then it perhaps took its rise amongst the sailors of the port of Bristol. For it is generally agreed that the "maid" is an euphemism for the witch who whistles up the winds to sink a ship, whilst her *hen crows* ominously, predicting death!

"The cuckoo flies when hay's cut; he can't abide the bustle."

"They've left the gate open at Bisley."

This saying is quite local. Bisley lies roughly north of Bussage, and the snow-wind reaches us from the direction of that high-lying, picturesque little town.

"A man from Nailsworth"—that is a liar. Why, no folklorist has put on record.

"A man from Cainscross"—he leaves the door open! Why? Again, I must admit ignorance. I was waiting my turn to "play the winners" at darts, one bitterly cold winter night, at the Bear—the famous old, and typically Cotswold inn—at Bisley, when a fellow decamped, leaving the door open. Hereupon, addressing the universe at large, everybody exclaimed, "He comes from Cainscross!"—when the delinquent returned, and shut it!

Another way of giving a discreet hint is to ask, "Do you live in a tent?" that is "Have you no doors at home?"

"This do make 'ee tell th' truth!" Spoken of an east wind; that is, this is torture! A proverbial saying dating doubtless from days when judicial torture was still practised.

"Hats off to the magpies!" combines homely wit and folk-lore. Owing to their predilection for gossip, these handsome black and white birds, the "prattling pies" of Elizabethan poets, are thought of collectively as feminine.

> One for sorrow,
> Two for mirth—

Yes, I know. But sorrow will not trouble you if you forestall it by raising your hat to them. Although they may not appear to notice your gesture, make no doubt about it, they do! They will think you a pleasant fellow, and a friend to the sex. Win the ladies to your side, and the battle is won!

"Put up a notice in your henhouse," says the farmer, "with NO EGGS—NO FOOD upon it." "Can hens *read*?" "They can read *that*," says he, laughing, "well enough!"

"Scratch Gloucestershire and find Rome." No county is richer than this in Roman remains.

"The Nightingale and the Blindworm were born one-eyed." "Lend me your eye, dear Blindworm," the great singer entreated, "I am invited to a party, and really I shall be ashamed to be seen at it if I go with only one eye."

"What you ask is a great matter, signorina," the Blindworm answered her, "but I am so enchanted with your singing that I can deny you nothing!"

And therewith he gave it her.

At the party, the Nightingale was a sensation, and the birds complimented her both upon her virtuosity and personal charm.

"How did the party go off?" inquired the Blindworm.

"Oh, admirably! I was the hit of the evening. I knew I should be!"

"Haven't you forgotten something?" inquired the Blindworm.

"N-no. I think not."

"My eye that you borrowed!"

"That I shall never return!"

"Then I shall take it back from you when you are asleep!"

"Thanks for telling me," says she; "to keep myself from going to sleep then, I shall sing all night!"

The moral is obvious. If you have fallen in love with a

woman for her singing, give her nothing at all until you have made inquiries as to her character of a magistrate, justice of the peace, barrister-at-law, commissioner for oaths, duly qualified solicitor, or her banker, upon the appropriate buff form, obtainable at any post-office. N.B.—Should any reader desire to compare my treatment of this excerpt from the Nightingale's history with my original, he should consult the duodecimo folio which lies in the great bay-window at Grasshopper Hall.

WANSWELL—the name implies "Well of Woden," that grotesque Germanic god who gave his name to Wednesday —is to be found half a mile east from Wanswell Green; or if you approach it from another direction, then one and a quarter miles north of the cross-roads at Berkeley. Like so many more of our Gloucestershire wells and springs, this doubtless was at one time sacred to the Roman nymphs, until they fled affrighted at the approach of the Hunnish Woden with his wolfish hankering after human sacrifices. Their terror reflects credit upon them.

The reputation of the waters for curative virtues, and for sanctity generally, clung to Wanswell throughout the Middle Ages and, unaffected by the dissolution of the monasteries, survived into comparatively modern times. Later the stream was converted into supplying the domestic requirements of Berkeley Castle, and the spot where the water is collected is covered by an unromantic iron shed. Vast was the resort of travellers to Wanswell. The girls there were buxom, blithe and compliant. The pilgrims were endowed with the holiday spirit. And the proverb arose that

> All the maids of Wanswell
> May dance in an eggshell!

"What is the meaning of 'he has *green fingers*'?" "Why! Don't you know that? It means 'everything he plants grows : he's a good gardener.'"

> Sheep for clover, and clover for bees,
> Wool and honey from clover leas;
> Sheep for wool, and wool for wealth,
> Bees for honey, and honey for health!

The gibes which are thrown out against many counties are often, rightly considered, rather complimentary than the reverse. The oft-quoted scoff that "Gloucestershire men are donkeys and long-eared 'uns" is of this type. As abuse, it carries an absurdity in the face of it for, to be "long-eared" is, in a donkey, a sign of breed. A short-eared donkey would be a monstrosity.

In the days before railways our Gloucestershire hill villages were self-contained communities. They baked their own bread, brewed their own beer, sheared their own sheep and wore the wool upon their backs, woven into imperishable broadcloth by cottage weavers. Such articles of refinement or luxury as the villages did not produce were brought from the towns in panniers by the hardy race of pack-donkeys. One such beast, particularly remarkable for the length of his silky ears, was purchased by a covetous rascal who shamefully overtasked him. So spirited was this beautiful creature that for one word of encouragement he would trudge another half-dozen miles. Only now and again he would look inquiringly at his master, as who should say, "Are we going on for ever?" And on such occasions of mute appeal, the rogue would answer, "Thee've only gone but one mile or under! Thee cassn't be tired already."

One day the poor beast had carried up the hills a dozen of claret for Squire, as much of burgundy for Parson, and 'baccy and brandy for the clerk. He bore a new spinning-wheel also for the cooper's wife who was industrious, and a new gown and French laces for the miller's daughter, who was a great beauty and wished to kill as many beaux as possible at the fair. Up the hills stumbled the poor donkey, and looked his question. "Thee hassn't bin but a mile yet," says the pedlar, mocking him. Suddenly with a lurch the poor beast rolls over and, in the authentic burr of the county, utters his last—and first—words.

Glaascestershire miles be long 'uns.

Which became the proverb you will have heard. Then why blush to be a "long-eared 'un"? The Gloucestershire donkey was shrewd, for he suspected the trick put upon him. He showed grit. And he died game. He was also intelligent, for although most donkeys are suspected of understanding English, I will maintain it against an oracle that not one in a thousand speaks it. The Gloucestershire donkey did. And what he said was to the point.

From the sayings of the people, to their sports, the transition is easy.

Trainers of Commandos in search of novel strenuosities might do worse than visit Cooper's Hill, two miles from Birdlip village, upon the occasion of the annual Cheese Rolling on Whit-Monday. You turn off by the Stone House from the road which runs between Birdlip and Cranham Corner, walk along a pleasant country stile-path, and then round, or over, the ancient camp, built, it is believed, by the Britons (but modernized by the Romans), to the opposite side. So far there has been nothing to remind us that we are on a hill; there has been no extensive view about us, and the going has been over tolerably level ground. But now abruptly we find ourselves at a point beyond which the ground falls away, in semi-precipitous slopes, to the fertile valley of the Severn below. A glorious panorama confronts us. We are in oldest England. Antiquity and modernity meet and intermingle. The juncture of two Roman roads comes into view, the Foss Way and Irmin Street. To the right, spread out there like a map, lies the extensive aerodrome of Brockworth. A sunlit plane takes off. Another lands.

A maypole marks the rallying-point of the Cheese Rollers. It is not a gay painted affair like that at Whiteshill six miles away, but a pleasing relic for all that, with a weathercock for a crown. The Master of the Ceremonies stands by in smock-frock and beaver hat. An enormous crowd eye him intently, and await the signal. The rope which holds them back drops. His pistol rings out sharp and clear, a cheese goes bowling down the slopes, and a horde of rustic sportsmen precipitate themselves forwards and downwards after their singular quarry.

The sport dates back to the early Middle Ages, when it was inaugurated to protect the common-land about the maypole with its valuable grazing rights from inclosure. My theory is that this sport was in effect, in the first instance, a species of *acted* round-robin. The object of that form of petition is to make it impossible to guess who first applied his signature. So with the rolling. It must have been a keen-sighted man who detected the first trespasser amongst a hundred roaring rustics hunting a cheese!

I was given a tip by a knowing road-mender who formerly, in the teeth of the most furious competition, achieved the coveted prize.

"Wear spiked boots," said he. "Unless you wear spiked boots, there's no keeping your footing on they slopes. It bean't to be done."

"Good," thought I, "until you set your heel upon the other fellow's uppers!"

"Will cheese-rolling survive this second world war?"

"Of course!" chimes in a friendly hedger-and-ditcher, "Us were cheese-rolling bevore new-fangled vootball an' cricket were thought on!"

The Master of the Ceremonies, that sturdy old man who has officiated for the last twenty-three years, hospitably invited me into his cottage, and regaled me with a host of interesting and sometimes lurid details. On one occasion a would-be spectator made the grievous mistake of coming out to witness the conflict, not from the hill downwards, but from the valley upwards. Obeying the mysterious laws of gravity as it leaped and bounded, the flying cheese caught this unhappy gentleman in the pit of the stomach and killed him outright. How came the village epitaph-maker to neglect this golden opportunity for his art?

> Here lies Billy if you please,
> Hit in the stomach with a cheese;
> Cheese is holsum fare they say—
> It turned Billy into clay!

The famous cheese itself, once a fat Double Gloster, is to-day a mere symbol. It is, I blush to say, a rubber cheese, and even this may yet go for salvage!

My old M.C. shows me the uniform in which he officiates : his smock-frock. Surely his must be the last garment of this type throughout the length and breadth of England to be publicly worn. The front is ornamented with curious stitching, and dating, as it does, from that honest epoch before the politicians began to promise us, at our own expense, the last of their batch of brave new worlds, it still shows little trace of wear.

"Is Bill showing you his 'shimmy'?" his old lady chaffs him. And "Bill" shows me his hat, which is not, as invariably reported, a "topper," but a genuine white beaver contemporary with the smock. In hats of this type Regency Bucks, if they favoured the "Fancy," would dash off in their curricles to see the "Black Diamond" mill Bob Gregson or Jem Belcher go down in a dust-up with the "Game Chicken." About the hatband, "Bill" has knotted six gay ribbons. "One for each of my mourners," says he, "when I pass on : favours for remembrance." Once, Bill tells me, long ago, a tragedy turned the mirth at one of these meetings into mourning. Whilst the young fellows chased the cheese, the young women were racing, upon the flat ground, for a smock. One light-heeled wench easily outdistanced all her fellows, caught the smock, flourished it about her head in triumph, and even as the cheering burst out, suddenly fell stone-dead !

"To-day," says Bill, "the cheese is rolled, and there'll be a tug-o'-war an' such, an' there be an' end. But in my young days, every brewery for miles about sent us a barrelful *free* ! So soon as the beer-wagon came in sight the fun began, and not one of us dreamed of leaving whilst a single drop o' that remained. After the cheese had been rolled, there were donkey-races, and dancing and gallivanting; and the boys and girls never thought about going home until it were breakfast time the morning after. Happy days !"

Chapter XI

THE COTSWOLD BACCHUS

One does not to-day think of England as a wine-producing country. So-called "British wines" are made from grapes which are pulped on the Continent. After a certain time the effervescence is artificially checked, when the results are sent to England. Here the effervescence is artificially provoked once more. This, I am told, is the process. To my mind, the result is not a drink for the discriminating winelover, but a chemical experiment, of interest only to the scientist. "We'll drink a good bottle," I pictured him saying, "come into the *laboratory*!"

But there was—incredible though it may seem to-day—an English wine-producing county *par excellence*. That county was Gloucestershire. Nowhere else does one find so many ancient houses whose names recall the tradition, and indeed often date back to the great eras of Gloucestershire wine-making: "The Vines," "The Vineyard." I was looking the other day at one of our hills which stretches in an undulating curve from east to west, in such a fashion as to catch both the early morning and late afternoon sun.

An old man, whose approach I had not noticed, observed, "That bank used to be called the 'Monks' Vineyard.'"

"Where did they get their vines from?"

"Gascony: by ship."

This statement he made categorically, and I see no reason to question its truth. Tradition dies hard in this county. The innkeeper of a neighbouring village said, as he pointed me out an aged yew in his garden, "They used to make bows of that tree!" Many and many a time have the traditions of a village proved to be well founded to the confusion of academic sceptics.

Probus, a late Roman Emperor—he was only assassinated A.D. 282—"granted to all Gauls, to the men of Spain, and to the Britons, the right to have vines and to make wine, as a reward for having refused to help Bonosus and Proculus, in their revolt of the Germans." In his *The History of the Wine Trade in England* M. André Simon scouts the belief that Probus is to be regarded, in consequence of this passage, as the father of English viticulture—a notion to which I must confess I was always tenderly attached. "The Britanni," says this author, "was a name applied by the Romans to the Gauls settled in the extreme west of France, and to some German tribes who, in this instance, were the most likely to be of any help to Probus or the revolted generals in Germany."

But as I am unwilling to throw Probus overboard, let us see what may be said for the other side of the question. There may well have been British levies in the imperial army and these men Probus might later desire to reward. He would hardly neglect Britain in raising levies, for Probus fought on the grand scale. When, for instance, he turned his arms against the Sarmatians, those enemies of the Empire, he had already—apart from wounded and the fliers —left dead upon the field four hundred thousand other Barbarians. Astounding figures! We might be studying the days of enlightenment, of mass education, and not the pre-gas, pre-tank and pre-plane pagan world!

M. Simon quotes Tacitus as saying that neither the olive nor the vine was grown in Britain. True; but we must bear in mind that Tacitus antedates Probus. The latter died one hundred and four years after Tacitus published his *Agricola,* the history in which we find this statement. That *humor terrarum cœlique*—that is the British *weather*—of which Tacitus speaks as inimical to the vine, by no means proves that no attempts at viticulture were made above a century *after* his death. I myself despite the *humor terrarum* have smoked British tobacco grown in Norfolk and am unlikely to forget its effects upon my throat! One further point. Vopiscus, who tells us about Probus, the Britons, and their vines, was that Emperor's *biographer*. As such he would obviously be at pains to sift evidence and verify facts. All turns, of course, upon our interpretation of the word *Britanni*. This *may* refer to the then dwellers in modern Brittany : it *may* refer to the members of some Germanic tribe living south of the Rhine. But in the absence of any qualifying epithet it seems, to me at least, more probable that the best-known of the "Britons," the Britanni of Britannia, are those implied. Whilst protesting myself pro-Probus, let me take this opportunity of expressing my unqualified admiration of M. Simon's authoritative *History of the Wine Trade in England*, a work as fascinatingly lucid as it is superlatively well documented.

That the early Christian missionaries drank wine appears certain, and may be regarded upon evidence which M. Simon puts forward as proved. If the Saxon invaders destroyed or merely neglected the vines they found growing at the time of their incursions, later they must have repented of their folly and made good their destruction, for when William the Norman made his famous survey he scheduled in Domesday Book, in an England of four or five millions, no less than thirty-eight vineyards. A chronicler of King Stephen's day for whose accuracy modern historians vouch testifies to the quality and abundance of English wine. "Gloster, with its Vale, can show richer vineyards than can any other county, the wine of which is by no means disagreeable to the palate, and has no disagreeable sharpness of taste, being little inferior in sweetness to that of France."

After describing, in his virile and vivid style, a flock of Cotswold sheep—its ram and bell-wether being crowned, in Elizabethan festal fashion, with garlands—Drayton, in his *Polyolbion*, goes on to give us the merrymaking. The shepherd whose flock has yielded the first lamb of the year is King of the Feast.

But Muse, returne to tell, how there the Sheepheards
    King,
Whose flock hath chanc't that yeere the earliest Lambe
    to bring,
In his gay Bauldrick sits at his lowe grassie Bord,
With Flawns, Curds, Clowted-creame, and Country
    dainties stor'd :
And, whilst the Bag-pipe playes, each lustie jocund
    Swaine
Quaffes Sillibubs in Kans, to all upon the Plaine,

And to their Country-girles, whose Nosegays they doe
  weare,
Some Roundelayes doe sing; the rest the burthen beare.

There you have the Cotswolds of pre-Puritan England.
That light-heartedness and freedom from self-consciousness
in rejoicing we Englishmen have never recaptured. The
"roundelayes," when not ballads with a refrain in which
everybody could join, would be those lyrics of the song books,
which were *poetry*, for the excellent reason that as verse had
not as yet been mechanized, only the poets wrote it. It comes
as something like a shock of pleasant surprise when one
reads, in Walton's *Compleat Angler*, of the milkmaid's singing that song of beautiful magic, Marlowe's "Come live with
me, and be my love." That we were then a singing people we
know from the independent testimony of many foreign, no
less than of native observers. There was then neither the
wolf-like howling, nor the shocking sentimentality of the still
lingering Victorian songs of the village pubs, nor the dusty
teetotalism of those little affairs in that Avalon of the old
maid, the village hall of to-day.

As round dances the Elizabethan were more interesting
to look at than the modern, although they were not, therefore, necessarily more enjoyable to dance. And there would
be kissing, of course, an integral part of the older English
country dance. Here parenthetically is the last figure of
"Paul's Steeple," as it is set forth in a polite, illiterate little
manual of 1651 (though the dance was old then) for the
"sons of ingenious gentlemen."

"First man takes his woman in his left hand. Lead her
down to 2 woman. Take the 2 woman in your right hand,
and setting them back to back, kisses the two, then your own
woman, turning off into your places."

Well might Dutch Erasmus say of England, in a letter to
a friend at Leyden, "The girls here are soft, winning, and
beautiful as the Muses," and "*quocumque te moveas, undique
basiatur* (whithersoever you betake yourself, there's kissing
on all sides)."

Such were the songs and such the dances in Drayton's
Cotswold shepherds' feast. An element of bathos intrudes

itself when we come to the drinkables. His "lustie swaines" drink "sillibubs," or wine, cream, and sugar mixed, from "kans"; which speaks little for their palates, but the world for their digestive systems !

"We'll to the tavern, and snap up a pint or two of wine," a rustic tells his lass, in a sunshiny comedy of the "spacious days," by Robert Greene. How have we declined from the amenities ! To-day the country labourer never tastes the juice of the vine, unless it be that travesty upon port which is sometimes to be met with in country alehouses—and then it will assuredly not be a "pint or two," but a very small glass at a very stiff price !

Yes, in Elizabeth's days the vine-dresser still earned his keep.

> In her days every man shall eat in safety,
> Under his own vine.

Wine gave the adventurers dash, the poets brilliance ! The flowers of the English Renaissance had their roots in wine. In the long gallery of his portraits, Shakespeare presents us with but one teetotaller, Adam, in *As You Like It.* After boasting, as they always do, of his aberration—to everybody's intense inconvenience—this trying peasant swoons away in a forest, and has to be borne to a place of security by a young gentleman of normal diet.

The decline of our Cotswold vineyards was already in sight, as Drayton himself laments.

> For Gloster in times past her selfe did highly prize,
> When in her pride of strength she nourisht goodly
>   Vines,
> And oft her cares represt with her delicious Wines.

Gloucestershire was still producing wine, but there was not the "frequencie of this benefit as in the old time." The cause of this decline is variously attributed to "the soil's old age . . . like a woman growing sterile," to some "change of place" on the part of the earth itself; to the "influence of the planets," and to the "sun's declination from us."

Meteorology is a science of late growth. Our forebears neither systematized nor recorded their observations upon weather conditions. The soil can hardly have changed. It is still thin, and this is what is wanted, for vines prefer the scanty nourishment of a rough hillside. They like air too and plenty of it. They must not be crowded together. Well, these conditions could be perfectly satisfied to-day. But more is needed. A combination of temperate climate with a high summer temperature, if viticulture is to be a success, is a *sine qua non*. Now, in England to-day the mean temperature is not lower than that of some wine-producing countries, but our normal summer is insufficiently sunny; and less so, I fancy, in the Cotswolds than in East Anglia or the south. It follows that one or other of two things must have happened, either our ancestors in the Middle Ages enjoyed a hotter summer—balanced, no doubt, by a colder winter—than we do to-day, or else that they were contented with very inferior drink. This second alternative is, surely, inadmissible. Through our Norman kings we were then closely linked up with France. Normandy was English ground. Its towns had English names. Our rich men at least must have known what good wine was. A hotter summer and a colder winter must be the true answer to our English vine-growing. William FitzStephen, in his twelfth-century *Description of London*— a fascinating document—gives us a vivid picture of the London boys skating, with bone skates, over the frozen marsh which is to-day Moorfields. FitzStephen speaks as though this was a normal winter occurrence. Bone skates, it may be added, have been dug up in Moorfields in modern times. On the other hand, this winter of our ancestors' being balanced with a hotter average summer is at least arguable from the projecting eaves of so many ancient houses—those of the Inns of Court, for example. Was not this style of construction intended originally to provide shade?

"Bristol Milk" we hear of in King Charles II's glorious days, and, despite Dutchmen in the Thames, glorious they were both in arts and arms. But whereas the term denotes to-day a sherry of surpassing excellence, it is now generally agreed that the drink which, under that name, delighted old-time Bristolians was not wine at all, but a milk punch made with that Jamaica rum which (together with the turtle) was a product of our trade with the West Indies. Mr Pepys

became acquainted with this beverage at the house of one
Mr Butts, with whose appearance, as a solid, reliable
burgher, he was much impressed. He closely resembled "one
of our grave London merchants." Fortunately this "gravity"
cast no languishing spell over the kitchen staff : "And so
brought us back by surprise to his house, where a substantial
good house, and well-furnished, and did give us good enter-
tainment of strawberries, and a whole venizon-pasty, cold,
and brave wine, and above all Bristol Milk."

Well, the Cotswold vines yielded up their last rubies, but
our tradition in wines is a sound one. A noted wine shop,
still flourishing, opened in Cirencester in 1760, the year when
George III ascended the throne, "amiable in manners, pure
in character, and full of good intentions." Later he became
mental : Cupid's revenge perhaps on too much virtue ! They
founded a Bristol branch in 1788. Another noted firm, also
still flourishing, opened up at Bristol in 1793, the year when
Britain joined the "First Coalition" against Napoleon's
France.

As native wine-growing decreased in Gloucestershire, the
manufacture of perry and cider began to take its place.
Cromwell's adherents, "ces imbéciles les puritains," as
Alexandre Dumas somewhere calls them, were the first to
impose taxes upon wines, spirits, cider and perry. The cider-
makers survived, however. But in 1763 the short-lived
ministry of Lord Bute patched up peace with France, and to
fill up the deficit caused by the war secured the passing of an
Act to impose something almost modern in the way of an
excise duty upon cider. Both the peace and the tax were
abhorrent to the Diehards of the West. Instead of the peace
proclamation being hailed with the crash of joybells, the
churches tolled as though for a funeral ! At Cheltenham, we
learn from the *Bristol Journal* of 23rd April 1763, the official
document was read by "a youth in mourning." Many farmers
are said to have given away cider gratis to the populace
rather than pay the tax. To give the detested gaugers no
pretext for visiting him one extremist dug up his apple-
orchards ! Unsapped as yet by the omnipresent tentacles of
our modern bureaucracy everybody kicked. The following
appears in *Felix Farley's Journal* of 22nd July 1763 :

"Great Numbers of Excisemen took up their Qualifications at our Quarter Sessions last Week. Some of the Subterranean Gentry [the miners] of the Forest of Dean are determined to take all that come within their Reach to the Regions below. One of the Brethren of the Stick [gaugers] was last Week catched by these Sons of Darkness in going his Rounds to the Cyder-Mills, and was instantaneously hurried down two or three hundred feet under Ground, where he now takes up his Abode. The Colliers, it is said, use him well, and he lives as they do; but they swear the Day of his Resurrection shall not come to pass till the Cyder-Act is repealed, or, at least, till Cyder-Making is over."

Four days later *The Bristol Journal* returns to the case again: "The Cyder Exciseman, who was some time since seized by the Colliers in Gloucestershire and carried into their Subterranean Regions, is still in the Pit with them; and they positively declare he shall not be at Liberty till the Act is repealed." The ultimate fate of the rascally gauger is not recorded. He is lucky to have been able to obtain from the colliers the same provisions as they enjoyed themselves. I am confident I have read in some early journal or pamphlet of a gauger's being caught and given no eatables at all during his term of imprisonment, being forced, as a reprisal, to subsist solely upon gin.

At Ledbury the anti-cider-tax demonstrators organized a mock funeral on a Homeric scale. "A procession was made through the principal parts of the town by the servants of the cider merchants, coopers, farmers, and some poor labourers, with numbers of poor people, the day the Cider Act took place; men with drums covered with black crape beating the dead march, drumsticks reverted; two mutes with crape hatbands and black cloaks; an empty barrel upon a bier carried by six poor farmers. Two men followed, the one with an empty can upon his head, upon the top of which was a branch of an apple tree with apples growing on it, both bough and can covered with crape. The other bore upon his shoulder the tools made use of by the woodmen when they fell trees. He wore funereal black. The church bells were rung muffled all day.

"Others moved in the matter besides the poor. The High

View from the Cotswold Escarpment at Frocester
Duntisbourne Rous, a farm

Sheriffs and the Grand Jury at the summer assizes subscribed their names to an address to their Parliamentary representatives. Later the High Sheriff called a meeting to consider 'the most proper method for obtaining a redress of those grievances which the makers of cyder and perry are subject to by the late Act.' "

As always in the eighteenth century, we find the clergy forward to prevent the exploitation of legitimate and moderate drinkers. A meeting of protest was called, the rendezvous chosen being the still flourishing Bell in Gloucester. But so many of the "principal gentlemen, clergy, and freeholders" put in an appearance that no inn could have contained them. So they repaired instead to the Booth Hall. The agitation proved successful, and as a direct result of the spirited opposition of all parties and classes of the community, in 1766 the hated impost was abolished. Cider is still brewed in Gloucestershire, and is a favourite beverage with many at the country inns. But it is no longer, as in the past, a thing taken for granted, like bread or salt. Modern taxation has put it yet again into the category of luxuries.

A fireside tale comes from Chalford village. In some time not exactly specified, but generally given as Victorian, a workman was called in to carry out repairs upon the understructure of an ancient house. Whilst he was at work in the cellar the fore half of his pick slipped astonishingly through the wall. Devoured by a very human curiosity, he had soon so improved the hole as to be able to insert his body and survey the secret chamber at his ease with candle and matches. Three mighty vats he viewed, filled to their very brims with golden liquor : vats in which a man might drown. Sampling their contents after the fashion of a thirsty horse which has at last discovered a cattle trough, he arrived at the conclusion that he had brought to light a long-forgotten hoard of perry of a degree of potency never before known to man ! Several hours passed before he emerged from the profound slumber into which his experimental researches had plunged him. He prepared to leave, but before he did so he had sufficient wit to cover the hole he had made in the cellar wall with sacking. Then and then only did he revisit the upper air. He arrived for work next morning with a couple of

Cottages at Bibury
Broadway Church

"empties" concealed amongst the tools in his canvas bag, and he returned with two "fulls" for supper that evening. Fundamentally a good fellow, he could not refrain from borrowing a bottle from a friend, assuring him at the same time, with a prodigious air of secrecy, that he should "have he back at night, villed wi' zummat good!"

But the recipient of the gift was also inquisitive. The favour being repeated, the friend could not fail to observe that, although his benefactor never went to the tavern, yet he never wanted for liquor. *Ergo*, he must obtain his supplies at the house where he worked. It was soon to be a case of other friends, other bottles! Labour upon the foundations of the old house proceeded slowly, with frequent intervals for refreshment. That the ladies should long be excluded from the secret was manifestly impossible. Men are such poor dissemblers that the "mere male" who endeavours to appear virtuous might *ipso facto* serve as artist's model for an Academy picture to be entitled "Richard Turpin before the Lord Chief Justice."

Oh, stony Chalford, how art thou about to be transformed! In the grim and gardenless village every face began now to wear a smile, and many a good fellow planted an unsteady foot as he returned home of an evening from his labours. But are we to credit the schoolmaster who, as he no-heeled his fifth brimmer, declared that it was Bacchus himself whom he beheld, his glowing curls interwreathed with vine-tendrils and ivy-buds, reclining, in godlike ease, beside the innermost vat? Was it not said that even now, after Heaven knows how many centuries, the god still appeared with a cup, which he proffered to hunters in the Forest of Dean, so soon as they reached a certain haunted grove and exclaimed, "I thirst!" But what inclined the thoughtful to embrace the schoolmaster's opinion that there was something more than mortal about these vats of perry was that the village began to wear now a veritable air of carnival. All was quaffing, laughing, backchat, and song! But the spectacle of so much human happiness was as gall to the "unco' guid"! With face as long as the proverbial violin, at dusk when his comrades the bats were flying, an informer stole forth and denounced the merrymakers. Top-hatted "peelers" arrived whilst a great moon climbed slowly aloft and watched regretfully.

They entered the secret chamber by the hole in the wall, desecrated the laughing lakes with buckets, and sent the ambrosial liquor, aflame now with a thousand witching tints and moonshiny sparkles, swirling away down the gutters. Alas! . . .

The recipe for "Gloucestershire Punch" I owe to Dr and Mrs Hoffman of Cranham, at whose hospitable home, when seeing in the New Year, I have sampled its merits upon more occasions than one. It is excellent: it is old: it is English. *Experto crede.* Our Georgian forefathers brewed it, as the Doctor brews it to-day.

Ingredients.—Two bottles whisky, half-bottle Jamaica rum, one bottle sherry, two large glasses orange curaçao, water in quantity equal to above.

Method.—Bring the water to the boil, and put in six sliced lemons in a muslin bag, together with one quarter of a pound of sugar. Add the whisky, rum and sherry. Bring to the simmer. (N.B.—It is important that the curaçao be added last.) Remove lemons and add more sugar to taste. Punch is an essentially midwinter drink, and when there is snow on our hills and a knife-blade in the air, "Gloucestershire Punch" has only to be tasted to be appreciated. It should, of course, be served "hotter than hot."

Punch will naturally remind Dickensians of Mr Pickwick, whose predilection for that beverage and the somnolence which it induced led upon one unforgettable occasion to his incarceration in the pound. But Dickens also shows us his hero in Gloucestershire regaling with Mr Bob Sawyer, Mr Benjamin Allen, and his servant Sam Weller at one of the noblest of our ancient inns.

"At the Hop Pole at Tewkesbury, they stopped to dine; upon which occasion there was more bottled ale, with some more Madeira, and some Port besides; and here the case-bottle was replenished for the fourth time. Under the influence of these combined stimulants, Mr Pickwick and Mr Ben Allen fell fast asleep for thirty miles, while Bob and Mr Weller sang duets in the dickey."

Many of our farmers brew their own home-made wine.

I have tasted elderberry, cowslip, dandelion and so forth. I have heard our old men declare that "turnip can be made stronger than any whisky!" Though not to be thought of in comparison with the genuine grape-wines of the wine-producing countries, these flower-wines have a distinctive flavour, can be exhilarating, and are not unpalatable. For the benefit of the curious, I will give the recipe for dandelion wine.

Ingredients.—Four quarts of dandelion heads; four quarts of boiling water, three pounds loaf sugar, one inch whole ginger, one lemon, thinly peeled rind of one orange, one tablespoonful of brewers' yeast, moistened with water.

Method.—Put the petals of the flowers into the bowl, pour the boiling water over them, and let the bowl remain covered several days, meanwhile stirring well and frequently. Strain the liquid into the preserving-pan, add the rinds of the orange and lemon both peeled off into thin strips, the sugar, ginger, and the lemon proper, having first thinly sliced it and stripped it of every particle of pith. Boil gently for about an hour and, when cool, add the yeast upon a slice of toast. Allow it to stand for two weeks when the effervescence should be over, or sufficiently so for the liquid to be transferred to the cask. Keep well bunged down for a year. Then bottle and keep for one to two years before drinking.

So late as Edwardian times, when spirits were not sold at prices prohibitive to the poor, the country custom was to add two pints of brandy to the liquid whilst it was in the preserving-pan, both to fortify and to accelerate fermentation, and one additional pint when the time came for casking. The result was, according to an old recipe-book I came upon the other day, "a refreshing and inexpensive drink." Three *pints* of brandy "*inexpensive*"? They *lived*, those ancestors of ours!

Chapter XII

COTSWOLD FARE

THE days of culinary adventures in Gloucestershire are
almost, although not quite, over. Speed, villainous speed,
hurries the specialities of a district into the remotest corners
of the land, and of other lands. One takes German mustard
with Argentine beef. One consumes *bouillabaise* in Soho.
There was a time when the devil avoided Cornwall. He
dreaded neither the holiness of hermit nor the piety of priest,
no; but he was terrified lest he might, by some wily
manœuvre, be kidnapped and smuggled into that pie of mystery, the Cornish pasty. He has outgrown, in our time, this
more than Freudian complex. All this might happen to him
now in the Mile End Road—so standardized do we all
become.

The only proverb which has to do with the *res culinaria*
of Gloucestershire does us less than justice.

> At Stow-on-the-Wold
> The wind blows cold,
> And the cooks have nothing to cook.

Let us hope that the allusion is to the poverty of the soil,
and consequent rarity of the more luscious of the fruits of
the earth, for there is no lack of cunning on the part of the
artists.

But if you are in doubt as to where to dine in any Gloucestershire market town, here is a suggestion. Find out, if
the market be on, when it will be "Farmers' Day"; then
inquire where the farmers go, and dine there. They may not
affect what a misogynistic friend once referred to as
"Women's food—Jazz and purple lobster!" but what you
do eat will be sterling stuff. Farmers know all about meat
and vegetables, and they prefer the carving-knife to the tin-
opener.

There are traditions in food to be met with. A lady of

this county informs me that her father always had his meat roasted with the jack. Further, that he was curious in the woods he employed, and would not, for example, eat roast beef if it had not been roasted before oak. For other dishes he preferred other woods. All this is a thing of the past, but by no means of the long-distant past. I have myself seen, in a wayside alehouse, that curious contrivance the double-jack. This instrument, so the landlady told me, they made use of only at Christmas, but then they roasted, at one and the same time, a sirloin and a fowl. By the same token, I remember the horse-pistol which hung on the taproom wall. When I taxed mine hostess with hanging up curiosities where they might be "discovered" and purchased by tourists, she replied with some heat, "That pistol were there when I were a child, and nobody have moved it zince!"

What is sometimes referred to as "good, old-fashioned, English cooking"—by which the genuine grills and roasts are implied—is rapidly becoming extinct, even with us in the country. The limited but excellent bill of fare of Regency to Edwardian days is still to be met with, I am assured, but in Australia. I understand, however, that tea is drunk with it *horresco referens!* One may bake, and well, in the gas-cooker, those joints which would formerly have been roasted before the open fire, but for the tin-opener there is nothing to be said whatever. It is a slovenly instrument which I should like to see as obsolete as the stone hatchet. Robbed of all its life-giving properties, much of the nation's vegetables, fish and meat (even the national roast beef!) comes from the tin. It will be a bad day for the national health if we—the beef and beer people *par excellence*—come to acquire a sentiment for eating rubbish. And now experiments are in progress for the wholesale dehydration of vegetables. This may be food for the crews of submarines when engaged upon active service, but Heaven forbid that we should regale them with it when they come ashore. Cookery is an art. It has nothing to do with science. The scientist should rule in his own laboratory. Were a scientist to put his nose within my kitchen more than once, I should buy a very fine, and fierce, Alsatian dog.

A farmer of a trifle under sixty gives me the following

particulars of his diet as a boy. "I was one of nine children, and as my father kept his own cows we had all the milk we could drink : gallons of it. We made our own cheese and butter, and my mother baked all our bread. None of us ever dreamed then of going to the baker's. We brewed our own beer too, which now would never be allowed : none of this chemical stuff ! We knew what went into it. As we kept fowls, there were always eggs, and roast chicken was to be had for the asking. Pigs too. We had those racks which you often see in the older style of farmhouse—those battens fixed beneath the kitchen ceiling—for hanging hams on to on hooks. Some people laughed at us for doing this. But it was the old way and—depend upon it—the right way. In course of time the hams became cured from the puffs of smoke which reached them day in, day out, from the fire. Wood-smoke, of course. We never burned anything but timber from our own trees. We made plenty of soup from fresh vegetables and milk. Our milk was always thick in cream. There's *fresh* milk you know and 'fresh'—ours wasn't *that* kind ! A quart of onion soup made with milk, and taken last thing before turning in, as supper, we thought a sovereign cure for a cold."

That may be taken as typical of a farmer's diet on the Cotswold hills in the years preceding the first World War. Not perhaps imaginative, but immensely sterling. In 1914 a car appeared in the village for the first time, a monstrous and ominous engine propelled by—I forget the name of the adventurous pioneer. Before then there had not even been the omnibus. Shoppers footed out the four-odd miles to our nearest town, made their purchases, and slogged back, their walk concluding with a stiffish climb as they drew towards home. Bread, however, dress materials, and such gear as pedlars commonly sell, kettles and saucepans and the like, were brought to us by the hardy race of pack-donkeys. For their better accommodation there was a regular *donkey-park,* where numbers were to be seen tethered, whilst their masters were regaling at the Rams and Lambs. This was before I settled here, but I *have* seen a woman on a pony with saddle-bags, and was informed that she regularly did her shopping in that fashion, riding from her house on the Cheltenham-

Stroud road to Gloucester town three times a week. And I have seen the last of the whole tribe of pack-donkeys, together with her packs into which, for they were deep, a very considerable quantity of loaves might be stowed away. This creature attained the unique distinction of being twice photographed professionally for two distinct series of picture-postcards. The poses chosen were admirable, but candour compels me to say that she was a dour brute who resented petting. Her name was Rose.

I return to farmers' fare. Most farmers and even farm-hands possessed sporting guns, and plentiful rabbits and an occasional hare helped to provide a welcome change of food. But I fancy the man was an original who was saying the other day, "I leave butcher's meat to my wife who likes it. I don't think it fresh. I shoot rabbits, starlings, blackbirds, sparrows and such, and she cooks them." And all those "smalé fowlés" to be plucked and prepared for table : a labour for Hercules !

A market gardener, the owner of a three-acre field, assures me that it is the rarest thing for any of his family to go into a shop to purchase foodstuff. "I grow all my own vegetables," he tells me, "and delicate stuff too—asparagus and such—the children love it. And we have ducks and their eggs, for a stream runs through my ground."

But the urbanization of the countryside proceeds apace. Except for the population of the big towns, and the miners of the Forest of Dean, Gloucestershire was formerly almost exclusively concerned with agriculture. To-day sixty thousand persons are engaged—in peacetime—in industries, and only twenty-five thousand in agriculture. With industrialization the instinct for keeping a good kitchen seems to die out. Tea is fast ousting supper as the last solid meal of the day, when tinned salmon will be followed by tinned fruit salad, and the *pièce de résistance* will be one of those florid cakes with margarine and plaster of paris sugar. Such grocers' delicacies grow in popularity. They must prove a boon to doctors and dentists.

I have often heard the older women complain that their children's teeth are not "what their own were," that the younger generation "live at the dentist's." Whether these statements are statistically sound or not, I am in no position to say, but they are current comment, and the reason given is always the same, namely the change from "honest food and home cooking" to the "tinned stuff."

The farmer whom I quoted above as giving me particulars of his diet as a boy explained to me also the method employed by his parents in pickling their hams. A Cranham lady who prepares a ham in this fashion every year, so as to have it ready against Christmas, gives me the recipe. Tewkesbury ham, it is called, when thus pickled.

"Rub thoroughly for ten consecutive days, daily, with salt, if the ham be a twenty-pounder. Place in a milk-pan or other large receptacle, and mix thoroughly one and a half ounces of saltpetre, one ounce bay salt, one ounce black pepper, one and a half ounces black treacle. When the above ingredients are thoroughly blended, baste your ham with them twice a day for three weeks. Now remove from the pickle, and hang a full day to drain. Smoke in peat. Allow two months to mature. Soak in cold water for twelve hours. Thus prepared, this ham will, with reasonable precautions, keep indefinitely. Now make a paste of flour and water, coat the ham with the paste, and bake, allowing twenty minutes to the pound."

From Painswick hails "Puppy-dog Pie." The reader having involuntarily turned pale, I hasten to reassure him. We Gloucestrians rarely eat dog. "Puppy-dog pie" is an ordinary meat pie, the peculiarity of which is that amongst the ingredients there must be a china dog. This is as essential as the ring and threepenny-piece are to the Christmas pudding. "Puppy-dog pie" is eaten once a year, on the day of the "Clipping of the Yews" in Painswick churchyard, when a special hymn is sung. (When last I witnessed the ceremony, a small boy in the crowd took fright. "What are they singing about, Father?" he cried in panic. "A wee song about a fox," his father replied. The child forwent his first intention of bellowing and smiled.) In the "Clipping" we are witnessing a pagan feast which the mellow wisdom of our ancestors incorporated with the Christian scheme. So late as the eighteenth century ale-mugs were carried into the churchyard—a trim and garden-like enclosure, in no way depressing—to mellow the throats of vocal rustics, whilst, crowned with flowers, the village girls danced. To-day the ancient love element is suppressed. Children, not marriageable maidens, wear the garlands and—does it not go without saying?—in this thin-faced time, the beer is banished.

"But why 'Puppy-dog pie'?" The china dog is symbolic of that live dog which the Romanized Cotswold shepherds once annually sacrificed during the *Faunalia*, or festival days of Faunus, the Latin Pan. In a well-known ode the poet Horace implores the god's protection for the young of his flock, promising that he, the poet, will have wine in plenty against the feast-day, and will fill those bowls which are the "companions of Venus." For the god was not only a patron of shepherds and their sheepwalks, but of their loves. For he himself was a wooer of the "flying nymphs," and to the eye of faith was accompanied in his progresses through wildest Gloucestershire with his train of satyrs. That those brimming cups which Horace thought of as love-potions yet found hazy survival in the ale-stoups of our Georgian rustics hardly admits of doubt. Alas! both girls and beer were banished by the Neo-Puritan pietist Robert Raikes (1735–1811), the sole representative of Gloucestershire's long and honourable list of men of thought and action to have his statue set up in the public gardens of the county's capital city.

Yet, honour where honour is due. Raikes visited the prisons of the old town, where smallpox and gaol-fever were rife. He administered moral and spiritual counsel to the inmates. He fed debtors. He distributed works of piety. He paid carefully selected old women a shilling per day to give Sunday Bible-readings to street urchins dragged from their games. He attempted to arouse, in all and sundry, *his* conception of the Higher Life. . . .

Let me confess and be hanged. I have met philanthropists both in books and life, but never have I met with one who seemed to me to be, in the amplest sense of the word, a *man*. In their enervating earnestness the type lack the saving grace of laughter. Fundamentally they are not quite human. What philanthropist would not heartily detest, as did Shakespeare's Malvolio, the burly manliness of Sir Toby, the femininity and wit of Maria, the catches and songs of bittersweet Feste, and all the strange power which they exercise over the heart?

You must not ask a poet to forgive the reformer who exorcized Venus, and proscribed Pan! . . .

"What were you telling me, Charlie, about 'Puppy-dog pie' in the old days your way?"

Thick-set, stocky Charlie, blue-eyed veteran of the '14–'18 war, smiles slowly.

"Doan't mention it then in Painswick of a Saturday night. They'm apt to be touchy like. You know the china dog which they puts in the pie once a year, when they clip the yews in the churchyard? Well, it were forty-five years ago, the Conservative Association held their annual banquet on that day. And there were fifty sat down to dinner in the hotel. As the pie were the seasonable dish, naturally that took first place, and a magnificent veal-and-ham were what it looked like. But the cook, who weren't from these parts, were wishful for to have a laugh of us, so he kills and skins a real puppy-dog, cooks it wi' all his art, look, and puts it in the pie.

"'How did you like the pie, gentlemen?' he asks the guests after dinner.

"'Fine!' says one.

"'Capital!' says another.

"'First-rate,' says a third gentleman. 'No one have never done us prouder than what you have to-night, William!'"

"And then it leaked out?"

"Yes; the truth comed out."

"But didn't they savage this culinary Mephistopheles for playing such a trick on them?"

"Well," says Charlie thoughtfully, "they'd said that they *liked* the pie, so they couldn't go back on their word now, could they? Besides," he adds, with just a touch of the gourmet's curiosity, "why shouldn't the pie be good? It was a *young* dog he'd cooked. . . . And you mustn't call Forest of Dean men 'bear-killers.'"

"How's that, Charlie?"

"Well, th' old lady only died a few weeks ago, at the age of eighty, and her father knew the man who killed the bear. Eighty's a good age for a woman, bean't it, zur?"

How tortuously complex is rustic simplicity!

"But, Charlie, if your old lady's father married young,

and lived to be eighty, like the daughter, that would *still* take him back no further than late Victorian times : so what about bears in the Forest of Dean ! "

"It weren't that. Th' bear were a performer, an' used to carry a pole around, an' dance, an' amuse people. His keeper had brought him to Gloucester, when th' bear an' he got separated somehow, and th' bear kept running up an' down amongst th' crowd, looking for his master. All th' ladies shrieked ! Not that they were frightened at all—they knew he were a tame bear—but to be interesting. An' then th' butcher—it were he were from th' Forest of Dean; an he didn't understand women at all—comed out from his shop wi' a gun, an' *shot* th' bear ! Then they all glared at him an' said 'You *brute* !' Well, they couldn't leave th' bear lying in the middle of th' street, so they carried it into th' butcher's shop and dumped it there. An' that were th' signal for all to make game of th' butcher who were wishful so to do.

" 'Oh, butcher,' says one on 'em, 'bean't bear in season now ? What about a nice bear steak ?'

" 'Or a nice loin chop then ? I'm told your bear chops be th' juiciest in town.'

"He were nigh mad before they'd done wi' him.

" 'Butcher,' says th' vlash barmaid o' th' Bell-wether, 'my sailor-lover's come home from sea——'

" 'From all th' seven seas, if it's your lovers !'

" 'Don't be cruel to a poor girl who's come to you for a helping hand ! I've got some red-currant jelly at home. Now do you think he would fancy some nice saddle of bear ?'

"But just then a lord comed along, an' offered the butcher money if he'd skin th' bear neatly an' sell him th' skin, which, of course, he did, to th' lord's satisfaction. I did hear how much money he got by it, but I forget just exactly : sovereigns an' all in gold : pounds which were pounds in they days, when beer were six pints to th' shilling ! So don't ever call th' Forest of Dean men bear-killers, nor mention bears when they're about. They'm touchy : an' they'm tough ! "

Lamprey pie is—or was—a Gloucestershire speciality. It is, as its name informs us, a pie in which the lamprey is the main ingredient. For centuries—dating from some hazy period in the Middle Ages—the city of Gloucester had the honour of supplying the reigning sovereign with an outstanding sample of this speciality. "A *royal* fish is the *lamphrey*," a Gloucestershire fisherman once assured me. Edward VII, who visited the town in an open victoria drawn by two superb bay horses—in the days of wasp-waists and picture-hats—was the last English king to receive the Pie.

Driving its plough between past and present, sharply dividing epoch from epoch, the first World War broke down the custom of centuries. But Mrs Smith, hostess of the Spread Eagle by Gloucester Market, has obligingly shown me the wooden moulds in which the crust was shaped, and which she preserves as a relic.

Whilst we are speaking of old customs, this would seem to be the place to mention those "courting spoons," several specimens of which are to be seen in the Bishop Hooper Museum, Gloucester. These are large wooden spoons, often ornamented with elaborate carving. They were widely used in Wales, and also in Gloucestershire in the Forest of Dean. When a courting youth judged the moment propitious for making his declaration, he did it by gesture: he handed her a spoon. The symbolism was perfectly understood: Rule my kitchen! Be my wife! Unless they come from the West, few of my readers will have heard of "courting spoons." But they may perhaps be acquainted with divers expressions, venerable by ancient custom, though rarely to be heard in Court circles: "A young spoony!" "He's spoony!" or "He's *spoons* on *her*!"

Elvers make their appearance in the Severn, and may be had in season in all fishmongers' shops. They must be thoroughly scoured by washing several times in salt and water, a thing commonly done in a muslin bag. Sometimes they are eaten simply after a rapid frying. A moment too long in the pan and the flavour is lost. Sometimes they are made into pies with other convenient ingredients, and sometimes potted. Here is a recipe from Brockworth and Witcombe villages as chronicled in *Gleanings from Gloucestershire Housewives*, a work with which no antiquary who likes his dinner will quarrel:

Ingredients.—One pound of elvers, two slices of bacon, two eggs.

Method.—Wash the elvers several times in salt water. Cook the bacon in the frying-pan. Break two eggs into the pan, and stir well. Cook until the elvers turn white. Dish up on the slices of bacon, and serve with a dash of vinegar.

We associate that not very exciting fruit, the banana, with Gloucestershire, and with reason, for in peacetime Avonmouth Port, Bristol, besides ten per cent of our grain and twenty-five per cent of our tobacco, imports its five millions of bananas annually. The Jamaicans who send us them make a very tolerable dish by frying them with eggs and rice, and flavouring them with saffron.

A large variety of edible snails often astonishes visitors to this county, as either these creatures do not thrive, or are less frequently to be observed, elsewhere. According to an uncontested tradition, these snails are the descendants of those formerly cultivated here by the Romans. Wherever we find Roman remains, there also we come upon the shells of oysters and of these edible snails. Pliny the Younger, if I recollect right, enumerates sea-urchins, eggs, lettuce and snails as hors d'œuvre to a dinner of which the intellectual element was to be, according to his guest's taste, an interlude, music, or declamations from Homer and Vergil. But to this exalted fare, combining snails and epic song, the expected friend preferred a supper of oysters with Spanish dancing-girls and never turned up.

The poet Spenser gives us a grimly humorous recipe for snails, which suggests that the Elizabethans—perhaps only those of them who lived in Gloucestershire—were not insensible to these creatures' charms as items in a bill of fare.

> With our sharp weapons we shal thee fray,
> And take the castill that thou liest in;
> We shal thee flay out of thy foule skin,
> And in a dish with onyons and peper,
> We shal thee dresse with strong vynegar.

I cannot pretend to know any Gloucestershire gentleman of repute whom curiosity has impelled to sample our Roman snails. But I have watched a tramp outside Birdlip village spearing them beneath the hedgerows with a pin and stick.

"You wouldn't like to give me sixpence, would you, gov'nor?"

"I should hate to," said I, "unless," I added hastily, for he had turned to go, "you tell me what you propose to do with those snails."

"*Do* with 'em? 'Borrow' a screw of salt, boil them in salt water in a tin, and *eat* them!" From emperors and pro-consuls and philosophers to tramps! Truly the decline of the snail in the world's regard is matter for tragedy!

The month for Severn salmon, as for all English salmon, is, of course, May. It is one of the beauties of that time of the year. Gloucestrians prefer this fish to its Scotch cousin, for its rich creaminess, and indeed for its freshness, as it does not reach us only after long train journeys. Severn, Queen of Rivers, seeks us out in the very heart of our country and regales us with her incomparable gifts. One may cook the treasure in many ways. I have even eaten it in the form of grilled steaks, the dryness imparted by the grilling being corrected by a rich Dutch or mousseline sauce. But such treatment betrays a certain wantonness. In normal times this might be done for the sake of variety. At the time of writing, the Government have long since "zoned" the fish, and at the word "zone," as though a spell had been cast, the salmon swam away in panic and have not been heard of since! They will return in due course, I will not suffer myself to doubt. My own vote is for salmon cold, after boiling in a well-thought-out stock, and then served with capers, cucumber, strips of anchovy, and home-made mayonnaise.

One thing more. As the salmon is a lady of rank, she herself would be the first to say "Since I see you are bent upon eating me, why, then, gentlemen, for the credit of human dignity and good manners, wash me down with a white wine of character; something full and flavoury, round and sound; of excellent bouquet, and not too sweet!"

CHAPTER XIII

SCHOOLS — BRISTOL GLASS

SCHOOLS

THE motto of the arms of Cheltenham is *Salubritas et eruditio*. It is happily selected, for besides its famous spa Cheltenham—as also Bristol—is nationally known as an educational centre.

To take Bristol first, we have of course its University, the importance and extent of which place it beyond the scope of a book of this nature. Within a comparatively short space of time Clifton College established a reputation as one of the leading public schools, although it was only founded in 1862, obtaining its Royal Charter fifteen years later. The ages of the pupils are from seven to eighteen; their number exceeds seven hundred. Clifton takes day-boys as well as boarders, and of the latter a substantial proportion are sons of Englishmen serving in professional capacities overseas. The Preparatory School buildings occupy a site facing the Downs, their dominating feature architecturally being the hexagonal lantern of the Chapel which lends dignity to the group. There are two quadrangles. Clifton possesses an Art School, Music School, library, gymnasium and swimming-bath. The Science School which dates from 1927, when it was opened by H.R.H. the Prince of Wales, is one of the best in the country. Clifton aims at providing a thoroughly sound general education with facilities for specialization in its later stages. The War Memorial takes the form of a gateway upon which the names of the five hundred and seventy-eight Old Cliftonians who made the supreme sacrifice are recorded. This monument was unveiled in 1922 by Earl Haig. More than three thousand Old Boys served with the forces in the 1914–18 war, of whom the two most distinguished were the Earl himself and Field-Marshal Birdwood. A statue to Earl Haig has been erected near the Memorial Gateway.

From Bristol to Cheltenham; Dean Close School was

144

Avon Gorge
Parish Church, Cirencester

founded in 1886 by a group of Evangelical Churchmen to be a memorial to the Reverend Francis Close, D.D., who had been incumbent of Cheltenham for many years before he became Dean of Carlisle. Doctor Close was for many years an outstanding figure in Cheltenham, and was himself one of the founders of Cheltenham College. Dean Close School, therefore, has always had, as was intended, an Evangelical tradition. Another aim of the founders was to provide a boarding-school education at "moderate cost." With this object in view the school was from the outset organized centrally on the dormitory system, and did not possess separate houses. The numbers in the first were not to exceed three hundred, and the first headmaster, Dr W. H. Flecker, and his wife established the tradition of a "family school," which has been maintained ever since. Dr Flecker was headmaster from 1886 to 1924, an exceptionally long term of office of thirty-eight years. The school is open to a limited number of day-boys proportioned to the boarders. In recent years, a Junior School has been created. Dean Close has an open-air theatre which was built by the boys themselves, and completed in 1937.

Cheltenham College, founded in 1841, occupies a group of buildings in a free but by no means unpleasing adaptation of the Tudor style. To this a handsome chapel has been added as a memorial to the six hundred and seventy-five Old Cheltonians who gave their lives in the first World War. The college is equipped for all the purposes of a great public school. The average number of boys is six hundred, the majority of whom are boarders. Cheltenham College possesses extensive playing-fields, upon the largest of which the annual county cricket matches are played. The most ancient scholastic foundation in the town is the Grammar School for boys which dates back to 1576, and owes its endowment to Richard Pate, one time Recorder of Gloucester. This institution is now included in the list of public schools. It offers students many valuable scholarships, including several to boys passing on to the universities.

The School of Arts and Crafts is one of the most important art schools in the West of England. The building is modern, and the studios are fitted up with the most up-to-

The ninety-nine Yew Trees in Painswick Churchyard
Painswick

date system of lighting and equipment. It is divided into four departments—for drawing and painting; for modelling and sculpture; for architecture; and for design and crafts—which provide instruction during the day and evening. In the summer term there is a special course for landscape painting. The Technical College at the Lypiatts has been considerably developed in recent years. The students number approximately one thousand.

Cheltenham Ladies' College is the best-known school for girl students in England, and probably in the world. It was founded in 1853, and incorporated in 1935 by Royal Charter. Miss Dorothea Beale, L.L.D., one of the pioneers of public boarding-schools for girls, was principal from 1858 to 1906. In 1873 the first block of the present buildings was erected, large additions being subsequently made. These include the Music Wing, in 1882; the Library Wing, in 1894; Princess Hall, which contains a room amply large enough for public lectures and concerts; the Science Wing, in 1904; the Gymnasium, in 1927; and the New Junior School—connected with the main college by a covered way—in 1936. The style of building is a free treatment of Gothic; the material, the handsome Cotswold stone. It goes without saying that the college contains the usual music-rooms, art studios, laboratories, with gymnasium, and swimming-bath, but—what is a unique feature—it can also boast its own observatory. Cheltenham College possesses its own sanatorium, its private hospital to which any pupil who develops an infectious complaint can be immediately removed and isolated. The Preparatory School takes boys and girls from four to eight years old. Division III is for pupils from four to eight; Division II for those from ten to thirteen years; Division I for those over thirteen. Above these is Upper College, where pupils are prepared for School Certificate and Higher Certificate Examinations, and the First Medical Examination.

One reads in the College History section of *The Cheltenham Ladies' College* magazine that the belief which the founders of the institution held and acted upon was that the "education of girls is of no less importance than that of boys." No doubt; girls have always been educated, but the point would seem to be that, since the destinies of boys and girls are different, the preparation for their destinies should be different also. These reflections are general and have no application to Cheltenham College in particular, or to any specific training institution for young women. What was the nature of feminine education throughout the centuries which preceded the Victorian epoch? It was concerned mainly with imparting such graces as should put a gloss upon Nature, and thus render it easier for a pupil to attract suitors and marry. Such was the type of education given to the women of my own family of three generations back. They were forbidden absolutely to read the sort of trash with which to-day every bookstall teems and were kept solidly to English literature, particular attention being given to Dryden and Pope. In this way it was intended that they should speak and write their own language not only with grammatical exactitude, but with easy mastery, with delicacy, if possible with wit. Music and French, of course, were not neglected. The "accomplishments" were also taught in Paris, as I remember, shortly before the 1914–18 war. And, whatever may be thought to the contrary over here, there is infinitely less sex antagonism in France and Belgium to-day than there is in England. I had found the daughter of my hostess absorbed apparently in Romain Rolland's *Michel Ange*.

"I had no idea," said I, "that you were interested in Michelangelo."

"I'm not," said she, with Gallic frankness, "but I must acquire *some* general knowledge of art and science. If I didn't, how on earth should I be able to hold my own in intelligent conversation? Father says I *must*; and Father is right!" Her mother told me : "Tante Berthe is coming to see us this afternoon. Draw her out—you will be the gainer —and listen to every word she says. You will hear the French language spoken in its utmost purity!" Even after the 1914–18 war the tradition of the "accomplishments" reigned upon the Continent, unperturbed by the feministic theory that women should be educated like men. I was in hospital in Switzerland, and a Swiss lady wrote me a letter to cheer me up, mentioning to a woman friend that she had done so. "What superb letters she writes!" cried this second lady with enthusiasm, "you could imagine you were hearing from some *grande dame* of the eighteenth century!" The modern theory of training women for men's courses of study at the universities is certainly an innovation, for it breaks not only the tradition of Europe, but all that experience has delivered to us on the subject from classical antiquity and the convictions of the whole eastern hemisphere of the world

I am no devotee of Victorian stuffiness, but have we nothing to learn from the "spacious days"? What need had the women of Shakespeare for the Mathematical Tripos? They took a shorter cut to life than that! What says Marina?

> I can sing, weave, sew, and dance,
> With other virtues, which I'll keep from boast.

And what the enchantingly feminine Viola in *Twelfth Night*?

> I can sing,
> And speak to him in many sort of music.

Latin was taught to women; but this too as an "accomplishment." We can see Lucentio, in *The Taming of the Shrew*, pay his court to Bianca. His is a lesson in masquerade to cover his wooing, but it is with Ovid he makes pretence of opening his course of studies. A knowledge of classical mythology was then an essential for her, if a young woman were to take her part in conversation, or to enjoy to the full the contemporary poems and plays, Shakespeare's own amongst them. The "Virgin Queen" learned Hebrew, and remained a virgin.

The woman who takes up a career commonly remains celibate. The nun inflicts no injury upon the community : she retires from it. The feminine careerist, on the other hand, ousts from a post the man who, had he obtained it, would have looked to it to support a wife and children. Women teachers are, for the most part, celibate. This being so, is it not possible that they may tend to lay too little stress upon marriage, a state of which they know nothing, as an end to be kept steadily in view?

We are at the close of a *second* world war. The loss in man-power has been shattering. Whole civilizations have perished as a result of the destruction of their fighting men. After its wars with the Turks, from 1453 until 1718, Venice.

the head state of an empire, sank slowly to the status of an unimportant provincial town. After the 1914–18 war, when England sent the expedition to assist the Russians of the White party against the Reds, their Russian captors—at such pains were they to keep up the numbers of their citizens!—adopted, amongst others, the expedient of releasing suitable English prisoners of war on the condition of their marrying Russian women. Their foresight bore fruit in that army which was able to—the expression is Mr Churchill's—"tear the guts out of" the invading Huns. These Huns also made the raising of the birthrate a prime consideration of national policy. A trifle before this second World War a German girl said to me, "A German woman looks forward to a family as her birthright. The German man comes home to them after his work of an evening. What does an upper-class Englishman come home to? His wife, his dog, and his wireless set."

I am the reverse of a misogynist, but I maintain that to hand on life and to inspire life are a woman's true functions; and both partake of the divine. It is for man to defend the community when it is in peril; it is for women to see to it that there is a community to defend.

To revert from general considerations to Cheltenham Ladies' College. Although this happens to be in Cheltenham, it is unique in being imperial. Many of the pupils come from Canada, others from Australia, New Zealand, South Africa, some from America. One of the aims of the college is to "give the girls a wide vision of life, a sense of adventure, and a desire to go out into all parts of the world." This ideal is of the happiest augury. Before the last war, in England and Wales, in a population of eight million women between the ages of twenty and fifty, there were no fewer than three million spinsters! In 1918 I was seeing a friend off from London Docks. He was bound for Africa to plant flax. There were aboard his smallish ship 14,000 men and one *married* woman! Had a "sense of adventure and a desire to go out into all parts of the world" inspired a like number of young women to undertake the voyage, it must have fallen to the first officer to attend to the navigation of the boat. The captain would have been too busy conducting marriages.

BRISTOL GLASS

One of our famous products of former times was that Bristol glass which is still eagerly sought after by collectors. In 1696 when "William was our royal King," but James II was keeping sharp watch upon our affairs from "across the water"—in the little Bristol of that day there were no fewer than nine glass-houses or manufacturies. The trade flourished and by 1760, when Sir Joshua Reynolds was giving immortality to the aristocracy—Hogarth having already done as much for the citizens, footpads and women of the town—the number of these installations had risen to fifteen.

Like every other period which has proved itself prolific in genius the eighteenth century was a day of wine-lovers. Tavern life throve extraordinarily and there was no public-house too small to have its club. For the latter coarse glass was preferable as being less likely to break; yet something solid withal, English and comfortable, hardy ware for the world of Hogarth's sitters; but "flint-glass" crystal clear and delicately cut for the politer topers of Sir Joshua Reynolds.

When the Demon Gin began to make his appearance, Bristol, moving with the times, began to produce those double-knopped, bucket-bowled gin glasses which to-day command high prices.

Then what do you say to these glasses fine?
Oh, they shall have no praise of mine.

Field workers had small use for drinking vessels which flew to pieces when dropped or roughly handled. The "leather bottels," or "black jacks," pleased the less delicate taste of the haymakers and their sun-browned lasses. (In Elizabethan times, of course, when "Venice glasses," or those made from fern in Sussex, were still a novelty, leather served the thirsty of all classes. So Fletcher shows us :

Body o' me, I'm dry still; give me the jack, boy;
This wooden skilt holds nothing !)

By the same token, Cheltenham Museum possesses a cider

tankard in *oak*! "Heart of oak were their men"; and not inappropriately their mugs were also.

This same collection can boast a curiosity in a two-gallon ale-jack in *copper*, which looks unhygienic. Unfortunately it is undated and experts cannot place it to within half a century. It may have been made any time between 1750 and 1800. To return to our glasses : Perhaps I ought already to have cautioned the reader against conceiving a prejudice against Bristol glass from the number of grotesque objects in this fine material which are all too much in evidence. Many a Gloucestershire public-house can show examples of these freaks. The Union Inn, Stroud, for example, displays a few. The Trouble-House Inn, on the Cirencester-Tetbury road, possessed, when last I visited it, a veritable museum. But they tell me that the landlord has since migrated to Hunters' Hall—can you beat the names of our Gloucestershire hostelries?—and he will doubtless have taken his glass with him.

Those who are curious may view a few examples of these wares in Cheltenham Museum. They may see, for instance, two walking-sticks with ornamental air-twists, the one in red, the other in greyish-green. You would expect them to break if walked with, and sure enough one of the pair lies broken in its showcase. Wherever the nature of things admits, Art should be *functional*—a platitude, but often forgotten. Other exhibits are a glass rolling-pin and a pipe.

Even for glass the products of the Bristol factories were brittle. Were that rolling-pin to break in the using, it would not merely cut the cook's fingers, it would fill her pie with that least digestible of ingredients—broken glass! As for the pipe, one sees but one objection; were one to apply a match to the bowl, it would shiver in pieces! Some experts maintain that these absurdities were not made in Bristol at all, but at Nailsea which, in Georgian days, was a village nine miles beyond that town. But Mr Newport of Cheltenham, an eminent collector and specialist in fine old glass, believes that both Bristol and Nailsea were equally guilty. It is generally believed that these objects were fashioned not as officially recognized products of the glass-houses, but by the hands in their spare time. They represent what the art of glass-blowing really meant to the *ignobile vulgus*. In some instances their plebeian origin is revealed in their inscriptions. "I love a Sailor!" or "Jack's the Boy" suggest that pieces which bear such mottoes were intended for love-tokens. But enough of these vitreous atrocities!

Bristol made not only the choicest table-glass, but pieces of many varieties: candlesticks, tea-trays, flower vases, essence or scent bottles and the like, and that in an agreeable diversity of colour. One finds such articles produced in green or greenish-blue, in opal, purple, red, or "cherry-red," and also in a glowing blue which one must look through towards the light if one is to appreciate its rich translucence fully. Cheltenham Museum possesses a cup in opal glass, also a green scent-bottle which is ornamented with an inset cameo of Lord Byron (although Mr Newport inclines to the view that this exhibit originated not from Bristol but London). How flattered that most impressionable of poets would have felt could he have divined that his portrait in miniature was gracing the toilet-table of a fair admirer!

One of the most characteristic colours in this glass is that "Bristol milk-white" which was designed at first in imitation of and rivalry with Chinese porcelain. Yet this lovely glass is not to be regarded simply as imitation, but as an æsthetic achievement of its own of high distinction. One finds it fashioned into vases, candlesticks, or toilet-boxes, either plain or ornamented with blossoms, butterflies, or other dainty devices; and such pieces are no less exquisite in form than hue.

Towards the end of the eighteenth century English experimenters discovered a true porcelain, capable of receiving any decoration, or of being moulded into any reasonable shape, while possessing the essential quality of translucence. In this preparation calcined ox-bones were added to the clay and ground rock. This distinctively English porcelain proved second to none. It was perfected about the year 1800, and its manufacture has been adopted—says Mr N. Hudson Moore in his *Old Glass, European and American*—to some extent in "France, Germany, Sweden and U.S.A."

One of the most famous enamellers of Bristol glass was Michael Edkin. One reads of his receiving the small sum of

eightpence for his designs, delicate delineations of pastoral
scenes with sheep and shepherd, set in a framework of dainty
filigree. We read that he painted with the finest brushes
made from hairs taken from the nostrils and eyelashes of
oxen. His reputation as craftsman grew steadily, and between
1762 and 1787 no fewer than five glass firms of repute secured
his services. This was as well, for there were expenses at
home. His wife presented him with thirty-six children!

One may still come upon genuine bottles of Bristol glass in
the antique shops, those more especially which were intended
to hold spirits, and are labelled accordingly "Brandy" or
"Rum" or "Hollands" in gilt lettering too often half-effaced
by time or rough usage. One gets the impression that our
Georgian forebears avoided using one bottle for any but one
liquor. Sometimes the word "Cider" appears upon a glass
no bigger than a modern wineglass. This is not astonishing
when one remembers that, even in living memory, one could
purchase cider long matured and heady—a drink for men,
which had nothing in common with the mothers' meeting
beverage sold under that name to-day. One reads of cider
used as an apéritif, and this no doubt would be as strong as
that Calvados which farmers drink so freely in the cider-
producing districts of modern Normandy. Witness Sir John
English in *The Country Lasses* of 1715 :

"Will your Grace taste a glass of old hock, with a little,
little dash of palm, before you eat? A Seville orange squeezed
into a glass of noble, racy, old canary? Or a glass of our
right Southam cyder, sweetened with a little old mead, and a
hard toast?"

Sometimes a man of substance would have his glass specially designed for him. Mechanization was unknown. There
was variety everywhere! Of this species, Mr Newport
possesses an outstandingly fine specimen of glass tankard.
The metal is heavily leaded which makes for brilliance, and
this effect is considerably heightened by an admixture of
antimony. This piece was fashioned to a farmer's wishes, and
displays his initials in a monogram upon one side of it. Upon
the other appear a wheatsheaf, and ingenious designs in
barley-stalks. One sees moreover the implements of the
farmer's craft—scythes, axe, a flail, a harrow, hay-fork, rake

and reaping-hook. This piece its owner assigns approximately to 1800. Not seldom contemporary heroes appear upon the mugs or glasses from which their healths would be drunk. Lord Nelson was frequently thus honoured. Now and again one finds the "Sailor King," dear to topers, and celebrated in vulgar rhyme :

> So let us sing,
> Live Billy, the King,
> For bating the tax upon beer !

Or that other William, hero of the Glorious Revolution, or—for the list is a long one—Admiral Byng, hanging from a gallows in full uniform, cocked hat and all. This unfortunate who had previously attacked and destroyed the Spanish fleet which he had found cruising off Cape Pessaro, failed to destroy the French fleet besieging Minorca, to relieve which island he had been sent with a wholly inadequate force. He was shot upon his own quarter-deck. But the verdict of history is that he was made the scapegoat of an incompetent ministry and that he was deficient in neither honour nor courage.

Mr Newport possesses two Jacobite glasses : pieces rarer than rare, and deserving of a place in a prince's cabinet. The one displays the Stuart Rose, with two buds symbolizing the young Charles Edward, the Pretender, and the younger brother Henry Benedict, Duke of York, who was later created a cardinal. The latter's acceptance of a cardinal's hat precluded the possibility of his ever becoming King of England. A second drinking-glass, made after that event, shows us in consequence only one rosebud. But a Star, symbolic of Hope, still shines. It need hardly be said that these glasses were never designed for the *hoi polloi*, and that whether for design or quality of glass, perfection has been attained as far as is humanly possible. The betrayal of the possession of the glasses by a Whig might have laid their Jacobite owner open to a charge of treason. What a world of history is recorded in the drinking-vessels of that virile and convivial England of the Georges !

Mr Newport is also the possessor of two specimens of those receptacles which are termed *par excellence* "Bristol bottles." Both were made to contain ale as is shown by the hops and barley of which the designer has made becoming use in his decoration, and both are of interest; but one more particularly so. This sets out in panorama the sport of hare-hunting. First runs the hare, then a first and then a second hound. There follow two huntsmen in the long coats and cocked hats of the period, bearing poles which might, one fancies, be used for beating bushes. In bold letters, as though this gave the clue to the design, one reads S E E O H E.

"I am completely mystified! What on earth does 'Seeohe' mean?"

"It was the cry of the hare-hunters, and the word survives in the modern 'Soho.'"

"What! The quarter of London where one finds all the French and Italian restaurants?"

"Yes."

"Were there hares in Soho, then, in the seventeen hundreds?"

My host smiles at my astonishment.

"It was simply *running* with them!"

Whether you are an artist who prizes an object for its æsthetic value, or a lover of history who takes pleasure in whatever speaks eloquently of the past, you will find the study of Bristol glass to be fraught with delightful surprises.

CHAPTER XIV

HISTORIC HOUSES

THE Priory of SS. Mary and Peter—"Prinknash Priory"—
now the home of the Caldey Benedictines stands in grounds
of idyllic beauty, although the war has taken sad toll of the
ancient trees. Yet even to-day beeches centuries old and of
immense height form a barrier of foliage which screens the
park from the main road with its traffic of motor-cycles,
cars, and double-decker omnibuses bound for Stroud, Gloucester, or Cheltenham. Singing birds, as one enters the
grounds from the din of the road, fill the air with music
varied by the soft crooning of the wood-doves, whilst the
occasional shrill screams of a jay supply discords which are
by no means unpleasing.

A printed notice introduces a less agreeable train of reflections. It warns me that the bull is usually loose, and that
the public use this park which is strictly private at their own
risk. I raise my eyes from this sinister intimation to find myself gazing into those of the creature against whom I have
been warned. Doped with the summer heat, he regards me
wistfully. I leave him to his meditations. Arrived at the old
mansion, grey with the greyness of an Oxford college, I ring,
and whilst waiting for admittance inhale the fragrance of
roses, which seems to come over me in waves from one of
those formally laid-out gardens which were the delight of
our Tudor ancestors. I am ushered into a cool parlour with
oak furniture and stone floor. The Sub-prior, with whom I
find myself in conversation, appears taken aback for a
moment when I explain that I am a pressman, but he bids
me be seated, while he leaves me to consult with the Father
Prior. This gentleman now in turn introduces himself to me
but informs me that he is anxious to avoid publicity.

I explained that I was interested in the reconditioning of
the house by members of his community, and in the Cotswold
style in architecture to which they had adhered throughout.
Assured that my mission was non-polemical, I was most

hospitably invited to dine with their community in the refectory, and handed over to the good offices of the guest-
master. Dinner over, Dom Christopher, who was formerly a
naval officer but has since specialized in the crafts of tiling
and carpentry, was deputed to take me on a tour of inspec-
tion.

A hunting-box in Chaucer's day when Cranham Woods,
beloved of picnickers was virgin forest, it was subsequently
enlarged so as to form a country retreat and rest-house for
the abbots of Gloucester. My guide drew my attention to a
handsome Gothic window which experts ascribe to the
fifteenth century, and which is still called "Abbot Parker's
Window." So to later, and to later ages. A bust in a niche
of the wall overlooking the courtyard is supposed to represent Henry VIII who in company with Anne Boleyn visited
one of the abbots, not on sinister machinations intent, but as
my host jovially expressed it "Just calling."

Another Tudor relic—a recent acquisition, however—is a
Madonna in Flemish oak which is believed to have once
belonged to Sir Thomas More, of whom the donor, a Mrs
Sutcliffe, is a collateral descendant. During the Civil War
Prince Rupert made Prinknash his headquarters during the
disastrous siege of Gloucester. The relief of that city by the
Roundheads formed the turning-point in that grim conten-
tion. From the day the siege was raised, the fortunes of the
Royalists declined. (Hard by at Castle Combe, one of the
King's children inquired of him why he did not go home.
To which Charles replied he had no home to go to.)

The eighteenth century saw much embellishment at Prinknash. But in quite modern times both the ancient fireplaces
and the oak panelling throughout the building were sold out
of the country to enable their then owners to pay death
duties. (Having held up the coach, the Turpins of Government waylaid the hearse.) On the removal of an Adam fireplace from one of the rooms yet a second fireplace was un-
expectedly brought to light. This was of the early Tudor
period possibly of the reign of Henry VII, which offered
some measure of compensation for other losses.

I gather that it is far from easy to convert a dwelling-
house into a monastery. In a private house only a very few

small rooms are required; in a monastery many, to provide cells for the monks. In a private house many *tolerably large* rooms are desirable; very few in a monastery. But in a monastery a few *really large* rooms are a necessity : for chapel, chapter-house, refectory, and library. For the sub-division of the older bedrooms into cells, thousands of feet of battens together with a large quantity of wall-board were acquired for the rapid running-up of partitions.

To obtain further space, the fourteenth-century chimney-stack had to be demolished, the more so as the introduction of central heating had rendered it superfluous. This proved a labour of Hercules. The walls of the chimney were in some places but little under three feet thick, and the weight of masonry to be removed was estimated at the astonishing figure of fifty tons. By means of a stout rope the monks lowered the largest stones down inside the chimney itself, to the ground-floor level. Others they carried downstairs. The lesser stones and rubble were unceremoniously dropped. In the sacristy below, two or three other monks were kept busy with wheelbarrows clearing the rapidly filling fireplace, and transporting the fallen masonry to the west court, whence a horse and cart conveyed it to a convenient dumping-place. As much of the weight of the old stone-tiled roof was sup-ported by this chimney, struts of immense strength and steel girders were employed to take the strain.

The conversion of small rooms into large I have already spoken of as an occasional necessity. My guide informed me that the refectory where I had dined—a most imposing apartment—had been, when they took the house over, a passage, a wash-house, and a coal cellar. The old roof, long neglected, gaped with chinks. (The roof repair was under-taken, 1931–2; the chimney, 1933–4.)

The process of retiling was entered upon in earnest, and my informant, who has made a specialist's study of the local style and has written a learned article upon the subject, was deputed master carpenter and directed the work. A carica-ture by Heath Robinson viewing the activities of the brothers from the Heath-Robinsonian angle, adorns the novices' common-room. As it is the older and now passing generation of builders who alone appear to understand the craft of tiling

roofs with "slats," or huge tiles of the seasoned local stone,
I plied my kind host with questions. Having had no previous
connection with building until necessity drew his attention to
it, he had been forced to study every detail of the technique
for himself.

"Were I layman," said he, "a bachelor, say, without
family ties, I should tile my house if I were to build one with
asbestos, which is guaranteed to last ten years. But we build
not for an individual but a community. We hope that our
house will outlast many generations of men."

"That," thought I, "is how Englishmen should build."
When we cease to, England will cease to be England and
Englishmen to be Englishmen. To such an extent as the
mechanizing processes of our day allow, let us emulate the
past and strive in our books and in our lives, if we may not
always in our buildings, to be *oak and stone*!

"Now the tiles of Cotswold stone," my host continued,
"if properly seasoned, may be *guaranteed* to last a hundred
years, and have been known to last three hundred. But good
material in one medium demands good material in all. One
cannot rest stone tiles—as we speak of them in the Cotswolds, although, to be sure, geologically they are more like
slates than tiles—upon deal battens. These would decay and
the tiler's labour be in vain. The timber which is to take the
strain of the tiles must be *oak*, and with this to support the
stone, you will have a roof to defy the centuries. And that
the result is as beautiful as it is durable is universally allowed.
Beauty is not a sauce added to indifferent cooking, but ordinary cooking well done."

An excellent aphorism.

My host speaks of the qualities of woods with the enthusiasm of one who has made for himself interesting discoveries.
I learn, not without astonishment, that *unseasoned* timber
was often used in preference to *seasoned* in the construction
of our ancient "black and white" buildings. Thus did the
Tudors construct those houses the solidity and beauty of
which delight us to-day. They cut their timber locally, built
with it, and let it season *in situ*. The beech, oak, and ash of
Prinknash were felled in what now is Prinknash Park or its
immediate vicinity. In this way the wood seasons, as my host

wittily phrases it, "in the climate it has been accustomed to from its youth up."

Dom Christopher carries this principle so far as to maintain that wood from the north of England should not be employed for building in the south, or vice versa, where locally grown timber is available. American oak employed to-day in quantity in this country will not last here as it would in the land of its origin. And it has been observed time and again that old furniture purchased in sound condition in England has gone to pieces rapidly in the very different climatic conditions of New York.

In one instance only has my informant declined the use of oak where its use was sanctified by tradition. In the past, oak pegs driven nail-fashion through previously drilled holes attached the tiles to the timbers below. Exposed to the weather these pegs rot, so that sometimes, when a peg has ceased altogether to support a tile the latter is held in its place upon the roof solely by the "torching," or bed of lime mixed with hair on which it lies : an unsettling reflection during the equinoctial gales. What then? Commonplace iron nails instead of oaken pegs? Worse and worse. There is acid in the sap of oak which rusts iron quickly.

Dom Christopher favours *brass* pegs. These are tough as need be and defy corrosion by the rain. Where weather is not to be feared, for interior beams and battens, for instance, he prefers oaken pegs in the style of our ancestors. Here again there is much to learn. Round pegs are undesirable. If they are sufficiently small to drive in easily they are too loose to hold tightly. If they are larger they are apt to break in the driving. Square pegs with slightly rounded edges are the ideal. They do not break even when driven home with a sledge; *and* driven home, they hold fast. Let the devil shift them if he can! Whence it would appear that the proverb derived from mediæval carpentry is only partially true. If a "square peg in a round hole" is *wrong*, that same peg slightly rounded is *right*.

I took reluctant leave of my kind host in the late afternoon. In this age when—whatever their historical or æsthetic value—old buildings are destroyed without protest on every side; when the societies which arise to prevent such vandal-

ism are rendered impotent from lack of funds, it is invigorating to find, at Prinknash, this Priory in which both the national and local styles are jealously preserved. It exemplifies, in its rejection of the shoddy and slipshod, that love of the sterling which was once regarded as a pre-eminently English characteristic. As I regain the park gates my watch reminds me that I must waste no time if I am not to miss my connections. I take a last glance at the scene of the Homeric labours of the monks. The stately old mansion has dissolved already in the blue and silver haze of the shimmering and dewy dusk. The wood-doves croon as they did when I was entering the grounds. And the bull favours me with an abstracted stare as though he were a philosopher revolving at his leisure a system of bovine metaphysics.

I made my way to Daneways House by way of Sapperton village. On the church door, written in a neat hand upon a card, I read: "Please close the door behind you, so that birds do not fly in and become trapped." Surely a country where such a notice can be exhibited and its admonition respected is, in a very high degree indeed, civilized! I went in, carefully closing the door.

The first word which flashed upon my mind on viewing the interior was one which must rarely occur to anyone when visiting a sacred place: that word was "charm." And yet, why not? The sun shone brightly through the windows and there was a cleanly comeliness about everything which made an immediate appeal to the heart. Even here the bird-song from the outer world penetrated. One distinguished the blackbird's flute, the scraped 'cellos of the rooks, the slight enchanted reed-pipe of the yellowhammer. They might all of them each in his distinctive musical idiom be expressing gratitude to the godly man who was at pains to prevent their kind from becoming trapped.

Yes, charm: let me be allowed the word. In a crowded town the sooty church stands up amongst the huddled graves, and a spiked railing imprisons those who sleep in God, as though the citizens still went in fear of bodysnatchers. In the country it is not so. In such green nooks as these the Old Destroyer comes no longer in the guise of a goblin, to shock and harry. We think of him rather as an ancient man, white-robed, white-bearded. Venerable, but not intimidating.

The church contains effigies to the local notabilities. Sir Henry Poole, in armour and full breeches, kneels opposite Anne, his wife : she in jewelled bodice, Elizabethan ruff, and long ropes of pearls. And there are other members of the Poole family. But the monument which most captivated me was that to Sir Robert Atkyns of Sapperton, county historian and father to all the county historians who have written since his day. He lies on his left side and rests his left elbow on a cushion. His shirt is open at the throat, its sleeves terminate in ruffles. Clean-shaven and in full-bottom wig, he gazes—elegantly—heavenwards, as though for inspiration.

"So," thought I, "could I wish—yet without this touch of quaintness—to be myself, some day, presented in effigy. And the epitaph enumerating those of my qualities which the world judged praiseworthy should be composed in such English as Addison was master of; or in such Latin as that of the younger Pliny."

I left Sapperton church, and by way of the stile-path which crosses the valley sought out the object of my quest, mellow Daneways House,

> Bosom'd high in tufted trees.

As I pass the little Bricklayers' Arms it is a new landlady whom I see through the open door, darning a sock.

"Good afternoon."

"Good afternoon."

"I haven't been this way for years. Have you still got the jack which roasts a fowl and a sirloin at the same time? And the flintlock pistol?"

"Oh!" says she, with a touch of condescension in her voice, "all those *old relics* went when *we* took over management."

How this age hates tradition. Why this rage for destruction? I wonder where the "relics" *went*? To America? To some junkshop? Why still these mute witnesses to the way of life of the past? If the havoc continue but long enough, we shall lose all racial memory, all tradition, and live confined as grossly within the limits of the present hour as those cattle in the meadow yonder, or this cur sleeping in the sun. Yet why vex oneself over trifles? To our muddling modern bureaucracy we have sacrificed that personal liberty for which our ancestors were prepared to hazard their lives : a legacy better worth preserving than their jacks and pistols ! But I deliberately break this train of thought. Why ruffle the tranquillity of this sunlit hour?

If you were overseas and feeling homesick you might recreate your spirit by sending it forth to roam abroad over England's green spaces. And if on this spiritual pilgrimage your desire were to visit a dwelling which should stand as a symbol of pre-industrial culture and dignity, where could you find one more to your purpose than sober, beautiful Daneways House? Like every building wherever it be which delights the eye Daneways is constructed of local material; in this case of Cotswold stone, which seems to absorb the sunlight and acquire with the centuries a tint of honey.

The house—for it is not of sufficient size for one to call it mansion—is, as I have intimated, English of the English. No one in his senses could mistake it for a German schloss or French château. The lack of planning alone would establish Daneways as child of the Gloucestershire countryside. It scouts symmetry : it achieves harmony. Generation after generation of men have slightly reshaped or added to it, to meet the shifting requirements of their day. By wellnigh imperceptible gradations, Chaucer's age becomes Shakespeare's, and this again merges into that of Bolingbroke and Pope; and one finds oneself reading this date upon the wall of the summer-house

TH

1753

Another inscription :

R.W.W.N.H

1866

A descendant of the Hancox family, now an old man, who sometimes visits Daneways, said, looking at this inscription, "There has often been a Nathanial in the family."

Yet the furniture, handsome product of such modern craftsmen as Gimson, seems always *right*; neither do the present-day carpets upon the ancient stone flags nor the electric lights which hang from black oak beams suffice in any way to destroy the *atmosphere*. A decent conservatism has welded past into present, and left no seam.

"Daneways has been lucky," says Mr Fletcher my delightful host, "in never having been the property of a very rich man, or it might have been pulled down and a new house built."

"Or a very poor one," I suggested, "or it might have been allowed to go derelict. How long have there been people at Daneways?"

"Since the Stone Age at least," says Mr Fletcher, smiling : "if you speak of the locality and not the house. Whilst digging to put a rose tree in the garden I dug up a flint hatchet and the experts believe, as I do myself, that it was shaped on the spot, and not imported. The same advantages obtained then as now; shelter from the winds and a spring of pure water. You see our well there? Come, I'll show you the outside of the house first, if you care to?"

"I should love to !"

"That was the fifteenth-century lancet window that you passed on your way to the front door; your guess was right. But here we are at the oldest portion. Look in at this window and see the thickness of the wall !"

"Why, it must be anything up to four feet through."

"Not much under. You can get an idea by measuring with your stick. Every window, you see, is barred."

"Modern banking was not introduced much before—what?—the seventeenth century. Most men kept their money in gold in their own homes. Hence most crime took the form of robbery with violence, and the typical criminals were the highwayman and footpad. Violence was resisted by violence, so that the Englishman's home was, in a literal sense, his castle."

"That is so. I didn't like the idea of having every window barred, in case of fire. Now besides the doors we have an additional window by which one could escape, if necessary. See, this bar comes out."

My host removes and then replaces it. . . .

The south aspect is *sui generis*. In the centre between the two wings is the main door—rounded, classical, supposedly Tudor—surmounted by a dripstone of traditional Cotswold and Gothic style. To the left of this door the double-gabled left wing rises but two stories in height. To its right the right wing soars up a whole *five* stories and is surmounted by a gable of totally different type; single, but with a two-way facing façade.

Do I seem to you to describe something wholly fantastic: a Walt Disney design of a palace for Mickey Mouse? So it might seem. But in point of fact, the High Building, as this right wing is called, is set against an abruptly rising hillock, and this detracts appreciably from the effect of height. Into this steep bank, the right wing merges with something of the inevitability of a beautiful object not of art, but of Nature.

We go indoors.

"Here you see the interior of the room in the outer wall of which you remarked a fifteenth-century lancet window. There it is, and there, opposite, a trefoil opening. There's a letter extant of very early date in which the then owner of Daneways asks the Bishop of Gloucester's permission for him to have a private chapel. It is believed that this was the chapel in question but we cannot establish this with any certainty as unfortunately the Bishop's reply is not forthcoming.

"Now here is the dining-room, with an Elizabethan ceiling of oak timbers. In Victoria's time these were painted white which was a fashion about the time that Walter Pater was writing. Later, somebody must have said 'But these timbers are *oak*! Therefore let them resemble oak.' And he had them painted with a very light grain resembling wood. Some time later yet a third connoisseur must have observed 'These timbers are of *old* oak! *Then*, they ought to *resemble* old oak!'

"So *he* had the old oak timbers painted to resemble *old* oak! I had all the paint taken off again."

My host's blue eyes sparkle with merriment.

"Glorious! One could almost fancy it a Government job and that half a hundred forms had to be applied for, waited for, attested and despatched before the applicants were able to obtain the different paints!

"Now for upstairs. Perhaps I had better go first to show you the way? Here we are in the room immediately over the dining-room we were in just now. Does anything strike you as odd about it?"

"Yes, decidedly. The floor slopes down from a centre line towards the extremities, like an old-style ship's deck or a road towards its gutters!"

"When the Elizabethans refashioned the older dining-hall they lowered it to about one-half of its original height. The floor of this room is the upper side of the newer classical ceiling below; it follows the up-and-down of the timbers, and nobody so much as bothered to make it level! Above us you can see the *original Gothic* ceiling and the oldest timbering in the house. That is one of the louvres of which, of course, there were several. The fires in the Middle Ages—as you no doubt know—were made upon the floor against a screen, and the smoke escaped by vents in the roof. The blackening and charring of these timbers is caused by soot. I have examined them with a magnifying-glass!"

"I don't know whether you have read William Harrison, sir, the Elizabethan parson who gave an account of his own times? He expresses his dislike of the new—Tudor—fire-places, and chimneys. He prefers the older style, with the fire in the centre of the hall and the smoke wandering upwards towards the roof-vents. Of course, 'sea-coal' was rarely burnt then. They had fuel and to spare in their woodlands. Harrison declares that the breathing of wood-smoke fortifies the lungs, and preserves the breather from the 'quack' and 'pose' which the *cognoscenti*, I believe, interpret as 'cold in the head' and 'catarrh.'"

"I didn't know that. Now here we are in the 'Trout Room.' It's called that from this stucco fish on the cornice. Set in the centre you see, between conventionalized lilies."

"If the fish—which might be almost *any* fish—can be taken for a *pike*—the 'luce' of our ancestors—then I fancy the 'flower-de-luces' to right and left express the same idea : the name of 'Lucy.'"

"Why, it might be so! And apropos, it is believed that a

family of the name of 'Lucy' *did* live here once; so your theory seems plausible : the 'luces' may symbolize the family name."

My host shows me, by two different chimney-pieces, two foot-square cupboards where they kept salt when salt was a high-priced luxury, and gunpowder.

"There is no tale of a ghost at Daneways, and anyway such tales are all bunkum!"

I am sorry to hear this. I must confess to regretting that no mailed warrior is reputed to scowl at visitors so soon as midnight has struck; no maiden is to be surprised in some rarely used room sitting upon her highbacked chair, with glimmering locks so long as to form a pool behind her upon the ground, weeping or crooning, as she turns her gossamer spinning-wheel.

You will not I suppose expect me to recount in guide-book style the names of the historical notabilities who at one time or another have inhabited either the Daneways House that we know or those which presumably were its remote ancestors? You will not desire to hear that Ulf—the Dane or Anglicized Dane—was ejected from his possessions by Ralph de Todeni, the Standard-bearer in 1066 to the Norman Hitler, William the Conqueror? No? I thought not. There were the Cliffords, the Leys, the Husseys, the Flemings, and many, many others; some knights, some yeomen.

"Dead!—See, see!—he drew a good bow—and dead!—he shot a good shoot : John of Gaunt loved him well, and betted much money on his head . . . Dead!"

Let Shakespeare's Justice Shallow pronounce the general epitaph.

I can discover but two things which reflect discreditably upon the fair fame of this noble building. One is the country-side tradition that a squire of Daneways, whose estate was being rapidly cleared of game by gangs of poachers, set up one of those sinister mantraps that one may sometimes come across in museums. In the mirk night he heard an appalling yell. "Ha!" thought he, "that's one of them!" He was mistaken. Setting out with lantern and a stout cudgel he perceived his son and heir in the trap! The young man had gone out courting, and had taken a short-cut home through the woods. No date is given for this improbable occurrence, which savours strangely of the Victorian "villain of the piece," with his mephistophelian laugh and black moustaches!

There is, however, a more serious charge brought this time against an historical character. Upon a brass plate, removed from a gravestone and now upon a wall of Bisley church, one reads this inscription :

"Here lyeth the body of William Hancox of Denway, Yeoman, who departed this life the 27th of December 1672. A Cavalier under Oliver Cromwell."

So the cat is out. Daneways once harboured a *Puritan*. For a long while the rebel's sword, rapier, gloves, jerkin, and two brass tobacco-boxes were preserved as heirlooms, and vaguely referred to as "Elizabethan." But the truth came to light at last : antiquaries are so damned inquisitive. *Then* there was nothing for it but to attempt to mitigate the backslider's enormities by reference to the tobacco-boxes. With disarming smile or deprecating shrug, one could just carry it off by observing of the black sheep,

"He kept tobacco-boxes, so at any rate the fellow wasn't a non-smoker."

I bade good-bye to my host whose courtesy and hospitality had given me an enchanting afternoon, and paused at some distance from the grounds for a last look back. An aged countryman joined me.

"Bin looking over th' great house, zur? That house have entertained many famous people in its time!"

"Indeed? And who?"

"Fair Rosamund and Bernard Shaw."

I walk Stroudwards by what was once the famous Thames and Severn canal. It had been constructed at prodigious cost and labour but no sooner was it completed to the last lock-gate than the railways began to be perfected. In competition with the Demon Speed the waterway was allowed to go derelict. Stroud is, I suppose, some eight miles or thereabouts from Daneways and

> It is allowed
> That Stroud
> Holds naught that's pretty,
> Wise nor witty.

In fact such historic or beautiful buildings as they do possess they are at pains to destroy.

But this by-way of the world, the canal walk, is an unmixed joy. For once speed proves an aid to beauty, for fervent youth takes the high-roads upon a motor-bike and the once well-trod field-paths are so forsaken that one might fancy oneself back in the England of Shakespeare. Here a broadish water-sheet remains, its crystal surface carpeted with those green rafts, leaves of the cream or yellow water-lilies which June will see in blossom. The copses are full of wild hyacinths and these too caress the eye with an effect of blue water as they overflow the dingles.

But farther on the old bed of the stream runs so dry that their masters have tethered two she-goats to feast upon the bristly reeds which only goats can digest. A young calf wanders up to them : lies down between them pining for company. Lovers meet here at dusk and in a world so far remote from life's fever-fret, Shakespeare's Puck, one feels, might start up to affright a village girl; or those "pretty, light, fantastic maids" of Michael Drayton, tricked out in all the finery of gossamer ruffs and gloves, might foregather with laughter to dance the "Hays" by moonlight.

I close my eyes to recapture from memory a last impression of Daneways. Age-old gables rise above an orchard where the winds wander, flinging fragrance. Blossom is everywhere; and the blue air is alive with birdsong. As in a microcosm I behold a country worth fighting for. Its name is England.

CHAPTER XV

GREAT GLOUCESTRIANS

How could one better head a chapter on "Great Gloucestrians" than with the name of Richard Whittington who was Gloucestershire born and bred? Immortal Dick, the prototype of all poor boys who "make good."

Since brevity is the word to-day, let me give his data as though for "Who Was Who"—"Whittington, Richard; died 1423. 3rd *s.* of Sir William Whittington of Pauntley, Glos, and Joan his wife. The latter was *d.* of William Mansell, Sheriff of Gloucestershire, and widow of Thomas Berkeley of Cobberley, Glos : who held the office of Sheriff of this county three times. Married Alice Fitzwarren, *d.* of his Master, having left Glos for London, and enrolled 'prentice of the Mercer's Company. In 1379 contributed 5 marks towards a City loan. In 1385 supplied velvets and damasks to the household of the Earl of Derby, later King Henry IV. 1385, sat in the Common Council as representative of Coleman Street ward; ditto 1387. In 1389 became surety for £10 to the Lord Chamberlain towards the defence of the City. 1389, Alderman for Bread Street ward. 1393-4, Sheriff. Temporarily appointed by King Richard II Lord Mayor of London until the next election in place of Adam Bamme, deceased during his term of office. Supplied wedding trousseaux to the Princesses Blanche and Philippa, daughters of King Henry IV. Loans to Crown include £1,000 (equivalent, Victorian currency, £10,000) to King Henry IV; and 700 gold marks ((?) equivalent as many Victorian pounds) to King Henry V. Lord Mayor of London 1397, 1406 and 1419. For public benefactions, see the Histories."

Alongside with the above, which is factual, the legend grew up and was traditionally handed down which everybody knows. Against this legend scientific historians and others have brought a broadside of criticism to bear. May I state quite frankly that their arguments leave me unconvinced? One Riley, for instance, is responsible for the following which has found favour with many : "In the fourteenth and beginning of the fifteenth century trading, or buying and selling at a profit, was known to the more educated classes under the French name of *achat*, which in English was written, and probably pronounced, *acat*. To a *cat* of this nature Whittington was indebted for his wealth."

But on this showing, *every* London merchant and tradesman who made money owed his fortune, equally with Whittington, to "a cat of this nature"! One of these mediæval Lord Mayors entertained, on some occasion, no fewer than four kings to dinner, with their respective queens. But *he* was never associated with "a cat"! And, parenthetically, one doubts whether the word ever was pronounced "a cat." It is more commonly written with an *e* final, and this *e* would be *pronounced*, so often as it came before a consonant. There is no proof either that the word was ever in very general use. It occurs but twice in the voluminous works of Chaucer, even including the pseudo-Chaucerian *Romaunt of the Rose*. Then again the folklorists are at it, explaining the cat away on the strength of other extant tales, Russian or Scandinavian, in which cats are traded against large sums of money. But don't these gentlemen see that this argument cuts both ways? If they prove anything it is that cats were saleable! Well, if others did it, why not Whittington? But what the folklorists do not say is that Whittington's is the *sole* case of the sale of a cat's being associated with an authentic historical character. Another argument used to demolish the cat is that Dick's pet does not appear in print before the seventeenth century. It is to be found in the British Museum blackletter ballad of 1641 entitled *London's glory and Whittington's renown . . . a remarkable story how Sir Richard Whittington . . . came to be three times Lord Mayor of London, and how his rise was by a cat.* But if this be the first *extant* reference can we safely infer from that that it was the *first*?

How turbulent is the history of Old London : and of New! How many books perished in the Dissolution of the Monasteries, in the Great Rebellion, and (in those days of scanty water supply, and of wooden houses) by conflagrations, of which the Great Fire, though an outstanding was by no means a unique example! But if, which is unlikely, the 1641 ballad were, in fact, the first to introduce the cat, would that prove it to have had no earlier existence in *oral* tradition? When country folk were unable to read, *all* knowledge was so handed down. The cat may have been a byword before it was a ballad! Then again, where is the fundamental objection? Why should the cat not make the first beginnings of its owner's fortune? (I like to think of Felix "making good.") Both Lysons, the antiquary, and Sir Walter Besant, the historian of London, rightly emphasize the point that domestic cats in Whittington's day were excessively rare. And, therefore, the more valuable. Rare they assuredly were at the later Renaissance. Though such may exist, I can think of no family group of this time in which a cat figures. The "Last Supper" of the Flemish master Quentin Metsys shows us a great lady whose pet *squirrel* is attached by a chain to a small weight. The poet Politiziano, in his "Angelo ad Puellam Suam," compares his merry mistress to a *squirrel* frolicking in a young maid's white bosom. The painters present us with *monkeys* in plenty, often carried by jesters, but cats no! Nor did they come into their own under James I. They were cold-shouldered by reason of their keeping bohemian company with witches!

John Stow, of the *Survey of London*, gives us a lengthy account of the rules and regulations by which the hospital which Whittington founded was to be administered. He transcribes Whittington's epitaph from his tomb in St Michael de Pater Noster church, which was later destroyed in the Great Fire. "But," object the iconoclasts, "Stow says nothing about the cat, which he assuredly would have done had he known about it." I doubt that "assuredly"! Historians, unless they happen to be Hume or Gibbon, are apt to be plodding fellows! John Stow enters church after church, copies epitaph after epitaph, but he never enters the Mermaid Tavern to call for a pint of sack! He may simply have thought the cat not worth while. Let me use the same argument as the John Stowists. John Stow never mentions his *supposed* contemporary William Shakespeare, which he *assuredly* would have done had the poet existed!

Now considering all this, is it really so unreasonable to fancy that the people may be right and the professors wrong?

That Dick's master, Fitzwarren, or the captain of his ship the *Unicorn*, may have traded a cat, when cats were rare, to some Moroccan plutocrat, who both as the owner of a palace infested with mice and as a purchaser taken with what, in his eyes at least, was a unique curiosity, might be willing to pay a fancy price for it?

Sober history confirms two points in the "legend." Richard Whittington did marry his master's daughter, the beautiful —or was she only rich?—Alice Fitzwarren. And, knight's son though he was, did begin life as a poor boy! How so? Why, very simply! His father Sir William married *without licence* Berkeley's widow—the lady of the effigy of Cobberley church—and for this he was *outlawed*. And *that* meant the payment of a crippling fine to redeem his outlawry. The selling of rich widows was then a lucrative branch of commerce. It was also a prerogative of the Crown. And Dick, remember, was the third of three sons. Yes, no doubt of it, he began life poor.

Henry V required prodigious supplies for his wars in France, and against the sums borrowed he issued his bonds. Legend—or tradition—has it that Whittington entertained this prince—Shakespeare's King Harry, the hero of Agincourt—to dinner in the Guildhall. Whilst his royal guest was inhaling with delight the fragrance of the rare woods and spices roaring up in flames from the mediæval hearth, Whittington cast upon the fire the royal bonds to the extent of thirty-seven thousand gold marks, which he had been at the pains to buy up *ad hoc*! This sum would equal sixty thousand Victorian pounds, and, if he reads this book, the Astronomer Royal shall tell us what it equals in these flimsy impostors which do duty with us moderns for pounds to-day. When King Harry saw his debts vanishing in smoke, he is said to have exclaimed "Never had prince such a subject!" To which Whittington replied "Never had subject such a prince!" Whether truth or fable, the writer of Whittington's epitaph *might* have had this incident in mind when he describes him as *regia spes et pres*, or, "hope and prop of kings"!

Men have won places in history as monsters. When we read the lives of Nero or Caligula or Tiberius we are amazed at the extent to which they found it possible to debase the human currency. Others, again, new-mint and enrich it. Although he knew poverty at first hand, so soon as he had attained to affluence Whittington exercised a princely liberality. Yet never did he suffer riches to corrupt his heart. Whether feasting kings or in the thick of great affairs he found time to pity the prisoners of Newgate, whose sufferings the world viewed with callous disregard. And he rebuilt their gaol, paying every penny of its reconstruction, so that, if it were in his power to help them, poor wretches should no longer die through "contagion of air." From his monkish epitaph I cull the following : "The Flower of Merchants"; "A Father to the Poor"; and this, with which I close, "Like fragrant spikenard was this Richard's fame."

Whilst Chaucer's pilgrims were telling tales upon the road to Canterbury, in due course it fell to the Monk's lot to tell his. He proceeded to regale his fellow-travellers with a series of sublime but lugubrious tragedies, and would probably have continued sermonizing the day through had not the Host protested. Harry Bailey says, in effect, "Don't tell us about men who were born to high estate, but perished miserably. It's depressing ! Reverse the process and let's hear something of the many others who began life miserably but ended happily !" Harry Bailey is the man in the street. His is every man's philosophy.

If you desire to entertain yourself as mine Host of the Tabard would have liked the Monk to entertain *him*, you have only to read the *Autobiography of a Super-Tramp*, the famous self-portrait of the late W. H. Davies the poet. To be sure Davies never attained to great estate, but then he never wished to. What he most desired in that roving life of his was time for study and reflection in order that he might tranquilly devote himself to literary creation. He desired books and a room with a fire. He also wished (what poet does not?) to see his masterpieces in print, to obtain a reasonable measure of public appreciation.

All this he achieved, as we shall see, in liberal measure. At the outset of his life it may be said without fear of contradiction that Davies was a self-taught man, for the school from which he played truant so often would appear to have exercised no formative influence upon his genius. His school and university would be the nearest available public library when he could spare time from tramping for his living, or fruit-picking, or herding plunging oxen on to ships for the munificent pay of his passage and ten or even thirty shillings at the end of the voyage. Sometimes in these early days he bought books but at the cost of ascetic deprivations. There would be so much the less beer, tea, sugar or butter : possibly no food at all !

Had this great lyric genius survived into the projected utopia of the educationalists and been kept at school willy-nilly until he had attained the age of eighteen, it is to be doubted if he would have written a line ! For instead of that mine of experience which he made his to draw from, he would have been kept poring over books in the dusty form-room dominated by some pedant with less knowledge of life than his own cat : a state-appointed interpreter of interpretations. But *life* is the raw material of art, and of all books worthy of the name. It is the prodigious quantity of first-hand experience that distinguishes the Elizabethan tragedies and comedies from all others, gives them their cutting edge, mints them as true !

When the time came for Davies to write he had a world of experience from which to draw. He had become acquainted, like Trinculo, with "strange bedfellows." He had met Klondyke gold-seekers, corrupt justices, and filthy Jews travelling steerage. He had encountered harlots and mad-women, farmers, down-and-outs, pedlars, drovers, tramps, deck-hands, gentlemen even, and at least one murderer ! He tells us of a character aboard ship who "smoked, chewed tobacco, swaggered, and swore like a trooper," and yet sang like any mermaid ! "His voice was of surprising sweetness; not of great power, but the softest voice I have ever heard from a man, although his aim seemed to be to make it rough and loud, as though ashamed of its sweetness." One day the herdmen were hoisting bales of fodder for the cattle when something went wrong. There was a shout of "Look below !" and down came a heavy bundle. It struck the singer on the shoulder. He spun round and fell unconscious. He was carried aft for examination by the ship's doctor, who discovered him to be a woman! She had worked her passage from Baltimore as a cattleman.

Now with all possible respect to the universities, one meets with few *characters* within their age-old walls, and with fewer than ever to-day, I'm told, when the influx of women into these quondam celibate haunts has transformed the port-bibbing, authoritative, downright don into an ornamental adjunct for afternoon teas! I blush to have to confess that, in the Oxford of my time, I met with *no* murderer—democracy was so young then!—and I was introduced to but one undergraduate tramp. He made money wherewith to pay his various fees by singing "Lead, Kindly Light" to pit queues outside the theatres, by hop-picking, and by the sale of sacred art. He had oleographs of the Prophet Daniel in a den of margarine lions, and others of the infant Samuel disguised as Little Lord Fauntleroy. He drove a brisk trade in these wares, and informed me, for he was a psychologist, that the urge on the part of his customers to buy them was not prompted by piety. They believed that to reject these icons was to court bad luck. Turn down Samuel or Daniel and you are up against the sublime originals of these pictorial representations, so look out for shocks! *Tantæne animis—?*

Alas! for my street-vendor. He got into a spot of bother in Paris through using the cathedral of Notre Dame for eight consecutive nights as his bedroom. The authorities somehow got it into their heads that he meditated decamping with some object of value. Their surmise may have been correct, but the most covetable object there, the Madonna of Michelangelo, is obviously too large to be removed except by van.

Admirably descriptive is the kitchen scene in Davies's autobiography with the grandfather, a retired sea-captain, tramping up and down the passage just outside the door as he had been accustomed to pace it, in former days, on the deck of his small schooner. He would throw open the front door to look at the stars, and inform himself from what latitude the wind blew. It "never changed without his knowledge; for the wary mariner invariably surprised it in the act of doing so."

River Avon at Twyning Ferry
Elkstone

Davies continues : "Three or four times in the evening he would open the kitchen door, as though he had just made his way from the hurricane deck to inquire after the welfare of passengers in the cabin. When this was done, the old lady would sometimes say, 'Francis, do sit down for a minute or two.' Then he would answer gruffly, but not unkindly, 'Avast there, Lydia,' closing the door, to begin again his steady pacing to and fro." The poet's elder brother was a simpleton, although honest and inoffensive. Such sports has Nature to make one boy a natural, his brother a genius!

"My grandmother having to answer the door, ordered my brother to watch some fish which was being prepared for dinner. When she returned the cat was enjoying a good meal under the sofa. To the old lady's cry of 'Francis, did I not tell you to watch the fish?' my brother answered truthfully—for he always told the truth and did what he was told —'So I did, Grandmother, and the cat took it.'"

But every page of this autobiography, so lucid in expression, so intellectually honest, so essentially great-souled, makes excellent reading. Apart from a minor blemish, the occasional misuse of adjective for adverb (as "previous" where custom demands "previously"), it has strange quality, this prose. It is so detached, so unhurrying, so Olympian! It puts me in mind of the novel *Manon Lescaut*, in which even a mutiny or an assassination will be related calmly. When Davies relates his fall from a truck he failed to board, and his loss of a leg beneath the wheels, or the foul language he utters under the anæsthetic during the subsequent amputation, he appears as little ruffled by emotion as though his subject were fishing in some shady Thames backwater.

Yet what a sure eye he has for Nature! In prose or paint it would be difficult to better this winter scene.

"How the snow falls in the north! Flake on flake falling incessantly, until the small dingles are almost on a level with the uplands. It throws itself on the leaves of autumn, and holds them down in security from the strongest winds. It piles great banks against people's doors, and mothers and daughters are made prisoners to their own hearths, until fathers and sons set to and cut a path to the open thoroughfare. Special snow-trains are at work clearing the track to

The old steps, Tetbury
The stone footbridge, Eastleach

make the way easier for passenger-trains and freight-trains that run on passenger lines, being loaded with cattle or other perishable goods; whilst other freight is often delayed for days, and sometimes weeks."

I could wager that this vivid passage, apparently so simple, was written and rewritten, perhaps several times! Sometimes Davies's prose approaches the sublime. He is on the tramp again and yet—vagabond amongst vagabonds—he follows his star and dreams of future fame.

"When I suffered most from lack of rest, or bodily sustenance, as my actual experience become darker, the thoughts of the future became brighter, as the stars shine to correspond with the night's shade."

Could human wit better that simile?

The following too is noble. His emotion vitalizes it for his subject is himself. Only the shallow declaim against egotism in the poets! Never does Milton more unquestionably attain to the sublime than when he treats—whether in *Sampson Agonistes* or *Paradise Lost*—of his own blindness. When Chaucer tells us that he loves the "dayeseye," he helps us to know him better; and to know him is to love him. It is always so. When Horace humorously execrates the tree which fell on his head, or tells us of the wolf who, coming upon him whilst he was singing of his Lalage in a wood, yet fled from him although he was unarmed, we are delighted. And why are we? The egotism of the poet stimulates that of his reader, and it is good to be stimulated. "Why! *I too* love flowers!" says the reader of Chaucer. "*I too* might go blind : how terrible!" he thinks, when deep in Milton. "A tree might fall on *my* head!" is his reaction to Horace. The centuries are bridged. The note of common humanity has been struck. We become tremblingly aware of life's vicissitudes and of its joys.

Crippled by his fall from the train, Davies gives up his tramp to Klondyke perforce and returns instead to England and his old home. Despite poverty, indeed penury, he is determined to fight for recognition as a poet, and more than recognition : fame! His task would have been arduous in Elizabethan or Georgian times, it was to prove Herculean under industrial democracy! In place of the patron who usually affected and often did love culture, and came to the assistance of its exponents, he had to deal with the "public." He had, by hook or crook, to penetrate the grocer-like mentality of the million to whom no form of success is conceivable which is not to be measured in terms of cash. "What did he *give* you for it?" How often have I myself met with that crushing comment! And Davies, poor fellow, had really no cards to play. He was no colossus of publicity like Bernard Shaw; nor could he impress sentimentalists in the role of romantic foreigner, and superimpose upon that of Gaudier a name like Brzeska!

"I was now," says Davies, "more content with my lot, determined that as my body failed, my brains should now have the chance they had longed for, when the spirit had been bullied into submission by the body's activity. . . . A far different Klondyke opened up before my eyes, which corresponded with the dreams of my youth. I pictured myself returning home, not with gold nuggets from the far West, but with literary fame, wrested from no less a place than mighty London. . . .

"Determined to lose no time in the conquest of that city, which I expected would be surrendered to me some time within twelve months, I began, without wasting more time in dreams, to make preparations for this journey. Alas! how many greater men failed in a lifetime at this attempt, although they now stand triumphant in death, holding in their spiritual hands the freedom and keys of the whole world's cities!"

In his slow climb into recognition Davies had to struggle harder than Dr Johnson ever had. Both men were poor, both abstinent. But we do not read of the doctor studying or composing in an overcrowded doss-house amidst the fumes of a coke-stove which took the playfulness out of a kitten, and slowly but surely asphyxiated the lodgers. But besides genius, Nature had endowed Davies with superb physique. She gave him tenacity in overflowing measure. The metal which might so easily have broken upon the anvil endured the blows, and became thrice as tough. England was spared the disgrace of causing the death of a second Chatterton; not this time a boy, but a man in the maturity of his powers. Yet though the

natural bent of Davies's soul was towards joy, his poems, as
we should guess, record not a few black moments :

> But rain without a break succeeding rain,
> Will wash the buried seed out, rot the grain,
> Make genius blind whose mind is with the lark
> To see the dawn while others are in dark.

> The man doth choose his star, and if he fail
> Inhabit that, what shall to him avail
> A thousand others that would give him home?
> Give him his star, or let the darkness come !

> He ceased : he who had fallen in the strife,
> And might have sucked some honey out of life
> And lodged it in the world's hive to its joy—
> But failed, since none would give his brain employ.

We had been speaking of the poet's vision, and in the copy
of his autobiography which he gave me Davies wrote this
epigram which admirably expresses that something of excite-
ment with which, in common with children, poets view
Nature. The child cannot express what he feels, and when he
has achieved power of expression, intensity of emotion fails
him, the vision fades, he has nothing to express. Not so the
poet :

> Fools have their second childhood, but the great
> Still keep their first, and have no second state.

This assuredly was true of Davies himself, whose directness,
dewy freshness, and intensity of joyful utterance were his to
the last.

> My youth was my old age,
>   Weary and long;
> It had too many cares
>   To think of song;
> My moulting days all came
>   When I was young.

> Now, in life's prime, my soul
>   Comes out in flower;

Late, as with Robin, comes
My singing power;
I was not born to joy
Till this late hour.

W. H. Davies had achieved his goal. Not riches, for those
he never sought. Yet he obtained a good deal more, even
upon the material plane, than the simple room he had
dreamed of with its fire and shelf of books. He had a
pleasant house at Nailsworth with a sufficiency of all neces-
sities, and of what for him would be luxuries. There was a
tolerably large garden at the back with a view over the roofs
of the town below and the green meadows beyond. In the
garden—true countryman that he was!—he loved to work
despite the handicap of that artificial leg. He took a spade
in the midst of our talk, to show me how well he could dig,
and whilst thus employed you would not have suspected his
infirmity.

"When you write a lyric," I remember asking him, "do
you write quickly, or keep it by you and polish it?"

"Sometimes a single line, or two, or three, will dart into
my mind. I think them too good to lose, so I keep them, and
build up the poem to them. It will be a long while then
before the piece is perfected. But the first lines *were essentially* the poem; and the whole thing will be of a piece. At
other times, the poem seems to start into my brain practically
complete. I remember once, in my bachelor days, putting on
an egg to boil, when an idea struck me. It *possessed* me! I
ferreted out paper and pencil, and wrote my lyric then and
there : literally in the 'boiling of an egg'! Although I'm willing to admit," adds Davies, with his Ben Jonsonian smile,
"it was an *uncommonly* hard-boiled egg when I came to eat
it!" That after-thought is typical both of his humour and his
rectitude. He was not out to dazzle or astonish, but to tell
truth, as even a trifle like this shows.

We returned from the garden. Davies produced a decanter
of port, and we spent an agreeable hour turning over books
and manuscripts. I saw upon his walls his portrait by William
Rothenstein; upon its pedestal a bronze head of him by
Epstein. The poet was now *laudatus a laudandis*, and found

in his work and its growing appreciation by poetry-lovers a
settled philosophical content.

"I said to Flecker, 'You *must* see Kenneth Hare. You're
both poets, and genuine poets are rare.' I brought him yester-
day to your digs in Beaumont Street. Where were you? We
waited a whole hour. In any case, look him up, there's a
good fellow. He's at Trinity, you know. You'll find him an
extraordinarily interesting chap, and a personality!"

"But I can't just march in on him!" I protested.

"Oh, yes, you can! Why on earth not? You've got his
Bridge of Fire, haven't you? Well, if you want an excuse—
which you don't—take that round with you, and ask him to
autograph it."

How often later was I to regret that I never took my
friend's advice! Why didn't I? I fancy I suffered from a
delusion characteristic of youth, that we all have time and to
spare; that we were bound to meet some time, so what was
the hurry? By argument from analogy it seemed a possible
inference that we should ourselves grow old some day : and
even die! Yet practically speaking, there was no hurry about
anything. We might postpone all reflections upon old age if
not *sine die*, yet for a blissfully indefinite period! We had all
our lives before us to meet in, and age was academic. Age
was for *dons*!

Oxford lay far behind me when I next heard of Flecker.
This was in 1910. He was in the Consular Service, I was
told, and abroad. Still I never doubted that he would return
home on leave, and that then we should meet. Then came
1914, when the Germans overran Belgium, deluging Europe
with blood. The still lingering, still vital Edwardian age with
its aristocracy, its ability and its wit, went down into the
whirlpool. Civilization itself was threatened. And, in 1915,
one of its lights was prematurely extinguished. Flecker died
at Leysin, Switzerland, of tuberculosis.

Although Flecker was born at Lewisham, London, on 5th
November 1884, yet Gloucestershire justifiably claims him;
for it was in Cheltenham that he passed his childhood—that
period rich in formative impressions—and here too that he
received his early education, at Dean Close School, where

his father, Dr Flecker, was headmaster. It was of his childhood in Gloucestershire that he was thinking when he composed, as he lay dying in Switzerland, his posthumously published "November Eves."

Flecker has suffered perhaps some loss of reputation by
the reprinting of too many of his juvenilia which, had his life
been longer spared, he would in all probability have suppressed. His translation of that conversation-piece of
Catullus—

> Varus me meus ad suos amores—

is a poor affair indeed compared with his last rendering from
a Latin original. Thus, his reinterpretation of Vergil's Book
VI, which he was at work upon when already sick and in a
sanatorium, is masterly.

When once Flecker attains the maturity of his powers, no
false quantity mars the rhythm, no assonance the music of
his verse. One can no more detect a slip of the pen in such
a lyric as "Glion—Noon" than one can that of the needle
in a Thames-side etching by Whistler. ("Glion—Evening"
pleases me less, since, although no less flawless technically, it
betrays overmuch the influence of Théophile Gautier.)

But poetry is the most consummate of the arts. More goes
to it than observation, however accurate, technique, however
brilliant, more even than passion. I mean that *magic* which
it has baffled critics to define. This quality made the Greeks
suppose that a poet was in touch with ultramundane agencies,
that he had access to the bed of a nymph, or was breathed
on by a god. This quality of magic, like ecstasy, cannot be
long sustained. It glimmers for a moment—strange wandering fire!—and vanishes as soon.

NOVEMBER EVES

November evenings! Damp and still
They used to cloak Leckhampton hill,
And lie down close on the grey plain,
And dim the dripping window-pane,
And send queer winds like Harlequins
That seized our elms for violins
And struck a note so sharp and low
Even a child could feel the woe.

Now fire chased shadow round the room;
Tables and chairs grew vast in gloom:
We crept about like mice, while Nurse
Sat mending, solemn as a hearse,
And even our unlearned eyes
Half closed with choking memories.

Is it the mist or the dead leaves,
Or the dead men—November eves?

The reader of Flecker's collected poems will be rewarded by not a few of those flawless pieces which will bear reading, re-reading, and reading yet again; lyrics wherein the power of genius has indissolubly wrought music, form and colour into a perfect whole. There is "Brumana," for instance, in which the poet gives such poignant expression to home-sickness. There are "Hyali," "Areiya," "The Old Ships," "The Painter's Mistress"—this last surely as delicately colourful a nude study as verse can show! Or he may prefer "In Pheacia," a poem only to be understood by youth, a thing not for critics but for lovers.

"To a Poet a Thousand Years Hence" expresses a thought which lurks in the hearts of all poets, since their imaginations enable them to sense the actuality of the past and to live, by anticipation, in the future. A noble enthusiasm inspires the grand sonnet, "On Turner's Polyphemus," though some may regard as a flaw the obviously Miltonic inspiration of the last line. In his "War Song of the Saracens" Flecker triumphs where, in a piece of similar purport, "How They brought the Good News from Ghent," Robert Browning may be said to have failed. Both poets attempt, by a cunning clash of syllables, to evoke in the minds of their readers the idea of galloping horses; but Flecker's lines are animated by an incomparably joyous spontaneity, whereas Browning's are marred by a certain theatricality and self-consciousness.

In the Epilogue to his Arabian romance "Hassan," where we see the merchants crowding about the "Gate of the Sun" in preparation for their great symbolic journey to Samarcand, Flecker combines, in one and the same composition, the very gold of poetry and humour! This combination, it will be remembered, William Morris maintained to be impossible.

Let me conclude this study with a few stanzas from "Oak and Olive" which, though hardly comparable with some of the poems mentioned, is yet characteristically Flecker with his humour and his vivid outline. It should possess a further appeal for those who love Gloucestershire, for the county is its inspiration.

When I go down the Gloucester lanes
    My friends are deaf and blind :
Fast as they turn their foolish eyes,
    The Mænads leap behind,
And when I hear the fire-winged feet,
    They only hear the wind.

Have I not chased the fluting Pan
    Through Cranham's sober trees?
Have I not sat on Painswick Hill
    With a nymph upon my knees,
And she as rosy as the dawn,
    And naked as the breeze?

But when I lie in Grecian fields,
    Smothered in asphodel,
Or climb the blue and barren hills,
    Or sing in woods that smell
With such hot spices of the South
    As mariners might sell—

Then my heart turns where no sun burns,
    To lands of glittering rain,
To fields beneath low-clouded skies
    New-widowed of their grain,
And Autumn leaves like blood and gold
    That strew a Gloucester lane.

Oh well I know sweet Hellas now,
    And well I knew it then,
When I with starry lads walked out—
    But ah, for home again !
Was I not bred in Gloucestershire,
    One of the Englishmen !

Flecker lies buried at Leckhampton hard by Cheltenham with its shady Promenade, its Regency air, and its gardens of flowering trees. Let us hope that this charming town will honour with a permanent memorial one of the most brilliant of her sons.

Roger Bacon (1214–94), who knew the composition of gunpowder, gave an account of spectacles and understood, though he perhaps never constructed, a telescope, is believed, on the faith of long tradition, to have lived at some period of his life at Toadsmoor, a hamlet about four miles from Stroud. Whilst at Oxford he was highly appreciated by the men of learning of that university. Later he migrated to Paris. Here, with other subjects, he studied alchemy and optics. In 1250 he returned to England, enjoyed the friendship of Robert Grostete, Bishop of Lincoln, and acquired an outstanding reputation for his scientific inquiries.

He joined the Franciscans, and John of Fedanza, better known as Bonaventura, being its General, fell under that bane of all men of original genius in the Middle Ages, suspicion of practising magic. He was placed under restraint. For ten whole years of his life, and men's lives were shorter then than now, he was kept in solitary confinement in Paris, where the most jealous care was taken that he should have no communication with the outside world. The philosopher was forbidden the use of writing materials, books and scientific instruments, including of course his own. This infamous treatment of the English Leonardo da Vinci brings to mind that sarcastic reflection of Heinrich Heine upon the restraint to which great minds were subjected in the Middle Ages, so wittily rendered by Hugh Kingsmill:

> The crowd had liberty of thought,
> Unfettered were the masses;
> We only gagged a paltry few,
> To wit, the *thinking* asses!

Roger Bacon was not set free until 1392. He died at Oxford the same year; from which it is presumed that it was only because he *was* dying that he was released.

His masterpiece is the *Opus Majus*, of which it has been said that it is the combined "*Encyclopædia* and *Novum Organum* of the thirteenth century." A universal spirit, Roger Bacon's studies included grammar (not excepting *Greek* grammar, in which he was a pioneer two centuries before his time), logic, mathematics, the *Calendar*—he suggested its reformation five centuries before Lord Chesterfield brought in his Bill for that purpose—physics, optics, alchemy (the ancestor of modern chemistry), moral philosophy and *experimental* science.

Centuries passed and the world no longer menaced scientists; then centuries and scientists became a menace to the world.

John Cabot (?–1498) was by birth a Genoese whose passion was exploration. He sought to obtain patronage at the Courts of Spain and of Portugal, failed in both attempts, came to England and settled in Bristol as a merchant, probably as early as 1472. On 5th March 1496 he applied to the English king Henry VII for letters-patent for himself and his three sons, Lewis, Sebastian and Sanco, entitling him to take possession on behalf of England of any unknown countries which he might discover. His request was granted—such being, in those days, the Bohemian freedom of the seas. John Cabot must now be regarded as an Englishman, for he lived as an English merchant in Bristol and took service under the English king.

With his new commission, in the spring of 1497, the adventurer sailed from the great port of the West in two ships, the name of one of which, the *Mathew*, has come down to us. They were English-built and manned by English seamen. Glorious success attended the enterprise. He viewed the coast of Newfoundland (or Labrador) at this day "unknown to all Christians," and sailed along nine hundred miles of coastline before breaking off and returning to England to report progress.

The log, if such there were, has not survived, and the feats of John Cabot and his son Sebastian have sometimes been confused owing to the lack of contemporary memoranda. It seems, however, probable that it was John who, at the happy conclusion of this voyage, presented his royal patron with presents which, however worthy of a king's acceptance, must have been a trifle embarrassing. They included three savages. Everybody was devoured with curiosity about these men, who ate raw flesh, garbed themselves in "beasts' skins" and were, in their demeanour, like "brute beasts" themselves. Amongst other souvenirs of their travels, King Henry, then resident at Richmond, was to receive such touching symbols of the loyalty of the returning mariners as "hawks, wildcats, and popinjays."

Raimondo di Soncino, writing on 18th December 1497, declares that John Cabot recorded his discoveries upon both a map and a globe. Both unhappily are lost. Were they extant to-day we should be the better able to establish John's title to fame with exactitude. On 3rd February 1498 King Henry granted him letters-patent again, this time in the name of John Cabot only. In the early summer of that year John sailed from Bristol—not this time with two, but as admiral of a small fleet of five good ships—upon the second expedition to the scene of his triumphs. The banners fluttered out, the trumpeters blew a flourish, the thronged quayside cheered; the crews cheered back. Now they are out of earshot! Now out of sight, lost in the shimmer between blue sky and blue water. Lost effectively : for not a man nor a plank of the expedition was ever seen or heard of again! The adventurer had sailed beyond longitude and latitude. But Fame still publishes him as father of the fearless race of Tudor voyagers.

Sebastian Cabot (1474?–1557) was the worthy son of the great father from whom he inherited his roving disposition, his gifts as cosmographer, cartographer, and —one might add—linguist, since Sebastian would appear to have attained easy mastery both in Spanish and Italian. We must think of him also as not a little of a courtier, for he would appear to have ingratiated himself with Henry VIII as his father, John, had with Henry's father. Certain it is that, putting his gifts as cartographer to account, Henry commissioned him to map Gascony and Guienne.

Sebastian, however, had looked for something more exciting.

> He wonder'd that your lordship
> Would suffer him to spend his youth at home,
> While other men, of slender reputation,
> Put forth their sons to seek preferment out :
> Some to the wars, to try their fortune there;
> Some to discover islands far away.

To one whose father had given this king's father wild men, wildcats and painted paraquitoes from lands no Christian had ever before heard of, mapping Guienne must have seemed very small potatoes indeed!

Lord Willoughby suggested that Sebastian should apply to the court of Spain. He did so, and with greater success than his father had experienced. He was eagerly entertained by King Ferdinand the Catholic, and, like many another Englishman of genius, was lost—luckily for a few years only—to the country of his birth. King Ferdinand gave Sebastian the rank of captain, a yearly pension of 50,000 maravedis, made him his Cartographer Royal and a member of the Council of the New Indies. Before the close of the year he had fallen in love with and married a Spanish girl, Catalina Medrano. On 23rd January 1515 Ferdinand the Catholic died, and Sebastian returned to the country of his birth. Whilst cartographer to his Spanish patron Sebastian had made a map of the world. This must have been made in several "states," for one "cut by Clement Adams" was shortly to be seen "in the privie gallery at Westminster, and in many other ancient merchants' houses." One likes to think of it as one of those gorgeous Renaissance affairs, bright as a monkish missal with azure and gold, and with whales or mermaids at the more important rivers' mouths.

Some assert that in the year 1517 Sebastian sailed from Bristol and discovered the bay and strait now known as Hudson Bay and Hudson Strait. Certain it is that Englishmen had become very much alive to this great navigator's genius. He had not, for example, to return to Bristol at his own expense. A warrant was issued to one Peckham to convey him—"to come out of Hispain and inhabit in England." He settled in his native Bristol and in the January of 1548 was awarded a pension of £166 13s 4d. How this compared with the late King Ferdinand's maravedis in purchasing power I fancy there's nobody to-day who could even approximately determine.

If England had become conscious of an acquisition in Sebastian's returning to the fold, Spain was exasperated at his loss. The Spanish monarch made a peremptory demand of the English Ambassador in Spain for the fugitive's return; he was the King of Spain's servant : he was in receipt of a pension from the Spanish Crown. The Privy Council's reply was spirited; they declared that Sebastian *didn't want to go.* Two governments were quarrelling over the possession of our Bristolian. He had most certainly "arrived."

Sebastian was made first Governor of the Merchant Adventurers, and in this capacity proved inaugurator of a new era in the history of commerce and English merchant shipping. He induced his company to strive after the "search and discoverie of the northern part of the world by sea, to open a way and passage to Cathay by the North East." The formation of the Merchant Adventurers Company was taking shape. On 18th December 1551 it was definitely incorporated, Sebastian's governorship of it being granted for life. In May 1553 under his supervision three vessels were fitted out for the Cathay project, "Sir H. Willoughby" being appointed Admiral and "R. Chancellor" Chief Pilot. The expedition was superlatively successful, the adventurers making in 1553 the *accidental* discovery of Russia. This enabled Antony Jenkinson five years later to open up the first trade-route to Central Asia across the Caspian Sea.

Within a week of the entry into London of "Armada Philip"—the pastry-complexioned husband of our Queen Mary—Sebastian's pension was recalled, for his having displayed so marked a preference for his own country over Spain : a gesture beneath the dignity of a king! Perhaps Philip sensed the odium this move was bringing upon himself, for two days later the victim was allowed to *share* his pension with one William Worthington. Despite this parsimonious protest from the least popular of monarchs, the Governor of the Company of Merchant Adventurers, whether as cartographer, navigator, or discoverer enjoyed ever increasing repute both at home and abroad, exercising towards the latter half of his life the office of Chief Pilot of England. Sebastian died at Bristol in 1557.

Gloucestershire is second to no county in the roll of men eminent in the realms of letters, action and science, but as my endeavour in this book is to be rather evocative than exhaustive, I will mention a few only. The historians include Robert of Gloucester, composer of a rhymed *Chronicle of Britain* in the days of Edward I. Richard of Cirencester (died 1401) who became a monk at Westminster, where he wrote his *Historia ab Hengista*. Sir Robert Atkyns of Sapperton (1647–1711), historian of the county, has his effigy in Sapperton church, which has already been mentioned. Samuel Rudder (1726–1801), who made various corrections upon his great original Atkyns and brought the earlier history up to date. Rudder's folio, published 1779, bears the motto "*Sit par fortuna labori.*" We owe it both to Atkyns and Rudder to remember that they laboured for their own credit and the public good. Neither can have enjoyed the least pecuniary profit from his scholarship or indefatigable hard work. Indeed Atkyns's monumental folio saw the light the year after its author's death.

William Grocyn (1442–1519), the tutor of Sir Thomas More and Erasmus, introduced the study of Greek into Oxford. He was born at Bristol, educated at Winchester and New College, Oxford, and as Greek was practically unknown in the England of his day he went to Italy when in his forty-sixth year to perfect himself in his subject. (We must remember that the "Sir John Cheke" of Milton's sonnet, who "taught Cambridge and King Edward Greek," came later into the field—b. 1514, d. 1557.) All credit then to the pioneer. Every Englishman to whom Greek means anything is in the debt of William Grocyn, not least the poets—the Elizabethans, Chapman and Ben Jonson, those of the eighteenth century, that age rich in classical culture, and later—amongst how many others!—Shelley, Swinburne, Mathew Arnold, and Robert Bridges.

Thomas Chatterton (1752–70)—how short a span of life his dates reveal!—was the son of a sub-chanter of St Mary Redcliffe, Bristol. He anticipated, and in great measure created, the romantic movement in poetry, both at home and abroad. He suffered the fate of so many pioneers, that of dying before the slow world had had time to appraise his merits. Poverty and semi-starvation—occasioned in part by the astuteness of some editors who accepted the boy's articles with no intention of paying for them—drove him, after a stubborn fight, to poison himself with arsenic when he was only seventeen years and nine months old.

Robert Southey (1774–1843) was the son of a linen-draper of Bristol. His verse, particularly his blank verse, is quite unbelievably bad—I am not sure that it is not even flatter than that of Mr Bernard Shaw, in his "The Admirable Bashville"—but he is the author of at least two excellent works in prose, his *Life of Nelson* and his nursery classic, translated into many languages, *Goldilocks and the Three Bears*.

In the realm of the fine arts we have Sir Thomas Lawrence, the portrait-painter (1769–1833). He was knighted in 1815, and in 1820 became President of the Royal Academy. His reputation would be higher had he not had so brilliant a contemporary as Gainsborough.

Under the head of action I have already spoken at length of the two Cabots, father and son. I will add one more, Sir William Penn (1621–70), father of William Penn, the founder of Pennsylvania. Sir William, born at Bristol, rose to the rank of Admiral, distinguished himself in the Dutch wars, and captured the island of Jamaica, which has remained ever since a British possession.

Amongst Gloucestershire scientists, I have already spoken of James Bradley (1693–1762). In 1742 he became Astronomer Royal. Edward Jenner (1749–1823) was born at Berkeley. He was the discoverer of vaccination and pioneer of modern sero-therapy. John Caxton, F.R.S. (1718–72), electrician, was the first to make powerful magnets. He was born at Stroud. There is no memorial to him. Jonathan Hulls is to-day a name almost forgotten, yet he was one of those who helped to shape the course of things to come, for he was the inventor of the steamboat. Hulls was the son of a mechanic of Aston Magna, a hamlet near Moreton. He settled at Broad Campden as a clock-repairer. He died in London in obscurity and poverty. Sir Mathew

Gloucester Cathedral
Cotswold Landscape

Hale (1609–76) became (1671) Chief Justice of the King's Bench.

And shall we pass Maskelyne over in silence? John Nevil Maskelyne of the St George's Hall who gilded the lapses of time—as somebody most inadequately tells us Shakespeare did—with "innocent delusion"! The mighty magician was born at Cheltenham of a Cheltenham mother, and was at it already at the age of sixteen. He exposed Davenport Brothers' Cabinet and Dark Séance—bogus spiritualism. He claimed indeed that spiritualists could produce *no* phenomena which, after a reasonable delay for thinking the problem out, he would not produce himself upon his stage. Still this though amazing is not by any means proof. If John Nevil Maskelyne can draw the cork without touching the champagne bottle, this does not absolutely dispense with the outside-chance possibility that a poltergeist or the ghost of a mischievous—and bibulous—butler may not be able to perform the same feat.

What a man he was! What could he *not* call from the "vasty deep," or pack off so soon as he had had enough of it into the infinite, the seventh sphere, or possibly even into the wings! One remembers the mulatto driving his donkey. Crack! Snap! went the whip, and the noise made by the donkey's hoofs might have disturbed the passers-by in the street outside. And then—*hey presto!*—both had vanished before your eyes! And do you remember the "Haunted House"? In a container the size of one of those sentry-boxes before Buckingham Palace ghost after ghost appeared: a miser counting his gold, a spectral house-painter with his brush! And this on a stage where the public had been lounging and studying, and playing Nosey Parker not a couple of minutes before. For the "Haunted House" stood upon a table, and the inquisitive had been allowed to thrust between its legs with sticks and umbrellas. Their knowing thrusts encountered only air!

"Do you see how I do it?" Maskelyne asked me, for, as a dramatic critic, I had pressed forward with the crowd.

"Not the remotest, Mr Maskelyne!"

He smiled like Mephistopheles.

o

Ozleworth Valley
Tetbury

Let me relate an anecdote which was told of him when I was in the twenties. Maskelyne, on a train journey, found himself in a railway carriage with two men opposite him, and one in the corner farthest from him, on the same side as himself.

"What about a game of cards?" says one of the men opposite. "Would you care to join us?"

"Who, I?" asks the ingenuous lamb of a confederate, "but I am so poor a player!"

"Well, it's only for small stakes, you know. Don't be a kill-joy, sir!"

"Well then, just for the sake of sport!"

"And you, sir?"

"I?" said Maskelyne, who had been studying them—but unostentatiously—"I'm a very poor hand at cards!"

"Well, we're no good; only just learning, in fact!"

"Well," says Maskelyne, "perhaps I will then: but cash *on the table*."

Was there, or was there not, something sinister in this?

Of course he took all their money!

"*You*, gentlemen, are card-sharpers: but *I*, gentlemen, am *Maskelyne*! No! I won't dream of returning a ha'penny! But I feel like a magnum of champagne, and if you care to join me——"

Let me, by way of conclusion, revert again to the "spacious days" and present a character who never fails to make an appeal to Englishmen the world over—the sportsman. Nor is this, after all, so very unreasonable, for sport, if it does nothing more, promotes physical health and where *that* is lacking mental health is impossible, as Juvenal reminds us in the most universally quoted of all Latin epigrams.

Captain Robert Dover, then (1575–1641), must have had solid no less than social qualities, for he is the subject of some laudatory verses by Ben Jonson—with the possible exception of Milton—the most learned of all our poets. Dover inaugurated the famous Cotswold "Olympic" games, and directed them for nearly forty years. He had practised as an attorney at Barton-on-the-Heath, Warwickshire (he was not a Gloucestershire man by birth), but was poles removed from the popular conception of the wrangling lawyer. He was consulted only twice and succeeded on both occasions in making peace between the litigants. His true interest was in athletics. He obtained from James I permission to select a site suitable for the contests he had in view, and chose a conveniently open stretch of country between Evesham and Stow-on-the-Wold. This still bears the name of Dover's Hill. James was ready enough to forward the scheme, both as loving field sports and as hating Puritans. And these last were now raising their customary hullabaloo about the "Cotswold Olympics" as "wicked and horrid sin"!

The Groom of the Chamber to James, Endymion Porter, presented the sportsman on behalf of Royalty with sundry suits, together with such trifles as a hat, ruff, and feathers. If such gifts appear to-day to savour of the ludicrous, it is because in this age of drab attire we are in danger of forgetting what his suits cost a gentleman of rank at the English Renaissance, more particularly, of course, if he desired to shine. In Buckingham's stricture of the clothes worn by the English nobles at the Field of the Cloth of Gold we may find the clue to Dover's ruff, hat and feathers :

> Oh, many
> Have broke their backs with laying manors on them
> For this great journey!

And I recall a passage in an old chronicle in which the loss by shipwreck of divers suits of cloth-of-gold which belonged to a nobleman is recorded as an item not beneath the dignity of a serious historian.

Mounted as he invariably was upon a white horse and tailored by royalty, hatted, ruffed, feathered, Captain Robert Dover unquestionably "filled the bill." The crowds were enormous. Nobles and commoners flocked to take part in or to watch the sports from as much as sixty miles away. A castle of carpenters' work, so constructed as to turn, windmill-fashion, upon a pivot, was set up upon a commanding height. Watchers kept a sharp look-out and so soon as they saw Dover come galloping up, the ostrich feathers fluttering gallantly in that hat which had been the King of England's, cannon from the festal fortress thundered out the announcement that the "Olympicks" were now to begin.

It was a democratic field with items for all tastes, gentle or plebeian. There was cudgel-play, for instance, in which rustic swashbucklers gave or received bloody heads. There were wrestling, jumping and pitching the hammer and the bar. Horsemen could compete at "quintain," when riders who failed at full gallop to spear the small ring fair and square were precipitated by a revolving beam from the saddle. There was "balloon," a sort of mixed foot and handball. As with football the game was played between rival teams. One struck the flying ball or kicked it, as opportunity served, and hands were protected by guards called "balloon-brassers."

There was horse-racing along a course of several miles. There was hare-hunting. Thanks to that same kind heart which made Dover, when attorney, compound his clients' quarrels, so soon as the timorous creatures were fairly run down their lives were spared. Addison must surely have had Dover in mind when he makes his Sir Roger de Coverley save the hares he hunted from the hounds, and preserve them unmolested for the remainder of their lives in a "veterans' park." Yellow badges were sported in sign of victory. We read of "five hundred gentlemen wearing Dover's favours." Neither must you suppose that so gallant a fellow as the Captain would forget the ladies. There were "country dances for virgins" and for these, as for the other items, valuable prizes were offered. There were tents to feast in and no prohibitions—depend upon it!—either upon liquor or hours. To read of Dover's doing is to forget the industrial present, and to find oneself as though by magic in the "merrie England" of tradition.

It was not to be for long. King James died, and under increasing Puritan pressure the "wicked and horrid Cotswold Olympics" were suppressed. With the accession to the throne of the "Merry Monarch" Dover's games were revived, and, with some few breaks, were continued until 1852. Queen Victoria's reign being hardly less puritanical than Cromwell's they were then finally discontinued.

CHAPTER XVI

COTSWOLD VILLAGES (I)

COBBERLEY——MISERDEN——BOURTON-ON-THE-WATER

COBBERLEY

"S I N C E you like walking," says my old cottager of Foston's Ash, "why don't you go to Cobberley?"

"What's to be seen there?"

"There's statues to Dick Whittington's father and mother in Cobberley church, and Dick himself, and the cat."

"Really!"

"Yes! I thought everybody knew that Dick were born at Cobberley!"

So I set out, skirting the fringe of glorious Cranham Woods, unspoilt and unenclosed; past the Royal George at Birdlip—where stood a posting-house centuries upon centuries ago, where Roman and Romanized Briton changed horses; past the Golden Hart—where in the same polished but remote time thirsty legionaries slaked their thirst: for there was a tavern there even then!—past Stockwell, sacred to the memory of "Farmer" George; and so by sunny fields and shady lanes to the Cobberley of my pilgrimage.

"Were you looking vor someone?"

"I want to see the church."

I am shown the sacristan's cottage: "If 'a be out, just go into th' shed. You'll find th' key on th' oak-stub where he does his hammering. He be a carpenter, look."

"Will you show me the monuments in the church?"

There are the effigies sure enough, the man, the woman and the child lying fast in stone. On Dick's gown stands a scuttle full of coke. From the stone face of the mother I take an aged copy of the *News of the World*. There's fame for you!

Vain the ambition of Kings
Who seek by trophies and dead things,
To leave a living name behind,
And weave but nets to catch the wind.

I remove the coal-scuttle, and study. Chins, ears and noses
have been ground flat, and the expressions which the sculptor
hoped, for his fame and theirs, should be eternal have been
rendered meaningless as pudding-basins. There is the *cat*. So
I have been assured. And I can see for myself that it is not
an owl.

"I suppose there is no doubt that these effigies *are* those
of the Whittingtons?"

"They might be."

"But *are* they?"

"Some say they are Berkeleys."

"Have the Berkeleys a connection with the Whittingtons?"

"They might have."

"These effigies are terribly defaced. Did you have the
Puritans at Cobberley?"

"We might have."

Behind a deal staircase—a very modern affair indeed
—which leads up to the organ I discover another effigy
half-blotted out, as though he had been interned in an
oubliette.

"Hullo! And this figure? Not in armour, I see. Was he a
priest?"

"He might be."

I might as well question an ox. I seek out the post-
office.

"Have you any postcards of the effigies of the Whittingtons?"

"There's no call for them."

"Where did the house stand where Dick Whittington was
born?"

"I can tell you," says a woman who has just come in with
a chip basket, "did you see the vicarage, just by the church?
It stood there."

"I'm immensely obliged."

"Quite welcome."

How remote this Arcadia seemed. Hitler might be a myth,

bestial and grotesque as his own Thor or Woden. Mussolini might exist but as the profile upon a coin, or pathetic dust from an urn in Herculaneum.[1] Cattle browse the wayside grass. Ducks appraise me with bright, cunning little eyes. *"Quick: a stranger!"* The drake shepherds his mistresses to the stream. They walk uncouthly, but take the water with dignity, confident of their precarious element, cut the clear stream, put a distance between us and leave in their wakes a transient galaxy of sparkling diamonds.

By a plank in the outskirts a fellow volunteers the information, "That be th' mechanical milking-shed."

"Wasn't Dick Whittington born hereabouts?"

"Ay."

"Do they know *where* he was born?"

"Th' house stood on th' same ground that th' post-office do to-day."

"Thanks."

There is no pub at Cobberley, which explains why adventurous Whittington migrated to London. I tramp to Birdlip. In the saloon bar of the Royal George I catch the words: "I'm joining the Wrens. I shall be leaving Cobberley soon."

Heaven-sent chance! She will know whether the cowman or the chip-basket woman was right as to Dick's birthplace.

"Excuse me; you mentioned Cobberley?"

"Yes?" (helpfully).

"I wanted to find out some particulars about Dick Whittington's birthplace. The sacristan wasn't very helpful."

My young lady smiles her scorn.

"Oh! *He.* What should *he* know about Dick Whittington? He's a *stranger.* He's only been at Cobberley eight years."

"Oh! A parvenu."

Her patriotism, her pride delight me.

"Now I was *born* at Cobberley!"

"'A citizen of no mean city.' What's it to be?" She favours a gin-and-lime, her boy in the Air Force a pint.

"Then *you* can tell me where Dick's birthplace stood?"

[1] Written in 1943.

"It stood," says my young friend, "on the site of the mechanical milking-shed."

MISERDEN

Sturdy, stone-built Miserden. The original name of this pretty place was Green Hampstead, but its being made over, after the Conquest, to one Musard, a Norman, it was re-christened "Musard-den"—*den*=a valley—with the inevitable result. "He shan't get away with *that*!" said Farmer Hodge, in the idiom and dialect of that distant day. So he pronounced the new word "Mizzerden," and gave his village a name no whit less English-sounding than that which it had enjoyed before the outlandish foreigner had begun monkeying with it.

You should pay Miserden a visit, if only to see the effigies to Sir William Sandys and his wife in the little bluff-towered church of St Andrew. Of the good knight himself it will suffice to say that nothing in his life became him better than his having this monument put up to himself after it. He was an admirable Lord of the Manor no doubt, a petty king in his day, but he left no message for after-times; he never raised the temperature of the Thames.

He was not—as one book has the effrontery to assert—the "honest country lord" whom Shakespeare represents as kissing Anne Boleyn at the banquet given by Wolsey in *Henry VIII*. This Sandys of the effigy died in the same year as Oliver Cromwell, and, though records are somewhat contradictory, appears to have lived to the age of seventy. This fact, if fact it be, would date him back not to Henry VIII's reign but to that of Elizabeth. Even so, he would have been too young to play a part upon that glittering stage. He would have been a boy of nine when the Invincible Armada sailed, and was defeated.

The knight before us was descended from a much earlier Sir William Sandys of Rottenby Castle in the parish of St Bees, Cumberland. This ancestor lived in the tumultuous days of Henry VI. The Sir William whom this monument immortalizes obtained his house and lands at Miserden by the unromantic method of purchase from the then owners, the Jerninghams, a Norfolk family. One regrets that the effigy could not have shown us the sculptor rather than the knight. For this artist makes stone speak. We are at the late Renaissance and have bidden no tearful farewell to the Middle Ages with its conventional mysticism, which gives to every Gothic knight so tedious a resemblance to all his fellows. This piece is a portrait and a convincingly true one! The Renaissance is the day for those who love life and love to behold life cunningly portrayed whether in static stone or paint, or in flux across the poets' mirror of the stage. Observe the beard, the eyebrows; notice the exquisite detail of that left hand where the veins show through the transparent-seeming skin; there is character in all. One finger steadies the scabbard of the sword, which one may imagine slipping: the other is half-concealed within the folds of the scarf. Notice the studs of the breastplate: the hinges of the greaves: the very claws of that allegorical bird, the griffin, against which the mailed shoes rest. Lady Sandys lies beside her lord, cut, she also, in alabaster. Notice the lacework of her cape: what perfection of detail! She holds her book of prayers with its loose-lying ribbons. At first glance, one perceives that the binding is vellum, not leather, so smoothly is the surface wrought up. But do not suppose, if I seem to harp upon detail, that the composition as a whole has been sacrificed to minutiæ. Nothing could be farther from the truth.

Sir William, or whichever of his descendants it waswho caused this monument to be erected, was less successful in his quest of a poet for the epitaph. The words seem stilted. But fashion affects even verse, so perhaps they may not have seemed so to a contemporary.

Here in this cabanet Earth's Richest Treasure
A pair unparable [incomparable] and therefore reader
Expect not phrases in sad elegyes
To clame [claim] thy fancy but to thaw thyne eyes—
    etc.

But my eyes refuse to "thaw"; and I can only hope that the sculptor was as happy in his knight as the knight was in his sculptor.

A word now as to that sculptor, for it is the height of

ingratitude to take pleasure in a man's handiwork yet not trouble to inquire as to his name. Nicholas Stone (1586–1647) was one of those variously gifted men who were characteristic of the Renaissance, whether at home here or abroad. No soul then was forced into a narrow rut by the necessity for specialization. Shakespeare himself, not contented with shining with the utmost lustre both at tragedy and comedy— dramatists amongst the ancients had confined themselves to one only of these two fields—contrived to outstrip all his forerunners and make a new *genre* of the historical play. Nicholas Stone was born, the son of a quarryman, in the year that witnessed Sir Philip Sidney's death. He died in that which saw Charles I a prisoner to the Puritans in his own favourite palace of Hampton Court. Stone's birthplace was Exmouth, but he was sent up to London as a youth and apprenticed to one Isaac James, a mason. He must always have been an ambitious boy, for after two years we read of him in Holland. To go so far afield must have required money and, since his father can hardly have been in a position to do much for him, it is reasonable to suppose that the young mason put by a sufficient sum from his slender earnings.

To be thrifty in youth generally denotes character. It is all the more creditable in a case like the present, when the economist is a raw country boy visiting for the first time a capital city with its multifarious enticements to dissipation. Although many men possessed both of genius and character have failed to win recognition in their lifetime, perhaps no man, however superlatively endowed, has succeeded without character in imposing himself upon his age. We are now to see the young stonemason in Amsterdam working 'prentice to one Pieter de Keyser, the son of Hendrik de Keyser, a sculptor. Despite the handicap arising from his not being a native of the country Nicholas Stone is entrusted with the design and execution of a work of importance, the portico of the Westkerke. His success must have been remarkable, for he gained not only money and reputation but that traditional prize of the good 'prentice of tradition, his master's daughter !

Nicholas Stone was back in England again some time

before 1614, and from now until his death he enjoyed a high and deserved reputation in the triple role of mason, sculptor and architect. The quarryman's son was employed by James I upon most of his royal palaces : Holyrood, Greenwich, Theobalds, Nonsuch, Whitehall, St James's, and Somerset House. He carried out, as mason, several designs for the great Inigo Jones, such as the Banqueting House at Whitehall, the water-gates of Somerset House—with the assistance of his brother—and the portico of Old St Paul's. As his own master, Stone designed and executed a work widely known, though not always remembered as his, the porch of St Mary's church in the High Street, Oxford. In 1619, he was honoured with the office of Master Mason to James I. (I fancy that in Renaissance English, the term "master mason" is sometimes interchangeable with that of "architect." Certainly across the Channel the term *maître maçon* is so used. We read of the *maître maçon* who designed that poem in stone, the château of *Azay-le-Rideau*.) Charles I—the most discriminating art-lover of all our English kings—gave Stone the royal patent as Master Mason and architect at Windsor Castle. Stone's two mansions I have not seen in any pictorial reproduction. Tart Hall which once stood in St James's Park was long since demolished, and so, I believe, was his Cornbury, Oxfordshire.

But Stone is remembered by many other effigies besides this thing of beauty, the Sandys monument, in the side-chapel of an obscure country church. Westminster Abbey contains no fewer than six effigies by him, whilst St Helen's, Bishopsgate, can boast of one which many esteem his masterpiece, that to Sir Julius Cæsar, Master of the Rolls, and friend of Lord Bacon.

In the astonishing little church at Miserden other monuments deserve more than a glance. I will mention one more. It represents Sir William Kingston of Miserden, who died —four years before the legal murder of Sir Walter Raleigh —at the early age of thirty-nine. In this short span of life he found time to become High Sheriff of the county. In the unpretentious prose of his epitaph we learn that he was "faithfvll to his Prince, and loving to his Covntry." During the two world wars how many thousands of men have we seen who possessed just these sterling qualities; and so long as England can produce them, England will endure.

The glass is modern and of less than average merit with the exception of one diminutive fragment, which dates from the fifteenth century and has survived to surmount a window in the north side of the nave. This portrays the Falcon and Fetterlock of which device the following is related. Edward IV, the hero of Tewkesbury, had three mistresses to whom he was unfaithfully attached. He would appear, however, to have set some store by *their* fidelity to *him*. The best-loved of the three entreated him to send her a badge with which to help out the decoration of her summer pavilion. His answer must have astonished her, for he met her request with this pictorial pun, the enigma of which is not hard to guess. He warns her, in the blunt French of a soldier, that he will punish inconstancy with lock and key.

BOURTON-ON-THE-WATER

It is at Malvern Road Station, Cheltenham, that a young fellow with whom I am passing traveller's comments observes: "If you're going to Bourton-on-the-Water, whatever you do, don't miss the miniature village. You get to it through the New Inn. It's a Bourton in little. All done by local masons and in local material. I've never seen the like of it; and I've been in the building line myself. It's only sixpence to go in, but it must have cost the old boy who built it every penny of a thousand pounds!"

Then, abruptly changing the subject, "What do you think," says he, " of this cocker of mine? All golden! And she's had eleven pups, all golden like herself, and not a spot on any one of them!"

But now my train steams in, so I bid my young sportsman farewell, and pass through stretches of gently undulating country which has remained wonderfully unspoiled, and through stations, gay in true rustic style with beds of flowers. The names of the villages where we stop smell as sweetly of England as do the bushes of red roses on the platforms: Leckhampton, Andoversford, Charlton Kings, Notgrove. Behind one of the rose bushes a pair of lovers, forgetting that it is only four feet high and that a train has come in and is now at the platform, stand in a tranced embrace, temporarily oblivious of such cramping limitations as space and time.

Bourton-on-the-Water is of early British origin. A Roman camp enclosing some sixty acres was situated here, hard by that famous Roman road the Foss Way. The enclosure, which was quadrangular in shape and partly surrounded by a paved aqueduct, has yielded the antiquaries a rich harvest of Roman coins together with a gold signet-ring. This last is something of a puzzle, for the ring space is too small to admit of its being slipped upon a finger. It weighs, we learn from Rudder, a trifle less than an ounce. The impression displays a Roman soldier with a spear in his left hand, a Victory in his right, and the Roman eagle sitting at his feet. The figure is seated and (this is singular) not upon a chair or throne, but on a *tripod*. When such out-of-the-way Roman ornaments were discovered by the men of the Middle Ages, they were commonly, but erroneously, presumed to have been used as charms.

Bourton-on-the-Water derives its name from the sparkling Windrush, one of the head streams of the Thames, which I seem to have read somewhere averages where it flows through the village some thirty feet across by eighteen inches deep. Were I a rich man I should long to present Bourton with at least one pair of swans! These princely birds would add the one touch needed to grace the scene. Upon either side of this enchanting waterway stretch admirably kept grass-plots, upon which at the moment a host of London visitors lie picknicking, for the local hostelries cannot accommodate another soul. One crosses the Windrush by those bridges which have given Bourton the nickname of the Venice of the Cotswolds. I suppose this is a good advertising slogan, but, whilst premising that these bridges are beautiful and *sui generis*, they are as little Venetian as it is possible to imagine. They are so unornamented, so unostentatious. Recall to your imagination, for example, the Bridge of Sighs, and see if you can pick up its like at Bourton. The bridges of the City of the Doges stand high that traffic may pass beneath, whereas these Bourton bridges do little more than clear the surface of the stream. The centre bridge, however, is of loftier construction than its fellows, a graceful three-arched affair of freestone, which was built in 1756.

The grassy spaces with their convenient wooden seats enable a spectator to study unharassed the handsome mansions of mellow Cotswold stone. Harrington House is an admirable example of Georgian domestic architecture. Near the Victoria Hall stands another attractive building, that with the sundials; this dates from 1698. I love the *space* at Bourton which enables us to admire the beauty of her ancient buildings without having to crane one's neck or, by taking just that one step beyond the kerb, court death or mutilation beneath the wheels of a passing lorry!

Give us space! Of what use is the nobility of the architect's design or the loving patience of the craftsman if there be no corner from which we may view in tranquillity the beauty they so liberally afford us? But at *spacious* Bourton-on-the-Water trim grass-plots take the place of those Continental squares with which every provincial town across the Channel is provided after the centuries-old tradition of the Roman forum. The new buildings harmonize with the old at Bourton, for all but an insignificant few are built of local stone. The quaintly named Old New Inn of 1718—how many of our *New* Inns are *old*!—stands at the southern end of the village. Its interesting sundial shows the quarter-hours : but do not, in a fine frenzy of enthusiasm for the days of the stage-coach, fall into the mistake of consulting it when making for the last 'bus back to Cheltenham!

It is through the gardens of the Old New Inn that one goes to see the miniature village, a reproduction of Bourton-on-the-Water, but *doll's-house size*! The dimensions of the houses are exactly to scale, all measurements having been made and nothing left to guesswork. A Lilliputian Windrush, not still but in motion and perhaps a yard wide, enters the village by a fall beside the mill. A stickleback would be a pike in such a stream. A rather unconvincing stone miller—he should at least have been painted in natural colours!—stands with folded arms in the doorway of his house. Everything which has delighted us in Bourton *Major* finds its counterpart here in *Bourton Minor*! Shops, police-station, library, the handsome manor house with its seven gables, all are here, even to the village hall which makes so stately a feature of the world outside with its twin chimneys used for decorative effect and its black and gold clock. And what colour in the miniature flowers in the gardens! What quaintness in the pigmy trees and shrubs! The gardener's toil must be never-ending, for so soon as shrub or tree evinces signs of becoming too high for its surroundings, up it must come and one smaller be put in its place! This village in duodecimo is being kept up to date; there stands its war memorial.

A section of the wall of the church has been made to open, so as to enable us to look within; we see the pews, hassocks, hymn-books. As we move away we hear music, as of a service. A concealed gramophone is playing "Hear My Prayer." The illusion is complete. I should have liked to stay on to see the model village at nightfall : the moon casting blue shadows from the elfin gable-ends : the reflections of the tiny street-lamps in the running waters. Time makes this impossible, but I can view it all in my imagination, and the effect is bewitching!

CHAPTER XVII

COTSWOLD VILLAGES (II)

MINCHINHAMPTON

A MARKET-PLACE need not be spacious, but it should be sufficiently so for one to view the houses about it in reasonable comfort. In this matter Minchinhampton—the Village of the Nuns—satisfies all reasonable requirements. Too often in England some huge building, corn-exchange or what-not, is set up in the centre of the one open space in the town, scientifically blocking the view from every quarter. I cannot forgive even so great a genius as Sir Christopher Wren for planting his Radcliffe Camera fairly and squarely in the middle of what might otherwise have been one of the noblest public squares in Europe.

Every house that abuts upon little Minchinhampton market-place is of Cotswold stone; and this is *right*. An intrinsically ugly building may possess a certain charm when the neighbourhood has provided the materials for its construction. A building beautiful in itself may prove an eyesore when contrived from imported material. It refuses to sink into its setting as an integral part of the scene.

Across the square stands the Crown, with three irregularly spaced dormer windows cutting its high-pitched roof of mellow tiles. And though I could wish a signboard bearing the pictorial representation of a crown rather than the mere word in prosaic letters, yet the bracket which is there to support it is of handsome smithied iron. All the other buildings about, some little bigger than cottages, are stone-walled also and stone-tiled; and they achieve a harmony.

At our backs is the old Market House, which I have often heard described locally as "Elizabethan." In point of fact, as the date upon it proclaims, it was erected in 1698 in the reign of William III, nearly a hundred years after the great

208

queen's death. The mistake nevertheless is understandable. When all travel was on horseback or afoot, and local craftsmen sufficed to local needs, it took more than a trifle to draw our ancestors from their "high wild hills and rough uneven ways." The nearest county town was *town* then *par excellence*, new fashions and new ideas were tardy in their arrival; and architects clung to traditional methods and the known style of earlier days. After a visit to the church we will return to the Market House with its steep roof and stone pillars.

The primitive church was Norman, but successive centuries have demolished, enlarged and transformed it in a thousand ways. In 1842 the iconoclasts had a veritable field-day, and the ancient structure underwent one of those curious "restorations" dear to the Victorian heart. They reformed away, for example, two minute Norman windows of the primitive church of only six inches in width! Four Norman arches went next, with their circular supporting pillars each with its indented capital. And as though all this were not enough they destroyed and rebuilt the nave and shortened the original chancel.

They were now in their element, and were on the point of consigning the glorious window of the south transept to the willing working-men, with their picks, shovels, and wheelbarrows when a Fellow of the Society of Antiquaries—a certain Dr Dalton who understood something about history and churches—successfully pleading with these architectural Tamburlaines, persuaded them to desist: *not*, however, too soon. The new brooms had swept mighty clean!

Most ancient churches present a not-unpleasing agglomeration of styles. What did the builders of Chaucer's merry day care about *Norman work*? As little as these very Normans had for the fortress-like Saxon-English style. Neither were the Elizabethans pedantic about respecting the peculiarities of the fourteenth-century church-builders, or those of the fifteenth century either. And doubtless my Lord Chesterfield and Mr Alexander Pope regarded all as *Gothic* which failed to come up to the polite standards of their own day when great ladies brought their lapdogs and their snuff-boxes to church with them, or refreshed themselves—such at least

P 209

Lower Slaughter

was the practice of *one* eighteenth-century dame, a regular worshipper at Gloucester Cathedral—with a glass of sherry during service.

Why then should we reproach the Victorians if they in their turn were cavalier in their attitude to the architectural styles of the ages which had preceded them? The reason is twofold. They had no style of their own to superimpose upon those which had gone before; only a soulless jumble of half a dozen earlier styles. And when it came to restoring, they knew nothing of archæology. In 1865, the process of reforming the work of the reformers began in earnest. The conservative iconoclasts of the new order abolished the "three-decker" pulpit, and removed the galleries which ran along three sides of the nave. They also rebuilt the east end of the chancel to bring it into harmony with its presumed original proportions. The organ, which in a huge gallery had blocked up the whole west end of the church, was next removed to its present unobtrusive position in the north transept.

It is, of course, by no means an impossibility that a generation may arise who will regret the disappearance of what the men of 1865 regarded as incongruities and disfigurements. The "three-decker" pulpit is already a rare curiosity. Those older galleries are seldom to be met with to-day outside a Hogarth print. Still, the captious critic is a perennial type. We need not take his lamentations very seriously. The men of 1865 brought the *lines* of the church into view. Its *design* became again apparent. And it is inconceivable that an architect could regard the changes which brought this about as otherwise than an improvement. The south transept is exceedingly impressive. Its high-pitched roof is not, as one might expect, of timber but all of stone. Stone ribs underprop stone flags, so that one is astonished that the walls are adequate to the strain. The mystery is solved when we view the exterior and realize the purpose of the external buttresses. In alcoves, which are part of the original design of this transept, one sees the recumbent effigies of Sir Peter de la Mere and his wife, of late thirteenth- or early fourteenth-century work. At the knight's feet lies a lion, as symbol of his courage; at the lady's a dog, emblematical of fidelity.

The modern glass of the window above them is both rich

in colour and graceful in design. The whole effect is noble
and worthy of this superb corner of the church. This glass
was executed by Messrs Hardman of Birmingham. It was
dedicated by H. D. Ricardo and his sister. So far, so good.
But I for one should like to know the name not only of the
firm but of its designer. This I was unable to discover either
by inquiry of the man who showed me round or by consulting
the excellent descriptive booklet of Mr A. T. Playne.

The tone of the bells is exceedingly clear and pleasing.
And this fact has given rise to the frequently expressed belief
that the ring is not composed of bells at all but of metal
tubes of different calibres, which are struck bell-fashion with
hammers. There is no truth in this fantastic notion. With
the exception of a sanctus bell which—the sexton tells me—
was recently retrieved from the valley into which it had
perhaps been thrown at the "Reformation," the oldest bell in
the peal is inscribed "1719 Messrs Rudhall Gloucester
fecerunt." The fourth bell and the tenor were recast by this
same firm of Rudhall in 1797 and again in 1825. The second
was recast in 1842 by Mears & Co, of the Whitechapel
Bell Foundry, London. When the bells are heard at a great
distance the weatherwise declare that rain will shortly
follow.

In the south transept one may see a brass plate to James
Bradley who was born at Sherborne, Gloucestershire, in
March 1693. He was admitted Fellow of the Royal Society
in 1718; appointed Savilian Professor of Astronomy at
Oxford in 1721; Lecturer on Experimental Philosophy in
1729; and succeeded Halley as Astronomer Royal in 1742,
in which capacity Sir Isaac Newton termed him "the greatest
astronomer in Europe." The immense mass of accurate observations made by him at Greenwich and published as
"Observations" formed the basis of the *Fundamenta Astro-
nomiæ* of the German astronomer Bessel. Bradley made his
discovery of the *aberration of light* in 1728, and that of the
nutation of the earth's axis in 1747. These discoveries made
exact knowledge of the position of the fixed stars possible
and laid the foundation of all modern observational astronomy.

The brass plate in the south transept sets forth his skill in the *arcana* of science, the veneration in which he was held by those best able to judge of his achievements, and the personal modesty of this great genius himself. The inscription is composed in the elegant Latin of the English "Augustan Age" —our "Second Renaissance"—and is a pleasure to read after the black-letter barbarity of the Middle Age with its puerile contractions. What benefit did their scribes propose to themselves in contracting *super* to *sup'* or *misericordia* to *m'cordia*, and the like? They effected a minimum of labour-saving to achieve a maximum of obscurity.

I say that Bradley's inscription is a joy to read: I should have said "might be." The need for relettering is obvious, and the plaque is placed a good yard too high. One does not enter a church with opera-glasses. Outside in the churchyard Bradley's tomb is a mediocre, not to say shabby, affair. An ordinary table-tomb like any of half a million others, one looks for the epitaph:

"Here lyeth John Hodge of the parish, yeoman; and Sarah, his faithful wife."

It is not thus that the great should lie.

To-day when the English school of sculptors have shown themselves capable of producing work of real distinction— the War Memorial at Paddington Station, the "Prospero and Ariel" of Broadcasting House—is it too much to suggest that the Minchinhampton folk should consider the setting up of a permanent memorial to their most distinguished citizen, in "his habit as he lived"? In these words a Latin author records his reactions on hearing that the Senate is to commission a statue to his personal friend:

"For the sake of the public therefore I am glad that a statue is decreed to Cottius. . . . It will be a great satisfaction to me ever and anon to view this likeness of him—to look back towards it—to halt beneath it—to pass it as I go along. For if we derive consolation from images of the departed set up in their own homes, how much more comforting are they . . . when, erected in a place of public resort, they are not only memorials of our lost ones' air and countenance, but of their glory and honour."

And is not all this equally true to-day?

If the little town of Bruges can—in a square dedicated to

him—erect a statue to Simon Stevin, the discoverer of the
parallelogram of forces, surely the relatively richer town of
Minchinhampton might do more for the founder of modern
astronomy than a tomb similar to any of a hundred thousand
others, and a half-obliterated brass tablet ten feet up on a
wall?

During the last ten years of his laborious life, Bradley was
in receipt of a Government pension of £250. Although this
represented a far greater purchasing power in the seventeen-
hundreds than it does to-day, one can hardly call it munificent. Still, it set a man of simple tastes decently above
poverty. James Bradley died in Chalford, Gloucestershire, in
1762.

And now, to return to the Market House.

That high-pitched roof is typical of the Cotswold style in
architecture. So also are those stone pillars; you will see the
like at the Bear Inn, Bisley; these last were removed from
the now demolished Bisley town hall. There is a very lively
tradition, which, however, I have not as yet seen confirmed in
any authentic record, that the supreme tragic actress Sarah
Siddons—the "Tragic Muse" of Sir Joshua Reynolds's
famous portrait—once acted in this building. It appears very
probable that the tradition is true. She was born into a family
of strolling players, or, if this sounds better, an "itinerant
company." We know that she appeared at many places
where a theatre had to be improvised and licensing regulations by-passed. Thus, for instance, at Worcester in her
'prentice days, she appeared at the King's Head, admission
to the performance being granted only to those would-be
spectators who had purchased packets of tooth-powder! The
play presented was entitled *Love in a Village*, and the great
actress—not Siddons as yet, her maiden name was Kemble—
played the heroine Rosetta, to the Meadows of her husband-
to-be.

Her connection with the West of England was long preserved. In 1744 for instance, at fashionable Cheltenham, she
played Belvidera the heroine of Otway's long-famous but
over-melodramatic tragedy, *Venice Preserved*. On this occasion, so it is said, a party of young aristocrats turned up
prepared to quiz the show. And it must be conceded that

the play contains passages which might, at least if overacted by provincials, arouse the reverse of tragic emotions.

JAFFEIR : Hark thee, my friend—Priuli—is—a Senator !
PIERRE : A dog !
JAFFEIR :   Agreed.
PIERRE :   Shoot him.
JAFFEIR :   With all my heart.

But the Siddons's brilliant acting, as the pathetic Belvidera, bewitched her audience. There was no longer the remotest disposition to laugh, and when the show was at an end the daughter of Lord Dungarvan helped out the struggling young beauty with gifts of cast-off dresses; for Sarah was still tormented in these struggling days with the perennial feminine nightmare of "having nothing to wear."

It may well have been from Cheltenham that Sarah visited Minchinhampton, for the roads were good and the distance such as even at that time could be travelled comfortably enough in a day. We must not picture the great tragedienne's progress through life as a triumphal march along a highway strewn with roses. Very much the contrary. In fact, if I may be permitted to parody Mr G. K. Chesterton,

> There were still strange barns to storm, and stages to
> be stamped on,
> Before she went to Drury Lane, by way of Minchin-
> hampton !

The "Tragic Muse"—*now* for an anticlimax—was born at the Shoulder of Mutton Inn, Brecon. From her earliest days her juvenile beauty attracted admiration, and though "the stage hath been seldom thought the school of innocence," no scandal attaches to her name. In her teens she fell in love with William Siddons of her father's company, a young fellow of versatility who could play anything from King Lear to Dick Whittington's cat. And as he succeeded in capturing the young beauty's affections from a host of rivals it may be assumed that in the role of lover he was no nonentity either. But the parents lacked cordiality. The girl's mother boxed young Siddons's ears, and her father expelled him from the company. Was it to keep the pair apart that Sarah was now sent as personal maid to a

lady of quality, a Mrs Greathead of Guy's Cliff, Warwickshire? It seems highly probable. Wherever they go actresses
carry the atmosphere of the stage about with them, and
young Sarah was no exception to the rule. She would regale
the servants' hall with recitations from Shakespeare, Milton,
and Rowe : the last of whom, now fallen into oblivion, was
the author of the long-popular tragedy *Jane Shore*, Poet-
laureate to George I, and translator of Lucan's *Pharsalia,*
for which work, after his death, his widow received a pension
from the Crown.

Can one not picture the looks of astonishment upon the
faces of Mrs Greathead's domestics when the newly engaged
lady's maid rose to declaim her "pieces" ! The bewigged
butler, the horse-faced footman, the chubby parlourmaids,
the bulging cook?

> O thou that with surpassing glory crown'd,
> Looks from thy sole dominion like the God
> Of this new world; at whose sight all the stars
> Hide their diminish'd heads.

"Lord ! Did you ever hear the like !" says the cook.

"They ought to give her money for that," cry the parlourmaids in chorus.

"Hark at young Sarah," cries the horse-faced footman.
The butler, in whose soul a genuine spring of poetry has been
loosed, feels tears start involuntarily to his eyes. Hastily he
buries his face in a quart-pot, and a trickle of double-X
escapes down his waistcoat. Sometimes, as such gifts as
Sarah's cannot long lie *perdu*, the young lady's-maid would
be *had up* to the drawing-room to entertain Mrs Greathead's
aristocratic friends.

The future star was as plentifully endowed with character
as with histrionic ability, for, "screwing her courage to the
sticking-place," whilst still only eighteen she wrung from her
parents their reluctant consent to her marriage with young
William Siddons. The ceremony took place at Coventry,
26th November 1773. They were upon the boards again very
soon afterwards, Sarah playing now for the first time as
Mrs Siddons.

Garrick, who kept an eye upon the provinces with a view

to securing new talent, sent a fellow-actor, King, to see her play. His report was favourable and Sarah was engaged for Drury Lane to play Portia, at five pounds a week; better money then than now. But her powers were slow maturing, her performance was mediocre, and after five nights the part was given to a man, Lamash.

On 1st February 1776 she played the First Julia in Bates's totally forgotten farce, the *Blackamoor Washed White*. The piece was "damned," its fourth performance occasioning a "riot." Our ancestors were always so curiously resentful of being bored. To-day an audience yawn and doze through the dullest pictures, but so far from rioting it never so much as occurs to them that they are free men who have the option of getting up and going out. The discovery of these times that water is cheap and can be used for drinking may account, in part, for this mule-like passivity.

As Lady Ann in Shakespeare's *Richard III*—tinkered up and vulgarized by Garrick and others—Sarah Siddons failed yet again to grip the spectators. Although her appearance must always have been striking, yet the best that the critic of the *Morning Chronicle* could find to say was: "She speaks sensibly, but her powers are not equal to a London theatre." It is, however, something to speak sensibly; by no means every Shakespearian actor does so even to-day! Another critic was less kind. He styled her rendering of Lady Ann as "lamentable." Garrick had no further use for her, and as no other London manager had either, she left the metropolis for the country once more.

But she had character, as we have seen, and she doubtless applied herself more strenuously to improving her technique. In any case, this same year of her retreat from London saw her first outstanding success at Manchester. In the year following, 1777, she won all hearts at York as Euphrasia in the *Grecian Daughter*. Perhaps she was more attractive physically as a maturer woman than she had been as a young girl. Her marriage may have increased her sex appeal for we find her fellow-player, Tate Wilkinson, declaring: "I recollect her fall and figure after the dying scene was noticed as most elegant!" Rarely does the pageant of Death inspire such genial reflections.

In fashionable Bath, Sarah seems to have clinched her former successes, and to have begun now to be recognized as England's major tragic actress. Lady Macbeth, Queen Katherine, Constance, in *King John*, The Lady in Milton's *Comus*, she played them all, enthralling her public and finding in the aristocracy of the day many generous patrons. In 1781 she played Hamlet, as a later Sarah was destined to do; and London now was all anxiety to have her back.

As she had been asked to leave, the situation was nice; there was much heavy diplomacy, much haggling over terms, and by way of smoothing over a tricky situation she was billed now at Drury Lane as "Mrs Siddons from Bath." How did she look at this time with the fickle goddess smiling on her, and the metropolis at her feet? A critic in *Dramatic Miscellanies* gives us this pen-portrait:

"The person of Mrs Siddons is greatly in her favour, just rising above middle stature, she looks, walks, and moves like a woman of superior rank. Her countenance is expressive, her eye so full of information that the passion is told from a look before she speaks. Her voice, though not so harmonious as Mrs Cibber's, is strong and pleasing; nor is a word lost for want of due articulation. She excels all persons in paying attention to the business of the scene; her eye never wanders from the person she speaks to or should look at when she is silent.

"Her modulation of grief, and her plaintive pronunciation of the interjection 'Oh!' is sweetly moving and reaches the heart. Her madness in Belvidera is terribly affecting. The many accidents of spectators falling into fainting fits in the time of her acting bear testimony to the effect of her exertions."

Minchinhampton was not again to catch sight of this very rare bird. But what of that? One cannot even if one would divest the "Elizabethan" Market House of its traditions. The quaint pillared building by which you wait to catch the bus for Stroud has known its moment of immortality.

LOWER SLAUGHTER

All the way as I walk by the stile-path to Lower Slaughter, drifting earthward from sunny clouds or from the sapphire

lakes between them, comes the drone of a plane. When that
sound was new how hateful it was to us. How it shattered
the hush : that eloquent silence, which the bark of the
farmer's dog or the lazy murmur of the chaffcutter seemed
rather to intensify than diminish : as a master adds discords
to grace his melody. To-day the throb of the propellers—
bass to the treble of all those larks—seems to me to be no
less one of the authentic voices of Nature than the singing
of the wind in the foliage, or the humming of the bees. Man
is an infinitely adaptable animal.

Lower Slaughter was built before Industrialism, the be-
trousered goddess, had scattered from her oily blouse corru-
gated iron, blue slates and standardized "roofing material"
—*O procul este profani!*—to oust our honey-coloured Cotswold tiles. This village, however, escaped degradation by its
very remoteness : a stile-path is no approach to tempt a
busy man.

How admirably did those older builders combine the practical with the æsthetically delightful. These high-pitched
gables, and dripstones, and dormers are there to throw off
the rain and superexcellently do they do their work. If,
during a shower, I open my study window in this modern
cottage where I sit writing, in comes the rain driven by the
wind and the room is flooded ! The machine and mass education have destroyed the old sterling style, and what but ugly
futility have we to put in its place?

I will not attempt to describe this object of my pilgrimage
lest I should detract from the beauty of my original. Lower
Slaughter is, to my mind, absolutely the loveliest village in
all England ! I have been here before, and there is commonly a sense of disillusionment when one visits for the
second time a place that one has loved. But I experience
none to-day. Lower Slaughter is the ideal English village.
It is a masterpiece. And I shall define a masterpiece as a
work of art that one can *live* with. If one is jaded by a
Botticelli, if the Venus of Milo grows stale, depend upon it
one has wearied of life.

The Lower Slaughter folk are great lovers of flowers, and
roses blow in all their gardens. I make for a seat in the open,
built about the trunk of an aged tree. Two old men are seated

there, the one communicative, the other drowsing in the sun. From this vantage-point I watch the Slaughter Brook which meanders through the village, a Marlovian waterway if ever there was one, and such as might have inspired those idyllic lines :

> By shallow rivers, to whose falls,
> Melodious birds sing madrigals.

A *goose* followed by a flotilla of ducklings swims into view. I look inquiringly at my old man.

"We put the goose egg in with the duck's," says he, "so now she swims around along with her pals. She *were* going to be killed for last Christmas dinner but she weren't fat enough. So she'll have to wait for *that* till next !" Heartless humorist ! But, attended by her singular train, the goose swims on regardless of destiny. Suddenly she plunges her bill beneath the surface, searching for some object beneath the broad leaves of the glistening water-lilies. She raises her head, snaps down a diminutive, bright-scaled fish, resumes her progress. A sudden breeze ruffles the crystal surface, bright with bird-song, fragrant with privet, rose, and honeysuckle. Heedless of Fate and unperturbed by any theory of living this goose *lives*. Perhaps she esteems herself to be immortal. For her peace of mind, I hope she may.

BIBLIOGRAPHY

ATKYNS, Sir ROBERT, Knt. ("Sir Robert Atkyns of Sapperton"), *The Ancient and Present State of Gloucestershire, etc.*, 2nd edition. (London, 1712.)

AUSTIN, ROLAND, *Transactions of the Bristol and Gloucestershire Archæological Society* for 1925, vol. xlvii. (Kendal, printed for the Society by Titus Wilson and Son, June 1926.)

BADDELEY, W. ST CLAIR, *History of Cirencester*. (Cirencester Newspaper Company Ltd, 1931.)

Biography, Dictionary of National, passim.

BRUCE, JOHN, F.S.A., *Historie of Edward IV in England, etc.* Edited for the Camden Society. (London, John Boyer Nichols and Son, 1838.)

BRUDIGAN, Lieutenant-Colonel F., *Historical Records of the North Gloucestershire Regiment.* (London, Blackfriars Printing and Publishing Co Ltd, 1884.)

Cheltenham Ladies' College, The, 1944. (A College production.)

Davies, W. H., The Collected Poems of. (London, Jonathan Cape, 1928.)

DRAYTON, MICHAEL, *Polyolbion*. Edited by J. William Hebel. (Oxford, printed at the Shakespeare Head Press, and published by Basil Blackwood, 1913.)

Educational Facilities in the County of Gloucestershire. Issued with the co-operation of the leading educational authorities. (Printed and published by British Isles Publicity Ltd, Bristol and London.)

ELLIS, Sir HENRY K. H., *Three books of Polydore Vergil's English History, etc.* Camden Society. (London, 1844.)

EVANS, HERBERT A., M.A., *Gloucestershire.* (Cambridge University Press, 1909.)

Flecker, James Elroy, The Collected Poems of, edited with an introduction by J. C. Squire. (London, Martin Secker, undated.)

FOSBROOKE, THOMAS DUDLEY, *Abstracts of the Records and Manuscripts respecting the County of Gloucester, formed into a History*. (Gloucester, printed by Jos. Harris, 1807.)

Gloucestershire Regiment, a Short History of the. (Gale and Polden, Aldershot; also at London and Portsmouth; undated.)

Historical Records of the Sixty-first, or the South Gloucestershire Regiment of Foot. (London, Parker, Furnivall and Parker, 1844.)

HOLINSHED, RAPHAEL, *The . . . Chronicles . . . augmented to the yeare* 1577, by John Hooker, or Vowell, and others.

HUME AND SMOLLETT, *The People's History of England*, with continuation to 1847 by J. C. Campbell. (London, Thomas Kelly, undated.)

LEWIS, J. SYDNEY, *Old Glass and How to Collect It*. (London, T. Werner Laurie, Ltd, 1925.)

Martial, M. V. (Epigrammatist), Delphin Edition. (Paris, 1680.)

"MERCURIUS MELANCHOLICUS" (? Pseudonym of Marchmont Nedham), "Loyalty Speaks Truth," etc. (Quarto, 1647.)

NEDHAM, MARCHMONT, *Mercurius Politicus*. Nos. 1–7 printed by R. White; Nos. 8–30 printed by M. Simmons; Nos. 31–254 printed by T. Newcomb.

NEDHAM, MARCHMONT (?), *Mercurius Pragmaticus*, No. 13, December 21–8, 1647.

PLAYNE, ARTHUR TWISDEN, B.A., *The Churches of Minchinhampton and Avening*. (Gloucester, John Bellows, 1921.)

RUDDER, SAMUEL, *New History of Gloucestershire, etc*. (based on Atkyns, whom Rudder corrects, augments, and brings up to date). (Printed by Samuel Rudder, 1779, Folio.)

RYVES, BRUNO, Dean of Windsor, later of Chichester, *Mercurius Rusticus*. (19 numbers from August 1642; the whole republished, 1646, 1647 and 1685.)

SAWYER, JOHN, *The Story of Gloucestershire*, 2nd edition. (Cheltenham, Norman Sawyer and Co.)

SMITH, REGINALD A., B.A., F.S.A., *A Late-Celtic Mirror*. (London, printed by J. B. Nichols and Sons, Westminster, 1909.)

INDEX

Abercrombie, Sir Ralph, 67
Alaric, 21, 22, 23
Alexandria, Battle of, 67, 68
Alfred the Great, 24
American War of Independence, the, 65
Amulet, 3
Anglo-Saxon Chronicle, the, 24
Astley, Sir Jacob, 58, 59, 61
Atkyns, Sir Robert, of Sapperton, 191
Attila, 22

Bacon, Roger, 186–7
Barnet, Battle of, 27, 28, 29
Bavaria, Elector of, 64
"Bear-killers," the, 139, 140
Beauchamp, Richard, 33
Bede, the Venerable, 24
Bellasis, Colonel, 50
Berkeley Castle, 26
Besant, Sir Walter, 172
Birch, Colonel, 58
Birdlip, 9; Mirror, 11, 12
"Bloody Meadow," the, 37
Bourton-on-the-Water, 204–7
Bradley, James, 192, 211, 212, 213
Brentford, Lord, 54
Brereton, Sir William, 58
Brictric, 26
Bristol, 32; Glass, 150, 155; Siege of, 50, 51
Bristollium (Bristova), 20
British-made baskets, 15
Brythons, 6, 7
Buck, Captain, 45, 46
"Buffs," the, 64

Cabot, John, 109, 187, 188
Cabot, Sebastian, 188–91
Caedmon, 24
Cæsar, Claudius, 10
Cæsar, Julius, 8
Caractacus, 10
Catullus, 11, 18, 19
Caxton, John, F.R.S., 192
Chalford, 129
Charles I, 44, 49, 51–7
Charlton Abbots, 9
Chatterton, Thomas, 191, 192
Chaucer, Geoffrey, 36, 174
Chedworth Villa, 20
Cheese-rolling, the, 118–20
Cheke, Sir John, 191
Cheltenham, 34; College, 145; Ladies' College, 146–9, 182

Christopher, Dom, 157–60
Cider tax, the, 127–9
Cirencester, 31, 32; Abbey of, 16; Bull-ring at, 16
Clarendon, Lord, 53
Cleeve Hill, 9
Clifton College, 144
"Clipping the Yews," 137
Clive, Robert, 79
Cobberley, 197
Connell, Private Andrew, 67
Cooper's Hill, 118
Corinium, 15–19, 23, 24
Courting spoons, 141
Courtney, Thomas, Earl of Devonshire, 29
Coxe, Judge, 95–7
Crickley, 9
Crofts, Sir Richard, 38
Cromwell, Oliver, 61, 62

Dandelion wine, 132
Daneways House, 161–9
Davies, W. H., 174–82
Dean Close School, 144–5
Dean, Forest of, 7–10
Delhi, Siege of, 73
Dover, Captain Robert, 194–6
Draper, Lieutenant-General Sir William, K.B., 65
Drayton, Michael, 123, 124
Druidesses, 8
Druids, 8
Dyrham, 10

Edkin, Michael, 152, 153
Edmund, Duke of Somerset, 29, 35, 37
Edward (Lancastrian) Prince of Wales, 37, 38
Edward II, 26, 27
Edward IV, 49, 27–41, 204
Edward VII, 141
Elvers, cooking of, 141, 142
Epstein, Jacob, 181
Erasmus, Desiderius, 124

Fairfax, Thomas, Lord, 10, 56, 57, 58
Fairford, 23
Falcon and Fetterlock, the, 204
Felix Farley's Journal, 127
Fireside tale, a, 129–31
First Stone Age, 1, 2
FitzStephen, William, 126
Fitzwarren, Alice, 173

Flecker, James Elroy, 182–6
Flecker, Dr W. H., 145, 183
Fleetwood, Colonel, 60
"Flowers of Toulouse," the, 72
Folklore, 93–108
Foss-way, the, 12, 118
Frith Wood, 100, 101

Garrick, David, 215, 216
Glevum, 9, 15, 20, 54
Gloucester, 23, 26, 33; Cathedral, 27
    and *passim*; Robert of, 191; its
    Roman layout, 15; Siege of, 51–5
Gloucestershire dialect, 81–92; *idem*
    Donkey, 117–18; *idem* Punch,
    131; *idem* Regiment, 65–8; 74–8
Goidels, 7
"Golden Farmer," the, 13
Goths, the, 21, 22
Grammar School, the, Cheltenham,
    145
Grandison, Lord, 50
Grocyn, William, 191

Hale, Sir Mathew, 193
Hangman's Stone, 87
Haresfield Beacon, 10
Heart, the Golden, 197
Henry V, 173
Hewson, Colonel, 49
Honey Beer, 7
Honorius, Emperor, 23
Hop Pole, the, 131
Hopson, Major-General, 65
Horace, 138
Hulls, Jonathan, 192
Hulse, General, 71

Irmin Street, 12, 34
Isabella, Queen of Edward II, 27

Jasper, Earl of Pembroke, 30, 33, 35,
    39
Jenner, Edward, 192
Jonson, Ben, 42, 194

King Arthur's Cave, 1

Ladysmith, 73
Lamprey pie, 141
Lansdown, 10
Lawrence, Sir Thomas, 192
Leckhampton, 9, 183
Lombard's Kop, 73
Long barrows, 3

Maida, Battle of, 69
Margaret, Queen of Henry VI, 28, 29,
    32–8
Marlborough, Great Duke, the, 64

Marten, Henry, 62
Martial, 15
Martinique, 65
Maskelyne, John Nevil, 193, 194
Massey, Colonel, 44, 52, 53, 63
Matilda, Queen of William the Con-
    queror, 26
Merchant Adventurers, 190
Milton, John, 42, 178, 215
Minchinhampton, 208–17
Minorca, 65
Mirror, the Birdlip, 11, 12
Miserden, 200–4
Model village, Bourton, 206, 207
Mons, Retreat from, 75
Moore, Commodore, 65
Morgan, Colonel, 56
Murray, James, the Hon., 65

New Inn, 27
New Stone Age, 3–6
Nonnos, 1
Northbroke, John, 49
Nottingham Hill, 9

"Old Bragg's," the, 72
"Old" Parr, 7
Otway, Thomas, 48, 213

Paget, Colonel, 68
Painswick, 137–9
Penn, Sir William, 192
Pentreath, Dolly, 6
Pepys, Samuel, 126, 127
Pickwickians, the, in Gloucestershire,
    131, 132
Plautius, Aulus, 9
Popular sayings, 109–18
Powell, Vavasour, 49
Prinknash Priory, 156–61
Probus, 13, 121–3
Prynne, William, 48
"Puppy-dog pie," 139

Raikes, Robert, 138
Richard III, 35, 36, 38
Rietfontein, 73
Roads, Roman, 12, 13, 15, 118
Robert of Gloucester, 191
Rollright Stones, 105–8
Roman camp, Bourton, 205
Rothenstein, William, 181
Royal George Hotel, 13, 14, 34
Rudder, Samuel, 191
Rupert, Prince, 50, 56
Ryves, Bruno, 42

Salamanca, 71
Salmon, Severn, 143
Sandys, Sir William, 200, 201

Sapperton, 161
Scapula, Ostorius, 9
School of Arts and Crafts, the, Cheltenham, 145, 146
Shakespeare, 31, 82, 83, 91, 125, 148, 172
Siddons, Sarah, 213–17
Silures, the, 9, 10
Silver-tailed, Dandies, the, 72
Slashers, the, 72
Slaughter, Lower, 217–19
Snails, edible, 142, 143
Sodbury, 10, 32
South African War, 73
Southey, Robert, 192
Spenser, Edmund, 142
Stanton, 9
Stillico, 21
Stinchcombe Hill, 10
Stone, Nicholas, 202, 203
Stow, John, 172
Stow-on-the-Wold, Battle of, 59; Cooks at, 133
Stuart, Major-General, 70
Sudeley Castle, 42

Talavera, 71
Tewkesbury, Battle of, 35–40; Abbey, 40; Ham, 137

Thokey, John, Abbot of Gloucester, 27
Toulouse, 71
Trouble-House Inn, 151

Uley Bury, 3, 10

Valens, 21
Vandals, the, 22, 23
Vavasour, Sir William, 54
Villeroy, Marshal, 64
Vineyards in Gloucestershire, 125, 126

Wanswell, 116
Warwick the King-maker, 27, 28
Wenlock, Lord, 37
Westridge, 10
White-way, 12
Whittington, Sir Richard, 170–4, 197–200
Wilhelm II, 22
Willersley, 9
William the Conqueror, 25, 26
Willoughby, Sir Hugh, 190
Windrush, 205
Wines, Cotswold, 125, 126
Wise woman, a, 98–100
Wolfe, James, Major-General, 69
Woodchester, Roman villa at, 20, 21